Baltimore and Ohio Railroad Company

Routes and Rates for Summer Tours via Picturesque B. & O. 1892

Baltimore and Ohio Railroad Company

Routes and Rates for Summer Tours via Picturesque B. & O. 1892

ISBN/EAN: 9783337193249

Printed in Europe, USA, Canada, Australia, Japan

Cover: Foto ©ninafisch / pixelio.de

More available books at **www.hansebooks.com**

FOR

Summer Tours

VIA

Picturesque B. & O.

1892.

PASSENGER DEPARTMENT,
BALTIMORE & OHIO RAILROAD,
BALTIMORE, MD.

PRESS OF
JOHN COX'S SONS,
(BALTIMORE, MD.)

We are told that "the proper study of Mankind is man." Good advice, truly, but there is better. The proper study of American mankind is his own splendid country. Don't go across the Atlantic and spend time and money in the Old World, until you know more of the wondrous New World; the glorious land of your nativity, whose picturesque loveliness cannot pale before the boasted beauty of all Europe's famed places. The average American abroad, questioned as to the scenic beauty of his own country, must either draw upon his imagination, or give hearsay evidence regarding the subjects wherewith he should be familiar through personal knowledge. Such a man is an unworthy dweller in a land of surpassing beauty, and of ample means of access thereto. Such a man feels that he has made the mistake of his life in not studying the United States before opening his Baedecker abroad.

From such errors, good Lord deliver us! Into such an error no man or woman can fall who will read and obey this, the Baltimore and Ohio Railroad's Invitation.

It's goodly main trunk, and its wide-reaching arms, beckon you to come forth in this summer of the year of Grace, 1892. To come forth from your homes and your offices, and learn of your fair land in a way that will make the lesson a luxury as well as a life-long gratification.

The succeeding pages tell you their own story, briefly, tersely, and in a business-like way. There is no place worthy of a summer's visit, from the game-filled forests and streams of Canada in the North, to the pine-scented mountains and lakes of the South, whereunto the "Picturesque B. & O." and its connections will not bear you swiftly and safely. At no time in the history of this great highway, or in the history of the Republic, has it been so easy to reach a multitude of delightful, health-giving summer resorts, over the B. & O. road, as is now the case. The road, under the fostering influence of a wise and yet liberal management, has availed itself of every plan and appliance that will conduce to the comfort and convenience of its patrons. It is needless, here, to specify, or enumerate, the resorts which are accessible *via* the B. & O. That is the province of the pages which follow. It is only to be added, that with such a road as the Baltimore & Ohio, there is no excuse for any American remaining in ignorance of the supreme beauty of his native land, or for his hesitating in the matter of summer travel. The latter has been made a luxury by the B. & O., with its perfectly appointed trains of the finest Pullman and other cars; its superb road-bed, its faultless train service and its efficient men in every department. Let the era of American benightedness give way before the acceptance of this general but less hearty invitation!

INDEX

	PAGE		PAGE
Abingdon, Va.	1	Block Island, R. I.	44 45
Adirondack Mountains, N. Y.	1 9	Bluefield, W. Va.	333
Afton, Va.	9 10	Blue Mountain, Md.	46
Agencies	xvii	Blue Mountain House (Adirondacks), N. Y.	5 4
Alburgh Springs (Lake Champlain), Vermont	143 144	Blue Mountain Lake (Adirondacks), N. Y.	5
Alexandria Bay (Thousand Islands), N. Y.	14 16	Blue Ridge Station, Pa.	48
Alleghany Springs (Shawsville), Va.	10 11	Blue Ridge Springs, Va.	46 47
All Round Muskoka Lakes (Muskoka Lakes), Ont.	250	Bluff Point (Lake Champlain), N. Y.	144 145
Alton Bay, N. H.	16 17	Bonsack (see Coyner's Spgs.), Va.	82
Arkville (Catskill Mountains), N. Y.	65	Boothbay, Me.	48 49
Asbury Park (Ocean Grove), N. J.	252 254	Boston, Mass.	49
Asheville, N. C.	17 19	Boston (feeding forms), Mass.	50 55
Atlantic City, N. J.	20 22	Bramwell, W. Va.	333
Auburn, N. Y.	22	Bridgehampton, N. Y.	56
Au Sable Chasm (Adirondacks), N. Y.	3	Bristol, Tenn.	333
Babylon, L. I.	23	Broadheads (Catskill Mountains), N. Y.	65
Bala (Muskoka Lakes), Ont.	250	Brown's (Catskill Mountains), N. Y.	65
Baldwin (Lake George), N. Y.	155 156	Buchanan, Va.	333
Bar Harbor (Mt. Desert Island), Me.	23 31	Buena Vista, Va.	333
Bases	xvi	Buena Vista Springs, Md.	56
Basic, Va.	333	Burlington (Lake Champlain), Vt.	145 149
Bedford Springs, Pa.	31 33	Cairo (Catskill M'ntains), N. Y.	66
Beech Glen (for Beaver Dam), Pa.	35	Caldwell (Lake George), N. Y.	156 157
Belmar (Ocean Beach), N. J.	35	Campobello, N. B.	56 58
Berkeley Springs, W. Va.	36 38	Capon Lake (Home), Va.	58
Bethlehem (White Mountains), N. H.	39 42	Capon Springs, Va.	59 62
Big Indian (Catskill Mountains), N. Y.	65	Catskill (Catskill Mountains), N. Y.	64
Big Spring (see Elliston, Va.)	333	Catskill Mountains, N. Y.	65 66
Big Tunnel (for Montgomery White Sulphur Springs, Va.)	184 185	Centre Harbor, N. H.	50 51
Black Mountain, N. C.	43	Chautauqua (Chautauqua Lake), N. Y.	67 68
		Chautauqua Lake, N. Y.	66 70
		Chichester (Catskill Mountains), N. Y.	65

(v)

	PAGE		PAGE
Chicontimi, P. Q.	277	Great Barrington (Berkshire Hills), Mass.	118-120
Childwold Park House (Adirondacks), N. Y.	4-5	Greenville, Tenn.	353
Chilhowie, Va.	353	Griffin's (Catskill Mountains), N. Y., see Fleischmann's	65
Christiansburg, Va.	72	Grottoes, Va.	120-121
Clayton (Thousand Islands), N. Y.	54-55	Ha-Ha Bay, P. Q.	277
Cloverdale, Va.	353	Haines' Corners (Catskill Mountains), N. Y.	65
Cold Sulphur Springs, Va.	75-76	Halcottville (Catskill Mountains), N. Y.	65
Cooperstown, N. Y.	56-58
Cottage City (Martha's Vineyard), Mass.	78-79	Harper's Ferry, W. Va.	121
Covington, Va.	80	Harrogate, Tenn.	121-122
Coyner's Spr'gs (Bonsack), Va.	82	Healing Springs, Va.	123
Crawford House (White Mountains), N. H.	82-86	Highfield, Md.	124
Davis, W. Va.	87	Highgate Springs, Vt.	124-125
Deer Park, Md.	87-89	Highland Lake, Pa.	125
Doubling Gap Springs, Pa.	89-90	High Point, N. J.	126-127
Dublin, Va.	353	Hobart (Catskill Mountains), N. Y.	65
Eagle's Mere, Pa.	90	Hot Springs, Va.	128-129
Eastport, Me.	90	Hot Springs, N. C.	129-130
Edgewood (Catskill Mountains), N. Y.	65	Hotel Champlain (see Bluff Point), N. Y.	144-145
Eggleston Springs (see Staytide), Va.	90-92	Howe's Cave, N. Y.	131
Elberon, N. J.	92-93	Hunter (Catskill Mountains), N. Y.	65
Elkins, W. Va.	93	Instructions and information.	ix-xi
Elliston (Big Springs), Va.	353	Isles of Shoals, N. H.	132-134
Elmira, N. Y.	93	Ithaca, N. Y.	134-135
Ephrata, Pa.	94	Jamestown (Chautauqua Lake), N. Y.	68-70
Fabyan House (White Mountains), N. H.	94-110	Jefferson (White Mountains), N. H.	135-138
Fauquier White Sulphur Sp'gs, Va.	94	Johnson's City, Tenn.	353
Fire Island, N. Y.	110	Jonesboro, Tenn.	353
Fleischmann's-Griffin's, Catskill Mountains, N. Y.	65	Jordan's White Sulphur Sp'gs, Va.	139-140
Forked Lake Carry (Adirondacks), N. Y.	5	Kanawha Falls, W. Va.	140-141
Fortress Monroe (Old Point Comfort), Va.	257-259	Kaaterskill (Catskill Mountains), N. Y.	65
Foster Falls, Va.	353	Kennebunkport, Me.	141-142
Frostburg, Md.	110	Kingston (Catskill Mount'ns), N. Y.	64-65
Geneva, N. Y.	110-111	Lake Champlain, N. Y.	142-153
Gettysburg, Pa.	111-112	Lake George, N. Y.	154-157
Glade Springs, Va.	112-113	Lake Hopatcong, N. J.	158
Glens Falls, N. Y.	143-144	Lake Minnewaska, N. Y.	158
Glen House (White Mount'ns), N. H.	144-146	Lake Mohonk, N. Y.	159-160
Gorman, Md.	117	Lake Placid (Adirondacks), N. Y.	5
Gloucester, Mass.	116-117	Lakewood (Chautauqua Lake), N. Y.	70
Goshen, Va.	118	Lancaster (White Mountains), N. H.	160-164
Grand Gorge (Catskill Mountains), N. Y.	65	Lanesville (Catskill Mountains), N. Y.	65
Grand Hotel Station (Catskill Mountains), N. Y.	65		

	PAGE		PAGE
La Porte, Pa.	164	New Bedford, Mass.	222
Laurel House (Catskill Mountains), N. Y.	65	Newport, R. I.	226-227
Lawrenceville (Catskill Mountains), N. Y.	66	Newport, Vt.	227-228
Lebanon Springs, N. Y.	164-165	New River, Va.	228
Lee (Berkshire Hills), Mass.	165-166	Niagara Falls, N. Y.	229-249
Leeds (Catskill Mountains), N. Y.	66	Niagara Falls feeding forms, N. Y.	249
Lenox (Berkshire Hills), Mass.	166-168	North Conway (White Mountains), N. H.	250-251
Lititz, Pa.	168	North Creek (Adirondacks), N. Y.	5
Lisbon (White Mountains), N. H.	168-169	Oak Bluffs, Mass. (see Cottage City)	78-79
Littleton (White Mountains), N. H.	169	Oakland, Md.	252
Long Branch, N. J.	169-171	Ocean Beach, N. J. (see Belmar)	35
Loon Lake House (Adirondacks), N. Y.	5	Ocean Grove (Asbury Park), N. J.	252-254
Luray, Va.	175	Ohio Pyle, Pa.	255-256
Luray Caverns, Va.	171-175	Old Orchard, Me.	256-257
Manchester-by-the-sea, Mass.	175-176	Old Point Comfort (Fortress Monroe), Va.	257-259
Maplewood (White Mountains), N. H.	176-180	Olive Branch (Catskill Mountains), N. Y.	65
Marion, N. C.	181-182	Ontario Beach (Lake Ontario), N. Y.	259-260
Marion, Va.	333	Orkney Springs, Va.	261-262
Markleton, Pa.	182	Otis Junction (Catskill Mountains), N. Y.	66
Massanetta Springs, Va.	182	Ottawa, Canada.	262-264
Mayville (Chautauqua Lake), N. Y.	68-70	Otsego Lake, N. Y.	76-78
Millboro, Va.	183-184	Palenville (Catskill Mountains), N. Y.	66
Monterey, Pa.	184	Parry Sound (Muskoka Lakes), Ontario	220
Montgomery White Sulphur Sp'gs (Big Tunnel Sta'ion), Va.	184-185	Patchogue (Long Island), N. Y.	264
Montreal, P. Q.	186-205	Paul Smith's (Adirondacks), N. Y.	6-7
Montrose, Pa.	205	Pen-Mar, Md.	256
Morganton, N. C.	205	Phoenicia (Catskill Mountains), N. Y.	65
Morristown, Tenn.	333	Pine Hill (Catskill Mountains), N. Y.	65
Mountain House Stat'n (Catskill Mountains), N. Y.	66	Plattsburgh (Lake Champl'n), N. Y.	149-151
Mountain Lake Park, Md.	208-212	Plymouth (White Mountains), N. H.	265
Movements of Steamer Lines, 355-363		Pocahontas, Va.	333
Mt. Desert Island (Bar Harbor), Me.	23-31	Poland Springs, Me.	266-267
Mt. Kineo House (Moosehead Lake), Me.	207-208	Port Cockburn (Muskoka Lakes), Ontario	220
Mt. Pleasant (Catskill Mountains), N. Y.	65	Port Kent, N. Y.	268
Mt. Washington (White Mountains), N. H.	212-218	Profile House, N. H.	268-275
Murray Bay, P. Q.	218	Pulaski, Va.	333
Muskoka Lakes, Ontario	218-221	Québec, P. Q.	256-257
Nantasket Beach, Mass.	221	Radford, Va.	333
Nantucket, Mass.	221		
Narragansett Pier, R. I.	222-224		
Natural Bridge, Va.	224-225		
Natural Bridge Station, Va.	225		

	PAGE		PAGE
Randolph, Vt.	278	Shenandoah Alum Sprgs, Va.	311 312
Rangeley Lakes, Me.	279 281	Shokan (Catskill Mountains),	
Raquette Lake (Adirondacks),		N. Y.	65
N. Y.	7	Somerset, Pa.	311
Rawley Springs, Va.	281 282	Sorrento, Me.	313 314
Red Sulphur Springs, W. Va.	282 283	South Cairo (Catskill Mountains),	
Richfield Springs, N. Y.	284 285	N. Y.	65
Riviere du Loup, P. Q.	278	South Harpswell, Me.	315
Roan Mountain, Tenn.	285 286	Stamford (Catskill Mount'ns),	
Roanoke, Va.	333	N. Y.	65
Roanoke Red Sulphur Springs		Staunton, Va.	316
(Salem), Va.	302 303	Stayside (Eggleston Springs),	
Roberval (Lake St. Johns),		Va.	10 12
P. Q.	286	Steamer Lines Movements	
Rockbridge Alum Sp'gs, Va.	286 288	of	355 363
Rockbridge Baths, Va.	289	Stockbridge (Berkshire Hills),	
Rock Enon Springs, Va.	290 291	Mass.	316 318
Rockingham Mineral Spr'gs,		Stribling Springs, Va.	319 321
Va.	291	Stony Clove (Catskill Mount-	
Rockland, Me.	295 295	ains), N. Y.	65
Rockport, Mass.	296	Stopovers	xii xv
Rosseau (Muskoka Lakes), On-		Summit (see Grand Hotel Sta-	
tario	290	tion), N. Y.	65
Round Knob, N. C.	296	Summit (Mt. Washington),	
Roxbury (Catskill Mount'ns),		N. H.	218
N. Y.	65	Sweet Chalybeate Sprgs, Va.	322 323
Rural Retreat, Va.	332	Sweet Springs, W. Va.	324 326
Rye Beach, N. H.	297	Switchback, Pa.	326 328
St. Andrew's, N. B.	299 50	Tadousac, P. Q.	278
St. John, N. B.	301	Tannersville (Catskill Mount-	
Sackett's Harbor, N. Y.	302	ains), N. Y.	65
Salem (Roanoke Red Sulphur		Tazewell, Va.	333
Springs), Va.	302 303	Tupper Lake (Adirondacks),	
Salt Sulphur Springs, W. Va.	304 304	N. Y.	9
Saltville, Va.	304	Twin Mountain House (White	
Santa Clara (Adirondacks),		Mountains), N. H.	329 331
N. Y.	7	Upper Chateaugay Lake (Ad-	
Saranac Inn Station (Adiron-		irondacks), N. H.	9
dacks), N. Y.	8	Valley View Springs, Va.	332
Saranac Inn (Adirondacks),		Virginia Beach, Va.	332 334
N. Y.	7 8	Warm Springs, Va.	334 335
Saranac Lake (Adirondacks),		Watch Hill, R. I.	336
N. Y.	8	Watkins Glen, N. Y.	337 340
Saratoga Springs, N. Y.	304 308	Waynesville, N. C.	340 341
Scarboro Beach, Me.	308 309	Wernersville, Pa.	341
Schroon Lake (Adirondacks),		West End, N. J.	342
N. Y.	8	West Hurley (Catskill Mount-	
Seneca Lake, N. Y.	337 340	ains), N. Y.	65
Seven Mile Ford, Va.	333	West Ossipee, N. H.	342 343
Shandaken (Catskill Mount-		West Point, N. Y.	343
ains), N. Y.	65	Whitefield, N. H.	343 346
Sharon Springs, N. Y.	309 310	White Sulphur Sp'gs, W. Va.	346 348
Sharon Sp'gs-Wytheville, Va.	350 351	Willow Grove, Va.	348
Shawsville (for Alleghany		Winter Harbor, Me.	349 350
Springs), Va.	10 11	Wytheville-Sharon Sp'gs, Va.	350 351
Sheldrake, N. Y.	310	York Beach, Me.	351 352
Shelter Island, N. Y.	312 313	York Harbor, Me.	352 353

SPECIAL INSTRUCTIONS TO AGENTS

AND

INFORMATION FOR THE PUBLIC.

1. Tickets herein described are sold from June 1st to September 30th, inclusive, and are good for return trip until October 31st, 1892, inclusive, and should be so limited with an "L" punch, except when otherwise noted.

2. Excursion tickets to Asheville and Hot Springs, N. C., and Harrogate, Tenn., are good for passage three (3) months from date of sale, and are good for use south-bound only within fifteen (15) days from date of issue as stamped on back of ticket; they must be presented at the ticket agency of the initial line at the destination point for identification and stamping before they can be used for the return trip, and are then good returning only within fifteen (15) days from such date as stamped on the back of ticket; in all cases, however, tickets must be used within the extreme limit.

3. The Asheville, N. C., tickets via Richmond & Danville R. R. may be validated at Hot Springs and *vice versa*.

4. Children under five years of age, free, between five and twelve (both ages inclusive), half fare.

5. Purchasers of Summer Excursion Tickets secure all the privileges accorded to passengers holding other First Class Tickets.

6. Transfers between stations are not included in Excursion Tickets except where specially noted, or transfer coupon is printed in ticket.

7. Passengers can purchase transfer checks for self and baggage through New York north-bound on application to Baltimore & Ohio Railroad agents. The agent, however, will not be permitted to sell transfer tickets for use south-bound.

8. In cases where transfer is included through Boston and New York, in both directions, as noted after routes, two transfer tags will be issued. Where transfer one way only is included, but one transfer tag will be delivered to passenger. Transfer tags, Form T. 15 (baggage only), will be furnished for transfer through Boston, and transfer tags, Form T. 2 (passenger and baggage), will be furnished for transfer through New York.

9. Baggage to the extent of one hundred and fifty (150) pounds will be checked free on Full-Fare Summer Excursion Tickets, and seventy-five (75) pounds on Half-Fare (Children's) Excursion Tickets.

10. Tickets between Cooperstown and Richfield Springs by the Otsego Lake Steamers and Stage are for passage only; baggage will be charged extra.

11. These routes embrace, in addition to those owned and operated by the Baltimore & Ohio Railroad Company, many other railway, stage, and steamboat lines; but while this Company issues tickets for passage over other lines in addition to its own, it acts only as *AGENT FOR THE SALE*, and is not responsible for the carriage of passengers or baggage beyond its own system of roads, such tickets being subject to use in accordance with the rules of the respective companies over which they read.

12. Stop-over may be made at any point named on the tickets; but should passengers desire to leave a train or boat at a station intermediate to those mentioned on a coupon, they should notify the proper official of the train or boat, who will either issue a stop-over check, or mark the ticket, as may be the practice of his company, provided the line on which station is located allows stop-over privileges. For rules of the various lines herein represented see pages xii to xv.

13. On the Richelieu & Ontario Navigation Company's Steamers, meals and berth are included in the rate on west-bound tickets between Montreal and Toronto, but are not included on east-bound tickets. On all other divisions of this line, meals and berths extra.

14. Tickets reading via New York Central & Hudson River Railroad between Canandaigua and Niagara Falls will be accepted for passage either via Lockport or via Buffalo.

15. Tickets reading via New York Central & Hudson River or West Shore Railroads will be accepted for passage on Hudson River Day Line Steamers between New York and Albany without extra charge. To avail themselves of this privilege, north-bound passengers will be required to have their rail tickets exchanged by purser on steamer. South-bound passengers, if via New York Central & Hudson River Railroad, either by conductor before arrival at Albany, or at Depot Ticket Office in that city. If via West Shore Railroad, exchange must be made by conductor before reaching Voorheesville. Rail tickets between Albany and New York will not be accepted for passage on People's (night) Line of Steamers.

16. Tickets reading via Stonington Line will be accepted for passage via Providence Line, and tickets reading via Providence Line will be accepted for passage via Stonington Line.

17. Tickets reading via Day Line Steamers on Hudson River between New York and Albany are good for passage on People's Line.

18. Tickets reading via People's (night) Line Steamers on Hudson River, between New York and Albany, will be accepted for passage on Day Line Steamers, on payment of one ($1.00) dollar additional in each direction, but will not be accepted for passage via rail lines.

19. Passengers holding through tickets via either Delaware & Hudson R. R. or Champlain Transportation Co. may use them via rail or lake between Fort Ticonderoga and Plattsburgh, or Hotel Champlain (Bluff Point), at their option.

20. Tickets reading over the Mount Washington Railroad are usually not available before the middle of June or after the middle of September. Purchasers should consult the proper advertising matter on this subject.

21. Purchasers should consult the proper advertising matter before buying tickets.

22. Tourists should remember that many of the steamer lines cease running or make irregular trips on or about October 1st.

23. Tickets via Sound Line Steamers between New York and Boston include a berth.

24. The coupons of tickets reading via Grand Trunk Railway or steamer between Toronto and Kingston; Kingston and Prescott; Prescott and Montreal; and Montreal and Quebec, —are valid either by rail or by the Richelieu & Ontario Navigation Company's (Royal Mail Line) Steamers.

25. The coupons of tickets reading via Grand Trunk Railway between Niagara Falls and Toronto read by Lewiston and steamer, but can be exchanged (without extra charge), on application to the agents at Niagara Falls, for tickets via rail to Toronto, Grand Trunk Railway (G. W. Division).

26. Tickets via Merchants & Miners' Transportation Company include berth in main saloon. Berths on upper deck extra; one way, $1.50; round trip, $3.00. Berths should be secured in advance.

27. † Rates from Philadelphia and Baltimore marked thus (†), are for basing purposes only.

28. In case application for rate is made to agents at stations from which no rate is quoted herein, advise this office promptly, stating the form number and destination of ticket for which rate is desired; and in case tickets are required make requisition on C. W. Woolford, Ticket Supply Clerk, Camden Station, Baltimore.

NOTE.—Movements of boat lines for season of 1892 will be found on pages 355 to 365.

STOP-OVER PRIVILEGES.

NOTICE.—In case passengers desire to obtain stop-over privileges when the local regulations of any line authorize such concessions, particular care should be observed to take passage on trains or boats scheduled to stop at the desired stopping-place.

ADIRONDACK RAILWAY,	Stop-over allowed on notice to conductor.
BALTIMORE & OHIO R. R.	Stop-over allowed at all stations unless otherwise noted in contract of ticket. Tickets to Deer Park, Md., Mountain Lake Park, Md., and Oakland, Md., sold at stations east of Washington are good to stop at Harper Ferry, Hancock and Cumberland only.
BALTIMORE & EASTERN SHORE R. R.	Stop-over allowed at any station on notice to conductor.
BANGOR & PISCATAQUIS R. R.	Stop-over allowed at any station on notice to conductor.
BATH & HAMMONDSPORT R. R.	Stop-over allowed at any station on notice to conductor.
BENNINGTON & RUTLAND R. R.	Stop-over checks good for 30 days issued upon application to conductor.
BOSTON & ALBANY R. R.	Stop-over allowed for 10 days on notice to conductor.
BOSTON & BANGOR STEAMSHIP LINE.	Stop-over allowed at any station on notice to purser.
BOSTON & MAINE R. R.	Stop-over for 10 days allowed at any station on notice to conductor, except between Salem, (Eastern Division) Reading (Western Division) or Wilmington and Ware (Southern Division) and Boston.
BURLINGTON & LAMOILLE R. R. (See Central Vermont R. R.)	
CANADIAN PACIFIC R. R.	Stop-over allowed on notice to conductor.
CATSKILL MOUNTAIN R. R.	Stop-over allowed at any station on notice to conductor.
CENTRAL R. R. of N. J.	Stop-over allowed on notice to conductor at any point except between New York & Elizabeth.
CENTRAL VERMONT R. R.	Stop-over allowed at any station on notice to conductor.
CHAMPLAIN TRANSPORTATION LINE (Steamer on Lake Champlain).	Stop-over allowed on notice to purser.

ROUTES AND RATES FOR SUMMER TOURS.   xiii

CHATEAUGAY R. R.	Stop-over allowed on notice to conductor.
CHAUTAUQUA STEAMBOAT CO. . . .	No stop-over privileges.
CHESAPEAKE & OHIO RY.	Stop-over allowed at any station on notice to conductor.
CHESHIRE R. R. (See Fitchburg R. R.)	
CITIZENS' LINE STEAMERS (on Hudson River).	Steamers make no intermediate landing.
CONCORD & MONTREAL R. R. . . .	Stop-over allowed at any station on notice to conductor.
CONNECTICUT RIVER R. R.	Stop-over allowed at any station on notice to conductor.
COOPERSTOWN & CHARLOTTE V'Y. R.R.	Stop-over allowed at any station on notice to conductor.
CUMBERLAND VALLEY R. R.	Stop-over allowed at any station on notice to conductor.
DAY LINE STEAMERS (on Hudson R.)	Stop-over allowed on notice to purser.
DELAWARE & HUDSON R. R.	Stop-over allowed at any station on notice to conductor.
DEL., LACKA. & WESTERN R. R. . .	Stop-over allowed at any station on notice to conductor.
DETROIT & CLEVE. STEAM NAV. CO. . .	Stop-over allowed on up trip only at Detroit, St. Clair Springs and Alpena.
FALL BROOK COAL CO.	Stop-over allowed at any station on notice to conductor.
FALL R. LINE (Old Col. S. B. Line) .	Stop-over allowed at Newport, R. I., in either direction on notice to purser.
FITCHBURG R. R.	Stop-over allowed on notice to conductor.
GRAND TRUNK R. R.	Stop-over allowed at any station on notice to conductor.
INLAND & SEABOARD COASTING CO.	(See People's Washington & Norfolk Steamboat Co.)
INTERCOLONIAL RY.	Stop-over allowed at any station on notice to conductor.
KAATERSKILL R. R.	Stop-over allowed at any station on notice to conductor.
KNOX & LINCOLN RY.	(See Maine Central R. R.)
LEHIGH VALLEY R. R.	Stop-over allowed at any station on notice to conductor.
LONG ISLAND R. R.	No stop-over privileges.
MAINE CENTRAL R. R.	Stop-over allowed at any station on notice to conductor, except on special Bar Harbor excursion tickets, which are limited to continuous passage in each direction.
MICHIGAN CENTRAL R. R.	Stop-over allowed at Bay City, Saginaw, and points north thereof.
MT. WASHINGTON R. R.	No intermediate stops.

NARRAGANSETT PIER R. R.	No stopover privileges.
NEW BEDFORD, MARTHA'S VINEYARD & NANTUCKET S. B. LINE	Stopover allowed for 10 days on notice to purser.
NEW LONDON NORTHERN R. R.	(See Central Vermont R. R.)
N. Y. CEN. & HUDSON RIVER R. R.	Stopover allowed at any station on notice to conductor.
N. Y., LAKE ERIE & WEST. R. R.	Stopover allowed on notice to conductor.
N. Y. & NEW ENGLAND R. R.	Stopover allowed on notice to conductor.
N. Y., NEW HAVEN & HART. R. R.	Stopover allowed on notice to conductor.
N. Y., ONTARIO & WESTERN R. R.	Stopover allowed on notice to conductor.
N. Y., PROVIDENCE & BOSTON R. R.	Stopover privileges allowed on application to conductor.
NORFOLK & WESTERN R. R.	Stopover allowed at any station on notice to conductor.
NORTHERN ADIRONDACK R. R.	Stopover allowed at any station on notice to conductor.
NORWICH LINE (Norwich & N. Y. Trans. Line).	Steamers make no intermediate landings.
OLD COLONY R. R.	One stopover allowed at any station on notice to conductor.
OLD COLONY STEAMBOAT LINE (Fall River Line).	Stopover allowed at Newport, R. I., in either direction on notice to purser.
PENNSYLVANIA R. R.	Stopover allowed at any station on notice to conductor, except on iron-clad (or signature) tickets.
PEOPLE'S (NIGHT) LINE STEAMERS (on Hudson River).	Steamers make no intermediate landing.
PEOPLE'S WASHINGTON & NORFOLK STEAMBOAT CO.	No stopover privileges allowed.
PHILADELPHIA & READING R. R.	Stopover allowed at any station on notice to conductor.
PORTLAND, MT. DESERT & MACHIAS STEAMBOAT LINE.	Stopover allowed at any landing on notice to purser.
PORTLAND & ROCHESTER R. R.	Stopover allowed at any station on notice to conductor.
PORTLAND STEAM PACKET LINE.	Steamers make no intermediate landings.
PROFILE & FRANCONIA NOTCH R. R.	Stopover allowed at any station on notice to conductor.
PROVIDENCE LINE (Providence & Stonington Steamship Co.).	Steamers make no intermediate landing.
PROVIDENCE & WORCESTER R. R.	(See N. Y., Providence & Boston R. R.)
RICHELIEU & ONTARIO NAVIGATION CO.	Stopover allowed on notice to purser.
RICHMOND & DANVILLE R. R.	Stopover allowed at any station on notice to conductor.

ROUTES AND RATES FOR SUMMER TOURS. xv

ROME, WATER'N & OGDENS'G R. R. (N. Y. C. & H. R. R., Lessee)...	Stopover checks issued on notice to conductor.
SCHROON LAKE STEAMBOAT LINE...	Stopover allowed on notice to captain.
SHENANDOAH VALLEY R. R. (See Norfolk and Western R. R.)	
STEAMERS BETWEEN CLAYTON AND ALEXANDRIA BAY..........	Stopover allowed for 30 days.
STEAMER ON CAYUGA LAKE......	Stopover allowed at any station on notice to captain.
STEAMER ON LAKE CHAMPLAIN (Champlain Transportation Co.)	Stopover allowed on notice to purser.
STEAMER ON LAKE GEORGE......	Stopover allowed on notice to purser.
STEAMER ON OTSEGO LAKE......	Stopover allowed at all landings on notice to captain.
STEAMER ON SENECA LAKE (Seneca Lake Steam Nav. Line).....	Stopover allowed at all landings.
STEAMER "MARY POWELL".....	No stopover privileges.
STONINGTON LINE (Prov. & Stonington Steamship Co.)........	Steamers make no intermediate landing.
STONY CLOVE & CATS. MOUN. R. R.	Stopover allowed at any station on notice to conductor.
SYRACUSE, GEN. & CORNING R. R.	(See Fall Brook Coal Co.)
ULSTER & DELAWARE R. R.....	Stopover allowed at any station on notice to conductor.
VERMONT VALLEY R. R........	Stopover allowed at any station on notice to conductor.
WALKILL VALLEY R. R.........	Stopover allowed at any station on notice to conductor.
WESTERN MARYLAND R. R.	One stopover each way allowed on notice to conductor.
WEST SHORE R. R.	Stopover allowed at any station on notice to conductor.
WESTERN N. Y. & PENNA. R. R...	One stopover allowed on notice to conductor.
WILLIAMSPORT & NORTH BRANCH R. R...............	Stopover allowed at any station on notice to conductor.
YORK HARBOR & BEACH R. R. (See Boston & Maine.)	

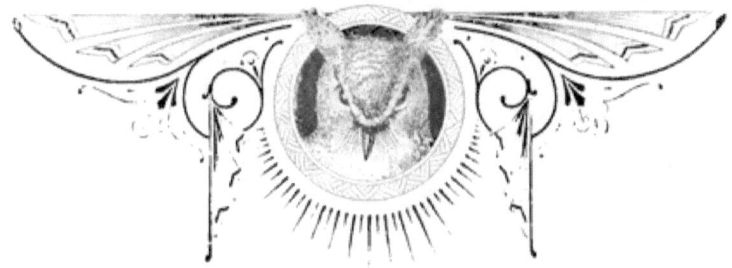

Bases for Constructing Through Rates from Coupon Ticket Stations to Summer Excursion Resorts reached VIA PHILADELPHIA.

Agents at Chester, Pa., Wilmington, Del., Newark, Del., and Havre de Grace, Md., will add the basing rates as quoted below *to Philadelphia* to the basing rates quoted herein *from Philadelphia*, such combined rates not to exceed Baltimore rates published herein.

Agents at the following stations, not including the above, will add the basing rates as given below *to Philadelphia or Baltimore* to the rates quoted herein *from Philadelphia or Baltimore* and adopt the lower rate, unless such rate exceeds rate quoted herein from point mentioned in right-hand column.

The basing rates quoted below to New York are to be used in constructing rates to Montreal, P. Q., and return only, basis for which is given on page 203.

FROM		Basing Rate to Baltimore and return.	Basing Rate to Philadelphia and return.	Basing Rate to New York and return.	NOT TO EXCEED
Baltimore	Md.		$4 00	$8 00	
Bellaire	Ohio	$16 05	20 05	24 05	
Berkeley Springs	W.Va.	5 75	9 75	13 75	
Cameron	W.Va.	14 60	18 60	22 60	Wheeling.
Charlestown	W.Va.	4 30	8 30	12 30	
Chester	Pa.		50	4 50	Baltimore.
Clarksburg	W.Va.	12 65	16 65	20 65	Parkersburg.
Connellsville	Pa.	11 40	15 40	19 40	Pittsburgh.
Cumberland	Md.	7 50	11 50	15 50	Pittsburgh.
Deer Park	Md.	9 00	13 00	17 00	Wheeling.
Fairmont	W.Va.	12 60	16 60	20 60	Wheeling.
Frederick	Md.	2 45	6 45	10 45	
Grafton	W.Va.	11 75	15 75	19 75	Wheeling.
Hagerstown	Md.	4 50	8 50	12 50	Pittsburgh.
Harper's Ferry	W.Va.	3 80	7 80	11 80	Pittsburgh.
Harrisonburg	Va.	8 80	12 80	16 80	
Havre de Grace	Md.		2 35	6 35	Baltimore.
Johnstown	Pa.	11 45	15 45	19 45	$1.35 more than Pittsburgh.
Keyser	W.Va.	8 60	12 60	16 60	Wheeling.
Lexington	Va.	11 90	15 90	19 90	
McKeesport	Pa.	13 15	16 60	20 60	Pittsburgh.
Martinsburg	W.Va.	4 65	8 65	12 65	Pittsburgh.
Meyersdale	Pa.	9 20	13 20	17 20	Pittsburgh.
Morgantown	W.Va.	13 65	17 65	21 65	90 cts. more than Wheeling.
Moundsville	W.Va.	15 40	19 40	23 40	Wheeling.
Mountain Lake Park	Md.	9 15	13 15	17 15	Wheeling.
Mt. Pleasant	Pa.	11 90	15 90	19 90	30 cts. more than Pittsburgh.
Newark	Del.		1 50	5 50	Baltimore.
Oakland	Md.	9 25	13 25	17 25	Wheeling.
Parkersburg	W.Va.	15 75	19 75	23 75	
Piedmont	W.Va.	8 80	12 80	16 80	Wheeling.
Pittsburgh	Pa.	13 70	16 60	20 60	
Rockwood	Pa.	9 65	13 65	17 65	Pittsburgh.
Somerset	Pa.	10 05	14 05	18 05	30 cts. more than Pittsburgh.
Staunton	Va.	10 10	14 10	18 10	
Strasburg	Va.	6 45	10 45	14 45	
Uniontown	Pa.	11 85	15 85	19 85	Pittsburgh.
Washington	D.C.	2 00	6 00	10 00	
Washington	Pa.	14 80	18 20	22 20	$1.30 more than Pittsburgh.
Wheeling	W.Va.	15 75	19 75	23 75	
Wilmington	Del.		1 00	5 00	Baltimore.
Winchester	Va.	5 40	9 40	13 40	

The above rates are for basing purposes only, and must not be used in selling tickets to Baltimore, Philadelphia and New York.

SUMMER EXCURSION TICKETS

AND ANY FURTHER INFORMATION THAT MAY BE DESIRED CAN BE OBTAINED BY APPLYING TO OR ADDRESSING THE FOLLOWING AGENTS OF THE COMPANY:

NEW YORK CITY.

C. P. CRAIG	Gen. East'n Pass. Agt.	No. 415 Broadway.
C. B. JONES	Ticket Agent	No. 415 Broadway.
THOS. COOK & SON	Ticket Agents	No. 261 Broadway.
H. G. FABOAT	Ticket Agent	No. 1140 Broadway.
A. J. OESTERLA	Ticket Agent	No. 172 Broadway.
FRANK L. WHITCOMB	Ticket Agent	No. 31 E. 14th St.

PHILADELPHIA, PA.

C. R. MACKENZIE	Dist. Passenger Agent	No. 833 Chestnut St.
FRANK W. CARPENTER	Ticket Agent	No. 833 Chestnut St.
C. D. GLADDING	Ticket Agent	Station 20th and Chestnut Streets.
M. ROSENBAUM	Ticket Agent	No. 609 South Third St. and 1290 N. Second St.
W. H. McCORMICK	Ticket Agent	N. E. Cor. Broad and Chestnut Streets.

BALTIMORE, MD.

B. F. BOND	Div. Passenger Agent	Central Building.
E. B. JONES	Ticket Agent	Camden Station.
G. D. CRAWFORD	Ticket Agent	Central Building.
G. LEIMBACH	Ticket Agent	No. 220 S. Broadway.

WASHINGTON, D. C.

S. B. HEGE	Passenger Agent	No. 1351 Penna. Ave.
CHAS. H. KEIDEL	Ticket Agent	No. 1351 Penna. Ave.
H. R. BOWSER	Ticket Agent	No. 619 Penna. Ave.
J. LEWIS, Jr.	Ticket Agent	Station, New Jersey Av. and C St.

PITTSBURGH, PA.

E. D. SMITH	Div. Passenger Agent	Fifth Ave. & Wood St.
C. E. GREGORY	Ticket Agent	Fifth Ave. & Wood St.
J. J. McCORMICK	Ticket Agent	No. 639 Smithfield St.
S. J. HUTCHINSON	Ticket Agent	B. & O. Station.

And all other Agents of the Company.

CHAS. O. SCULL,
    Gen'l Passenger Agent,
        Baltimore, Md.

J. M. SCHRYVER,
    Ass't Gen'l Passenger Agent,
        Baltimore, Md.

Baggage Checked from Hotel and Private Residence.

Summer Excursion Routes and Rates.

ABINGDON, VA.

FORM EX. 20. ABINGDON, VA. AND RETURN.

Baltimore & Ohio R. R. . . . . to Shenandoah Junc.
Norfolk & Western R. R. . . . . to Abingdon.

Returning, same route.

THROUGH RATES.

Baltimore, Md.	$19 15	Morgantown, W. Va.	$25 40
Bellaire, O.	27 80	Moundsville, W. Va.	27 40
Berkeley Springs, W. Va.	17 90	Mountain Lake Park, Md.	21 55
Cameron, W. Va.	26 90	Mt. Pleasant, Pa.	23 65
Chester, Pa.	22 95	Newark, Del.	21 75
Clarksburg, W. Va.	24 40	New York, N. Y.	27 15
Connellsville, Pa.	23 15	Oakland, Md.	21 05
Cumberland, Md.	19 65	Parkersburg, W. Va.	27 50
Deer Park, Md.	21 40	Philadelphia, Pa.	23 15
Fairmont, W. Va.	24 40	Piedmont, W. Va.	20 60
Frederick, Md.	17 20	Pittsburgh, Pa.	23 15
Grafton, W. Va.	23 50	Rockwood, Pa.	21 10
Harper's Ferry, W. Va.	16 40	Somerset, Pa.	21 80
Havre de Grace, Md.	20 90	Uniontown, Pa.	23 60
Johnstown, Pa.	23 20	Washington, D. C.	17 15
Keyser, W. Va.	20 40	Washington, Pa.	26 55
McKeesport, Pa.	24 90	Wheeling, W. Va.	27 50
Martinsburg, W. Va.	16 30	Wilmington, Del.	22 15
Meyersdale, Pa.	20 95		

ADIRONDACKS.

The general elevation of the Adirondacks surpasses any range east of the Rocky Mountains. More than five hundred mountains, wild and savage in appearance, range themselves in picturesque confusion, for the most part covered with primeval forests, the highest only exposing their rock-bare summits. Hundreds of beautiful lakes lie in the valleys, at high elevations above the sea. A writer in "Picturesque America" describes the lakes as "all lovely and romantic in everything except their names; and the scenery they offer, in combination with the towering mountains and the old and savage forest, is not surpassed on earth." Fine hotels and well-kept boarding-houses are now found throughout the region, and every year witnesses an increased number of tourists, while there is a very large yearly addition to the number who make their summer homes in this delightful wilderness. Chief among the attractive resorts are Blue Mountain Lake, Raquette Lake, Forked Lake and Long Lake, reached by the picturesque Adirondack Railway.

ROUTES AND RATES FOR SUMMER TOURS. 3

FORM EX. 121.—AU SABLE CHASM, N. Y., AND RETURN.

Baltimore & Ohio R. R. . . . . to Philadelphia.
Philadelphia & Reading R. R. . . . . to Bound Brook.
Central R. R. of New Jersey . . . . to New York.
New York Central & Hudson River R. R. . . . to Troy.
Delaware & Hudson R. R. . . . . to Port Kent.
Keeseville, Au Sable Chasm & L. Champlain R. R. to Au Sable Chasm.

Returning, same route.

THROUGH RATES.

Baltimore, Md. . . . . $22 50 | Washington, D. C. $24 50
†Philadelphia, Pa. . . . . 18 50 |

FORM EX. 122.—AU SABLE CHASM, N. Y., AND RETURN.

Baltimore & Ohio R. R. . . . . to Philadelphia.
Philadelphia & Reading R. R. . . . . to Bound Brook.
Central R. R. of New Jersey . . . . to New York.
West Shore R. R. . . . . to Albany.
Delaware & Hudson R. R. . . . . to Port Kent.
Keeseville, Au Sable Chasm & L. Champlain R. R. to Au Sable Chasm.

Returning, same route.
Transfer through New York in both directions, included.

THROUGH RATES.

Baltimore, Md. . . . . $22 50 | Washington, D. C. $24 50
†Philadelphia, Pa. . . . . 18 50 |

FORM EX. 805.—AU SABLE CHASM, N. Y., AND RETURN.

Baltimore & Ohio R. R. . . . . to Philadelphia.
Philadelphia & Reading R. R. . . . . to Bound Brook.
Central R. R. of New Jersey . . . . to New York.
Day or People's Line Steamers . . . . to Albany.
Delaware & Hudson R. R. . . . . to Port Kent.
Keeseville, Au Sable Chasm & L. Champlain R. R. to Au Sable Chasm.

Returning, same route.

THROUGH RATES.

Baltimore, Md. . . . . $20 50 | Washington, D. C. $22 50
†Philadelphia, Pa. . . . . 16 50 |

FORM EX. 731.—BLUE MOUNTAIN LAKE, N. Y., AND RETURN.

Adirondack Ry. . . . . Saratoga to North Creek.
Stage . . . . to Blue Mountain Lake.

Returning, same route.

To be sold only in connection with summer excursion forms passing through or terminating at Saratoga.

Rate $9 50

FORM EX. 732.—BLUE MOUNTAIN HOUSE, N. Y., AND RETURN.

Baltimore & Ohio R. R. . . . . to Philadelphia.
Philadelphia & Reading R. R. . . . . to Bound Brook.
Central R. R. of New Jersey . . . . to New York.
New York Central & Hudson River R. R. . . . to Utica.
Rome, Watertown & Ogdensburg R. R. . . . . to Norwood.
Central Vermont R. R. (O. & L. C. Div.) . . . to Moira.
Northern Adirondack R. R. . . . . to Spring Cove.
Stage . . . . to Blue Mountain House.

Returning, same route.

AU SABLE CHASM.

THROUGH RATES.

Baltimore, Md. . . . . . . $28.50 | Washington, D. C. $30.50
Philadelphia, Pa. . . . . . 24.50 |

FORM EX. 733.—CHILDWOLD PARK HOUSE, N. Y., AND RETURN.

Baltimore & Ohio R. R. . . . . to Philadelphia.
Philadelphia & Reading R. R. . . . . . . to Bound Brook.
Central R. R. of New Jersey . . . . to New York.
New York Central & Hudson River R. R. . to Utica.

```
Rome, Watertown & Ogdensburg R. R. . . . to Norwood.
Central Vermont R. R. (O. & L. C. Div.) . . to Moira.
Northern Adirondack R. R. . . . . . . . . to Childwold Station.
Stage . . . . . . . . . . . . . . . . . . . to Childwold Park House.
                        Returning, same route.
                          THROUGH RATES.
Baltimore, Md. . . . . . $31 85 | Washington, D. C. . . . . $33 85
†Philadelphia, Pa. . . . . 27 85 |
```

Form Ex. 172.—Forked Lake Carry, N. Y., and Return.

```
Baltimore & Ohio R. R. . . . . . . . . . . to Philadelphia.
Philadelphia & Reading R. R. . . . . . . . to Bound Brook.
Central R. R. of New Jersey . . . . . . . . to New York.
New York Central & Hudson River R. R. . to Troy.
Delaware & Hudson R. R. . . . . . . . . . to Saratoga.
Adirondack Ry. . . . . . . . . . . . . . . to North Creek.
Stage . . . . . . . . . . . . . . . . . . . to Blue Mount'n Lake.
Blue Mountain and Raquette Lake Steamb't Line, to Forked Lake Carry.
                        Returning, same route.
                          THROUGH RATES.
Baltimore, Md. . . . . . $28 50 | Washington, D. C. . . . . $30 50
†Philadelphia, Pa. . . . . 24 50 |
```

Form Ex. 173.—Forked Lake Carry, N. Y., and Return.

```
Baltimore & Ohio R. R. . . . . . . . . . . to Philadelphia.
Philadelphia & Reading R. R. . . . . . . . to Bound Brook.
Central R. R. of New Jersey . . . . . . . . to New York.
West Shore R. R. . . . . . . . . . . . . . to Albany.
Delaware & Hudson R. R. . . . . . . . . . to Saratoga.
Adirondack Ry. . . . . . . . . . . . . . . to North Creek.
Stage . . . . . . . . . . . . . . . . . . . to Blue Mount'n Lake.
Blue Mountain and Raquette Lake Steamb't Line, to Forked Lake Carry.
                        Returning, same route.
    Transfer through New York, in both directions, included.
                          THROUGH RATES.
Baltimore, Md. . . . . . $28 50 | Washington, D. C. . . . . $30 50
†Philadelphia, Pa. . . . . 24 50 |
```

Form Ex. 730.—Lake Placid, N. Y., and Return.

```
Chateaugay R. R. . . . . . . . . . Plattsburgh to Saranac Lake.
O'Brien's Stage Line . . . . . . . . . . . to Lake Placid.
                        Returning, same route.
   To be sold only in connection with summer excursion forms passing
through or terminating at Plattsburgh.
Rate . . . . . . . . . . . . . . . . . . . . . . . . . . . . $7 00
```

Form Ex. 727.—Loon Lake House, N. Y., and Return.

```
Chateaugay R. R. . . . . . . . . . Plattsburgh to Loon Lake Station.
Chase's Stage (4 miles) . . . . . . . . . . to Loon Lake House.
                        Returning, same route.
   To be sold only in connection with summer excursion forms passing
through or terminating at Plattsburgh.
Rate . . . . . . . . . . . . . . . . . . . . . . . . . . . . $4 80
```

Form Ex. 804.—North Creek, N. Y., and Return.

```
Adirondack Ry . . . . . . . . . . . . Saratoga to North Creek.
                        Returning, same route.
   Sold in connection with any ticket passing through or terminating
at Saratoga.
Rate . . . . . . . . . . . . . . . . . . . . . . . . . . . . $3 50
```

FORM EX. 225. PAUL SMITH'S, N. Y., AND RETURN.

Baltimore & Ohio R. R. . . . . to Philadelphia.
Philadelphia & Reading R. R. . . . . to Bound Brook.
Central R. R. of New Jersey . . . . to New York.
New York Central & Hudson River R. R. . . . . to Utica.
Rome, Watertown & Ogdensburg R. R. . . . . . to Norwood.
Central Vermont R. R. (O. & L. C. Div.) . . . . to Moira.
Northern Adirondack R. R. . . . . to Paul Smith's Stat'n
Paul Smith's Stages . . . . to Paul Smith's.
Returning, same route.

THROUGH RATES.

Baltimore, Md. . . . . . $29 00 | Washington, D. C. $31 00
|Philadelphia, Pa. . . . . 25 00 |

FORM EX. 227. PAUL SMITH'S, N. Y., AND RETURN.

Baltimore & Ohio R. R. . . . . to Philadelphia.
Philadelphia & Reading R. R. . . . . to Bound Brook.
Central R. R. of New Jersey . . . . to New York.
West Shore R. R. . . . . to Utica.
Rome, Watertown & Ogdensburg R. R. . . . . . to Norwood.
Central Vermont R. R. (O. & L. C. Div.) . . . . to Moira.
Northern Adirondack R. R. . . . . to Paul Smith's Stat'n
Paul Smith's Stages . . . . to Paul Smith's.
Returning, same route.
Transfer through New York, in both directions, included.

THROUGH RATES.

Baltimore, Md. . . . . . $29 00 | Washington, D. C. $31 00
|Philadelphia, Pa. . . . . 25 00 |

FORM EX. 229. PAUL SMITH'S, N. Y., AND RETURN.

Baltimore & Ohio R. R. . . . . to Philadelphia.
Philadelphia & Reading R. R. . . . . to Bound Brook.
Central R. R. of New Jersey . . . . to New York.
New York Central & Hudson River R. R. . . . . to Troy.
Fitchburg R. R. . . . . to White Creek.
Bennington & Rutland R. R. . . . . to Rutland.
Central Vermont R. R. (O. & L. C. Div.) . . . . to Moira.
Northern Adirondack R. R. . . . . to Paul Smith's Stat'n
Paul Smith's Stages . . . . to Paul Smith's.
Returning, same route.

THROUGH RATES.

Baltimore, Md. . . . . . $29 00 | Washington, D. C. $31 00
|Philadelphia, Pa. . . . . 25 00 |

FORM EX. 230. PAUL SMITH'S, N. Y., AND RETURN.

Baltimore & Ohio R. R. . . . . to Philadelphia.
Philadelphia & Reading R. R. . . . . to Bound Brook.
Central R. R. of New Jersey . . . . to New York.
West Shore R. R. . . . . to Albany.
Delaware & Hudson R. R. . . . . to Troy.
Fitchburg R. R. . . . . to White Creek.
Bennington & Rutland R. R. . . . . to Rutland.
Central Vermont R. R. (O. & L. C. Div.) . . . . to Moira.
Northern Adirondack R. R. . . . . to Paul Smith's Stat'n
Paul Smith's Stages . . . . to Paul Smith's.
Returning, same route.
Transfer through New York, in both directions, included.

THROUGH RATES.

Baltimore, Md. . . . . . $29 00 | Washington, D. C. $31 00
|Philadelphia, Pa. . . . . 25 00 |

| Philadelphia, Pa | 25 00 |

ROUTES AND RATES FOR SUMMER TOURS.

FORM EX. 805.—PAUL SMITH'S, N. Y., AND RETURN.

Chateaugay R. R. . . . . .Plattsburg to Bloomingdale.
St. Regis Stage Co. (6 miles) . . . . .to Paul Smith's.
Returning, same route.

Sold in connection with any ticket passing through or terminating at Plattsburgh.

Rate $6 25

FORM EX. 806.—RAQUETTE LAKE, N. Y., AND RETURN.

Adirondack Ry. . . . . .Saratoga to North Creek.
Stage (29 miles) . . . . .to Blue Mountain Lake.
Blue Mountain & Raquette Lake Steamers . . .to Raquette Lake.
Returning, same route.

Sold in connection with any ticket passing through or terminating at Saratoga.

Rate $12 00

FORM EX. 734.—SANTA CLARA, N. Y., AND RETURN.

Baltimore & Ohio R. R. . . . . .to Philadelphia.
Philadelphia & Reading R. R. . . . . .to Bound Brook.
Central R. R. of New Jersey . . . . .to New York.
New York Central & Hudson River R. R. . . .to Utica.
Rome, Watertown & Ogdensburg R. R. . . . .to Norwood.
Central Vermont R. R. (O. & L. C. Div.) . . .to Moira.
Northern Adirondack R. R. . . . . .to Santa Clara.
Returning, same route.

THROUGH RATES.

Baltimore, Md. . . . . . $26 30 | Washington, D. C. $28 30
Philadelphia, Pa. . . . . 22 30 |

FORM EX. 234.—SARANAC INN, N. Y., AND RETURN.

Baltimore & Ohio R. R. . . . . .to Philadelphia.
Philadelphia & Reading R. R. . . . . .to Bound Brook.
Central R. R. of New Jersey . . . . .to New York.
New York Central & Hudson River R. R. . . .to Utica.
Rome, Watertown & Ogdensburg R. R. . . . .to Norwood.
Central Vermont R. R. (O. & L. C. Div.) . . .to Moira.
Northern Adirondack R. R. . . . . .to Saranac Inn Station
Stage . . . . .to Saranac Inn.
Returning, same route.

THROUGH RATES.

Baltimore, Md. . . . . . $30 00 | Washington, D. C. $32 00
Philadelphia, Pa. . . . . 26 00 |

FORM EX. 235.—SARANAC INN, N. Y., AND RETURN.

Baltimore & Ohio R. R. . . . . .to Philadelphia.
Philadelphia & Reading R. R. . . . . .to Bound Brook.
Central R. R. of New Jersey . . . . .to New York.
West Shore R. R. . . . . .to Utica.
Rome, Watertown & Ogdensburg R. R. . . . .to Norwood.
Central Vermont R. R. (O. & L. C. Div.) . . .to Moira.
Northern Adirondack R. R. . . . . .to Saranac Inn Station
Stage . . . . .to Saranac Inn.
Returning, same route.

Transfer through New York, in both directions, included.

THROUGH RATES.

Baltimore, Md. . . . . . $30 00 | Washington, D. C. $32 00
Philadelphia, Pa. . . . . 26 00 |

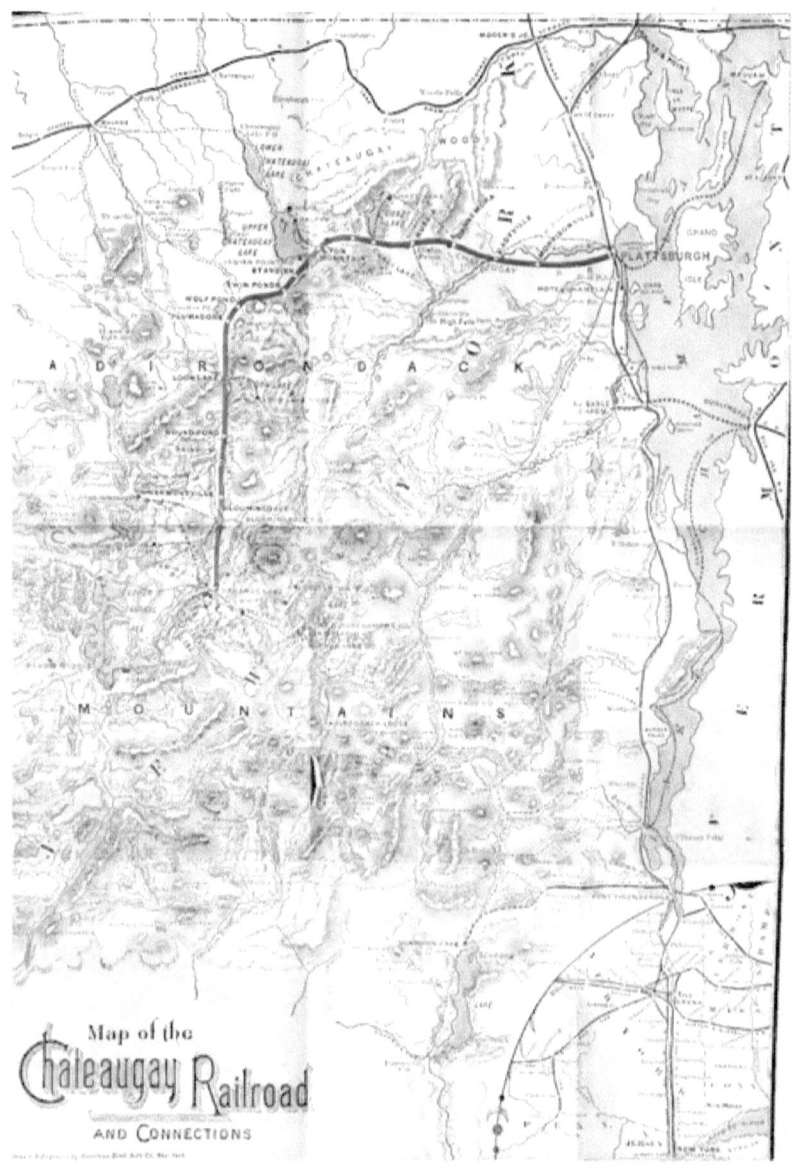

FORM EX. 728.— SARANAC INN, N. Y., AND RETURN.
Chateaugay R. R. . . . . Plattsburgh to Saranac Lake.
Saranac Inn Stage Line . . . . to Saranac Inn.
                    Returning, same route.
   To be sold only in connection with summer excursion forms passing through or terminating at Plattsburgh.
Rate $7 25

FORM EX. 735.— SARANAC INN STATION, N. Y., AND RETURN.
Baltimore & Ohio R. R. . . . . to Philadelphia.
Philadelphia & Reading R. R. . . . . to Bound Brook.
Central R. R. of New Jersey . . . . to New York.
New York Central & Hudson River R. R. . . . to Utica.
Rome, Watertown & Ogdensburg R. R. . . . . to Norwood.
Central Vermont R. R. (O. & L. C. Div.) . . . . to Moira.
Northern Adirondack R. R. . . . . to Saranac Inn Stat'n.
                    Returning, same route.
                    THROUGH RATES.
Baltimore, Md. . . . . . . $28 00 | Washington, D. C. $30 00
| Philadelphia, Pa. . . . . 24 00 |

FORM EX. 807.— SARANAC LAKE, N. Y., AND RETURN.
Chateaugay R. R. . . . . Plattsburg to Saranac Lake.
                    Returning, same route.
   Sold in connection with any ticket passing through or terminating at Plattsburgh.
Rate $5 65

SCHROON LAKE.

FORM EX. 808.— SCHROON LAKE, N. Y., AND RETURN.
Adirondack Ry. . . . . Saratoga to Riverside.
Leavitt's Stage Line . . . . to Pottersville.
Schroon Lake Steamers . . . . to Schroon Lake.
                    Returning, same route.
   Sold in connection with any ticket passing through or terminating at Saratoga.
Rate $6 50

FORM EX. 736. TUPPER LAKE, N. Y., AND RETURN.

Baltimore & Ohio R. R. . . . . to Philadelphia.
Philadelphia & Reading R. R. . . . . to Bound Brook.
Central R. R. of New Jersey . . . . to New York.
New York Central & Hudson River R. R. . . . to Utica.
Rome, Watertown & Ogdensburg R. R. . . . . to Norwood.
Central Vermont R. R., O. & L. C. Div. . . . . to Moira.
Northern Adirondack R. R. . . . . to Tupper Lake.
Returning, same route.

THROUGH RATES.

Baltimore, Md. . . . . . . $29 05 | Washington, D. C. $31 00
Philadelphia, Pa. . . . . . 25 00 |

FORM EX. 869. UPPER CHATEAUGAY LAKE, N. Y., AND RETURN.

Chateaugay R. R. . . . . . . Plattsburgh to Lyon Mountain.
Stage, 6 miles . . . . to Upper Chateaugay Lake.
Returning, same route.

Sold in connection with any ticket passing through or terminating at Plattsburgh.
Rate. $3 40

AFTON, VA.

FORM EX. 13. AFTON, VA., AND RETURN.

Baltimore & Ohio R. R. . . . . to Staunton.
Chesapeake & Ohio Ry. . . . . to Afton.
Returning, same route.

THROUGH RATES.

Baltimore, Md.	$11 40	Meyersdale, Pa.	$12 70
Bellaire, O.	19 50	Morgantown, W. Va.	17 15
Berkeley Springs, W. Va.	9 25	Moundsville, W. Va.	18 80
Cameron, W. Va.	18 40	Mountain Lake Park, Md.	13 25
Charlestown, W. Va.	6 80	Mt. Pleasant, Pa.	15 40
Chester, Pa.	14 60	Newark, Del.	13 40
Clarksburg, W. Va.	16 15	New York, N. Y.	19 40
Connellsville, Pa.	14 00	Oakland, Md.	13 35
Cumberland, Md.	11 20	Parkersburg, W. Va.	19 50
Deer Park, Md.	13 40	Philadelphia, Pa.	15 40
Fairmont, W. Va.	16 15	Piedmont, W. Va.	12 30
Frederick, Md.	8 35	Pittsburgh, Pa.	17 20
Grafton, W. Va.	15 25	Rockwood, Pa.	15 15
Hagerstown, Md.	8 45	Somerset, Pa.	15 55
Harper's Ferry, W. Va.	7 30	Strasburg, Va.	4 65
Harrisonburg, Va.	2 30	Uniontown, Pa.	15 55
Havre de Grace, Md.	12 55	Washington, D. C.	9 30
Johnstown, Pa.	14 95	Washington, Pa.	18 30
Keyser, W. Va.	12 40	Wheeling, W. Va.	19 30
Lexington, Va.	2 80	Wilmington, Del.	14 40
McKeesport, Pa.	16 65	Winchester, Va.	5 70
Martinsburg, W. Va.	8 05		

FORM EX. 14. AFTON, VA., AND RETURN.

Baltimore & Ohio R. R. . . . . to Shenandoah June.
Norfolk & Western R. R. . . . . to Basic.
Chesapeake & Ohio Ry. . . . . to Afton.
Returning, same route.

THROUGH RATES.

Baltimore, Md.	$9 90	New York, N. Y.	$17 90
Chester, Pa.	13 40	Philadelphia, Pa.	13 90
Havre de Grace, Md.	11 35	Washington, D. C.	7 90
Newark, Del.	12 90	Wilmington, Del.	12 90

FORM EX. 115. AFTON, VA., AND RETURN.

Baltimore & Ohio R. R. . . . . to Washington.
Transfer. . . . . B. & O. Depot to C. & O. Depot.
Chesapeake & Ohio Ry. . . . . to Afton.

Returning, same route.

THROUGH RATES.

Baltimore, Md.	$9 30	Meyersdale, Pa.	$15 40
Bellaire, O.	22 25	Morgantown, W. Va.	19 85
Berkeley Springs, W. Va.	11 85	Moundsville, W. Va.	21 50
Cameron, W. Va.	20 85	Mountain Lake Park, Md.	15 15
Charlestown, W. Va.	10 50	Mt. Pleasant, Pa.	18 40
Chester, Pa.	12 80	Newark, Del.	11 60
Clarksburg, W. Va.	18 85	New York, N. Y.	17 30
Connellsville, Pa.	17 60	Oakland, Md.	15 55
Cumberland, Md.	13 90	Parkersburg, W. Va.	21 95
Deer Park, Md.	15 30	Philadelphia, Pa.	13 30
Fairmont, W. Va.	18 85	Piedmont, W. Va.	15 00
Frederick, Md.	10 10	Pittsburgh, Pa.	19 90
Grafton, W. Va.	17 95	Rockwood, Pa.	15 80
Hagerstown, Md.	10 90	Somerset, Pa.	16 25
Harper's Ferry, W. Va.	10 00	Uniontown, Pa.	18 05
Havre de Grace, Md.	10 75	Washington, Pa.	21 00
Johnstown, Pa.	17 65	Wheeling, W. Va.	21 95
Keyser, W. Va.	14 80	Wilmington, Del.	12 30
McKeesport, Pa.	19 35	Winchester, Va.	11 00
Martinsburg, W. Va.	10 75		

ALLEGHANY SPRINGS (SHAWSVILLE) VA.

FORM EX. S10.—ALLEGHANY SPRINGS (SHAWSVILLE), VA., AND RETURN.

Baltimore & Ohio R. R. . . . . to Washington.
Transfer. . . . . B. & O. Depot to R. & D. Depot.
Richmond & Danville R. R. . . . . to Lynchburg.
Norfolk & Western R. R. . . . . to Shawsville.

Returning, same route.

THROUGH RATES.

Baltimore, Md.	$15 85	New York, N. Y.	$21 85
Chester, Pa.	17 35	Philadelphia, Pa.	17 85
Havre de Grace, Md.	15 30	Washington, D. C.	11 85
Newark, Del.	16 15	Wilmington, Del.	16 85

Stages from Shawsville to Alleghany Springs, distance three miles.

FORM EX. 2.—ALLEGHANY SPRINGS (SHAWSVILLE), VA., AND RETURN.

Baltimore & Ohio R. R. . . . . to Shenandoah June.
Norfolk & Western R. R. . . . . to Shawsville.

Returning, same route.

THROUGH RATES.

Baltimore, Md.	$15 85	Havre de Grace, Md.	$15 30
Bellaire, O.	22 75	Johnstown, Pa.	18 15
Berkeley Springs, W. Va.	12 85	Keyser, W. Va.	15 95
Cameron, W. Va.	21 35	McKeesport, Pa.	19 85
Chester, Pa.	17 35	Martinsburg, W. Va.	11 25
Clarksburg, W. Va.	19 35	Meyersdale, Pa.	15 90
Connellsville, Pa.	18 10	Morgantown, W. Va.	20 35
Cumberland, Md.	14 40	Moundsville, W. Va.	22 05
Deer Park, Md.	16 35	Mountain Lake Park, Md.	16 30
Fairmont, W. Va.	19 35	Mt. Pleasant, Pa.	18 60
Frederick, Md.	12 15	Newark, Del.	16 15
Grafton, W. Va.	18 45	New York, N. Y.	21 85
Harper's Ferry, W. Va.	11 05	Oakland, Md.	16 00

Parkersburg, W. Va.	$22 15	Uniontown, Pa.	$18 55
Philadelphia, Pa.	17 85	Washington, D. C.	14 80
Piedmont, W. Va.	15 55	Washington, Pa.	21 30
Pittsburgh, Pa.	20 40	Wheeling, W. Va.	22 6
Rockwood, Pa.	16 35	Wilmington, Del.	16 85
Somerset, Pa.	16 75		

Stages from Shawsville to Alleghany Springs, distance three miles.

ALEXANDRIA BAY (THOUSAND ISLANDS).

This is the chief summer resort of the unrivaled Thousand Islands. The islands are very numerous, extending from Lake Ontario down the river for a distance of forty miles. On many of the larger islands there are elegant villas. The boating is good and the fishing is fine. Pickerel, mus-kallonge, black bass, and dory reward the angler. As a health resort the Thousand Islands rank very high, and the scenic attractions of Alexandria Bay, with the excellent hotel accommodations available, certainly assure its permanent popularity. Steamers make frequent trips between Clayton, twelve miles distant, and Alexandria Bay.

FORM EX. 280. ALEXANDRIA BAY, N. Y., AND RETURN.

Baltimore & Ohio R. R. . . . . to Philadelphia.
Philadelphia & Reading R. R. . . . . to Bound Brook.
Central R. R. of New Jersey . . . . to New York.
New York, Ontario & Western Ry . . . . to Central Square.
Rome, Watertown & Ogdensburg R. R. . . . . to Clayton.
Thousand Island Steamboat Co. . . . . to Alexandria Bay.

Returning, same route.

THROUGH RATES.

Baltimore, Md. . . . . . $24 00   Washington, D. C. $26 00
Philadelphia, Pa. 20 00

12   BALTIMORE & OHIO RAILROAD COMPANY

FORM EX. 282. ALEXANDRIA BAY, N. Y., AND RETURN.

Baltimore & Ohio R. R. . . . . to Philadelphia.
Philadelphia & Reading R. R. . . . . to Bound Brook.
Central R. R. of New Jersey . . . . to New York.
New York Central & Hudson River R. R. . . . . to Utica.
Rome, Watertown & Ogdensburg R. R. . . . . . to Clayton.
Thousand Island Steamboat Co. . . . . to Alexandria Bay.

Returning, same route.

THROUGH RATES.

Baltimore, Md. . . . . . $24 00 | Washington, D. C. 26 00
Philadelphia, Pa. . . . . 20 00 |

FORM EX. 283. ALEXANDRIA BAY, N. Y., AND RETURN.

Baltimore & Ohio R. R. . . . . to Philadelphia.
Philadelphia & Reading R. R. . . . . to Bound Brook.
Central R. R. of New Jersey . . . . to New York.
West Shore R. R. . . . . to Utica.
Rome, Watertown & Ogdensburg R. R. . . . . . to Clayton.
Thousand Island Steamboat Co. . . . . to Alexandria Bay.

Returning, same route.

Transfer through New York, in both directions, included.

THROUGH RATES.

Baltimore, Md. . . . . . $24 00 | Washington, D. C. 26 00
Philadelphia, Pa. . . . . 20 00 |

FORM EX. 284. ALEXANDRIA BAY, N. Y., AND RETURN.

Baltimore & Ohio R. R. . . . . to Philadelphia.
Philadelphia & Reading R. R. . . . . to Bound Brook.
Central R. R. of New Jersey . . . . to New York.
Delaware, Lackawanna & Western R. R. . . . . to Utica.
Rome, Watertown & Ogdensburg R. R. . . . . . to Clayton.
Thousand Island Steamboat Co. . . . . to Alexandria Bay.

Returning, same route.

THROUGH RATES.

Baltimore, Md. . . . . . $24 00 | Washington, D. C. 26 00
Philadelphia, Pa. . . . . 20 00 |

FORM EX. 554. ALEXANDRIA BAY, N. Y., AND RETURN.

Baltimore & Ohio R. R. . . . . to Philadelphia.
Philadelphia & Reading R. R. . . . . to Bethlehem.
Lehigh Valley R. R. . . . . to Sterling.
Rome, Watertown & Ogdensburg R. R. . . . . . to Clayton.
Thousand Island Steamboat Co. . . . . to Alexandria Bay.

Returning, same route.

THROUGH RATES.

Baltimore, Md. . . . . . $23 85 | Washington, D. C. 25 85
Philadelphia, Pa. . . . . 19 85 |

FORM EX. 555. ALEXANDRIA BAY, N. Y., AND RETURN.

Baltimore & Ohio R. R. . . . . to Philadelphia.
Philadelphia & Reading R. R. . . . . to Bethlehem.
Lehigh Valley R. R. . . . . to Sterling.
Rome, Watertown & Ogdensburg R. R. . . . . . to Clayton.
Thousand Island Steamboat Co. . . . . to Alexandria Bay.

ROUTES AND RATES FOR SUMMER TOURS.   13

Thousand Island Steamboat Co. . . . . to Clayton.
Rome, Watertown & Ogdensburg R. R. . . . . . to Utica.
New York Central & Hudson River R. R. . . . . to New York.
Central R. R. of New Jersey . . . . to Bound Brook.
Philadelphia & Reading R. R. . . . . to Philadelphia.
Baltimore & Ohio R. R. . . . . to starting point.

THROUGH RATES.

Baltimore, Md. . . . . . . $26 00   Washington, D. C. $28 00
†Philadelphia, Pa. 22 00

FORM EX. 556.—ALEXANDRIA BAY, N. Y., AND RETURN.

Baltimore & Ohio R. R. . . . . to Philadelphia.
Philadelphia & Reading R. R. . . . . to Bethlehem.
Lehigh Valley R. R. . . . . to Waverly.
New York, Lake Erie & Western R. R. . . . . . to Niagara Falls.
New York Central & Hudson River R. R. . . . . to Utica.
Rome, Watertown & Ogdensburg R. R. . . . . . to Clayton.
Thousand Island Steamboat Co. . . . . to Alexandria Bay.
Thousand Island Steamboat Co. . . . . to Clayton.
Rome, Watertown & Ogdensburg R. R. . . . . . to Utica.
New York Central & Hudson River R. R. . . . . to Schenectady.
Delaware & Hudson R. R. . . . . to Saratoga.
Delaware & Hudson R. R. . . . . to Albany.
New York & Albany Day Line . . . . to New York.
Central R. R. of New Jersey . . . . to Bound Brook.
Philadelphia & Reading R. R. . . . . to Philadelphia.
Baltimore & Ohio R. R. . . . . to starting point.

THROUGH RATES.

Baltimore, Md. . . . . . . $31 75   Washington, D. C. $33 75
†Philadelphia, Pa. 27 75

FORM EX. 557.—ALEXANDRIA BAY, N. Y., AND RETURN.

Baltimore & Ohio R. R. . . . . to Philadelphia.
Philadelphia & Reading R. R. . . . . to Bethlehem.
Lehigh Valley R. R. . . . . to Waverly.
New York, Lake Erie & Western R. R. . . . . . to Niagara Falls.
West Shore R. R. . . . . to Utica.
Rome, Watertown & Ogdensburg R. R. . . . . . to Clayton.
Thousand Island Steamboat Co. . . . . to Alexandria Bay.
Thousand Island Steamboat Co. . . . . to Clayton.
Rome, Watertown & Ogdensburg R. R. . . . . . to Utica.
West Shore R. R. . . . . to South Schenectady.
Delaware & Hudson R. R. . . . . to Saratoga.
Delaware & Hudson R. R. . . . . to Albany.
New York & Albany Day Line Steamers . . . . to New York.
Central R. R. of New Jersey . . . . to Bound Brook.
Philadelphia & Reading R. R. . . . . to Philadelphia.
Baltimore & Ohio R. R. . . . . to starting point.

THROUGH RATES.

Baltimore, Md. . . . . . . $31 75 | Washington, D. C. $33 75
†Philadelphia, Pa. . . . . . 27 75 |

FORM EX. 558.—ALEXANDRIA BAY, N. Y., AND RETURN.

Baltimore & Ohio R. R. . . . . to Philadelphia.
Philadelphia & Reading R. R. . . . . to Bethlehem.
Central R. R. of New Jersey . . . . to Scranton.
Delaware, Lackawanna & Western R. R. . . . . to Utica.
Rome, Watertown & Ogdensburg R. R. . . . . . to Clayton.
Thousand Island Steamboat Co. . . . . to Alexandria Bay.

LAKE YOUGHIOGHENY ON PICTURESQUE B. & O.

ROUTES AND RATES FOR SUMMER TOURS.   15

Thousand Island Steamboat Co. . . . . to Clayton.
Rome, Watertown & Ogdensburg R. R. . . . . . to Utica.
New York Central & Hudson River R. R. . . . . to New York.
Central R. R. of New Jersey . . . . to Bound Brook
Philadelphia & Reading R. R. . . . . to Philadelphia.
Baltimore & Ohio R. R. . . . . to starting point.

THROUGH RATES.

Baltimore, Md. . . . . . $24 55 | Washington, D. C. $26 55
†Philadelphia, Pa. 20 55

FORM EX. 757.—ALEXANDRIA BAY, N. Y., AND RETURN.

Baltimore & Ohio R. R. . . . . to Philadelphia.
Philadelphia & Reading R. R. . . . . to Bethlehem.
Lehigh Valley R. R. . . . . to Waverly.
New York, Lake Erie & Western R. R. . . . . . to Binghamton
Delaware, Lackawanna & Western R. R. . . . . to Utica.
Rome, Watertown & Ogdensburg R. R. . . . . . to Clayton.
Thousand Island Steamboat Co. . . . . to Alexandria Bay.
Thousand Island Steamboat Co. . . . . to Clayton.
Rome, Watertown & Ogdensburg R. R. . . . . . to Utica.
New York Central & Hudson River R. R. . . . . to Geneva.
Seneca Lake Steam Navigation Co. . . . . to Watkins.
Pennsylvania R. R. . . . . to Elmira.
New York, Lake Erie & Western R. R. . . . . . to Waverly.
Lehigh Valley R. R. . . . . to Bethlehem
Philadelphia & Reading R. R. . . . . to Philadelphia.
Baltimore & Ohio R. R. . . . . to starting point.

THROUGH RATES.

Baltimore, Md. . . . . . $24 35 | Washington, D. C. $26 35
†Philadelphia, Pa. 21 95

FORM EX. 646.—ALEXANDRIA BAY, N. Y., AND RETURN.

Baltimore & Ohio R. R. . . . . to Philadelphia.
Philadelphia & Reading R. R. . . . . to Bound Brook.
Central R. R. of New Jersey . . . . to New York.
New York & Albany Day Line . . . . to Albany.
New York Central & Hudson River R. R. . . . . to Utica.
Rome, Watertown & Ogdensburg R. R. . . . . . to Clayton.
Thousand Island Steamboat Co. . . . . to Alexandria Bay.

Returning, same route.

THROUGH RATES.

Baltimore, Md. . . . . . $22 00 | Washington, D. C. $24 00
†Philadelphia, Pa. 18 00

FORM EX. 647.—ALEXANDRIA BAY, N. Y., AND RETURN.

Baltimore & Ohio R. R. . . . . to Philadelphia.
Philadelphia & Reading R. R. . . . . to Bound Brook.
Central R. R. of New Jersey . . . . to New York.
New York & Albany Day Line . . . . to Albany.
West Shore R. R. . . . . to Utica.
Rome, Watertown & Ogdensburg R. R. . . . . . to Clayton.
Thousand Island Steamboat Co. . . . . to Alexandria Bay

Returning, same route.

THROUGH RATES.

Baltimore, Md. . . . . . $22 00 | Washington, D. C. $24 00
†Philadelphia, Pa. 18 00

FORM EX. 1051.—ALEXANDRIA BAY, AND RETURN.

(For routes to Niagara Falls see page 249.)

Grand Trunk Ry. . . . . Niagara Falls to Toronto.
Grand Trunk Ry. . . . . to Kingston.
Richelieu & Ontario Navigation Co. . . . . . to Alexandria Bay.
Thousand Islands Steamboat Co. . . . . to Clayton.
Rome, Watertown & Ogdensburg R. R. . . . to Utica.
New York Central & Hudson River R. R. . . to New York.
Central R. R. of N. J. . . . . to Bound Brook.
Philadelphia & Reading R. R. . . . . to Philadelphia.
Baltimore & Ohio R. R. . . . . to starting point.

THROUGH RATES.

Baltimore, Md. . . . . . . $30 00 | Washington, D. C. $32 00
[Philadelphia, Pa. . . . . . 26 00 |

FORM EX. 1060.—ALEXANDRIA BAY, N. Y., AND RETURN.

(For routes to Niagara Falls see page 249.)

Grand Trunk Ry. . . . . to Toronto.
Grand Trunk Ry. . . . . to Gananoque Junc.
Thousand Islands Ry. . . . . to Gananoque.
Deseronto Navigation Co. . . . . to Alexandria Bay.
Thousand Island Steamboat Co. . . . . to Clayton.
Rome, Watertown & Ogdensburg R. R. . . to Utica.
New York Central & Hudson River R. R. . . to New York.
Central R. R. of New Jersey . . . . to Bound Brook.
Philadelphia & Reading R. R. . . . . to Philadelphia.
Baltimore & Ohio R. R. . . . . to starting point.

THROUGH RATES.

Baltimore, Md. . . . . . . $30 00 | Washington, D. C. $32 00
[Philadelphia, Pa. 26 00

ALTON BAY, N. H.

FORM EX. 811.—TO ALTON BAY, N. H., AND RETURN.

(Via Sound Lines and Boston in both directions.)

Baltimore & Ohio R. R. . . . . to Philadelphia.
Philadelphia & Reading R. R. . . . . to Bound Brook.
Central R. R. of New Jersey . . . . to New York.
Sound Lines (see pages 50 to 55 for route) . . . to Boston.
Boston & Maine R. R. . . . . to Alton Bay.

Returning, same route.

THROUGH RATES.

Baltimore, Md. . . . . . . $20 80 | Washington, D. C. $22 80
[Philadelphia, Pa. . . . . . 16 80 |

FORM EX. 811.—TO ALTON BAY, N. H., AND RETURN.

(Via Rail Lines and Boston in both directions.)

Baltimore & Ohio R. R. . . . . to Philadelphia.
Rail Lines (see pages 50 to 55 for route) . . . to Boston.
Boston & Maine R. R. . . . . to Alton Bay.

Returning, same route.

THROUGH RATES.

Baltimore, Md. . . . . . . $22 80 | Washington, D. C. $24 80
[Philadelphia, Pa. . . . . . 18 80 |

ROUTES AND RATES FOR SUMMER TOURS. 17

FORM EX. SH.—TO ALTON BAY, N. H., AND RETURN.

(Via Rail Lines and Boston; returning via Boston and Sound Lines.)

Baltimore & Ohio R. R. . . . . to Philadelphia.
Rail Lines (see pages 50 to 55 for routes) . . . . . to Boston.
Boston & Maine R. R. . . . . to Alton Bay.
Boston & Maine R. R. . . . . to Boston.
Sound Lines (see pages 50 to 55 for routes) . . . . to New York.
Central R. R. of New Jersey . . . . to Bound Brook.
Philadelphia & Reading R. R. . . . . to Philadelphia.
Baltimore & Ohio R. R. . . . . to starting point.

THROUGH RATES.

Baltimore, Md. . . . . . . $24 80 Washington, D. C. . . . $25 80
†Philadelphia, Pa. 17 80

FORM EX. SH.—TO ALTON BAY, N. H., AND RETURN.

(Via Sound Lines and Boston; returning, all rail.)

Baltimore & Ohio R. R. . . . . to Philadelphia.
Philadelphia & Reading R. R. . . . . to Bound Brook.
Central R. R. of New Jersey . . . . to New York.
Sound Lines (see pages 50 to 55 for routes) . . . . to Boston.
Boston & Maine R. R. . . . . to Alton Bay.
Boston & Maine R. R. . . . . to Boston.
Rail Lines (see pages 50 to 55 for routes) . . . . . to Philadelphia.
Baltimore & Ohio R. R. . . . . to starting point.

THROUGH RATES.

Baltimore, Md. . . . . . . $24 80 Washington, D. C. . . . $25 80
†Philadelphia, Pa. 17 80

ASHEVILLE, N. C.

FORM EX. 45.—ASHEVILLE, N. C., AND RETURN.

Limited to three (3) months from date of sale.

Baltimore & Ohio R. R. . . . . to Washington.
Transfer . . . . B. & O. Depot to R. & D. Depot.
Richmond & Danville R. R. . . . . to Asheville.

Returning, same route.

THROUGH RATES.

Baltimore, Md.	$22 00	Meyersdale, Pa.	$28 10
Bellaire, O.	31 95	Morgantown, W. Va.	32 55
Berkeley Springs, W. Va.	21 65	Moundsville, W. Va.	31 20
Cameron, W. Va.	33 50	Mountain Lake Park, Md.	28 15
Charlestown, W. Va.	23 20	Mt. Pleasant, Pa.	30 80
Chester, Pa.	25 50	Newark, Del.	24 30
Clarksburg, W. Va.	31 55	New York, N. Y.	30 00
Connellsville, Pa.	30 30	Oakland, Md.	28 25
Cumberland, Md.	26 60	Parkersburg, W. Va.	31 65
Deer Park, Md.	28 00	Philadelphia, Pa.	26 00
Fairmont, W. Va.	31 55	Piedmont, W. Va.	27 70
Frederick, Md.	22 80	Pittsburgh, Pa.	32 60
Grafton, W. Va.	30 65	Rockwood, Pa.	28 55
Hagerstown, Md.	23 00	Somerset, Pa.	28 95
Harper's Ferry, W. Va.	22 70	Uniontown, Pa.	30 75
Havre de Grace, Md.	23 15	Washington, Pa.	33 70
Johnstown, Pa.	30 55	Wheeling, W. Va.	31 65
Keyser, W. Va.	27 50	Wilmington, Del.	25 00
McKeesport, Pa.	32 05	Winchester, Va.	24 30
Martinsburg, W. Va.	23 15		

FORM EX. 16.—ASHEVILLE, N. C., AND RETURN.
Limited to three (3) months from date of sale.

Baltimore & Ohio R. R. . . . . to Shenandoah June.
Norfolk & Western R. R. . . . . to Bristol.
East Tennessee, Virginia & Georgia R. R. . . . . to Paint Rock.
Richmond & Danville R. R. . . . . to Asheville.
Returning, same route.

ROUTES AND RATES FOR SUMMER TOURS. 19

THROUGH RATES.

Baltimore, Md.	$22 00	Morgantown, W. Va.	$29 55
Bellaire, O.	31 95	Moundsville, W. Va.	31 25
Berkeley Springs, W. Va.	24 75	Mountain Lake Park, Md.	25 70
Cameron, W. Va.	30 55	Mt. Pleasant, Pa.	27 80
Chester, Pa.	25 50	Newark, Del.	24 30
Clarksburg, W. Va.	28 55	New York, N. Y.	30 00
Connellsville, Pa.	27 30	Oakland, Md.	25 80
Cumberland, Md.	23 60	Parkersburg, W. Va.	31 65
Deer Park, Md.	25 55	Philadelphia, Pa.	26 00
Fairmont, W. Va.	28 55	Piedmont, W. Va.	24 75
Frederick, Md.	20 65	Pittsburgh, Pa.	29 00
Grafton, W. Va.	27 65	Rockwood, Pa.	25 55
Harper's Ferry, W. Va.	20 00	Somerset, Pa.	25 95
Havre de Grace, Md.	23 45	Uniontown, Pa.	27 75
Johnstown, Pa.	27 55	Washington, D. C.	29 00
Keyser, W. Va.	24 55	Washington, Pa.	30 70
McKeesport, Pa.	29 05	Wheeling, W. Va.	31 65
Martinsburg, W. Va.	20 45	Wilmington, Del.	25 00
Meyersdale, Pa.	25 10		

FORM EX. 5.—ASHEVILLE, N. C., AND RETURN.
Limited to three (3) months from date of sale.

Baltimore & Ohio R. R. . . . . to Lexington.
Chesapeake & Ohio R. R. . . . . to Lynchburg.
Richmond & Danville R. R. . . . . to Asheville.
Returning, same route.

THROUGH RATES.

Baltimore, Md.	$22 00	Morgantown, W. Va.	$29 55
Bellaire, O.	31 95	Moundsville, W. Va.	31 25
Berkeley Springs, W. Va.	24 75	Mountain Lake Park, Md.	25 70
Cameron, W. Va.	30 55	Mt. Pleasant, Pa.	27 80
Charlestown, W. Va.	20 00	Newark, Del.	24 30
Chester, Pa.	25 50	New York, N. Y.	30 00
Clarksburg, W. Va.	28 55	Oakland, Md.	25 80
Connellsville, Pa.	27 30	Parkersburg, W. Va.	31 65
Cumberland, Md.	23 60	Philadelphia, Pa.	26 00
Deer Park, Md.	25 55	Piedmont, W. Va.	24 75
Fairmont, W. Va.	28 55	Pittsburgh, Pa.	29 00
Frederick, Md.	20 65	Rockwood, Pa.	25 55
Grafton, W. Va.	27 65	Somerset, Pa.	25 95
Hagerstown, Md.	20 00	Staunton, Va.	17 30
Harper's Ferry, W. Va.	20 00	Strasburg, Va.	20 00
Harrisonburg, Va.	18 00	Uniontown, Pa.	27 75
Havre de Grace, Md.	23 45	Washington, D. C.	29 00
Johnstown, Pa.	27 55	Washington, Pa.	30 70
Keyser, W. Va.	24 55	Wheeling, W. Va.	31 65
McKeesport, Pa.	29 05	Wilmington, Del.	25 00
Martinsburg, W. Va.	20 45	Winchester, Va.	20 00
Meyersdale, Pa.	25 10		

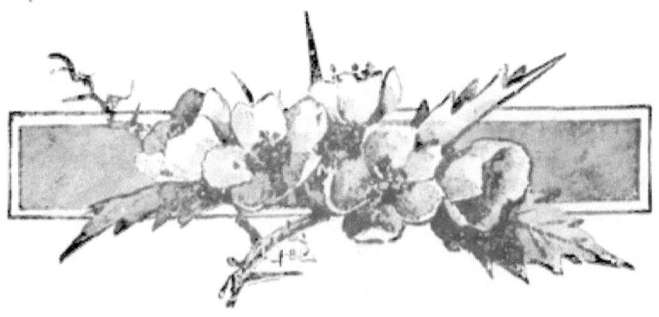

ATLANTIC CITY, N. J.

This seaside city has acquired such prominence as a summer and winter resort that a description of its many attractions seems to be unnecessary. Thousands are attracted to

SAND FORTS.

this famous resort, in summer, to enjoy the magnificent surf bathing and avail themselves of the unequaled opportunities for sailing and fishing, while in winter the numerous hotels and cottages are filled with pleasure-seekers and those who desire to escape the rigor of Northern and Western latitudes. Beautiful avenues lined with shade trees afford excellent opportunities for driving and riding, and a stroll through the markets, well supplied from the surrounding large cities and the waters of the ocean, would gladden the heart of an epicure. The sewerage system is exceptionally good and the supply of pure, wholesome water from the mainland is apparently inexhaustible. Through connections are made at Philadelphia with the Atlantic City R. R., thus making this resort the most accessible of any of its seaside rivals.

FORM EX. 657.—ATLANTIC CITY, N. J., AND RETURN.
Limited to six (6) months from date of sale.
Baltimore & Ohio R. R. . . . . to Philadelphia.
Transfer, (Passenger only) B. & O. R. R. Depot to P. & R. R. R. (A. C. Line Pier.)
Philadelphia & Reading R. R. (A. C. Line) . . . . to Atlantic City.
Returning, same route.

THROUGH RATES.

Baltimore, Md.	$ 6 30	Martinsburg, W. Va.	$10 25
Bellaire, O.	22 35	Meyersdale, Pa.	15 30
Berkeley Springs, W. Va.	12 05	Morgantown, W. Va.	19 95
Cameron, W. Va.	20 90	Moundsville, W. Va.	21 70
Charlestown, W. Va.	10 60	Mountain Lake Park, Md.	15 15
Chester, Pa.	2 80	Mt. Pleasant, Pa.	18 50
Clarksburg, W. Va.	18 95	Newark, Del.	3 80
Connellsville, Pa.	17 70	Oakland, Md.	15 55
Cumberland, Md.	14 00	Parkersburg, W. Va.	22 05
Deer Park, Md.	15 30	Piedmont, W. Va.	15 20
Fairmont, W. Va.	18 90	Pittsburgh, Pa.	18 90
Frederick, Md.	8 75	Rockwood, Pa.	15 95
Grafton, W. Va.	18 05	Somerset, Pa.	16 55
Hagerstown, Md.	9 50	Staunton, Va.	16 40
Harper's Ferry, W. Va.	9 70	Strasburg, Va.	12 75
Harrisonburg, Va.	15 40	Uniontown, Pa.	18 15
Havre de Grace, Md.	4 65	Washington, D. C.	8 30
Johnstown, Pa.	17 75	Washington, Pa.	20 50
Keyser, W. Va.	14 80	Wheeling, W. Va.	22 05
Lexington, Va.	18 20	Wilmington, Del.	3 30
McKeesport, Pa.	18 90	Winchester, Va.	11 70

FORM SPL. EX. 272.—ATLANTIC CITY, N. J., AND RETURN.
Limited to ten (10) days after date of sale.
Baltimore & Ohio R. R. . . . . to Philadelphia.
Transfer, (Passenger only) B. & O. R. R. Depot to P. & R. R. R. (A. C. Line Pier.)
Philadelphia & Reading R. R. (A. C. Line) . . . . to Atlantic City.
Returning, same route.

THROUGH RATES.
Chester, Pa. . . . . $2 30 Wilmington, Del. $2 80

22 BALTIMORE & OHIO RAILROAD COMPANY

ATLANTIC CITY, N. J. EXCURSION FORM EX. 715.

Limited to six (6) months from date of sale.

Baltimore & Ohio R. R. . . . . to Philadelphia.
Philadelphia & Reading R. R. (A. C. Lines) . . . to Atlantic City.

Returning, same route.

THROUGH RATES.

Baltimore, Md.	$6 00	Martinsburg, W. Va.	$9 35
Bellaire, O.	22 05	Meyersdale, Pa.	15 20
Berkeley Springs, W. Va.	11 75	Morgantown, W. Va.	19 65
Cameron, W. Va.	20 60	Moundsville, W. Va.	21 10
Charlestown, W. Va.	10 50	Mountain Lake Park, Md.	15 15
Chester, Pa.	2 50	Mt. Pleasant, Pa.	17 80
Clarksburg, W. Va.	18 65	Newark, Del.	3 50
Connellsville, Pa.	17 10	Oakland, Md.	15 25
Cumberland, Md.	13 70	Parkersburg, W. Va.	24 75
Deer Park, Md.	15 00	Piedmont, W. Va.	11 80
Fairmont, W. Va.	18 00	Pittsburgh, Pa.	18 00
Frederick, Md.	8 45	Rockwood, Pa.	15 65
Grafton, W. Va.	17 75	Somerset, Pa.	16 65
Hagerstown, Md.	9 20	Staunton, W. Va.	16 10
Harper's Ferry, W. Va.	9 10	Strasburg, Va.	12 15
Harrisonburg, Va.	14 80	Uniontown, Pa.	17 85
Havre de Grace, Md.	4 35	Washington, D. C.	8 00
Johnstown, Pa.	17 45	Washington, Pa.	20 20
Keyser, W. Va.	11 60	Wheeling, W. Va.	21 75
Lexington, Va.	17 80	Wilmington, Del.	3 00
McKeesport, Pa.	18 60	Winchester, Va.	11 10

ATLANTIC CITY, N. J. EXCURSION FORM EX. 865.

Limited to ten (10) days after date of sale.

Baltimore & Ohio R. R. . . . . to Philadelphia.
Philadelphia & Reading R. R. (A. C. Lines) . . . to Atlantic City.

Returning, same route.

THROUGH RATES.

Chester, Pa. . . . . $2 00 Wilmington, Del. $2 50

AUBURN, N. Y.

FORM EX. 739.—AUBURN, N. Y., AND RETURN.

Baltimore & Ohio R. R. . . . . to Philadelphia.
Philadelphia & Reading R. R. . . . . to Bethlehem.
Lehigh Valley R. R. . . . . to Auburn.

Returning, same route.

THROUGH RATES.

Baltimore, Md. . . . . $16 00 Washington, D. C. $18 00
†Philadelphia, Pa. . . . . . 12 00 |

FORM EX. 812. AUBURN, N. Y., AND RETURN.

Baltimore & Ohio R. R. . . . . to Philadelphia.
Philadelphia & Reading R. R. . . . . to Bethlehem.
Lehigh Valley R. R. . . . . to Cayuga.
New York Central & Hudson River R. R. . . . . . to Auburn.
Lehigh Valley R. R. . . . . to Bethlehem.
Philadelphia & Reading R. R. . . . . to Philadelphia.
Baltimore & Ohio R. R. . . . . to starting point.

THROUGH RATES.

Baltimore, Md. . . . . $17 10 Washington, D. C. $19 10
†Philadelphia, Pa. . . . . . 13 10 |

BABYLON, L. I.

FORM EX. 815. BABYLON, LONG ISLAND, N. Y., AND RETURN.

Baltimore & Ohio R. R. . . . . to Philadelphia.
Philadelphia & Reading R. R. . . . . to Bound Brook.
Central R. R. of New Jersey . . . . to New York.
Metropolitan Ferry Co., James' Slip or 34th Street
   Ferry . . . . to Long Island City.
Long Island R. R. . . . . to Babylon.
           Returning, same route.

THROUGH RATES.

Baltimore, Md. . . . . . $10 40   Washington, D. C. . . . $12 40
Philadelphia, Pa. 6 40

BAR HARBOR MT. DESERT ISLAND, ME.

Mount Desert Island lies off the coast of Maine, one hundred and ten miles east of Portland. It is about fourteen miles in length by eight in breadth, and covers an area of one hundred square miles; yet within this limited compass there is a wonderful variety of scenery and a pro-

fuse wealth of natural beauties. Mountain, valley, ocean and lake, silver stream and dancing cascade, all unite to form the character of this curious isle. There are thirteen mountain peaks on the island, some of them towering up to great height, and one of them—Green Mountain—the highest on the North Atlantic coast, commands from its summit a vast, varied and grand view.

FORM EX. 504.—BAR HARBOR, ME., AND RETURN.

(Via rail to Rockland, returning by Sound Lines from Boston.)

Baltimore & Ohio R. R.	to Philadelphia.
Rail Lines (see pages 50 to 55 for routes)	to Boston.
Boston & Maine R. R.	to Portland.
Maine Central R. R.	to Rockland.
Boston & Bangor S. S. Line	to Bar Harbor.
Boston & Bangor S. S. Line	to Rockland.
Maine Central R. R.	to Portland.
Boston & Maine R. R.	to Boston.
Sound Lines (see pages 50 to 55 for routes)	to New York.
Central R. R. of New Jersey	to Bound Brook.
Philadelphia & Reading R. R.	to Philadelphia.
Baltimore & Ohio R. R.	to starting point.

THROUGH RATES.

Baltimore, Md. . . . . . $27 00   Washington, D. C. $26 00
†Philadelphia, Pa. 23 00

FORM EX. 504.—BAR HARBOR, ME., AND RETURN.

(Via Sound Lines to Boston, thence rail to Rockland; returning by rail.)

Baltimore & Ohio R. R.	to Philadelphia.
Philadelphia & Reading R. R.	to Bound Brook.
Central R. R. of New Jersey	to New York.
Sound Lines (see pages 50 to 55 for routes)	to Boston.
Boston & Maine R. R.	to Portland.
Maine Central R. R.	to Rockland.
Boston & Bangor S. S. Line	to Bar Harbor.
Boston & Bangor S. S. Line	to Rockland.
Maine Central R. R.	to Portland.
Boston & Maine R. R.	to Boston.
Rail Lines (see pages 50 to 55 for routes)	to Philadelphia.
Baltimore & Ohio R. R.	to starting point.

THROUGH RATES.

Baltimore, Md. . . . . . $27 00   Washington, D. C. $26 00
†Philadelphia, Pa. 23 00

FORM EX. 504.—BAR HARBOR, ME., AND RETURN.

(Via Rail Lines and Rockland in both directions.)

Baltimore & Ohio R. R.	to Philadelphia.
Rail Lines (see pages 50 to 55 for routes)	to Boston.
Boston & Maine R. R.	to Portland.
Maine Central R. R.	to Rockland.
Boston & Bangor S. S. Line	to Bar Harbor.

Returning, same route.

THROUGH RATES.

Baltimore, Md. . . . . . $28 00   Washington, D. C. $30 00
†Philadelphia, Pa. 24 00

FORM EX. 504.—BAR HARBOR, ME., AND RETURN.

(Via Sound Lines to Boston, and rail to Rockland in both directions.)

Baltimore & Ohio R. R.	to Philadelphia.
Philadelphia & Reading R. R.	to Bound Brook.
Central R. R. of New Jersey	to New York.
Sound Lines (see pages 50 to 55 for routes)	to Boston.
Boston & Maine R. R.	to Portland.
Maine Central R. R.	to Rockland.
Boston & Bangor S. S. Line	to Bar Harbor.

Returning, same route.

THROUGH RATES.

Baltimore, Md.	$26 00	Washington, D. C.	$28 00
Philadelphia, Pa.	22 00		

FORM EX. 505.—BAR HARBOR, ME., AND RETURN.

(Via rail to Rockland, returning via Sound Lines from Boston.)

Baltimore & Ohio R. R.	to Philadelphia.
Rail Lines (see pages 50 to 55 for routes)	to Boston.
Boston & Maine R. R.	to Portland.
Maine Central R. R.	to Rockland.
Portland, Mt. Desert & Machias Steamboat Line	to Bar Harbor.
Portland, Mt. Desert & Machias Steamboat Line	to Rockland.
Maine Central R. R.	to Portland.
Boston & Maine R. R.	to Boston.
Sound Lines (see pages 50 to 55 for route)	to New York.
Central R. R. of New Jersey	to Bound Brook.
Philadelphia & Reading R. R.	to Philadelphia.
Baltimore & Ohio R. R.	to starting point.

THROUGH RATES.

Baltimore, Md.	$27 00	Washington, D. C.	$29 00
Philadelphia, Pa.	23 00		

FORM EX. 506.—BAR HARBOR, ME., AND RETURN.

(Via Sound Lines to Boston, thence rail to Rockland; returning by rail.)

Baltimore & Ohio R. R.	to Philadelphia.
Philadelphia & Reading R. R.	to Bound Brook.
Central R. R. of New Jersey	to New York.
Sound Lines (see pages 50 to 55 for route)	to Boston.
Boston & Maine R. R.	to Portland.
Maine Central R. R.	to Rockland.
Portland, Mt. Desert & Machias Steamboat Line	to Bar Harbor.
Portland, Mt. Desert & Machias Steamboat Line	to Rockland.
Maine Central R. R.	to Portland.
Boston & Maine R. R.	to Boston.
Rail Lines (see pages 50 to 55 for route)	to Philadelphia.
Baltimore & Ohio R. R.	to starting point.

THROUGH RATES.

Baltimore, Md.	$27 00	Washington, D. C.	$29 00
Philadelphia, Pa.	23 00		

ROUTES AND RATES FOR SUMMER TOURS.

FORM EX. 505. BAR HARBOR, ME., AND RETURN.
(Via Rail Lines and Rockland in both directions.)

Baltimore & Ohio R. R. . . . . to Philadelphia.
Rail Lines (see pages 50 to 55 for routes) . . . to Boston.
Boston & Maine R. R. . . . . to Portland.
Maine Central R. R. . . . . to Rockland.
Portland, Mt. Desert & Machias Steamboat Line, to Bar Harbor.
Returning, same route.

THROUGH RATES.

Baltimore, Md. . . . . . $28 00 | Washington, D. C. $30 00
Philadelphia, Pa. . . . . 24 00 |

FORM EX. 505. BAR HARBOR, ME., AND RETURN.
(Via Sound Lines to Boston, thence rail to Rockland in both directions.)

Baltimore & Ohio R. R. . . . . to Philadelphia.
Philadelphia & Reading R. R. . . . . to Bound Brook.
Central R. R. of New Jersey . . . . to New York.
Sound Lines (see pages 50 to 55 for routes) . . . to Boston.
Boston & Maine R. R. . . . . to Portland.
Maine Central R. R. . . . . to Rockland.
Portland, Mt. Desert & Machias Steamboat Line, to Bar Harbor.
Returning, same route.

THROUGH RATES.

Baltimore, Md. . . . . . $26 00 | Washington, D. C. $28 00
Philadelphia, Pa. . . . . 22 00 |

FORM EX. 506. BAR HARBOR, ME., AND RETURN.
(Via rail to Boston, steamer to Portland, and rail to Rockland; returning by Sound Lines from Boston.)

Baltimore & Ohio R. R. . . . . to Philadelphia.
Rail Lines (see pages 50 to 55 for routes) . . . to Boston.
Portland Steam Packet Line . . . . to Portland.
Maine Central R. R. . . . . to Rockland.
Portland, Mt. Desert & Machias Steamboat Line, to Bar Harbor.
Portland, Mt. Desert & Machias Steamboat Line, to Rockland.
Maine Central R. R. . . . . to Portland.
Portland Steam Packet Line . . . . to Boston.
Sound Lines (see pages 50 to 55 for routes) . . . to New York.
Central R. R. of New Jersey . . . . to Bound Brook.
Philadelphia & Reading R. R. . . . . to Philadelphia.
Baltimore & Ohio R. R. . . . . to starting point.

THROUGH RATES.

Baltimore, Md. . . . . . $26 00 | Washington, D. C. $28 00
Philadelphia, Pa. . . . . 22 00 |

FORM EX. 506. BAR HARBOR, ME., AND RETURN.
(Via Sound Lines to Boston, steamer to Portland, and rail to Rockland; returning by rail from Boston.)

Baltimore & Ohio R. R. . . . . to Philadelphia.
Philadelphia & Reading R. R. . . . . to Bound Brook.
Central R. R. of New Jersey . . . . to New York.
Sound Lines (see pages 50 to 55 for routes) . . . to Boston.
Portland Steam Packet Line . . . . to Portland.
Maine Central R. R. . . . . to Rockland.
Portland, Mt. Desert & Machias Steamboat Line, to Bar Harbor.
Portland, Mt. Desert & Machias Steamboat Line, to Rockland.

Maine Central R. R. . . . . to Portland.
Portland Steam Packet Line . . . . to Boston.
Rail Lines (see pages 50 to 55 for route) . . . . . to Philadelphia.
Baltimore & Ohio R. R. . . . . to starting point.

THROUGH RATES.

Baltimore, Md.	$26 00	Washington, D. C.	$28 00
†Philadelphia, Pa.	22 00		

FORM EX. 505.—BAR HARBOR, ME., AND RETURN.

(Via Rail Lines to Boston, steamer to Portland, and rail to Rockland in both directions.)

Baltimore & Ohio R. R. . . . . to Philadelphia.
Rail Lines (see pages 50 to 55 for route) . . . . . to Boston.
Portland Steam Packet Line . . . . to Portland.
Maine Central R. R. . . . . to Rockland.
Portland, Mt. Desert & Machias Steamboat Line . to Bar Harbor.

Returning, same route.

THROUGH RATES.

Baltimore, Md.	$27 00	Washington, D. C.	$29 00
†Philadelphia, Pa.	23 00		

FORM EX. 506.—BAR HARBOR, ME., AND RETURN.

(Via Sound Lines to Boston, steamer to Portland, and rail to Rockland in both directions.)

Baltimore & Ohio R. R. . . . . to Philadelphia.
Philadelphia & Reading R. R. . . . . to Bound Brook.
Central R. R. of New Jersey. . . . . to New York.
Sound Lines (see pages 50 to 55 for route) . . . . to Boston.
Portland Steam Packet Line. . . . . to Portland.
Maine Central R. R. . . . . to Rockland.
Portland, Mt. Desert & Machias Steamboat Line . to Bar Harbor.

Returning, same route.

THROUGH RATES.

Baltimore, Md.	$25 00	Washington, D. C.	$27 00
†Philadelphia, Pa.	21 00		

FORM EX. 507 OR SPL. EX. 545. BAR HARBOR, ME., AND RETURN.

(Via rail to Bar Harbor, returning by same route to Boston, thence via Sound Lines from Boston.)

Baltimore & Ohio R. R. . . . . to Philadelphia.
Rail Lines (see pages 50 to 55 for route) . . . . . to Boston.
Boston & Maine R. R. . . . . to Portland.
Maine Central R. R. . . . . to Bar Harbor.
Maine Central R. R. . . . . to Portland.
Boston & Maine R. R. . . . . to Boston.
Sound Lines (see pages 50 to 55 for route) . . . . to New York.
Central R. R. of New Jersey . . . . to Bound Brook.
Philadelphia & Reading R. R. . . . . to Philadelphia.
Baltimore & Ohio R. R. . . . . to starting point.

Special Excursion, Form Spl. Ex. 545, is good for continuous passage only, east of Portland, and the rates for same are $2.50 less than the rates for the regular excursion as quoted below.

THROUGH RATES.

Baltimore, Md.	$31 00	Washington, D. C.	$33 00
†Philadelphia, Pa.	27 00		

A QUIET DAY ON THE POTOMAC.

FORM EX. 507 OR SPL. EX. 515.—BAR HARBOR, ME., AND RETURN.

(Via Sound Lines to Boston, rail to Bar Harbor, returning by same route to Boston, thence via rail.)

Baltimore & Ohio R. R. . . . . to Philadelphia.
Philadelphia & Reading R. R. . . . . to Bound Brook.
Central R. R. of New Jersey. . . . . to New York.
Sound Lines (see pages 50 to 55 for route) . . . to Boston.
Boston & Maine R. R. . . . . to Portland.
Maine Central R. R. . . . . to Bar Harbor.
Maine Central R. R. . . . . to Portland.
Boston & Maine R. R. . . . . to Boston.
Rail Lines (see pages 50 to 55 for route) . . . . to Philadelphia.
Baltimore & Ohio R. R. . . . . to starting point.

Special Excursion Form, Spl. Ex. 515, is good for continuous passage only, east of Portland, and the rates for same are $2.50 less than rates for the regular excursion as quoted below.

THROUGH RATES.

Baltimore, Md. . . . . . . $34 00 | Washington, D. C. $35 00
Philadelphia, Pa. . . . . . 27 00 |

FORM EX. 507 OR SPL. EX. 515.—BAR HARBOR, ME., AND RETURN.

(Via Rail Lines to Bar Harbor in both directions.)

Baltimore & Ohio R. R. . . . . to Philadelphia.
Rail Lines (see pages 50 to 55 for route) . . . . to Boston.
Boston & Maine R. R. . . . . to Portland.
Maine Central R. R. . . . . to Bar Harbor.

Returning, same route.

Special Excursion, Form Spl. Ex. 515, is good for continuous passage only, east of Portland, and the rates for same are $2.50 less than rates for the regular excursion as quoted below.

THROUGH RATES.

Baltimore, Md. . . . . . . $32 00 | Washington, D. C. $34 00
Philadelphia, Pa. . . . . . 28 00 |

FORM EX. 507 OR SPL. EX. 515.—BAR HARBOR, ME., AND RETURN.

(Via Sound Lines to Boston, rail to Bar Harbor, and return to Boston, thence via Sound Lines.)

Baltimore & Ohio R. R. . . . . to Philadelphia.
Philadelphia & Reading R. R. . . . . to Bound Brook.
Central R. R. of New Jersey. . . . . to New York.
Sound Lines (see pages 50 to 55 for route) . . . to Boston.
Boston & Maine R. R. . . . . to Portland.
Maine Central R. R. . . . . to Bar Harbor.

Returning, same route.

Special Excursion, Form Spl. Ex. 515, is good for continuous passage only, east of Portland, and the rates for same are $2.50 less than rates for the regular excursion as quoted below.

THROUGH RATES.

Baltimore, Md. . . . . . . $30 00 | Washington, D. C. $32 00
Philadelphia, Pa. . . . . . 26 00 |

FORM EX. 510.—BAR HARBOR, ME., AND RETURN.

(Via rail to Rockland, returning by Sound Lines from Boston.)

Baltimore & Ohio R. R. . . . . to Philadelphia.
Rail Lines (see pages 50 to 55 for route) . . . . to Boston.
Portland Steam Packet Line . . . . to Portland.
Maine Central R. R. . . . . to Rockland.
Boston & Bangor S. S. Line . . . . to Bar Harbor.

ROUTES AND RATES FOR SUMMER TOURS. 31

Boston & Bangor S. S. Line . . . . to Rockland.
Maine Central R. R. . . . . to Portland.
Portland Steam Packet Line . . . . to Boston.
Sound Lines (see pages 30 to 35 for route) . . . . to New York.
Central R. R. of New Jersey . . . . to Bound Brook.
Philadelphia & Reading R. R. . . . . to Philadelphia.
Baltimore & Ohio R. R. . . . . to starting point.

THROUGH RATES.

Baltimore, Md. . . . . . $26.00 | Washington, D. C. $28.00
Philadelphia, Pa. 22.00

FORM EX. 510. BAR HARBOR, ME., AND RETURN.

(Via Sound Lines to Boston, rail to Rockland; returning by rail.)

Baltimore & Ohio R. R. . . . . to Philadelphia.
Philadelphia & Reading R. R. . . . . to Bound Brook.
Central R. R. of New Jersey . . . . to New York.
Sound Lines (see pages 30 to 35 for route) . . . . to Boston.
Portland Steam Packet Line . . . . to Portland.
Maine Central R. R. . . . . to Rockland.
Boston & Bangor S. S. Line . . . . to Bar Harbor.
Boston & Bangor S. S. Line . . . . to Rockland.
Maine Central R. R. . . . . to Portland.
Portland Steam Packet Line . . . . to Boston.
Rail Lines (see pages 30 to 35 for route) . . . . to Philadelphia.
Baltimore & Ohio R. R. . . . . to starting point.

THROUGH RATES.

Baltimore, Md. . . . . . $26.00 | Washington, D. C. $28.00
Philadelphia, Pa. 22.00

FORM EX. 510.—BAR HARBOR, ME., AND RETURN.

(Via Rail Lines and Rockland in both directions.)

Baltimore & Ohio R. R. . . . . to Philadelphia.
Rail Lines (see pages 30 to 35 for route) . . . . to Boston.
Portland Steam Packet Line . . . . to Portland.
Maine Central R. R. . . . . to Rockland.
Boston & Bangor S. S. Line . . . . to Bar Harbor.

Returning, same route.

THROUGH RATES.

Baltimore, Md. . . . . . $27.00 | Washington, D. C. $29.00
Philadelphia, Pa. 23.00

FORM EX. 510. BAR HARBOR, ME., AND RETURN.

(Via Sound Lines to Boston, thence rail to Rockland in both directions.)

Baltimore & Ohio R. R. . . . . to Philadelphia.
Philadelphia & Reading R. R. . . . . to Bound Brook.
Central R. R. of New Jersey . . . . to New York.
Sound Lines (see pages 30 to 35 for route) . . . . to Boston.
Portland Steam Packet Line . . . . to Portland.
Maine Central R. R. . . . . to Rockland.
Boston & Bangor S. S. Line . . . . to Bar Harbor.

Returning, same route.

THROUGH RATES.

Baltimore, Md. . . . . . $25.00 | Washington, D. C. $27.00
Philadelphia, Pa. 21.00

FORM EX. 511.—BAR HARBOR, ME., AND RETURN.

(Via rail to Boston, thence by steamer; returning by Sound Lines from Boston.)

Baltimore & Ohio R. R. . . . . to Philadelphia.
Rail Lines (see pages 50 to 55 for route) . . . . . to Boston.
Boston & Bangor S. S. Line . . . . to Bar Harbor.
Boston & Bangor S. S. Line . . . . to Boston.
Sound Lines (see pages 50 to 55 for route) . . . . to New York.
Central R. R. of New Jersey . . . . to Bound Brook.
Philadelphia & Reading R. R. . . . . to Philadelphia.
Baltimore & Ohio R. R. . . . . to starting point.

THROUGH RATES.

Baltimore, Md. . . . . . . $24 50 | Washington, D. C. $26 50
Philadelphia, Pa. . . . . . 20 50 |

FORM EX. 511.—BAR HARBOR, ME., AND RETURN.

(Via Sound Lines to Boston, thence steamer from Boston; returning by rail from Boston.)

Baltimore & Ohio R. R. . . . . to Philadelphia.
Philadelphia & Reading R. R. . . . . to Bound Brook.
Central R. R. of New Jersey . . . . to New York.
Sound Lines (see pages 50 to 55 for route) . . . . to Boston.
Boston & Bangor S. S. Line . . . . to Bar Harbor.
Boston & Bangor S. S. Line . . . . to Boston.
Rail Lines (see pages 50 to 55 for route) . . . . . to Philadelphia.
Baltimore & Ohio R. R. . . . . to starting point.

THROUGH RATES.

Baltimore, Md. . . . . . . $24 50 | Washington, D. C. $26 50
Philadelphia, Pa. . . . . . 20 50 |

FORM EX. 511.—BAR HARBOR, ME., AND RETURN.

(Via Rail Lines to Boston, thence steamer in both directions.)

Baltimore & Ohio R. R. . . . . to Philadelphia.
Rail Lines (see pages 50 to 55 for route) . . . . . to Boston.
Boston & Bangor S. S. Line . . . . to Bar Harbor.

Returning, same route.

THROUGH RATES.

Baltimore, Md. . . . . . . $25 50 | Washington, D. C. $27 50
Philadelphia, Pa. . . . . . 21 50 |

FORM EX. 511.—BAR HARBOR, ME., AND RETURN.

(Via Sound Lines to Boston, thence Steamer in both directions.)

Baltimore & Ohio R. R. . . . . to Philadelphia.
Philadelphia & Reading R. R. . . . . to Bound Brook.
Central R. R. of New Jersey . . . . to New York.
Sound Lines (see pages 50 to 55 for route) . . . . to Boston.
Boston & Bangor S. S. Line . . . . to Bar Harbor.

Returning, same route.

THROUGH RATES.

Baltimore, Md. . . . . . . $23 50 | Washington, D. C. $25 50
Philadelphia, Pa. . . . . . 19 50 |

FORM EX. 512.—BAR HARBOR, ME., AND RETURN.

(Via rail to Bar Harbor; returning via Sound Lines from Boston.)

Baltimore & Ohio R. R. . . . . to Philadelphia.
Rail Lines (see pages 50 to 55 for route) . . . . . to Boston.
Boston & Maine R. R. . . . . to Portland.
Maine Central R. R. . . . . to Bar Harbor.

Boston & Bangor S. S. Line . . . . to Rockland.
Maine Central R. R. . . . . to Portland.
Boston & Maine R. R. . . . . to Boston.
Sound Lines (see pages 50 to 55 for routes) . . . . to New York.
Central R. R. of New Jersey . . . . to Bound Brook.
Philadelphia & Reading R. R. . . . . to Philadelphia.
Baltimore & Ohio R. R. . . . . to starting point.

THROUGH RATES.

Baltimore, Md. . . . . . . $29 00 | Washington, D. C. . . . $31 00
(Philadelphia, Pa. 25 00)

FORM EX. 512.—BAR HARBOR, ME., AND RETURN.

(Via Sound Lines to Boston, rail to Bar Harbor; returning via rail from Boston.)

Baltimore & Ohio R. R. . . . . to Philadelphia.
Philadelphia & Reading R. R. . . . . to Bound Brook.
Central R. R. of New Jersey . . . . to New York.
Sound Lines (see pages 50 to 55 for routes) . . . . to Boston.
Boston & Maine R. R. . . . . to Portland.
Maine Central R. R. . . . . to Bar Harbor.
Boston & Bangor S. S. Line . . . . to Rockland.
Maine Central R. R. . . . . to Portland.
Boston & Maine R. R. . . . . to Boston.
Rail Lines (see pages 50 to 55 for routes) . . . . to Philadelphia.
Baltimore & Ohio R. R. . . . . to starting point.

THROUGH RATES.

Baltimore, Md. . . . . . . $29 00 | Washington, D. C. . . . $31 00
(Philadelphia, Pa. 25 00)

FORM EX. 512.—BAR HARBOR, ME., AND RETURN.

(Via rail to Bar Harbor; returning via rail from Boston.)

Baltimore & Ohio R. R. . . . . to Philadelphia.
Rail Lines (see pages 50 to 55 for routes) . . . . to Boston.
Boston & Maine R. R. . . . . to Portland.
Maine Central R. R. . . . . to Bar Harbor.
Boston & Bangor S. S. Line . . . . to Rockland.
Maine Central R. R. . . . . to Portland.
Boston & Maine R. R. . . . . to Boston.
Rail Lines (see pages 50 to 55 for routes) . . . . to Philadelphia.
Baltimore & Ohio R. R. . . . . to starting point.

THROUGH RATES.

Baltimore, Md. . . . . . . $30 00 | Washington, D. C. . . . $32 00
(Philadelphia, Pa. 26 00)

FORM EX. 512.—BAR HARBOR, ME., AND RETURN.

(Via Sound Lines to Boston, rail to Bar Harbor; returning via Sound Lines from Boston.)

Baltimore & Ohio R. R. . . . . to Philadelphia.
Philadelphia & Reading R. R. . . . . to Bound Brook.
Central R. R. of New Jersey . . . . to New York.
Sound Lines (see pages 50 to 55 for routes) . . . . to Boston.
Boston & Maine R. R. . . . . to Portland.
Maine Central R. R. . . . . to Bar Harbor.
Boston & Bangor S. S. Line . . . . to Rockland.
Maine Central R. R. . . . . to Portland.
Boston & Maine R. R. . . . . to Boston.
Sound Lines (see pages 50 to 55 for routes) . . . . to New York.
Central R. R. of New Jersey . . . . to Bound Brook.
Philadelphia & Reading R. R. . . . . to Philadelphia.
Baltimore & Ohio R. R. . . . . to starting point.

THROUGH RATES.

Baltimore, Md. . . . . . . $28 00 | Washington, D. C. . . . $30 00
(Philadelphia, Pa. 24 00)

FORM EX. 1195. BAR HARBOR, ME., AND RETURN.

Baltimore & Ohio R. R. . . . . to Philadelphia.
Philadelphia & Reading R. R. . . . . to Bound Brook.
Central R. R. of New Jersey . . . . to New York.
Mallory Steamship Line . . . . to Bar Harbor.
Returning, same route.

THROUGH RATES.

Baltimore, Md. . . . . . $26 00 | Washington, D. C. $28 00
Philadelphia, Pa. . . . . 22 00 |

Steamers of the Mallory Line will leave New York, Pier 21, East River, Saturdays, commencing June 4th, at 3.00 P. M. Above rates include berth on steamer. Staterooms from $1.00 to $5.00 extra, according to location. Meals: Breakfast and supper, 75 cents; dinner, $1.00.

BEDFORD SPRINGS, PA.

FORM EX. 705. BEDFORD SPRINGS, PA., AND RETURN.
Baltimore & Ohio R. R. . . . . to Cumberland
Pennsylvania R. R. (Bedford Div.) . . . . to Bedford.
Returning, same route.

THROUGH RATES.

Baltimore, Md.	$ 9 55	Meyersdale, Pa.	$ 3 35
Bellaire, O.	10 25	Morgantown, W. Va.	7 80
Berkeley Springs, W. Va.	1 55	Moundsville, W. Va.	9 35
Cameron, W. Va.	8 80	Mountain Lake Park, Md.	3 90
Charlestown, W. Va.	6 45	Mt. Pleasant, Pa.	6 05
Chester, Pa.	12 75	Newark, Del.	11 85
Clarksburg, W. Va.	6 80	New York, N. Y.	16 75
Connellsville, Pa.	5 35	Oakland, Md.	4 00
Cumberland, Md.	1 85	Parkersburg, W. Va.	9 90
Deer Park, Md.	3 75	Philadelphia, Pa.	12 75
Fairmont, W. Va.	6 80	Piedmont, W. Va.	2 95
Frederick, Md.	6 80	Pittsburgh, Pa.	6 65
Grafton, W. Va.	5 90	Rockwood, Pa.	3 80
Hagerstown, Md.	6 80	Somerset, Pa.	4 45
Harper's Ferry, W. Va.	5 75	Staunton, Va.	12 05
Harrisonburg, Va.	10 75	Strasburg, Va.	8 40
Havre de Grace, Md.	11 00	Uniontown, Pa.	5 95
Johnstown, Pa.	5 05	Washington, D. C.	7 95
Keyser, W. Va.	2 75	Washington, Pa.	8 45
Lexington, Va.	13 85	Wheeling, W. Va.	9 90
McKeesport, Pa.	6 65	Wilmington, Del.	12 55
Martinsburg, W. Va.	5 00	Winchester, Va.	7 35

In addition to the above, Form Ex. 129, reading via Hyndman, may be sold from all Stations east of Cumberland, at above rates.
Baggage should be checked via Hyndman only.
Sell Form Ex. 129 only.

FORM EX. 789.—BEDFORD SPRINGS, PA., AND RETURN.

Baltimore & Ohio R. R. . . . . to Cumberland
Baltimore & Ohio R. R. . . . . to Hyndman.
Pennsylvania R. R. . . . . to Bedford.
Pennsylvania R. R. . . . . to Cumberland.
Baltimore & Ohio R. R. . . . . to Pittsburgh.
Rate from Pittsburgh . . . . $6.65.

BEECH GLEN, PA.

FORM EX. 598. BEECH GLEN, PA. (OR BEAVER DAM), AND RETURN.

Baltimore & Ohio R. R. . . . . to Philadelphia.
Philadelphia & Reading R. R. . . . . to Halls.
Williamsport & North Branch R. R. . . . to Beech Glen.
Returning, same route.

THROUGH RATES.

Baltimore, Md. . . . . . . $11.75 | Washington, D. C. . . $13.75
Philadelphia, Pa. . . . . $8.25 |

BELMAR, N. J. (OCEAN BEACH).

Ten years ago the site of Belmar (formerly Ocean Beach) was a dreary stretch of land— the "haunts of coot and hern." To-day it is a flourishing watering-place, whose present population is but a foretaste of its future prosperity.

Shark River, near which Belmar is situated, was probably so named because there are no sharks to be caught there; but there are plenty of other fish to be had for the taking. From May to October bluefish and weakfish abound; in June come the sheep's-head, and striped bass offer royal sport at all seasons of the year.

Belmar is eight miles south of Long Branch.

FORM EX. 594. BELMAR, N. J. (OCEAN BEACH), AND RETURN.

Baltimore & Ohio R. R. . . . . to Philadelphia.
Philadelphia & Reading R. R. . . . . to Bound Brook.
Central R. R. of New Jersey . . . . to Belmar (Ocean Beach).
Returning, same route.

THROUGH RATES.

Baltimore, Md. . . . . . $8.00 | Washington, D. C. . . $10.00
Philadelphia, Pa. . . . . $4.00 |

In addition to the above, excursion tickets, Form Ex. 594, Belmar, N. J. (Ocean Beach), may be sold from the following stations at rates as quoted below.

Tickets should be limited with an "L" punch to sixteen (16) days including day of issue.

THROUGH RATES.

Baltimore, Md. . . . . . $7.50 | Philadelphia, Pa. $3.50
Chester, Pa. . . . . 4.00 | Washington, D. C. . . . 9.50
Havre de Grace, Md. . . 5.85 | Wilmington, Del. 4.50
Newark, Del. . . . . 5.00 |

BERKELEY SPRINGS, W. VA.,

Is situated in a high and healthy mountain district, and widely known as a most healthful, charming, and popular summer resort, and as one of the oldest springs in the Alle-

BERKELEY SPRINGS.

ghany range, having long years ago been favored by the Washingtons, the Fairfaxes, and other families of historic fame. Aside from the capacious hotel buildings, the lawn studded with stately elms, the bath-houses nestling beneath the overhanging trees, and the happily situated cottages, Berkeley's location, with the gifts bestowed upon it by Nature, is alone worthy of remark. Yet not in this instance is it true that nature unadorned is most adorned, for human skill and ingenuity have been exercised to enhance the beauty of the place with the best possible success. From the road, as one descends the mountain, the dell in which the structures have been reared appears to be hardly any larger than the palm of the hand, and, contrasted with the great face of the range which locks the valley in close embrace, the simile is relatively sustained. The volume and unceasing supply of water at these springs are remarkable. The discharge is from no less than five principal sources, besides numerous tributary ones, and is upward of two thousand gallons per minute. It is clear and crystalline, tasteless, and of a uniform and invariable temperature of 74° Fahrenheit. Its medicinal properties are of such a high and unequivocal standard that the State went to a large expense in fitting up bath-houses and providing them with every known appurtenance for securing the greatest benefit from their use. Any form of bath may be taken as best suits the bather. There are stone swimming-pools of large dimensions both for ladies and gentlemen, the supply being so vast that virtually each person has fresh water, and always at a normal temperature. There are also a dozen or more private baths, ten feet by four and five feet deep, for gentlemen; and as many are furnished for the use of ladies. The component parts of the water from the main springs are carbonate of lime, crenate, iron, chloride of sodium, calcium, sulphate of magnesia and silicate of lime. There are also springs largely impregnated with sulphur, offering a fine tonic for drinking or for bathing. The accommodations are upon an extensive scale, and at the height of the season Berkeley is a very animated and brilliant resort. Balls are given nightly, and the social attractions are all that the most fastidious could wish. The air during the hottest summer weather is pure and salubrious, the temperature rarely, if ever, reaching high figures, and the nights are ever such as to require blankets to render sleep agreeable. During the proper season the hunting about Berkeley is fine; deer, wild turkey, pheasant, partridge, and other game abounding. Fishermen have the mountain streams near by where they can tempt trout with fly, and a distance of two miles brings them to the Potomac, than which for black bass fishing there are no better waters on the continent.

FORM EX. 124. BERKELEY SPRINGS, W. VA., AND RETURN.

Baltimore & Ohio R. R. . . . . to Berkeley Springs.
Returning, same route.

THROUGH RATES.

Baltimore, Md.	$5.75	Morgantown, W. Va.	$8.50
Bellaire, O.	10.95	Moundsville, W. Va.	10.45
Cameron, W. Va.	9.50	Mountain Lake Park, Md.	1.60
Charlestown, W. Va.	2.45	Mt. Pleasant, Pa.	6.75
Chester, Pa.	9.25	Newark, Del.	8.05
Clarksburg, W. Va.	7.50	New York, N. Y.	13.75
Connellsville, Pa.	6.25	Oakland, Md.	1.70
Cumberland, Md.	2.55	Parkersburg, W. Va.	10.60
Deer Park, Md.	1.45	Philadelphia, Pa.	9.75
Fairmont, W. Va.	7.50	Piedmont, W. Va.	3.05
Frederick, Md.	3.00	Pittsburgh, Pa.	8.55
Grafton, W. Va.	6.60	Rockwood, Pa.	1.50
Hagerstown, Md.	3.00	Somerset, Pa.	1.90
Harper's Ferry, W. Va.	1.95	Staunton, Va.	8.25
Harrisonburg, Va.	6.95	Strasburg, Va.	1.65
Havre de Grace, Md.	7.20	Uniontown, Pa.	6.70
Johnstown, Pa.	6.30	Washington, D. C.	1.45
Keyser, W. Va.	3.45	Washington, Pa.	9.65
Lexington, Va.	10.05	Wheeling, W. Va.	10.60
McKeesport, Pa.	8.00	Wilmington, Del.	8.75
Martinsburg, W. Va.	1.20	Winchester, Va.	3.55
Meyersdale, Pa.	1.65		

In addition to the season tickets for which rates are quoted above, special tickets, Form Ex. 877, will be sold from the following stations to Berkeley Springs, W. Va., and return, for use going on train No. 1 on Fridays, and all trains on Saturday and Sunday of each week, good to return on any train leaving Berkeley Springs on the following Monday.

EXCURSION RATES.

Baltimore, Md.	$4.00	Washington, D. C.	$3.50

BETHLEHEM (WHITE MOUNTAINS), N. H.

This village is said to be the highest of any east of the Rocky Mountains, being 1,500 feet above the level of the ocean. Pure air, convenience to the many attractive resorts in the Presidential range of the White Mountains, and the facilities offered by a good sized village are only a few of the claims of this pretty region.

FORM EX. 815. BETHLEHEM, N. H., AND RETURN.
(Via rail and Boston; returning by Sound Lines.)

Baltimore & Ohio R. R.	to Philadelphia.
Rail Lines (see pages 50 to 55 for routes)	to Boston.
Boston & Maine R. R.	to North Conway.
Maine Central R. R.	to Zealand Junction
Profile & Franconia Notch R. R.	to Bethlehem.
Profile & Franconia Notch R. R.	to Zealand Junction
Maine Central R. R.	to North Conway.
Boston & Maine R. R.	to Boston.
Sound Lines (see pages 50 to 55 for routes)	to New York.
Central R. R. of New Jersey	to Bound Brook.
Philadelphia & Reading R. R.	to Philadelphia.
Baltimore & Ohio R. R.	to starting point

Transfer through Boston, returning, included.

THROUGH RATES.

Baltimore, Md.	$27 40	Washington, D. C.	$29 40
Philadelphia, Pa.	23 40		

FORM EX. 815. BETHLEHEM, N. H., AND RETURN.
(Via Sound Lines and Boston; returning via all rail.)

Baltimore & Ohio R. R.	to Philadelphia.
Philadelphia & Reading R. R.	to Bound Brook.
Central R. R. of New Jersey	to New York.
Sound Lines (see pages 50 to 55 for routes)	to Boston.
Boston & Maine R. R.	to North Conway.
Maine Central R. R.	to Zealand Junction.
Profile & Franconia Notch R. R.	to Bethlehem.
Profile & Franconia Notch R. R.	to Zealand Junction.
Maine Central R. R.	to North Conway.
Boston & Maine R. R.	to Boston.
Rail Lines (see pages 50 to 55 for routes)	to Philadelphia.
Baltimore & Ohio R. R.	to starting point.

Transfer through Boston, going, included.

THROUGH RATES.

Baltimore, Md.	$27 40	Washington, D. C.	$29 40
Philadelphia, Pa.	23 40		

FORM EX. 815. BETHLEHEM, N. H., AND RETURN.
(Via Rail Lines and Boston, in both directions.)

Baltimore & Ohio R. R.	to Philadelphia
Rail Lines (see pages 50 to 55 for routes)	to Boston.
Boston & Maine R. R.	to North Conway.
Maine Central R. R.	to Zealand Junction
Profile & Franconia Notch R. R.	to Bethlehem.

Returning, same route.

THROUGH RATES.

Baltimore, Md.	$28 75	Washington, D. C.	$30 75
Philadelphia, Pa.	24 75		

FORM Ex. 815. BETHLEHEM, N. H., AND RETURN.

(Via Sound Lines and Boston, in both directions.)

Baltimore & Ohio R. R. . . . . to Philadelphia.
Philadelphia & Reading R. R. . . . . to Bound Brook.
Central R. R. of New Jersey . . . . to New York.
Sound Lines (see pages 50 to 55 for routes) . . . to Boston.
Boston & Maine R. R. . . . . to North Conway.
Maine Central R. R. . . . . to Zealand Junction
Profile & Franconia Notch R. R. . . . . to Bethlehem.

Returning, same route.

Transfer through Boston, in both directions, included.

THROUGH RATES.

Baltimore, Md. . . . . . $24 00   Washington, D. C. . $26 00
(Philadelphia, Pa. . . . 20 00)

FORM Ex. 816. BETHLEHEM, N. H., AND RETURN.

(Via rail and Portland; returning via Sound Lines.)

Baltimore & Ohio R. R. . . . . to Philadelphia.
Rail Lines (see pages 50 to 55 for routes) . . . . to Boston.
Boston & Maine R. R. . . . . to Portland.
Maine Central R. R. . . . . to Zealand Junc.
Profile & Franconia Notch R. R. . . . . to Bethlehem.
Profile & Franconia Notch R. R. . . . . to Zealand Junc.
Maine Central R. R. . . . . to Portland.
Boston & Maine R. R. . . . . to Boston.
Sound Lines (see pages 50 to 55 for routes) . . . to New York.
Central R. R. of New Jersey . . . . to Bound Brook.
Philadelphia & Reading R. R. . . . . to Philadelphia.
Baltimore & Ohio R. R. . . . . to starting point.

Transfer through Boston, returning, included.

THROUGH RATES.

Baltimore, Md. . . . . . $27 10   Washington, D. C. . . $29 10
(Philadelphia, Pa. . . . 23 10)

FORM Ex. 816. BETHLEHEM, N. H., AND RETURN.

(Via Sound Lines and Portland; returning by rail.)

Baltimore & Ohio R. R. . . . . to Philadelphia.
Philadelphia & Reading R. R. . . . . to Bound Brook.
Central R. R. of New Jersey . . . . to New York.
Sound Lines (see pages 50 to 55 for routes) . . . to Boston.
Boston & Maine R. R. . . . . to Portland.
Maine Central R. R. . . . . to Zealand Junc.
Profile & Franconia Notch R. R. . . . . to Bethlehem.
Profile & Franconia Notch R. R. . . . . to Zealand Junction
Maine Central R. R. . . . . to Portland.
Boston & Maine R. R. . . . . to Boston.
Rail Lines (see pages 50 to 55 for routes) . . . . to Philadelphia.
Baltimore & Ohio R. R. . . . . to starting point.

Transfer through Boston, going, included.

THROUGH RATES.

Baltimore, Md. . . . . . $27 10   Washington, D. C. . . $29 10
(Philadelphia, Pa. . . . 23 10)

ROUTES AND RATES FOR SUMMER TOURS   41

FORM EX. 846.   BETHLEHEM, N. H., AND RETURN.
(Via Rail Lines and Portland, in both directions.)

Baltimore & Ohio R. R. . . . . to Philadelphia.
Rail Lines (see pages 50 to 55 for route) . . . . to Boston.
Boston & Maine R. R. . . . . to Portland.
Maine Central R. R. . . . . to Zealand Junction.
Profile & Franconia Notch R. R. . . . . to Bethlehem.
Returning, same route.

THROUGH RATES.

Baltimore, Md. . . . . . . $28 75 | Washington, D. C. . . $29 75
(Philadelphia, Pa. . . . 24 75 |

FORM EX. 846.   BETHLEHEM, N. H., AND RETURN.
(Via Sound Lines and Portland, in both directions.)

Baltimore & Ohio R. R. . . . . to Philadelphia.
Philadelphia & Reading R. R. . . . . to Bound Brook.
Central R. R. of New Jersey . . . . to New York.
Sound Lines (see pages 50 to 55 for route) . . . to Boston.
Boston & Maine R. R. . . . . to Portland.
Maine Central R. R. . . . . to Zealand Junction.
Profile and Franconia Notch R. R. . . . . . . to Bethlehem.
Returning, same route.
Transfer through Boston, in both directions, included.

THROUGH RATES.

Baltimore, Md. . . . . . . $24 00 | Washington, D. C. . . $26 00
(Philadelphia, Pa. . . . 20 00 |

FORM EX. 544.   BETHLEHEM, N. H., AND RETURN.
(Via rail and Boston; returning by Sound Lines.)

Baltimore & Ohio R. R. . . . . to Philadelphia.
Rail Lines (see pages 50 to 55 for route) . . . . to Boston.
Boston & Maine R. R. . . . . to Nashua.
Concord & Montreal R. R. . . . . to Bethlehem June.
Profile & Franconia Notch R. R. . . . . to Bethlehem.
Profile & Franconia Notch R. R. . . . . to Bethlehem June.
Concord & Montreal R. R. . . . . to Nashua.
Boston & Maine R. R. . . . . to Boston.
Sound Lines (see pages 50 to 55 for route) . . . to New York.
Central R. R. of New Jersey . . . . to Bound Brook.
Philadelphia & Reading R. R. . . . . to Philadelphia.
Baltimore & Ohio R. R. . . . . to starting point.
Transfer through Boston, returning, included.

THROUGH RATES.

Baltimore, Md. . . . . . . $26 00 | Washington, D. C. . . $28 00
(Philadelphia, Pa. . . . 22 00 |

FORM EX. 544.   BETHLEHEM, N. H., AND RETURN.
(Via Sound Lines and Boston; returning via all rail.)

Baltimore & Ohio R. R. . . . . to Philadelphia.
Philadelphia & Reading R. R. . . . . to Bound Brook.
Central R. R. of New Jersey . . . . to New York.
Sound Lines (see pages 50 to 55 for route) . . . to Boston.
Boston & Maine R. R. . . . . to Nashua.
Concord & Montreal R. R. . . . . to Bethlehem June.
Profile & Franconia Notch R. R. . . . . to Bethlehem.
Profile & Franconia Notch R. R. . . . . to Bethlehem June.
Concord & Montreal R. R. . . . . to Nashua.
Boston & Maine R. R. . . . . to Boston.
Rail Lines (see pages 50 to 55 for route) . . . . to Philadelphia.
Baltimore & Ohio R. R. . . . . to starting point.
Transfer through Boston, going, included.

THROUGH RATES.

Baltimore, Md. . . . . . . $26 00 | Washington, D. C. $28 00
Philadelphia, Pa. 22 00

FORM EX. 511.—BETHLEHEM, N. H., AND RETURN.

(Via Rail Lines and Boston in both directions.)

Baltimore & Ohio R. R. . . . . to Philadelphia.
Rail Lines (see pages 50 to 55 for routes) . . . to Boston.
Boston & Maine R. R. . . . . to Nashua.
Concord & Montreal R. R. . . . . to Bethlehem June.
Profile & Franconia Notch R. R. . . . . to Bethlehem.

Returning, same route.

THROUGH RATES.

Baltimore, Md. . . . . . . $28 75 | Washington, D. C. $30 75
Philadelphia, Pa. 24 75

FORM EX. 544.—BETHLEHEM, N. H., AND RETURN.

(Via Sound Lines and Boston in both directions.)

Baltimore & Ohio R. R. . . . . to Philadelphia.
Philadelphia & Reading R. R. . . . . to Bound Brook.
Central R. R. of New Jersey . . . . to New York.
Sound Lines (see pages 50 to 55 for routes) . . to Boston.
Boston & Maine R. R. . . . . to Nashua.
Concord & Montreal R. R. . . . . to Bethlehem June.
Profile & Franconia Notch R. R. . . . . to Bethlehem.

Returning, same route.

Transfer through Boston, in both directions, included.

THROUGH RATES.

Baltimore, Md. . . . . . . $23 00 | Washington, D. C. $25 00
Philadelphia, Pa. 19 00

FORM EX. 608.—BETHLEHEM, N. H., AND RETURN.

Baltimore & Ohio R. R. . . . . to Philadelphia.
Philadelphia & Reading R. R. . . . . to Bound Brook.
Central R. R. of New Jersey . . . . to New York.
New York, New Haven & Hartford R. R. . . . to Springfield.
Connecticut River R. R. . . . . to South Vernon.
Central Vermont R. R. . . . . to Brattleboro.
Vermont Valley R. R. . . . . to Windsor.
Central Vermont R. R. . . . . to White River June.
Boston & Maine R. R. . . . . to Wells' River.
Concord & Montreal R. R. . . . . to Bethlehem June.
Profile & Franconia Notch R. R. . . . . to Bethlehem.

Returning, same route.

THROUGH RATES.

Baltimore, Md. . . . . . . $25 00 | Washington, D. C. $27 00
Philadelphia, Pa. 21 00

BLACK MOUNTAIN, N. C.

FORM EX. 57. BLACK MOUNTAIN, N. C., AND RETURN.

Baltimore & Ohio R. R. . . . . to Washington
Transfer . . . . B. & O. Depot to R. & D. Depot
Richmond & Danville R. R. . . . . to Black Mountain

Returning, same route.

THROUGH RATES.

Baltimore, Md.	$24 50	Meyersdale, Pa.	$27 90
Bellaire, O.	31 15	Morgantown, W. Va.	32 05
Berkeley Springs, W. Va.	24 15	Moundsville, W. Va.	33 70
Cameron, W. Va.	33 00	Mountain Lake Park, Md.	27 05
Charlestown, W. Va.	22 70	Mt. Pleasant, Pa.	30 30
Chester, Pa.	25 00	Newark, Del.	23 80
Clarksburg, W. Va.	31 05	New York, N. Y.	29 70
Connellsville, Pa.	29 80	Oakland, Md.	27 25
Cumberland, Md.	26 10	Parkersburg, W. Va.	31 15
Deer Park, Md.	27 70	Philadelphia, Pa.	25 00
Fairmont, W. Va.	31 05	Piedmont, W. Va.	27 20
Frederick, Md.	22 70	Pittsburgh, Pa.	32 10
Grafton, W. Va.	30 15	Rockwood, Pa.	28 05
Hagerstown, Md.	23 10	Somerset, Pa.	28 15
Harper's Ferry, W. Va.	22 20	Uniontown, Pa.	30 25
Havre de Grace, Md.	22 95	Washington, Pa.	33 20
Johnstown, Pa.	29 85	Wheeling, W. Va.	31 15
Keyser, W. Va.	27 00	Wilmington, Del.	24 50
McKeesport, Pa.	31 55	Winchester, Va.	23 80
Martinsburg, W. Va.	22 95		

FORM EX. E. — BLACK MOUNTAIN, N. C., AND RETURN.

Baltimore & Ohio R. R. . . . . to Lexington.
Chesapeake & Ohio R. R. . . . . to Lynchburg.
Richmond & Danville R. R. . . . . to Black Mountain.

Returning, same route.

THROUGH RATES.

Baltimore, Md.	$21 50	Morgantown, W. Va.	$29 35
Bellaire, O.	31 75	Moundsville, W. Va.	31 00
Berkeley Springs, W. Va.	24 15	Mountain Lake Park, Md.	25 15
Cameron, W. Va.	30 30	Mt. Pleasant, Pa.	27 00
Charlestown, W. Va.	19 50	Newark, Del.	25 80
Chester, Pa.	25 00	New York, N. Y.	29 50
Clarksburg, W. Va.	28 35	Oakland, Md.	25 55
Connellsville, Pa.	27 10	Parkersburg, W. Va.	31 50
Cumberland, Md.	23 10	Philadelphia, Pa.	25 50
Deer Park, Md.	25 20	Piedmont, W. Va.	24 50
Fairmont, W. Va.	28 35	Pittsburgh, Pa.	29 40
Frederick, Md.	20 15	Rockwood, Pa.	25 35
Grafton, W. Va.	27 15	Somerset, Pa.	25 75
Hagerstown, Md.	20 50	Staunton, Va.	16 00
Harper's Ferry, W. Va.	19 50	Strasburg, Va.	19 50
Harrisonburg, Va.	17 90	Uniontown, Pa.	27 55
Havre de Grace, Md.	22 95	Washington, D. C.	19 50
Johnstown, Pa.	27 15	Washington, Pa.	30 50
Keyser, W. Va.	24 30	Wheeling, W. Va.	31 50
McKeesport, Pa.	28 85	Wilmington, Del.	26 50
Martinsburg, W. Va.	20 25	Winchester, Va.	19 50
Meyersdale, Pa.	24 90		

BLOCK ISLAND, R. I.

"There is that lovely island fair;
 And the pale health-seeker findeth there
 The wine of life in its pleasant air.

"No greener valleys the sun invite;
 On smoother beaches no sea-birds light;
 No blue waves shatter to foam more white.'"

The peculiar advantage of Block Island lies in this, that it is not only a resort at the sea, but in the sea. Situated ten miles south of Point Judith, it is washed on every side by the waters of the Atlantic Ocean. No land breeze, bearing pestiferous mosquitoes and choking dust can find its way to this guarded spot. No impurities from neighboring cities defile the clearness of its surf. The thermometer rarely registers over 75°.

The hotels are amply provided with all modern improvements, and the social life of the place, while not lacking in spirit, does not obtrude itself to the annoyance of those whose chief objects are quiet and health.

FORM EX. 609.—BLOCK ISLAND, R. I., AND RETURN.

Baltimore & Ohio R. R. . . . . to Philadelphia.
Philadelphia & Reading R. R. . . . . to Bound Brook.
Central R. R. of New Jersey . . . . to New York.
Old Colony Steamboat Co. (Fall River Line). . to Newport.
Fall River & Providence Steamship Co. . . . . to Block Island.
Returning, same route.

THROUGH RATES.

Baltimore, Md. . . . . . . $14 75 | Washington, D. C. $16 75
{Philadelphia, Pa. . . . . 10 75 |

FORM EX. 710.—BLOCK ISLAND, R. I., AND RETURN.

Baltimore & Ohio R. R. . . . . to Philadelphia.
Philadelphia & Reading R. R. . . . . to Bound Brook.
Central R. R. of New Jersey . . . . to New York.
Stonington Line . . . . to Stonington.
Watch Hill Ferry . . . . to Watch Hill.
Steamer "Block Island" . . . . to Block Island.
Returning, same route.

THROUGH RATES.

Baltimore, Md. . . . . . . $12 30 | Washington, D. C. $14 30
{Philadelphia, Pa. . . . . 8 30 |

FORM EX. 711.—BLOCK ISLAND, R. I., AND RETURN.

Baltimore & Ohio R. R. . . . . to Philadelphia.
Philadelphia & Reading R. R. . . . . to Bound Brook.
Central R. R. of New Jersey . . . . to New York.
New York, New Haven & Hartford R. R. . . . . to New London.
Steamer "Block Island" . . . . to Block Island.
Returning, same route.

THROUGH RATES.

Baltimore, Md. . . . . . . $15 00 | Washington, D. C. $17 00
{Philadelphia, Pa. . . . . 11 00 |

FORM EX. 712.—BLOCK ISLAND, R. I., AND RETURN.

Baltimore & Ohio R. R. . . . . to Philadelphia.
Philadelphia & Reading R. R. . . . . to Bound Brook.
Central R. R. of New Jersey . . . . to New York.
Norwich Line . . . . to New London.
Steamer "Block Island" . . . . to Block Island.
Returning, same route.

THROUGH RATES.

Baltimore, Md. . . . . . . $12 30 | Washington, D. C. $14 30
{Philadelphia, Pa. . . . . 8 30 |

BLUE MOUNTAIN, MD.

FORM EX. 725. BLUE MOUNTAIN, MD., AND RETURN.

Baltimore & Ohio R. R. . . . . to Baltimore.
Transfer, B. & O. R. R. Depot . . . to Western Md. R. R., Fulton Station.
Western Maryland R. R. . . . . to Blue Mountain.
Returning, same route.

THROUGH RATES.

Baltimore, Md.	$5 00	Philadelphia, Pa.	$7 00
Chester, Pa.	7 10	Washington, D. C.	5 00
New York, N. Y.	11 00	Wilmington, Del.	6 00

FORM EX. 678. BLUE MOUNTAIN, MD., AND RETURN.

Baltimore & Ohio R. R. . . . . to Hagerstown.
Transfer, B. & O. Depot . . . . to W. M. R. R. Depot.
West. Md. R. R. (via Short Line) . . . . to Blue Mountain.
Returning, same route.

THROUGH RATES.

Bellaire, O.	$14 00	Moundsville, W. Va.	$13 20
Berkeley Springs, W. Va.	3 65	Mountain Lake Park, Md.	7 65
Charlestown, W. Va.	2 80	Mt. Pleasant, Pa.	9 80
Clarksburg, W. Va.	10 55	Oakland, Md.	7 75
Connellsville, Pa.	9 30	Parkersburg, W. Va.	13 65
Cumberland, Md.	5 60	Piedmont, W. Va.	6 70
Deer Park, Md.	7 50	Pittsburgh, Pa.	11 00
Fairmont, W. Va.	10 55	Rockwood, Pa.	7 55
Grafton, W. Va.	9 65	Somerset, Pa.	7 95
Harper's Ferry, W. Va.	2 30	Staunton, Va.	8 60
Harrisonburg, Va.	7 30	Uniontown, Pa.	9 75
Johnstown, Pa.	9 35	Washington, D. C.	1 35
Keyser, W. Va.	6 50	Washingt'n via Pittsb'h, Pa	12 70
Lexington, Va.	10 10	Wheeling, W. Va.	13 65
Meyersdale, Pa.	7 10	Winchester, Va.	3 90
Morgantown, W. Va.	11 55		

BLUE RIDGE SPRINGS, VA.

FORM EX. 32. BLUE RIDGE SPRINGS, VA., AND RETURN.

Baltimore & Ohio R. R. . . . . to Washington.
Transfer . . . . B. & O. Depot to R. & D. Depot.
Richmond & Danville R. R. . . . . to Lynchburg.
Norfolk & Western R. R. . . . . to Blue Ridge Springs.
Returning, same route.

THROUGH RATES.

Baltimore, Md.	$12 10	Meyersdale, Pa.	$18 20
Bellaire, O.	25 05	Morgantown, W. Va.	22 65
Berkeley Springs, W. Va.	14 75	Moundsville, W. Va.	24 30
Cameron, W. Va.	23 60	Mountain Lake Park, Md.	18 25
Charlestown, W. Va.	13 30	Mt. Pleasant, Pa.	20 90
Chester, Pa.	15 60	Newark, Del.	14 10
Clarksburg, W. Va.	21 65	New York, N. Y.	20 10
Connellsville, Pa.	20 40	Oakland, Md.	18 35
Cumberland, Md.	16 70	Parkersburg, W. Va.	24 75
Deer Park, Md.	18 10	Philadelphia, Pa.	16 10
Fairmont, W. Va.	21 65	Piedmont, W. Va.	17 80
Frederick, Md.	12 90	Pittsburgh, Pa.	22 70
Grafton, W. Va.	20 75	Rockwood, Pa.	18 65
Hagerstown, Md.	13 70	Somerset, Pa.	19 05
Harper's Ferry, W. Va.	12 80	Uniontown, Pa.	20 85
Havre de Grace, Md.	13 55	Washington, Pa.	23 80
Johnstown, Pa.	20 45	Wheeling, W. Va.	24 75
Keyser, W. Va.	17 60	Wilmington, Del.	15 10
McKeesport, Pa.	22 15	Winchester, Va.	14 10
Martinsburg, W. Va.	13 55		

Form Ex. 35.— BLUE RIDGE SPRINGS, VA., AND RETURN.

Baltimore & Ohio R. R. . . . . to Shenandoah June
Norfolk & Western R. R. . . . . to Blue Ridge Station
Returning, same route.

THROUGH RATES.

Baltimore, Md.	$12 80	Morgantown, W. Va.	$19 05
Bellaire, O.	21 45	Moundsville, W. Va.	20 75
Berkeley Springs, W. Va.	11 25	Mountain Lake Park, Md.	15 20
Cameron, W. Va.	20 05	Mt. Pleasant, Pa.	17 50
Chester, Pa.	16 30	Newark, Del.	15 40
Clarksburg, W. Va.	18 65	New York, N. Y.	20 80
Connellsville, Pa.	16 80	Oakland, Md.	15 50
Cumberland, Md.	13 40	Parkersburg, W. Va.	21 15
Deer Park, Md.	15 05	Philadelphia, Pa.	16 80
Fairmont, W. Va.	18 05	Piedmont, W. Va.	11 25
Frederick, Md.	10 85	Pittsburgh, Pa.	19 40
Grafton, W. Va.	17 40	Rockwood, Pa.	15 05
Harper's Ferry, W. Va.	9 75	Somerset, Pa.	15 45
Havre de Grace, Md.	11 25	Uniontown, Pa.	17 25
Johnstown, Pa.	16 85	Washington, D. C.	10 80
Keyser, W. Va.	11 05	Washington, Pa.	20 20
McKeesport, Pa.	18 55	Wheeling, W. Va.	21 15
Martinsburg, W. Va.	9 95	Wilmington, Del.	15 80
Meyersdale, Pa.	14 60		

BLUE RIDGE STATION, PA.

Form Ex. 756.—Blue Ridge Station, Pa., and Return.

Baltimore & Ohio R. R. . . . . to Baltimore.
Transfer, B. & O. Depot . . . . to W. Md. R. R., Fulton Station
Western Maryland R. R. . . . . to Blue Ridge Station

Returning, same route.

THROUGH RATES.

Baltimore, Md.	$5.70	Philadelphia, Pa.	$7.50
Chester, Pa.	7.00	Washington, D. C.	5.70
New York, N. Y.	11.50	Wilmington, Del.	6.50

BOOTHBAY, ME.

Form Ex. 925.—Boothbay, Me., and Return.

(Via rail to Bath, thence by steamer; returning via Sound Lines from Boston.)

Baltimore & Ohio R. R. . . . . to Philadelphia.
Rail Lines (see pages 50 to 55 for routes) . . . . . to Boston.
Boston & Maine R. R. . . . . to Portland.
Maine Central R. R. . . . . to Bath.
Eastern Steamboat Co. . . . . to Boothbay.
Eastern Steamboat Co. . . . . to Bath.
Maine Central R. R. . . . . to Portland.
Boston & Maine R. R. . . . . to Boston.
Sound Lines (see pages 50 to 55 for routes) . . . . to New York.
Central R. R. of New Jersey . . . . to Bound Brook.
Philadelphia & Reading R. R. . . . . to Philadelphia.
Baltimore & Ohio R. R. . . . . to starting point.

THROUGH RATES.

Baltimore, Md.	$25.75	Washington, D. C.	$25.75
Philadelphia, Pa.	19.75		

Form Ex. 925.—Boothbay, Me., and Return.

(Via Sound Lines to Bath, thence by steamer; returning by rail from Boston.)

Baltimore & Ohio R. R. . . . . to Philadelphia.
Philadelphia & Reading R. R. . . . . to Bound Brook.
Central R. R. of New Jersey . . . . to New York.
Sound Lines (see pages 50 to 55 for routes) . . . to Boston.
Boston & Maine R. R. . . . . to Portland.
Maine Central R. R. . . . . to Bath.
Eastern Steamboat Co. . . . . to Boothbay.
Eastern Steamboat Co. . . . . to Bath.
Maine Central R. R. . . . . to Portland.
Boston & Maine R. R. . . . . to Boston.
Rail Lines (see pages 50 to 55 for routes) . . . . to Philadelphia.
Baltimore & Ohio R. R. . . . . to starting point.

THROUGH RATES.

Baltimore, Md.	$25.75	Washington, D. C.	$25.75
Philadelphia, Pa.	19.75		

Form Ex. 925.—Boothbay, Me., and Return.

(Via Rail Lines, Bath and steamer in both directions.)

Baltimore & Ohio R. R. . . . . to Philadelphia.
Rail Lines (see pages 50 to 55 for routes) . . . . to Boston.
Boston & Maine R. R. . . . . to Portland.
Maine Central R. R. . . . . to Bath.
Eastern Steamboat Co. . . . . to Boothbay.

Returning, same route.

ROUTES AND RATES FOR SUMMER TOURS. 49

THROUGH RATES.

Baltimore, Md. . . . . . . $24 75 | Washington, D. C. 26 75
Philadelphia, Pa. . . . . 20 75 |

FORM EX. 925. BOOTHBAY, ME., AND RETURN.

(Via Sound Lines, Bath and steamer in both directions.)

Baltimore & Ohio R. R. . . . . to Philadelphia.
Philadelphia & Reading R. R. . . . . to Bound Brook
Central R. R. of New Jersey . . . . to New York.
Sound Lines (see pages 50 to 55 for routes) . . . to Boston.
Boston & Maine R. R. . . . . to Portland.
Maine Central R. R. . . . . to Bath.
Eastern Steamboat Co. . . . . to Boothbay.

Returning, same route.

THROUGH RATES.

Baltimore, Md. . . . . . . $22 75 | Washington, D. C. 24 75
Philadelphia, Pa. . . . . 18 75 |

BOSTON, MASS.

FORM EX. 667. —TO BOSTON, MASS., AND RETURN.

Baltimore & Ohio R. R. . . . . to Baltimore.
Omnibus Transfer, one passenger and ordinary
   baggage . . . . to M. & M. T. Co.'s Long Dock
Merchants' and Miners' Transportation Co. . . . to Boston.

Returning, same route.

Rate from Baltimore (including transfer) $23 00

FORM EX. 668.—BOSTON, MASS., AND RETURN.

Baltimore & Ohio R. R. . . . . to Baltimore.
Omnibus Transfer, one passenger and ordinary
   baggage . . . . to M. & M. T. Co.'s Long Dock.
Merchants' and Miners' Transportation Co. . . . to Boston.
Old Colony R. R. . . . . to Fall River.
Old Colony Steamboat Co. (Fall River Line) . . . to New York.
New York Transfer Co. . . . . to Depot C. R. R. of New Jersey
Central R. R. of New Jersey . . . . to Bound Brook.
Philadelphia & Reading R. R. . . . . to Philadelphia.
Baltimore & Ohio R. R. . . . . to starting point.

Rate from Baltimore (including transfers) $22 80

FORM EX. 669.—BOSTON, MASS., AND RETURN.

Baltimore & Ohio R. R. . . . . to Baltimore.
Omnibus Transfer, one passenger and ordinary
   baggage . . . . to M. & M. T. Co.'s Long Dock.
Merchants' and Miners' Transportation Co. . . . to Boston.
Boston & Albany R. R. . . . . to Springfield.
New York, New Haven & Hartford R. R. . . . . to New Haven.
New York, New Haven & Hartford R. R. . . . . to New York.
New York Transfer Co. . . . . to Depot C. R. R. of New Jersey.
Central R. R. of New Jersey . . . . to Bound Brook.
Philadelphia & Reading R. R. . . . . to Philadelphia.
Baltimore & Ohio R. R. . . . . to starting point.

Rate from Baltimore (including transfers) $23 80

FEEDING FORMS TO AND FROM BOSTON, MASS.

which have been prepared for use in connection with extension tickets of Baltimore & Ohio R. R. issue, from Boston to Boston, thus making complete round-trip tickets from point of sale. These forms are not for sale except in connection with the extension tickets.

TO BOSTON AND RETURN.

Form Ex. 197.—Boston, Mass., and Return.

Baltimore & Ohio R. R. . . . . to Philadelphia.
Philadelphia & Reading R. R. . . . . to Bound Brook.
Central R. R. of New Jersey . . . . to New York.
Old Colony Steamboat Co. (Fall River Line) . . to Fall River.
Old Colony R. R. . . . . to Boston.
Returning, same route.

Form Ex. 198.—Boston, Mass., and Return.

Baltimore & Ohio R. R. . . . . to Philadelphia.
Philadelphia & Reading R. R. . . . . to Bound Brook.
Central R. R. of New Jersey . . . . to New York.
New York, New Haven & Hartford R. R. . . . to New Haven.
New York, New Haven & Hartford R. R. . . . to Springfield.
Boston & Albany R. R. . . . . to Boston.
Returning, same route.

Form Ex. 199.—Boston, Mass., and Return.

Baltimore & Ohio R. R. . . . . to Philadelphia.
Philadelphia & Reading R. R. . . . . to Bound Brook.
Central R. R. of New Jersey . . . . to New York.
New York, New Haven & Hartford R. R. . . . to New Haven.
New York, New Haven & Hartford R. R. (S. L. D.) to New London.
New York, Providence & Boston R. R. . . . . to Providence.
Old Colony R. R. . . . . to Boston.
Returning, same route.

Form Ex. 771.—Boston, Mass., and Return.

Baltimore & Ohio R. R. . . . . to Philadelphia.
Philadelphia & Reading R. R. . . . . to Bethlehem.
Central R. R. of New Jersey . . . . to Easton.
Lehigh & Hudson River R. R. . . . . to Belvidere.
Lehigh & Hudson River R. R. . . . . to Maybrook.
Central, New England and Western R. R. . . to Simsbury.
New York, New Haven & Hartford R. R. . . . to Northampton.
Boston & Maine R. R. . . . . to Boston.
Returning, same route.

Form Ex. 926.—Boston, Mass., and Return.

Baltimore & Ohio R. R. . . . . to Philadelphia.
Philadelphia & Reading R. R. . . . . to Bound Brook.
Central R. R. of New Jersey . . . . to New York.
New York, New Haven & Hartford R. R. . . . to Hartford.
New York & New England R. R. . . . . to Boston.
Returning, same route.

Form Ex. 927.—Boston, Mass., and Return.

Baltimore & Ohio R. R. . . . . to Philadelphia.
Philadelphia & Reading R. R. . . . . to Bound Brook.
Central R. R. of N. J. . . . . to New York.
New York, New Haven & Hartford R. R. . . . to New Haven.
New York, New Haven & Hartford R. R. (Air
  Line Division) . . . . to Willimantic.
New York & New England R. R. . . . . to Boston.
Returning, same route.

FORM EX. 928. BOSTON, MASS., AND RETURN.

Baltimore & Ohio R. R. . . . . to Philadelphia.
Philadelphia & Reading R. R. . . . . to Bound Brook.
Central R. R. of New Jersey . . . . to New York.
Norwich Line. . . . . to New London.
New York & New England R. R. (N. & W. Div.) to Putnam.
New York & New England R. R. . . . . to Boston.

Returning, same route.

FORM EX. 929. BOSTON, MASS., AND RETURN.

Baltimore & Ohio R. R. . . . . to Philadelphia.
Philadelphia & Reading R. R. . . . . to Bound Brook.
Central R. R. of New Jersey . . . . to New York.
Stonington Line. . . . . to Stonington.
New York, Providence & Boston R. R. . . . . . . to Providence.
Old Colony R. R. to Boston.

Returning, same route.

FORM EX. 930. BOSTON, MASS., AND RETURN.

Baltimore & Ohio R. R. . . . . to Philadelphia.
Philadelphia & Reading R. R. . . . . to Bound Brook.
Central R. R. of New Jersey . . . . to New York.
Providence Line . . . . to Providence.
Old Colony R. R. to Boston.

Returning, same route.

TO BOSTON.

FORM EX. 931.—TO BOSTON, MASS.

Baltimore & Ohio R. R. . . . . to Philadelphia.
Philadelphia & Reading R. R. . . . . to Bethlehem.
Central R. R. of N. J. . . . . to Easton.
Lehigh & Hudson River R. R. . . . . to Belvidere.
Lehigh & Hudson River R. R. . . . . to Maybrook.
Central New England & Western R. R. . . . . . to Simsbury.
New York, New Haven & Hartford R. R. . . . . to Northampton
Boston & Maine R. R. . . . . to Boston.

FORM EX. 932.—TO BOSTON, MASS.

Baltimore & Ohio R. R. . . . . to Philadelphia.
Philadelphia & Reading R. R. . . . . to Bound Brook.
Central R. R. of New Jersey . . . . to New York.
New York, New Haven & Hartford R. R. . . . . to New Haven.
New York, New Haven & Hartford R. R. (S. L. D.) to New London.
New York, Providence & Boston R. R. . . . . . . to Providence.
Old Colony R. R. to Boston.

FORM EX. 933.—TO BOSTON, MASS.

Baltimore & Ohio R. R. . . . . to Philadelphia.
Philadelphia & Reading R. R. . . . . to Bound Brook.
Central R. R. of New Jersey . . . . to New York.
New York, New Haven & Hartford R. R. . . . . to New Haven.
New York, New Haven & Hartford R. R. (Air
  Line Div.) . . . . to Willimantic.
New York & New England R. R. . . . . to Boston.

FORM EX. 934.—TO BOSTON, MASS.

Baltimore & Ohio R. R. . . . . to Philadelphia.
Philadelphia & Reading R. R. . . . . to Bound Brook.
Central R. R. of New Jersey . . . . to New York.
New York, New Haven & Hartford R. R. . . . . to Hartford.
New York & New England R. R. . . . . to Boston.

NORTH FORK, POTOMAC.

FORM EX. 935.—To BOSTON, MASS.

Baltimore & Ohio R. R. . . . . to Philadelphia.
Philadelphia & Reading R. R. . . . . to Bound Brook.
Central R. R. of New Jersey . . . . to New York.
New York, New Haven & Hartford R. R. . . . to Springfield.
Boston & Albany R. R. . . . . to Boston.

FORM EX. 936.—To BOSTON, MASS.

Baltimore & Ohio R. R. . . . . to Philadelphia.
Philadelphia & Reading R. R. . . . . to Bound Brook.
Central R. R. of New Jersey . . . . to New York.
Old Colony Steamboat Co. (Fall River Line) . to Fall River.
Old Colony R. R. . . . . to Boston.

FORM EX. 937.—To BOSTON, MASS.

Baltimore & Ohio R. R. . . . . to Philadelphia.
Philadelphia & Reading R. R. . . . . to Bound Brook.
Central R. R. of New Jersey . . . . to New York.
Providence Line . . . . to Providence.
Old Colony R. R. . . . . to Boston.

FORM EX. 938.—To BOSTON, MASS.

Baltimore & Ohio R. R. . . . . to Philadelphia.
Philadelphia & Reading R. R. . . . . to Bound Brook.
Central R. R. of New Jersey . . . . to New York.
Stonington Line . . . . to Stonington.
New York, Providence & Boston R. R. . . . . to Providence.
Old Colony R. R. . . . . to Boston.

FORM EX. 939.—To BOSTON, MASS.

Baltimore & Ohio R. R. . . . . to Philadelphia.
Philadelphia & Reading R. R. . . . . to Bound Brook.
Central R. R. of New Jersey . . . . to New York.
Norwich Line . . . . to New London.
New York & New England R. R. (N. & W. Div.) to Putnam.
New York & New England R. R. . . . . to Boston.

FROM BOSTON.

FORM EX. 940.—FROM BOSTON, MASS.

Boston & Maine R. R. . . . . Boston to Northampton.
New York, New Haven & Hartford R. R. . . . to Simsbury.
Central New England & Western R. R. . . . . to Maybrook.
Lehigh & Hudson River R. R. . . . . to Belvidere.
Lehigh & Hudson River R. R. . . . . to Easton.
Central R. R. of N. J. . . . . to Bethlehem.
Philadelphia & Reading R. R. . . . . to Philadelphia.
Baltimore & Ohio R. R. . . . . to starting point.

FORM EX. 941.—FROM BOSTON, MASS.

Old Colony R. R. . . . . Boston to Providence.
New York, Providence & Boston R. R. . . . . to New London.
New York, New Haven & Hartford R. R. (S. L.
    Div.) . . . . to New Haven.
New York, New Haven & Hartford R. R. . . . to New York.
Central R. R. of New Jersey . . . . to Bound Brook.
Philadelphia & Reading R. R. . . . . to Philadelphia.
Baltimore & Ohio R. R. . . . . to starting point.

ROUTES AND RATES FOR SUMMER TOURS.   55

FORM EX. 942.— FROM BOSTON, MASS.

New York & New England R. R. . . . . . Boston to Willimantic.
New York, New Haven & Hartford (Air Line
   Div.) . . . . to New Haven.
New York, New Haven & Hartford R. R. . . . . to New York.
Central R. R. of New Jersey . . . . to Bound Brook.
Philadelphia & Reading R. R. . . . . to Philadelphia.
Baltimore & Ohio R. R. . . . . to starting point.

FORM EX. 943.— FROM BOSTON, MASS.

New York & New England R. R. . . . . . Boston to Hartford.
New York, New Haven & Hartford R. R. . . . . to New York.
Central R. R. of New Jersey . . . . to Bound Brook.
Philadelphia & Reading R. R. . . . . to Philadelphia.
Baltimore & Ohio R. R. . . . . to starting point.

FORM EX. 944.— FROM BOSTON, MASS.

Boston & Albany R. R. . . . . Boston to Springfield.
New York, New Haven & Hartford R. R. . . . . to New York.
Central R. R. of New Jersey . . . . to Bound Brook.
Philadelphia & Reading R. R. . . . . to Philadelphia.
Baltimore & Ohio R. R. . . . . to starting point.

FORM EX. 945.— FROM BOSTON, MASS.

Old Colony R. R. . . . . Boston to Fall River.
Old Colony Steamboat Co. (Fall River Line) . . to New York.
Central R. R. of New Jersey . . . . to Bound Brook.
Philadelphia & Reading R. R. . . . . to Philadelphia.
Baltimore & Ohio R. R. . . . . to starting point.

FORM EX. 946.— FROM BOSTON, MASS.

Old Colony R. R. . . . . Boston to Providence.
Providence Line . . . . to New York.
Central R. R. of New Jersey . . . . to Bound Brook.
Philadelphia & Reading R. R. . . . . to Philadelphia.
Baltimore & Ohio R. R. . . . . to starting point.

FORM EX. 947.— FROM BOSTON, MASS.

Old Colony R. R. . . . . Boston to Providence.
New York, Providence & Boston R. R. . . . . to Stonington.
Stonington Line . . . . to New York.
Central R. R. of New Jersey . . . . to Bound Brook.
Philadelphia & Reading R. R. . . . . to Philadelphia.
Baltimore & Ohio R. R. . . . . to starting point.

FORM EX. 948.— FROM BOSTON, MASS.

New York & New England R. R. . . . . . Boston to Putnam.
New York & New England R. R., N. & W. Div. to New London.
Norwich Line . . . . to New York.
Central R. R. of New Jersey . . . . to Bound Brook.
Philadelphia & Reading R. R. . . . . to Philadelphia.
Baltimore & Ohio R. R. . . . . to starting point.

BRIDGEHAMPTON, N. Y.

FORM EX. 919. BRIDGEHAMPTON (LONG ISLAND), N. Y., AND RETURN.

Baltimore & Ohio R. R. . . . . to Philadelphia.
Philadelphia & Reading R. R. . . . . to Bound Brook
Central R. R. of New Jersey . . . . to New York.
Metropolitan Ferry Co., James' Slip or 34th Street
    Ferry . . . . to Long Island City.
Long Island R. R. to Bridgehampton.

Returning, same route.

THROUGH RATES.

Baltimore, Md. . . . . $15 15 | Washington, D. C. $15 15
Philadelphia, Pa. . . . . . .   9 15 |

BUENA VISTA SPRINGS, MD.

FORM EX. 826. BUENA VISTA SPRINGS, MD., AND RETURN.

Baltimore & Ohio R. R. . . . . to Hagerstown.
Transfer, Baltimore & Ohio R. R. Depot . . . to W. M. R. R. Depot
Western Maryland R. R. . . . . to Buena Vista Spr'gs

Returning, same route.

THROUGH RATES.

Bellaire, O.	$11 40	Morgantown, W. Va.	$11 65
Berkeley Springs, W. Va.	3 75	Moundsville, W. Va.	13 30
Cameron, W. Va.	12 65	Mountain Lake Park, Md.	7 75
Charlestown, W. Va.	2 90	Mt. Pleasant, Pa.	9 10
Clarksburg, W. Va.	10 65	Oakland, Md.	7 85
Connellsville, Pa.	9 10	Parkersburg, W. Va.	13 75
Cumberland, Md.	5 70	Piedmont, W. Va.	6 80
Deer Park, Md.	7 60	Pittsburgh, Pa.	11 70
Fairmont, W. Va.	10 65	Rockwood, Pa.	7 65
Grafton, W. Va.	9 75	Somerset, Pa.	8 05
Harper's Ferry, W. Va.	2 40	Staunton, Va.	8 70
Harrisonburg, Va.	7 40	Strasburg, Va.	5 05
Johnstown, Pa.	9 15	Uniontown, Pa.	9 85
Keyser, W. Va.	6 00	Washington, D. C.	4 15
Lexington, Va.	10 50	Washington, Pa.	12 80
McKeesport, Pa.	11 15	Wheeling, W. Va.	13 75
Martinsburg, W. Va.	2 55	Winchester, Va.	4 00
Meyersdale, Pa.	7 20		

CAMPOBELLO, N. B.

FORM EX. 960.—CAMPOBELLO, N. B., AND RETURN.

(Via Rail and Boston, returning by Sound Lines.)

Baltimore & Ohio R. R. . . . . to Philadelphia.
Rail Lines (see pages 50 to 55 for routes) . . . to Boston.
Boston & Maine R. R. . . . . to Portland.
International Steamship Line. . . . . to Campobello.
International Steamship Line. . . . . to Portland.
Boston & Maine R. R. . . . . to Boston.
Sound Lines (see pages 50 to 55 for routes) . to New York.
Central R. R. of New Jersey . . . . to Bound Brook.
Philadelphia & Reading R. R. . . . . to Philadelphia.
Baltimore & Ohio R. R. . . . . to starting point.

THROUGH RATES.

Baltimore, Md. . . . . $27 50 Washington, D. C. $29 50
Philadelphia, Pa. 23 50

ROUTES AND RATES FOR SUMMER TOURS. 57

Form Ex. 950. —CAMPOBELLO, N. B., AND RETURN.
(Via Sound Lines and Boston, returning by Rail Lines.)

Baltimore & Ohio R. R. . . . . to Philadelphia.
Philadelphia & Reading R. R. . . . . to Bound Brook.
Central R. R. of New Jersey . . . . to New York.
Sound Lines (see pages 50 to 55 for routes) . . to Boston.
Boston & Maine R. R. . . . . to Portland.
International Steamship Co. . . . . to Campobello.
International Steamship Co. . . . . to Portland.
Boston & Maine R. R. . . . . to Boston.
Rail Lines (see pages 50 to 55 for routes) . . . to Philadelphia.
Baltimore & Ohio R. R. . . . . to starting point.

THROUGH RATES.

Baltimore, Md. . . . . . . $27 50   Washington, D. C. . . . $29 50
†Philadelphia, Pa. 23 50

Form Ex. 950. —CAMPOBELLO, N. B., AND RETURN.
(Via Rail and Boston in both directions.)

Baltimore & Ohio R. R. . . . . to Philadelphia.
Rail Lines (see pages 50 to 55 for routes) . . . to Boston.
Boston & Maine R. R. . . . . to Portland.
International Steamship Line . . . . to Campobello.
Returning, same route.

THROUGH RATES.

Baltimore, Md. . . . . . . $28 50   Washington, D. C. . . . $30 50
†Philadelphia, Pa. 24 50

Form Ex. 950. —CAMPOBELLO, N. B., AND RETURN.
(Via Sound Lines and Boston in both directions.)

Baltimore & Ohio R. R. . . . . to Philadelphia.
Philadelphia & Reading R. R. . . . . to Bound Brook.
Central R. R. of New Jersey . . . . to New York.
Sound Lines (see pages 50 to 55 for routes) . . to Boston.
Boston & Maine R. R. . . . . to Portland.
International Steamship Line . . . . to Campobello.
Returning, same route.

THROUGH RATES.

Baltimore, Md. . . . . . . $26 50   Washington, D. C. . . . $28 50
†Philadelphia, Pa. 22 50

Form Ex. 951. —CAMPOBELLO, N. B., AND RETURN.
(Rail to Boston, returning via Sound Lines.)

Baltimore & Ohio R. R. . . . . to Philadelphia.
Rail Lines (see pages 50 to 55 for routes) . . . to Boston.
International Steamship Line . . . . to Campobello.
International Steamship Line . . . . to Boston.
Sound Lines (see pages 50 to 55 for routes) . . to New York.
Central R. R. of New Jersey . . . . to Bound Brook.
Philadelphia & Reading R. R. . . . . to Philadelphia.
Baltimore & Ohio R. R. . . . . to starting point.

THROUGH RATES.

Baltimore, Md. . . . . . . $24 50   Washington, D. C. . . . $26 50
†Philadelphia, Pa. 20 50

58   BALTIMORE & OHIO RAILROAD COMPANY

FORM EX. 954. CAMPOBELLO, N. B., AND RETURN.
(Sound Lines to Boston, returning via rail.)
Baltimore & Ohio R. R. . . . . to Philadelphia.
Philadelphia & Reading R. R. . . . . to Bound Brook.
Central R. R. of New Jersey . . . . to New York.
Sound Lines (see pages 50 to 55 for routes) . . . . to Boston.
International Steamship Line . . . . to Campobello.
International Steamship Line . . . . to Boston.
Rail Lines (see pages 50 to 55 for routes) . . . . . to Philadelphia.
Baltimore & Ohio R. R. . . . . to starting point.

THROUGH RATES.
Baltimore, Md. . . . $24 50   Washington, D. C. $26 50
†Philadelphia, Pa. . . 20 50

FORM EX. 954.—CAMPOBELLO, N. B., AND RETURN.
(Via Sound Lines and Boston in both directions.)
Baltimore & Ohio R. R. . . . . to Philadelphia.
Philadelphia & Reading R. R. . . . . to Bound Brook.
Central R. R. of New Jersey . . . . to New York.
Sound Lines (see pages 50 to 55 for routes) . . . . to Boston.
International Steamship Line . . . . to Campobello.
Returning, same route.

THROUGH RATES.
Baltimore, Md. . . . $23 50   Washington, D. C. $25 50
†Philadelphia, Pa. . . 19 50

FORM EX. 954.—CAMPOBELLO, N. B., AND RETURN.
(Via rail and Boston in both directions.)
Baltimore & Ohio R. R. . . . . to Philadelphia.
Rail Lines (see pages 50 to 55 for routes) . . . . . to Boston.
International Steamship Line . . . . to Campobello.
Returning, same route.

THROUGH RATES.
Baltimore, Md. . . . $25 50   Washington, D. C. $27 50
†Philadelphia, Pa. . . 21 50

CAPON LAKE HOME, VA.

FORM EX. 208.—CAPON LAKE HOME, VA., AND RETURN.
Baltimore & Ohio R. R. . . . . to Winchester.
Stage (27 miles) . . . . to Capon Lake Home.
Returning, same route.

THROUGH RATES.

Baltimore, Md.	$10 40	Meyersdale, Pa.	$12 00
Bellaire, O.	18 85	Morgantown, W. Va.	10 45
Berkeley Springs, W. Va.	8 55	Moundsville, W. Va.	18 40
Cameron, W. Va.	17 40	Mountain Lake Park, Md.	12 55
Charlestown, W. Va.	6 40	Mt. Pleasant, Pa.	14 70
Chester, Pa.	13 90	Newark, Del.	12 70
Clarksburg, W. Va.	15 45	New York, N. Y.	18 40
Connellsville, Pa.	14 20	Oakland, Md.	12 65
Cumberland, Md.	10 70	Parkersburg, W. Va.	18 60
Deer Park, Md.	12 40	Philadelphia, Pa.	14 40
Fairmont, W. Va.	15 45	Piedmont, W. Va.	11 00
Frederick, Md.	7 65	Pittsburgh, Pa.	16 50
Grafton, W. Va.	14 55	Rockwood, Pa.	12 45
Hagerstown, Md.	7 65	Somerset, Pa.	12 85
Harper's Ferry, W. Va.	6 60	Staunton, Va.	9 70
Harrisonburg, Va.	8 40	Strasburg, Va.	6 65
Havre de Grace, Md.	11 85	Uniontown, Pa.	14 65
Johnstown, Pa.	14 25	Washington, D. C.	8 80
Keyser, W. Va.	11 40	Washington, Pa.	17 60
Lexington, Va.	11 50	Wheeling, W. Va.	18 40
McKeesport, Pa.	15 95	Wilmington, Del.	13 10
Martinsburg, W. Va.	7 55		

CAPON SPRINGS, VA.

Any one in search of a really medicinal mineral water and baths of any temperature, a most charming and attractive summer resort, at very moderate rates of charge, will find it at Capon Springs. Besides the Capon fountain, there are here two as fine iron springs as there are on the globe. Also an excellent white sulphur spring in the neigborhood.

These springs gush forth in bold streams from a gorge in North Mountain, and are surrounded by picturesque scenery, presenting on every hand varied and striking views. Aside from the known medicinal value of the waters, there is a cool, dry and most salubrious climate. The ordinary range of the mercury throughout the day, in the summer months, is between 60 and 75 degrees, contrasting delightfully with the hot air of the cities and lowlands; in fact, there is a charm about the air of this region that none can fail to appreciate and enjoy. The attractive walks and rambles, amounting in the aggregate to several miles in extent, cannot fail to add to the enjoyment of the guests. One can hardly imagine anything more delightful to the lowlander or the denizen of cities than a climb to the heights of the white cliffs above the spring, or a

ramble down Brent's leafy avenue, or a stroll to Point Lookout, or along the crest of Ward's Ridge, or a horseback ascent to Eagles' Rock, on the summit of the great North Mountain.

From some of these the view is limited to the little vale at your feet, embosoming the mountain house and its surroundings, or to the winding valley of Cacapon river beyond. From others the scope of vision reaches westward to the Alleghanies, and embraces scenes of wild and varied beauty, but it is from the grand elevation of Eagles' Rock that the outlook grows sublime. One seems to stand on an island peak, surrounded on every hand by a boundless ocean, whose green waves in the near and middle distance fade into azure hues where the far-off horizon melts into the sky. The view from this point is bounded only by the Blue Ridge on the east and the countless spurs and ranges of the Alleghanies on the west, and thus includes within its scope a *coup d'œil* of almost the entire breadth of the great Appalachian chain.

On closer inspection, the beholder looks down into the far-famed valley of the Shenandoah, the "Great Valley of Virginia," as designated in geography. And if the day be propitious and the atmosphere transparent, he will descry Winchester to the northeast, Kearnstown and Strasburg and other villages of the Valley before him, and off to the southwest; and then turning his gaze to the setting sun, he will behold the vast expanse of mountain and valley and primeval forest bathed in floods of violet and purple light, through which the wavy outline of the earth is dimly drawn against the evening sky.

The new walks and rides opened up for the guests afford great satisfaction and delight, and especially is the splendid view from Eagles' Rock admired and enjoyed. Ladies and gentlemen of extensive travel abroad, as well as in America, pronounce it, in some of its features, unsurpassed, if equalled, by anything they have ever seen. There has been opened up a horseback route to the "Pinnacle," via Eagles' Rock, a still

loftier peak of the North Mountain range, which in addition to the superb panorama spread from Eagles' Rock, commands views of Harper's Ferry and regions of the upper Potomac; also one to Potter's View, to the south of these two points, commanding a splendid view of the Capon river valley many miles away.

FORM EX. 576. CAPON SPRINGS, VA., AND RETURN.

Baltimore & Ohio R. R. . . . . to Capon Road.
Stage (16 miles) . . . . to Capon Springs.
Returning, same route.

THROUGH RATES.

Baltimore, Md.	$14 30	Meyersdale, Pa.	$12 90
Bellaire, O.	19 75	Morgantown, W. Va.	17 35
Berkeley Springs, W. Va.	9 45	Moundsville, W. Va.	19 00
Cameron, W. Va.	18 30	Mountain Lake Park, Md.	13 15
Charlestown, W. Va.	7 00	Mt. Pleasant, Pa.	15 00
Chester, Pa.	14 80	Newark, Del.	13 00
Clarksburg, W. Va.	16 35	New York, N. Y.	19 30
Connellsville, Pa.	15 40	Oakland, Md.	13 55
Cumberland, Md.	11 40	Parkersburg, W. Va.	19 70
Deer Park, Md.	13 30	Philadelphia, Pa.	15 30
Fairmont, W. Va.	16 35	Piedmont, W. Va.	12 20
Frederick, Md.	8 35	Pittsburgh, Pa.	17 10
Grafton, W. Va.	15 45	Rockwood, Pa.	13 35
Hagerstown, Md.	8 55	Somerset, Pa.	13 75
Harper's Ferry, W. Va.	7 30	Staunton, Va.	8 80
Harrisonburg, Va.	7 30	Strasburg, Va.	5 20
Havre de Grace, Md.	12 75	Uniontown, Pa.	15 25
Johnstown, Pa.	15 45	Washington, D. C.	9 70
Keyser, W. Va.	12 30	Washington, Pa.	18 30
Lexington, Va.	10 00	Wheeling, W. Va.	19 10
McKeesport, Pa.	16 85	Wilmington, Del.	14 30
Martinsburg, W. Va.	8 25	Winchester, Va.	5 90

MUSIC STAND & SPRING.

CATSKILL MOUNTAINS, N. Y.

Of the many delightful localities accessible by the Baltimore & Ohio R. R., few can surpass in grandeur the towering Catskills.

"This enchanted region of perpetual coolness and refreshing breezes, where sparkling streams dash and tumble through mossy forest and shady glen, and wind-swept heights uplift themselves far above the heat and worry of the every-day life of the plains."

That's how an enthusiast once spoke, and there are many thousands who declare he knew whereof he spoke.

When all the rest of the world is hot and muggy, the Catskills are cool and refreshing.

There brisk breezes are always to be found, and shady nooks and lonely walks and fine drives.

It is, indeed, an enchanted region.

And there, just as everywhere, active preparations are being made for the accommodation of the thousands who will fly to these rocky fastnesses for pure, invigorating mountain air when the suns of summer blister and scorch.

Form Ex. 115. Catskill, N. Y., and Return.

Baltimore & Ohio R. R. . . . . to Philadelphia.
Philadelphia & Reading R. R. . . . . to Bound Brook.
Central R. R. of New Jersey . . . . to New York.
West Shore R. R. to Catskill.
Returning, same route.
Transfer through New York, in both directions, included.

Through Rates.

Baltimore, Md. . . . . . . $11 75   Washington, D. C. . . . $13 75
‡Philadelphia, Pa. 7 75

Form Ex. 116. Catskill, N. Y., and Return.

Baltimore & Ohio R. R. . . . . to Philadelphia.
Philadelphia & Reading R. R. . . . . to Bound Brook.
Central R. R. of New Jersey . . . . to New York.
New York & Albany Day Line . . . . to Catskill.
Returning, same route.

Through Rates.

Baltimore, Md. . . . . . . $10 75   Washington, D. C. . . . $12 75
‡Philadelphia, Pa. 6 75

Form Ex. 118. Catskill, N. Y., and Return.

Baltimore & Ohio R. R. . . . . to Philadelphia.
Philadelphia & Reading R. R. . . . . to Bound Brook.
Central R. R. of New Jersey . . . . to New York.
West Shore R. R. to Catskill.
New York & Albany Day Line . . . . to New York.
Central R. R. of New Jersey . . . . to Bound Brook.
Philadelphia & Reading R. R. . . . . to Philadelphia.
Baltimore & Ohio R. R. . . . . to starting point.
Transfer through New York, going, included.

Through Rates.

Baltimore, Md. . . . . . . $11 70   Washington, D. C. . . . $13 50
‡Philadelphia, Pa. 7 70

Form Ex. 117. Kingston, N. Y., and Return.

Baltimore & Ohio R. R. . . . . to Philadelphia.
Philadelphia & Reading R. R. . . . . to Bound Brook.
Central R. R. of New Jersey . . . . to New York.
West Shore R. R. to Kingston.
Returning, same route.
Transfer through New York, in both directions, included.

Through Rates.

Baltimore, Md. . . . . . . $11 25   Washington, D. C. . . . $13 25
‡Philadelphia, Pa. 7 25

FORM EX. 750. KINGSTON, N. Y., AND RETURN.

Baltimore & Ohio R. R. . . . . to Philadelphia.
Philadelphia & Reading R. R. . . . . to Bound Brook.
Central R. R. of New Jersey . . . . to New York.
Steamer "Mary Powell" . . . . to Kingston.

Returning, same route.

THROUGH RATES.

Baltimore, Md. . . . . $9.50 | Washington, D. C. $11.50
Philadelphia, Pa. . . . . . . 5.50 |

CATSKILL MOUNTAIN RESORTS.

	Rates from Kingston.
Form Ex. 111—Arkville, N. Y., and return	$2.75
Form Ex. 112—Big Indian, N. Y., and return	2.05
Form Ex. 113—Brown's, N. Y., and return	.80
Form Ex. 114—Broadhead's, N. Y., and return	.95
Form Ex. 115—Grand Gorge, N. Y., and return	3.80
Form Ex. 116—Grand Hotel Station, N. Y. (Summit), and return, for Grand Hotel	2.35
Form Ex. 118—Fleischmann's (Griffin's), N. Y., and return	2.50
Form Ex. 119—Halcottville, N. Y., and return	3.05
Form Ex. 120—Hobart, N. Y., and return	4.55
Form Ex. 121—Mt. Pleasant, N. Y., and return	1.50
Form Ex. 122—Olive Branch, N. Y., and return	.70
Form Ex. 123—Phoenicia, N. Y., and return	1.50
Form Ex. 124—Pine Hill, N. Y., and return	2.28
Form Ex. 125—Roxbury, N. Y., and return	3.10
Form Ex. 126—Shandaken, N. Y., and return	1.85
Form Ex. 127—Shokan, N. Y., and return	.95
Form Ex. 128—Stamford, N. Y., and return	4.50
Form Ex. 129—West Hurley, N. Y., and return	.50

The above forms read as follows:

Ulster & Delaware R. R., Kingston . . . . to destination.
Ulster & Delaware R. R., destination . . . . . . to Kingston.

	Rates from Kingston.
Form Ex. 130—Chichester, N. Y., and return	$1.65
Form Ex. 131—Lanesville, N. Y., and return	2.25
Form Ex. 132—Edgewood, N. Y., and return	2.05
Form Ex. 133—Stony Clove, N. Y., and return	3.15
Form Ex. 134—Hunter, N. Y., and return	3.55

The above forms read as follows:

Ulster & Delaware R. R., Kingston . . . . to Phoenicia.
Stony Clove & Catskill Mountain R. R., Phoenicia to destination.

Returning, same route.

	Rates from Kingston.
Form Ex. 135—Tannersville, N. Y., and return	$4.05
Form Ex. 136—Haines' Corners, N. Y., and return	4.45
Form Ex. 137—Laurel House, N. Y., and return	4.85
Form Ex. 138—Kaaterskill, N. Y., and return	5.05

The above forms read as follows:

Ulster & Delaware R. R., Kingston . . . . to Phoenicia.
Stony Clove & Catskill Mountain R. R., Phoenicia to Kaaterskill Junc.
Kaaterskill R. R., Kaaterskill Junction . . . . . to destination.

Returning, same route.

The above Catskill Mountain excursion forms reading from Kingston should be issued as a side-trip in connection with tickets passing through Kingston, at rates from Kingston quoted above, or, in connection with excursion ticket to Kingston, at rate arrived at by adding the excursion fare to Kingston and return to the rate quoted above from Kingston.

		Rates from Catskill.
Form Ex. 110	Lawrenceville, N. Y., and return	$2 00
Form Ex. 111	Leeds, N. Y., and return	80
Form Ex. 112	Mountain House Station, N. Y., and return (for Catskill Mountain House)	2 00
Form Ex. 1086	Otis Junction, N. Y., and return (connection with Otis Elevating Ry. for Catskill Mountain Station)	$2 00
Form Ex. 113	Palenville, N. Y., and return	2 00
Form Ex. 114	South Cairo, N. Y., and return	1 50

The above forms read as follows:
Catskill Mountain R. R., Catskill . . . . to destination.
Returning, same route.

Form Ex. 139 Cairo, N. Y., and return, from Catskill $2 00

Catskill Mountain R. R., Catskill . . . . to Cairo Junction.
Cairo R. R., Cairo Junction . . . . to Cairo.
Returning, same route.

The above Catskill Mountain excursion forms reading from Catskill should be issued as a side-trip in connection with tickets passing through Catskill, at rates from Catskill quoted above, or in connection with excursion ticket to Catskill at rate arrived at by adding the excursion fare to Catskill and return to the rate quoted above from Catskill.

CHAUTAUGUA LAKE.

This, the farthest west of the New York lakes, is situated in Chautauqua county, and is the highest navigable body of water on the continent, being fourteen hundred feet above the sea. The lake is eighteen miles long and from one to three miles wide. Its invigorating air, clear waters, excellent bathing, boating and fishing, and the charming drives which the vicinity affords, have all combined to make it a very popular resort. Here the *Chautauqua Assembly*, organized in 1874, holds its annual meeting every July and August. It is an enterprise designed to combine the recreations of a summer resort with intellectual culture and improvement. It comprises a series of diversified exercises in popular lectures and concerts, brilliant stereopticon exhibitions, organ recitals, Athenian watch-fires, &c. The Chautauqua Assembly also implies a well-graded system of education, leading up from its "*Teachers' Retreat*" and "*School of Languages*" to the C. L. S. C. (Chautauqua Literary and Scientific Circle) and *Chautauqua University*. The "*Teachers' Retreat*" is a three-weeks' meeting, held every summer, at which lectures are given and scientific subjects discussed by able specialists, while the *School of Languages* is a summer school of six weeks, designed to illustrate the best method of teaching languages. The C. L. S. C. is an association for social and intellectual improvement, with a four years' course of reading in history, literature, science and art, so judiciously arranged as to embrace the principal subjects of a college curriculum. *Chautauqua University* is a provision for non-resident students who desire to take a thorough university education while at home and engaged in business, and who are able to devote two or more hours daily to earnest study. But the reader must not be impressed with the idea that life at this beautiful lake is all study, nor must he expect to meet with serious-faced, deep-brown-study-countenanced people only. While Point Chautauqua and Chautauqua are preferred by the more serious, *Lakewood*, a few miles distant, is more congenial to the lover of harmless gaiety. The stranger will enjoy the shady drive from Jamestown to Mayville, and he will miss a beautiful sight should he omit to take the trip by steamer from Jamestown through *The Narrows*.

FORM EX. 236. CHAUTAUQUA, N. Y., AND RETURN.

Baltimore & Ohio R. R.	to Philadelphia.
Philadelphia & Reading R. R.	to Bound Brook.
Central R. R. of New Jersey	to New York.
New York Central & Hudson River R. R.	to Buffalo.
Western New York & Pennsylvania R. R.	to Mayville.
Chautauqua Lake Ry.	to Chautauqua.

Returning, same route.

THROUGH RATES.

Baltimore, Md.	$26 50	Washington, D. C.	$28 00
Philadelphia, Pa.	22 50		

FORM EX. 591. CHAUTAUQUA, N. Y. AND RETURN.

Baltimore & Ohio R. R. .... to Philadelphia.
Philadelphia & Reading R. R. .... to Bound Brook.
Central R. R. of New Jersey .... to New York.
West Shore R. R. .... to Buffalo.
Western New York & Pennsylvania R. R. .... to Mayville.
Chautauqua Steamboat Co. .... to Chautauqua.

Returning, same route.
Transfer through New York, in both directions, included.

THROUGH RATES.

Baltimore, Md. .... $25 00   Washington, D. C. $27 00
†Philadelphia, Pa. 21 00

FORM EX. 592.—CHAUTAUQUA, N. Y., AND RETURN.

Baltimore & Ohio R. R. .... to Philadelphia.
Philadelphia & Reading R. R. .... to Bound Brook.
Central R. R. of New Jersey .... to New York.
Delaware, Lackawanna & Western R. R. .... to Buffalo.
Western New York & Pennsylvania R. R. .... to Mayville.
Chautauqua Steamboat Co. .... to Chautauqua.

Returning, same route.

THROUGH RATES.

Baltimore, Md. .... $26 50   Washington, D. C. $28 50
†Philadelphia, Pa. 22 50

FORM EX. 593. CHAUTAUQUA LAKE AND RETURN.

Baltimore & Ohio R. R. .... to Philadelphia.
Philadelphia & Reading R. R. .... to Bound Brook.
Central R. R. of New Jersey .... to New York.
New York, Lake Erie & Western R. R. .... to Lakewood or Jamestown.
Chautauqua Steamboat Co. .... to any point on the lake.

Returning, same route.

THROUGH RATES.

Baltimore, Md. .... $25 00   Washington, D. C. $27 00
†Philadelphia, Pa. 21 00

FORM EX. 611.—JAMESTOWN, N. Y. (CHAUTAUQUA LAKE) AND RETURN.

Baltimore & Ohio R. R. .... to Philadelphia.
Philadelphia & Reading R. R. .... to Bethlehem.
Lehigh Valley R. R. .... to Waverly.
New York, Lake Erie & Western R. R. .... to Salamanca.
New York, Lake Erie & Western R. R. .... to Jamestown.

Returning, same route.

THROUGH RATES.

Baltimore, Md. .... $18 80   Washington, D. C. $20 80
†Philadelphia, Pa. 17 00

FORM EX. 500.—MAYVILLE, N. Y., AND RETURN.

Baltimore & Ohio R. R. .... to Philadelphia.
Philadelphia & Reading R. R. .... to Bound Brook.
Central R. R. of New Jersey .... to New York.
West Shore R. R. .... to Buffalo.
Western New York & Pennsylvania R. R. .... to Mayville.

Returning, same route.
Transfer through New York, in both directions, included.

THROUGH RATES.

Baltimore, Md. .... $25 00   Washington, D. C. $27 00
†Philadelphia, Pa. 21 00

ROUTES AND RATES FOR SUMMER TOURS. 69

FORM EX. 747.—MAYVILLE, N. Y. (CHAUTAUQUA LAKE), AND RETURN.

Baltimore & Ohio R. R. . . . . to Philadelphia.
Philadelphia & Reading R. R. . . . . to Bethlehem.
Lehigh Valley R. R. . . . . to Waverly.
New York, Lake Erie & Western R. R. . . . to Jamestown.
Chautauqua Steamboat Co. . . . . to Mayville.
Western New York & Pennsylvania R. R. . . to Buffalo.
New York, Lake Erie & Western R. R. . . . to Niagara Falls.
New York Central & Hudson River R. R. . . to Geneva.
Seneca Lake Steam Navigation Co. . . . . . to Watkins.
Pennsylvania R. R. . . . . to Elmira.
New York, Lake Erie & Western R. R. . . . to Waverly.
Lehigh Valley R. R. . . . . to Bethlehem.
Philadelphia & Reading R. R. . . . . to Philadelphia.
Baltimore & Ohio R. R. . . . . to starting point.

THROUGH RATES.

Baltimore, Md., ... $23.50   Washington, D. C. . . . $25.00
†Philadelphia, Pa. . . . 19.50

FORM EX. 338.—MAYVILLE, N. Y., AND RETURN.

Baltimore & Ohio R. R. . . . . to Philadelphia.
Philadelphia & Reading R. R. . . . . to Bound Brook.
Central R. R. of New Jersey . . . . to New York.
New York Central & Hudson River R. R. . . to Niagara Falls.
New York Central & Hudson River R. R. . . to Buffalo.

Western New York & Pennsylvania R. R. . . . . to Mayville.
Western New York & Pennsylvania R. R. . . . . to Buffalo.
New York Central & Hudson River R. R. . . . . to New York.
Central R. R. of New Jersey . . . . to Bound Brook.
Philadelphia & Reading R. R. . . . . to Philadelphia.
Baltimore & Ohio R. R. . . . . to starting point.

THROUGH RATES.

Baltimore, Md. . . . . $27 00 | Washington, D. C. $29 00
†Philadelphia, Pa. . . . . . 23 00 |

FORM EX. 83.—LAKEWOOD OR JAMESTOWN, N. Y., AND RETURN.

Baltimore & Ohio R. R. . . . . to Pittsburgh.
Pittsburgh Transfer Co., B. & O. R. R. Depot to P. & L. E. R. R. Depot.
Pittsburgh & Lake Erie R. R. . . . . to Youngstown.
New York, Lake Erie & Western R. R. . . to Lakewood or Jamestown.
Returning, same route.

THROUGH RATES.

Baltimore, Md.	$24 70	Martinsburg, W. Va.	$17 45
Bellaire, O.	11 40	Meyersdale, Pa.	12 50
Berkeley Springs, W. Va.	16 50	Morgantown, W. Va. (via	
Cameron, W. Va. (via Wheeling)	11 40	Wheeling)	11 90
Charlestown, W. Va.	18 30	Moundsville, W. Va. (via Wheeling)	11 25
Chester, Pa.	23 60	Mountain Lake Park, Md.	
Clarksburg, W. Va. (via Wheeling)	13 65	(via Cumberland)	10 05
Connellsville, Pa.	10 30	Mt. Pleasant, Pa.	10 60
Cumberland, Md.	11 00	Newark, Del.	23 60
Deer Park, Md. (via Cumberland)	9 90	New York, N. Y.	27 60
		Oakland, Md. (via Cumberland)	10 15
Fairmont, W. Va. (via Wheeling)	13 30	Philadelphia, Pa.	23 60
Frederick, Md.	18 85	Piedmont, W. Va.	13 40
Grafton, W. Va. (via Wheeling)	11 80	Rockwood, Pa.	12 05
		Somerset, Pa.	12 40
		Staunton, Va.	21 30
Hagerstown, Md.	18 85	Strasburg, Va.	20 35
Harper's Ferry, W. Va.	17 90	Uniontown, Pa.	10 80
Harrisonburg, Va.	22 80	Washington, D. C.	20 40
Havre de Grace, Md.	23 15	Washington, Pa.	9 50
Keyser, W. Va.	11 80	Wheeling, W. Va.	10 80
Lexington, Va.	26 00	Wilmington, Del.	23 60
McKeesport, Pa.	8 60	Winchester, Va.	19 50

CENTRE HARBOR, N. H.

FORM EX. 1104.—CENTRE HARBOR, N. H., AND RETURN.

(Via rail and Boston; returning via Boston and Sound Lines.)

Baltimore & Ohio R. R. . . . . to Philadelphia.
Rail Lines (see pages 50 to 55 for routes) . . . to Boston.
Boston & Maine R. R. . . . . to Nashua.
Concord & Montreal R. R. . . . . to Weirs.
Lake Winnipesaukee Steamboat Co. . . . . . . to Centre Harbor.
Lake Winnipesaukee Steamboat Co. . . . . . . to Weirs.
Concord & Montreal R. R. . . . . to Nashua.
Boston & Maine R. R. . . . . to Boston.
Sound Lines (see pages 50 to 55 for routes) . . to New York.
Central R. R. of New Jersey . . . . to Bound Brook.
Philadelphia & Reading R. R. . . . . to Philadelphia.
Baltimore & Ohio R. R. . . . . to starting point.

THROUGH RATES.

Baltimore, Md. . . . . . . $22 50 | Washington, D. C. $24 50
†Philadelphia, Pa. . . . . 18 50 |

Transfer through Boston, returning, included.

ROUTES AND RATES FOR SUMMER TOURS.

FORM EX. 1104.—CENTRE HARBOR, N. H., AND RETURN.
(Via Sound Lines and Boston; returning via Boston and Rail Lines.)

Baltimore & Ohio R. R.	to Philadelphia.
Philadelphia & Reading R. R.	to Bound Brook.
Central R. R. of New Jersey	to New York.
Sound Lines (see pages 50 to 55 for route)	to Boston.
Boston & Maine R. R.	to Nashua.
Concord & Montreal R. R.	to Weirs.
Lake Winnipesaukee Steamboat Co.	to Centre Harbor.
Lake Winnipesaukee Steamboat Co.	to Weirs.
Concord & Montreal R. R.	to Nashua.
Boston & Maine R. R.	to Boston.
Rail Lines (see pages 50 to 55 for route)	to Philadelphia.
Baltimore & Ohio R. R.	to starting point.

THROUGH RATES.
Baltimore, Md. .... $22.50   Washington, D. C. $24.50
†Philadelphia, Pa. 18.50

Transfer through Boston, going, included.

FORM EX. 1104.—CENTRE HARBOR, N. H., AND RETURN.
(Via Rail Lines and Boston in both directions.)

Baltimore & Ohio R. R.	to Philadelphia.
Rail Lines (see pages 50 to 55 for route)	to Boston.
Boston & Maine R. R.	to Nashua.
Concord & Montreal R. R.	to Weirs.
Lake Winnipesaukee Steamboat Co.	to Centre Harbor.

Returning, same route.

THROUGH RATES.
Baltimore, Md. .... $25.00   Washington, D. C. $25.00
†Philadelphia, Pa. 19.00

FORM EX. 1104.—CENTRE HARBOR, N. H., AND RETURN.
(Via Sound Lines and Boston in both directions.)

Baltimore & Ohio R. R.	to Philadelphia.
Philadelphia and Reading R. R.	to Bound Brook.
Central R. R. of New Jersey	to New York.
Sound Lines (see pages 50 to 55 for route)	to Boston.
Boston & Maine R. R.	to Nashua.
Concord & Montreal R. R.	to Weirs.
Lake Winnipesaukee Steamboat Co.	to Centre Harbor.

Returning, same route.

THROUGH RATES.
Baltimore, Md. .... $19.00   Washington, D. C. $24.00
†Philadelphia, Pa. 15.00

CHRISTIANSBURG, VA.

FORM EX. 8.—CHRISTIANSBURG, VA., AND RETURN.

Baltimore & Ohio R. R. . . . . to Shenandoah June.
Norfolk & Western R. R. . . . . to Christiansburg.

Returning, same route.

THROUGH RATES.

Baltimore, Md.	$14 50	Morgantown, W. Va.	$20 75
Bellaire, O.	23 45	Moundsville, W. Va.	22 45
Berkeley Springs, W. Va.	12 95	Mountain Lake Park, Md.	16 90
Cameron, W. Va.	21 75	Mt. Pleasant, Pa.	19 00
Chester, Pa.	17 80	Newark, Del.	16 60
Clarksburg, W. Va.	19 75	New York, N. Y.	22 30
Connellsville, Pa.	18 50	Oakland, Md.	17 00
Cumberland, Md.	14 80	Parkersburg, W. Va.	22 85
Deer Park, Md.	16 75	Philadelphia, Pa.	18 30
Fairmont, W. Va.	19 75	Piedmont, W. Va.	15 95
Frederick, Md.	12 55	Pittsburgh, Pa.	20 80
Grafton, W. Va.	18 85	Rockwood, Pa.	16 75
Harper's Ferry, W. Va.	11 45	Somerset, Pa.	17 15
Havre de Grace, Md.	15 75	Uniontown, Pa.	18 95
Johnstown, Pa.	18 55	Washington, D. C.	12 30
Keyser, W. Va.	15 75	Washington, Pa.	21 90
McKeesport, Pa.	20 25	Wheeling, W. Va.	22 85
Martinsburg, W. Va.	11 65	Wilmington, Del.	17 30
Meyersdale, Pa.	16 30		

FORM EX. 88.—CHRISTIANSBURG, VA., AND RETURN.

Baltimore & Ohio R. R. . . . . to Washington.
Transfer . . . . B. & O. Depot to R. & D. Depot.
Richmond & Danville R. R. . . . . to Lynchburg.
Norfolk & Western R. R. . . . . to Christiansburg.

Returning, same route.

THROUGH RATES.

Baltimore, Md.	$14 30	Meyersdale, Pa.	$20 40
Bellaire, O.	27 25	Morgantown, W. Va.	24 85
Berkeley Springs, W. Va.	16 95	Moundsville, W. Va.	26 50
Cameron, W. Va.	25 80	Mountain Lake Park, Md.	20 45
Charlestown, W. Va.	15 50	Mt. Pleasant, Pa.	23 10
Chester, Pa.	17 80	Newark, Del.	16 60
Clarksburg, W. Va.	23 85	New York, N. Y.	22 30
Connellsville, Pa.	22 60	Oakland, Md.	20 35
Cumberland, Md.	18 90	Parkersburg, W. Va.	26 95
Deer Park, Md.	20 20	Philadelphia, Pa.	18 30
Fairmont, W. Va.	23 85	Piedmont, W. Va.	20 00
Frederick, Md.	15 10	Pittsburgh, Pa.	24 90
Grafton, W. Va.	22 95	Rockwood, Pa.	20 85
Hagerstown, Md.	15 90	Somerset, Pa.	21 25
Harper's Ferry, W. Va.	15 00	Uniontown, Pa.	23 05
Havre de Grace, Md.	15 75	Washington, Pa.	26 00
Johnstown, Pa.	22 65	Wheeling, W. Va.	26 95
Keyser, W. Va.	19 80	Wilmington, Del.	17 30
McKeesport, Pa.	24 35	Winchester, Va.	16 00
Martinsburg, W. Va.	15 75		

CLAYTON, N. Y.

Clayton is a charming village of about 3,000 inhabitants, and during the season of summer travel is a gay and animated town. It is at this point that tourists embark on the Royal Mail steamers for the trip among the islands and through the rapids to Montreal and Quebec. Here, too, passengers for Round Island, Thousand Island Park, Central Park and Alexander Bay take passage on the Thousand Island Steamboat Company's popular line of steamers, for the famous resorts down the river. Geographically considered, the location of Clayton is unsurpassed. It is situated on a bold peninsula jutting out into the pure waters of the most majestic of American rivers. Broad bays, both to the east and west, afford a variety of coast suited to the various wants of man.

Its three hotels—the Hubbard House, the West End and the Walton House—are well and favorably known to all acquainted with the beauties of this region. They are conducted with the utmost care and skill, and guests will find them both comfortable and home-like.

Directly in front of the town beautiful islands, upon which summer houses have been erected, form a most pleasing contrast to the wide stretch of water above.

FORM EX. 274. CLAYTON, N. Y., AND RETURN.

Baltimore & Ohio R. R. . . . . to Philadelphia.
Philadelphia & Reading R. R. . . . . to Bound Brook.
Central R. R. of New Jersey . . . . to New York.
New York Central & Hudson River R. R. . to Utica.
Rome, Watertown & Ogdensburg R. R. . . to Clayton.
Returning, same route.

THROUGH RATES.

Baltimore, Md. . . . . . . $23 25   Washington, D. C. $25 25
Philadelphia, Pa. 19 25

FORM EX. 275. CLAYTON, N. Y., AND RETURN.

Baltimore & Ohio R. R. . . . . to Philadelphia.
Philadelphia & Reading R. R. . . . . to Bound Brook.
Central R. R. of New Jersey . . . . to New York.
West Shore R. R. . . . . to Utica.
Rome, Watertown & Ogdensburg R. R. . . to Clayton.
Returning, same route.
Transfer through New York, in both directions, included.

THROUGH RATES.

Baltimore, Md. . . . . . . $23 25   Washington, D. C. $25 25
Philadelphia, Pa. 19 25

FORM EX. 276. CLAYTON, N. Y., AND RETURN.

Baltimore & Ohio R. R. . . . . to Philadelphia.
Philadelphia & Reading R. R. . . . . to Bound Brook.
Central R. R. of New Jersey . . . . to New York.
Delaware, Lackawanna & Western R. R. . to Utica.
Rome, Watertown & Ogdensburg R. R. . . to Clayton.
Returning, same route.

THROUGH RATES.

Baltimore, Md. . . . . . . $23 25   Washington, D. C. $25 25
Philadelphia, Pa. 19 25

FORM EX. 278. CLAYTON, N. Y., AND RETURN.

Baltimore & Ohio R. R. . . . . to Philadelphia.
Philadelphia & Reading R. R. . . . . to Bound Brook.
Central R. R. of New Jersey . . . . to New York.
Delaware, Lackawanna & Western R. R. . to Syracuse.
Rome, Watertown & Ogdensburg R. R. . . to Clayton.
Returning, same route.

THROUGH RATES.

Baltimore, Md. . . . . . . $23 25   Washington, D. C. $25 25
Philadelphia, Pa. 19 25

ROUTES AND RATES FOR SUMMER TOURS.

FORM EX. 279.—CLAYTON, N. Y., AND RETURN.

Baltimore & Ohio R. R. . . . . to Philadelphia.
Philadelphia & Reading R. R. . . . . to Bound Brook.
Central R. R. of New Jersey . . . . to New York.
New York, Ontario & Western R. R. . . . . . . to Central Square.
Rome, Watertown & Ogdensburg R. R. . . . . to Clayton.

Returning, same route.

THROUGH RATES.

Baltimore, Md.	$23 25	Washington, D. C.	$25 25
Philadelphia, Pa.	19 25		

COLD SULPHUR SPRINGS, VA.

FORM EX. 51.—COLD SULPHUR SPRINGS, VA., AND RETURN.

Baltimore & Ohio R. R. . . . . to Shenandoah June.
Norfolk & Western R. R. . . . . to Basic.
Chesapeake & Ohio Ry. . . . . to Goshen.
Stage (2 miles) . . . . to Cold Sulphur Springs.

Returning, same route.

THROUGH RATES.

Baltimore, Md.	$13 30	New York, N. Y.	$21 30
Chester, Pa.	16 80	Philadelphia, Pa.	17 30
Havre de Grace, Md.	14 75	Washington, D. C.	11 30
Newark, Del.	15 60	Wilmington, Del.	16 30

FORM EX. 179.—COLD SULPHUR SPRINGS, VA., AND RETURN.

Baltimore & Ohio R. R. . . . . to Staunton.
Chesapeake & Ohio Ry. . . . . to Goshen.
Stage (2 miles) . . . . to Cold Sulphur Springs.

Returning, same route.

THROUGH RATES.

Baltimore, Md.	$13 30	Meyersdale, Pa.	$14 00
Bellaire, O.	21 15	Morgantown, W. Va.	19 05
Berkeley Springs, W. Va.	11 15	Moundsville, W. Va.	20 70
Cameron, W. Va.	20 00	Mountain Lake Park, Md.	15 15
Charlestown, W. Va.	8 70	Mt. Pleasant, Pa.	17 30
Chester, Pa.	16 80	Newark, Del.	15 60
Clarksburg, W. Va.	18 05	New York, N. Y.	21 30
Connellsville, Pa.	16 80	Oakland, Md.	15 25
Cumberland, Md.	13 10	Parkersburg, W. Va.	21 20
Deer Park, Md.	15 00	Philadelphia, Pa.	17 30
Fairmont, W. Va.	18 05	Piedmont, W. Va.	11 20
Frederick, Md.	10 25	Pittsburgh, Pa.	19 40
Grafton, W. Va.	17 15	Rockwood, Pa.	15 05
Hagerstown, Md.	10 25	Somerset, Pa.	15 45
Harper's Ferry, W. Va.	9 20	Strasburg, Va.	6 55
Harrisonburg, Va.	4 20	Uniontown, Pa.	17 25
Havre de Grace, Md.	14 75	Washington, D. C.	11 30
Johnstown, Pa.	16 85	Washington, Pa.	20 20
Keyser, W. Va.	11 00	Wheeling, W. Va.	21 20
Lexington, Va.	4 70	Wilmington, Del.	16 30
McKeesport, Pa.	18 55	Winchester, Va.	7 60
Martinsburg, W. Va.	9 95		

FORM EX. 264.—COLD SULPHUR SPRINGS, VA., AND RETURN.

Baltimore & Ohio R. R. . . . . to Washington.
Transfer . . . . B. & O. Depot to C. & O. Depot.
Chesapeake & Ohio Ry. . . . . to Goshen.
Stage (2 miles) . . . . to Cold Sulphur Springs.

Returning, same route.

THROUGH RATES.

Baltimore, Md.	$13 30	Meyersdale, Pa.	$19 40
Bellaire, O.	26 25	Morgantown, W. Va.	22 85
Berkeley Springs, W. Va.	15 95	Moundsville, W. Va.	25 50
Cameron, W. Va.	24 80	Mountain Lake Park, Md.	19 45
Charlestown, W. Va.	14 50	Mt. Pleasant, Pa.	22 10
Chester, Pa.	16 80	Newark, Del.	15 60
Clarksburg, W. Va.	22 85	New York, N. Y.	21 50
Connellsville, Pa.	21 00	Oakland, Md.	19 55
Cumberland, Md.	17 90	Parkersburg, W. Va.	25 95
Deer Park, Md.	19 30	Philadelphia, Pa.	17 30
Fairmont, W. Va.	22 85	Piedmont, W. Va	19 00
Frederick, Md.	14 40	Pittsburgh, Pa.	23 90
Grafton, W. Va.	21 95	Rockwood, Pa.	19 85
Hagerstown, Md.	14 80	Somerset, Pa.	20 25
Harper's Ferry, W. Va.	14 00	Uniontown, Pa.	22 05
Havre de Grace, Md.	14 75	Washington, Pa.	25 00
Johnstown, Pa.	21 65	Wheeling, W. Va.	25 95
Keyser, W. Va.	18 50	Wilmington, Del.	16 30
McKeesport, Pa.	23 55	Winchester, Va.	15 00
Martinsburg, W. Va.	14 75		

COOPERSTOWN OTSEGO LAKE, N. Y.

This popular resort is situated at the foot of Otsego Lake, near the outlet of the Susquehanna River. The town is beautifully located high up in the mountains; possesses a clear, bracing atmosphere and charming scenery, and attracts annually thousands of visitors. "It is one of the Meccas of America," for here was once the home of J. Fenimore Cooper, and amid these scenes he wrote those wonderful American stories which have given him imperishable renown.

ROUTES AND RATES FOR SUMMER TOURS. 77

FORM EX. 304.—COOPERSTOWN, N. Y., AND RETURN.

Baltimore & Ohio R. R. . . . . to Philadelphia.
Philadelphia & Reading R. R. . . . . to Bound Brook.
Central R. R. of New Jersey . . . . to New York.
New York Central & Hudson River R. R. . . . to Albany.
Delaware & Hudson R. R. . . . . to C. & C. V. June.
Cooperstown & Charlotte Valley R. R. . . . . to Cooperstown.
Returning, same route.

THROUGH RATES.

Baltimore, Md. . . . . . . $19 15 | Washington, D. C. $21 15
†Philadelphia, Pa. . . . . 15 15 |

FORM EX. 305.—COOPERSTOWN, N. Y., AND RETURN.

Baltimore & Ohio R. R. . . . . to Philadelphia.
Philadelphia & Reading R. R. . . . . to Bound Brook.
Central R. R. of New Jersey . . . . to New York.
Delaware, Lackawanna & Western R. R. . . . to Richfield Springs.
Otsego Lake Steamboat Co. and Stage . . . . to Cooperstown.
Returning, same route.

THROUGH RATES.

Baltimore, Md. . . . . . . $19 65 | Washington, D. C. $21 65
†Philadelphia, Pa. . . . . 15 65 |

Tickets between Cooperstown and Richfield Springs by the Otsego Lake steamer and stage are for passage only; baggage will be charged extra.

FORM EX. 306.—COOPERSTOWN, N. Y., AND RETURN.

Baltimore & Ohio R. R. . . . . to Philadelphia.
Philadelphia & Reading R. R. . . . . to Bound Brook.
Central R. R. of New Jersey . . . . to New York.
Delaware, Lackawanna & Western R. R. . . . to Binghamton.
Delaware & Hudson R. R. . . . . to C. & C. V. June.
Cooperstown & Charlotte Valley R. R. . . . . to Cooperstown.
Otsego Lake Steamboat Co. and Stage . . . . to Richfield Springs.
Delaware, Lackawanna & Western R. R. . . . to New York.
Central R. R. of New Jersey . . . . to Bound Brook.
Philadelphia & Reading R. R. . . . . to Philadelphia.
Baltimore & Ohio R. R. . . . . to starting point.

THROUGH RATES.

Baltimore, Md. . . . . . . $19 75 | Washington, D. C. $21 75
†Philadelphia, Pa. . . . . 15 75 |

Tickets between Cooperstown and Richfield Springs by the Otsego Lake steamer and stage are for passage only; baggage will be charged extra.

FORM EX. 718.—COOPERSTOWN, N. Y., AND RETURN.

Baltimore & Ohio R. R. . . . . to Philadelphia.
Philadelphia & Reading R. R. . . . . to Bethlehem.
Lehigh Valley R. R. . . . . to Waverly.
New York, Lake Erie & Western R. R. . . . . to Binghamton.
Delaware & Hudson R. R. . . . . to C. & C. V. June.
Cooperstown & Charlotte Valley R. R. . . . . to Cooperstown.
Returning, same route.

THROUGH RATES.

Baltimore, Md. . . . . . . $17 30 | Washington, D. C. $19 30
†Philadelphia, Pa. . . . . 13 30 |

FORM EX. 508. COOPERSTOWN, N. Y., AND RETURN.

Baltimore & Ohio R. R.	to Philadelphia.
Philadelphia & Reading R. R.	to Bound Brook.
Central R. R. of New Jersey	to New York.
New York Central & Hudson River R. R.	to Albany.
Delaware & Hudson R. R.	to C. & C. V. Junc.
Cooperstown & Charlotte Valley R. R.	to Cooperstown.
Otsego Lake Steamboat Co. and Stage	to Richfield Springs.
Delaware, Lackawanna & Western R. R.	to Utica.
New York Central & Hudson River R. R.	to New York.
Central R. R. of New Jersey	to Bound Brook.
Philadelphia & Reading R. R.	to Philadelphia.
Baltimore & Ohio R. R.	to starting point.

THROUGH RATES.

Baltimore, Md.	$20 85	Washington, D. C.	$22 85
Philadelphia, Pa.	16 85		

Tickets between Cooperstown and Richfield Springs by the Otsego Lake steamer and stage are for passage only; baggage will be charged extra.

FORM EX. 78L. COOPERSTOWN, N. Y., AND RETURN.

Baltimore & Ohio R. R.	to Philadelphia.
Philadelphia & Reading R. R.	to Bound Brook.
Central R. R. of New Jersey	to New York.
People's Line	to Albany.
Delaware & Hudson R. R.	to C. & C. V. Junc.
Cooperstown & Charlotte Valley R. R.	to Cooperstown.

Returning, same route.

THROUGH RATES.

Baltimore, Md.	$16 15	Washington, D. C.	$18 15
Philadelphia, Pa.	12 15		

Tickets between Cooperstown and Richfield Springs by the Otsego Lake steamer and stage are for passage only; baggage will be charged extra.

COTTAGE CITY MARTHA'S VINEYARD, MASS.

Like Ocean Grove, N. J., Oak Bluffs owes its existence to the zeal of a religious denomination desiring to work among the thousands who every summer leave the city churches bare and flock to the seaside. The Baptists have here erected a tabernacle capable of seating five thousand people, and laid out the surrounding grounds in an inviting manner. It is estimated that twenty-five thousand people may be found here during the season. The island of Martha's Vineyard (twenty-one miles by six) is separated from Barnstable County, Massachusetts, by Vineyard Sound, four miles wide. At its southwestern extremity lies Gay Head, where occurred the wreck of the "City of Columbus."

FORM EX. 625.—COTTAGE CITY (MARTHA'S VINEYARD, MASS.,
AND RETURN.

Baltimore & Ohio R. R. . . . . to Philadelphia.
Philadelphia & Reading R. R. . . . . to Bound Brook.
Central R. R. of New Jersey . . . . to New York.
Old Colony Steamboat Co. (Fall River Line) . . to Fall River.
Old Colony R. R. . . . . to New Bedford.
New Bedford, Martha's Vineyard & Nantucket
    Steamboat Line . . . . to Cottage City.
              Returning, same route.

THROUGH RATES.

Baltimore, Md.	$15 25	Washington, D. C.	$17 25
Philadelphia, Pa.	11 25		

FORM EX. 952.—COTTAGE CITY (MARTHA'S VINEYARD, MASS., AND
RETURN.

(Via Newport and New Bedford, returning via Wood's Holl and Boston.)
Baltimore & Ohio R. R. . . . . to Philadelphia.
Philadelphia & Reading R. R. . . . . to Bound Brook.
Central R. R. of New Jersey . . . . to New York.
Old Colony Steamboat Co. (Fall River Line) . . to Newport.
Old Colony R. R. . . . . to New Bedford.
New Bedford, Martha's Vineyard & Nantucket
    Steamboat Line . . . . to Cottage City.
New Bedford, Martha's Vineyard & Nantucket
    Steamboat Line . . . . to Wood's Holl.
Old Colony R. R. . . . . to Boston.
Rail or Sound Lines (see pages 50 to 55 for route) . to Philadelphia.
Baltimore & Ohio R. R. . . . . to starting point.

FORM EX. 997.—COTTAGE CITY (MARTHA'S VINEYARD), MASS.

Reverse of preceding excursion.

THROUGH RATES.

	Via Sound.	Via Rail.
Baltimore, Md.	$17 75	$20 35
Philadelphia, Pa.	13 75	16 35
Washington, D. C.	19 75	22 35

Transfer through Boston included via Sound Lines only.

This ticket will be accepted by Old Colony Railroad, between New
York and Boston, via either Fall River or Newport.

FORM EX. 1105.—COTTAGE CITY (MARTHA'S VINEYARD), MASS.

Baltimore & Ohio R. R. . . . . to Philadelphia.
Philadelphia & Reading R. R. . . . . to Bound Brook.
Central R. R. of New Jersey . . . . to New York.
Maine Steamship Co. . . . . to Cottage City.
              Returning, same route.

THROUGH RATES.

Baltimore, Md.	$15 00	Washington, D. C.	$17 00
Philadelphia, Pa.	11 00		

Steamers of Maine Steamship Co. leave Pier 38, East River, N. Y.,
Mondays, Wednesdays and Saturdays at 5 P. M.

The above rates include berth in state room. Meals 75 cents each.

COVINGTON, VA.

FORM EX. 58.— COVINGTON, VA., AND RETURN.

Baltimore & Ohio R. R. . . . . to Shenandoah June.
Norfolk & Western R. R. . . . . to Basic.
Chesapeake & Ohio Ry. . . . . to Covington.
Returning, same route.

THROUGH RATES.

Baltimore, Md.	$14 00	New York, N. Y.	$22 00
Chester, Pa.	17 50	Philadelphia, Pa.	18 00
Havre de Grace, Md.	15 15	Washington, D. C.	12 00
Newark, Del.	16 30	Wilmington, Del.	17 00

FORM EX. 70L.— COVINGTON, VA., AND RETURN.

Baltimore & Ohio R. R. . . . . to Staunton.
Chesapeake & Ohio Ry. . . . . to Covington.
Returning, same route.

THROUGH RATES.

Baltimore, Md.	$14 00	Meyersdale, Pa.	$15 90
Bellaire, O.	22 75	Morgantown, W. Va.	20 55
Berkeley Springs, W. Va.	12 15	Moundsville, W. Va.	22 00
Cameron, W. Va.	21 30	Mountain Lake Park, Md.	16 15
Charlestown, W. Va.	10 00	Mt. Pleasant, Pa.	18 00
Chester, Pa.	17 50	Newark, Del.	16 30
Clarksburg, W. Va.	19 35	New York, N. Y.	22 00
Connellsville, Pa.	18 10	Oakland, Md.	16 55
Cumberland, Md.	14 40	Parkersburg, W. Va.	22 50
Deer Park, Md.	16 30	Philadelphia, Pa.	18 00
Fairmont, W. Va.	19 35	Piedmont, W. Va.	15 50
Frederick, Md.	11 55	Pittsburgh, Pa.	20 40
Grafton, W. Va.	18 45	Rockwood, Pa.	16 35
Hagerstown, Md.	11 55	Somerset, Pa.	16 75
Harper's Ferry, W. Va.	10 50	Strasburg, Va.	7 85
Harrisonburg, Va.	5 50	Uniontown, Pa.	18 55
Havre de Grace, Md.	15 15	Washington, D. C.	12 00
Johnstown, Pa.	18 45	Washington, Pa.	21 50
Keyser, W. Va.	15 30	Wheeling, W. Va.	22 50
Lexington, Va.	6 00	Wilmington, Del.	17 00
McKeesport, Pa.	19 85	Winchester, Va.	8 90
Martinsburg, W. Va.	11 25		

FORM EX. 171.— COVINGTON, VA., AND RETURN.

Baltimore & Ohio R. R. . . . . to Washington.
Transfer . . . . B. & O. Depot to C. & O. Depot.
Chesapeake & Ohio Ry. . . . . to Covington.
Returning, same route.

THROUGH RATES.

Baltimore, Md.	$14 00	Meyersdale, Pa.	$20 10
Bellaire, O.	26 95	Morgantown, W. Va.	24 55
Berkeley Springs, W. Va.	16 65	Moundsville, W. Va.	26 20
Cameron, W. Va.	25 50	Mountain Lake Park, Md.	20 15
Charlestown, W. Va.	15 20	Mt. Pleasant, Pa.	22 80
Chester, Pa.	17 50	Newark, Del.	16 30
Clarksburg, W. Va.	23 55	New York, N. Y.	22 00
Connellsville, Pa.	22 30	Oakland, Md.	20 25
Cumberland, Md.	18 60	Parkersburg, W. Va.	26 65
Deer Park, Md.	20 00	Philadelphia, Pa.	18 00
Fairmont, W. Va.	23 55	Piedmont, W. Va.	19 70
Frederick, Md.	11 80	Pittsburgh, Pa.	24 00
Grafton, W. Va.	22 65	Rockwood, Pa.	20 55
Hagerstown, Md.	15 60	Somerset, Pa.	20 95
Harper's Ferry, W. Va.	14 70	Uniontown, Pa.	22 75
Havre de Grace, Md.	15 15	Washington, Pa.	25 70
Johnstown, Pa.	22 65	Wheeling, W. Va.	26 65
Keyser, W. Va.	19 50	Wilmington, Del.	17 00
McKeesport, Pa.	24 05	Winchester, Va.	16 30
Martinsburg, W. Va.	15 45		

FALLS OF THE NORTH FORK

COYNER'S SPRINGS (BONSACK), VA.

Form Ex. 3.—Coyner's Springs, (Bonsack) Va., and Return.

Baltimore & Ohio R. R. . . . . to Shenandoah June.
Norfolk & Western R. R. . . . . to Bonsack.

Returning, same route.

Coyner's Springs three-quarters mile distant from Bonsack, Va.

THROUGH RATES.

Baltimore, Md.	$12 80	Morgantown, W. Va.	$19 05
Bellaire, O.	21 45	Moundsville, W. Va.	20 75
Berkeley Springs, W. Va.	11 25	Mountain Lake Park, Md.	15 20
Cameron, W. Va.	20 05	Mt. Pleasant, Pa.	17 30
Chester, Pa.	16 30	Newark, Del.	15 10
Clarksburg, W. Va.	18 05	New York, N. Y.	20 80
Connellsville, Pa.	16 80	Oakland, Md.	15 30
Cumberland, Md.	13 40	Parkersburg, W. Va.	21 45
Deer Park, Md.	15 05	Philadelphia, Pa.	16 80
Fairmont, W. Va.	18 05	Piedmont, W. Va.	14 25
Frederick, Md.	10 85	Pittsburgh, Pa.	19 10
Grafton, W. Va.	17 15	Rockwood, Pa.	15 05
Harper's Ferry, W. Va.	9 75	Somerset, Pa.	15 15
Havre de Grace, Md.	14 25	Uniontown, Pa.	17 25
Johnstown, Pa.	16 85	Washington, D. C.	10 80
Keyser, W. Va.	14 05	Washington, Pa.	20 20
McKeesport, Pa.	18 55	Wheeling, W. Va.	21 45
Martinsburg, W. Va.	9 95	Wilmington, Del.	15 80
Meyersdale, Pa.	14 00		

CRAWFORD HOUSE (WHITE MOUNTAINS), N. H.

The Crawford House stands upon the site of the old Notch House, one of the earliest inns erected in the White Mountains. It is situated on a plateau 2,000 feet above the sea, and commands a magnificent view of Mt. Washington (6,293 feet), and Mt. Monroe (5,349 feet). The bridle-path hence up Mt. Washington passes over Mounts Pleasant, Monroe, Franklin and Clinton, and is said to afford finer views than any other route.

Within easy reach of the Crawford House are the Notch, a huge chasm in the mountains, which rises 2,000 feet on either side; Silver Cascade and Sylvan Glade Cataract, between which it is hard to award the palm; and Mount Willard, commanding a view down the Notch, which, says Bayard Taylor, "cannot be surpassed in Switzerland."

Form Ex. 516.—Crawford House, N. H., and Return.

(Via rail and North Conway; returning by Sound Lines.)

Baltimore & Ohio R. R. . . . . to Philadelphia.
Rail Lines (see pages 50 to 55 for route) . . . . . to Boston.
Boston & Maine R. R. . . . . to North Conway.
Maine Central R. R. . . . . to Crawford House.
Maine Central R. R. . . . . to North Conway.
Boston & Maine R. R. . . . . to Boston.

ROUTES AND RATES FOR SUMMER TOURS. 83

Sound Lines (see pages 50 to 55 for route) . . . . to New York.
Central R. R. of New Jersey . . . . to Bound Brook.
Philadelphia & Reading R. R. . . . . to Philadelphia.
Baltimore & Ohio R. R. . . . . to starting point.

Transfer through Boston, returning, included.

THROUGH RATES.

Baltimore, Md. . . . . . . $25 85 | Washington, D. C. . . . $27 85
†Philadelphia, Pa. . . . . 21 85 |

FORM EX. 516.—CRAWFORD HOUSE, N. H., AND RETURN.

(Via Sound Lines and North Conway; returning all rail.)

Baltimore & Ohio R. R. . . . . to Philadelphia.
Philadelphia & Reading R. R. . . . . to Bound Brook.
Central R. R. of New Jersey . . . . to New York.
Sound Lines (see pages 50 to 55 for route) . . . to Boston.
Boston & Maine R. R. . . . . to North Conway.
Maine Central R. R. . . . . to Crawford House.
Maine Central R. R. . . . . to North Conway.
Boston & Maine R. R. . . . . to Boston.
Rail Lines (see pages 50 to 55 for route) . . . . to Philadelphia.
Baltimore & Ohio R. R. . . . . to starting point.

Transfer through Boston, going, included.

THROUGH RATES.

Baltimore, Md. . . . . . . $25 85 | Washington, D. C. . . . $27 85
†Philadelphia, Pa. . . . . 21 85 |

FORM EX. 516.—CRAWFORD HOUSE, N. H., AND RETURN.

(Via Rail Lines and North Conway, in both directions.)

Baltimore & Ohio R. R. . . . . to Philadelphia.
Rail Lines (see pages 50 to 55 for route) . . . . to Boston.
Boston & Maine R. R. . . . . to North Conway.
Maine Central R. R. . . . . to Crawford House.

Returning, same route.

THROUGH RATES.

Baltimore, Md. . . . . . . $27 75 | Washington, D. C. . . . $29 75
†Philadelphia, Pa. . . . . 23 75 |

FORM EX. 516.—CRAWFORD HOUSE, N. H., AND RETURN.

(Via Sound Lines and North Conway, in both directions.)

Baltimore & Ohio R. R. . . . . to Philadelphia.
Philadelphia & Reading R. R. . . . . to Bound Brook.
Central R. R. of New Jersey . . . . to New York.
Sound Lines (see pages 50 to 55 for route) . . . to Boston.
Boston & Maine R. R. . . . . to North Conway.
Maine Central R. R. . . . . to Crawford House.

Returning, same route.

Transfer through Boston, in both directions, included.

THROUGH RATES.

Baltimore, Md. . . . . . . $23 00 | Washington, D. C. . . . $25 00
†Philadelphia, Pa. . . . . 19 00 |

84   BALTIMORE & OHIO RAILROAD COMPANY

FORM EX. 517.—CRAWFORD HOUSE, N. H., AND RETURN.
(Via rail and Portland; returning via Sound Lines.)

Baltimore & Ohio R. R. . . . . to Philadelphia.
Rail Lines (see pages 50 to 55 for route) . . . . . to Boston.
Boston & Maine R. R. . . . . to Portland.
Maine Central R. R. . . . . to Crawford House.
Maine Central R. R. . . . . to Portland.
Boston & Maine R. R. . . . . to Boston.
Sound Lines (see pages 50 to 55 for route) . . . . to New York.
Central R. R. of New Jersey . . . . to Bound Brook.
Philadelphia & Reading R. R. . . . . to Philadelphia.
Baltimore & Ohio R. R. . . . . to starting point.

Transfer through Boston, returning, included.

THROUGH RATES.

Baltimore, Md. . . . . . . $25 85 | Washington, D. C. . . . $27 85
(Philadelphia, Pa. . . . . 24 85 |

FORM EX. 517.—CRAWFORD HOUSE, N. H., AND RETURN.
(Via Sound Lines and Portland; returning all rail.)

Baltimore & Ohio R. R. . . . . to Philadelphia.
Philadelphia & Reading R. R. . . . . to Bound Brook.
Central R. R. of New Jersey . . . . to New York.
Sound Lines (see pages 50 to 55 for route) . . . . to Boston.
Boston & Maine R. R. . . . . to Portland.
Maine Central R. R. . . . . to Crawford House.
Maine Central R. R. . . . . to Portland.
Boston & Maine R. R. . . . . to Boston.
Rail Lines (see pages 50 to 55 for route) . . . . . to Philadelphia.
Baltimore & Ohio R. R. . . . . to starting point.

Transfer through Boston, going, included.

THROUGH RATES.

Baltimore, Md. . . . . . . $25 85 | Washington, D. C. . . . $27 85
(Philadelphia, Pa. . . . . 24 85 |

FORM EX. 517.—CRAWFORD HOUSE, N. H., AND RETURN.
(Via Rail Lines and Portland, in both directions.)

Baltimore & Ohio R. R. . . . . to Philadelphia.
Rail Lines (see pages 50 to 55 for route) . . . . . to Boston.
Boston & Maine R. R. . . . . to Portland.
Maine Central R. R. . . . . to Crawford House.

Returning, same route.

THROUGH RATES.

Baltimore, Md. . . . . . . $27 75 | Washington, D. C. . . . $29 75
(Philadelphia, Pa. . . . . 23 75 |

FORM EX. 517.—CRAWFORD HOUSE, N. H., AND RETURN.
(Via Sound Lines and Portland, in both directions.)

Baltimore & Ohio R. R. . . . . to Philadelphia.
Philadelphia & Reading R. R. . . . . to Bound Brook.
Central R. R. of New Jersey . . . . to New York.
Sound Lines (see pages 50 to 55 for route) . . . . to Boston.
Boston & Maine R. R. . . . . to Portland.
Maine Central R. R. . . . . to Crawford House.

Returning, same route.
Transfer through Boston, in both directions, included.

THROUGH RATES.

Baltimore, Md. . . . . . . $25 00 | Washington, D. C. . . . $25 00
(Philadelphia, Pa. . . . . 19 00 |

ROUTES AND RATES FOR SUMMER TOURS.   85

FORM EX. 955. CRAWFORD HOUSE, N. H., AND RETURN.
(Via rail and Portland; returning via Sound Lines.)

Baltimore & Ohio R. R. . . . . to Philadelphia.
Rail Lines (see pages 50 to 55 for route) . . . . to Boston.
Boston & Maine R. R. . . . . to Nashua.
Concord & Montreal R. R. . . . . to Fabyans.
Maine Central R. R. . . . . to Crawford House.
Maine Central R. R. . . . . to Fabyans.
Concord & Montreal R. R. . . . . to Nashua.
Boston & Maine R. R. . . . . to Boston.
Sound Lines (see pages 50 to 55 for route) . . . to New York.
Central R. R. of New Jersey . . . . to Bound Brook.
Philadelphia & Reading R. R. . . . . to Philadelphia.
Baltimore & Ohio R. R. . . . . to starting point.

Transfer through Boston, returning, included.

THROUGH RATES.

Baltimore, Md. . . . . . $27 45 | Washington, D. C. $29 45
(Philadelphia, Pa. . . . . 23 45 |

FORM EX. 955. CRAWFORD HOUSE, N. H., AND RETURN.
(Via Sound Lines and Portland; returning all rail.)

Baltimore & Ohio R. R. . . . . to Philadelphia.
Philadelphia & Reading R. R. . . . . to Bound Brook.
Central R. R. of New Jersey . . . . to New York.
Sound Lines (see pages 50 to 55 for route) . . . to Boston.
Boston & Maine R. R. . . . . to Nashua.
Concord & Montreal R. R. . . . . to Fabyans.
Maine Central R. R. . . . . to Crawford House.
Maine Central R. R. . . . . to Fabyans.
Concord & Montreal R. R. . . . . to Nashua.
Boston & Maine R. R. . . . . to Boston.
Rail Lines (see pages 50 to 55 for route) . . . . to Philadelphia.
Baltimore & Ohio R. R. . . . . to starting point.

Transfer through Boston, going, included.

THROUGH RATES.

Baltimore, Md. . . . . . $27 45 | Washington, D. C. $29 45
(Philadelphia, Pa. . . . . 23 45 |

FORM EX. 955.—CRAWFORD HOUSE, N. H., AND RETURN.
(Via Rail Lines and Portland, in both directions.)

Baltimore & Ohio R. R. . . . . to Philadelphia.
Rail Lines (see pages 50 to 55 for route) . . . . to Boston.
Boston & Maine R. R. . . . . to Nashua.
Concord & Montreal R. R. . . . . to Fabyans.
Maine Central R. R. . . . . to Crawford House.

Returning, same route.

THROUGH RATES.

Baltimore, Md. . . . . . $28 00 | Washington, D. C. $30 00
(Philadelphia, Pa. . . . . 24 00 |

FORM EX. 955.—CRAWFORD HOUSE, N. H., AND RETURN.
(Via Sound Lines, Nashua and Fabyans, in both directions.)

Baltimore & Ohio R. R. . . . . to Philadelphia.
Philadelphia & Reading R. R. . . . . to Bound Brook.
Central R. R. of New Jersey . . . . to New York.
Sound Lines (see pages 50 to 55 for route) . . . to Boston.

Boston & Maine R. R.,..............to Nashua.
Concord & Montreal R. R.............to Fabyans.
Maine Central R. R.................to Crawford House.
Returning, same route.
Transfer through Boston, in both directions, included.

THROUGH RATES.
Baltimore, Md.......$25 00 | Washington, D. C.....$25 00
|Philadelphia, Pa.....19 00 |

FORM EX. 612. CRAWFORD HOUSE, N. H., AND RETURN.

Baltimore & Ohio R. R..............to Philadelphia.
Philadelphia & Reading R. R..........to Bound Brook.
Central R. R. of New Jersey..........to New York.
New York, New Haven & Hartford R. R....to Springfield.
Connecticut River R. R..............to South Vernon.
Central Vermont R. R...............to Brattleboro.
Vermont Valley R. R................to Windsor.
Central Vermont R. R...............to White River June.
Boston & Maine R. R...............to Wells River.
Concord & Montreal R. R.............to Fabyan House.
Maine Central R. R................to Crawford House.
Returning, same route.

THROUGH RATES.
Baltimore, Md.......$25 00 | Washington, D. C.....$27 00
|Philadelphia, Pa.....21 00 |

FORM EX. 953. CRAWFORD HOUSE (WHITE MOUNTAINS), N. H.,
AND RETURN.

(Via New York and Connecticut Valley; returning via Boston.)
Baltimore & Ohio R. R..............to Philadelphia.
Philadelphia & Reading R. R..........to Bound Brook.
Central R. R. of N. J..............to New York.
New York, New Haven & Hartford R. R....to Springfield.
Connecticut River R. R.............to South Vernon.
Central Vermont R. R...............to Brattleboro.
Vermont Valley R. R................to Windsor.
Central Vermont R. R...............to White River Jc.
Boston & Maine R. R................to Wells River.
Concord & Montreal R. R.............to Fabyan House.
Maine Central R. R................to Crawford House.
Maine Central R. R................to Portland.
Boston & Maine R. R................to Boston.
Rail or Sound Lines (see pages 50 to 55 for routes) to Philadelphia.
Baltimore & Ohio R. R..............to starting point.

FORM EX. 954. CRAWFORD HOUSE (WHITE MOUNTAINS), N. H.,
AND RETURN.

Reverse of preceding excursion.
Transfer through Boston included, via Sound Lines.

THROUGH RATES.
                        Via Sound. Via Rail.
Baltimore, Md.............$24 75 $27 10
|Philadelphia, Pa..........20 75   23 10
Washington, D. C..........26 75   29 10

FORM EX. 957. CRAWFORD HOUSE, N. H., AND RETURN.

Maine Central R. R..........Fabyan House to Crawford House.
Returning by same route.
Sold in connection with any ticket passing through or terminating at Fabyans.
Rate........................$0 60

DAVIS, W. VA.

FORM EX. 720.—DAVIS, W. VA., AND RETURN.

Baltimore & Ohio R. R. . . . . to Cumberland.
West Virginia Central Ry. . . . . to Davis.
     Returning, same route.

THROUGH RATES.

Baltimore, Md.	$11 10	Meyersdale, Pa.	$7 90
Berkeley Springs, W. Va.	5 85	Mt. Pleasant, Pa.	7 60
Charlestown, W. Va.	7 80	Newark, Del.	13 10
Chester, Pa.	14 60	New York, N. Y.	19 10
Connellsville, Pa.	7 10	Philadelphia, Pa.	15 10
Frederick, Md.	8 35	Pittsburgh, Pa.	9 10
Hagerstown, Md.	8 55	Rockwood, Pa.	5 35
Harper's Ferry, W. Va.	7 30	Somerset, Pa.	5 70
Harrisonburg, Va.	12 30	Staunton, Va.	13 60
Havre de Grace, Md.	12 55	Strasburg, Va.	9 95
Johnstown, Pa.	7 15	Uniontown, Pa.	7 50
Keyser, W. Va.	1 50	Washington, D. C.	9 50
Lexington, Va.	15 10	Washington, Pa.	11 85
McKeesport, Pa.	8 80	Wilmington, Del.	14 10
Martinsburg, W. Va.	6 30	Winchester, Va.	8 90

FORM EX. 65.—DAVIS, W. VA., AND RETURN.

Baltimore & Ohio R. R. . . . . to Piedmont.
West Virginia Central R. R. . . . . to Davis.
     Returning, same route.

THROUGH RATES.

Bellaire, O.	$9 50	Morgantown, W. Va.	$7 15
Cameron, W. Va.	8 10	Moundsville, W. Va.	8 80
Clarksburg, W. Va.	6 15	Mountain Lake Park, Md.	3 20
Deer Park, Md.	3 10	Oakland, Md.	3 35
Fairmont, W. Va.	6 10	Parkersburg, W. Va.	9 10
Grafton, W. Va.	5 25	Wheeling, W. Va.	9 20
Keyser, W. Va.	2 50		

DEER PARK, MD.

ON THE CREST OF THE ALLEGHANIES, THE PEER OF SUMMER RESORTS.

This famous mountain resort is situated on the line of the Baltimore & Ohio R. R., in the heart of the Alleghanies, and has the advantage of the vestibule express train service between the East and West. All trains stop at the hotel station during the season. Electric lights have been introduced throughout the houses and grounds; Turkish and Russian baths and large swimming pools provided for ladies and gentlemen; suitable grounds for lawn tennis; bowling-alleys and billiard-rooms are here; fine riding and driving horses, carriages, mountain wagons, tally-ho coaches, &c., are kept for hire; in short, all the necessary adjuncts for the comfort, health, or pleasure of patrons.

Address Passenger Department, Baltimore & Ohio R. R., for illustrated book descriptive of Deer Park.

ROUTES AND RATES FOR SUMMER TOURS. 89

FORM EX. 5 OR EX.—DEER PARK, MD., AND RETURN.

Baltimore & Ohio R. R. . . . . to Deer Park.
Returning, same route.

THROUGH RATES.

Baltimore, Md.	$9 00	Moundsville, W. Va.	$5 70
Bellaire, O.	6 50	Mountain Lake Park, Md.	15
Berkeley Springs, W. Va.	4 45	Mt. Pleasant, Pa.	6 40
Cameron, W. Va.	5 00	Newark, Del.	11 30
Charlestown, W. Va.	6 30	New York, N. Y.	17 00
Chester, Pa.	12 30	Oakland, Md.	25
Clarksburg, W. Va.	3 05	Parkersburg, W. Va.	6 30
Connellsville, Pa.	5 00	Philadelphia, Pa.	13 00
Cumberland, Md.	1 90	Piedmont, W. Va.	80
Fairmont, W. Va.	3 05	Pittsburgh, Pa.	7 90
Frederick, Md.	6 85	Relay, Md.	9 00
Grafton, W. Va.	2 45	Rockwood, Pa.	3 85
Hagerstown, Md.	6 85	Somerset, Pa.	4 25
Harper's Ferry, W. Va.	5 80	Staunton, Va.	12 40
Harrisonburg, Va.	10 80	Strasburg, Va.	8 45
Havre de Grace, Md.	10 45	Uniontown, Pa.	6 05
Johnstown, Pa.	5 65	Washington, D. C.	8 00
Keyser, W. Va.	1 00	Washington, Pa. (via Wheeling)	7 50
Lexington, Va.	13 90		
McKeesport, Pa.	7 35	Wheeling, W. Va.	6 45
Martinsburg, W. Va.	5 00	Wilmington, Del.	12 00
Meyersdale, Pa.	3 40	Winchester, Va.	7 40
Morgantown, W. Va.	4 05		

In addition to the season tickets for which rates are quoted above, special signature contract tickets Form Ex. 800 will be sold from the following stations to Deer Park, Md., and return, for use going on train No. 3 on Fridays and all trains on Saturday and Sunday of each week, good to return on any train leaving Deer Park on the following Monday.

EXCURSION RATES.

Baltimore, Md.	$5 00	Washington, D. C.	$5 00
Philadelphia, Pa.	8 00		

DOUBLING GAP SPRINGS, PA.

FORM EX. 642.—DOUBLING GAP SPRINGS, PA., AND RETURN.

Baltimore & Ohio R. R. . . . . to Hagerstown.
Transfer (B. & O. R. R. Depot) . . . . to C. V. R. R. Depot.
Cumberland Valley R. R. . . . . to Newville.
Stage . . . . to Doubling Gap Spgs.
Returning, same route.

THROUGH RATES.

Baltimore, Md.	$8 25	Newark, Del.	$10 55
Charlestown, W. Va.	5 50	Staunton, Va.	11 40
Frederick, Md.	5 70	Strasburg, Va.	7 45
Harper's Ferry, W. Va.	4 80	Washington, D. C.	6 80
Harrisonburg, Va.	9 80	Wilmington, Del.	11 25
Havre de Grace, Md.	9 70	Winchester, Va.	6 45
Lexington, Va.	12 90		

FORM EX. 645.—DOUBLING GAP SPRINGS, PA., AND RETURN.

Baltimore & Ohio R. R. . . . . to Martinsburg.
Transfer (B. & O. R. R. Depot) . . . . to C. V. R. R. Depot.
Cumberland Valley R. R. . . . . to Newville.
Stage . . . . to Doubling Gap Spgs.
Returning same route.

THROUGH RATES.

Baltimore, Md.	$9 20	Morgantown, W. Va.	$13 05
Bellaire, O.	16 40	Moundsville, W. Va.	15 30
Berkeley Springs, W. Va.	5 75	Mountain Lake Park, Md.	9 75
Cameron, W. Va.	14 65	Mt. Pleasant, Pa.	11 90
Charlestown, W. Va.	5 80	Newark, Del.	11 45
Clarksburg, W. Va.	12 65	Oakland, Md.	9 85
Connellsville, Pa.	11 40	Parkersburg, W. Va.	15 75
Cumberland, Md.	7 70	Piedmont, W. Va.	8 80
Deer Park, Md.	9 60	Pittsburgh, Pa.	13 70
Fairmont, W. Va.	12 65	Rockwood, Pa.	9 65
Frederick, Md.	6 35	Somerset, Pa.	10 05
Grafton, W. Va.	11 75	Staunton, Va.	11 00
Harper's Ferry, W. Va.	5 30	Strasburg, Va.	7 90
Harrisonburg, Va.	10 30	Uniontown, Pa.	11 80
Havre de Grace, Md.	10 60	Washington, D. C.	7 20
Johnstown, Pa.	11 45	Washington, Pa.	11 80
Keyser, W. Va.	8 60	Wheeling, W. Va.	15 75
Lexington, Va.	13 40	Wilmington, Del.	11 95
McKeesport, Pa.	13 45	Winchester, Va.	6 50
Meyersdale, Pa.	9 20		

EAGLES MERE, PA.

FORM EX. 558.—EAGLES MERE, PA., AND RETURN.

Baltimore & Ohio R. R.	to Philadelphia
Philadelphia & Reading R. R.	to Halls
Williamsport & North Branch R. R.	to Eagles Mere

Returning same route.

THROUGH RATES.

Baltimore, Md.	$10 50	Washington, D. C.	$12 50
†Philadelphia, Pa.	9 20		

Baggage will be checked through to Muncy Valley only on these tickets. From Muncy Valley stages convey passengers and baggage to Eagles Mere. Stage transportation of passengers included in ticket, but an extra charge will be made for transporting baggage from Muncy Valley to Eagles Mere.

EASTPORT, ME.

FORM EX. 956.—EASTPORT, ME., AND RETURN.

Baltimore & Ohio R. R.	to Philadelphia
Philadelphia & Reading R. R.	to Bound Brook
Central R. R. of New Jersey	to New York
Mallory Steamship Line	to Eastport

Returning, same route.

THROUGH RATES.

Baltimore, Md.	$25 00	Washington, D. C.	
†Philadelphia, Pa.	22 00		

The steamers of the Mallory Steamship Line leave New York, Pier 21 East River, Saturdays at 3.00 P. M. for Eastport, Me. The above rates include berth on steamer. Staterooms from $1.00 to $2.00 each extra, according to location. Meals: Breakfast and supper, 75 cents each; dinner, $1.00.

EGGLESTON SPRINGS, VA.

FORM EX. 50.—EGGLESTON SPRINGS (STAYTIDE), VA., AND RETURN.

Baltimore & Ohio R. R.	to Shenandoah June.
Norfolk & Western R. R.	to Staytide.

Returning, same route.

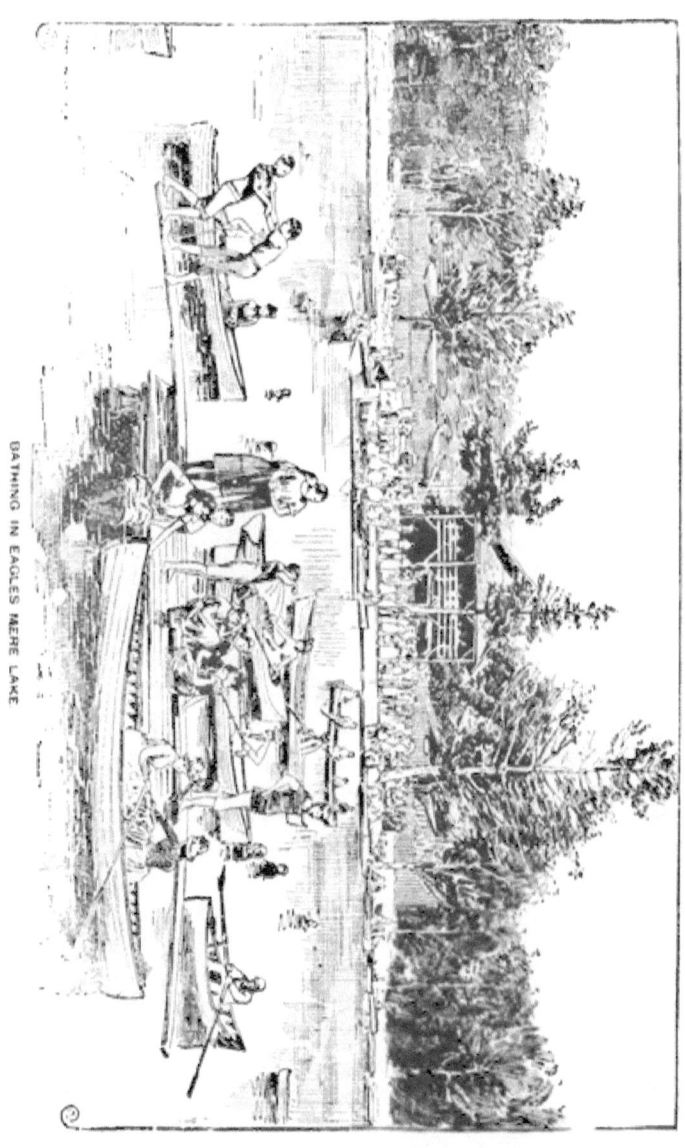
BATHING IN EAGLES MERE LAKE

THROUGH RATES.

Baltimore, Md.	$15 65	Morgantown, W. Va.	$21 95
Bellaire, O.	24 35	Moundsville, W. Va.	23 65
Berkeley Springs, W. Va.	14 45	Mountain Lake Park, Md.	18 10
Cameron, W. Va.	22 95	Mt. Pleasant, Pa.	20 20
Chester, Pa.	19 15	Newark, Del.	17 95
Clarksburg, W. Va.	20 95	New York, N. Y.	23 05
Connellsville, Pa.	19 70	Oakland, Md.	18 00
Cumberland, Md.	16 00	Parkersburg, W. Va.	25 95
Deer Park, Md.	17 95	Philadelphia, Pa.	19 65
Fairmont, W. Va.	20 95	Piedmont, W. Va.	17 25
Frederick, Md.	15 75	Pittsburgh, Pa.	22 60
Grafton, W. Va.	20 05	Rockwood, Pa.	20 75
Harper's Ferry, W. Va.	12 65	Somerset, Pa.	22 35
Havre de Grace, Md.	17 40	Uniontown, Pa.	21 50
Johnstown, Pa.	19 75	Washington, D. C.	15 65
Keyser, W. Va.	16 95	Washington, Pa.	25 10
McKeesport, Pa.	21 45	Wheeling, W. Va.	22 05
Martinsburg, W. Va.	12 85	Wilmington, Del.	18 65
Meyersdale, Pa.	17 50		

FORM EX. 165.—EGGLESTON SPRINGS (STAYSIDE), VA. AND RETURN.

Baltimore & Ohio R. R. .... to Washington
Transfer .... B. & O. Depot to R. & D. Depot.
Richmond & Danville R. R. .... to Lynchburg
Norfolk & Western R. R. .... to Stayside.

Returning, same route.

THROUGH RATES.

Baltimore, Md.	$15 65	Meyersdale, Pa.	$21 50
Bellaire, O.	28 00	Morgantown, W. Va.	23 30
Berkeley Springs, W. Va.	18 30	Moundsville, W. Va.	27 85
Cameron, W. Va.	27 15	Mountain Lake Park, Md.	21 10
Charlestown, W. Va.	16 85	Mt. Pleasant, Pa.	29 35
Chester, Pa.	19 15	Newark, Del.	17 95
Clarksburg, W. Va.	25 20	New York, N. Y.	23 05
Connellsville, Pa.	23 95	Oakland, Md.	21 10
Cumberland, Md.	20 25	Parkersburg, W. Va.	28 20
Deer Park, Md.	21 65	Philadelphia, Pa.	10 65
Fairmont, W. Va.	25 20	Piedmont, W. Va.	21 35
Frederick, Md.	16 15	Pittsburgh, Pa.	28 25
Grafton, W. Va.	24 30	Rockwood, Pa.	22 30
Hagerstown, Md.	17 25	Somerset, Pa.	22 00
Harper's Ferry, W. Va.	16 35	Uniontown, Pa.	24 40
Havre de Grace, Md.	17 40	Washington, Pa.	27 35
Johnstown, Pa.	21 00	Wheeling, W. Va.	28 30
Keyser, W. Va.	21 45	Wilmington, Del.	18 85
McKeesport, Pa.	25 70	Winchester, Va.	17 05
Martinsburg, W. Va.	17 40		

ELBERON, N. J.

FORM EX. 636.—ELBERON, N. J., AND RETURN.

Baltimore & Ohio R. R. .... to Philadelphia.
Philadelphia & Reading R. R. .... to Bound Brook.
Central R. R. of New Jersey .... to Elberon.

Returning same route.

THROUGH RATES.

Baltimore, Md.	$8 00	Washington, D. C.	$10 00
†Philadelphia, Pa.	4 00		

In addition to the above, excursion tickets, Form Ex. 636, Elberon, N. J., may be sold from the following stations at rates as quoted below. Tickets should be limited with an "L" punch to 16 days, including day of issue.

THROUGH RATES.

Baltimore, Md.	$7 50	Philadelphia, Pa.		$8 50
Chester, Pa.	4 00	Washington, D. C.		9 50
Havre de Grace, Md.	5 85	Wilmington, Del.		4 50
Newark, Del.	5 00			

ELKINS, W. VA.

FORM EX. 724.—ELKINS, W. VA., AND RETURN.

Baltimore & Ohio R. R. . . . . to Cumberland.
West Virginia Central R. R. . . . . to Elkins.
Returning, same route.

THROUGH RATES.

Baltimore, Md.	$12 25	Meyersdale, Pa.		$6 05
Berkeley Springs, W. Va.	7 00	Mt. Pleasant, Pa.		8 75
Charlestown, W. Va.	8 95	Newark, Del.		14 25
Chester, Pa.	15 25	New York, N. Y.		20 25
Connellsville, Pa.	8 25	Philadelphia, Pa.		16 25
Frederick, Md.	9 50	Pittsburgh, Pa.		10 55
Hagerstown, Md.	9 50	Rockwood, Pa.		6 50
Harper's Ferry, W. Va.	8 15	Somerset, Pa.		6 85
Harrisonburg, Va.	13 45	Staunton, Va.		14 75
Havre de Grace, Md.	13 70	Strasburg, Va.		11 10
Johnstown, Pa.	8 20	Uniontown, Pa.		8 65
Keyser, W. Va.	5 15	Washington, D. C.		10 65
Lexington, Va.	16 25	Washington, Pa.		13 00
McKeesport, Pa.	9 95	Wilmington, Del.		15 25
Martinsburg, W. Va.	7 65	Winchester, Va.		10 05

FORM EX. 62.—ELKINS, W. VA., AND RETURN.

Baltimore & Ohio R. R. . . . . to Piedmont.
West Virginia Central R. R. . . . . to Elkins.
Returning, same route.

THROUGH RATES.

Bellaire, Ohio	$10 65	Morgantown, W. Va.		$8 30
Cameron, W. Va.	9 25	Moundsville, W. Va.		9 95
Clarksburg, W. Va.	7 50	Mountain Lake Park, Md.		4 55
Deer Park, Md.	4 25	Oakland, Md.		4 50
Fairmount, W. Va.	7 25	Parkersburg, W. Va.		10 55
Grafton, W. Va.	6 10	Wheeling, W. Va.		10 35
Keyser, W. Va.	3 65			

ELMIRA, N. Y.

Elmira is a flourishing city of nearly twenty-five thousand inhabitants and is a great manufacturing centre. On a hill east of the city is the noted Elmira Water Cure. The Elmira Female College, the State Reformatory, and the Southern Tier Orphans' Home are also located here.

FORM EX. 539.—ELMIRA, N. Y., AND RETURN.

Baltimore & Ohio R. R. . . . . to Philadelphia.
Philadelphia & Reading R. R. . . . . to Bethlehem.
Lehigh Valley R. R. . . . . to Waverly.
New York, Lake Erie & Western R. R. . . . . to Elmira.
Returning, same route.

THROUGH RATES.

Baltimore, Md.	$12 70	Washington, D. C.		$14 70
Philadelphia, Pa.	10 70			

EPHRATA, PA.

FORM EX 655. EPHRATA, PA., AND RETURN.

Baltimore & Ohio R. R. . . . . to Philadelphia
Philadelphia & Reading R. R. . . . . to Ephrata.
Returning, same route.

THROUGH RATES.

	Limit.	Rate.		Limit.	Rate.
Baltimore, Md.	11 days.	$7 11	†Philadelphia, Pa.	6 days.	$3 11
Chester, Pa.	6 days.	3 61	Washington, D. C.	11 days.	9 11
Havre de Grace, Md.	6 days.	5 46	Wilmington, Del.	6 days.	4 11
Newark, Del.	6 days.	4 61			

FAUQUIER WHITE SULPHUR SPRINGS, VA.

FORM EX. 281.—FAUQUIER WHITE SULPHUR SPRINGS, VA., AND RETURN.

Baltimore & Ohio R. R. . . . . to Washington.
Transfer . . . . B. & O. Depot to R. & D. Depot
Richmond & Danville R. R. . . . . to Warrenton.
Stage (7 miles) . . . . to Fauquier White Sulphur Springs.
Returning, same route.

THROUGH RATES.

Baltimore, Md.	$6 25		Meyersdale, Pa.	$12 35
Bellaire, O.	19 20		Morgantown, W. Va.	16 80
Berkeley Springs, W. Va.	8 90		Moundsville, W. Va.	18 45
Cameron, W. Va.	17 75		Mountain Lake Park, Md.	12 10
Charlestown, W. Va.	7 15		Mt. Pleasant, Pa.	15 05
Chester, Pa.	9 75		Newark, Del.	8 55
Clarksburg, W. Va.	15 80		New York, N. Y.	11 25
Connellsville, Pa.	11 55		Oakland, Md.	12 70
Cumberland, Md.	10 85		Parkersburg, W. Va.	18 90
Deer Park, Md.	12 25		Philadelphia, Pa.	10 25
Fairmont, W. Va.	15 80		Piedmont, W. Va.	11 95
Frederick, Md.	7 05		Pittsburgh, Pa.	16 85
Grafton, W. Va.	14 90		Rockwood, Pa.	12 80
Hagerstown, Md.	7 85		Somerset, Pa.	13 20
Harper's Ferry, W. Va.	6 95		Uniontown, Pa.	15 00
Havre de Grace, Md.	7 70		Washington, Pa.	17 95
Johnstown, Pa.	14 60		Wheeling, W. Va.	18 90
Keyser, W. Va.	11 75		Wilmington, Del.	9 25
McKeesport, Pa.	16 30		Winchester, Va.	8 55
Martinsburg, W. Va.	7 70			

FABYAN HOUSE (WHITE MOUNTAINS), N. H.

The Fabyan is one of the largest and most finely-appointed hotels in the White Mountains. In it are to be found all the conveniences of modern times, and from its windows one may command an imposing view of the entire White Mountain range.

The Fabyan is the nearest hotel on the mountains to what is known as the Base, where the Mt. Washington R. R. connects with the Mt. Washington Branch of the Concord & Montreal. The White Mountains Division of the Maine Central R. R. crosses the Concord & Montreal R. R. near the Fabyan House, thus making it the most important railroad centre, and most accessible resort in the mountains.

FORM EX. 518.—FABYAN HOUSE, N. H., AND RETURN.

(Via rail, Boston and North Conway; returning via Sound Lines.)

Baltimore & Ohio R. R. . . . . to Philadelphia.
Rail Lines (see pages 50 to 55 for route) . . . . . to Boston.
Boston & Maine R. R. . . . . to North Conway.
Maine Central R. R. to Fabyan House.
Maine Central R. R. to North Conway.
Boston & Maine R. R. . . . . to Boston.
Sound Lines (see pages 50 to 55 for route) . . . to New York.
Central R. R. of New Jersey . . . . to Bound Brook.
Philadelphia & Reading R. R. . . . . to Philadelphia.
Baltimore & Ohio R. R. . . . . to starting point.

Transfer through Boston, returning, included.

THROUGH RATES.

Baltimore, Md. . . . . . . $26 10 | Washington, D. C. $28 10
†Philadelphia, Pa. . . . . 22 10 |

FORM EX. 518.—FABYAN HOUSE, N. H., AND RETURN.

(Via Sound Lines, Boston, and North Conway; returning via rail.)

Baltimore & Ohio R. R. . . . . to Philadelphia.
Philadelphia & Reading R. R. . . . . to Bound Brook.
Central R. R. of New Jersey . . . . to New York.
Sound Lines (see pages 50 to 55 for route) . . . to Boston.
Boston & Maine R. R. . . . . to North Conway.
Maine Central R. R. to Fabyan House.
Maine Central R. R. to North Conway.
Boston & Maine R. R. . . . . to Boston.
Rail Lines (see pages 50 to 55 for route) . . . . . to Philadelphia.
Baltimore & Ohio R. R. . . . . to starting point.

Transfer through Boston, going, included.

THROUGH RATES.

Baltimore, Md. . . . . . . $26 10 | Washington, D. C. $28 10
†Philadelphia, Pa. . . . . 22 10 |

FORM EX. 518.—FABYAN HOUSE, N. H., AND RETURN.

(Via Rail Lines and North Conway in both directions.)

Baltimore & Ohio R. R. . . . . to Philadelphia.
Rail Lines (see pages 50 to 55 for route) . . . . . to Boston.
Boston & Maine R. R. . . . . to North Conway.
Maine Central R. R. to Fabyan House.

Returning, same route.

THROUGH RATES.

Baltimore, Md. . . . . . . $27 75 | Washington, D. C. $29 75
†Philadelphia, Pa. . . . . 23 75 |

FORM EX. 518.—FABYAN HOUSE, N. H., AND RETURN.

(Via Sound Lines and North Conway in both directions.)

Baltimore & Ohio R. R. . . . . to Philadelphia.
Philadelphia & Reading R. R. . . . . to Bound Brook.
Central R. R. of New Jersey . . . . to New York.
Sound Lines (see pages 50 to 55 for route) . . . to Boston.
Boston & Maine R. R. . . . . to North Conway.
Maine Central R. R. to Fabyan House.

Returning, same route.

Transfer through Boston, in both directions, included.

THROUGH RATES.

Baltimore, Md. . . . . . . $23 00 | Washington, D. C. $25 00
†Philadelphia, Pa. . . . . 19 00 |

FORM EX. 549.—FABYAN HOUSE, N. H., AND RETURN.
(Via rail, Boston and Portland; returning via Sound Lines.)

Baltimore & Ohio R. R. . . . . to Philadelphia.
Rail Lines (see pages 50 to 55 for routes) . . . . . to Boston.
Boston & Maine R. R. . . . . to Portland.
Maine Central R. R. to Fabyan House.
Maine Central R. R. to Portland.
Boston & Maine R. R. . . . . to Boston.
Sound Lines (see pages 50 to 55 for routes) . . . . to New York.
Central R. R. of New Jersey . . . . to Bound Brook.
Philadelphia & Reading R. R. . . . . to Philadelphia.
Baltimore & Ohio R. R. . . . . to starting point.

Transfer through Boston, returning, included.

THROUGH RATES.

Baltimore, Md. . . . . . $26 40 | Washington, D. C. $28 40
†Philadelphia, Pa. . . . . 22 40 |

FORM EX. 549.—FABYAN HOUSE, N. H., AND RETURN.
(Via Sound Lines, Boston and Portland; returning via rail.)

Baltimore & Ohio R. R. . . . . to Philadelphia.
Philadelphia & Reading R. R. . . . . to Bound Brook.
Central R. R. of New Jersey . . . . to New York.
Sound Lines (see pages 50 to 55 for routes) . . . . to Boston.
Boston & Maine R. R. . . . . to Portland.
Maine Central R. R. to Fabyan House.
Maine Central R. R. to Portland.
Boston & Maine R. R. . . . . to Boston.
Rail Lines (see pages 50 to 55 for routes) . . . . . to Philadelphia.
Baltimore & Ohio R. R. . . . . to starting point.

Transfer through Boston, going, included.

THROUGH RATES.

Baltimore, Md. . . . . . $26 40 | Washington, D. C. $28 40
†Philadelphia, Pa. . . . . 22 40 |

FORM EX. 549.—FABYAN HOUSE, N. H., AND RETURN.
(Via Rail Lines and Portland in both directions.)

Baltimore & Ohio R. R. . . . . to Philadelphia.
Rail Lines (see pages 50 to 55 for routes) . . . . . to Boston.
Boston & Maine R. R. . . . . to Portland.
Maine Central R. R. to Fabyan House.

Returning, same route.

THROUGH RATES.

Baltimore, Md. . . . . . $27 75 | Washington, D. C. $29 75
†Philadelphia, Pa. . . . . 23 75 |

FORM EX. 549.—FABYAN HOUSE, N. H., AND RETURN.
(Via Sound Lines and Portland in both directions.)

Baltimore & Ohio R. R. . . . . to Philadelphia.
Philadelphia & Reading R. R. . . . . to Bound Brook.
Central R. R. of New Jersey . . . . to New York.
Sound Lines (see pages 50 to 55 for routes) . . . . to Boston.
Boston & Maine R. R. . . . . to Portland.
Maine Central R. R. to Fabyan House.

Returning, same route.
Transfer through Boston, in both directions, included.

THROUGH RATES.

Baltimore, Md. . . . . . $23 00 | Washington, D. C. $25 00
†Philadelphia, Pa. . . . . 19 00 |

Form Ex. 520. Fabyan House, N. H., and Return.

(Via rail, Boston, Concord and Bethlehem Junction; returning via North Conway and Sound Lines.)

Baltimore & Ohio R. R.	to Philadelphia.
Rail Lines (see pages 50 to 55 for routes)	to Boston.
Boston & Maine R. R.	to Nashua.
Concord & Montreal R. R.	to Bethlehem Junc.
Profile & Franconia Notch R. R.	to Profile House.
Profile & Franconia Notch R. R.	to Zealand Junc.
Maine Central R. R.	to Fabyan House.
Maine Central R. R.	to North Conway.
Boston & Maine R. R.	to Boston.
Sound Lines (see pages 50 to 55 for routes)	to New York.
Central R. R. of New Jersey	to Bound Brook.
Philadelphia & Reading R. R.	to Philadelphia.
Baltimore & Ohio R. R.	to starting point.

Transfer through Boston, returning, included.

Through Rates.

Baltimore, Md.	$29 10	Washington, D. C.	$31 10
Philadelphia, Pa.	25 10		

Form Ex. 520. Fabyan House, N. H., and Return.

(Via Sound Lines, Boston, Concord and Bethlehem Junction; returning via North Conway and rail.)

Baltimore & Ohio R. R.	to Philadelphia.
Philadelphia & Reading R. R.	to Bound Brook.
Central R. R. of New Jersey	to New York.
Sound Lines (see pages 50 to 55 for routes)	to Boston.
Boston & Maine R. R.	to Nashua.
Concord & Montreal R. R.	to Bethlehem Junc.
Profile & Franconia Notch R. R.	to Profile House.
Profile & Franconia Notch R. R.	to Zealand Junc.
Maine Central R. R.	to Fabyan House.
Maine Central R. R.	to North Conway.
Boston & Maine R. R.	to Boston.
Rail Lines (see pages 50 to 55 for routes)	to Philadelphia.
Baltimore & Ohio R. R.	to starting point.

Transfer through Boston, going, included.

Through Rates.

Baltimore, Md.	$29 10	Washington, D. C.	$31 10
Philadelphia, Pa.	25 10		

Form Ex. 520. — Fabyan House, N. H., and Return.

(Via rail, Boston, Concord and Bethlehem Junction; returning via North Conway and rail.)

Baltimore & Ohio R. R.	to Philadelphia.
Rail Lines (see pages 50 to 55 for routes)	to Boston.
Boston & Maine R. R.	to Nashua.
Concord & Montreal R. R.	to Bethlehem Junc.
Profile & Franconia Notch R. R.	to Profile House.
Profile & Franconia Notch R. R.	to Zealand Junc.
Maine Central R. R.	to Fabyan House.
Maine Central R. R.	to North Conway.
Boston & Maine R. R.	to Boston.
Rail Lines (see pages 50 to 55 for routes)	to Philadelphia.
Baltimore & Ohio R. R.	to starting point.

Through Rates.

Baltimore, Md.	$31 20	Washington, D. C.	$33 20
Philadelphia, Pa.	27 20		

98   BALTIMORE & OHIO RAILROAD COMPANY

FORM EX. 520.—FABYAN HOUSE, N. H., AND RETURN.
(Via Sound Lines, Boston, Concord and Bethlehem Junction; returning
via North Conway and Sound Lines.

Baltimore & Ohio R. R. .... to Philadelphia.
Philadelphia & Reading R. R. .... to Bound Brook.
Central R. R. of New Jersey .... to New York.
Sound Lines (see pages 50 to 55 for routes) .... to Boston.
Boston & Maine R. R. .... to Nashua.

Concord & Montreal R. R. . . . . to Bethlehem June.
Profile & Franconia Notch R. R. . . . . to Profile House.
Profile & Franconia Notch R. R. . . . . to Zealand June.
Maine Central R. R. . . . . to Fabyan House.
Maine Central R. R. . . . . to North Conway.
Boston & Maine R. R. . . . . to Boston.
Sound Lines (see pages 50 to 55 for route) . . . to New York.
Central R. R. of New Jersey . . . . to Bound Brook.
Philadelphia & Reading R. R. . . . . to Philadelphia.
Baltimore & Ohio R. R. . . . . to starting point.

Transfer through Boston, in both directions, included.

THROUGH RATES.

Baltimore, Md. . . . . . . $26 50 | Washington, D. C. $28 50
†Philadelphia, Pa. . . . . 22 50 |

FORM EX. 521.—FABYAN HOUSE, N. H., AND RETURN.

(Via rail and North Conway ; returning via Bethlehem Junction, Concord and Sound Lines.)

Baltimore & Ohio R. R. . . . . to Philadelphia.
Rail Lines (see pages 50 to 55 for route) . . . to Boston.
Boston & Maine R. R. . . . . to North Conway.
Maine Central R. R. . . . . to Fabyan House.
Maine Central R. R. . . . . to Zealand June.
Profile & Franconia Notch R. R. . . . . to Profile House.
Profile & Franconia Notch R. R. . . . . to Bethlehem June.
Concord & Montreal R. R. . . . . to Nashua.
Boston & Maine R. R. . . . . to Boston.
Sound Lines (see pages 50 to 55 for route) . . . to New York.
Central R. R. of New Jersey . . . . to Bound Brook.
Philadelphia & Reading R. R. . . . . to Philadelphia.
Baltimore & Ohio R. R. . . . . to starting point.

Transfer through Boston, returning, included.

THROUGH RATES.

Baltimore, Md. . . . . . . $29 10 | Washington, D. C. $31 10
†Philadelphia, Pa. . . . . 25 10 |

FORM EX. 524.—FABYAN HOUSE, N. H., AND RETURN.

(Via Sound Lines and North Conway ; returning via Bethlehem Junction, Concord and rail.)

Baltimore & Ohio R. R. . . . . to Philadelphia.
Philadelphia & Reading R. R. . . . . to Bound Brook.
Central R. R. of New Jersey . . . . to New York.
Sound Lines (see pages 50 to 55 for route) . . . to Boston.
Boston & Maine R. R. . . . . to North Conway.
Maine Central R. R. . . . . to Fabyan House.
Maine Central R. R. . . . . to Zealand June.
Profile & Franconia Notch R. R. . . . . to Profile House.
Profile & Franconia Notch R. R. . . . . to Bethlehem June.
Concord & Montreal R. R. . . . . to Nashua.
Boston & Maine R. R. . . . . to Boston.
Rail Lines (see pages 50 to 55 for route) . . . to Philadelphia.
Baltimore & Ohio R. R. . . . . to starting point.

Transfer through Boston, going, included.

THROUGH RATES.

Baltimore, Md. . . . . . . $29 10 | Washington, D. C. $31 10
†Philadelphia, Pa. . . . . 25 10 |

Form Ex. 521.—FABYAN HOUSE, N. H., AND RETURN.

(Via rail, Boston and North Conway; returning via Bethlehem Junction, Concord and rail.)

Baltimore & Ohio R. R.	to Philadelphia.
Rail Lines (see pages 50 to 55 for route)	to Boston.
Boston & Maine R. R.	to North Conway.
Maine Central R. R.	to Fabyan House.
Maine Central R. R.	to Zealand Junc.
Profile & Franconia Notch R. R.	to Profile House.
Profile & Franconia Notch R. R.	to Bethlehem Junc.
Concord & Montreal R. R.	to Nashua.
Boston & Maine R. R.	to Boston.
Rail Lines (see pages 50 to 55 for route)	to Philadelphia.
Baltimore & Ohio R. R.	to starting point.

THROUGH RATES.

Baltimore, Md.	$34 20	Washington, D. C.	$33 20
†Philadelphia, Pa.	27 20		

Form Ex. 521.—FABYAN HOUSE, N. H., AND RETURN.

(Via Sound Lines and North Conway; returning via Bethlehem Junction, Concord, and Sound Lines.)

Baltimore & Ohio R. R.	to Philadelphia.
Philadelphia & Reading R. R.	to Bound Brook.
Central R. R. of New Jersey	to New York.
Sound Lines (see pages 50 to 55 for route)	to Boston.
Boston & Maine R. R.	to North Conway.
Maine Central R. R.	to Fabyan House.
Maine Central R. R.	to Zealand Junc.
Profile & Franconia Notch R. R.	to Profile House.
Profile & Franconia Notch R. R.	to Bethlehem Junc.
Concord & Montreal R. R.	to Nashua.
Boston & Maine R. R.	to Boston.
Sound Lines (see pages 50 to 55 for route)	to New York.
Central R. R. of New Jersey	to Bound Brook.
Philadelphia & Reading R. R.	to Philadelphia.
Baltimore & Ohio R. R.	to starting point.

Transfer through Boston, in both directions, included.

THROUGH RATES.

Baltimore, Md.	$26 50	Washington, D. C.	$28 50
†Philadelphia, Pa.	22 50		

Form Ex. 522.—FABYAN HOUSE, N. H., AND RETURN.

(Via rail, Boston and Concord; returning via Sound Lines.)

Baltimore & Ohio R. R.	to Philadelphia.
Rail Lines (see pages 50 to 55 for route)	to Boston.
Boston & Maine R. R.	to Nashua.
Concord & Montreal R. R.	to Fabyan House.
Concord & Montreal R. R.	to Nashua.
Boston & Maine R. R.	to Boston.
Sound Lines (see pages 50 to 55 for route)	to New York.
Central R. R. of New Jersey	to Bound Brook.
Philadelphia & Reading R. R.	to Philadelphia.
Baltimore & Ohio R. R.	to starting point.

Transfer through Boston, returning, included.

THROUGH RATES.

Baltimore, Md.	$26 40	Washington, D. C.	$28 40
†Philadelphia, Pa.	22 40		

FORM EX. 522.—FABYAN HOUSE, N. H., AND RETURN.
(Via Sound Lines, Boston and Concord; returning via rail.)

Baltimore & Ohio R. R. . . . . to Philadelphia.
Philadelphia & Reading R. R. . . . . to Bound Brook.
Central R. R. of New Jersey . . . . to New York.
Sound Lines (see pages 50 to 55 for route) . . . to Boston.
Boston & Maine R. R. . . . . to Nashua.
Concord & Montreal R. R. . . . . to Fabyan House.
Concord & Montreal R. R. . . . . to Nashua.
Boston & Maine R. R. . . . . to Boston.
Rail Lines (see pages 50 to 55 for route) . . . . to Philadelphia.
Baltimore & Ohio R. R. . . . . to starting point.

Transfer through Boston, going, included.

THROUGH RATES.

Baltimore, Md. . . . . . . $26 40 | Washington, D. C. $28 40
†Philadelphia, Pa. . . . . 22 40 |

FORM EX. 522.—FABYAN HOUSE, N. H., AND RETURN.
(Via rail, Boston and Concord in both directions.)

Baltimore & Ohio R. R. . . . . to Philadelphia.
Rail Lines (see pages 50 to 55 for route) . . . . to Boston.
Boston & Maine R. R. . . . . to Nashua.
Concord & Montreal R. R. . . . . to Fabyan House.

Returning, same route.

THROUGH RATES.

Baltimore, Md. . . . . . . $27 75 | Washington, D. C. $29 75
†Philadelphia, Pa. . . . . 23 75 |

FORM EX. 522.—FABYAN HOUSE, N. H., AND RETURN.
(Via Sound Lines, Boston and Concord in both directions.)

Baltimore & Ohio R. R. . . . . to Philadelphia.
Philadelphia & Reading R. R. . . . . to Bound Brook.
Central R. R. of New Jersey . . . . to New York.
Sound Lines (see pages 50 to 55 for route) . . . to Boston.
Boston & Maine R. R. . . . . to Nashua.
Concord & Montreal R. R. . . . . to Fabyan House.

Returning, same route.
Transfer through Boston, in both directions, included.

THROUGH RATES.

Baltimore, Md. . . . . . . $23 00 | Washington, D. C. $25 00
†Philadelphia, Pa. . . . . 19 00 |

FORM EX. 613.—FABYAN HOUSE, N. H., AND RETURN.

Baltimore & Ohio R. R. . . . . to Philadelphia.
Philadelphia & Reading R. R. . . . . to Bound Brook.
Central R. R. of New Jersey . . . . to New York.
New York, New Haven & Hartford R. R. . . . . to Springfield.
Connecticut River R. R. . . . . to South Vernon.
Central Vermont R. R. . . . . to Brattleboro.
Vermont Valley R. R. . . . . to Windsor.
Central Vermont R. R. . . . . to White River Junc.
Boston & Maine R. R. . . . . to Wells River.
Concord & Montreal R. R. . . . . to Fabyan House.

Returning, same route.

THROUGH RATES.

Baltimore, Md. . . . . . . $24 40 | Washington, D. C. $26 40
†Philadelphia, Pa. . . . . 20 40 |

FORM EX. 614.—FABYAN HOUSE, N. H., AND RETURN.

Baltimore & Ohio R. R. . . . . to Philadelphia.
Philadelphia & Reading R. R. . . . . to Bound Brook.
Central R. R. of New Jersey . . . . to New York.
Old Colony Steamboat Co. (Fall River Line) . . to Fall River.
Old Colony R. R. to Lowell.
Boston & Maine R. R. . . . . to Nashua.
Concord & Montreal R. R. . . . . to Fabyan House.

Returning, same route.

THROUGH RATES.

Baltimore, Md. . . . . . $23 00 | Washington, D. C. . $25 00
†Philadelphia, Pa. . . . 19 00 |

FORM EX. 968.—FABYAN HOUSE, N. H., AND RETURN.

(Via New York and Connecticut Valley; returning via Portland and Boston.)

Baltimore & Ohio R. R. . . . . to Philadelphia.
Philadelphia & Reading R. R. . . . . to Bound Brook.
Central R. R. of New Jersey . . . . to New York.
New York, New Haven & Hartford R. R. . . . to Springfield.
Connecticut River R. R. . . . . to South Vernon.
Central Vermont R. R. . . . . to Brattleboro.
Vermont Valley R. R. . . . . to Windsor.
Central Vermont R. R. . . . . to White River Junc.
Boston & Maine R. R. . . . . to Wells River.
Concord & Montreal R. R. . . . . to Fabyan House.
Maine Central R. R. . . . . to Portland.
Boston & Maine R. R. . . . . to Boston.
Rail or Sound Lines (see pages 50 to 55 for route) to Philadelphia.
Baltimore & Ohio R. R. . . . . to starting point.

FORM EX. 969.—FABYAN HOUSE, N. H., AND RETURN.

Reverse of preceding excursion.

THROUGH RATES.

	Via Sound.	Via Rail.
Baltimore, Md.	$24 70	$23 80
†Philadelphia, Pa.	20 70	22 80
Washington, D. C.	26 70	28 80

Transfer through Boston included via Sound Lines only.

FORM EX. 960.—FABYAN HOUSE, N. H., AND RETURN.

(Via New York, Lake Champlain and Montreal; returning via Portland and Boston.)

Baltimore & Ohio R. R. . . . . to Philadelphia.
Philadelphia & Reading R. R. . . . . to Bound Brook.
Central R. R. of New Jersey . . . . to New York.
New York Central & Hudson River R. R. . . . to Troy.
Delaware & Hudson R. R. (via Saratoga and
   Plattsburg.) . . . . to Rouse's Point.
Grand Trunk R. R. . . . . to Montreal.
Grand Trunk R. R. . . . . to St. John's.
Central Vermont R. R. . . . . to Montpelier.
Montpelier & Wells River R. R. . . . . to Wells River.
Concord & Montreal R. R. . . . . to Fabyan House.
Maine Central R. R. . . . . to Portland.
Boston & Maine R. R. . . . . to Boston.
Rail or Sound Lines (see pages 50 to 55 for route) to Philadelphia.
Baltimore & Ohio R. R. . . . . to starting point.

FORM EX. 961.—FABYAN HOUSE, N. H.

Reverse of preceding excursion.

THROUGH RATES.

	Via Sound.	Via Rail.
Baltimore, Md.	$31 50	$32 00
Philadelphia, Pa.	27 50	28 00
Washington, D. C.	33 50	34 00

Transfer through Boston included via Sound Lines only.

FORM EX. 1002.—FABYAN HOUSE, N. H., AND RETURN.

(Via New York, Lake George and Lake Champlain; returning via Portland and Boston.)

Baltimore & Ohio R. R.	to Philadelphia.
Philadelphia & Reading R. R.	to Bound Brook.
Central R. R. of New Jersey	to New York.
West Shore R. R.	to Albany.
Delaware & Hudson R. R.	to Caldwell.
Champlain Transportation Co.(Lake George Strs.)	to Baldwin.
Delaware & Hudson R. R.	to Fort Ticonderoga.
Champlain Transportation Co.	to Burlington.
Central Vermont R. R.	to Cambridge Junc.
St. Johnsbury & Lake Champlain R. R.	to Lunenburg.
Maine Central R. R.	to Fabyan House.
Maine Central R. R.	to Portland.
Boston & Maine R. R.	to Boston.
Rail or Sound Lines (see pages 50 to 55 for routes)	to Philadelphia.
Baltimore & Ohio R. R.	to starting point.

Transfer through New York, going, included.

FORM EX. 1003.—FABYAN HOUSE, N. H., AND RETURN.

Reverse of preceding excursion.

Transfer through New York, returning, included.

THROUGH RATES.

	Via Sound.	Via Rail.
Baltimore, Md.	$28 70	$30 80
Philadelphia, Pa.	24 70	26 80
Washington, D. C.	30 70	32 80

Transfer through Boston included via Sound Lines only.

FORM EX. 964.—FABYANS, N. H., AND RETURN.

(Via New York, Lakes George and Champlain, and Montpelier; returning via Nashua and Boston.)

Baltimore & Ohio R. R.	to Philadelphia.
Philadelphia & Reading R. R.	to Bound Brook.
Central R. R. of New Jersey	to New York.
West Shore R. R.	to Albany.
Delaware & Hudson R. R.	to Caldwell.
Champlain Transportation Co.(Lake George Strs.)	to Baldwin.
Delaware & Hudson R. R.	to Ft. Ticonderoga.
Champlain Transportation Co.	to Burlington.
Central Vermont R. R.	to Montpelier.
Montpelier & Wells River R. R.	to Wells River.
Concord & Montreal R. R.	to Fabyans.
Concord & Montreal R. R.	to Nashua.
Boston & Maine R. R.	to Boston.
Rail or Sound Lines (see pages 50 to 55 for routes)	to Philadelphia.
Baltimore & Ohio R. R.	to starting point.

Transfer through New York, going, included.

FORM EX. 965.—FABYANS, N. H., AND RETURN.
Reverse of preceding excursion.
Transfer through New York, returning, included.
THROUGH RATES.

	Via Sound.	Via Rail.
Baltimore, Md.	$28 70	$30 80
†Philadelphia, Pa.	24 70	26 80
Washington, D. C.	30 70	32 80

Transfer through Boston included via Sound Lines only.

FORM EX. 966.—FABYAN HOUSE, N. H., AND RETURN.
(Via New York and Lake Champlain; returning via Portland and Boston.)

Baltimore & Ohio R. R.	to Philadelphia.
Philadelphia & Reading R. R.	to Bound Brook.
Central R. R. of New Jersey	to New York.
New York Central & Hudson River R. R.	to Troy.
Delaware & Hudson R. R.	to Ft. Ticonderoga.
Champlain Transportation Co.	to Burlington.
Central Vermont R. R.	to Cambridge Junc.
St. Johnsbury & Lake Champlain R. R.	to Lunenburg.
Maine Central R. R.	to Fabyan House.
Maine Central R. R.	to Portland.
Boston & Maine R. R.	to Boston.
Rail or Sound Lines (see pages 30 to 35 for route)	to Philadelphia.
Baltimore & Ohio R. R.	to starting point.

FORM EX. 967.—FABYAN HOUSE, N. H., AND RETURN.
Reverse of preceding excursion.
THROUGH RATES.

	Via Sound.	Via Rail.
Baltimore, Md.	$27 20	$29 30
†Philadelphia, Pa.	23 20	25 30
Washington, D. C.	29 20	31 30

Transfer through Boston included via Sound Lines only.

FORM EX. 968.—FABYAN HOUSE, N. H., AND RETURN.
(Via New York, Day Line Steamers on Hudson River, Lake George and Lake Champlain; returning via Portland and Boston.)

Baltimore & Ohio R. R.	to Philadelphia.
Philadelphia & Reading R. R.	to Bound Brook.
Central R. R. of New Jersey	to New York.
Day or People's Line Steamers	to Albany.
Delaware and Hudson R. R.	to Caldwell.
Champlain Transportation Co. (Lake George Strs.)	to Baldwin.
Delaware & Hudson R. R.	to Fort Ticonderoga.
Champlain Transportation Co.	to Burlington.
Central Vermont R. R.	to Cambridge Junc.
St. Johnsbury & Lake Champlain R. R.	to Lunenburg.
Maine Central R. R.	to Fabyan House.
Maine Central R. R.	to Portland.
Boston & Maine R. R.	to Boston.
Rail or Sound Lines (see pages 30 to 35 for route)	to Philadelphia.
Baltimore & Ohio R. R.	to starting point.

FORM EX. 969.—FABYAN HOUSE, N. H., AND RETURN.
Reverse of preceding excursion.
THROUGH RATES.

	Via Sound.	Via Rail.
Baltimore, Md.	$27 70	$29 80
†Philadelphia, Pa.	23 70	25 80
Washington, D. C.	29 70	31 80

Transfer through Boston included via Sound Lines only.

FALLS OF THE BLACKWATER.

FORM EX. 970.—FABYAN HOUSE, N. H., AND RETURN.

(Via New York, Day Line Steamers on Hudson River, Lake Champlain
and Montpelier; returning via Nashua and Boston.)

Baltimore & Ohio R. R.	to Philadelphia.
Philadelphia & Reading R. R.	to Bound Brook.
Central R. R. of New Jersey	to New York.
Day or People's Line Steamers	to Albany.
Delaware & Hudson R. R.	to Fort Ticonderoga
Champlain Transportation Co.	to Burlington.
Central Vermont R. R.	to Montpelier.
Montpelier & Wells River R. R.	to Wells River.
Concord & Montreal R. R.	to Fabyan House.
Concord & Montreal R. R.	to Nashua.
Boston & Maine R. R.	to Boston.
Rail or Sound Lines (see pages 50 to 55 for route)	to Philadelphia.
Baltimore & Ohio R. R.	to starting point.

FORM EX. 971.—FABYAN HOUSE, N. H., AND RETURN.

Reverse of preceding excursion.

THROUGH RATES.

	Via Sound.	Via Rail.
Baltimore, Md.	$26 20	$28 30
Philadelphia, Pa.	22 20	24 30
Washington, D. C.	28 20	30 30

Transfer through Boston included via Sound Lines only.

FORM EX. 972.—FABYAN HOUSE, N. H., AND RETURN.

(Via New York, Day Line Steamers on Hudson River and Lake Champlain; returning via Portland and Boston.)

Baltimore & Ohio R. R.	to Philadelphia.
Philadelphia & Reading R. R.	to Bound Brook.
Central R. R. of New Jersey	to New York.
Day or People's Line Steamers	to Albany.
Delaware & Hudson R. R.	to Fort Ticonderoga.
Champlain Transportation Co.	to Burlington
Central Vermont R. R.	to Cambridge Junc.
St. Johnsbury & Lake Champlain R. R.	to Lunenburg.
Maine Central R. R.	to Fabyan House.
Maine Central R. R.	to Portland.
Boston & Maine R. R.	to Boston.
Rail or Sound Lines (see pages 50 to 55 for route)	to Philadelphia.
Baltimore & Ohio R. R.	to starting point.

FORM EX. 973.—FABYAN HOUSE, N. H., AND RETURN.

Reverse of preceding excursion.

THROUGH RATES.

	Via Sound.	Via Rail.
Baltimore, Md.	$26 20	$28 30
Philadelphia, Pa.	22 20	24 30
Washington, D. C.	28 20	30 30

Transfer through Boston included via Sound Lines only.

FORM EX. 974.—FABYAN HOUSE, N. H., AND RETURN.

(Via Niagara Falls, Alexandria Bay, and Montreal; returning via
Montpelier and Boston.)

For route to Niagara Falls, see page 249.

New York Central & Hudson River R. R.	to Lewiston.
Rome, Watertown & Ogdensburg R. R.	to Clayton.
Richelieu & Ontario Navigation Co.	to Alexandria Bay.
Richelieu & Ontario Navigation Co.	to Prescott.

Richelieu & Ontario Navigation Co. or Grand
  Trunk R. R. . . . . to Montreal.
Grand Trunk R. R. . . . . to St. John's.
Central Vermont R. R. . . . . to Montpelier.
Montpelier & Wells River R. R. . . . . to Wells River.
Concord & Montreal R. R. . . . . to Fabyan House.
Maine Central R. R. . . . . to Portland.
Boston & Maine R. R. . . . . to Boston.
Rail or Sound Lines (see pages 50 to 55 for route) to Philadelphia.
Baltimore & Ohio R. R. . . . . to starting point.

THROUGH RATES.

	Via Sound.	Via Rail.
Baltimore, Md.	$40 25	$40 75
Philadelphia, Pa.	36 25	36 75
Washington, D. C.	42 25	42 75

Transfer through Boston included via Sound Lines only.

Form Ex. 975. Fabyan House, N. H., and Return.

(Via Niagara Falls, Toronto and Montreal; returning via Montpelier and Boston.)

For route to Niagara Falls, see page 249.

New York Central & Hudson River R. R. . . . . to Lewiston.
Niagara Navigation Co. . . . . to Toronto.
Richelieu & Ontario Navigation Co. or Grand
  Trunk R. R. . . . . to Kingston.
Richelieu & Ontario Navigation Co. or Grand
  Trunk R. R. . . . . to Prescott.
Richelieu & Ontario Navigation Co. or Grand
  Trunk R. R. . . . . to Montreal.
Grand Trunk R. R. . . . . to St. John's.
Central Vermont R. R. . . . . to Montpelier.
Montpelier & Wells River R. R. . . . . to Wells River.
Concord & Montreal R. R. . . . . to Fabyan House.
Maine Central R. R. . . . . to Portland.
Boston & Maine R. R. . . . . to Boston.
Rail or Sound Lines (see pages 50 to 55 for route) to Philadelphia.
Baltimore & Ohio R. R. . . . . to starting point.

THROUGH RATES.

	Via Sound.	Via Rail.
Baltimore, Md.	$40 25	$40 75
Philadelphia, Pa.	36 25	36 75
Washington, D. C.	42 25	42 75

Transfer through Boston included via Sound Lines only.

Form Ex. 976. Fabyan House, N. H., and Return.

(Via Niagara Falls, Alexandria Bay, Montreal and Quebec; returning via Boston.)

For route to Niagara Falls, see page 249.

New York Central & Hudson River R. R. . . . . to Lewiston.
Rome, Watertown & Ogdensburg R. R. . . . . . . to Clayton.
Richelieu & Ontario Navigation Co. . . . . to Alexandria Bay.
Richelieu & Ontario Navigation Co. . . . . to Prescott.
Richelieu & Ontario Navigation Co. or Grand
  Trunk R. R. . . . . to Montreal.
Richelieu & Ontario Navigation Co. or Grand
  Trunk R. R. . . . . to Quebec.
Grand Trunk R. R. . . . . to Groveton.
Concord & Montreal R. R. . . . . to Fabyan House.
Concord & Montreal R. R. . . . . to Nashua.
Boston & Maine R. R. . . . . to Boston.
Rail or Sound Lines (see pages 50 to 55 for route) to Philadelphia.
Baltimore & Ohio R. R. . . . . to starting point.

THROUGH RATES.

	Via Sound.	Via Rail.
Baltimore, Md.	$14 25	$14 75
Philadelphia, Pa.	10 25	10 75
Washington, D. C.	16 25	16 75

Transfer through Boston included via Sound Lines only.

FORM EX. 977.—FABYAN HOUSE, N. H., AND RETURN.

(Via Niagara Falls, Toronto, Montreal and Quebec; returning via Boston.)

For route to Niagara Falls, see page 249.

New York Central & Hudson River R. R. . . . . to Lewiston.
Niagara Navigation Co. . . . . to Toronto.
Richelieu & Ontario Navigation Co. or Grand
    Trunk R. R. . . . . to Kingston.
Richelieu & Ontario Navigation Co. or Grand
    Trunk R. R. . . . . to Prescott.
Richelieu & Ontario Navigation Co. or Grand
    Trunk R. R. . . . . to Montreal.
Richelieu & Ontario Navigation Co. or Grand
    Trunk R. R. . . . . to Quebec.
Grand Trunk R. R. . . . . to Groveton.
Concord & Montreal R. R. . . . . to Fabyan House.
Concord & Montreal R. R. . . . . to Nashua.
Boston & Maine R. R. . . . . to Boston.
Rail or Sound Lines (see pages 50 to 55 for route) to Philadelphia.
Baltimore & Ohio R. R. . . . . to starting point.

THROUGH RATES.

	Via Sound.	Via Rail.
Baltimore, Md.	$14 25	$14 75
Philadelphia, Pa.	10 25	10 75
Washington, D. C.	16 25	16 75

Transfer through Boston included via Sound Lines only.

FORM EX. 978.—FABYAN HOUSE, N. H., AND RETURN.

(Via Niagara Falls, Alexandria Bay and Montreal; returning via Boston.)

For route to Niagara Falls, see page 249.

New York Central & Hudson River R. R. . . . . to Lewiston.
Rome, Watertown & Ogdensburg R. R. . . . . to Clayton.
Richelieu & Ontario Navigation Co. . . . . . . to Alexandria Bay.
Richelieu & Ontario Navigation Co. . . . . . . to Prescott.
Richelieu & Ontario Navigation Co. or Grand
    Trunk R. R. . . . . to Montreal.
Grand Trunk R. R. . . . . to Groveton.
Concord & Montreal R. R. . . . . to Fabyan House.
Concord & Montreal R. R. . . . . to Nashua.
Boston & Maine R. R. . . . . to Boston.
Rail or Sound Lines (see pages 50 to 55 for route) to Philadelphia.
Baltimore & Ohio R. R. . . . . to starting point.

THROUGH RATES.

	Via Sound.	Via Rail.
Baltimore, Md.	$10 25	$10 75
Philadelphia, Pa.	36 25	36 75
Washington, D. C.	12 25	12 75

Transfer through Boston included via Sound Lines only.

FORM EX. 979.—FABYAN HOUSE, N. H., AND RETURN.

(Via Niagara Falls, Toronto and Montreal; returning via Boston.)

For route to Niagara Falls, see page 249.

New York Central & Hudson River R. R. . . . . to Lewiston.
Niagara Navigation Co. . . . . to Toronto.
Richelieu & Ontario Navigation Co. or Grand
 Trunk R. R. to Kingston.
Richelieu & Ontario Navigation Co. or Grand
 Trunk R. R. to Prescott.
Richelieu & Ontario Navigation Co. or Grand
 Trunk R. R. to Montreal.
Grand Trunk R. R. . . . . to Groveton.
Concord & Montreal R. R. . . . . to Fabyan House.
Concord & Montreal R. R. . . . . to Nashua.
Boston & Maine R. R. . . . . to Boston.
Rail or Sound Lines (see pages 50 to 55 for route) to Philadelphia.
Baltimore & Ohio R. R. . . . . to starting point.

THROUGH RATES.

	Via Sound.	Via Rail.
Baltimore, Md.	$40 25	$40 75
Philadelphia, Pa.	36 25	36 75
Washington, D. C.	42 25	42 75

Transfer through Boston included via Sound Lines only.

FORM EX. 980.—FABYAN HOUSE, N. H., AND RETURN.

(Via Niagara Falls; returning via Boston.)

For route to Niagara Falls, see page 249.

New York Central & Hudson River R. R. . . . . to Lewiston.
Rome, Watertown & Ogdensburg R. R. . . . . . to Norwood.
Central Vermont R. R. . . . . to Swanton.
St. Johnsbury & Lake Champlain R. R. . . . . . to Lunenburg.
Maine Central R. R. . . . . to Fabyan House.
Maine Central R. R. . . . . to Portland.
Boston & Maine R. R. . . . . to Boston.
Rail or Sound Lines (see pages 50 to 55 for route) to Philadelphia.
Baltimore & Ohio R. R. . . . . to starting point.

THROUGH RATES.

	Via Sound.	Via Rail.
Baltimore, Md.	$27 20	$29 30
Philadelphia, Pa.	33 20	35 30
Washington, D. C.	39 20	41 30

Transfer through Boston included via Sound Lines only.

FORM EX. 1049.—FABYAN HOUSE, N. H., AND RETURN.

(Via Niagara Falls; returning via Boston.)

For route to Niagara Falls see page 249.

New York Central & Hudson River R. R. . . . . to Lewiston.
Rome, Watertown & Ogdensburg R. R. . . . . . to Norwood.
Central Vermont R. R. . . . . to Montpelier.
Montpelier & Wells River R. R. . . . . to Wells River Junc.
Concord & Montreal R. R. . . . . to Fabyan House.
Concord & Montreal R. R. . . . . to Bethlehem Junc.
Profile & Franconia Notch R. R. . . . . to Profile House.
Pemmigewasset Valley Stage Line (10 miles) . . to North Woodstock.
Concord & Montreal R. R. . . . . to Nashua Junction.
Boston & Maine R. R. . . . . to Boston.
Sound or Rail Lines (see pages 50 to 55 for route) to Philadelphia.
Baltimore & Ohio R. R. . . . . to starting point.

THROUGH RATES.

	Via Sound.	Via Rail.
Baltimore, Md.	$20 00	$10 40
†Philadelphia, Pa.	35 00	36 40
Washington, D. C.	11 00	12 40

Transfer through Boston included via Sound Lines only.

FIRE ISLAND, N. Y.

FORM EX. 789.—FIRE ISLAND, N. Y., AND RETURN.

Baltimore & Ohio R. R. . . . . to Philadelphia.
Philadelphia & Reading R. R. . . . . to Bound Brook.
Central R. R. of New Jersey . . . . to New York.
Metropolitan Ferry Co. (35th St. or James' Slip), to Long Island City.
Long Island R. R. . . . . to Babylon.
Steamer . . . . to Fire Island.
Returning, same route.

THROUGH RATES.

Baltimore, Md. . . . . . $11 40 | Washington, D. C. $13 40
†Philadelphia, Pa. . . . 7 40 |

FROSTBURG, MD.

FORM EX. 102.—FROSTBURG, MD., AND RETURN.

Baltimore & Ohio R. R. . . . . to Cumberland.
Cumberland & Pennsylvania R. R. . . . . to Frostburg.
Returning, same route.

THROUGH RATES.

Baltimore, Md.	$9 00	New York, N. Y.	$17 00
Chester, Pa.	12 50	Philadelphia, Pa.	13 00
Havre de Grace, Md.	10 45	Washington, D. C.	7 00
Newark, Del.	11 50	Wilmington, Del.	12 00

GENEVA.

The Village of Geneva is one of the most attractive communities in the interior of the Empire State. It enjoys a large local trade, the stores being ranged chiefly along the wide main street beside the lake and upon several bisecting streets, the many handsome homes of its citizens occupying higher ground looking out upon the lake further to the south. Two very excellent hotels, the Kirkwood and Franklin, compete for the patronage of travelers. A powerful sulphur spring recently discovered at this point presages the erection of a sanitarium. Hobart College, one of the most influential and substantial of our educational institutions, occupies a very advantageous site fronting upon the lake.

FORM EX. 500.—GENEVA, N. Y., AND RETURN.

Baltimore & Ohio R. R. . . . . to Philadelphia.
Philadelphia & Reading R. R. . . . . to Bethlehem.
Lehigh Valley R. R. . . . . to Geneva.
Returning, same route.

THROUGH RATES.

Baltimore, Md. . . . . . $14 40 | Washington, D. C. . . . $16 40
†Philadelphia, Pa. . . . 12 85 |

ROUTES AND RATES FOR SUMMER TOURS. 111

FORM EX. 567.—GENEVA, N. Y., AND RETURN.

Baltimore & Ohio R. R. to Philadelphia.
Philadelphia & Reading R. R. . . . . to Bethlehem.
Lehigh Valley R. R. . . . . to Geneva.
Seneca Lake Steam Navigation Co. . . . . to Watkins.
Pennsylvania R. R. . . . . to Williamsport.
Philadelphia & Reading R. R. . . . . to Philadelphia.
Baltimore & Ohio R. R. . . . . to starting point.

THROUGH RATES.

Baltimore, Md. . . . . . $16 65 | Washington, D. C. . . . $18 65
†Philadelphia, Pa. . . . 14 00

FORM EX. 568.—GENEVA, N. Y., AND RETURN.

Baltimore & Ohio R. R. to Philadelphia.
Philadelphia & Reading R. R. . . . . to Williamsport.
Pennsylvania R. R. . . . . to Watkins.
Seneca Lake Steam Navigation Co. . . . . to Geneva.
New York Central & Hudson River R. R. . . . to Canandaigua.
Pennsylvania R. R. . . . . to Williamsport.
Philadelphia & Reading R. R. . . . . to Philadelphia.
Baltimore & Ohio R. R. . . . . to starting point.

THROUGH RATES.

Baltimore, Md. . . . . . $16 65 | Washington, D. C. . . . $18 65
†Philadelphia, Pa. . . . 14 00

GETTYSBURG, PA.

FORM EX. 644.—GETTYSBURG, PA., AND RETURN.

Limited to six (6) months from date of sale.

Baltimore & Ohio R. R. to Hagerstown.
Transfer, Baltimore & Ohio R. R. Depot . . . . to W. M. R. R. Depot.
Western Maryland R. R. (via Short Line) . . . to Gettysburg.

Returning, same route.

THROUGH RATES.

Bellaire, O.,	$15 10	Morgantown, W. Va.	. . .	$12 95
Cameron, W. Va.,	13 95	Moundsville, W. Va.	. . .	14 60
Charlestown, W. Va.,	4 10	Mountain Lake Park, Md.	. . .	9 05
Clarksburg, W. Va.,	11 95	Mt. Pleasant, Pa.	. . .	11 20
Connellsville, Pa.,	10 70	Oakland, Md.	. . .	9 45
Cumberland, Md.	7 00	Parkersburg, W. Va.	. . .	15 05
Deer Park, Md.,	8 90	Piedmont, W. Va.	. . .	8 40
Fairmont, W. Va.,	11 95	Pittsburgh, Pa.	. . .	11 95
Grafton, W. Va.,	11 05	Rockwood, Pa.	. . .	8 95
Harper's Ferry, W. Va.,	3 60	Somerset, Pa.	. . .	9 35
Harrisonburg, Va.,	8 60	Staunton, Va.	. . .	9 90
Johnstown, Pa.,	10 75	Strasburg, Va.	. . .	6 25
Keyser, W. Va.,	7 90	Uniontown, Pa.	. . .	11 15
Lexington, Va.,	11 70	Washington, D. C.	. . .	5 15
McKeesport, Pa.,	11 95	Washington, Pa.	. . .	13 35
Martinsburg, W. Va.,	3 85	Wheeling, W. Va.	. . .	15 05
Meyersdale, Pa.,	8 50	Winchester, Va.	. . .	5 25

FORM EX. 685.—GETTYSBURG, PA., AND RETURN.

Limited to six (6) months from date of sale.

Baltimore & Ohio R. R. to Baltimore.
Transfer, B. & O. R. R. Depot . . . . to W. M. R. R. (Fulton Station).
Western Maryland R. R. . . . . to Gettysburg.

Returning, same route.

GETTYSBURG AND VICINITY

COMPLIMENTS OF THE BALTIMORE & OHIO RAILROAD COMPANY

THROUGH RATES.

Bellaire, O.,	$9 65	Moundsville, W. Va.,		$9 00
Cameron, W. Va.,	18 20	Mountain Lake Park, Md.,		12 75
Charlestown, W. Va.,	7 90	Mt. Pleasant, Pa.,		15 50
Chester, Pa.,	6 00	New York, N. Y.,		9 65
Clarksburg, W. Va.,	16 25	Oakland, Md.,		12 85
Connellsville, Pa.,	15 00	Parkersburg, W. Va.,		19 35
Cumberland, Md.,	11 50	Philadelphia, Pa.,		6 00
Deer Park, Md.,	12 60	Piedmont, W. Va.,		12 10
Fairmont, W. Va.,	16 20	Pittsburgh, Pa.,		17 30
Grafton, W. Va.,	15 35	Rockwood, Pa.,		13 25
Harper's Ferry, W. Va.,	7 40	Somerset, Pa.,		13 65
Harrisonburg, Va.,	12 40	Staunton, Va.,		13 70
Johnstown, Pa.,	15 05	Strasburg, Va.,		10 05
Keyser, W. Va.,	12 20	Uniontown, Pa.,		15 15
Lexington, Va.,	15 50	Washington, D. C.,		5 00
McKeesport, Pa.,	16 75	Washington, Pa.,		18 40
Martinsburg, W. Va.,	8 25	Wheeling, W. Va.,		19 35
Meyersdale, Pa.,	12 80	Wilmington, Del.,		6 00
Morgantown, W. Va.,	17 25	Winchester, Va.,		9 00

FORM EX. 698.—GETTYSBURG, PA., AND RETURN.

Limited to six (6) months from date of sale.

Baltimore & Ohio R. R. . . . . to Shenandoah June.
Norfolk & Western R. R. . . . . to Hagerstown.
Western Maryland R. R. . . . . to Gettysburg.

Returning, same route.

THROUGH RATES.

Bellaire, O.,	$15 40	Morgantown, W. Va.,		$12 95
Cameron, W. Va.,	13 95	Moundsville, W. Va.,		11 60
Clarksburg, W. Va.,	11 95	Mountain Lake Park, Md.,		9 05
Connellsville, Pa.,	10 70	Mt. Pleasant, Pa.,		11 20
Cumberland, Md.,	7 00	Oakland, Md.,		9 15
Deer Park, Md.,	8 90	Parkersburg, W. Va.,		15 05
Fairmont, W. Va.,	11 95	Piedmont, W. Va.,		8 40
Grafton, W. Va.,	11 05	Pittsburgh, Pa.,		11 95
Johnstown, Pa.,	10 75	Rockwood, Pa.,		8 95
Keyser, W. Va.,	7 90	Somerset, Pa.,		9 35
McKeesport, Pa.,	11 95	Uniontown, Pa.,		11 15
Martinsburg, W. Va.,	3 85	Washington, Pa.,		13 55
Meyersdale, Pa.,	8 50	Wheeling, W. Va.,		15 05

GLADE SPRINGS, VA.

FORM EX. 100.—GLADE SPRINGS, VA., AND RETURN.

Baltimore & Ohio R. R. . . . . to Shenandoah June.
Norfolk & Western R. R. . . . . to Glade Springs.

Returning, same route.

THROUGH RATES.

Baltimore, Md.,	$18 80	Fairmont, W. Va.,		$25 80
Bellaire, O.,	27 20	Frederick, Md.,		16 60
Berkeley Springs, W. Va.,	17 00	Grafton, W. Va.,		22 90
Cameron, W. Va.,	25 80	Harper's Ferry, W. Va.,		15 50
Chester, Pa.,	22 30	Havre de Grace, Md.,		20 25
Clarksburg, W. Va.,	23 80	Johnstown, Pa.,		22 60
Connellsville, Pa.,	22 55	Keyser, W. Va.,		19 80
Cumberland, Md.,	18 85	McKeesport, Pa.,		24 30
Deer Park, Md.,	20 80	Martinsburg, W. Va.,		15 70

Meyersdale, Pa.	$20 35	Piedmont, W. Va.		$20 00
Morgantown, W. Va.	24 80	Pittsburgh, Pa.		24 85
Moundsville, W. Va.	26 50	Rockwood, Pa.		20 80
Mountain Lake Park, Md.	20 95	Somerset, Pa.		21 20
Mt. Pleasant, Pa.	23 05	Uniontown, Pa.		23 00
Newark, Del.	24 10	Washington, D. C.		16 80
New York, N. Y.	26 80	Washington, Pa.		25 95
Oakland, Md.	21 05	Wheeling, W. Va.		26 90
Parkersburg, W. Va.	26 90	Wilmington, Del.		24 80
Philadelphia, Pa.	22 80			

GLENS FALLS, N. Y.

This charming village takes its name from the picturesque falls of the Hudson, which tumble over a rocky precipice sixty-three feet high and nine hundred feet long, and is a much frequented summer resort. The island below the falls is associated with some of the most thrilling incidents of Cooper's "Last of the Mohicans."

FORM EX. 506.—GLENS FALLS, N. Y., AND RETURN.

Baltimore & Ohio R. R.	to Philadelphia.
Philadelphia & Reading R. R.	to Bound Brook.
Central R. R. of New Jersey	to New York.
New York Central & Hudson River R. R.	to Troy.
Delaware & Hudson R. R.	to Glens Falls.

Returning, same route.

THROUGH RATES.

Baltimore, Md.	$16 80	Washington, D. C.	$18 80
†Philadelphia, Pa.	12 80		

FORM EX. 310.—GLENS FALLS, N. Y., AND RETURN.

Baltimore & Ohio R. R. . . . . to Philadelphia.
Philadelphia & Reading R. R. . . . . to Bound Brook.
Central R. R. of New Jersey . . . . to New York.
West Shore R. R. . . . . to Albany.
Delaware & Hudson R. R. . . . . to Glens Falls.
Returning, same route.
Transfer through New York, in both directions, included.

THROUGH RATES.
Baltimore, Md. . . . . . . $16 50 | Washington, D. C. . . . $18 50
Philadelphia, Pa. 12 50

GLEN HOUSE, N. H.

FORM EX. 523.—GLEN HOUSE, N. H., AND RETURN.
(Via rail and North Conway; returning by Sound Lines.)

Baltimore & Ohio R. R. . . . . to Philadelphia.
Rail Lines (see pages 50 to 55 for route) . . . to Boston.
Boston & Maine R. R. . . . . to North Conway.
Maine Central R. R. . . . . to Glen Station.
Stage (14 miles). . . . . to Glen House.
Stage (14 miles). . . . . to Glen Station.
Maine Central R. R. . . . . to North Conway.
Boston & Maine R. R. . . . . to Boston.
Sound Lines (see pages 50 to 55 for route) . . to New York.
Central R. R. of New Jersey . . . . to Bound Brook.
Philadelphia & Reading R. R. . . . . to Philadelphia.
Baltimore & Ohio R. R. . . . . to starting point.
Transfer through Boston, returning, included.

THROUGH RATES.
Baltimore, Md. . . . . . . $29 50 | Washington, D. C. . . . $31 50
Philadelphia, Pa. 25 50

FORM EX. 523.—GLEN HOUSE, N. H., AND RETURN.
(Via Sound Lines and North Conway; returning by all rail.)

Baltimore & Ohio R. R. . . . . to Philadelphia.
Philadelphia & Reading R. R. . . . . to Bound Brook.
Central R. R. of New Jersey . . . . to New York.
Sound Lines (see pages 50 to 55 for route) . . to Boston.
Boston & Maine R. R. . . . . to North Conway.
Maine Central R. R. . . . . to Glen Station.
Stage (14 miles). . . . . to Glen House.
Stage (14 miles). . . . . to Glen Station.
Maine Central R. R. . . . . to North Conway.
Boston & Maine R. R. . . . . to Boston.
Rail Lines (see pages 50 to 55 for route) . . . to Philadelphia.
Baltimore & Ohio R. R. . . . . to starting point.
Transfer through Boston, going, included.

THROUGH RATES.
Baltimore, Md. . . . . . . $29 50 | Washington, D. C. . . . $31 50
Philadelphia, Pa. 25 50

FORM EX. 523.—GLEN HOUSE, N. H., AND RETURN.
(Via Rail Lines and North Conway in both directions.)

Baltimore & Ohio R. R. . . . . to Philadelphia.
Rail Lines (see pages 50 to 55 for route) . . . to Boston.
Boston & Maine R. R. . . . . to North Conway.
Maine Central R. R. . . . . to Glen Station.
Stage (14 miles). . . . . to Glen House.
Returning, same route.

THROUGH RATES.
Baltimore, Md. . . . . . . $29 50 | Washington, D. C. . . . $31 50
Philadelphia, Pa. 25 50

ROUTES AND RATES FOR SUMMER TOURS.

FORM EX. 523.—GLEN HOUSE, N. H., AND RETURN.

(Via Sound Lines and North Conway in both directions.)

Baltimore & Ohio R. R.	to Philadelphia.
Philadelphia & Reading R. R.	to Bound Brook.
Central R. R. of New Jersey	to New York.
Sound Lines (see pages 50 to 55 for route)	to Boston.
Boston & Maine R. R.	to North Conway.
Maine Central R. R.	to Glen Station.
Stage (11 miles)	to Glen House.

Returning, same route.

Transfer through Boston, in both directions, included.

THROUGH RATES.

Baltimore, Md. $26 00	Washington, D. C. $28 00
†Philadelphia, Pa. 22 00	

FORM EX. 524.—GLEN HOUSE, N. H., AND RETURN.

(Via rail, Boston and Portland; returning by Sound Lines.)

Baltimore & Ohio R. R.	to Philadelphia.
Rail Lines (see pages 50 to 55 for route)	to Boston.
Boston & Maine R. R.	to Portland.
Maine Central R. R.	to Glen Station.
Stage (11 miles)	to Glen House.
Stage (11 miles)	to Glen Station.
Maine Central R. R.	to Portland.
Boston & Maine R. R.	to Boston.
Sound Lines (see pages 50 to 55 for route)	to New York.
Central R. R. of New Jersey	to Bound Brook.
Philadelphia & Reading R. R.	to Philadelphia.
Baltimore & Ohio R. R.	to starting point.

Transfer through Boston, returning, included.

THROUGH RATES.

Baltimore, Md. $29 50	Washington, D. C. $31 50
†Philadelphia, Pa. 25 50	

FORM EX. 524.—GLEN HOUSE, N. H., AND RETURN.

(Via Sound Lines, Boston and Portland; returning all rail.)

Baltimore & Ohio R. R.	to Philadelphia.
Philadelphia & Reading R. R.	to Bound Brook.
Central R. R. of New Jersey	to New York.
Sound Lines (see pages 50 to 55 for route)	to Boston.
Boston & Maine R. R.	to Portland.
Maine Central R. R.	to Glen Station.
Stage (11 miles)	to Glen House.
Stage (11 miles)	to Glen Station.
Maine Central R. R.	to Portland.
Boston & Maine R. R.	to Boston.
Rail Lines (see pages 50 to 55 for route)	to Philadelphia.
Baltimore & Ohio R. R.	to starting point.

Transfer through Boston, going, included.

THROUGH RATES.

Baltimore, Md. $29 50	Washington, D. C. $31 50
†Philadelphia, Pa. 25 50	

FORM EX. 524. —GLEN HOUSE, N. H., AND RETURN.

(Via Rail Lines and Portland in both directions.)

Baltimore & Ohio R. R. . . . . to Philadelphia.
Rail Lines (see pages 50 to 55 for route) . . . . to Boston.
Boston & Maine R. R. . . . . to Portland.
Maine Central R. R. . . . . to Glen Station.
Stage (11 miles) . . . . to Glen House.

Returning, same route.

THROUGH RATES.

Baltimore, Md. . . . . . . $29.50 | Washington, D. C. $31.50
Philadelphia, Pa. . . . . . 25.50 |

FORM EX. 524. —GLEN HOUSE, N. H., AND RETURN.

(Via Sound Lines and Portland in both directions.)

Baltimore & Ohio R. R. . . . . to Philadelphia.
Philadelphia & Reading R. R. . . . . to Bound Brook.
Central R. R. of New Jersey . . . . to New York.
Sound Lines (see pages 50 to 55 for route) . . . to Boston.
Boston & Maine R. R. . . . . to Portland.
Maine Central R. R. . . . . to Glen Station.
Stage (11 miles) . . . . to Glen House.

Returning, same route.

Transfer through Boston, in both directions, included.

THROUGH RATES.

Baltimore, Md. . . . . . . $26.00 | Washington, D. C. $28.00
Philadelphia, Pa. . . . . . 22.00 |

GLOUCESTER, MASS.

FORM EX. 762.—GLOUCESTER, MASS., AND RETURN.

(Via Sound Lines and Boston in both directions.)

Baltimore & Ohio R. R. . . . . to Philadelphia.
Philadelphia & Reading R. R. . . . . to Bound Brook.
Central R. R. of New Jersey . . . . to New York.
Sound Lines (see pages 50 to 55 for route) . . . to Boston.
Boston & Maine R. R. . . . . to Gloucester.

Returning, same route.

THROUGH RATES.

Baltimore, Md. . . . . . . $17.50 | Washington, D. C. $19.50
Philadelphia, Pa. . . . . . 13.50 |

FORM EX. 762. —GLOUCESTER, MASS., AND RETURN.

(Via Rail Lines and Boston in both directions.)

Baltimore & Ohio R. R. . . . . to Philadelphia.
Rail Lines (see pages 50 to 55 for route) . . . . to Boston.
Boston & Maine R. R. . . . . to Gloucester.

Returning, same route.

THROUGH RATES.

Baltimore, Md. . . . . . . $19.50 | Washington, D. C. $21.50
Philadelphia, Pa. . . . . . 15.50 |

FORM EX. 762.—GLOUCESTER, MASS., AND RETURN.

(Via Rail Lines and Boston; returning via Boston and Sound Lines.)

Baltimore & Ohio R. R. . . . . to Philadelphia.
Rail Lines (see pages 50 to 55 for route) . . . . to Boston.
Boston & Maine R. R. . . . . to Gloucester.
Boston & Maine R. R. . . . . to Boston.

Sound Lines (see pages 50 to 55 for routes). . . . to New York.
Central R. R. of New Jersey . . . . to Bound Brook.
Philadelphia & Reading R. R. . . . . to Philadelphia.
Baltimore & Ohio R. R. . . . . to starting point.

THROUGH RATES.

Baltimore, Md. . . . . . . $18 50 | Washington, D. C. $20 50
†Philadelphia, Pa. . . . . 11 50 |

FORM EX. 762. GLOUCESTER, MASS., AND RETURN.

(Via Sound Lines and Boston; returning, all rail.)

Baltimore & Ohio R. R. . . . . to Philadelphia.
Philadelphia & Reading R. R. . . . . to Bound Brook.
Central R. R. of New Jersey . . . . to New York.
Sound Lines (see pages 50 to 55 for routes) . . . to Boston.
Boston & Maine R. R. . . . . to Gloucester.
Boston & Maine R. R. . . . . to Boston.
Rail Lines (see pages 50 to 55 for routes). . . . to Philadelphia.
Baltimore & Ohio R. R. . . . . to starting point.

THROUGH RATES.

Baltimore, Md. . . . . . . $18 50 | Washington, D. C. $20 50
†Philadelphia, Pa. . . . . 11 50 |

GORMAN, MD.

FORM EX. 722.—GORMAN, MD., AND RETURN.

Baltimore & Ohio R. R. . . . . to Cumberland.
West Virginia Central R. R. . . . . to Gorman.

Returning, same route.

THROUGH RATES.

Baltimore, Md.	$10 40	Meyersdale, Pa.	$3 00
Berkeley Springs, W. Va.	4 85	Mt. Pleasant, Pa	6 60
Charlestown, W. Va.	6 80	Newark, Del.	12 40
Chester, Pa.	13 60	New York, N. Y.	18 10
Connellsville, Pa.	6 10	Philadelphia, Pa	11 10
Frederick, Md.	7 35	Pittsburgh, Pa.	8 40
Hagerstown, Md.	7 35	Rockwood, Pa	4 35
Harper's Ferry, W. Va.	6 30	Somerset, Pa.	4 70
Harrisonburg, Va.	11 30	Staunton, Va.	12 00
Havre de Grace, Md.	11 55	Strasburg, Va.	8 95
Johnstown, Pa.	6 45	Uniontown, Pa.	6 50
Keyser, W. Va.	3 30	Washington, D. C.	8 20
Lexington, Va.	11 40	Washington, Pa.	10 85
McKeesport, Pa.	7 80	Wilmington, Del.	13 10
Martinsburg, W. Va.	5 50	Winchester, Va.	7 90

FORM EX. 744.—GORMAN, MD., AND RETURN.

Baltimore & Ohio R. R. . . . . to Piedmont.
West Virginia Central R. R. . . . . to Gorman.

Returning, same route.

THROUGH RATES.

Bellaire, O.	$8 50	Morgantown, W. Va.	$6 15
Cameron, W. Va.	7 40	Moundsville, W. Va.	7 80
Clarksburg, W. Va.	5 45	Mountain Lake Park, Md.	2 20
Deer Park, Md.	2 40	Oakland, Md.	2 35
Fairmont, W. Va.	5 10	Parkersburg, W. Va.	8 40
Grafton, W. Va.	4 25	Wheeling, W. Va.	8 20
Keyser, W. Va.	1 50		

GOSHEN, VA.

FORM EX. 64.—GOSHEN, VA., AND RETURN.

Baltimore & Ohio R. R. . . . . to Shenandoah June.
Norfolk & Western R. R. . . . . to Basic.
Chesapeake & Ohio Ry. . . . . to Goshen.

Returning, same route.

THROUGH RATES.

Baltimore, Md.	$12 50	New York, N. Y.	$20 50
Chester, Pa.	15 80	Philadelphia, Pa.	16 30
Havre de Grace, Md.	13 75	Washington, D. C.	10 50
Newark, Del.	14 60	Wilmington, Del.	15 30

FORM EX. 111.—GOSHEN, VA., AND RETURN.

Baltimore & Ohio R. R. . . . . to Staunton.
Chesapeake & Ohio Ry. . . . . to Goshen.

Returning, same route.

THROUGH RATES.

Baltimore, Md.	$12 50	Meyersdale, Pa.	$13 00
Bellaire, O.	20 45	Morgantown, W. Va.	18 05
Berkeley Springs, W. Va.	10 15	Moundsville, W. Va.	19 70
Cameron, W. Va.	19 00	Mountain Lake Park, Md.	11 15
Charlestown, W. Va.	7 70	Mt. Pleasant, Pa.	16 30
Chester, Pa.	15 80	Newark, Del.	14 60
Clarksburg, W. Va.	17 05	New York, N. Y.	20 50
Connellsville, Pa.	15 80	Oakland, Md.	11 25
Cumberland, Md.	12 10	Parkersburg, W. Va.	20 50
Deer Park, Md.	11 00	Philadelphia, Pa.	16 30
Fairmont, W. Va.	17 05	Piedmont, W. Va.	15 30
Frederick, Md.	9 25	Pittsburgh, Pa.	18 10
Grafton, W. Va.	16 15	Rockwood, Pa.	14 05
Hagerstown, Md.	9 25	Somerset, Pa.	14 15
Harper's Ferry, W. Va.	8 20	Strasburg, Va.	5 55
Harrisonburg, Va.	3 20	Uniontown, Pa.	16 25
Havre de Grace, Md.	13 75	Washington, D. C.	10 50
Johnstown, Pa.	15 85	Washington, Pa.	19 20
Keyser, W. Va.	14 00	Wheeling, W. Va.	20 20
Lexington, Va.	3 70	Wilmington, Del.	15 30
McKeesport, Pa.	17 55	Winchester, Va.	6 00
Martinsburg, W. Va.	8 75		

GREAT BARRINGTON, BERKSHIRE HILLS, MASS.

Which is one of the most charmingly attractive villages in or out of Berkshire. Its broad streets, numberless huge elms, neat and well-kept houses, and the bustle of its business centre, are all pleasant to the ear and eye, and have won for it much admiration both at home and abroad.

Good hotels and superior accommodations for guests from the cities, among village residents and farmers, are some of the attractive features which the town presents. Its elevation and perfect drainage secure the absence of malaria and mosquitoes, and as a point within four hours of New York, and convenient to other centres, it is regarded as one of the most healthful and attractive; and in its charming scenery, delightful drives over the finest gravel roads, shooting, boating and fishing, Great Barrington and its surroundings has few rivals in all New England.

The scenic beauties of the near vicinity are marked and striking, and the drives are widely admitted to be the finest known. This town, as do many of the adjoining

ones, takes pride in keeping its roadways in most excellent condition, and the nature of the soil is such that they are always good and always in order for enjoyable pleasure riding.

For the last fifty years Great Barrington has been known to many of our great masters of landscape painting. Lovers of beautiful scenery have sketched many of the picturesque views of the vicinity, and have done their share with Bryant to make the whole region classic. City people who remain here till the last week of September will be much interested to see a country fair. The fair of the Housatonic Agricultural Society, in this village, is next to the largest one in the State. The village of Great Barrington has unexcelled natural advantages in the picturesque and the beautiful. Variety is prolific and surprises are unceasing. Village neatness is conspicuous; the street fences are nearly all removed; handsome lawns, nice houses and graceful trees are on every hand; an air of thrift, comfort and well-being pervades.

Under the new life that has been given to Great Barrington within a few years, the town is coming into greater prominence than ever as a summer and autumn resort.

FORM EX. 981.—GREAT BARRINGTON, (BERKSHIRE HILLS) MASS.

Baltimore & Ohio R. R.,	to Philadelphia.
Philadelphia & Reading R. R.	to Bound Brook.
Central R. R. of New Jersey	to New York.
New York, New Haven & Hartford R. R.	to South Norwalk.
Housatonic R. R.	to Great Barrington.

Returning, same route.

THROUGH RATES.

Baltimore, Md.	$15 70	Washington, D. C.	$16 70
Philadelphia, Pa.	9 70		

Tickets limited to continuous passage on Housatonic R. R., and not good on Sunday trains over that line.

FORM EX. 982.—GREAT BARRINGTON, (BERKSHIRE HILLS) MASS.

Baltimore & Ohio R. R.	to Philadelphia.
Philadelphia & Reading R. R.	to Bound Brook.
Central R. R. of New Jersey	to New York.
New York, New Haven & Hartford R. R.	to Bridgeport.
Housatonic R. R.	to Great Barrington.

Returning, same route.

THROUGH RATES.

Baltimore, Md.	$14 20	Washington, D. C.	$16 20
Philadelphia, Pa.	10 20		

Tickets limited to continuous passage on Housatonic R. R., and not good on Sunday trains over that line.

GROTTOES, VA.

FORM EX. 983.—GROTTOES, VA., AND RETURN.

Baltimore & Ohio R. R.	to Shenandoah June.
Norfolk & Western R. R.	to Grottoes.

Returning, same route.

THROUGH RATES.

From	Rate	From	Rate
Baltimore, Md.	$10 40	Morgantown, W. Va.	$15 85
Bellaire, O.	18 25	Moundsville, W. Va.	17 55
Berkeley Springs, W. Va.	8 05	Mountain Lake Park, Md.	12 00
Cameron, W. Va.	16 85	Mt. Pleasant, Pa.	14 10
Chester, Pa.	13 90	Newark, Del.	12 70
Clarksburg, W. Va.	14 85	New York, N. Y.	18 40
Connellsville, Pa.	13 09	Oakland, Md.	12 10
Cumberland, Md.	9 90	Parkersburg, W. Va.	17 95
Deer Park, Md.	11 85	Philadelphia, Pa.	14 40
Fairmont, W. Va.	14 85	Piedmont, W. Va.	11 05
Frederick, Md.	7 65	Pittsburgh, Pa.	15 90
Grafton, W. Va.	13 95	Rockwood, Pa.	11 85
Harper's Ferry, W. Va.	6 55	Somerset, Pa.	12 25
Havre de Grace, Md.	11 85	Uniontown, Pa.	14 05
Johnstown, Pa.	13 65	Washington, D. C.	8 60
Keyser, W. Va.	10 85	Wheeling, W. Va.	17 00
McKeesport, Pa.	15 35	Wilmington, Del.	17 95
Martinsburg, W. Va.	6 75	Wilmington, Del.	13 40
Meyersdale, Pa.	11 10		

HARPER'S FERRY, W. VA.

Baltimore & Ohio R. R. . . . . to Harper's Ferry.
Returning, same route.

THROUGH RATES.

Baltimore, Md. . . . . . . $3 25 | Washington, D. C. . . . $2 25
Agents will use Excursion Book Tickets.

HARROGATE, TENN.

HARROGATE, TENN.—Excursion Form Ex. 104.
Limited to three (3) months from date of sale.

Baltimore & Ohio R. R. . . . . to Washington
Transfer . . . . B. & O. Depot to R. & D. Depot.
Richmond & Danville R. R. . . . . to Lynchburg.
Norfolk & Western R. R. . . . . to Norton.
Louisville & Nashville R. R. . . . . to Harrogate.

Returning, same route.

THROUGH RATES.

From	Rate	From	Rate
Baltimore, Md.	$22 00	Meyersdale, Pa.	$28 10
Bellaire, O.	31 95	Morgantown, W. Va.	32 55
Berkeley Spring, W. Va.	24 65	Moundsville, W. Va.	31 20
Cameron, W. Va.	33 50	Mountain Lake Park, Md.	28 15
Charlestown, W. Va.	23 20	Mt. Pleasant, Pa.	30 80
Chester, Pa.	25 50	Newark, Del.	24 30
Clarksburg, W. Va.	31 55	New York, N. Y.	30 00
Connellsville, Pa.	30 30	Oakland, Md.	28 25
Cumberland, Md.	26 60	Parkersburg, W. Va.	34 65
Deer Park, Md.	28 00	Philadelphia, Pa.	26 00
Fairmont, W. Va.	31 55	Piedmont, W. Va.	27 70
Frederick, Md.	22 80	Pittsburgh, Pa.	32 60
Grafton, W. Va.	30 65	Rockwood, Pa.	28 55
Hagerstown, Md.	23 60	Somerset, Pa.	28 95
Harper's Ferry, W. Va.	22 70	Uniontown, Pa.	30 75
Havre de Grace, Md.	23 45	Washington, Pa.	33 70
Johnstown, Pa.	30 35	Wheeling, W. Va.	34 65
Keyser, W. Va.	27 50	Wilmington, Del.	25 00
McKeesport, Pa.	32 05	Winchester, Va.	24 30
Martinsburg, W. Va.	23 45		

HARROGATE, TENN.--EXCURSION FORM EX. 1162.

Limited to three (3) months from date of sale.

Baltimore & Ohio R. R. . . . . to Shenandoah Jc.
Norfolk & Western R. R. . . . . to Norton.
Louisville & Nashville R. R. . . . . to Harrogate.

Returning, same route.

THROUGH RATES.

Baltimore, Md.	$22 00	Morgantown, W. Va.	$29 55
Bellaire, O.	31 95	Moundsville, W. Va.	31 25
Berkeley Springs, W. Va.	24 75	Mountain Lake Park, Md.	25 70
Cameron, W. Va.	30 55	Mt. Pleasant, Pa.	27 80
Chester, Pa.	25 30	Newark, Del.	24 50
Clarksburg, W. Va.	28 55	New York, N. Y.	30 00
Connellsville, Pa.	27 30	Oakland, Md.	25 80
Cumberland, Md.	23 60	Parkersburg, W. Va.	31 65
Deer Park, Md.	25 55	Philadelphia, Pa.	26 00
Fairmont, W. Va.	28 55	Piedmont, W. Va.	24 75
Frederick, Md.	20 65	Pittsburgh, Pa.	29 60
Grafton, W. Va.	27 65	Rockwood, Pa.	25 55
Harper's Ferry, W. Va.	20 00	Somerset, Pa.	25 95
Havre de Grace, Md.	23 45	Uniontown, Pa.	27 75
Johnstown, Pa.	27 55	Washington, D. C.	20 00
Keyser, W. Va.	24 55	Washington, Pa.	30 70
McKeesport, Pa.	29 05	Wheeling, W. Va.	31 65
Martinsburg, W. Va.	20 45	Wilmington, Del.	25 00
Meyersdale, Pa.	25 10		

HEALING SPRINGS, VA.

FORM EX. 65.—HEALING SPRINGS, VA., AND RETURN.

Baltimore & Ohio R. R.	to Shenandoah June
Norfolk & Western R. R.	to Basic
Chesapeake & Ohio Ry.	to Hot Springs.
Stage Line	to Healing Springs.

Returning, same route.

THROUGH RATES.

Baltimore, Md.	$18 00	New York, N. Y.	$26 00
Chester, Pa.	21 50	Philadelphia, Pa.	22 00
Havre de Grace, Md.	19 45	Washington, D. C.	16 00
Newark, Del.	20 30	Wilmington, Del.	21 00

FORM EX. 77.—HEALING SPRINGS, VA., AND RETURN.

Baltimore & Ohio R. R.	to Staunton.
Transfer Baltimore & Ohio R. R. Depot	to C. & O. R. R. Depot.
Chesapeake & Ohio Ry.	to Hot Springs.
Stage Line	to Healing Springs.

Returning, same route.

Add transfer through Staunton.

THROUGH RATES.

Baltimore, Md.	$18 00	Meyersdale, Pa.	$20 40
Bellaire, O.	27 25	Morgantown, W. Va.	24 85
Berkeley Springs, W. Va.	16 95	Moundsville, W. Va.	26 50
Cameron, W. Va.	25 80	Mountain Lake Park, Md.	20 95
Charlestown, W. Va.	14 50	Mt. Pleasant, Pa.	23 40
Chester, Pa.	21 50	Newark, Del.	20 30
Clarksburg, W. Va.	23 85	New York, N. Y.	26 00
Connellsville, Pa.	22 00	Oakland, Md.	21 05
Cumberland, Md.	18 90	Parkersburg, W. Va.	27 00
Deer Park, Md.	20 80	Philadelphia, Pa.	22 00
Fairmont, W. Va.	23 85	Piedmont, W. Va.	20 00
Frederick, Md.	16 05	Pittsburgh, Pa.	24 50
Grafton, W. Va.	22 95	Rockwood, Pa.	20 85
Hagerstown, Md.	16 05	Somerset, Pa.	21 25
Harper's Ferry, W. Va.	15 00	Strasburg, Va.	14 95
Harrisonburg, Va.	10 00	Uniontown, Pa.	23 05
Havre de Grace, Md.	19 45	Washington, D. C.	16 00
Johnstown, Pa.	22 65	Washington, Pa.	26 00
Keyser, W. Va.	19 80	Wheeling, W. Va.	27 00
Lexington, Va.	10 50	Wilmington, Del.	21 00
McKeesport, Pa.	24 35	Winchester, Va.	13 40
Martinsburg, W. Va.	15 75		

FORM EX. 342.—HEALING SPRINGS, VA., AND RETURN.

Baltimore & Ohio R. R.	to Washington.
Transfer Baltimore & Ohio R. R. Depot	to C. & O. R. R. Depot.
Chesapeake & Ohio Ry.	to Hot Springs.
Stage Line	to Healing Springs.

Returning, same route.

THROUGH RATES.

Baltimore, Md.	$18 00	New York, N. Y.	$26 00
Chester, Pa.	21 50	Philadelphia, Pa.	22 00
Havre de Grace, Md.	19 45	Wilmington, Del.	21 00
Newark, Del.	20 30		

HIGHFIELD, MD.

Form Ex. 857.—Highfield, Md., and Return.

Baltimore & Ohio R. R. . . . . to Hagerstown.
Transfer, Baltimore & Ohio R. R. Depot . . . . to W. M. R. R. Depot.
Western Maryland R. R. . . . . to Highfield.

Returning, same route.

THROUGH RATES.

Bellaire, O.	$11 10	Morgantown, W. Va.	$11 00
Berkeley Springs, W. Va.	3 75	Moundsville, W. Va.	13 35
Cameron, W. Va.	12 65	Mountain Lake Park, Md.	7 75
Charlestown, W. Va.	2 90	Mt. Pleasant, Pa.	9 30
Clarksburg, W. Va.	10 65	Oakland, Md.	7 85
Connellsville, Pa.	9 40	Parkersburg, W. Va.	13 75
Cumberland, Md.	5 70	Piedmont, W. Va.	6 80
Deer Park, Md.	7 60	Pittsburgh, Pa.	11 70
Fairmont, W. Va.	10 65	Rockwood, Pa.	7 65
Grafton, W. Va.	9 75	Somerset, Pa.	8 05
Harper's Ferry, W. Va.	2 40	Staunton, Va.	8 70
Harrisonburg, Va.	7 40	Strasburg, Va.	5 05
Johnstown, Pa.	9 45	Uniontown, Pa.	9 85
Keyser, W. Va.	6 60	Washington, D. C.	1 45
Lexington, Va.	10 50	Washington, Pa.	12 80
McKeesport, Pa.	11 15	Wheeling, W. Va.	13 75
Martinsburg, W. Va.	2 55	Winchester, Va.	1 00
Meyersdale, Pa.	7 20		

HIGHGATE SPRINGS, VT.

Form Ex. 984.—Highgate Springs, Vt., and Return.

(Via New York, Day Line Steamers, Saratoga Springs, Lake Champlain; returning via Connecticut Valley.)

Baltimore & Ohio R. R. . . . . to Philadelphia.
Philadelphia & Reading R. R. . . . . to Bound Brook.
Central R. R. of New Jersey . . . . to New York.
Day or People's Line Steamers . . . . to Albany.
Delaware & Hudson R. R. . . . . to Ft. Ticonderoga.
Champlain Transportation Co. . . . . to Burlington.
Central Vermont R. R. . . . . to Highgate Springs.
Central Vermont R. R. . . . . to Windsor.
Vermont Valley R. R. . . . . to Brattleboro.
Central Vermont R. R. . . . . to South Vernon.

Connecticut River R. R. . . . . to Springfield.
New York, New Haven & Hartford R. R. . . . to New York.
Central R. R. of New Jersey . . . . to Bound Brook.
Philadelphia & Reading R. R. . . . . to Philadelphia.
Baltimore & Ohio R. R. . . . . to starting point.

Form Ex. 985. Highgate Springs, Vt.

Reverse of preceding excursion.

Through Rates.

Baltimore, Md. . . . . . . $25 80 | Washington, D. C. $25 80
Philadelphia, Pa. . . . . 19 80 |

Form Ex. 986. Highgate Springs, Vt., and Return.

(Via Connecticut Valley in both directions.)

Baltimore & Ohio R. R. . . . . to Philadelphia.
Philadelphia & Reading R. R. . . . . to Bound Brook.
Central R. R. of New Jersey . . . . to New York.
New York, New Haven & Hartford R. R. . . . to Springfield.
Connecticut River R. R. . . . . to South Vernon.
Central Vermont R. R. . . . . to Brattleboro.
Vermont Valley R. R. . . . . to Windsor.
Central Vermont R. R. . . . . to Highgate Springs.

Returning, same route.

Through Rates.

Baltimore, Md. . . . . . . $22 85 | Washington, D. C. $24 85
Philadelphia, Pa. . . . . 18 85 |

Form Ex. 987. Highgate Springs, Vt., and Return.

Central Vermont R. R. . . . . Burlington to Highgate Springs.

Returning, same route.

Sold in connection with any ticket passing through or terminating at Burlington.

Rate $1 50

HIGHLAND LAKE, PA.

Form Ex. 984. Highland Lake, Pa., and Return.

Baltimore & Ohio R. R. . . . . to Philadelphia.
Philadelphia & Reading R. R. . . . . to Halls.
Williamsport & North Branch R. R. . . . . . to Chamouni.
Williamsport & North Branch Transfer . . . to Highland Lake.

Returning, same route.

Through Rates.

Baltimore, Md. . . . . . . $10 00 | Washington, D. C. $12 00
Philadelphia, Pa. . . . . 8 80 |

Baggage will be checked through to Chamouni only on these tickets. From Chamouni stages convey passengers and baggage to Highland Lake. Stage transportation of passengers included in ticket, but an extra charge will be made for transporting baggage from Chamouni to Highland Lake.

HIGH POINT, N. J.
POST OFFICE PORT JERVIS, N. Y.

The beauties of the valley of the Delaware River are quite familiar to tourists generally, and the region in the vicinity of Port Jervis has long been famous not only for its scenic charms, but for its bountiful entertainment for the gunner and angler also.

The mountains and valleys of Orange and adjacent counties have also an extended reputation for their garden and dairy products; in fact, most of the good things which go to make a summer sojourn completely satisfactory are abundant in this beautiful territory.

To mention the so well known natural productiveness of farm and lake and stream of this and the adjoining counties were superfluous, excepting so far as to identify this location—the Inn at High Point—as being situated in their very midst, and where all the advantages offered by them are directly at hand.

On the summit of the highest mountains in New Jersey, and within easy access of Port Jervis, by a well-kept and easy graded turnpike, has just been completed this mountain house—"The Inn at High Point."

The location is on the crest of the Kittatiny Range, in the wilds of a mountainous country, yet within forty-five minutes drive of Port Jervis. There are few places on the American Continent so closely surrounded by the development of civilization, where so much aboriginal nature, so much quiet beauty, and the scenery unmarred by the touch of man, can be found.

It is true that wealth and fashion have invaded this beautiful territory and erected commodious hotels and handsome chateaux where summer idlers pass their holiday in luxurious ease, but the quiet roads, the sparkling streams, and the beautiful Lake Marcia still remain.

"So wondrous wild, the whole might seem
The scenery of a fairy dream."

There are charming walks in every direction, delicate vistas of beauty and picturesque views of the lake, and the magnificent view displayed on every side is limited only in extent by the power of vision. Situated as it is at an altitude of 1967 feet above sea level, in the rarified air of the mountains, it must needs be healthful, and the invigorating breezes, which are not only ever active, but impregnated with the fragrance of surrounding pines and hemlocks, possess a peculiarly effective strengthening power.

Centered in the midst of so delightful and charming a region is to be found a happy combination of quiet solitude, pure air, mountain spring water, hand in hand with all the domestic comforts and conveniences of city homes.

FORM EX. 847.—HIGH POINT, N. J., AND RETURN.

Baltimore & Ohio R. R.	to Philadelphia.
Philadelphia & Reading R. R.	to Bound Brook.
Central R. R. of New Jersey	to New York.
New York, Lake Erie & Western R. R.	to Port Jervis.
High Point Stage Line (5 miles)	to Inn at High Point.

Returning, same route.

THROUGH RATES.

Baltimore, Md.	$15 10	Washington, D. C.	$15 10
Philadelphia, Pa.	9 10		

HOT SPRINGS, VA.

The location is a charming one, in a little pocket in the mountains, the gorges separating these acting as channels for the constant play of cool, fresh air. The aspect from either hotel or cottage is so varied and so animated that the opportunities for special studies are almost endless.

FORM EX. 96. HOT SPRINGS, VA., AND RETURN

Baltimore & Ohio R. R. . . . . to Shenandoah Junc.
Norfolk & Western R. R. . . . . to Basic.
Chesapeake & Ohio Ry. . . . . to Hot Springs.

Returning, same route.

THROUGH RATES.

Baltimore, Md.	$17.00	New York, N. Y.	$25.00
Chester, Pa.	20.50	Philadelphia, Pa.	21.00
Havre de Grace, Md.	18.45	Washington, D. C.	15.00
Newark, Del.	19.50	Wilmington, Del.	20.00

FORM EX. 75. HOT SPRINGS, VA., AND RETURN

Baltimore & Ohio R. R. . . . . to Staunton.
Transfer, Baltimore & Ohio R. R. Depot . . to C. & O. R. R. Depot
Chesapeake & Ohio Ry. . . . . to Hot Springs.

Returning, same route.

ROUTES AND RATES FOR SUMMER TOURS.   129

THROUGH RATES.

Baltimore, Md.	$17 00	Meyersdale, Pa.	$19 30
Bellaire, O.	26 15	Morgantown, W. Va.	23 75
Berkeley Springs, W.Va.	15 85	Moundsville, W. Va.	25 30
Cameron, W. Va.	24 70	Mountain Lake Park, Md.	19 85
Charlestown, W. Va.	13 40	Mt. Pleasant, Pa.	22 00
Chester, Pa.	20 50	Newark, Del.	19 30
Clarksburg, W. Va.	22 75	New York, N. Y.	25 00
Connellsville, Pa.	21 30	Oakland, Md.	19 45
Cumberland, Md.	17 80	Parkersburg, W. Va.	25 30
Deer Park, Md.	19 70	Philadelphia, Pa.	21 00
Fairmont, W. Va.	22 75	Piedmont, W. Va.	18 30
Frederick, Md.	14 95	Pittsburgh, Pa.	23 80
Grafton, W. Va.	21 85	Rockwood, Pa.	19 75
Hagerstown, Md.	14 95	Somerset, Pa.	20 15
Harper's Ferry, W. Va.	13 90	Strasburg, Va.	11 25
Harrisonburg, Va.	8 90	Uniontown, Pa.	21 80
Havre de Grace, Md.	18 45	Washington, D. C.	15 00
Johnstown, Pa.	21 55	Washington, Pa.	24 30
Keyser, W. Va.	18 70	Wheeling, W. Va.	25 30
Lexington, Va.	9 40	Wilmington, Del.	20 00
McKeesport, Pa.	23 25	Winchester, Va.	12 30
Martinsburg, W. Va.	14 65		

FORM EX. 622. —HOT SPRINGS, VA., AND RETURN.

Baltimore & Ohio R. R. .... to Washington.
Transfer. Baltimore & Ohio R. R. Depot .... to C. & O. R. R. Depot.
Chesapeake & Ohio Ry. .... to Hot Springs.
Returning, same route.

THROUGH RATES.

Baltimore, Md.	$17 00	New York, N. Y.	$25 00
Chester, Pa.	20 50	Philadelphia, Pa.	21 00
Havre de Grace, Md.	18 45	Wilmington, Del.	20 00
Newark, Del.	19 30		

HOT SPRINGS, N. C.

FORM EX. 17.—HOT SPRINGS, N. C. AND RETURN.
Limited to three (3) months from date of sale.

Baltimore & Ohio R. R. .... to Shenandoah June.
Norfolk & Western R. R. .... to Bristol.
East Tennessee, Virginia & Georgia R. R. ...... to Paint Rock.
Richmond & Danville R. R. .... to Hot Springs.
Returning, same route.

THROUGH RATES.

Baltimore, Md.	$22 00	Morgantown, W. Va.	$29 45
Bellaire, O.	31 35	Moundsville, W. Va.	31 25
Berkeley Springs, W.Va.	24 75	Mountain Lake Park, Md.	25 70
Cameron, W. Va.	30 55	Mt. Pleasant, Pa.	27 80
Chester, Pa.	25 50	Newark, Del.	24 30
Clarksburg, W. Va.	28 55	New York, N. Y.	30 00
Connellsville, Pa.	27 30	Oakland, Md.	25 80
Cumberland, Md.	23 60	Parkersburg, W. Va.	31 65
Deer Park, Md.	25 55	Philadelphia, Pa.	26 00
Fairmont, W. Va.	28 55	Piedmont, W. Va.	24 75
Frederick, Md.	20 65	Pittsburgh, Pa.	29 60
Grafton, W. Va.	27 65	Rockwood, Pa.	25 55
Harper's Ferry, W. Va.	20 00	Somerset, Pa.	25 95
Havre de Grace, Md.	23 45	Uniontown, Pa.	27 75
Johnstown, Pa.	27 55	Washington, D. C.	20 00
Keyser, W. Va.	24 55	Washington, Pa.	30 70
McKeesport, Pa.	29 05	Wheeling, W. Va.	31 65
Martinsburg, W. Va.	20 45	Wilmington, Del.	25 00
Meyersdale, Pa.	25 10		

130   BALTIMORE & OHIO RAILROAD COMPANY

Form Ex. 56.— Hot Springs, N. C., and Return.

Limited to three (3) months from date of sale.

Baltimore & Ohio R. R. . . . . to Washington
Transfer, B. & O. R. R. Depot . . . . to R. & D. Depot
Richmond & Danville R. R. . . . . to Hot Springs.

Returning, same route.

THROUGH RATES.

Baltimore, Md.	$22 00	Meyersdale, Pa.	$28 10
Bellaire, O.	31 95	Morgantown, W. Va.	32 55
Berkeley Springs, W. Va.	24 65	Moundsville, W. Va.	31 20
Cameron, W. Va.	33 50	Mountain Lake Park, Md.	28 15
Charlestown, W. Va.	23 20	Mt. Pleasant, Pa.	30 80
Chester, Pa.	25 50	Newark, Del.	24 30
Clarksburg, W. Va.	31 55	New York, N. Y.	30 00
Connellsville, Pa.	29 30	Oakland, Md.	28 25
Cumberland, Md.	26 60	Parkersburg, W. Va.	31 65
Deer Park, Md.	28 00	Philadelphia, Pa.	26 00
Fairmont, W. Va.	31 55	Piedmont, W. Va.	27 70
Frederick, Md.	22 80	Pittsburgh, Pa.	32 00
Grafton, W. Va.	30 65	Rockwood, Pa.	28 55
Hagerstown, Md.	23 60	Somerset, Pa.	28 95
Harper's Ferry, W. Va.	22 70	Uniontown, Pa.	30 75
Havre de Grace, Md.	23 45	Washington, Pa.	33 70
Johnstown, Pa.	30 55	Wheeling, W. Va.	31 65
Keyser, W. Va.	27 50	Wilmington, Del.	25 00
McKeesport, Pa.	32 05	Winchester, Va.	24 30
Martinsburg, W. Va.	23 45		

Form Ex. 57.— Hot Springs, N. C., and Return.

Limited to three (3) months from date of sale.

Baltimore & Ohio R. R. . . . . to Lexington.
Chesapeake & Ohio R. R. . . . . to Lynchburg.
Richmond & Danville R. R. . . . . to Hot Springs.

Returning, same route.

THROUGH RATES.

Baltimore, Md.	$22 00	Morgantown, W. Va.	$29 55
Bellaire, O.	31 95	Moundsville, W. Va.	31 25
Berkeley Springs, W. Va.	24 75	Mountain Lake Park, Md.	25 70
Cameron, W. Va.	30 55	Mt. Pleasant, Pa.	27 80
Charlestown, W. Va.	20 00	Newark, Del.	24 30
Chester, Pa.	25 50	New York, N. Y.	30 00
Clarksburg, W. Va.	28 55	Oakland, Md.	25 80
Connellsville, Pa.	27 30	Parkersburg, W. Va.	31 65
Cumberland, Md.	23 60	Philadelphia, Pa.	26 00
Deer Park, Md.	25 55	Piedmont, W. Va.	24 75
Fairmont, W. Va.	28 55	Pittsburgh, Pa.	29 00
Frederick, Md.	20 65	Rockwood, Pa.	25 55
Grafton, W. Va.	27 65	Somerset, Pa.	25 95
Hagerstown, Md.	20 00	Staunton, Va.	17 30
Harper's Ferry, W. Va.	20 00	Strasburg, Va.	20 00
Harrisonburg, Va.	18 60	Uniontown, Pa.	27 75
Havre de Grace, Md.	23 45	Washington, D. C.	20 00
Johnstown, Pa.	27 55	Washington, Pa.	30 70
Keyser, W. Va.	24 55	Wheeling, W. Va.	31 65
McKeesport, Pa.	30 05	Wilmington, Del.	25 00
Martinsburg, W. Va.	20 45	Winchester, Va.	20 00
Meyersdale, Pa.	25 10		

HOWE'S CAVE, N. Y.

This remarkable cave is situated on the line of the Delaware & Hudson R. R., and is a great natural curiosity. The entrance to the cave is but a few rods from the station, and is reached by a short walk through the handsomely laid out grounds belonging to the Pavilion Hotel. An irregular circular opening in the limestone leads to the "Reception Room," which is fantastically adorned with stalagmites, and furnished with curious rock formations. Cataract Hall, the Haunted Castle, Stygian Cave, and the Devil's Gateway are some of the main features of the cavern. The Pavilion Hotel and Cave House are constructed to accommodate a large number of guests, and contain every appliance of elegance and comfort.

Form Ex. 311. Howe's Cave, N. Y., and Return.

Baltimore & Ohio R. R.	to Philadelphia
Philadelphia & Reading R. R.	to Bound Brook
Central R. R. of New Jersey	to New York
New York Central & Hudson River R. R.	to Albany
Delaware & Hudson R. R.	to Howe's Cave

Returning, same route.

THROUGH RATES.

Baltimore, Md.	$15 80	Washington, D. C.	$17 80
†Philadelphia, Pa.	11 80		

Form Ex. 312. Howe's Cave, N. Y., and Return.

Baltimore & Ohio R. R.	to Philadelphia
Philadelphia & Reading R. R.	to Bound Brook
Central R. R. of New Jersey	to New York
West Shore R. R.	to Albany
Delaware & Hudson R. R.	to Howe's Cave

Returning, same route.
Transfer through New York, in both directions, included.

THROUGH RATES.

Baltimore, Md.	$15 80	Washington, D. C.	$17 80
†Philadelphia, Pa.	11 80		

ISLES OF SHOALS, N. H.

FORM EX. 874 TO ISLES OF SHOALS, N. H., AND RETURN.
(Via Sound Lines and Boston in both directions.)

Baltimore & Ohio R. R. . . . . to Philadelphia.
Philadelphia & Reading R. R. . . . . to Bound Brook.
Central R. R. of New Jersey . . . . to New York.
Sound Lines (see pages 50 to 55 for routes) . . to Boston.
Boston & Portsmouth Steamship Co. . . . . . to Isles of Shoals.
Returning, same route.

THROUGH RATES.

Baltimore, Md. . . . . $17.50   Washington, D. C. $19.50
Philadelphia, Pa. 15.50

FORM EX. 874 TO ISLES OF SHOALS, N. H., AND RETURN.
(Via Rail Lines and Boston in both directions.)

Baltimore & Ohio R. R. . . . . to Philadelphia.
Rail Lines (see pages 50 to 55 for routes) . . . to Boston.
Boston & Portsmouth Steamship Co. . . . . . to Isles of Shoals.
Returning, same route.

ROUTES AND RATES FOR SUMMER TOURS.

THROUGH RATES.

Baltimore, Md. . . . . . . $19 50   Washington, D. C. $21 00
 Philadelphia, Pa. 15 50

FORM EX. 874, TO ISLES OF SHOALS, N. H., AND RETURN.

(Via Rail Lines and Boston; returning via Boston and Sound Lines.)

Baltimore & Ohio R. R. . . . . to Philadelphia.
Rail Lines (see pages 50 to 55 for routes) . . . . . to Boston.
Boston & Portsmouth Steamship Co. . . . . . to Isles of Shoals.
Boston & Portsmouth Steamship Co. . . . . . . to Boston.
Sound Lines (see pages 50 to 55 for routes) . . . . to New York.
Central R. R. of New Jersey . . . . to Bound Brook.
Philadelphia & Reading R. R. . . . . to Philadelphia.
Baltimore & Ohio R. R. . . . . to starting point.

THROUGH RATES.

Baltimore, Md. . . . . . . $18 50   Washington, D. C. $20 50
 Philadelphia, Pa. 14 50

FORM EX. 874, TO ISLES OF SHOALS, N. H., AND RETURN.

(Via Sound Lines and Boston; returning all rail.)

Baltimore & Ohio R. R. . . . . to Philadelphia.
Philadelphia & Reading R. R. . . . . to Bound Brook.
Central R. R. of New Jersey . . . . to New York.
Sound Lines (see pages 50 to 55 for routes) . . . . to Boston.
Boston & Portsmouth Steamship Co. . . . . . to Isles of Shoals.
Boston & Portsmouth Steamship Co. . . . . . . to Boston.
Rail Lines (see pages 50 to 55 for routes) . . . . to Philadelphia.
Baltimore & Ohio R. R. . . . . to starting point.

THROUGH RATES.

Baltimore, Md. . . . . . . $18 50   Washington, D. C. $20 50
 Philadelphia, Pa. 14 50

FORM EX. 875, TO ISLES OF SHOALS, N. H., AND RETURN.

(Via Sound Lines and Boston in both directions.)

Baltimore & Ohio R. R. . . . . to Philadelphia.
Philadelphia & Reading R. R. . . . . to Bound Brook.
Central R. R. of New Jersey . . . . to New York.
Sound Lines (see pages 50 to 55 for routes) . . . . to Boston.
Boston & Maine R. R. . . . . to Portsmouth.
Boston & Portsmouth Steamship Co. . . . . . to Isles of Shoals.

Returning, same route.

THROUGH RATES.

Baltimore, Md. . . . . . . $20 00   Washington, D. C. $22 00
 Philadelphia, Pa. 16 00

FORM EX. 875, TO ISLES OF SHOALS, N. H., AND RETURN.

(Via Rail Lines and Boston in both directions.)

Baltimore & Ohio R. R. . . . . to Philadelphia.
Rail Lines (see pages 50 to 55 for routes) . . . . . to Boston.
Boston & Maine R. R. . . . . to Portsmouth.
Boston & Portsmouth Steamship Co. . . . . . to Isles of Shoals.

Returning, same route.

THROUGH RATES.

Baltimore, Md. . . . . . . $22 00   Washington, D. C. $24 00
 Philadelphia, Pa. 18 00

134   BALTIMORE & OHIO RAILROAD COMPANY

FORM EX. 875 TO ISLES OF SHOALS, N. H., AND RETURN.

(Via Rail Lines and Boston; returning via Boston and Sound Lines.)

Baltimore & Ohio R. R. . . . . to Philadelphia.
Rail Lines (see pages 50 to 55 for route) . . . . . to Boston.
Boston & Maine R. R. . . . . to Portsmouth.
Boston & Portsmouth Steamship Co. . . . . . to Isles of Shoals.
Boston & Portsmouth Steamship Co. . . . . . to Portsmouth.
Boston & Maine R. R. . . . . to Boston.
Sound Lines (see pages 50 to 55 for route) . . . . to New York.
Central R. R. of New Jersey . . . . to Bound Brook.
Philadelphia & Reading R. R. . . . . to Philadelphia.
Baltimore & Ohio R. R. . . . . to starting point.

THROUGH RATES.

Baltimore, Md. . . . . . . $21 00 | Washington, D. C. $21 00
| Philadelphia, Pa. 17 00

FORM EX. 875 TO ISLES OF SHOALS, N. H., AND RETURN.

(Via Sound Lines and Boston; returning, all rail.)

Baltimore & Ohio R. R. . . . . to Philadelphia.
Philadelphia & Reading R. R. . . . . to Bound Brook.
Central R. R. of New Jersey . . . . to New York.
Sound Lines (see pages 50 to 55 for route) . . . . to Boston.
Boston & Maine R. R. . . . . to Portsmouth.
Boston & Portsmouth Steamship Co. . . . . . to Isles of Shoals.
Boston & Portsmouth Steamship Co. . . . . . to Portsmouth.
Boston & Maine R. R. . . . . to Boston.
Rail Lines (see pages 50 to 55 for route) . . . . . to Philadelphia.
Baltimore & Ohio R. R. . . . . to starting point.

THROUGH RATES.

Baltimore, Md. . . . . . . $21 00 | Washington, D. C. $21 00
| Philadelphia, Pa. 17 00

ITHACA, N. Y.

FORM EX. 988. ITHACA, N. Y., AND RETURN.

Baltimore & Ohio R. R. . . . . to Philadelphia.
Philadelphia & Reading R. R. . . . . to Bethlehem.
Lehigh Valley R. R. . . . . to Ithaca.

Returning, same route.

THROUGH RATES.

Baltimore, Md. . . . . . . $15 35 | Washington, D. C. $17 35
| Philadelphia, Pa. . . . . 11 35 |

FORM EX. 989. ITHACA, N. Y., AND RETURN.

Baltimore & Ohio R. R. . . . . to Philadelphia.
Philadelphia & Reading R. R. . . . . to Bethlehem.
Lehigh Valley R. R. . . . . to Waverly.
New York, Lake Erie & Western R. R. . . . . to Elmira.
Elmira, Cortland & Northern R. R. . . . . . . to Ithaca.
Delaware, Lackawanna & Western R. R. . . . to Mauunka Chunk.
Pennsylvania R. R. . . . . to Philadelphia.
Baltimore & Ohio R. R. . . . . to starting point.

THROUGH RATES.

Baltimore, Md. . . . . . . $16 65 | Washington, D. C. $18 65
| Philadelphia, Pa. . . . . 12 65 |

ROUTES AND RATES FOR SUMMER TOURS.   135

FORM EX. 390.—ITHACA, N. Y., AND RETURN.

Baltimore & Ohio R. R. . . . . to Philadelphia.
Philadelphia & Reading R. R. . . . . to Bethlehem.
Lehigh Valley R. R. . . . . to Ithaca.
Delaware, Lackawana & Western R. R. . . . to Mauunka Chunk.
Pennsylvania R. R. . . . . to Philadelphia.
Baltimore & Ohio R. R. . . . . to starting point.

THROUGH RATES.

Baltimore, Md. . . . . . . $16 65   Washington, D. C. $18 65
†Philadelphia, Pa. 12 65

JEFFERSON, N. H.

FORM EX. 391.—JEFFERSON, N. H., AND RETURN.

(Via rail to Jefferson, N. H.; returning by same route to Boston, thence
via Sound Lines from Boston.)

Baltimore & Ohio R. R. . . . . to Philadelphia.
Rail Lines (see pages 50 to 55 for routes) . . . to Boston.
Boston & Maine R. R. . . . . to North Conway.
Maine Central R. R. . . . . to Jefferson.
Maine Central R. R. . . . . to North Conway.
Boston & Maine R. R. . . . . to Boston.
Sound Lines (see pages 50 to 55 for routes) . . to New York.
Central R. R. of New Jersey . . . . to Bound Brook.
Philadelphia & Reading R. R. . . . . to Philadelphia.
Baltimore & Ohio R. R. . . . . to starting point.

THROUGH RATES.

Baltimore, Md. . . . . . . $26 70   Washington, D. C. $28 70
†Philadelphia, Pa. 22 70

Transfer through Boston, returning, included.

FORM EX. 392.—JEFFERSON, N. H., AND RETURN.

(Via Sound Lines to Boston, rail to Jefferson; returning by same route
to Boston, thence via rail.)

Baltimore & Ohio R. R. . . . . to Philadelphia.
Philadelphia & Reading R. R. . . . . to Bound Brook.
Central R. R. of New Jersey . . . . to New York.
Sound Lines (see pages 50 to 55 for routes) . . to Boston.
Boston & Maine R. R. . . . . to North Conway.
Maine Central R. R. . . . . to Jefferson.
Maine Central R. R. . . . . to North Conway.
Boston & Maine R. R. . . . . to Boston.
Rail Lines (see pages 50 to 55 for routes) . . . to Philadelphia.
Baltimore & Ohio R. R. . . . . to starting point.

THROUGH RATES.

Baltimore, Md. . . . . . . $26 70   Washington, D. C. $28 70
†Philadelphia, Pa. 22 70

Transfer through Boston, going, included.

FORM EX. 393.—JEFFERSON, N. H., AND RETURN.

(Via Rail Lines to Jefferson, N. H., in both directions.)

Baltimore & Ohio R. R. . . . . to Philadelphia.
Rail Lines (see pages 50 to 55 for routes) . . . to Boston.
Boston & Maine R. R. . . . . to North Conway.
Maine Central R. R. . . . . to Jefferson.

Returning, same route.

THROUGH RATES.

Baltimore, Md. . . . . . . $28 00   Washington, D. C. $30 00
†Philadelphia, Pa. 24 00

136   BALTIMORE & OHIO RAILROAD COMPANY

FORM EX. 391.—JEFFERSON, N. H., AND RETURN.
(Via Sound Lines to Boston, rail to Jefferson, N. H., and return to Boston, thence via Sound Lines.)

Baltimore & Ohio R. R. . . . . to Philadelphia.
Philadelphia & Reading R. R. . . . . to Bound Brook.
Central R. R. of New Jersey . . . . to New York.
Sound Lines (see pages 50 to 55 for routes) . . . to Boston.
Boston & Maine R. R. . . . . to North Conway.
Maine Central R. R. . . . . to Jefferson.
                Returning, same route.
                  THROUGH RATES.

Baltimore, Md. . . . . . . $25 80 | Washington, D. C. . . . $25 80
(Philadelphia, Pa. . . . . 19 80 |
      Transfer through Boston, in both directions, included.

FORM EX. 392.—JEFFERSON, N. H., AND RETURN.
(Via rail to Jefferson, N. H.; returning by same route to Boston, thence via Sound Lines from Boston.)

Baltimore & Ohio R. R. . . . . to Philadelphia.
Rail Lines (see pages 50 to 55 for routes) . . . . to Boston.
Boston & Maine R. R. . . . . to Portland.
Maine Central R. R. . . . . to Jefferson.
Maine Central R. R. . . . . to Portland.
Boston & Maine R. R. . . . . to Boston.
Sound Lines (see pages 50 to 55 for routes) . . . to New York.
Central R. R. of New Jersey . . . . to Bound Brook.
Philadelphia & Reading R. R. . . . . to Philadelphia.
Baltimore & Ohio R. R. . . . . to starting point.
                  THROUGH RATES.

Baltimore, Md. . . . . . . $26 70 | Washington, D. C. . . . $28 70
(Philadelphia, Pa. . . . . 22 70 |
      Transfer through Boston, returning, included.

FORM EX. 393.—JEFFERSON, N. H., AND RETURN.
(Via Sound Lines to Boston, rail to Jefferson, N. H.; returning by same route to Boston, thence via rail.)

Baltimore & Ohio R. R. . . . . to Philadelphia.
Philadelphia & Reading R. R. . . . . to Bound Brook.
Central R. R. of New Jersey . . . . to New York.
Sound Lines (see pages 50 to 55 for routes) . . . to Boston.
Boston & Maine R. R. . . . . to Portland.
Maine Central R. R. . . . . to Jefferson.
Maine Central R. R. . . . . to Portland.
Boston & Maine R. R. . . . . to Boston.
Rail Lines (see pages 50 to 55 for routes) . . . . to Philadelphia.
Baltimore & Ohio R. R. . . . . to starting point.
                  THROUGH RATES.

Baltimore, Md. . . . . . . $26 70 | Washington, D. C. . . . $28 70
(Philadelphia, Pa. . . . . 22 70 |
      Transfer through Boston, going, included.

FORM EX. 392.—JEFFERSON, N. H.
(Via Rail Lines to Jefferson, N. H., in both directions.)

Baltimore & Ohio R. R. . . . . to Philadelphia.
Rail Lines (see pages 50 to 55 for routes) . . . . to Boston.
Boston & Maine R. R. . . . . to Portland.
Maine Central R. R. . . . . to Jefferson.
                Returning, same route.
                  THROUGH RATES.

Baltimore, Md. . . . . . . $28 00 | Washington, D. C. . . . $30 00
(Philadelphia, Pa. . . . . 24 00 |

ROUTES AND RATES FOR SUMMER TOURS 137

FORM EX. 362. JEFFERSON, N. H., AND RETURN.

(Via Sound Lines to Boston, rail to Jefferson, N. H., and return to Boston, thence via Sound Lines.)

Baltimore & Ohio R. R. . . . . to Philadelphia.
Philadelphia & Reading R. R. . . . . to Bound Brook.
Central R. R. of New Jersey . . . . to New York.
Sound Lines (see pages 50 to 55 for routes) . . . . to Boston.
Boston & Maine R. R. . . . . to Portland.
Maine Central R. R. . . . . to Jefferson.
Returning, same route.

THROUGH RATES.

Baltimore, Md. . . . . . . $23 80 | Washington, D. C. $25 80
(Philadelphia, Pa. . . . . 19 80 |

Transfer through Boston, in both directions, included.

FORM EX. 363. JEFFERSON, N. H.

(Via rail and Boston; returning via Sound Lines.)

Baltimore & Ohio R. R. . . . . to Philadelphia.
Rail Lines (see pages 50 to 55 for routes) . . . . to Boston.
Boston & Maine R. R. . . . . to Nashua.
Concord & Montreal R. R. . . . . to Jefferson.
Concord & Montreal R. R. . . . . to Nashua.
Boston & Maine R. R. . . . . to Boston.
Sound Lines (see pages 50 to 55 for route) . . . . to New York.
Central R. R. of New Jersey . . . . to Bound Brook.
Philadelphia & Reading R. R. . . . . to Philadelphia.
Baltimore & Ohio R. R. . . . . to starting point.

THROUGH RATES.

Baltimore, Md. . . . . . . $26 30 | Washington, D. C. $28 30
(Philadelphia, Pa. . . . . 22 30 |

Transfer through Boston, returning, included.

FORM EX. 364. JEFFERSON, N. H., AND RETURN.

(Via Sound Lines and Boston; returning all rail.)

Baltimore & Ohio R. R. . . . . to Philadelphia.
Philadelphia & Reading R. R. . . . . to Bound Brook.
Central R. R. of New Jersey . . . . to New York.
Sound Lines (see pages 50 to 55 for route) . . . . to Boston.
Boston & Maine R. R. . . . . to Nashua.
Concord & Montreal R. R. . . . . to Jefferson.
Concord & Montreal R. R. . . . . to Nashua.
Boston & Maine R. R. . . . . to Boston.
Rail Lines (see pages 50 to 55 for routes) . . . . to Philadelphia.
Baltimore & Ohio R. R. . . . . to starting point.

THROUGH RATES.

Baltimore, Md. . . . . . . $26 30 | Washington, D. C. $28 30
(Philadelphia, Pa. . . . . 22 30 |

Transfer through Boston, going, included.

FORM EX. 365. JEFFERSON, N. H., AND RETURN

(Via Rail Lines and Boston in both directions.)

Baltimore & Ohio R. R. . . . . to Philadelphia.
Rail Lines (see pages 50 to 55 for routes) . . . . to Boston.
Boston & Maine R. R. . . . . to Nashua.
Concord & Montreal R. R. . . . . to Jefferson.
Returning, same route.

THROUGH RATES.

Baltimore, Md. . . . . . . $24 00 | Washington, D. C. $26 00
(Philadelphia, Pa. . . . . 28 00 |

FORM EX. 303.—JEFFERSON, N. H., AND RETURN.

(Via Sound Lines and Boston in both directions.)

Baltimore & Ohio R. R. . . . . to Philadelphia.
Philadelphia & Reading R. R. . . . . to Bound Brook.
Central R. R. of New Jersey . . . . to New York.
Sound Lines (see pages 50 to 55 for routes) . . . to Boston.
Boston & Maine R. R. . . . . to Nashua.
Concord & Montreal R. R. . . . . to Jefferson.

Returning, same route.

THROUGH RATES.

Baltimore, Md. . . . . . . $25 00 | Washington, D. C. $25 00
(Philadelphia, Pa. 19 00

Transfer through Boston, in both directions, included.

FORM EX. 304.—JEFFERSON, N. H., AND RETURN.

(Via New York and Connecticut Valley in both directions.)

Baltimore & Ohio R. R. . . . . to Philadelphia.
Philadelphia & Reading R. R. . . . . to Bound Brook.
Central R. R. of New Jersey . . . . to New York.
New York, New Haven & Hartford R. R. . . . to Springfield.
Connecticut River R. R. . . . . to South Vernon.
Central Vermont R. R. . . . . to Brattleboro.
Vermont Valley R. R. . . . . to Windsor.
Central Vermont R. R. . . . . to White River Jc.
Boston & Maine R. R. . . . . to Wells River.
Concord & Montreal R. R. . . . . to Jefferson.

Returning, same route.

THROUGH RATES.

Baltimore, Md. . . . . . . $24 80 | Washington, D. C. $26 80
(Philadelphia, Pa. 20 80

FORM EX. 305.—JEFFERSON, N. H., AND RETURN.

(Via New York and Connecticut Valley; returning via Boston.)

Baltimore & Ohio R. R. . . . . to Philadelphia.
Philadelphia & Reading R. R. . . . . to Bound Brook.
Central R. R. of New Jersey . . . . to New York.
New York, New Haven & Hartford R. R. . . . to Springfield
Connecticut River R. R. . . . . to South Vernon.
Central Vermont R. R. . . . . to Brattleboro.
Vermont Valley R. R. . . . . to Windsor.
Central Vermont R. R. . . . . to White River Junct
Boston & Maine R. R. . . . . to Wells River.
Concord & Montreal R. R. . . . . to Jefferson.
Concord & Montreal R. R. . . . . to Nashua.
Boston & Maine R. R. . . . . to Boston.
Rail or Sound Lines (see pages 50 to 55 for routes) to Philadelphia.
Baltimore & Ohio R. R. . . . . to starting point.

FORM EX. 306.—JEFFERSON, N. H., AND RETURN.

Reverse of preceding excursion.

THROUGH RATES.

	Via Sound.	Via Rail.
Baltimore, Md.	$27 30	$27 30
(Philadelphia, Pa.	20 00	23 30
Washington, D. C.	25 30	29 30

Transfer through Boston included via Sound Lines only.

JORDAN'S WHITE SULPHUR SPRINGS, VA.

Jordan's White Sulphur Springs is situated one and one-half miles from Stephenson Station, in a most delightful district. The surrounding hills are covered with a luxuriant vegetation, and the climb to the top of almost any one of them is compensated by a series of magnificent views.

JORDAN'S SULPHUR.

The resort is an esteemed one for families. Here many of them regularly spend season after season, and enjoy as much as anything else these reunions of summer companions. The main spring, known as the White Sulphur, is in the centre of the grounds, and near by are wells of pure, sweet water, free from mineral qualities. To indulge in an extended dissertation on the medicinal virtues of the water would be but to repeat, in a condensed form, the pamphlets which are issued, giving not only analyses in full, but much interesting matter besides relative to the various forms of disease which are most benefited by its use. The whole country about Jordan's White Sulphur Springs lies some five hundred feet above the level of Harper's Ferry, and therefore the pure air, together with the fragrance of the pines which cover the surrounding hills, is refreshing and healthful. As the name implies, the water is largely impregnated with sulphur and the minerals usually accompanying it.

FORM EX. 507.—JORDAN'S WHITE SULPHUR SPRINGS, VA., AND RETURN.

Baltimore & Ohio R. R. . . . . . . to Stephenson's.
Stage (1½ miles) . . . . to Jordan's White Sulphur Springs.
Returning, same route.

THROUGH RATES.

Baltimore, Md.	$6 15	Meyersdale, Pa.	$7 75
Bellaire, O.	11 00	Morgantown, W. Va.	12 20
Berkeley Springs, W. Va.	4 20	Moundsville, W. Va.	13 85
Cameron, W. Va.	13 15	Mountain Lake Park, Md.	8 30
Charlestown, W. Va.	4 85	Mt. Pleasant, Pa.	10 45
Chester, Pa.	9 65	Newark, Del.	8 45
Clarksburg, W. Va.	11 20	New York, N. Y.	11 45
Connellsville, Pa.	9 95	Oakland, Md.	8 40
Cumberland, Md.	6 25	Parkersburg, W. Va.	14 55
Deer Park, Md.	8 45	Philadelphia, Pa.	10 45
Fairmont, W. Va.	11 20	Piedmont, W. Va.	7 55
Frederick, Md.	3 40	Pittsburgh, Pa.	12 25
Grafton, W. Va.	10 50	Rockwood, Pa.	8 30
Hagerstown, Md.	3 40	Somerset, Pa.	8 00
Harper's Ferry, W. Va.	2 35	Staunton, Va.	5 95
Harrisonburg, Va.	4 65	Strasburg, Va.	1 80
Havre de Grace, Md.	7 60	Uniontown, Pa.	10 40
Johnstown, Pa.	10 00	Washington, D. C.	4 55
Keyser, W. Va.	7 15	Washington, Pa.	13 35
Lexington, Va.	7 75	Wheeling, W. Va.	11 35
McKeesport, Pa.	11 70	Wilmington, Del.	9 45
Martinsburg, W. Va.	3 10	Winchester, Va.	1 20

KANAWHA FALLS, W. VA.

FORM EX. 67.—KANAWHA FALLS, W. VA., AND RETURN.

Baltimore & Ohio R. R. . . . . to Shenandoah June.
Norfolk & Western R. R. . . . . to Basic.
Chesapeake & Ohio Ry. . . . . to Kanawha Falls.
Returning, same route.

THROUGH RATES.

Baltimore, Md.	$18 30	New York, N. Y.	$26 30
Chester, Pa.	21 80	Philadelphia, Pa.	22 30
Havre de Grace, Md.	19 75	Washington, D. C.	16 30
Newark, Del.	20 60	Wilmington, Del.	21 30

FORM EX. 95.—KANAWHA FALLS, W. VA., AND RETURN.

Baltimore & Ohio R. R. . . . . to Washington.
Transfer B. & O. Depot . . . . to R. & D. Depot.
Chesapeake & Ohio Ry. . . . . to Kanawha Falls.
Returning, same route.

THROUGH RATES.

Baltimore, Md.	$18 50	New York, N. Y.	$26 50
Chester, Pa.	21 80	Philadelphia, Pa.	22 30
Havre de Grace, Md.	19 75	Wilmington, Del.	21 30
Newark, Del.	20 00		

FORM EX. 256. KANAWHA FALLS, W. VA., AND RETURN.

Baltimore & Ohio R. R. . . . . to Staunton.
Chesapeake & Ohio Ry. . . . . to Kanawha Falls.
Returning, same route.

THROUGH RATES.

Baltimore, Md.	$18 50	Meyersdale, Pa.	$20 80
Bellaire, O.	27 65	Morgantown, W. Va.	25 25
Berkeley Springs, W. Va.	17 35	Moundsville, W. Va.	28 30
Cameron, W. Va.	26 20	Mountain Lake Park, Md.	21 35
Charlestown, W. Va.	14 00	Mt. Pleasant, Pa.	23 50
Chester, Pa.	21 80	Newark, Del.	20 00
Clarksburg, W. Va.	24 25	New York, N. Y.	26 50
Connellsville, Pa.	23 00	Oakland, Md.	21 15
Cumberland, Md.	19 50	Parkersburg, W. Va.	27 10
Deer Park, Md.	21 20	Philadelphia, Pa.	22 30
Fairmont, W. Va.	21 25	Piedmont, W. Va.	20 10
Frederick, Md.	16 45	Pittsburgh, Pa.	25 30
Grafton, W. Va.	23 35	Rockwood, Pa.	24 25
Hagerstown, Md.	16 45	Somerset, Pa.	24 65
Harper's Ferry, W. Va.	15 40	Strasburg, Va.	12 75
Harrisonburg, Va.	10 40	Uniontown, Pa.	23 45
Havre de Grace, Md.	19 75	Washington, D. C.	16 20
Johnstown, Pa.	23 65	Washington, Pa.	26 10
Keyser, W. Va.	20 20	Wheeling, W. Va.	27 40
Lexington, Va.	10 80	Wilmington, Del.	21 30
McKeesport, Pa.	24 75	Winchester, Va.	13 80
Martinsburg, W. Va.	16 45		

KENNEBUNKPORT, ME.

FORM EX. 762. KENNEBUNKPORT, ME., AND RETURN.

(Via rail and Boston; returning by Sound Lines.)

Baltimore & Ohio R. R. . . . . to Philadelphia.
Rail Lines (see pages 50 to 55 for routes) . . . . . to Boston.
Boston & Maine R. R. . . . . to Kennebunkport.
Boston & Maine R. R. . . . . to Boston.
Sound Lines (see pages 50 to 55 for routes) . . . . to New York.
Central R. R. of New Jersey . . . . to Bound Brook.
Philadelphia & Reading R. R. . . . . to Philadelphia.
Baltimore & Ohio R. R. . . . . to starting point.

THROUGH RATES.

Baltimore, Md.	$20 90	Washington, D. C.	$22 90
Philadelphia, Pa.	16 90		

FORM EX. 762. — KENNEBUNKPORT, ME., AND RETURN.

(Via Sound Lines and Boston; returning by rail.)

Baltimore & Ohio R. R. . . . . to Philadelphia.
Philadelphia & Reading R. R. . . . . to Bound Brook.
Central R. R. of New Jersey . . . . to New York.
Sound Lines (see pages 50 to 55 for routes) . . . . to Boston.
Boston & Maine R. R. . . . . to Kennebunkport.
Boston & Maine R. R. . . . . to Boston.
Rail Lines (see pages 50 to 55 for routes) . . . . to Philadelphia.
Baltimore & Ohio R. R. . . . . to starting point.

THROUGH RATES.

Baltimore, Md.	$20 90	Washington, D. C.	$22 90
Philadelphia, Pa.	16 90		

FORM EN. 762. KENNEBUNKPORT, ME., AND RETURN.
Via Rail Lines and Boston in both directions.

Baltimore & Ohio R. R. . . . . to Philadelphia
Rail Lines (see pages 50 to 53 for routes) . . . . to Boston.
Boston & Maine R. R. . . . . to Kennebunkport
Returning, same route.

THROUGH RATES.

Baltimore, Md. . . . . $24 30 | Washington, D. C. $25 30
Philadelphia, Pa. 17 30

FORM EN. 762. KENNEBUNKPORT, ME.
Via Sound Lines and Boston in both directions.

Baltimore & Ohio R. R. . . . . to Philadelphia
Philadelphia & Reading R. R. . . . . to Bound Brook.
Central R. R. of New Jersey . . . . to New York.
Sound Lines (see pages 50 to 55 for routes) . . . . to Boston.
Boston & Maine R. R. . . . . to Kennebunkport
Returning, same route.

THROUGH RATES.

Baltimore, Md. . . . . $19 30 | Washington, D. C. $21 30
Philadelphia, Pa. 15 30

LAKE CHAMPLAIN.

Lake Champlain is a picturesque sheet of water lying between the States of New York and Vermont, and extends for a short distance into Canada. It is about one hundred and thirty miles in length and varies in breadth from half a mile to fifteen miles. This lake filling a valley inclosed by lofty mountains, is celebrated for its magnificent scenery, embracing the Green Mountains of Vermont on the east and the Adirondack Mountains of New York on the west. Its waters in some places are three hundred feet deep and abound with many varieties of fish. Not only are the shores of Lake Champlain attractive in themselves, but they contain many places of celebrity and historic interest. At the confluence of the outlet of Lake George with Lake Champlain, the ruins of old Fort Ticonderoga loom up upon a high rocky bluff. The remains of the fortress of Crown Point are still visible. The localities where Burgoyne held his council with the Indian tribes, and where Arnold and Carlton fought, are pointed out to the tourist. The naval battle in which Commodore Macdonough gained his signal victory over General Macomb and the British flotilla was fought off Plattsburgh, and many other points of nearly equal interest are within easy reach. Vermont's most beautiful city, Burlington, is located upon the eastern shore of the lake.

The Adirondacks, Au Sable Chasm, and other famous points full of interest to tourists are reached with facility from Port Kent on the western shore.

FORM EX. 268. ALBURGH SPRINGS, VT. AND RETURN.

Baltimore & Ohio R. R.	to Philadelphia.
Philadelphia & Reading R. R.	to Bound Brook.
Central R. R. of New Jersey	to New York.
New York Central & Hudson River R. R.	to Troy.
Fitchburg R. R.	to White Creek.
Bennington & Rutland R. R.	to Rutland.
Central Vermont R. R.	to Alburgh Springs

Returning, same route.

THROUGH RATES.

Baltimore, Md.	$22.90	Washington, D. C.	$24.90
Philadelphia, Pa.	18.90		

FORM EX. 269. ALBURGH SPRINGS, VT. AND RETURN.

Baltimore & Ohio R. R.	to Philadelphia
Philadelphia & Reading R. R.	to Bound Brook
Central R. R. of New Jersey	to New York.
West Shore R. R.	to Albany.
Delaware & Hudson R. R.	to Troy.
Fitchburg R. R.	to White Creek.
Bennington & Rutland R. R.	to Rutland.
Central Vermont R. R.	to Alburgh Springs.

Returning, same route.

Transfer through New York, in both directions, included.

THROUGH RATES.

Baltimore, Md.	$22.90	Washington, D. C.	$24.90
Philadelphia, Pa.	18.90		

FORM EX. 270.—ALBURGH SPRINGS, VT., AND RETURN.

Baltimore & Ohio R. R. . . . . to Philadelphia.
Philadelphia & Reading R. R. . . . . to Bound Brook.
Central R. R. of New Jersey . . . . to New York.
New York Central & Hudson River R. R. . . to Troy.
Delaware & Hudson R. R. . . . . to Rutland.
Central Vermont R. R. . . . . to Alburgh Springs.
            Returning, same route.

THROUGH RATES.
Baltimore, Md. . . . . . . $22 90 | Washington, D. C. . . . $24 90
| Philadelphia, Pa. 18 90

FORM EX. 273.—ALBURGH SPRINGS, VT., AND RETURN.

Baltimore & Ohio R. R. . . . . to Philadelphia.
Philadelphia & Reading R. R. . . . . to Bound Brook.
Central R. R. of New Jersey . . . . to New York.
West Shore R. R. to Albany.
Delaware & Hudson R. R. . . . . to Rutland.
Central Vermont R. R. . . . . to Alburgh Springs.
            Returning, same route.
    Transfer through New York, in both directions, included.

THROUGH RATES.
Baltimore, Md. . . . . . . $22 90 | Washington, D. C. . . . $24 90
| Philadelphia, Pa. 18 90

FORM EX. 713.—BLUFF POINT, N. Y. (HOTEL CHAMPLAIN), AND RETURN.

Baltimore & Ohio R. R. . . . . to Philadelphia.
Philadelphia & Reading R. R. . . . . to Bound Brook.
Central R. R. of New Jersey . . . . to New York.
New York & Albany Day Line . . . . to Albany.
Delaware & Hudson R. R. . . . . to Bluff Point.
            Returning, same route.

THROUGH RATES.
Baltimore, Md. . . . . . . $20 90 | Washington, D. C. . . . $22 90
| Philadelphia, Pa. 16 90

FORM EX. 714.—BLUFF POINT, N. Y. (HOTEL CHAMPLAIN), AND RETURN.

Baltimore & Ohio R. R. . . . . to Philadelphia.
Philadelphia & Reading R. R. . . . . to Bound Brook.
Central R. R. of New Jersey . . . . to New York.
New York Central & Hudson River R. R. . . to Troy.
Delaware & Hudson R. R. . . . . to Bluff Point.
            Returning, same route.

THROUGH RATES.
Baltimore, Md. . . . . . . $22 50 | Washington, D. C. . . . $24 50
| Philadelphia, Pa. 18 50

FORM EX. 1011.—BLUFF POINT (HOTEL CHAMPLAIN), N. Y., AND RETURN.

Baltimore & Ohio R. R. . . . . to Philadelphia.
Philadelphia & Reading R. R. . . . . to Bound Brook.
Central R. R. of New Jersey . . . . to New York.
West Shore R. R. to Albany.
Delaware & Hudson R. R. . . . . to Bluff Point.
            Returning, same route.
    Transfer through New York, in both directions, included.

THROUGH RATES.
Baltimore, Md. . . . . . . $22 50 | Washington, D. C. . . . $24 50
| Philadelphia, Pa. 18 50

ROUTES AND RATES FOR SUMMER TOURS. 145

FORM EX. 715. BLUFF POINT, N. Y. (HOTEL CHAMPLAIN), AND RETURN.

Baltimore & Ohio R. R. . . . . to Philadelphia.
Philadelphia & Reading R. R. . . . . to Bound Brook.
Central R. R. of New Jersey . . . . to New York.
People's Line. . . . . to Albany.
Delaware & Hudson R. R. . . . . to Bluff Point.

Returning, same route.

THROUGH RATES.

Baltimore, Md. . . . . . $19 90   Washington, D. C. $21 90
{Philadelphia, Pa. 15 90

FORM EX. 716. BLUFF POINT, N. Y. (HOTEL CHAMPLAIN), AND RETURN.

Baltimore & Ohio R. R. . . . . to Philadelphia.
Philadelphia & Reading R. R. . . . . to Bound Brook.
Central R. R. of New Jersey . . . . to New York.
New York Central & Hudson River R. R. . . . to Troy.
Fitchburg R. R. . . . . to White Creek.
Bennington & Rutland Ry . . . . to Rutland.
Central Vermont R. R. . . . . to Burlington.
Champlain Transportation Co. . . . . to Bluff Point.

Returning, same route.

THROUGH RATES.

Baltimore, Md. . . . . . $22 50   Washington, D. C. $24 50
{Philadelphia, Pa. 18 50

FORM EX. 1010.—BLUFF POINT (HOTEL CHAMPLAIN), N. Y., AND RETURN.

Baltimore & Ohio R. R. . . . . to Philadelphia.
Philadelphia & Reading R. R. . . . . to Bound Brook.
Central R. R. of New Jersey . . . . to New York.
New York, New Haven & Hartford R. R. . . . to Springfield.
Connecticut River R. R. . . . . to South Vernon.
Central Vermont R. R. . . . . to Brattleboro.
Vermont Valley R. R. . . . . to Windsor.
Central Vermont R. R. . . . . to Burlington.
Champlain Transportation Co. . . . . to Bluff Point.

Returning, same route.

THROUGH RATES.

Baltimore, Md. . . . . . $22 50   Washington, D. C. $24 50
{Philadelphia, Pa. 18 50

FORM EX. 285.—BURLINGTON, VT., AND RETURN.

Baltimore & Ohio R. R. . . . . to Philadelphia.
Philadelphia & Reading R. R. . . . . to Bound Brook.
Central R. R. of New Jersey . . . . to New York.
New York Central & Hudson River R. R. . . . to Troy.
Fitchburg R. R. . . . . to White Creek.
Bennington & Rutland R. R. . . . . to Rutland.
Central Vermont R. R. . . . . to Burlington.

Returning, same route.

THROUGH RATES.

Baltimore, Md. . . . . . $21 00   Washington, D. C. $23 00
{Philadelphia, Pa. 17 00

146   BALTIMORE & OHIO RAILROAD COMPANY

FORM EX. 286.—BURLINGTON, VT., AND RETURN.

Baltimore & Ohio R. R. . . . . to Philadelphia.
Philadelphia & Reading R. R. . . . . to Bound Brook.
Central R. R. of New Jersey . . . . to New York.
West Shore R. R. . . . . to Albany.
Delaware & Hudson R. R. . . . . to Troy.
Fitchburg R. R. to White Creek.
Bennington & Rutland R. R. . . . . to Rutland.
Central Vermont R. R. . . . . to Burlington.

Returning, same route.

Transfer through New York, in both directions, included.

THROUGH RATES.

Baltimore, Md. . . . . . . $21 00   Washington, D. C. $23 00
Philadelphia, Pa. 17 00

FORM EX. 287.—BURLINGTON, VT., AND RETURN.

Baltimore & Ohio R. R. . . . . to Philadelphia.
Philadelphia & Reading R. R. . . . . to Bound Brook.
Central R. R. of New Jersey . . . . to New York.
New York Central & Hudson River R. R. . . . to Troy.
Delaware & Hudson R. R. . . . . to Fort Ticonderoga.
Champlain Transportation Co. . . . . to Burlington.

Returning, same route.

THROUGH RATES.

Baltimore, Md. . . . . . . $21 00   Washington, D. C. $23 00
Philadelphia, Pa. 17 00

FORM EX. 288.—BURLINGTON, VT., AND RETURN.

Baltimore & Ohio R. R. . . . . to Philadelphia.
Philadelphia & Reading R. R. . . . . to Bound Brook.
Central R. R. of New Jersey . . . . to New York.
West Shore R. R. . . . . to Albany.
Delaware & Hudson R. R. . . . . to Fort Ticonderoga.
Champlain Transportation Co. . . . . to Burlington.

Returning, same route.

Transfer through New York, in both directions, included.

THROUGH RATES.

Baltimore, Md. . . . . . . $21 00   Washington, D. C. $23 00
Philadelphia, Pa. 17 00

FORM EX. 292.—BURLINGTON, VT., AND RETURN.

Baltimore & Ohio R. R. . . . . to Philadelphia.
Philadelphia & Reading R. R. . . . . to Bound Brook.
Central R. R. of New Jersey . . . . to New York.
New York Central & Hudson River R. R. . . . to Troy.
Delaware & Hudson R. R. . . . . to Rutland.
Central Vermont R. R. . . . . to Burlington.

Returning, same route.

THROUGH RATES.

Baltimore, Md. . . . . . . $21 00   Washington, D. C. $23 00
Philadelphia, Pa. 17 00

Form Ex. 297.—Burlington, Vt., and Return.

Baltimore & Ohio R. R. . . . . to Philadelphia.
Philadelphia & Reading R. R. . . . . to Bound Brook
Central R. R. of New Jersey . . . . to New York
West Shore R. R. . . . . to Albany.
Delaware & Hudson R. R. . . . . to Rutland.
Central Vermont R. R. . . . . to Burlington.

Returning, same route.
Transfer through New York, in both directions, included.

THROUGH RATES.

Baltimore, Md. . . . . . . $21 00   Washington, D. C. $23 00
Philadelphia, Pa. 17 00

Form Ex. 774.—Burlington, Vt., and Return.

Baltimore & Ohio R. R. . . . . to Philadelphia.
Philadelphia & Reading R. R. . . . . to Bound Brook.
Central R. R. of New Jersey . . . . to New York.
New York & Albany Day Line . . . . to Albany.
Delaware & Hudson R. R. . . . . to Rutland.
Central Vermont R. R. . . . . to Burlington.

Returning, same route.

THROUGH RATES.

Baltimore, Md. . . . . . . $19 50   Washington, D. C. $21 50
Philadelphia, Pa. 15 50

Form Ex. 775.—Burlington, Vt., and Return.

Baltimore & Ohio R. R. . . . . to Philadelphia.
Philadelphia & Reading R. R. . . . . to Bound Brook.
Central R. R. of New Jersey . . . . to New York.
New York & Albany Day Line . . . . to Albany.
Delaware & Hudson R. R. . . . . to Caldwell.
Champlain Transportation Co. (Lake George Strs.) to Baldwin.
Delaware & Hudson R. R. . . . . to Ft. Ticonderoga.
Champlain Transportation Co. . . . . to Burlington.
Champlain Transportation Co. . . . . to Ft. Ticonderoga.
Delaware & Hudson R. R. . . . . to Albany.
New York & Albany Day Line . . . . to New York.
Central R. R. of New Jersey . . . . to Bound Brook.
Philadelphia & Reading R. R. . . . . to Philadelphia.
Baltimore & Ohio R. R. . . . . to starting point.

THROUGH RATES.

Baltimore, Md. . . . . . . $21 00   Washington, D. C. $23 00
Philadelphia, Pa. 17 00

Form Ex. 776.—Burlington, Vt., and Return.

Baltimore & Ohio R. R. . . . . to Philadelphia.
Philadelphia & Reading R. R. . . . . to Bound Brook.
Central R. R. of New Jersey . . . . to New York.
People's Line Steamer . . . . to Albany.
Delaware & Hudson R. R. . . . . to Rutland.
Central Vermont R. R. . . . . to Burlington.

Returning, same route.

THROUGH RATES.

Baltimore, Md. . . . . . . $18 50   Washington, D. C. $20 50
Philadelphia, Pa. 14 50

FORM EX. 777.—BURLINGTON, VT., AND RETURN.

Baltimore & Ohio R. R.	to Philadelphia.
Philadelphia & Reading R. R.	to Bound Brook.
Central R. R. of New Jersey	to New York.
People's Line Steamer	to Albany.
Delaware & Hudson R. R.	to Caldwell.
Champlain Transportation Co. (Lake George Strs.)	to Baldwin.
Delaware & Hudson R. R.	to Ft. Ticonderoga.
Champlain Transportation Co.	to Burlington.
Champlain Transportation Co.	to Ft. Ticonderoga.
Delaware & Hudson R. R.	to Albany.
People's Line Steamer	to New York.
Central R. R. of New Jersey	to Bound Brook.
Philadelphia & Reading R. R.	to Philadelphia.
Baltimore & Ohio R. R.	to starting point.

THROUGH RATES.

Baltimore, Md. . . . . . $20 00   Washington, D. C. $22 00
†Philadelphia, Pa. 16 00

FORM EX. 778.—BURLINGTON, VT., AND RETURN.

Baltimore & Ohio R. R.	to Philadelphia.
Philadelphia & Reading R. R.	to Bound Brook.
Central R. R. of New Jersey	to New York.
New York Central & Hudson River R. R.	to Troy.
Delaware & Hudson R. R.	to Caldwell.
Champlain Transportation Co. (Lake George Strs.)	to Baldwin.
Delaware & Hudson R. R.	to Ft. Ticonderoga.
Champlain Transportation Co.	to Burlington.
Champlain Transportation Co.	to Ft. Ticonderoga.
Delaware & Hudson R. R.	to Troy.
New York Central & Hudson River R. R.	to New York.
Central R. R. of New Jersey	to Bound Brook.
Philadelphia & Reading R. R.	to Philadelphia.
Baltimore & Ohio R. R.	to starting point.

THROUGH RATES.

Baltimore, Md. . . . . . $22 50   Washington, D. C. $24 50
†Philadelphia, Pa. 18 50

FORM EX. 898.—BURLINGTON, VT., AND RETURN.

(Via Saratoga, Lake George, and Lake Champlain.)

Baltimore & Ohio R. R.	to Philadelphia.
Philadelphia & Reading R. R.	to Bound Brook.
Central R. R. of New Jersey	to New York.
West Shore R. R.	to Albany.
Delaware & Hudson R. R. (via Saratoga)	to Caldwell.
Champlain Transportation Co., Lake George Strs.	to Baldwin.
Delaware & Hudson R. R.	to Ft. Ticonderoga.
Champlain Transportation Co.	to Burlington.
Champlain Transportation Co.	to Ft. Ticonderoga.
Delaware & Hudson R. R.	to Albany.
West Shore R. R.	to New York.
Central R. R. of New Jersey	to Bound Brook.
Philadelphia & Reading R. R.	to Philadelphia.
Baltimore & Ohio R. R.	to starting point.

Transfer through New York, in both directions, included.

THROUGH RATES.

Baltimore, Md. . . . . . $22 50   Washington, D. C. $24 50
†Philadelphia, Pa. 18 50

FORM EX. 1025. BURLINGTON, VT., AND RETURN.

Baltimore & Ohio R. R.	to Philadelphia.
Philadelphia & Reading R. R.	to Bound Brook.
Central R. R. of New Jersey	to New York.
Day or People's Line Steamers	to Albany.
Delaware & Hudson R. R.	to Caldwell.
Champlain Transportation Co., Lake George Stmrs.	to Baldwin.
Delaware & Hudson R. R.	to Fort Ticonderoga.
Champlain Transportation Co.	to Burlington.
Central Vermont R. R.	to Montpelier.
Montpelier & Wells River R. R.	to Wells River.
Concord & Montreal R. R.	to Nashua Junction.
Boston & Maine R. R.	to Boston.
Rail or Sound Lines (see pages 50 to 55 for routes)	to Philadelphia.
Baltimore & Ohio R. R.	to starting point.

THROUGH RATES.

	Via Sound.	Via Rail.
Baltimore, Md.	$26 80	$27 80
Philadelphia, Pa.	22 80	23 80
Washington, D. C.	28 80	29 80

PLATTSBURGH, N. Y.

A beautiful town of about eight thousand inhabitants, situated on the west shore of Lake Champlain, at the mouth of the Saranac River. The Champlain Transportation Company's steamers ply daily between Fort Ticonderoga and Plattsburgh, and daily steamers cross the lake to St. Albans, a sail of twenty-five miles, and a most delightful trip.

FORM EX. 534. PLATTSBURGH, N. Y. AND RETURN.

Baltimore & Ohio R. R. . . . . to Philadelphia.
Philadelphia & Reading R. R. . . . . to Bound Brook.
Central R. R. of New Jersey . . . . to New York.
New York Central & Hudson River R. R. . . . to Troy.
Delaware & Hudson R. R. . . . . to Caldwell.
Champlain Transportation Co.(Lake George Strs.)to Baldwin.
Delaware & Hudson R. R. . . . . to Fort Ticonderoga.
Champlain Transportation Co. . . . . to Plattsburgh.

Returning, same route.

THROUGH RATES.

Baltimore, Md. . . . . . . $25 75 | Washington, D. C. . . . $27 75
†Philadelphia, Pa. . . . . 24 75 |

FORM EX. 754.—PLATTSBURGH, N. Y., AND RETURN.

Baltimore & Ohio R. R. . . . . to Philadelphia.
Philadelphia & Reading R. R. . . . . to Bound Brook.
Central R. R. of New Jersey . . . . to New York.
New York & Albany Day Line . . . . to Albany.
Delaware & Hudson R. R. . . . . to Plattsburgh.

Returning, same route.

THROUGH RATES.

Baltimore, Md. . . . . . . $21 10 | Washington, D. C. . . . $23 10
†Philadelphia, Pa. . . . . 17 10 |

FORM EX. 755. PLATTSBURGH, N. Y., AND RETURN.

Baltimore & Ohio R. R. . . . . to Philadelphia.
Philadelphia & Reading R. R. . . . . to Bound Brook.
Central R. R. of New Jersey . . . . to New York.
People's Line . . . . to Albany.
Delaware & Hudson R. R. . . . . to Plattsburgh.

Returning, same route.

THROUGH RATES.

Baltimore, Md. . . . . . . $20 10 | Washington, D. C. . . . $22 10
†Philadelphia, Pa. . . . . 16 10 |

FORM EX. 532.—PLATTSBURGH, N. Y., AND RETURN.

Baltimore & Ohio R. R. . . . . to Philadelphia.
Philadelphia & Reading R. R. . . . . to Bound Brook.
Central R. R. of New Jersey . . . . to New York.
New York Central & Hudson River R. R. . . . to Troy.
Delaware & Hudson R. R. . . . . to Plattsburg.

Returning, same route.

THROUGH RATES.

Baltimore, Md. . . . . . . $22 75 | Washington, D. C. . . . 24 75
†Philadelphia, Pa. . . . . 18 75 |

FORM EX. 533.—PLATTSBURGH, N. Y., AND RETURN.

Baltimore & Ohio R. R. . . . . to Philadelphia.
Philadelphia & Reading R. R. . . . . to Bound Brook.
Central R. R. of New Jersey . . . . to New York.
West Shore R. R. . . . . to Albany.
Delaware & Hudson R. R. . . . . to Plattsburg.

Returning, same route.

Transfer through New York, in both directions, included.

THROUGH RATES.

Baltimore, Md. . . . . . . $22 75 | Washington, D. C. . . . 24 75
†Philadelphia, Pa. . . . . 18 75 |

FORM EX. 534.—PLATTSBURGH, N. Y., AND RETURN.

Baltimore & Ohio R. R. . . . . to Philadelphia.
Philadelphia & Reading R. R. . . . . to Bound Brook.
Central R. R. of New Jersey . . . . to New York.
West Shore R. R. . . . . to Albany.
Delaware & Hudson R. R. . . . . to Caldwell.
Champlain Transportation Co. (Lake George Strs.) to Baldwin.
Delaware & Hudson R. R. . . . . to Fort Ticonderoga.
Champlain Transportation Co. . . . . to Plattsburgh.

Returning, same route.

Transfer through New York, in both directions, included.

THROUGH RATES.

Baltimore, Md. . . . . . . $25 75 | Washington, D. C. $27 75
Philadelphia, Pa. 24 75

FORM EX. 1012.—PLATTSBURGH, N. Y., AND RETURN.

(Via rail and Rutland in both directions.)

Baltimore & Ohio R. R. . . . . to Philadelphia.
Philadelphia & Reading R. R. . . . . to Bound Brook.
Central R. R. of New Jersey . . . . to New York.
New York Central & Hudson River R. R. . . . to Troy.
Fitchburg R. R. . . . . to White Creek.
Bennington & Rutland R. R. . . . . to Rutland.
Central Vermont R. R. . . . . to Burlington.
Champlain Transportation Co. . . . . to Plattsburgh.

Returning, same route.

THROUGH RATES.

Baltimore, Md. . . . . . . $22 75 | Washington, D. C. $24 75
Philadelphia, Pa. 18 75

FORM EX. 1013.—PLATTSBURGH, N. Y., AND RETURN.

(Via rail and Connecticut River Line in both directions.)

Baltimore & Ohio R. R. . . . . to Philadelphia.
Philadelphia & Reading R. R. . . . . to Bound Brook.
Central R. R. of New Jersey . . . . to New York.
New York, New Haven & Hartford R. R. . . . to Springfield.
Connecticut River R. R. . . . . to South Vernon.
Central Vermont R. R. . . . . to Brattleboro.
Vermont Valley R. R. . . . . to Windsor.
Central Vermont R. R. . . . . to Burlington.
Champlain Transportation Co. . . . . to Plattsburgh.

Returning, same route.

THROUGH RATES.

Baltimore, Md. . . . . . . $22 75 | Washington, D. C. $24 75
Philadelphia, Pa. 18 75

FORM EX. 1014.—PLATTSBURGH, N. Y., AND RETURN.

(Via West Shore Route, Saratoga and Lakes George and Champlain; returning via Saratoga and West Shore route direct.)

Baltimore & Ohio R. R. . . . . to Philadelphia.
Philadelphia & Reading R. R. . . . . to Bound Brook.
Central R. R. of New Jersey . . . . to New York.
West Shore R. R. . . . . to Albany.
Delaware & Hudson R. R. . . . . to Caldwell.
Champlain Transportation Co. (Lake George Strs.) to Baldwin.

Delaware & Hudson R. R. . . . . to Fort Ticonderoga.
Delaware & Hudson R. R. or Champlain Trans-
　　portation Co. . . . . to Plattsburgh.
Delaware & Hudson R. R. . . . . to Albany.
West Shore R. R. to New York.
Central R. R. of New Jersey . . . . to Bound Brook.
Philadelphia & Reading R. R. . . . . to Philadelphia.
Baltimore & Ohio R. R. . . . . to starting point.
　　Transfer through New York, in both directions, included.

THROUGH RATES.

Baltimore, Md. . . . . . . $24 25 ｜ Washington, D. C. $26 25
‡Philadelphia, Pa. . . . . 20 25 ｜

FORM EX. 1016.—PLATTSBURGH, N. Y., AND RETURN.

(Via New York, Saratoga and Lakes George and Champlain; returning all rail direct.)

Baltimore & Ohio R. R. . . . . to Philadelphia.
Philadelphia & Reading R. R. . . . . to Bound Brook.
Central R. R. of New Jersey. . . . . to New York.
New York Central and Hudson River R. R. . . to Troy.
Delaware & Hudson R. R. . . . . to Caldwell.
Champlain Transportation Co. (Lake George Strs.) to Baldwin.
Delaware & Hudson R. R. . . . . to Fort Ticonderoga.
Delaware & Hudson R. R. or Cham. Trans. Co. . to Plattsburgh.
Delaware & Hudson R. R. . . . . to Troy.
New York Central & Hudson River R. R. . . . to New York.
Central R. R. of New Jersey. . . . . to Bound Brook.
Philadelphia & Reading R. R. . . . . to Philadelphia.
Baltimore & Ohio R. R. . . . . to starting point.

FORM EX. 1017.—PLATTSBURGH, N. Y., AND RETURN.

Reverse of preceding excursion.

THROUGH RATES.

Baltimore, Md. . . . . . . $24 25 ｜ Washington, D. C. $26 25
‡Philadelphia, Pa. . . . . 20 25 ｜

FORM EX. 1018.—PLATTSBURGH, N. Y., AND RETURN.

(Via New York, Hudson River Steamers, Saratoga, and Lakes George
and Champlain; returning via Saratoga, Hudson River
Steamers and New York direct.)

Baltimore & Ohio R. R. . . . . to Philadelphia.
Philadelphia & Reading R. R. . . . . to Bound Brook.
Central R. R. of New Jersey. . . . . to New York.
Day or People's Line Steamers. . . . . to Albany.
Delaware & Hudson R. R. . . . . to Caldwell.
Champlain Trans. Co. (Lake George Strs.) . . to Baldwin.
Delaware & Hudson R. R. . . . . to Fort Ticonderoga.
Delaware & Hudson R. R. or Cham. Trans. Co. . to Plattsburgh.
Delaware & Hudson R. R. . . . . to Albany.
Day or People's Line Steamers. . . . . to New York.
Central R. R. of New Jersey. . . . . to Bound Brook.
Philadelphia & Reading R. R. . . . . to Philadelphia.
Baltimore & Ohio R. R. . . . . to starting point.

FORM EX. 1019.—PLATTSBURGH, N. Y., AND RETURN.

Reverse of preceding excursion.

THROUGH RATES.

Baltimore, Md. . . . . . . $22 00 ｜ Washington, D. C. $24 00
‡Philadelphia, Pa. . . . . 18 00 ｜

FORM EX. 1020.—PLATTSBURGH, N. Y., AND RETURN.
(Via rail; returning via Hudson River.)

Baltimore & Ohio R. R. . . . . to Philadelphia.
Philadelphia & Reading R. R. . . . . to Bound Brook.
Central R. R. of New Jersey . . . . to New York.
New York Central & Hudson River R. R. . . . to Troy.
Delaware & Hudson R. R. . . . . to Plattsburgh.
Delaware & Hudson R. R. . . . . to Albany.
Day or People's Line Steamers . . . . to New York.
Central R. R. of New Jersey . . . . to Bound Brook.
Philadelphia & Reading R. R. . . . . to Philadelphia.
Baltimore & Ohio R. R. . . . . to starting point.

FORM EX. 1021.—PLATTSBURGH, N. Y., AND RETURN.
Reverse of preceding excursion.

THROUGH RATES.

Baltimore, Md. . . . . $22 40 | Washington, D. C. $24 40
Philadelphia, Pa. . . . 18 40

FORM EX. 1022.—PLATTSBURGH, N. Y., AND RETURN.
(Via rail; returning via Hudson River.)

Baltimore & Ohio R. R. . . . . to Philadelphia.
Philadelphia & Reading R. R. . . . . to Bound Brook.
Central R. R. of New Jersey . . . . to New York.
West Shore R. R. . . . . to Albany.
Delaware & Hudson R. R. . . . . to Plattsburgh.
Delaware & Hudson R. R. . . . . to Albany.
Day or People's Line Steamers . . . . to New York.
Central R. R. of New Jersey . . . . to Bound Brook.
Philadelphia & Reading R. R. . . . . to Philadelphia.
Baltimore & Ohio R. R. . . . . to starting point.

Transfer through New York, going, included.

FORM EX. 1023.—PLATTSBURGH, N. Y., AND RETURN.
Reverse of preceding excursion.
Transfer through New York, returning, included.

THROUGH RATES.

Baltimore, Md. . . . . $22 40 | Washington, D. C. $24 40
Philadelphia, Pa. . . . 18 40

FORM EX. 1024.—PLATTSBURGH, N. Y., AND RETURN.

Baltimore & Ohio R. R. . . . . to Philadelphia.
Philadelphia & Reading R. R. . . . . to Bound Brook.
Central R. R. of New Jersey . . . . to New York.
Day or People's Line Steamers . . . . to Albany.
Delaware & Hudson R. R. . . . . to Caldwell.
Champlain Transportation Co.(Lake George Strs. to Baldwin.
Delaware & Hudson R. R. . . . . to Ft. Ticonderoga.
Champlain Transportation Co. . . . . to Plattsburgh.
Champlain Transportation Co. . . . . to Burlington.
Central Vermont R. R. . . . . to Montpelier.
Montpelier & Wells River R. R. . . . . to Wells River.
Concord & Montreal R. R. . . . . to Nashua.
Boston & Maine R. R. . . . . to Boston.
Rail or Sound Lines (see pages 50 to 55 for route) to Philadelphia.
Baltimore & Ohio R. R. . . . . to starting point.

THROUGH RATES.
                              Via Sound. Via Rail.
Baltimore, Md. $27 95 $28 95
Philadelphia, Pa. 23 95   24 95
Washington, D. C. 29 95   30 95

LAKE GEORGE.

This lake, which is four hundred and thirty miles from Washington, is a picturesque sheet of water in Warren and Washington counties, N. Y. It is three hundred and forty-six feet above sea-level, is about thirty-five miles long and from three-quarters of a mile to four miles wide. It is the most famous and popular of American lakes, and deservedly so. With the varied scenery on its banks —

here precipitous hills, with their wooded crests fading in the distance; there rugged cliffs lifting high their massive and time-worn bulks above the clear depths of the placid lake; smiling valleys hollowed out between the hills, revealing the proud majesty of more distant heights and the enchanting multitude of tiny islets (said to equal in number the days of the year) lying on its surface—one feels transported with the sublimity of the scene.

Many magnificent hotels, superior boarding-houses and summer homes are to be seen on every island and along the borders of the lake. Custom long since made it a condition binding upon those who visited Saratoga to spend some part of the season at Lake George, and hence it is that one in his rambles about Lake George meets so many faces that were familiar to him in Saratoga. Until within a year or two past the journey between Saratoga and Lake George was accomplished partly by rail and partly by stage-coach or carriage; but this has been superseded by the more advanced, civilized and comfortable method of travel by rail, for the iron bands of the Delaware & Hudson Canal Co. R. R. now cement and unite in a closer union these twin sisters of revolutionary renown. A sail over the lake between Caldwell and Baldwin is one of the most delightful episodes of a trip to Lake George, in contrast with which there is nothing more replete with charming reminiscences.

FORM EX. 315.—BALDWIN (LAKE GEORGE), N. Y., AND RETURN.

Baltimore & Ohio R. R.	to Philadelphia.
Philadelphia & Reading R. R.	to Bound Brook.
Central R. R. of New Jersey	to New York.
New York Central & Hudson River R. R.	to Troy.
Delaware & Hudson R. R.	to Caldwell.
Champlain Transportation Co., Lake George Str.	to Baldwin.
Delaware & Hudson R. R.	to Troy.
New York Central & Hudson River R. R.	to New York.
Central R. R. of New Jersey	to Bound Brook.
Philadelphia & Reading R. R.	to Philadelphia.
Baltimore & Ohio R. R.	to starting point.

THROUGH RATES.

Baltimore, Md.	$21 00	Washington, D. C.	$23 00
Philadelphia, Pa.	17 00		

FORM EX. 315.—BALDWIN (LAKE GEORGE), N. Y., AND RETURN.

Baltimore & Ohio R. R. . . . . to Philadelphia.
Philadelphia & Reading R. R. . . . . to Bound Brook.
Central R. R. of New Jersey . . . . to New York.
West Shore R. R. . . . . to Albany.
Delaware & Hudson R. R. . . . . to Caldwell.
Champlain Transportation Co. (Lake George Strs.) to Baldwin.
Delaware & Hudson R. R. . . . . to Albany.
West Shore R. R. . . . . to New York.
Central R. R. of New Jersey . . . . to Bound Brook.
Philadelphia & Reading R. R. . . . . to Philadelphia.
Baltimore & Ohio R. R. . . . . to starting point.

Transfer through New York, in both directions, included.

THROUGH RATES.

Baltimore, Md. . . . . . $21 00   Washington, D. C. $23 00
Philadelphia, Pa. 17 00

FORM EX. 316.—CALDWELL (LAKE GEORGE), N. Y., AND RETURN.

Baltimore & Ohio R. R. . . . . to Philadelphia.
Philadelphia & Reading R. R. . . . . to Bound Brook.
Central R. R. of New Jersey . . . . to New York.
New York Central & Hudson River R. R. . . . . to Troy.
Delaware & Hudson R. R. . . . . to Baldwin.
Champlain Transportation Co. (Lake George Strs.) to Caldwell.
Delaware & Hudson R. R. . . . . to Troy.
New York Central & Hudson River R. R. . . . . to New York.
Central R. R. of New Jersey . . . . to Bound Brook.
Philadelphia & Reading R. R. . . . . to Philadelphia.
Baltimore & Ohio R. R. . . . . to starting point.

THROUGH RATES.

Baltimore, Md. . . . . . $21 00   Washington, D. C. $23 00
Philadelphia, Pa. 17 00

FORM EX. 317.—CALDWELL (LAKE GEORGE), N. Y., AND RETURN.

Baltimore & Ohio R. R. . . . . to Philadelphia.
Philadelphia & Reading R. R. . . . . to Bound Brook.
Central R. R. of New Jersey . . . . to New York.
West Shore R. R. . . . . to Albany.
Delaware & Hudson R. R. . . . . to Baldwin.
Champlain Transportation Co. (Lake George Strs.) to Caldwell.
Delaware & Hudson R. R. . . . . to Albany.
West Shore R. R. . . . . to New York.
Central R. R. of New Jersey . . . . to Bound Brook.
Philadelphia & Reading R. R. . . . . to Philadelphia.
Baltimore & Ohio R. R. . . . . to starting point.

Transfer through New York, in both directions, included.

THROUGH RATES.

Baltimore, Md. . . . . . $21 00   Washington, D. C. $23 00
Philadelphia, Pa. 17 00

FORM EX. 318.—CALDWELL (LAKE GEORGE), N. Y., AND RETURN.

Baltimore & Ohio R. R. . . . . to Philadelphia.
Philadelphia & Reading R. R. . . . . to Bound Brook.
Central R. R. of New Jersey . . . . to New York.
New York Central & Hudson River R. R. . . . . to Troy.
Delaware & Hudson R. R. . . . . to Caldwell.

Returning, same route.

THROUGH RATES.

Baltimore, Md. . . . . . $18 05   Washington, D. C. $20 05
Philadelphia, Pa. 14 05

FORM EX. 716. CALDWELL (LAKE GEORGE), N. Y., AND RETURN.

Baltimore & Ohio R. R. . . . . to Philadelphia.
Philadelphia & Reading R. R. . . . . to Bound Brook.
Central R. R. of New Jersey . . . . to New York.
People's Line . . . . to Albany.
Delaware & Hudson R. R. . . . . to Caldwell.
　　　　　　Returning, same route.

THROUGH RATES.

Baltimore, Md. . . . . $15 10 | Washington, D.C. $17 10
{Philadelphia, Pa. . . . . . 11 10 |

FORM EX. 717.—CALDWELL (LAKE GEORGE), N. Y., AND RETURN.

Baltimore & Ohio R. R. . . . . to Philadelphia.
Philadelphia & Reading R. R. . . . . to Bound Brook.
Central R. R. of New Jersey . . . . to New York.
Citizens' Steamboat Company . . . . to Troy.
Delaware & Hudson R. R. . . . . to Caldwell.
　　　　　　Returning, same route.

THROUGH RATES.

Baltimore, Md. . . . . $15 05 | Washington, D.C. $17 05
{Philadelphia, Pa. . . . . . 11 05 |

FORM EX. 519. CALDWELL (LAKE GEORGE), N. Y., AND RETURN.

Baltimore & Ohio R. R. . . . . to Philadelphia.
Philadelphia & Reading R. R. . . . . to Bound Brook.
Central R. R. of New Jersey . . . . to New York.
West Shore R. R. . . . . to Albany.
Delaware & Hudson R. R. . . . . to Caldwell.
　　　　　　Returning, same route.

Transfer through New York, in both directions, included.

THROUGH RATES.

Baltimore, Md. . . . . $18 05 | Washington, D.C. $20 05
{Philadelphia, Pa. . . . . . 11 05 |

FORM EX. 614.—CALDWELL (LAKE GEORGE), N. Y., AND RETURN.

Baltimore & Ohio R. R. . . . . to Philadelphia.
Philadelphia & Reading R. R. . . . . to Bound Brook.
Central R. R. of New Jersey . . . . to New York.
New York & Albany Day Line . . . . to Albany.
Delaware & Hudson R. R. . . . . to Caldwell.
　　　　　　Returning, same route.

THROUGH RATES.

Baltimore, Md. . . . . $16 10 | Washington, D.C. $18 10
{Philadelphia, Pa. . . . . . 12 10 |

FORM EX. 1026.—LAKE GEORGE, N. Y.

Lake George, Lake Champlain and Fort Ticonderoga, N. Y., and return from Saratoga. Tourists purchasing Excursion Tickets to Saratoga Springs, N. Y., can visit Lake George, Lake Champlain and Fort Ticonderoga by purchasing in addition the following ticket:

Delaware & Hudson R. R. . . . . Saratoga to Caldwell.
Champlain Transportation Co. (Lake George Strs.) to Baldwin.
Delaware & Hudson R. R. . . . . to Saratoga.

FORM EX. 1027. LAKE GEORGE, N. Y.
　　　　　Reverse of preceding excursion.

Rate $5 50

LAKE HOPATCONG, N. J.

FORM EX. 654.—LAKE HOPATCONG, N. J., AND RETURN.

Baltimore & Ohio R. R. . . . . to Philadelphia.
Philadelphia & Reading R. R. . . . . to Bound Brook.
Central R. R. of New Jersey . . . . to Lake Hopatcong.

Returning, same route.

THROUGH RATES.

Baltimore, Md. . . . . . . $8 75 | Washington, D. C. $10 75
Philadelphia, Pa. . . . . . 4 75 |

LAKE MINNEWASKA, N. Y.

FORM EX. 320.—LAKE MINNEWASKA, N. Y., AND RETURN.

Baltimore & Ohio R. R. . . . . to Philadelphia.
Philadelphia & Reading R. R. . . . . to Bound Brook.
Central R. R. of New Jersey . . . . to New York.
West Shore R. R. . . . . to Kingston.
Wallkill Valley R. R. . . . . to New Paltz.
Smiley's Stage Line . . . . to Lake Minnewaska.

Returning, same route.

Transfer through New York, in both directions, included.

THROUGH RATES.

Baltimore, Md. . . . . . . $14 90 | Washington, D. C. $16 90
Philadelphia, Pa. . . . . . 10 90 |

FORM EX. 321.—LAKE MINNEWASKA, N. Y., AND RETURN.

Baltimore & Ohio R. R. . . . . to Philadelphia.
Philadelphia & Reading R. R. . . . . to Bound Brook.
Central R. R. of New Jersey . . . . to New York.
New York, Lake Erie & Western R. R. . . . . . . to Montgomery.
Wallkill Valley R. R. . . . . to New Paltz.
Smiley's Stage Line . . . . to Lake Minnewaska.

Returning, same route.

THROUGH RATES.

Baltimore, Md. . . . . . . $14 90 | Washington, D. C. $16 90
Philadelphia, Pa. . . . . . 10 90 |

FORM EX. 872.—LAKE MINNEWASKA, N. Y., AND RETURN.

Baltimore & Ohio R. R. . . . . to Philadelphia.
Philadelphia & Reading R. R. . . . . to Bethlehem.
Central R. R. of New Jersey . . . . to Easton.
Lehigh & Hudson River R. R. . . . . to Belvidere.
Lehigh & Hudson River R. R. . . . . to Maybrook.
Central New England & Western R. R. . . . . . to Loyd.
Smiley's Stage Line . . . . to Lake Minnewaska.

Returning, same route.

THROUGH RATES.

Baltimore, Md. . . . . . . $14 90 | Washington, D. C. $16 90
Philadelphia, Pa. . . . . . 10 90 |

Smiley's stage will meet trains at Loyd upon notification of Mr. A. K. Smiley, at Mohonk Lake, Ulster Co., N. Y., either by mail or telegraph.

TABLE ROCK, LAKE MOHONK.

LAKE MOHONK.

The Shawangunk Mountains are a sharp, narrow range, midway between the Catskills and the Highlands, extending in a southwesterly direction from Kingston, N. Y., for a distance of thirty miles into the northern portion of New Jersey. Mohonk Lake is located near the summit of Sky-Top, one of the highest of these mountains in Ulster County, N. Y., and is about fifteen miles west of Poughkeepsie on the Hudson, and six miles from New Paltz, a station on the Wallkill Valley Railroad.

FORM EX. 322. LAKE MOHONK, N. Y., AND RETURN.

Baltimore & Ohio R. R. . . . . to Philadelphia.
Philadelphia & Reading R. R. . . . . to Bound Brook.
Central R. R. of New Jersey. . . . . to New York
West Shore R. R. . . . . to Kingston.
Wallkill Valley R. R. . . . . to New Paltz.
Smiley's Stage Line . . . . to Lake Mohonk.

Returning, same route.

Transfer through New York, in both directions, included.

160 BALTIMORE & OHIO RAILROAD COMPANY

THROUGH RATES.

Baltimore, Md. . . . . . . $14 40 | Washington, D. C. $16 40
|Philadelphia, Pa. . . . . 10 40 |

FORM EX. 323.—LAKE MOHONK, N. Y., AND RETURN.

Baltimore & Ohio R. R. . . . . to Philadelphia.
Philadelphia & Reading R. R. . . . . to Bound Brook.
Central R. R. of New Jersey. . . . . to New York.
New York, Lake Erie & Western R. R. . . . . . to Montgomery.
Wallkill Valley R. R. . . . . to New Paltz.
Smiley's Stage Line. . . . . to Lake Mohonk.
                 Returning, same route.

THROUGH RATES.

Baltimore, Md. . . . . . . $14 40 | Washington, D. C. $16 40
|Philadelphia, Pa. . . . . 10 40 |

FORM EX. 873.—LAKE MOHONK, N. Y., AND RETURN.

Baltimore & Ohio R. R. . . . . to Philadelphia.
Philadelphia & Reading R. R. . . . . to Bethlehem.
Central R. R. of New Jersey. . . . . to Easton.
Lehigh & Hudson River R. R. . . . . to Belvidere.
Lehigh & Hudson River R. R. . . . . to Maybrook.
Central New England & Western R. R. . . . . . to Loyd.
Smiley's Stage Line. . . . . to Lake Mohonk.
                 Returning, same route.

THROUGH RATES.

Baltimore, Md. . . . . . . $14 40 | Washington, D. C. $16 40
|Philadelphia, Pa. . . . . 10 40 |

Smiley's stage will meet trains at Loyd upon notification of Mr. A. K. Smiley, at Mohonk Lake, Ulster Co., N. Y., either by mail or telegraph.

LANCASTER, N. H.

FORM EX. 1028.—LANCASTER, N. H., AND RETURN.

(Via rail to Lancaster, N. H.; returning by same route to Boston, thence via Sound Lines from Boston.)

Baltimore & Ohio R. R. . . . . to Philadelphia.
Rail Lines (see pages 50 to 55 for route) . . . . to Boston.
Boston & Maine R. R. . . . . to North Conway.
Maine Central R. R. . . . . to Lancaster.
Maine Central R. R. . . . . to North Conway.
Boston & Maine R. R. . . . . to Boston.
Sound Lines (see pages 50 to 55 for route) . . . to New York.
Central R. R. of New Jersey. . . . . to Bound Brook.
Philadelphia & Reading R. R. . . . . to Philadelphia.
Baltimore & Ohio R. R. . . . . to starting point.

THROUGH RATES.

Baltimore, Md. . . . . . . $26 15 | Washington, D. C. $28 15
|Philadelphia, Pa. . . . . 22 15 |
     Transfer through Boston, returning, included.

FORM EX. 1028.—LANCASTER, N. H., AND RETURN.

(Via Sound Lines to Boston, rail to Lancaster, N. H.; returning by same route to Boston, thence via rail.)

Baltimore & Ohio R. R. . . . . to Philadelphia.
Philadelphia & Reading R. R. . . . . to Bound Brook.
Central R. R. of New Jersey. . . . . to New York.
Sound Lines (see pages 50 to 55 for route) . . . to Boston.

ROUTES AND RATES FOR SUMMER TOURS. 161

Boston & Maine R. R. . . . . to North Conway.
Maine Central R. R. . . . . to Lancaster.
Maine Central R. R. . . . . to North Conway.
Boston & Maine R. R. . . . . to Boston.
Rail Lines (see pages 50 to 55 for route) . . . . . . to Philadelphia.
Baltimore & Ohio R. R. . . . . to starting point.

THROUGH RATES.

Baltimore, Md. . . . . $26 45 | Washington, D. C. $28 45
(Philadelphia, Pa. . . . . 22 45 |

Transfer through Boston, going, included.

FORM EX. 1028.—LANCASTER, N. H., AND RETURN.

(Via Rail Lines to Lancaster, N. H., in both directions.)

Baltimore & Ohio R. R. . . . . to Philadelphia.
Rail Lines (see pages 50 to 55 for route) . . . . . . to Boston.
Boston & Maine R. R. . . . . to North Conway.
Maine Central R. R. . . . . to Lancaster.

Returning, same route.

THROUGH RATES.

Baltimore, Md. . . . . $28 50 | Washington, D. C. $30 70
(Philadelphia, Pa. . . . . 24 50 |

FORM EX. 1028.—LANCASTER, N. H., AND RETURN.

(Via Sound Lines to Boston, rail to Lancaster, N. H., and return to Boston, thence via Sound Lines.)

Baltimore & Ohio R. R. . . . . to Philadelphia.
Philadelphia & Reading R. R. . . . . to Bound Brook.
Central R. R. of New Jersey . . . . to New York.
Sound Lines (see pages 50 to 55 for route) . . . . to Boston.
Boston & Maine R. R. . . . . to North Conway.
Maine Central R. R. . . . . to Lancaster.

Returning, same route.

THROUGH RATES.

Baltimore, Md. . . . . $25 30 | Washington, D. C. $25 30
(Philadelphia, Pa. . . . . 19 30 |

Transfer through Boston, in both directions, included.

FORM EX. 1029.—LANCASTER, N. H., AND RETURN.

(Via rail to Lancaster, N. H.; returning by same route to Boston, thence via Sound Lines from Boston.)

Baltimore & Ohio R. R. . . . . to Philadelphia.
Rail Lines (see pages 50 to 55 for route) . . . . . . to Boston.
Boston & Maine R. R. . . . . to Portland.
Maine Central R. R. . . . . to Lancaster.
Maine Central R. R. . . . . to Portland.
Boston & Maine R. R. . . . . to Boston.
Sound Lines (see pages 50 to 55 for route) . . . . to New York.
Central R. R. of New Jersey . . . . to Bound Brook.
Philadelphia & Reading R. R. . . . . to Philadelphia.
Baltimore & Ohio R. R. . . . . to starting point.

THROUGH RATES.

Baltimore, Md. . . . . $26 45 | Washington, D. C. $28 45
(Philadelphia, Pa. . . . . 22 45 |

Transfer through Boston, returning, included.

FORM EX. 1029. LANCASTER, N. H., AND RETURN.

(Via Sound Lines to Boston, rail to Lancaster, N. H.; returning by same route to Boston, thence via rail.)

Baltimore & Ohio R. R. . . . . to Philadelphia.
Philadelphia & Reading R. R. . . . . to Bound Brook.
Central R. R. of New Jersey . . . . to New York.
Sound Lines (see pages 50 to 55 for route). . . . to Boston.
Boston & Maine R. R. . . . . to Portland.
Maine Central R. R. . . . . to Lancaster.
Maine Central R. R. . . . . to Portland.
Boston & Maine R. R. . . . . to Boston.
Rail Lines (see pages 50 to 55 for route) . . . . to Philadelphia.
Baltimore & Ohio R. R. . . . . to starting point.

THROUGH RATES.

Baltimore, Md. . . . . . $26 45 | Washington, D. C. $28 45
†Philadelphia, Pa. . . . . 22 45 |

Transfer through Boston, going, included.

FORM EX. 1029. LANCASTER, N. H., AND RETURN.

(Via Rail Lines to Lancaster, N. H., in both directions.)

Baltimore & Ohio R. R. . . . . to Philadelphia.
Rail Lines (see pages 50 to 55 for route) . . . . to Boston.
Boston & Maine R. R. . . . . to Portland.
Maine Central R. R. . . . . to Lancaster.

Returning, same route.

THROUGH RATES.

Baltimore, Md. . . . . . $28 50 | Washington, D. C. $30 50
†Philadelphia, Pa. . . . . 24 50 |

FORM EX. 1029. LANCASTER, N. H., AND RETURN.

(Via Sound Lines to Boston, rail to Lancaster, N. H., and return to Boston, thence via Sound Lines.)

Baltimore & Ohio R. R. . . . . to Philadelphia.
Philadelphia & Reading R. R. . . . . to Bound Brook.
Central R. R. of New Jersey . . . . to New York.
Sound Lines (see pages 50 to 55 for route). . . . to Boston.
Boston & Maine R. R. . . . . to Portland.
Maine Central R. R. . . . . to Lancaster.

Returning, same route.

THROUGH RATES.

Baltimore, Md. . . . . . $23 50 | Washington, D. C. $25 50
†Philadelphia, Pa. . . . . 19 50 |

Transfer through Boston, in both directions, included.

FORM EX. 1029. LANCASTER, N. H., AND RETURN.

(Via rail and Boston; returning by Sound Lines.)

Baltimore & Ohio R. R. . . . . to Philadelphia.
Rail Lines (see pages 50 to 55 for route) . . . . to Boston.
Boston & Maine R. R. . . . . to Nashua.
Concord & Montreal R. R. . . . . to Lancaster.
Concord & Montreal R. R. . . . . to Nashua.
Boston & Maine R. R. . . . . to Boston.
Sound Lines (see pages 50 to 55 for route). . . . to New York.
Central R. R. of New Jersey . . . . to Bound Brook.
Philadelphia & Reading R. R. . . . . to Philadelphia.
Baltimore & Ohio R. R. . . . . to starting point.

THROUGH RATES.

Baltimore, Md. . . . . . $26 45 | Washington, D. C. $28 45
†Philadelphia, Pa. . . . . 22 45 |

Transfer through Boston, returning, included.

FORM EX. 1030. — LANCASTER, N. H., AND RETURN.

(Via Sound Lines and Boston; returning all rail.)

Baltimore & Ohio R. R. . . . . to Philadelphia.
Sound Lines (see pages 50 to 55 for routes) . . . . to Boston.
Boston & Maine R. R. . . . . to Nashua.
Concord & Montreal R. R. . . . . to Lancaster.
Concord & Montreal R. R. . . . . to Nashua.
Boston & Maine R. R. . . . . to Boston.
Rail Lines (see pages 50 to 55 for routes) . . . . . to Philadelphia.
Baltimore & Ohio R. R. . . . . to starting point.

THROUGH RATES.

Baltimore, Md. . . . . . . $26 45 | Washington, D. C. $28 45
†Philadelphia, Pa. . . . . 22 45 |

Transfer through Boston, going, included.

FORM EX. 1030. — LANCASTER, N. H., AND RETURN.

(Via Rail Lines and Boston in both directions.)

Baltimore & Ohio R. R. . . . . to Philadelphia.
Rail Lines (see pages 50 to 55 for routes) . . . . . to Boston.
Boston & Maine R. R. . . . . to Nashua.
Concord & Montreal R. R. . . . . to Lancaster.

Returning, same route.

THROUGH RATES.

Baltimore, Md. . . . . . . $28 50 | Washington, D. C. $30 50
†Philadelphia, Pa. . . . . 24 50 |

FORM EX. 1030. — LANCASTER, N. H., AND RETURN.

(Via Sound Lines and Boston in both directions.)

Baltimore & Ohio R. R. . . . . to Philadelphia.
Philadelphia & Reading R. R. . . . . to Bound Brook.
Central R. R. of New Jersey. . . . . to New York.
Sound Lines (see pages 50 to 55 for routes) . . . . to Boston.
Boston & Maine R. R. . . . . to Nashua.
Concord & Montreal R. R. . . . . to Lancaster.

Returning, same route.

THROUGH RATES.

Baltimore, Md. . . . . . . 23 50 | Washington, D. C. $25 50
†Philadelphia, Pa. . . . . $19 50 |

Transfer through Boston, in both directions, included.

FORM EX. 1031. — LANCASTER, N. H., AND RETURN.

(Via New York, Springfield and Wells River in both directions.)

Baltimore & Ohio R. R. . . . . to Philadelphia.
Philadelphia & Reading R. R. . . . . to Bound Brook.
Central R. R. of New Jersey . . . . to New York.
New York, New Haven & Hartford R. R. . . . . to Springfield.
Connecticut River R. R. . . . . to South Vernon.
Central Vermont R. R. . . . . to Brattleboro.
Vermont Valley R. R. . . . . to Windsor.
Central Vermont R. R. . . . . to White River June.
Boston & Maine R. R. . . . . to Wells River.
Concord & Montreal R. R. . . . . to Lancaster.

Returning, same route.

THROUGH RATES.

Baltimore, Md. . . . . . . $25 00 | Washington, D. C. $27 00
†Philadelphia, Pa. . . . . 21 00 |

FORM EX. 1032.—LANCASTER, N. H., AND RETURN.

(Via New York, Springfield and Boston.)

Baltimore & Ohio R. R. . . . . to Philadelphia.
Philadelphia & Reading R. R. . . . . to Bound Brook.
Central R. R. of New Jersey . . . . to New York.
New York, New Haven & Hartford R. R. . . . . to Springfield.
Connecticut River R. R. . . . . to South Vernon.
Central Vermont R. R. . . . . to Brattleboro.
Vermont Valley R. R. to Windsor.
Central Vermont R. R. . . . . to White River Junc.
Boston & Maine R. R. . . . . to Wells River.
Concord & Montreal R. R. . . . . to Lancaster.
Concord & Montreal R. R. . . . . to Nashua.
Boston & Maine R. R. . . . . to Boston.
Rail or Sound Lines (see pages 50 to 55 for route) to Philadelphia.
Baltimore & Ohio R. R. . . . . to starting point.

FORM EX. 1033.—LANCASTER, N. H., AND RETURN.

Reverse of preceding excursion.

THROUGH RATES.

	Via Sound.	Via Rail.
Baltimore, Md.	$25 00	$27 15
Philadelphia, Pa.	21 00	23 15
Washington, D. C.	27 00	29 15

Transfer through Boston included via Sound Lines only.

LA PORTE, PA.

FORM EX. 569.—LA PORTE, PA., AND RETURN.

Baltimore & Ohio R. R. . . . . to Philadelphia.
Philadelphia & Reading R. R. . . . . to Halls.
Williamsport & North Branch R. R. . . . . to La Porte.

Returning, same route.

THROUGH RATES.

Baltimore, Md. . . . . . . $11 75   Washington, D. C. $13 75
Philadelphia, Pa. 9 24

*⁂ Baggage will be checked through to Nordmont only on these tickets. An extra charge of twenty-five cents for each piece of baggage will be made on the stage line between Nordmont and La Porte.

LEBANON SPRINGS, N. Y.

These springs, famed for their medicinal properties, are located on the Bennington & Rutland R. R., one hundred and fifty-four miles from New York. The village is one thousand feet above the sea and the air is always fresh and invigorating. The Shaker Village near the springs is worth visiting, and strangers are always welcomed and politely entertained.

FORM EX. 524.—LEBANON SPRINGS, N. Y., AND RETURN.

Baltimore & Ohio R. R. . . . . to Philadelphia.
Philadelphia & Reading R. R. . . . . to Bound Brook.
Central R. R. of New Jersey . . . . to New York.

New York Central & Hudson River R. R. . . . . . . to Hudson.
Boston & Albany R. R. . . . . to Chatham.
Lebanon Springs R. R. . . . . to Lebanon Springs.

Returning, same route.

THROUGH RATES.

Baltimore, Md. . . . . . $11.00 Washington, D. C. . . . $16.00
Philadelphia, Pa. 10.00

FORM EX. 325. LEBANON SPRINGS, N. Y., AND RETURN.

Baltimore & Ohio R. R. . . . . to Philadelphia.
Philadelphia & Reading R. R. . . . . to Bound Brook.
Central R. R. of New Jersey. . . . . to New York.
New York Cent. & Hudson R. R. R. (Harlem Div.) to Chatham.
Lebanon Springs R. R. . . . . to Lebanon Springs.

Returning, same route.

THROUGH RATES.

Baltimore, Md. . . . . . $11.00 Washington, D. C. . . . $16.00
Philadelphia, Pa. 10.00

LEE BERKSHIRE HILLS, MASS.

Is a very small name for a beautiful, and what the Yankees call a smart, town. Nestling among the foot-hills of these mountain ranges, midway between old Greylock and Mount Washington, and divided by the swiftly-flowing Housatonic, Lee has enough beauty to satisfy the desires of its children. Many portions of Lee are exceedingly beautiful; indeed, the whole western portions of Lee are very beautiful, and much the same as Stockbridge and Lenox. On the east of the village, and in close proximity to it, rises the rocky eminence called "Fern Cliff," the summit of which is crowned with a beautiful grove of hemlocks. This is the trysting-place of the villagers, and no spot could be more charming for a pic-nic and walks by daylight and moonlight.

One of the most charming features in the scenery of Lee is "Laurel Lake," a beautiful sheet of water situated in the northeastern part of the town. The outline of this lakelet is marked by bays and capes, and its shores here and there beautiful with groves of pine, hemlock and maple. The land rises in gentle slopes from the water, furnishing beautiful sites for country seats.

FORM EX. 981.—LEE, BERKSHIRE HILLS, MASS.

Baltimore & Ohio R. R. . . . . to Philadelphia.
Philadelphia & Reading R. R. . . . . to Bound Brook.
Central R. R. of New Jersey . . . . to New York.
New York, New Haven & Hartford R. R. . . to South Norwalk.
Housatonic R. R. . . . . to Lee.

Returning, same route.

THROUGH RATES.

Baltimore, Md. . . . . . . $13 70   Washington, D. C. . . $15 70
Philadelphia, Pa. 9 70

Limited to continuous passage on Housatonic R. R., and not good on Sunday trains over that line.

FORM EX. 982.—LEE, BERKSHIRE HILLS, MASS.

Baltimore & Ohio R. R. . . . . to Philadelphia.
Philadelphia & Reading R. R. . . . . to Bound Brook.
Central R. R. of New Jersey . . . . to New York.
New York, New Haven & Hartford R. R. . . to Bridgeport.
Housatonic R. R. . . . . to Lee.

Returning, same route.

THROUGH RATES.

Baltimore, Md. . . . . . . $14 80   Washington, D. C. . . $16 80
Philadelphia, Pa. 10 80

Limited to continuous passage on Housatonic R. R., and not good on Sunday trains over that line.

LENOX BERKSHIRE HILLS, MASS.

One of the most fashionable resorts in New England, is located on hill-side and on hill-top, where pure air abounds, and overlooks the villages, farms and homes to the southward as far as the eye can reach. Stockbridge Bowl lies near at hand, with other miniature lakelets not far away. Wooded hills, cultivated fields, and villages without number dot the landscapes between Lenox and the Dome of the Taghkanics, which shut out the world from between here and the great beyond.

Wealthy New Yorkers, Philadelphians and Bostonians have here erected extensive villas and found a summer resort peculiar to itself, representing much aristocracy of wealth, refinement and culture. The elegant residences are open early, kept open late, and the season is a long one, the society being more exclusive and aristocratic even than that represented by the *ton* at Newport. The old town has been completely metamorphosed within the last quarter of a century, and palaces stand now where plain farm houses once had place.

Elegant equipages dash up and down the village streets, and out upon the hill-sides; club-houses for both sexes are well maintained, and the gayest of the gay, in its own way, is Lenox during the summer months. The drives and walks in and around Lenox are incomparably lovely. To characterize the peculiar charms of each one would take many pages. Whichever way one turns, the variety will be found inexhaustible and the beauty exquisite. The favorite game among the young people is tennis, which is played  at many private courts and at the court of the Lenox Club. Archery is indulged in to some extent. The appearance of Lenox village is that of the most exacting neatness and beauty. Not a blemish offends the eye. Tasteful homes, smooth lawns, flowers, graceful trees, the coming and going of handsome equipages, and many harmonizing accessories, please the sight constantly.

The season in Lenox used to end the first week in September. Now the height of the season is in October, and

many people remain till November or December. The
season is a very long one in Lenox, beginning in the early
summer, and making a round of summer, autumn and part
of winter. That Lenox is really what its admirers claim
for it is proved by the fact that people who come here have
most of them done extensive traveling where the finest
scenery in the world is found, and that they are people of
taste and culture, whose opinion is law.

FORM EX. 981.—LENOX (BERKSHIRE HILLS), MASS.

Baltimore & Ohio R. R. . . . . to Philadelphia.
Philadelphia & Reading R. R. . . . . to Bound Brook.
Central R. R. of New Jersey . . . . to New York.
New York, New Haven & Hartford R. R. . . to South Norwalk.
Housatonic R. R. . . . . to Lenox.
Returning, same route.

THROUGH RATES.

Baltimore, Md. . . . . . . $15 70   Washington, D. C. $15 70
Philadelphia, Pa. 9 70

Limited to continuous passage on Housatonic R. R., and not good
on Sunday trains over that line.

FORM EX. 982.—LENOX (BERKSHIRE HILLS), MASS.

Baltimore & Ohio R. R. . . . . to Philadelphia.
Philadelphia & Reading R. R. . . . . to Bound Brook.
Central R. R. of New Jersey . . . . to New York.
New York, New Haven & Hartford R. R. . . to Bridgeport.
Housatonic R. R. . . . . to Lenox.
Returning, same route.

THROUGH RATES.

Baltimore, Md. . . . . . . $14 80   Washington, D. C. $16 80
Philadelphia, Pa. 10 80

Limited to continuous passage on Housatonic R. R., and not good on
Sunday trains over that line.

LITITZ, PA.

FORM EX. 656. LITITZ, PA., AND RETURN.

Baltimore & Ohio R. R. . . . . to Philadelphia.
Philadelphia & Reading R. R. . . . . to Lititz.
Returning, same route.

THROUGH RATES.

	Limit.	Rate.		Limit.	Rate.
Baltimore, Md.	11 days,	$7 12	Philadelphia, Pa.	6 days,	$3 42
Chester, Pa.	6 days,	5 92	Washington, D. C.	11 days,	9 12
Havre de Grace, Md.	6 days,	5 77	Wilmington, Del.	6 days,	4 42
Newark, Del.	6 days,	4 92			

LISBON, N. H.

FORM EX. 959.—LISBON, N. H., AND RETURN.

Baltimore & Ohio R. R. . . . . to Philadelphia.
Philadelphia & Reading R. R. . . . . to Bound Brook.
Central R. R. of New Jersey . . . . to New York.
New York, New Haven & Hartford R. R. . . to Springfield.
Connecticut River R. R. . . . . to South Vernon.

Central Vermont R. R. . . . . to Brattleboro.
Vermont Valley R. R. . . . . to Windsor.
Central Vermont R. R. . . . . to White River Junc.
Boston & Maine R. R. . . . . to Wells River.
Concord & Montreal R. R. . . . . to Lisbon.
                    Returning, same route.

THROUGH RATES.
Baltimore, Md. . . . . . . $23 20   Washington, D. C. $24 20
 Philadelphia, Pa. . . .   19 20

LITTLETON, N. H.

FORM EX. 1001.—LITTLETON, N. H., AND RETURN.

Baltimore & Ohio R. R. . . . . to Philadelphia.
Philadelphia & Reading R. R. . . . . to Bound Brook.
Central R. R. of New Jersey . . . . to New York.
New York, New Haven & Hartford R. R. . . . to Springfield.
Connecticut River R. R. . . . . to South Vernon.
Central Vermont R. R. . . . . to Brattleboro.
Vermont Valley R. R. . . . . to Windsor.
Central Vermont R. R. . . . . to White River Junc.
Boston & Maine R. R. . . . . to Wells River.
Concord & Montreal R. R. . . . . to Littleton.
                    Returning, same route.

THROUGH RATES.
Baltimore, Md. . . . . . . $25 80   Washington, D. C. $25 80
 Philadelphia, Pa. . . .   19 80

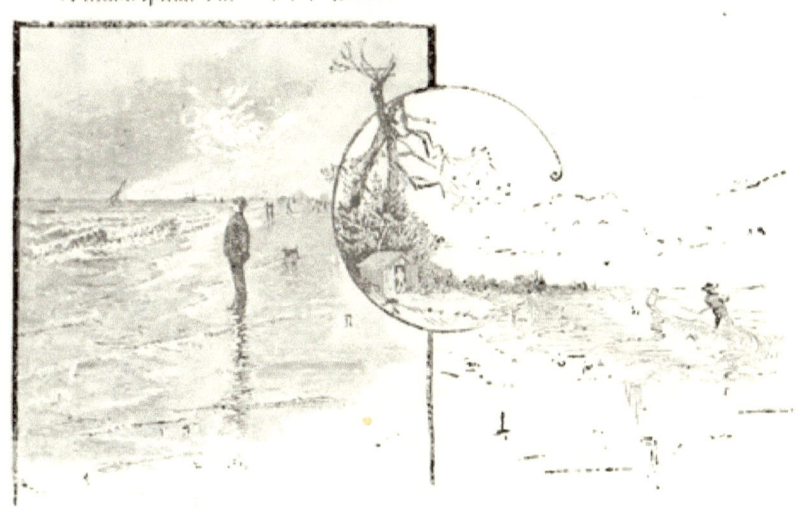

LONG BRANCH, N. J.

Long Branch is the summer capital of fashion on the New Jersey coast. Its proximity to New York, the intrinsic merits of the place, and the prestige it has won through years of recognition as the resort most favored by the representatives of wealth and fashion, has placed it in the front rank of American watering-places. The summer town is built upon a commanding bluff, overlooking the broad Atlantic; Ocean avenue, the principal boulevard, extends for miles along its crest, with only a narrow strip of green lawn and an occasional pavilion between it and the sea. The large hotels are built fronting on this great avenue, and the picture formed by passing equipages and richly dressed people in the foreground, with the blue expanse of ocean, flecked with white sails or dotted with the black speck of a passing steamer, spreading out to the horizon, is exceedingly fascinating. Landward the prospect is also pleasing, as the luxuriant growth of vegetation and the profusion of great trees give a pastoral aspect not usually found on the very strand of the sea. Palatial hotels and princely villas greet the eye on every hand. Both the ocean drives and the inland roads are so good that driving and horse-back riding are universally indulged in.

Pleasant neighbors surround Long Branch. To the south, Elberon, Deal Beach, Ocean Beach and Ocean Grove; to the north, North Long Branch, Monmouth Beach, Sea Bright and the Navesink Highlands, with a pretty chain of villas connecting them, form a succession of delightful resorts unsurpassed in attractiveness in the country. Untold wealth has been lavished in the construction of handsome villas and the embellishment of the grounds surrounding them, and it has made the barren sands of this strip of coast blossom like the rose.

The bathing at Long Branch is famous. Monmouth Park race course, one of the largest and best appointed in the land, is an exciting source of diversion to lovers of sport.

FORM EX. 570.—LONG BRANCH, N. J., AND RETURN.

Baltimore & Ohio R. R. . . . . to Philadelphia
Philadelphia & Reading R. R. . . . . to Bound Brook
Central R. R. of New Jersey . . . . to Long Branch.

Returning, same route.

THROUGH RATES.

Baltimore, Md. . . . . $8.00   Washington, D. C. $10.00
Philadelphia, Pa. 4.00

In addition to the above, excursion tickets, Form Ex. 570, Long Branch, N. J., may be sold from the following stations at rates as quoted below. Tickets should be limited with an "L" punch to 16 days, including day of issue.

THROUGH RATES.

Baltimore, Md. . . . . $7.50   Philadelphia, Pa. $3.50
Chester, Pa. . . . . 4.00   Washington, D. C. 9.50
Havre de Grace, Md. . . . 5.85   Wilmington, Del. 4.50
Newark, Del. 5.00

LURAY CAVERNS.

The Caverns of Luray are admitted by all who have visited them to be the most wonderful examples of nature's handiwork ever discovered. Experienced travelers, scientific explorers, geologists and men learned in the philosophy of nature, with one accord yield their unqualified admiration, and bear cheerful testimony to the supreme grandeur of these curious formations. Luray Cave is remarkable for its forms of stalagmites and stalactites, the latter being of great delicacy of shape and unique beyond all comparison. Mammoth Cave may be larger, but its attractions by no means compare with those of Luray, and while one may become satiated with the unearthly at the former in a day, it is no uncommon thing for tourists to remain at the latter, for daily visits to the cave, for a week or more. The introduction of the electric light within the caverns has been productive of wonderful results, presenting spectacles and effects which only the inspired hand of a Doré could reproduce. Descending the stone steps of the cave the visitor reaches the entrance hall, or vestibule, of this underground palace. A thrill of awe is the first sensation, as one finds himself immersed in gloom and surrounded by grotesque shapes, which an excited fancy clothes with ghostly appearances. This feeling, however, gives place at once to emotions of wonder and amazement. The entrance hall is a large compartment, supported by fluted columns, and adorned with snowy drapery and glittering stalactites. From this section avenues radiate to other portions of the cave. One leads to the Vegetable Garden, where the pend-

A CORNER OF THE BALL ROOM.

GIANT'S HALL.

ants assume the perfect form of vegetables; then through lesser rooms the way leads to the Fish Market, where the wall is hung with rows of fish, so natural in their likeness that the beholder is startled into a belief in their real existence. A succession of chambers, each named from some striking resemblance to well-known objects, and each filled with the curious creations of a subterranean world, are connected by passages which appear to have been carved by some giant hand; grottoes, adorned with the richest ornamentation; cascades of sparkling brilliancy; and forms and figures of infinite shape and variety inspire emotions of wonder, which grow with each new revelation. The Crystal Lake, with its flood of pellucid water; the Cathedral, with its silent organ, near which the Empress Column raises its head to the dome; the Bridal Chamber, with its alabaster figures in trailing drapery; the Giant's Hall, with its glittering arches and rows of mighty columns; the Elfin Ramble, a wide plateau resembling a play-ground for the princesses of this fairy realm; Pluto's Chasm, with its spectre clothed in crystalline draperies; Hovey's Hall, adorned with statuary; Hades, a dark abyss of impenetrable depth; the Ball-room, with its gorgeous furnishing — form but a small portion of wonders to be seen. Others there are equally worthy; but a detailed description is absolutely impossible in so short a sketch—they must be seen and studied to be appreciated. Nature has fashioned its wonders in her own inscrutable way. Man has done nothing except smooth the way for the explorer, and dispel the primal gloom by the power of electricity. The exploration can be made without serious difficulty, as there are few obstructions to impede the progress of the visitor, and these few are easily overcome by the most timid adventurer.

Not by any means the least attractive feature of Luray is the handsome Luray Inn, one of the prettiest and best-appointed hotels in the country.

FORM EX. 202.—LURAY (CAVERNS), VA., AND RETURN.

Limited to three (3) months from date of sale.

Baltimore & Ohio R. R. . . . . to Shenandoah June.
Norfolk & Western R. R. . . . . to Luray.
Luray Transfer Co., ... to Luray Caverns.
Luray Cave and Hotel Co. . . . . Admission to Caverns.

Returning, same route.

THROUGH RATES.

Baltimore, Md.	$8 70	Fairmont, W. Va.	$13 15
Bellaire, O.	16 55	Frederick, Md.	5 95
Berkeley Springs, W. Va.	6 35	Grafton, W. Va.	12 25
Cameron, W. Va.	15 45	Harper's Ferry, W. Va.	4 85
Chester, Pa.	12 20	Havre de Grace, Md.	10 15
Clarksburg, W. Va.	13 45	Johnstown, Pa.	11 95
Connellsville, Pa.	11 90	Keyser, W. Va.	9 15
Cumberland, Md.	8 20	McKeesport, Pa.	13 65
Deer Park, Md.	10 15	Martinsburg, W. Va.	5 65

Meyersdale, Pa.	$9 70	Piedmont, W. Va.	$9 35
Morgantown, W. Va.	11 15	Pittsburgh, Pa.	11 20
Moundsville, W. Va.	15 85	Rockwood, Pa.	10 15
Mountain Lake Park, Md.	10 30	Somerset, Pa.	10 55
Mt. Pleasant, Pa.	12 10	Uniontown, Pa.	12 35
Newark, Del.	11 00	Washington, D. C.	7 10
New York, N. Y.	16 15	Washington, Pa.	15 30
Oakland, Md.	10 10	Wheeling, W. Va.	16 25
Parkersburg, W. Va.	16 50	Wilmington, Del.	11 70
Philadelphia, Pa.	12 70		

FORM EX. 425.—LURAY, VA.

Limited to three (3) months from date of sale.

Baltimore & Ohio R. R. ....to Shenandoah Junc.
Norfolk & Western R. R. ....to Luray.

Returning, same route.

THROUGH RATES.

Baltimore, Md.	$7 35	Morgantown, W. Va.	$12 80
Bellaire, O.	15 20	Moundsville, W. Va.	14 50
Cameron, W. Va.	13 80	Mt. Pleasant, Pa.	11 05
Chester, Pa.	10 85	New York, N. Y.	15 10
Clarksburg, W. Va.	11 80	Oakland, Md.	9 65
Connellsville, Pa.	10 55	Parkersburg, W. Va.	11 30
Cumberland, Md.	6 85	Philadelphia, Pa.	11 35
Fairmont, W. Va.	11 80	Piedmont, W. Va.	8 00
Frederick, Md.	4 60	Pittsburgh, Pa.	12 85
Grafton, W. Va.	10 90	Rockwood, Pa.	8 80
Harper's Ferry, W. Va.	3 50	Somerset, Pa.	9 20
Johnstown, Pa.	10 62	Uniontown, Pa.	11 00
Keyser, W. Va.	7 80	Washington, D. C.	5 75
Martinsburg, W. Va.	3 70	Washington, Pa.	13 95
McKeesport, Pa.	12 20	Wilmington, Del.	10 35
Meyersdale, Pa.	8 35	Wheeling, W. Va.	11 90

These rates do not include transfer from Luray Station, nor admission to the caves.

MANCHESTER-BY-THE-SEA, MASS.

FORM EX. 762.—MANCHESTER-BY-THE-SEA, MASS., AND RETURN.

(Via Sound Lines and Boston in both directions.)

Baltimore & Ohio R. R. ....to Philadelphia.
Philadelphia & Reading R. R. ....to Bound Brook.
Central R. R. of New Jersey ....to New York.
Sound Lines (see pages 50 to 55 for routes) ....to Boston.
Boston & Maine R. R. ....to Manchester-by-the-Sea.

Returning, same route.

THROUGH RATES.

Baltimore, Md.	$17 20	Washington, D. C.	$19 20
Philadelphia, Pa.	13 20		

FORM EX. 762.—MANCHESTER-BY-THE-SEA, MASS., AND RETURN.

(Via Rail Lines and Boston in both directions.)

Baltimore & Ohio R. R. ....to Philadelphia.
Rail Lines (see pages 50 to 55 for routes) ....to Boston.
Boston & Maine R. R. ....to Manchester-by-the-Sea.

Returning, same route.

THROUGH RATES.

Baltimore, Md.	$19 20	Washington, D. C.	$21 20
Philadelphia, Pa.	15 20		

FORM EX. 762.— MANCHESTER-BY-THE-SEA, MASS., AND RETURN.

(Via Rail Lines and Boston; returning via Boston and Sound Lines.)

Baltimore & Ohio R. R. . . . . to Philadelphia.
Rail Lines (see pages 50 to 55 for route) . . . to Boston.
Boston & Maine R. R. . . . . to Manchester-by-the-Sea.
Boston & Maine R. R. . . . . to Boston.
Sound Lines (see pages 50 to 55 for route) . . to New York.
Central R. R. of New Jersey . . . . to Bound Brook.
Philadelphia & Reading R. R. . . . . to Philadelphia.
Baltimore & Ohio R. R. . . . . to starting point.

THROUGH RATES.

Baltimore, Md. . . . . . . $18 20 | Washington, D. C. $20 20
(Philadelphia, Pa. . . . . . 14 20 |

FORM EX. 762.— MANCHESTER-BY-THE-SEA, MASS., AND RETURN.

(Via Sound Lines and Boston; returning all rail.)

Baltimore & Ohio R. R. . . . . to Philadelphia.
Philadelphia & Reading R. R. . . . . to Bound Brook.
Central R. R. of New Jersey . . . . to New York.
Sound Lines (see pages 50 to 55 for route) . . to Boston.
Boston & Maine R. R. . . . . to Manchester-by-the-Sea.
Boston & Maine R. R. . . . . to Boston.
Rail Lines (see pages 50 to 55 for route) . . . to Philadelphia.
Baltimore & Ohio R. R. . . . . to starting point.

THROUGH RATES.

Baltimore, Md. . . . . . . $18 20 | Washington, D. C. $20 20
(Philadelphia, Pa. . . . . . 14 20 |

MAPLEWOOD, N. H.

One of the most charming mountain suburbs forming Bethlehem proper is Maplewood. It is in reality a part of Bethlehem, being but a mile south, and commanding one of the finest views of Mt. Washington, the Presidential and the Franconia ranges.

FORM EX. 1038.— MAPLEWOOD, N. H., AND RETURN.

(Via rail and Boston; returning by Sound Lines.)

Baltimore & Ohio R. R. . . . . to Philadelphia.
Rail Lines (see pages 50 to 55 for route) . . . to Boston.
Boston & Maine R. R. . . . . to Nashua.
Concord & Montreal R. R. . . . . to Bethlehem June.
Profile & Franconia Notch R. R. . . . . to Maplewood.
Profile & Franconia Notch R. R. . . . . to Bethlehem June.
Concord & Montreal R. R. . . . . to Nashua.
Boston & Maine R. R. . . . . to Boston.
Sound Lines (see pages 50 to 55 for route) . . to New York.
Central R. R. of New Jersey . . . . to Bound Brook.
Philadelphia & Reading R. R. . . . . to Philadelphia.
Baltimore & Ohio R. R. . . . . to starting point.

THROUGH RATES.

Baltimore, Md. . . . . . . $26 30 | Washington, D. C. $28 30
(Philadelphia, Pa. . . . . . 22 30 |

Transfer through Boston, returning, included.

FORM EX. 1638.—MAPLEWOOD, N. H., AND RETURN.

(Via Sound Lines and Boston; returning via all rail.)

Baltimore & Ohio R. R. . . . . to Philadelphia.
Philadelphia & Reading R. R. . . . . to Bound Brook.
Central R. R. of New Jersey . . . . to New York.
Sound Lines (see pages 50 to 55 for routes) . . to Boston.
Boston & Maine R. R. . . . . to Nashua.
Concord & Montreal R. R. . . . . to Bethlehem Junc.
Profile & Franconia Notch R. R. . . . . to Maplewood.
Profile & Franconia Notch R. R. . . . . to Bethlehem Junc.
Concord & Montreal R. R. . . . . to Nashua.
Boston & Maine R. R. . . . . to Boston.
Rail Lines (see pages 50 to 55 for routes) . . . to Philadelphia.
Baltimore & Ohio R. R. . . . . to starting point.

THROUGH RATES.

Baltimore, Md. . . . . . $26 30 | Washington, D. C. $28 30
Philadelphia, Pa. 22 30

Transfer through Boston, going, included.

FORM EX. 1638.—MAPLEWOOD, N. H., AND RETURN.

(Via Rail Lines and Boston, in both directions.)

Baltimore & Ohio R. R. . . . . to Philadelphia.
Rail Lines (see pages 50 to 55 for routes) . . . to Boston.
Boston & Maine R. R. . . . . to Nashua.
Concord & Montreal R. R. . . . . to Bethlehem Junc.
Profile & Franconia Notch R. R. . . . . to Maplewood.

Returning, same route.

THROUGH RATES.

Baltimore, Md. . . . . . $28 45 | Washington, D. C. $30 45
Philadelphia, Pa. 24 45

FORM EX. 1638.—MAPLEWOOD, N. H.

(Via Sound Lines and Boston, in both directions.)

Baltimore & Ohio R. R. . . . . to Philadelphia.
Philadelphia & Reading R. R. . . . . to Bound Brook.
Central R. R. of New Jersey . . . . to New York.
Sound Lines (see pages 50 to 55 for routes) . . to Boston.
Boston & Maine R. R. . . . . to Nashua.
Concord & Montreal R. R. . . . . to Bethlehem Junc.
Profile & Franconia Notch R. R. . . . . to Maplewood.

Returning, same route.

THROUGH RATES.

Baltimore, Md. . . . . . $22 70 | Washington, D. C. $24 70
Philadelphia, Pa. 18 70

Transfer through Boston, in both directions, included.

FORM EX. 1639.—MAPLEWOOD, N. H., AND RETURN.

(Via rail and Boston; returning by Sound Lines.)

Baltimore & Ohio R. R. . . . . to Philadelphia.
Rail Lines (see pages 50 to 55 for routes) . . . to Boston.
Boston & Maine R. R. . . . . to North Conway.
Maine Central R. R. . . . . to Zealand Junction.
Profile & Franconia Notch R. R. . . . . to Maplewood.
Profile & Franconia Notch R. R. . . . . to Zealand Junction.
Maine Central R. R. . . . . to North Conway.
Boston & Maine R. R. . . . . to Boston.
Sound Lines (see pages 50 to 55 for routes) . . to New York.
Central R. R. of New Jersey . . . . to Bound Brook.
Philadelphia & Reading R. R. . . . . to Philadelphia.
Baltimore & Ohio R. R. . . . . to starting point.

178   BALTIMORE & OHIO RAILROAD COMPANY

THROUGH RATES.
Baltimore, Md. . . . . . . $25 80 | Washington, D. C. $28 80
(Philadelphia, Pa. . . . . 22 80 |
Transfer through Boston, returning, included.

FORM EX. 1039.—MAPLEWOOD, N. H., AND RETURN.
(Via Sound Lines and Boston; returning via all rail.)

Baltimore & Ohio R. R. . . . . to Philadelphia.
Philadelphia & Reading R. R. . . . . to Bound Brook.
Central R. R. of New Jersey . . . . to New York.
Sound Lines (see pages 50 to 55 for route) . . . . to Boston.
Boston & Maine R. R. . . . . to North Conway.
Maine Central R. R. . . . . to Zealand Junction.
Profile & Franconia Notch R. R. . . . . to Maplewood.
Profile & Franconia Notch R. R. . . . . to Zealand Junction.
Maine Central R. R. . . . . to North Conway.
Boston & Maine R. R. . . . . to Boston.
Rail Lines (see pages 50 to 55 for route) . . . . . to Philadelphia.
Baltimore & Ohio R. R. . . . . to starting point.

THROUGH RATES.
Baltimore, Md. . . . . . . $25 80 | Washington, D. C. $28 80
(Philadelphia, Pa. . . . . 22 80 |
Transfer through Boston, going, included.

FORM EX. 1029.—MAPLEWOOD, N. H., AND RETURN.
(Via Rail Lines and Boston in both directions.)

Baltimore & Ohio R. R. . . . . to Philadelphia.
Rail Lines (see pages 50 to 55 for route) . . . . . to Boston.
Boston & Maine R. R. . . . . to North Conway.
Maine Central R. R. . . . . to Zealand Junction.
Profile & Franconia Notch R. R. . . . . to Maplewood.
Returning, same route.

THROUGH RATES.
Baltimore, Md. . . . . . . $28 45 | Washington, D. C. $30 45
(Philadelphia, Pa. . . . . 24 45 |

FORM EX. 1030.—MAPLEWOOD, N. H., AND RETURN.
(Via Sound Lines and Boston in both directions.)

Baltimore & Ohio R. R. . . . . to Philadelphia.
Philadelphia & Reading R. R. . . . . to Bound Brook.
Central R. R. of New Jersey . . . . to New York.
Sound Lines (see pages 50 to 55 for route) . . . . to Boston.
Boston & Maine R. R. . . . . to North Conway.
Maine Central R. R. . . . . to Zealand Junction.
Profile & Franconia Notch R. R. . . . . to Maplewood.
Returning, same route.

THROUGH RATES.
Baltimore, Md. . . . . . . $23 70 | Washington, D. C. $26 70
(Philadelphia, Pa. . . . . 19 70 |
Transfer through Boston, in both directions, included.

FORM EX. 1040.—MAPLEWOOD, N. H., AND RETURN.
(Via rail and Boston; returning by Sound Lines.)

Baltimore & Ohio R. R. . . . . to Philadelphia.
Rail Lines (see pages 50 to 55 for route) . . . . . to Boston.
Boston & Maine R. R. . . . . to Portland.

GARRETT COTTAGE, DEER PARK, MD.

Maine Central R. R. . . . . to Zealand Junction.
Profile & Franconia Notch R. R. . . . . to Maplewood.
Profile & Franconia Notch R. R. . . . . to Zealand Junction.
Maine Central R. R. . . . . to Portland.
Boston & Maine R. R. . . . . to Boston.
Sound Lines (see pages 50 to 55 for route) . . . to New York.
Central R. R. of New Jersey. . . . . to Bound Brook.
Philadelphia & Reading R. R. . . . . to Philadelphia.
Baltimore & Ohio R. R. . . . . to starting point.

THROUGH RATES.

Baltimore, Md. . . . . . . $26 80 | Washington, D. C. $28 80
†Philadelphia, Pa. . . . . 22 80 |
    Transfer through Boston, returning, included.

FORM EX. 1040.—MAPLEWOOD, N. H., AND RETURN.
    (Via Sound Lines and Boston; returning via all rail.)

Baltimore & Ohio R. R. . . . . to Philadelphia.
Philadelphia & Reading R. R. . . . . to Bound Brook.
Central R. R. of New Jersey. . . . . to New York.
Sound Lines (see pages 50 to 55 for route) . . . to Boston.
Boston & Maine R. R. . . . . to Portland.
Maine Central R. R. . . . . to Zealand Junction.
Profile & Franconia Notch R. R. . . . . to Maplewood.
Profile & Franconia Notch R. R. . . . . to Zealand Junction.
Maine Central R. R. . . . . to Portland.
Boston & Maine R. R. . . . . to Boston.
Rail Lines (see pages 50 to 55 for route) . . . . to Philadelphia.
Baltimore & Ohio R. R. . . . . to starting point.

THROUGH RATES.

Baltimore, Md. . . . . . . $26 80 | Washington, D. C. $28 80
†Philadelphia, Pa. . . . . 22 80 |
    Transfer through Boston, going, included.

FORM EX. 1040.—MAPLEWOOD, N. H., AND RETURN.
    (Via Rail Lines and Boston in both directions.)

Baltimore & Ohio R. R. . . . . to Philadelphia.
Rail Lines (see pages 50 to 55 for route) . . . . to Boston.
Boston & Maine R. R. . . . . to Portland.
Maine Central R. R. . . . . to Zealand Junction.
Profile & Franconia Notch R. R. . . . . to Maplewood.
            Returning, same route.

THROUGH RATES.

Baltimore, Md. . . . . . . $28 45 | Washington, D. C. $30 45
†Philadelphia, Pa. . . . . 24 45 |

FORM EX. 1040.—MAPLEWOOD, N. H., AND RETURN.
    (Via Sound Lines and Boston in both directions.)

Baltimore & Ohio R. R. . . . . to Philadelphia.
Philadelphia & Reading R. R. . . . . to Bound Brook.
Central R. R. of New Jersey. . . . . to New York.
Sound Lines (see pages 50 to 55 for route) . . . to Boston.
Boston & Maine R. R. . . . . to Portland.
Maine Central R. R. . . . . to Zealand Junction.
Profile and Franconia Notch R. R. . . . . to Maplewood.
            Returning, same route.

THROUGH RATES.

Baltimore, Md. . . . . . . $23 70 | Washington, D. C. $25 70
†Philadelphia, Pa. . . . . 19 70 |
    Transfer through Boston, in both directions, included.

MARION, N. C.

FORM EX. 39. MARION, N. C., AND RETURN.

Baltimore & Ohio R. R. . . . . to Washington.
Transfer . . . . , B. & O. to R. & D. Depot.
Richmond & Danville R. R. . . . . to Marion.
Returning, same route.

THROUGH RATES.

Baltimore, Md.	$20 50	Meyersdale, Pa.	$26 60
Bellaire, O.	33 15	Morgantown, W. Va.	31 05
Berkeley Springs, W. Va.	23 15	Moundsville, W. Va.	32 70
Cameron, W. Va.	32 00	Mountain Lake Park, Md.	26 65
Charlestown, W. Va.	21 70	Mt. Pleasant, Pa.	29 30
Chester, Pa.	24 00	Newark, Del.	22 80
Clarksburg, W. Va.	30 05	New York, N. Y.	28 50
Connellsville, Pa.	28 80	Oakland, Md.	26 75
Cumberland, Md.	25 10	Parkersburg, W. Va.	33 15
Deer Park, Md.	26 50	Philadelphia, Pa.	24 50
Fairmont, W. Va.	30 05	Piedmont, W. Va.	26 30
Frederick, Md.	21 30	Pittsburgh, Pa.	31 10
Grafton, W. Va.	29 15	Rockwood, Pa.	27 05
Hagerstown, Md.	22 10	Somerset, Pa.	27 15
Harper's Ferry, W. Va.	21 20	Uniontown, Pa.	29 25
Havre de Grace, Md.	21 95	Washington, Pa.	32 20
Johnstown, Pa.	28 85	Wheeling, W. Va.	33 15
Keyser, W. Va.	26 00	Wilmington, Del.	23 50
McKeesport, Pa.	30 55	Winchester, Va.	22 80
Martinsburg, W. Va.	21 95		

FORM EX. 45.—MARION, N. C., AND RETURN.

Baltimore & Ohio R. R. . . . . to Lexington.
Chesapeake & Ohio R. R. . . . . to Lynchburg.
Richmond & Danville R. R. . . . . to Marion.
Returning, same route.

THROUGH RATES.

Baltimore, Md.	$20 50	Meyersdale, Pa.	$25 00
Bellaire, O.	30 75	Morgantown, W. Va.	28 35
Berkeley Springs, W. Va.	20 15	Moundsville, W. Va.	30 00
Cameron, W. Va.	29 50	Mountain Lake Park, Md.	21 15
Charlestown, W. Va.	18 50	Mt. Pleasant, Pa.	26 60
Chester, Pa.	21 00	Newark, Del.	22 80
Clarksburg, W. Va.	27 35	New York, N. Y.	28 40
Connellsville, Pa.	26 10	Oakland, Md.	21 55
Cumberland, Md.	22 40	Parkersburg, W. Va.	30 50
Deer Park, Md.	21 50	Philadelphia, Pa.	21 50
Fairmont, W. Va.	27 35	Piedmont, W. Va.	23 50
Frederick, Md.	19 15	Pittsburgh, Pa.	28 10
Grafton, W. Va.	26 45	Rockwood, Pa.	24 35
Hagerstown, Md.	19 50	Somerset, Pa.	24 75
Harper's Ferry, W. Va.	18 50	Staunton, Va.	15 60
Harrisonburg, Va.	16 00	Uniontown, Pa.	26 55
Havre de Grace, Md.	21 95	Washington, D. C.	18 50
Johnstown, Pa.	26 45	Washington, Pa.	29 50
Keyser, W. Va.	23 50	Wheeling, W. Va.	30 50
McKeesport, Pa.	27 85	Wilmington, Del.	23 50
Martinsburg, W. Va.	19 25	Winchester, Va.	18 50

MARKLETON, PA.

EX. LOCAL, BALTIMORE & OHIO R. R. MARKLETON, PA., AND RETURN.

Use Local Excursion-book Tickets.

THROUGH RATES.

Connellsville, Pa.	$1 50	Pittsburgh, Pa.	$3 75
Cumberland, Md.	2 25	Rockwood, Pa.	35
Johnstown, Pa.	2 40	Somerset, Pa.	65
McKeesport, Pa.	3 45	Uniontown, Pa.	1 90
Meyersdale, Pa.	80	Washington, Pa.	4 90
Mt. Pleasant, Pa.	2 00		

MASSANETTA SPRINGS, VA.

FORM EX. 186. MASSANETTA SPRINGS, VA., AND RETURN.

Baltimore & Ohio R. R. . . . . to Harrisonburg.
Stage . . . . to Massanetta Springs.
Returning, same route.

THROUGH RATES.

Baltimore, Md.	$10 80	Morgantown, W. Va.	$16 85
Bellaire, O.	19 25	Moundsville, W. Va.	18 50
Berkeley Springs, W. Va.	8 95	Mountain Lake Park, Md.	12 95
Cameron, W. Va.	17 80	Mt. Pleasant, Pa.	15 10
Charlestown, W. Va.	6 50	Newark, Del.	13 10
Chester, Pa.	11 30	New York, N. Y.	18 80
Clarksburg, W. Va.	15 85	Oakland, Md.	13 05
Connellsville, Pa.	14 60	Parkersburg, W. Va.	19 00
Cumberland, Md.	10 90	Philadelphia, Pa.	11 80
Deer Park, Md.	12 80	Piedmont, W. Va.	12 00
Fairmont, W. Va.	15 85	Pittsburgh, Pa.	16 80
Frederick, Md.	8 95	Rockwood, Pa.	12 85
Grafton, W. Va.	14 95	Somerset, Pa.	13 25
Hagerstown, Md.	8 05	Staunton, Va.	3 20
Harper's Ferry, W. Va.	7 00	Strasburg, Va.	4 50
Havre de Grace, Md.	12 25	Uniontown, Pa.	15 05
Johnstown, Pa.	14 65	Washington, D. C.	9 20
Keyser, W. Va.	11 80	Washington, Pa.	18 00
Lexington, Va.	5 40	Wheeling, W. Va.	19 00
McKeesport, Pa.	16 35	Wilmington, Del.	13 80
Martinsburg, W. Va.	7 75	Winchester, Va.	5 40
Meyersdale, Pa.	12 40		

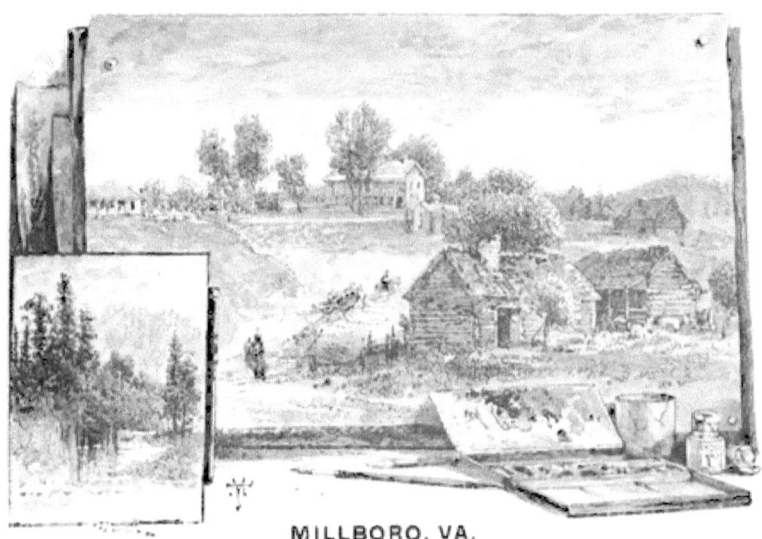

MILLBORO, VA.

FORM EX. 58.—MILLBORO, VA., AND RETURN.

Baltimore & Ohio R. R. . . . . to Shenandoah June.
Norfolk & Western R. R. . . . . to Basic.
Chesapeake & Ohio Ry. . . . . to Millboro.
Returning, same route.

THROUGH RATES.

Baltimore, Md.	$12 70	New York, N. Y.	$20 70
Chester, Pa.	16 20	Philadelphia, Pa.	16 70
Havre de Grace, Md.	14 15	Washington, D. C.	10 70
Newark, Del.	15 00	Wilmington, Del.	15 70

FORM EX. 176.—MILLBORO, VA., AND RETURN.

Baltimore & Ohio R. R. . . . . to Staunton.
Chesapeake & Ohio Ry. . . . . to Millboro.
Returning, same route.

THROUGH RATES.

Baltimore, Md.	$12 70	Meyersdale, Pa.	$14 00
Bellaire, O.	20 85	Morgantown, W. Va.	18 15
Berkeley Springs, W. Va.	10 55	Moundsville, W. Va.	20 40
Cameron, W. Va.	19 40	Mountain Lake Park, Md.	14 55
Charlestown, W. Va.	8 40	Mt. Pleasant, Pa.	16 70
Chester, Pa.	16 20	Newark, Del.	15 00
Clarksburg, W. Va.	17 15	New York, N. Y.	20 70
Connellsville, Pa.	16 20	Oakland, Md.	14 65
Cumberland, Md.	12 50	Parkersburg, W. Va.	20 15
Deer Park, Md.	14 40	Philadelphia, Pa.	16 70
Fairmont, W. Va.	17 65	Piedmont, W. Va.	13 60
Frederick, Md.	9 65	Pittsburgh, Pa.	18 50
Grafton, W. Va.	16 55	Rockwood, Pa.	14 15
Hagerstown, Md.	9 65	Somerset, Pa.	14 85
Harper's Ferry, W. Va.	8 00	Strasburg, Va.	5 95
Harrisonburg, Va.	2 60	Uniontown, Pa.	16 65
Havre de Grace, Md.	14 15	Washington, D. C.	10 70
Johnstown, Pa.	16 25	Washington, Pa.	19 60
Keyser, W. Va.	13 10	Wheeling, W. Va.	20 60
Lexington, Va.	1 40	Wilmington, Del.	15 70
McKeesport, Pa.	17 95	Winchester, Va.	7 00
Martinsburg, W. Va.	9 35		

FORM EX. 655.—MILLBORO, VA., AND RETURN.

Baltimore & Ohio R. R. . . . . to Washington.
Transfer B. & O. Depot . . . . to C. & O. Depot.
Chesapeake & Ohio Ry. . . . . to Millboro.
        Returning, same route.

THROUGH RATES.

Baltimore, Md.	$12 70	Meyersdale, Pa.	$18 80
Bellaire, O.	25 65	Morgantown, W. Va.	23 25
Berkeley Springs, W. Va.	15 35	Moundsville, W. Va.	24 90
Cameron, W. Va.	24 20	Mountain Lake Park, Md.	18 85
Charlestown, W. Va.	13 90	Mt. Pleasant, Pa.	21 50
Chester, Pa.	16 20	Newark, Del.	15 00
Clarksburg, W. Va.	22 25	New York, N. Y.	20 70
Connellsville, Pa.	21 00	Oakland, Md.	18 95
Cumberland, Md.	17 50	Parkersburg, W. Va.	25 25
Deer Park, Md.	18 70	Philadelphia, Pa.	16 70
Fairmont, W. Va.	22 25	Piedmont, W. Va.	18 40
Frederick, Md.	13 45	Pittsburgh, Pa.	23 30
Grafton, W. Va.	21 35	Rockwood, Pa.	19 25
Hagerstown, Md.	14 30	Somerset, Pa.	19 65
Harper's Ferry, W. Va.	13 40	Uniontown, Pa.	24 15
Havre de Grace, Md.	14 45	Washington, Pa.	24 40
Johnstown, Pa.	24 05	Wheeling, W. Va.	25 35
Keyser, W. Va.	18 20	Wilmington, Del.	15 70
McKeesport, Pa.	22 75	Winchester, Va.	15 00
Martinsburg, W. Va.	14 15		

MONTEREY, PA.

FORM EX. 658.—MONTEREY, PA., AND RETURN.

Baltimore & Ohio R. R. . . . . to Hagerstown.
Transfer . . . . to W. M. Depot.
Western Maryland R. R. . . . . to Monterey.
        Returning, same route.

THROUGH RATES.

Bellaire, O.	$14 20	Moundsville, W. Va.	$13 40
Berkeley Springs, W. Va.	3 85	Mountain Lake Park, Md.	7 85
Cameron, W. Va.	12 75	Mt. Pleasant, Pa.	10 00
Charlestown, W. Va.	3 00	New York, N. Y.	13 95
Clarksburg, W. Va.	10 75	Oakland, Md.	7 95
Connellsville, Pa.	9 50	Parkersburg, W. Va.	13 85
Cumberland, Md.	5 80	Philadelphia, Pa.	9 95
Deer Park, Md.	7 70	Piedmont, W. Va.	6 90
Fairmont, W. Va.	10 75	Pittsburgh, Pa.	11 80
Grafton, W. Va.	9 85	Rockwood, Pa.	7 75
Harper's Ferry, W. Va.	2 50	Somerset, Pa.	8 15
Harrisonburg, Va.	7 50	Staunton, Va.	8 80
Johnstown, Pa.	9 55	Strasburg, Va.	5 15
Keyser, W. Va.	6 70	Uniontown, Pa.	9 95
Lexington, Va.	10 60	Washington, D. C.	1 55
McKeesport, Pa.	11 25	Washington, Pa.	12 30
Martinsburg, W. Va.	2 70	Wheeling, W. Va.	13 85
Meyersdale, Pa.	7 20	Winchester, Va.	4 40
Morgantown, W. Va.	11 75		

MONTGOMERY WHITE SULPHUR SPRINGS, VA.

FORM EX. 87.—MONTGOMERY WHITE SULPHUR SPRINGS, VA., (BIG TUNNEL STATION), AND RETURN.

Baltimore & Ohio R. R. . . . . to Washington.
Transfer B. & O. Depot . . . . to R. & D. Depot.
Richmond & Danville R. R. . . . . to Lynchburg.
Norfolk & Western R. R. . . . . to Big Tunnel Station.
        Returning, same route.

ROUTES AND RATES FOR SUMMER TOURS   185

THROUGH RATES.

Baltimore, Md.	$14.05	Meyersdale, Pa.	$20.15
Bellaire, O.	27.00	Morgantown, W. Va.	21.00
Berkeley Springs, W. Va.	16.70	Moundsville, W. Va.	26.25
Cameron, W. Va.	25.55	Mountain Lake Park, Md.	20.20
Charlestown, W. Va.	15.25	Mt. Pleasant, Pa.	22.85
Chester, Pa.	17.55	Newark, Del.	16.35
Clarksburg, W. Va.	23.60	New York, N. Y.	22.05
Connellsville, Pa.	22.35	Oakland, Md.	20.30
Cumberland, Md.	18.05	Parkersburg, W. Va.	26.70
Deer Park, Md.	20.05	Philadelphia, Pa.	18.05
Fairmont, W. Va.	23.00	Piedmont, W. Va.	19.75
Frederick, Md.	14.85	Pittsburgh, Pa.	21.05
Grafton, W. Va.	22.70	Rockwood, Pa.	20.00
Hagerstown, Md.	15.65	Somerset, Pa.	21.00
Harper's Ferry, W. Va.	11.75	Uniontown, Pa.	22.80
Havre de Grace, Md.	15.50	Washington, Pa.	25.75
Johnstown, Pa.	22.10	Wheeling, W. Va.	26.70
Keyser, W. Va.	19.55	Wilmington, Del.	17.05
McKeesport, Pa.	21.10	Winchester, Va.	16.35
Martinsburg, W. Va.	15.50		

FORM EX. 289. MONTGOMERY WHITE SULPHUR SPRINGS, VA. (BIG TUNNEL STATION), AND RETURN.

Baltimore & Ohio R. R. . . . . to Shenandoah June.
Norfolk & Western R. R. . . . . to Big Tunnel.
Returning, same route.

THROUGH RATES.

Baltimore, Md.	$14.05	Morgantown, W. Va.	$20.55
Bellaire, O.	22.98	Moundsville, W. Va.	22.25
Berkeley Springs, W. Va.	12.75	Mountain Lake Park, Md.	16.70
Cameron, W. Va.	21.55	Mt. Pleasant, Pa.	18.80
Chester, Pa.	17.55	Newark, Del.	16.35
Clarksburg, W. Va.	19.55	New York, N. Y.	22.05
Connellsville, Pa.	18.30	Oakland, Md.	16.80
Cumberland, Md.	14.60	Parkersburg, W. Va.	22.65
Deer Park, Md.	16.55	Philadelphia, Pa.	18.05
Fairmont, W. Va.	19.55	Piedmont, W. Va.	15.75
Frederick, Md.	12.35	Pittsburgh, Pa.	20.00
Grafton, W. Va.	18.65	Rockwood, Pa.	16.55
Harper's Ferry, W. Va.	11.25	Somerset, Pa.	16.95
Havre de Grace, Md.	15.50	Uniontown, Pa.	18.75
Johnstown, Pa.	18.35	Washington, D. C.	12.05
Keyser, W. Va.	15.55	Washington, Pa.	22.00
McKeesport, Pa.	20.05	Wheeling, W. Va.	22.65
Martinsburg, W. Va.	11.45	Wilmington, Del.	17.05
Meyersdale, Pa.	16.40		

DOWN THE LACHINE RAPIDS.

MONTREAL.

Montreal, "The Queen of the St. Lawrence," ranks among the most beautiful cities of the continent. It is built on an island of the same name, at the confluence of the Ottawa and St. Lawrence Rivers, which, from its fertility, has been called the Garden of Canada. The St. Lawrence is one and a half miles wide at this point, and the entire river front is lined with lofty and massive walls, quays and terraces of gray limestone. The principal buildings are of the same material, which is of a delicate neutral tint, very pleasing to the eye. Architecturally, many of these are very fine, the Cathedral of Notre Dame especially, being of great size and elegant design, is well worth a visit. The view from one of the towers, in which hangs the great bell, is very extensive and interesting. Other places of note are: The Jesuit College, McGill College, the Post-office, New Court-house, Bank of Montreal, Bank of British North America, Champ de Mars, and Bon Pasteur Nunnery.

FORM EX. 327.—MONTREAL, P. Q., AND RETURN.

Baltimore & Ohio R. R.	to Philadelphia.
Philadelphia & Reading R. R.	to Bound Brook.
Central R. R. of New Jersey	to New York.
New York Central & Hudson River R. R.	to Troy.
Delaware & Hudson R. R.	to Caldwell.
Champlain Transportation Co. (Lake George Strs.)	to Baldwin.
Delaware & Hudson R. R.	to Ticonderoga.
Champlain Transportation Co.	to Plattsburgh.
Delaware & Hudson R. R.	to Rouse's Point.
Grand Trunk Ry.	to Montreal.
Grand Trunk Ry.	to Rouse's Point.
Delaware & Hudson R. R.	to Plattsburgh.
Champlain Transportation Co.	to Ticonderoga.
Delaware & Hudson R. R.	to Troy.
New York Central & Hudson River R. R.	to New York.
Central R. R. of New Jersey	to Bound Brook.
Philadelphia & Reading R. R.	to Philadelphia.
Baltimore & Ohio R. R.	to starting point.

THROUGH RATES.

Baltimore, Md. . . . . . . $27 75   Washington, D. C. . . $29 75
†Philadelphia, Pa. 23 75

FORM EX. 328.—MONTREAL, P. Q., AND RETURN.

Baltimore & Ohio R. R.	to Philadelphia.
Philadelphia & Reading R. R.	to Bound Brook.
Central R. R. of New Jersey	to New York.
New York Central & Hudson River R. R.	to Troy.
Delaware & Hudson R. R.	to Ticonderoga.
Champlain Transportation Co.	to Plattsburgh.
Delaware & Hudson R. R.	to Rouse's Point.
Grand Trunk Ry.	to Montreal.
Grand Trunk Ry.	to Rouse's Point.
Delaware & Hudson R. R.	to Plattsburgh.
Champlain Transportation Co.	to Ticonderoga.
Delaware & Hudson R. R.	to Baldwin.
Champlain Transportation Co. (Lake George Strs.)	to Caldwell.
Delaware & Hudson R. R.	to Troy.
New York Central & Hudson River R. R.	to New York.
Central R. R. of New Jersey	to Bound Brook.
Philadelphia & Reading R. R.	to Philadelphia.
Baltimore & Ohio R. R.	to starting point.

THROUGH RATES.

Baltimore, Md. . . . . . . $27 75   Washington, D. C.   29 75
†Philadelphia, Pa. 23 75

FORM EX. 329.—MONTREAL, P. Q., AND RETURN.

Baltimore & Ohio R. R.	to Philadelphia.
Philadelphia & Reading R. R.	to Bound Brook.
Central R. R. of New Jersey	to New York.
New York Central & Hudson River R. R.	to Troy.
Delaware & Hudson R. R.	to Rouse's Point.
Grand Trunk Ry.	to Montreal.

Returning, same route.

THROUGH RATES.

Baltimore, Md. . . . . . . $26 25   Washington, D. C.   28 25
†Philadelphia, Pa. 22 25

FORM EX. 330.—MONTREAL, P. Q., AND RETURN.

Baltimore & Ohio R. R.	to Philadelphia.
Philadelphia & Reading R. R.	to Bound Brook.
Central R. R. of New Jersey	to New York.
New York Central & Hudson River R. R.	to Troy.
Fitchburg R. R.	to White Creek.
Bennington & Rutland R. R.	to Rutland.
Central Vermont R. R.	to St. John's.
Grand Trunk Ry.	to Montreal.

Returning, same route.

THROUGH RATES.

Baltimore, Md.	$26 25	Washington, D. C.	$28 25
Philadelphia, Pa.	22 25		

FORM EX. 331.—MONTREAL, P. Q., AND RETURN.

Baltimore & Ohio R. R.	to Philadelphia.
Philadelphia & Reading R. R.	to Bound Brook.
Central R. R. of New Jersey	to New York.
New York Central & Hudson River R. R.	to Troy.
Delaware & Hudson R. R.	to Caldwell.
Champlain Transportation Co., Lake George Strs.	to Baldwin.
Delaware & Hudson R. R.	to Ticonderoga.
Champlain Transportation Co.	to Burlington.
Central Vermont R. R.	to St. John's.
Grand Trunk Ry.	to Montreal.
Grand Trunk Ry.	to St. John's.
Central Vermont R. R.	to Rutland.
Bennington & Rutland R. R.	to White Creek.
Fitchburg R. R.	to Troy.
New York Central & Hudson River R. R.	to New York.
Central R. R. of New Jersey	to Bound Brook.
Philadelphia & Reading R. R.	to Philadelphia.
Baltimore & Ohio R. R.	to starting point.

THROUGH RATES.

Baltimore, Md.	$28 70	Washington, D. C.	$30 70
Philadelphia, Pa.	24 70		

FORM EX. 332.—MONTREAL, P. Q., AND RETURN.

Baltimore & Ohio R. R.	to Philadelphia.
Philadelphia & Reading R. R.	to Bound Brook.
Central R. R. of New Jersey	to New York.
New York Central & Hudson River R. R.	to Troy.
Fitchburg R. R.	to White Creek.
Bennington & Rutland R. R.	to Rutland.
Central Vermont R. R.	to St. John's.
Grand Trunk Ry.	to Montreal.
Grand Trunk Ry.	to St. John's.
Central Vermont R. R.	to Burlington.
Champlain Transportation Co.	to Fort Ticonderoga.
Delaware & Hudson R. R.	to Baldwin.
Champlain Transportation Co., Lake George Strs.	to Caldwell.
Delaware & Hudson R. R.	to Troy.
New York Central & Hudson River R. R.	to New York.
Central R. R. of New Jersey	to Bound Brook.
Philadelphia & Reading R. R.	to Philadelphia.
Baltimore & Ohio R. R.	to starting point.

THROUGH RATES.

Baltimore, Md.	$28 70	Washington, D. C.	$30 70
Philadelphia, Pa.	24 70		

Form Ex. 344.—Montreal, P. Q., and Return.

Railroad	Destination
Baltimore & Ohio R. R.	to Philadelphia.
Philadelphia & Reading R. R.	to Bound Brook.
Central R. R. of New Jersey	to New York.
West Shore R. R.	to Albany.
Delaware & Hudson R. R.	to Caldwell.
Champlain Transportation Co., Lake George Strs.	to Baldwin.
Delaware & Hudson R. R.	to Ticonderoga.
Champlain Transportation Co.	to Plattsburgh.
Delaware & Hudson R. R.	to Rouse's Point.
Grand Trunk Ry.	to Montreal.
Grand Trunk Ry.	to Rouse's Point.
Delaware & Hudson R. R.	to Plattsburgh.
Champlain Transportation Co.	to Ticonderoga.
Delaware & Hudson R. R.	to Albany.
West Shore R. R.	to New York.
Central R. R. of New Jersey	to Bound Brook.
Philadelphia & Reading R. R.	to Philadelphia.
Baltimore & Ohio R. R.	to starting point.

Transfer through New York, in both directions, included.

THROUGH RATES.

Baltimore, Md. . . . . . $27 75 | Washington, D. C. $29 75
(Philadelphia, Pa. 23 75

Form Ex. 345.—Montreal, P. Q., and Return.

Railroad	Destination
Baltimore & Ohio R. R.	to Philadelphia.
Philadelphia & Reading R. R.	to Bound Brook.
Central R. R. of New Jersey	to New York.
West Shore R. R.	to Albany.
Delaware & Hudson R. R.	to Rouse's Point.
Grand Trunk Ry.	to Montreal.

Returning, same route.

Transfer through New York, in both directions, included.

THROUGH RATES.

Baltimore, Md. . . . . . $26 25 | Washington, D. C. $28 25
(Philadelphia, Pa. 22 25

Form Ex. 347.—Montreal, P. Q., and Return.

Railroad	Destination
Baltimore & Ohio R. R.	to Philadelphia.
Philadelphia & Reading R. R.	to Bound Brook.
Central R. R. of New Jersey	to New York.
West Shore R. R.	to Albany.
Delaware & Hudson R. R.	to Caldwell.
Champlain Transportation Co., Lake George Strs.	to Baldwin.
Delaware & Hudson R. R.	to Ticonderoga.
Champlain Transportation Co.	to Burlington.
Central Vermont R. R.	to St. John's.
Grand Trunk Ry.	to Montreal.
Grand Trunk Ry.	to St. John's.
Central Vermont R. R.	to Rutland.
Bennington & Rutland R. R.	to White Creek.
Fitchburg R. R.	to Troy.
Delaware & Hudson R. R.	to Albany.
West Shore R. R.	to New York.
Central R. R. of New Jersey	to Bound Brook.
Philadelphia & Reading R. R.	to Philadelphia.
Baltimore & Ohio R. R.	to starting point.

Transfer through New York, in both directions, included.

THROUGH RATES.

Baltimore, Md. . . . . . $28 70 | Washington, D. C. $30 70
(Philadelphia, Pa. 24 70

FORM EX. 348. — MONTREAL, P. Q., AND RETURN.

Baltimore & Ohio R. R.	to Philadelphia.
Philadelphia & Reading R. R.	to Bound Brook.
Central R. R. of New Jersey.	to New York.
West Shore R. R.	to Albany.
Delaware & Hudson R. R.	to Troy.
Fitchburg R. R.	to White Creek.
Bennington and Rutland R. R.	to Rutland.
Central Vermont R. R.	to St. John's.
Grand Trunk Ry.	to Montreal.
Grand Trunk Ry.	to St. John's.
Central Vermont R. R.	to Burlington.
Champlain Transportation Co.	to Fort Ticonderoga.
Delaware & Hudson R. R.	to Baldwin.
Champlain Transportation Co. (Lake George Strs.)	to Caldwell.
Delaware & Hudson R. R.	to Albany.
West Shore R. R.	to New York.
Central R. R. of New Jersey.	to Bound Brook.
Philadelphia & Reading R. R.	to Philadelphia.
Baltimore & Ohio R. R.	to starting point.

Transfer through New York, in both directions, included.

THROUGH RATES.

Baltimore, Md. . . . . . $28 70   Washington, D. C. $30 70
§Philadelphia, Pa. 24 70

FORM EX. 357. — MONTREAL, P. Q., AND RETURN.

Baltimore & Ohio R. R.	to Philadelphia.
Philadelphia & Reading R. R.	to Bound Brook.
Central R. R. of New Jersey.	to New York.
West Shore R. R.	to Oneida Castle.
New York, Ontario & Western Ry.	to Central Square.
Rome, Watertown & Ogdensburg R. R.	to Clayton.
Thousand Island Steamboat Co.	to Alexandria Bay.
Richelieu & Ontario Navigation Co.	to Montreal.
Grand Trunk Ry.	to Rouse's Point.
Delaware & Hudson R. R.	to Albany.
West Shore R. R.	to New York.
Central R. R. of New Jersey.	to Bound Brook.
Philadelphia & Reading R. R.	to Philadelphia.
Baltimore & Ohio R. R.	to starting point.

Transfer through New York, in both directions, included.

THROUGH RATES.

Baltimore, Md. . . . . . $31 50   Washington, D. C. $33 50
§Philadelphia, Pa. 27 50

FORM EX. 358. — MONTREAL, P. Q., AND RETURN.

Baltimore & Ohio R. R.	to Philadelphia.
Philadelphia & Reading R. R.	to Bound Brook.
Central R. R. of New Jersey.	to New York.
New York, Ontario & Western R. R.	to Central Square.
Rome, Watertown & Ogdensburg R. R.	to Clayton.
Thousand Island Steamboat Co.	to Alexandria Bay.
Richelieu & Ontario Navigation Co.	to Montreal.
Grand Trunk Ry.	to Rouse's Point.
Delaware & Hudson R. R.	to Albany.
New York and Albany Day Line Steamers.	to New York.
Central R. R. of New Jersey.	to Bound Brook.
Philadelphia & Reading R. R.	to Philadelphia.
Baltimore & Ohio R. R.	to starting point.

THROUGH RATES.

Baltimore, Md. . . . . . $31 10   Washington, D. C. $33 10
§Philadelphia, Pa. 27 10

FORM EX. 556. MONTREAL, P. Q. AND RETURN.

Baltimore & Ohio R. R.	to Philadelphia.
Philadelphia & Reading R. R.	to Bound Brook.
Central R. R. of New Jersey	to New York.
New York, Ontario & Western Ry.	to Central Square.
Rome, Watertown & Ogdensburg R. R.	to Clayton.
Thousand Island Steamboat Co.	to Alexandria Bay.
Richelieu & Ontario Navigation Co. Steamer.	to Montreal.
Grand Trunk Ry.	to Rouse's Point.
Delaware & Hudson R. R.	to Albany.
West Shore R. R.	to New York.
Central R. R. of New Jersey.	to Bound Brook.
Philadelphia & Reading R. R.	to Philadelphia.
Baltimore & Ohio R. R.	to starting point.

Transfer through New York, returning, included.

THROUGH RATES.

Baltimore, Md.	$31.50	Washington, D. C.	$33.50
Philadelphia, Pa.	27.50		

FORM EX. 567. MONTREAL, P. Q. AND RETURN.

Baltimore & Ohio R. R.	to Philadelphia.
Philadelphia & Reading R. R.	to Bound Brook.
Central R. R. of New Jersey	to New York.
Delaware, Lackawanna & Western R. R.	to Utica.
Rome, Watertown & Ogdensburg R. R.	to Clayton.
Richelieu & Ontario Navigation Co. Steamer	to Alexandria Bay.
Richelieu & Ontario Navigation Co. Steamer	to Montreal.

Returning, same route.

THROUGH RATES.

Baltimore, Md.	$31.75	Washington, D. C.	$33.75
Philadelphia, Pa.	27.75		

FORM EX. 589.—MONTREAL, P. Q. AND RETURN.

Baltimore & Ohio R. R.	to Philadelphia.
Philadelphia & Reading R. R.	to Bound Brook.
Central R. R. of New Jersey	to New York.
Delaware, Lackawanna & Western R. R.	to Utica.
Rome, Watertown & Ogdensburg R. R.	to Clayton.
Richelieu & Ontario Navigation Co. Steamer	to Alexandria Bay.
Richelieu & Ontario Navigation Co. Steamer	to Montreal.
Canadian Pacific Ry.	to Ottawa.
Canadian Pacific Ry.	to Prescott.
Ferry	to Ogdensburg.
Rome, Watertown & Ogdensburg R. R.	to Utica.
Delaware, Lackawanna & Western R. R.	to New York.
Central R. R. of New Jersey	to Bound Brook.
Philadelphia & Reading R. R.	to Philadelphia.
Baltimore & Ohio R. R.	to starting point.

THROUGH RATES.

Baltimore, Md.	$35.10	Washington, D. C.	$37.10
Philadelphia, Pa.	31.10		

FORM EX. 620. MONTREAL, P. Q. AND RETURN.

Baltimore & Ohio R. R.	to Philadelphia.
Philadelphia & Reading R. R.	to Bound Brook.
Central R. R. of New Jersey	to New York.
New York, New Haven & Hartford R. R.	to Springfield.
Connecticut River R. R.	to South Vernon.
Central Vermont R. R.	to Brattleboro.

192   BALTIMORE & OHIO RAILROAD COMPANY

Vermont Valley R. R. . . . . to Bellows Falls.
Central Vermont R. R. . . . . to St. John's.
Grand Trunk Ry. . . . . to Montreal.

Returning, same route.

THROUGH RATES.

Baltimore, Md. . . . . . . $26 25 Washington, D. C. $28 25
†Philadelphia, Pa. 22 25

FORM EX. 634.—MONTREAL, P. Q., AND RETURN.

For route to Niagara Falls, see page 249.

New York Central & Hudson River R. R. . . . . to Lewiston.
Niagara Navigation Co. . . . . to Toronto.
Grand Trunk Ry. or Richelieu & Ontario Nav. Co. to Kingston.
Grand Trunk Ry. or Richelieu & Ontario Nav. Co. to Prescott.
Grand Trunk Ry. or Richelieu & Ontario Nav. Co. to Montreal.
Grand Trunk Ry. . . . . to Rouse's Point.
Delaware & Hudson R. R. . . . . to Plattsburgh.
Champlain Transportation Co. . . . . to Ticonderoga.
Delaware & Hudson R. R. . . . . to Albany.
New York & Albany Day Line . . . . to New York.
Central R. R. of New Jersey . . . . to Bound Brook.
Philadelphia & Reading R. R. . . . . to Philadelphia.
Baltimore & Ohio R. R. . . . . to starting point.

THROUGH RATES.

Baltimore, Md. . . . . . . $36 35 Washington, D. C. $38 35
†Philadelphia, Pa. 32 35

FORM EX. 635.—MONTREAL, P. Q., AND RETURN.

For route to Niagara Falls, see page 249.

New York Central & Hudson River R. R. . . . . to Lewiston.
Rome, Watertown & Ogdensburg R. R. . . . . . . to Clayton.
Richelieu & Ontario Navigation Co. . . . . to Alexandria Bay.
Richelieu & Ontario Navigation Co. . . . . to Montreal.
Grand Trunk Ry. . . . . to Rouse's Point.
Delaware & Hudson R. R. . . . . to Plattsburgh.
Champlain Transportation Co. . . . . to Ticonderoga.
Delaware & Hudson R. R. . . . . to Albany.
New York & Albany Day Line . . . . to New York.
Central R. R. of New Jersey . . . . to Bound Brook.
Philadelphia & Reading R. R. . . . . to Philadelphia.
Baltimore & Ohio R. R. . . . . to starting point.

THROUGH RATES.

Baltimore, Md. . . . . . . $36 35 Washington, D. C. $38 35
†Philadelphia, Pa. 32 35

FORM EX. 636.—MONTREAL, P. Q., AND RETURN.

For route to Niagara Falls, see page 249.

New York Central & Hudson River R. R. . . . . to Lewiston.
Rome, Watertown & Ogdensburg R. R. . . . . . . to Clayton.
Richelieu & Ontario Navigation Co. . . . . to Alexandria Bay.
Richelieu & Ontario Navigation Co. . . . . to Montreal.
Grand Trunk Ry. . . . . to Rouse's Point.
Delaware & Hudson R. R. . . . . to Plattsburgh.
Champlain Transportation Co. . . . . to Ticonderoga.
Delaware & Hudson R. R. . . . . to Baldwin.
Champlain Transportation Co., Lake George Strs. to Caldwell.
Delaware & Hudson R. R. . . . . to Albany.
New York & Albany Day Line . . . . to New York.
Central R. R. of New Jersey . . . . to Bound Brook.

ROUTES AND RATES FOR SUMMER TOURS.   193

Philadelphia & Reading R. R. . . . . to Philadelphia.
Baltimore & Ohio R. R. . . . . to starting point.

THROUGH RATES.

Baltimore, Md. . . . . . . $37 85 | Washington, D. C. $39 85
†Philadelphia, Pa. . . . . 33 85 |

FORM EX. 637.—MONTREAL, P. Q., AND RETURN.

For route to Niagara Falls, see page 219.

New York Central & Hudson River R. R. . . . to Lewiston.
Rome, Watertown & Ogdensburg R. R. . . . . to Clayton.
Richelieu & Ontario Navigation Co. . . . . . to Alexandria Bay.
Richelieu & Ontario Navigation Co. . . . . . to Montreal.
Grand Trunk Ry. . . . . to Rouse's Point.
Delaware & Hudson R. R. . . . . to Plattsburgh.
Champlain Transportation Co. . . . . to Ticonderoga.
Delaware & Hudson R. R. . . . . to Troy.
New York Central & Hudson River R. R. . . . to New York.
Central R. R. of New Jersey . . . . to Bound Brook.
Philadelphia & Reading R. R. . . . . to Philadelphia.
Baltimore & Ohio R. R. . . . . to starting point.

THROUGH RATES.

Baltimore, Md. . . . . . . $36 75 | Washington, D. C. $38 75
†Philadelphia, Pa. . . . . 32 75 |

FORM EX. 638.—MONTREAL, P. Q., AND RETURN.

For route to Niagara Falls, see page 219.

New York Central & Hudson River R. R. . . . to Lewiston.
Rome, Watertown & Ogdensburg R. R. . . . . to Clayton.
Richelieu & Ontario Navigation Co. . . . . . to Alexandria Bay.
Richelieu & Ontario Navigation Co. . . . . . to Montreal.
Grand Trunk Ry. . . . . to St. John's.
Central Vermont R. R. . . . . to White River Junc.
Boston & Maine R. R. . . . . to Concord.
Concord & Montreal R. R. . . . . to Nashua.
Boston & Maine R. R. . . . . to Boston.
Old Colony R. R. . . . . to Fall River.
Old Colony Steamboat Co. (Fall River Line) . to New York.
Central R. R. of New Jersey . . . . to Bound Brook.
Philadelphia & Reading R. R. . . . . to Philadelphia.
Baltimore & Ohio R. R. . . . . to starting point.

THROUGH RATES.

Baltimore, Md. . . . . . . $40 25 | Washington, D. C. $42 25
†Philadelphia, Pa. . . . . 36 25 |

Transfer through Boston included.

FORM EX. 639.—MONTREAL, P. Q., AND RETURN.

For route to Niagara Falls, see page 219.

New York Central & Hudson River R. R. . . . to Lewiston.
Rome, Watertown & Ogdensburg R. R. . . . . to Clayton.
Richelieu & Ontario Navigation Co. . . . . . to Alexandria Bay.
Richelieu & Ontario Navigation Co. . . . . . to Montreal.
Grand Trunk Ry. . . . . to Sherbrooke.
Boston & Maine R. R. . . . . to Concord.
Concord & Montreal R. R. . . . . to Nashua.
Boston & Maine R. R. . . . . to Boston.
Old Colony R. R. . . . . to Fall River.
Old Colony Steamboat Co. (Fall River Line) . to New York.
Central R. R. of New Jersey . . . . to Bound Brook.
Philadelphia & Reading R. R. . . . . to Philadelphia.
Baltimore & Ohio R. R. . . . . to starting point.

THROUGH RATES.

Baltimore, Md. . . . . . . $40 25 | Washington, D. C. $42 25
†Philadelphia, Pa. . . . . 36 25 |

Transfer through Boston included.

BALTIMORE & OHIO RAILROAD COMPANY

Form Ex. 610.—Montreal, P. Q., and Return.

For route to Niagara Falls, see page 249.

New York Central & Hudson River R. R.	to Lewiston.
Rome, Watertown & Ogdensburg R. R.	to Clayton.
Richelieu & Ontario Navigation Co.	to Alexandria Bay.
Richelieu & Ontario Navigation Co.	to Montreal.
Grand Trunk Ry.	to Rouse's Point.
Delaware & Hudson R. R.	to Plattsburgh.
Champlain Transportation Co.	to Ticonderoga.
Delaware & Hudson R. R.	to Baldwin.
Champlain Transportation Co., Lake George Strs.	to Caldwell.
Delaware & Hudson R. R.	to Troy.
New York Central & Hudson River R. R.	to New York.
Central R. R. of New Jersey	to Bound Brook.
Philadelphia & Reading R. R.	to Philadelphia.
Baltimore & Ohio R. R.	to starting point.

THROUGH RATES.

Baltimore, Md.	$38 25	Washington, D. C.	$40 25
†Philadelphia, Pa.	34 25		

Form Ex. 754.—Montreal, P. Q., and Return.

Baltimore & Ohio R. R.	to Philadelphia.
Philadelphia & Reading R. R.	to Bound Brook.
Central R. R. of New Jersey	to New York.
New York & Albany Day Line	to Albany.
Delaware & Hudson R. R.	to Rouse's Point.
Grand Trunk Ry.	to Montreal.

Returning, same route.

THROUGH RATES.

Baltimore, Md.	$24 25	Washington, D. C.	$26 25
†Philadelphia, Pa.	20 25		

MONTREAL, P. Q.

The following forms of tickets reading *to Montreal* are intended to be sold in connection with forms reading *from Montreal* at through excursion rates, arrived at by method defined on page 203. These forms as well as forms reading *from Montreal must not be sold separately.*

FORM EX. 326.— MONTREAL, P. Q.

Baltimore & Ohio R. R.	to Philadelphia.
Philadelphia & Reading R. R.	to Bound Brook.
Central R. R. of New Jersey	to New York.
New York Central & Hudson River R. R.	to Troy.
Delaware & Hudson R. R.	to Caldwell.
Champlain Transportation Co. (Lake George Strs.)	to Baldwin.
Delaware & Hudson R. R.	to Ticonderoga.
Champlain Transportation Co.	to Plattsburgh.
Delaware & Hudson R. R.	to Rouse's Point.
Grand Trunk Ry.	to Montreal.

Rate from New York $11.70

FORM EX. 333.— MONTREAL, P. Q.

Baltimore & Ohio R. R.	to Philadelphia.
Philadelphia & Reading R. R.	to Bound Brook.
Central R. R. of New Jersey	to New York.
New York Central & Hudson River R. R.	to Utica.
Rome, Watertown & Ogdensburg R. R.	to Clayton.
Richelieu & Ontario Navigation Co. Steamer	to Alexandria Bay.
Richelieu & Ontario Navigation Co. Steamer	to Montreal.

Rate from New York $13.50

FORM EX. 334.— MONTREAL, P. Q.

Baltimore & Ohio R. R.	to Philadelphia.
Philadelphia & Reading R. R.	to Bound Brook.
Central R. R. of New Jersey	to New York.
New York Central & Hudson River R. R.	to Niagara Falls.
New York Central & Hudson River R. R.	to Syracuse.
Rome, Watertown & Ogdensburg R. R.	to Clayton.
Richelieu & Ontario Navigation Co. Steamer	to Alexandria Bay.
Richelieu & Ontario Navigation Co. Steamer	to Montreal.

Rate from New York $20.00

FORM EX. 335.— MONTREAL, P. Q.

Baltimore & Ohio R. R.	to Philadelphia.
Philadelphia & Reading R. R.	to Bound Brook.
Central R. R. of New Jersey	to New York.
New York Central & Hudson River R. R.	to Niagara Falls.
New York Central & Hudson River R. R.	to Lewiston.
Rome, Watertown & Ogdensburg R. R.	to Clayton.
Richelieu & Ontario Navigation Co. Steamer	to Alexandria Bay.
Richelieu & Ontario Navigation Co. Steamer	to Montreal.

Rate from New York $20.00

Form Ex. 336.—Montreal, P. Q.

Baltimore & Ohio R. R.	to Philadelphia.
Philadelphia & Reading R. R.	to Bound Brook.
Central R. R. of New Jersey	to New York.
New York Central & Hudson River R. R.	to Niagara Falls.
New York Central & Hudson River R. R.	to Lewiston.
Niagara Navigation Co., Steamer	to Toronto.
Grand Trunk Ry. or Richelieu & Ontario Navigation Co.	to Kingston.
Grand Trunk Ry. or Richelieu & Ontario Navigation Co.	to Prescott.
Grand Trunk Ry. or Richelieu & Ontario Navigation Co.	to Montreal.
Rate from New York	$20 00

Form Ex. 337.—Montreal, P. Q.

Baltimore & Ohio R. R.	to Philadelphia.
Philadelphia & Reading R. R.	to Bound Brook.
Central R. R. of New Jersey	to New York.
New York Central & Hudson River R. R. (via Niagara Falls)	to Suspension Bridge.
Grand Trunk Ry.	to Toronto.
Grand Trunk Ry. or Richelieu & Ontario Navigation Co., Steamer	to Kingston.
Grand Trunk Ry. or Richelieu & Ontario Navigation Co., Steamer	to Prescott.
Grand Trunk Ry. or Richelieu & Ontario Navigation Co., Steamer	to Montreal.
Rate from New York	$20 00

Form Ex. 340.—Montreal, P. Q.

Baltimore & Ohio R. R.	to Philadelphia.
Philadelphia & Reading R. R.	to Bound Brook.
Central R. R. of New Jersey	to New York.
New York Central & Hudson River R. R.	to Niagara Falls.
New York Central & Hudson River R. R.	to Lewiston.
Niagara Navigation Co.	to Toronto.
Canadian Pacific Ry.	to Smith's Falls.
Canadian Pacific Ry.	to Ottawa.
Canadian Pacific Ry. or Ottawa River Nav. Co.	to Montreal.
Rate from New York	$20 00

Form Ex. 340 must not be sold in connection with forms from Montreal reading via Grand Trunk Railway.

Form Ex. 341.—Montreal, P. Q.

Baltimore & Ohio R. R.	to Philadelphia.
Philadelphia & Reading R. R.	to Bound Brook.
Central R. R. of New Jersey	to New York.
New York Central & Hudson River R. R.	to Niagara Falls.
New York Central & Hudson River R. R.	to Lewiston.
Niagara Navigation Co.	to Toronto.
Canadian Pacific Ry.	to Smith's Falls.
Canadian Pacific Ry.	to Ottawa.
Canadian Pacific Ry.	to Prescott.
Richelieu & Ontario Navigation Co.	to Montreal.
Rate from New York	$20 00

Form Ex. 341 must not be sold in connection with forms from Montreal reading via Grand Trunk Railway.

SOUTH BRANCH, POTOMAC.

FORM EX. 343. MONTREAL, P. Q.

Baltimore & Ohio R. R. . . . . to Philadelphia.
Philadelphia & Reading R. R. . . . . to Bound Brook.
Central R. R. of New Jersey . . . . to New York.
West Shore R. R. to Albany.
Delaware & Hudson R. R. . . . . to Caldwell.
Champlain Transportation Co. (Lake George Strs. to Baldwin.
Delaware & Hudson R. R. . . . . to Ticonderoga.
Champlain Transportation Co. . . . . to Plattsburg.
Delaware & Hudson R. R. . . . . to Rouse's Point.
Grand Trunk Ry. to Montreal.

Rate from New York $11.70

FORM EX. 350. MONTREAL, P. Q.

Baltimore & Ohio R. R. . . . . to Philadelphia.
Philadelphia & Reading R. R. . . . . to Bound Brook.
Central R. R. of New Jersey . . . . to New York.
West Shore R. R. to Utica.
Rome, Watertown & Ogdensburg R. R. . . . . . . to Clayton.
Richelieu & Ontario Navigation Co. Steamer . . to Alexandria Bay.
Richelieu & Ontario Navigation Co. Steamer . . to Montreal.

Rate from New York $13.50

FORM EX. 352. MONTREAL, P. Q.

Baltimore & Ohio R. R. . . . . to Philadelphia.
Philadelphia & Reading R. R. . . . . to Bound Brook.
Central R. R. of New Jersey . . . . to New York.
West Shore R. R. to Niagara Falls.
New York Central & Hudson River R. R. . . . . to Lewiston.
Rome, Watertown & Ogdensburg R. R. . . . . . . to Clayton.
Richelieu & Ontario Navigation Co. Steamer . . to Alexandria Bay.
Richelieu & Ontario Navigation Co. Steamer . . to Montreal.

Rate from New York $19.50

FORM EX. 353. MONTREAL, P. Q.

Baltimore & Ohio R. R. . . . . to Philadelphia.
Philadelphia & Reading R. R. . . . . to Bound Brook.
Central R. R. of New Jersey . . . . to New York.
West Shore R. R. to Suspension Bridge.
Grand Trunk Ry. to Port Dalhousie.
Steamer "Empress of India" . . . . to Toronto.
Grand Tr. Ry. or Richelieu & Ontario Nav. Co. Str. to Kingston.
Grand Tr. Ry. or Richelieu & Ontario Nav. Co. Str. to Prescott.
Grand Tr. Ry. or Richelieu & Ontario Nav. Co. Str. to Montreal.

Rate from New York $19.50

FORM EX. 354. MONTREAL, P. Q.

Baltimore & Ohio R. R. . . . . to Philadelphia.
Philadelphia & Reading R. R. . . . . to Bound Brook.
Central R. R. of New Jersey . . . . to New York.
West Shore R. R. to Suspension Bridge.
Grand Trunk Ry. to Toronto.
Grand Tr. Ry. or Richelieu & Ontario Nav. Co. Str. to Kingston.
Grand Tr. Ry. or Richelieu & Ontario Nav. Co. Str. to Prescott.
Grand Tr. Ry. or Richelieu & Ontario Nav. Co. Str. to Montreal.

Rate from New York $19.70

Form Ex. 355. Montreal, P. Q.

Baltimore & Ohio R. R. . . . . to Philadelphia.
Philadelphia & Reading R. R. . . . . to Bound Brook.
Central R. R. of New Jersey . . . . to New York.
West Shore R. R. . . . . to Niagara Falls.
New York Central & Hudson River R. R. . . . to Lewiston.
Niagara Navigation Co. . . . . to Toronto.
Canadian Pacific Ry. . . . . to Smith's Falls.
Canadian Pacific Ry. . . . . to Ottawa.
Canadian Pacific Ry. or Ottawa River Nav. Co. . to Montreal.

Rate from New York $49.50

Form Ex. 355 must not be sold in connection with forms from Montreal reading via Grand Trunk Railway.

Form Ex. 356. Montreal, P. Q.

Baltimore & Ohio R. R. . . . . to Philadelphia.
Philadelphia & Reading R. R. . . . . to Bound Brook.
Central R. R. of New Jersey . . . . to New York.
West Shore R. R. . . . . to Niagara Falls.
New York Central & Hudson River R. R. . . . to Lewiston.
Niagara Navigation Co. . . . . to Toronto.
Canadian Pacific Ry. . . . . to Smith's Falls.
Canadian Pacific Ry. . . . . to Ottawa.
Canadian Pacific Ry. . . . . to Prescott.
Richelieu & Ontario Navigation Co. Steamer . . to Montreal.

Rate from New York $49.50

Form Ex. 356 must not be sold in connection with forms from Montreal reading via Grand Trunk Railway.

Form Ex. 360. Montreal, P. Q.

Baltimore & Ohio R. R. . . . . to Philadelphia.
Philadelphia & Reading R. R. . . . . to Bound Brook.
Central R. R. of New Jersey . . . . to New York.
New York, Lake Erie & Western R. R. . . . . to Suspension Bridge.
Grand Trunk Ry. . . . . to Port Dalhousie.
Steamer "Empress of India" . . . . to Toronto.
Grand Tr. Ry. or Richelieu & Ontario Nav. Co. Str. to Kingston.
Grand Tr. Ry. or Richelieu & Ontario Nav. Co. Str. to Montreal.

Rate from New York $49.50

Form Ex. 361. Montreal, P. Q.

Baltimore & Ohio R. R. . . . . to Philadelphia.
Philadelphia & Reading R. R. . . . . to Bound Brook.
Central R. R. of New Jersey . . . . to New York.
New York, Lake Erie & Western R. R. . . . . to Niagara Falls.
New York Central & Hudson River R. R. . . . to Lewiston.
Niagara Navigation Co's Steamer . . . . to Toronto.
Grand Trunk Ry. or Richelieu & Ontario Navigation Co. Steamer . . . . to Kingston.
Grand Trunk Ry. or Richelieu & Ontario Navigation Co. Steamer . . . . to Montreal.

Rate from New York $49.50

Form Ex. 362. Montreal, P. Q.

Baltimore & Ohio R. R. . . . . to Philadelphia.
Philadelphia & Reading R. R. . . . . to Bound Brook.
Central R. R. of New Jersey . . . . to New York.
New York, Lake Erie & Western R. R. . . . . to Suspension Bridge.
Grand Trunk Ry. . . . . to Toronto.
Grand Trunk Ry. or Richelieu & Ontario Navigation Co. Steamer . . . . to Kingston.
Grand Trunk Ry. or Richelieu & Ontario Navigation Co. Steamer . . . . to Montreal.

Rate from New York $49.50

FORM EX. 363. MONTREAL, P. Q.

Baltimore & Ohio R. R. . . . . to Philadelphia.
Philadelphia & Reading R. R. . . . . to Bound Brook.
Central R. R. of New Jersey. . . . . to New York.
New York, Lake Erie & Western R. R. . . . . . to Niagara Falls.
New York Central & Hudson River R. R. . . . to Lewiston.
Niagara Navigation Co. Steamer . . . . to Toronto.
Canadian Pacific Ry. . . . . to Ottawa.
Canadian Pacific Ry. or Ottawa River Navigation
 Co. Steamer, ... to Montreal.

Rate from New York $19.70

Form Ex. 363 must not be sold in connection with forms from Montreal reading via Grand Trunk Railway.

FORM EX. 364. —MONTREAL, P. Q.

Baltimore & Ohio R. R. . . . . to Philadelphia.
Philadelphia & Reading R. R. . . . . to Bound Brook.
Central R. R. of New Jersey. . . . . to New York.
New York, Lake Erie & Western R. R. . . . . . to Niagara Falls.
New York Central & Hudson River R. R. . . . to Lewiston.
Niagara Navigation Co. Steamer . . . . to Toronto.
Canadian Pacific Ry. . . . . to Ottawa.
Canadian Pacific Ry. . . . . to Prescott.
Richelieu & Ontario Navigation Co. Steamer . . to Montreal.

Rate from New York $19.50

Form Ex. 364 must not be sold in connection with forms from Montreal reading via Grand Trunk Railway.

FORM EX. 365. —MONTREAL, P. Q.

Baltimore & Ohio R. R. . . . . to Philadelphia.
Philadelphia & Reading R. R. . . . . to Bound Brook.
Central R. R. of New Jersey. . . . . to New York.
New York, Lake Erie & Western R. R. . . . . . to Niagara Falls.
New York Central & Hudson River R. R. . . . to Lewiston.
Niagara Navigation Co. Steamer . . . . to Toronto.
Canadian Pacific Ry. . . . . to Sharbot Lake.
Kingston & Pembroke Ry. . . . . to Kingston.
Richelieu & Ontario Navigation Co. Steamer . . to Montreal.

Rate from New York $19.50

Form Ex. 365 must not be sold in connection with forms from Montreal reading via Grand Trunk Railway.

FORM EX. 366.—MONTREAL, P. Q.

Baltimore & Ohio R. R. . . . . to Philadelphia.
Philadelphia & Reading R. R. . . . . to Bound Brook.
Central R. R. of New Jersey. . . . . to New York.
New York, Lake Erie & Western R. R. . . . . . to Binghamton.
Delaware & Hudson R. R. . . . . to C. & C. V. June.
Cooperstown & Charlotte Valley R. R. . . . . . to Cooperstown.
Otsego Lake Steamer and Stage. . . . . to Richfield Springs.
Delaware, Lackawanna & Western R. R. . . . . to Utica.
Rome, Water, & Ogdens. R. R. (via Trenton Falls) to Clayton.
Richelieu & Ontario Navigation Co. Steamer . . to Alexandria Bay.
Richelieu & Ontario Navigation Co. Steamer . . to Montreal.

Rate from New York $17.20

Tickets between Cooperstown and Richfield Springs by the Otsego Lake Steamer and stage are for passage only; baggage will be charged extra.

Form Ex. 370.—Montreal, P. Q.

Baltimore & Ohio R. R.	to Philadelphia.
Philadelphia & Reading R. R.	to Bound Brook.
Central R. R. of New Jersey	to New York.
Delaware, Lackawanna & Western R. R.	to Buffalo.
New York Central & Hudson River R. R.	to Niagara Falls.
New York Central & Hudson River R. R.	to Lewiston.
Niagara Navigation Co. Steamer	to Toronto.
Canadian Pacific Ry.	to Ottawa.
Canadian Pac. Ry. or Ottawa River Nav. Co. Str.	to Montreal.
Rate from New York	$49.50

Form Ex. 370 must not be sold in connection with forms from Montreal reading via Grand Trunk Railway.

Form Ex. 372.—Montreal, P. Q.

Baltimore & Ohio R. R.	to Philadelphia.
Philadelphia & Reading R. R.	to Bound Brook.
Central R. R. of New Jersey	to New York.
Delaware, Lackawanna & Western R. R.	to Buffalo.
New York Central & Hudson River R. R.	to Niagara Falls.
New York Central & Hudson River R. R.	to Lewiston.
Niagara Navigation Co. Steamer	to Toronto.
Gr. Trunk Ry. or Richelieu & Ont. Nav. Co. Str.	to Kingston.
Gr. Trunk Ry. or Richelieu & Ont. Nav. Co. Str.	to Prescott.
Gr. Trunk Ry. or Richelieu & Ont. Nav. Co. Str.	to Montreal.
Rate from New York	$49.50

Form Ex. 375.—Montreal, P. Q.

Baltimore & Ohio R. R.	to Philadelphia.
Philadelphia & Reading R. R.	to Bound Brook.
Central R. R. of New Jersey	to New York.
Delaware, Lackawanna & Western R. R.	to Buffalo.
New York, Lake Erie & Western R. R.	to Suspension Bridge.
Grand Trunk Ry.	to Port Dalhousie.
Steamer "Empress of India"	to Toronto.
Gr. Trunk Ry. or Richelieu & Ont. Nav. Co. Str.	to Kingston.
Gr. Trunk Ry. or Richelieu & Ont. Nav. Co. Str.	to Prescott.
Gr. Trunk Ry. or Richelieu & Ont. Nav. Co. Str.	to Montreal.
Rate from New York	$49.50

Form Ex. 377.—Montreal, P. Q.

Baltimore & Ohio R. R.	to Philadelphia.
Philadelphia & Reading R. R.	to Bound Brook.
Central R. R. of New Jersey	to New York.
Delaware, Lackawanna & Western R. R.	to Buffalo.
New York Central & Hudson River R. R.	to Niagara Falls.
Grand Trunk Ry.	to Toronto.
Gr. Trunk Ry. or Richelieu & Ont. Nav. Co. Str.	to Kingston.
Gr. Trunk Ry. or Richelieu & Ont. Nav. Co. Str.	to Prescott.
Gr. Trunk Ry. or Richelieu & Ont. Nav. Co. Str.	to Montreal.
Rate from New York	$49.50

Form Ex. 378.—Montreal, P. Q.

Baltimore & Ohio R. R.	to Philadelphia.
Philadelphia & Reading R. R.	to Bound Brook.
Central R. R. of New Jersey	to New York.
Delaware, Lackawanna & Western R. R.	to Buffalo.
New York Central & Hudson River R. R.	to Niagara Falls.
New York Central & Hudson River R. R.	to Lewiston.
Rome, Watertown & Ogdensburg R. R.	to Clayton.
Richelieu & Ontario Navigation Co. Steamer	to Alexandria Bay.
Richelieu & Ontario Navigation Co. Steamer	to Montreal.
Rate from New York	$49.50

Form Ex. 346.—Montreal, P. Q.

Baltimore & Ohio R. R. . . . . to Philadelphia.
Philadelphia & Reading R. R. . . . . to Bound Brook.
Central R. R. of New Jersey . . . . to New York.
Delaware, Lackawanna & Western R. R. . . . to Utica.
Rome, Watertown & Ogdensburg R. R. . . . . to Clayton.
Richelieu & Ontario Navigation Co. Steamer . . to Alexandria Bay.
Richelieu & Ontario Navigation Co. Steamer . . to Montreal.

Rate from New York $13.40

Form Ex. 379.—Montreal, P. Q.

Baltimore & Ohio R. R. . . . . to Philadelphia.
Philadelphia & Reading R. R. . . . . to Bound Brook.
Central R. R. of New Jersey . . . . to New York.
Delaware, Lackawanna & Western R. R. . . . to Richfield Springs.
Delaware, Lackawanna & Western R. R. . . . to Utica.
Rome, Watertown & Ogdensburg R. R. . . . . to Clayton.
Richelieu & Ontario Navigation Co. Steamer . . to Alexandria Bay.
Richelieu & Ontario Navigation Co. Steamer . . to Montreal.

Rate from New York $14.40

Form Ex. 380.—Montreal, P. Q.

Baltimore & Ohio R. R. . . . . to Philadelphia.
Philadelphia & Reading R. R. . . . . to Bound Brook.
Central R. R. of New Jersey . . . . to New York.
Delaware, Lackawanna & Western R. R. . . . to Syracuse.
Rome, Watertown & Ogdensburg R. R. . . . . to Clayton.
Richelieu & Ontario Navigation Co. Steamer . . to Alexandria Bay.
Richelieu & Ontario Navigation Co. Steamer . . to Montreal.

Rate from New York $14.40

Form Ex. 381.—Montreal, P. Q.

Baltimore & Ohio R. R. . . . . to Philadelphia.
Philadelphia & Reading R. R. . . . . to Bound Brook.
Central R. R. of New Jersey . . . . to New York.
Delaware, Lackawanna & Western R. R. . . . to Oswego.
Rome, Watertown & Ogdensburg R. R. . . . . to Clayton.
Richelieu & Ontario Navigation Co. Steamer . . to Alexandria Bay.
Richelieu & Ontario Navigation Co. Steamer . . to Montreal.

Rate from New York $14.70

Form Ex. 326.—Montreal, P. Q.

Baltimore & Ohio R. R. . . . . to Philadelphia.
Philadelphia & Reading R. R. . . . . to Bound Brook.
Central R. R. of New Jersey . . . . to New York.
New York, New Haven & Hartford R. R. . . . to Springfield.
Connecticut River R. R. . . . . to South Vernon.
Central Vermont R. R. . . . . to Brattleboro.
Vermont Valley R. R. . . . . to Bellows Falls.
Central Vermont R. R. . . . . to St. John's.
Grand Trunk Ry. . . . . to Montreal.

Rate from New York $10.00

The following forms of tickets reading *from Montreal* are intended to be sold in connection with any of the foregoing tickets reading to and terminating at Montreal.

The going and returning routes desired should be selected, and the basing rate for the round trip *from New York* should be made by a combination of the fares from and to New York as quoted immediately after each route. To the rates so determined, agents will add their excursion basing fare to New York and return, as quoted herein, on page xxi, thereby arriving at the through rates from their respective stations to Montreal, P. Q., and return.

Thus, for example, in case passenger at Baltimore selects Form Ex. 326 going and Ex. 382 returning from Montreal, a combination of the rates quoted via these routes to and from Montreal would be $24.50 (the basing rate from New York); to this rate the agent at Baltimore will add $8.00 (his excursion basing rate to New York), making the through fare from Baltimore for the tour $32.50.

FORM EX. 382.—FROM MONTREAL, P. Q.

Grand Trunk Ry.	to St. John's.
Central Vermont R. R.	to Bellows Falls.
Cheshire R. R.	to Fitchburg.
Fitchburg R. R.	to Boston.
Old Colony R. R.	to Fall River.
Old Colony Steamboat Co. (Fall River Line)	to New York.
Central R. R. of New Jersey	to Bound Brook.
Philadelphia & Reading R. R.	to Philadelphia.
Baltimore & Ohio R. R.	to destination.
Rate from Montreal to New York	$13.00

FORM EX. 383.—FROM MONTREAL, P. Q.

Grand Trunk Ry.	to St. John's.
Central Vermont R. R.	to White River Junc.
Boston & Maine R. R.	to Boston.
Old Colony R. R.	to Fall River.
Old Colony Steamboat Co. (Fall River Line)	to New York.
Central R. R. of New Jersey	to Bound Brook.
Philadelphia & Reading R. R.	to Philadelphia.
Baltimore & Ohio R. R.	to destination.
Rate from Montreal to New York	$13.00

FORM EX. 384.—FROM MONTREAL, P. Q.

Grand Trunk Ry.	to Rouse's Point.
Delaware & Hudson R. R.	to Plattsburgh.
Champlain Transportation Co.	to Fort Ticonderoga.
Delaware & Hudson R. R.	to Baldwin.
Champlain Transportation Co. (Lake George Strs.)	to Caldwell.
Delaware & Hudson R. R.	to Saratoga.
Fitchburg R. R.	to Boston.

Old Colony R. R. .... to Fall River.
Old Colony Steamboat Co. (Fall River Line) ... to New York.
Central R. R. of New Jersey .... to Bound Brook.
Philadelphia & Reading R. R. .... to Philadelphia.
Baltimore & Ohio R. R. .... to destination.

Rate from Montreal to New York $17 15

FORM EX. 385.—FROM MONTREAL, P. Q.

Grand Trunk Ry. .... to Portland.
Boston & Maine R. R. .... to Boston.
Old Colony R. R. .... to Fall River.
Old Colony Steamboat Co. (Fall River Line) ... to New York.
Central R. R. of New Jersey .... to Bound Brook.
Philadelphia & Reading R. R. .... to Philadelphia.
Baltimore & Ohio R. R. .... to destination.

Rate from Montreal to New York $13 00

FORM EX. 386.—FROM MONTREAL, P. Q.

Canadian Pacific Ry. .... to Newport, Vt.
Boston & Maine R. R. .... to Wells' River.
Concord & Montreal R. R. .... to Concord.
Boston & Maine R. R. .... to Boston.
Old Colony R. R. .... to Fall River.
Old Colony Steamboat Co. (Fall River Line) ... to New York.
Central R. R. of New Jersey .... to Bound Brook.
Philadelphia & Reading R. R. .... to Philadelphia.
Baltimore & Ohio R. R. .... to destination.

Rate from Montreal to New York $13 00

Form Ex. 386 must not be sold in connection with forms to Montreal reading via Grand Trunk Railway.

FORM EX. 387.—FROM MONTREAL, P. Q.

Canadian Pacific Ry. .... to Newport, Vt.
Boston & Maine R. R. .... to Wells' River.
Concord & Montreal R. R. .... to Fabyan's.
Boston & Maine R. R. .... to North Conway.
Boston & Maine R. R. .... to Boston.
Old Colony R. R. .... to Fall River.
Old Colony Steamboat Co. (Fall River Line) ... to New York.
Central R. R. of New Jersey .... to Bound Brook.
Philadelphia & Reading R. R. .... to Philadelphia.
Baltimore & Ohio R. R. .... to destination.

Rate from Montreal to New York $13 00

Form Ex. 387 must not be sold in connection with forms to Montreal, reading via Grand Trunk Railway.

FORM EX. 388.—FROM MONTREAL, P. Q.

Grand Trunk Ry. .... to Rouse's Point.
Delaware & Hudson R. R. .... to Plattsburgh.
Champlain Transportation Co. .... to Burlington.
Central Vermont R. R. .... to Montpelier.
Montpelier & Wells' River R. R. .... to Wells' River.
Concord & Montreal R. R. .... to Concord.
Boston & Maine R. R. .... to Boston.
Old Colony R. R. .... to Fall River.
Old Colony Steamboat Co. (Fall River Line) ... to New York.
Central R. R. of New Jersey .... to Bound Brook.
Philadelphia & Reading R. R. .... to Philadelphia.
Baltimore & Ohio R. R. .... to destination.

Rate from Montreal to New York $13 85

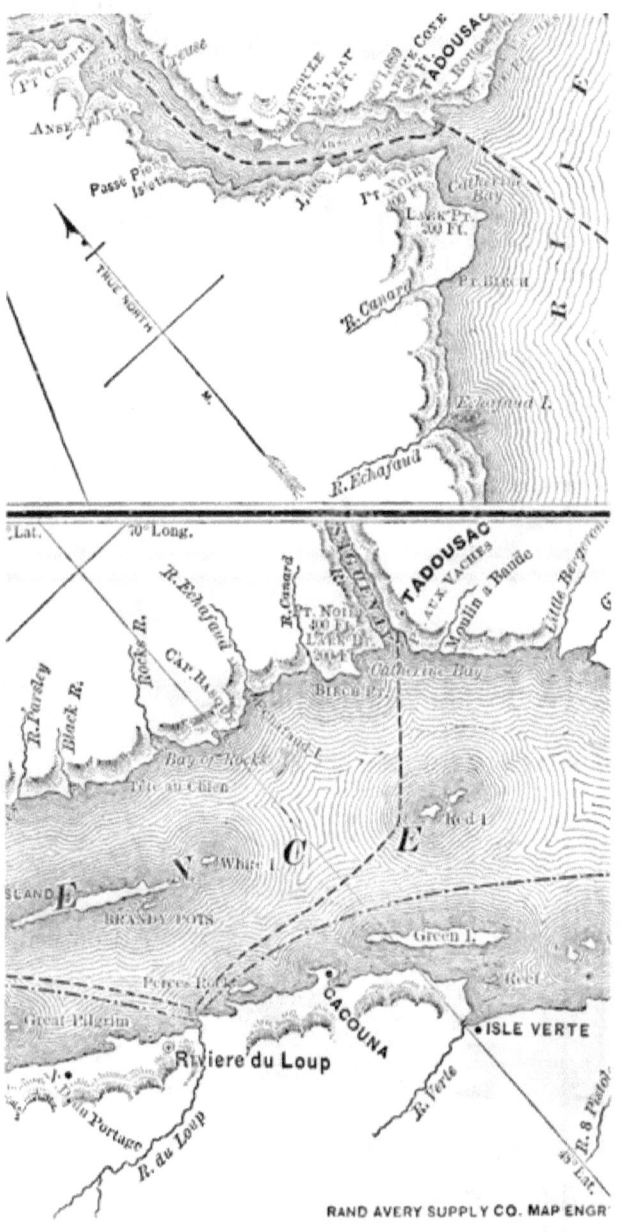

SAGUENAY RIVER LINE

OFFICIAL TIME-TABLE.

From the 21st of June to the 16th of September, 1892

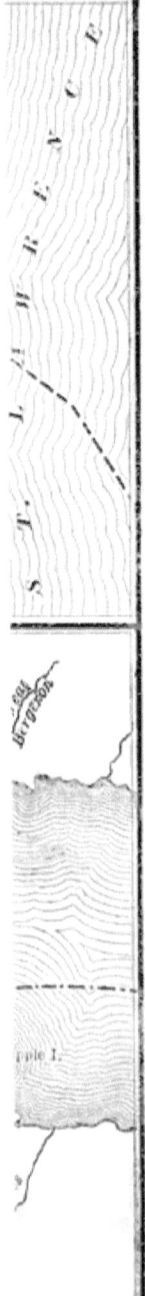

Distance	PORTS	Steamer CANADA. Leaves Tuesday.	Steamer SAGUENAY. Lvs. Wednesday.	Steamer CANADA. Leaves Friday.	Steamer SAGUENAY. Lvs. Saturday.
	Lve. Quebec	7.30 AM	7.30 AM	7.30 AM	7.30 AM
85	Arr. Bay St. Paul	11.30 AM	11.30 AM	11.30 AM	11.30 AM
82	" Eboulement	12.30 PM	12.30 PM	12.30 PM	12.30 PM
112	" Murray Bay	2.00 PM	2.00 PM	2.00 PM	2.00 PM
131	" Rivière du Loup	5.00 PM	5.00 PM	5.00 PM	5.00 PM
165	" Tadousac	7.00 PM	7.00 PM	7.00 PM	7.00 PM
196	" L'Anse St. Jean	*Wednes. AM	*Thurs. AM	*Saturday AM	*Sunday AM
205	" Ha! Ha! Bay	" R "	" R "	" R "	" R "
225	" Chicoutimi	Rt'n			
Rt'n	Lve. Chicoutimi				
62	Arr. L'Anse St. Jean				
101	" Tadousac	Wed. 2.30 PM	Thur. 2.30 PM	Sat'y 2.30 PM	Monday 2.30 PM
134	" Rivière du Loup	" 5.00 PM	" 5.00 PM	" 5.00 PM	" 5.00 PM
153	" Murray Bay	" 10.00 PM	" 10.00 PM	" 10.00 PM	" 10.00 PM
180	" Eboulements	" 11.30 PM	" 11.30 PM	" 11.30 PM	" 11.30 PM
225	" Bay St. Paul				
	" Quebec	Thu. 7.00 AM	Friday 7.00 AM	Sun. 7.00 AM	Monday 7.00 AM

* Indicates that the steamer arrives and leaves according to the tide.

When the tide suits, the steamer proceeds to Chicoutimi before calling at Ha! Ha! Bay.

P. S.—From the 3d of May to the 15th of November a steamer will leave Quebec on Tuesday and Friday at 7.30 a. m., and from June 21st to September 16th an additional steamer will leave on Wednesdays and Saturdays.

Steamer "SAGUENAY" will commence on or about May 3d, will run until about November 15th, and call at all the Ports.

Steamer "CANADA" will commence about June 24th, and run until about September 16th, inclusive; will call at all the Ports except Bay St. Paul and Eboulments.

Returning, the departure from Murray Bay will be at 10 p. m., stopping at the way Ports.

☞ For the convenience of families, etc., commencing July 4th to the 12th of September, one steamer will leave Quebec for Murray Bay every Monday at 10 o'clock a. m.; returning, leave Murray Bay on Tuesdays at 7 a. m., touching at all the intermediate ports.

FORM EX. 388.—FROM MONTREAL, P. Q.

Grand Trunk Ry.	to Groveton Junction.
Concord & Montreal R. R.	to Concord.
Boston & Maine R. R.	to Boston.
Old Colony R. R.	to Fall River.
Old Colony Steamboat Co. (Fall River Line)	to New York.
Central R. R. of New Jersey	to Bound Brook.
Philadelphia & Reading R. R.	to Philadelphia.
Baltimore & Ohio R. R.	to destination.
Rate from Montreal to New York	$13.00

FORM EX. 389.—FROM MONTREAL, P. Q.

Canadian Pacific Ry.	to Newport, Vt.
Boston & Maine R. R.	to Wells River.
Concord & Montreal R. R.	to Fabyan's.
Maine Central R. R.	to Portland.
Boston & Maine R. R.	to Boston.
Old Colony R. R.	to Fall River.
Old Colony Steamboat Co. (Fall River Line)	to New York.
Central R. R. of New Jersey	to Bound Brook.
Philadelphia & Reading R. R.	to Philadelphia.
Baltimore & Ohio R. R.	to destination.
Rate from Montreal to New York	$13.00

Form Ex. 389 must not be sold in connection with forms to Montreal, reading via Grand Trunk Railway.

FORM EX. 391.—FROM MONTREAL, P. Q.

Grand Trunk Ry.	to St. John's.
Central Vermont R. R.	to Bellows Falls.
Vermont Valley R. R.	to Brattleboro.
Central Vermont R. R.	to South Vernon.
Connecticut River R. R.	to Springfield.
New York, New Haven & Hartford R. R.	to New York.
Central R. R. of New Jersey	to Bound Brook.
Philadelphia & Reading R. R.	to Philadelphia.
Baltimore & Ohio R. R.	to destination.
Rate from Montreal to New York	$10.00

FORM EX. 392.—FROM MONTREAL, P. Q.

Grand Trunk Ry.	to St. John's.
Central Vermont R. R.	to Swanton.
Boston & Maine R. R.	to Lunenburg.
Maine Central R. R.	to Portland.
Boston & Maine R. R.	to Boston.
Old Colony R. R.	to Fall River.
Old Colony Steamboat Co. (Fall River Line)	to New York.
Central R. R. of New Jersey	to Bound Brook.
Philadelphia & Reading R. R.	to Philadelphia.
Baltimore & Ohio R. R.	to destination.
Rate from Montreal to New York	$13.00

MONTROSE, PA.

FORM EX. 395.—MONTROSE, PA., AND RETURN.

Baltimore & Ohio R. R.	to Philadelphia.
Philadelphia & Reading R. R.	to Bethlehem.
Lehigh Valley R. R.	to Tunkhannock.
Montrose Ry.	to Montrose.

Returning, same route.

THROUGH RATES.

Baltimore, Md.	$13.50	Washington, D. C.	$15.50
Philadelphia, Pa.	9.50		

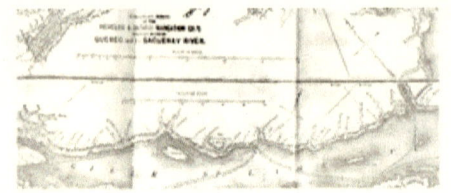

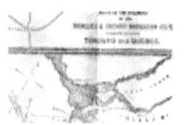

MORGANTON, N. C.

Form Ex. 10.—Morganton, N. C. and Return.

Baltimore & Ohio R. R.	to Washington.
Transfer B. & O. Depot.	to R. & D. Depot.
Richmond & Danville R. R.	to Morganton.

Returning, same route.

THROUGH RATES.

Baltimore, Md.	$19 70	Meyersdale, Pa.	$25 60
Bellaire, O.	32 15	Morgantown, W. Va.	30 05
Berkeley Springs, W. Va.	22 15	Moundsville, W. Va.	31 70
Cameron, W. Va.	31 00	Mountain Lake Park, Md.	25 65
Charlestown, W. Va.	20 70	Mt. Pleasant, Pa.	28 30
Chester, Pa.	25 00	Newark, Del.	23 80
Clarksburg, W. Va.	30 05	New York, N. Y.	29 70
Connellsville, Pa.	27 80	Oakland, Md.	25 75
Cumberland, Md.	24 10	Parkersburg, W. Va.	32 15
Deer Park, Md.	25 70	Philadelphia, Pa.	25 70
Fairmont, W. Va.	29 05	Piedmont, W. Va.	25 30
Frederick, Md.	20 30	Pittsburgh, Pa.	30 10
Grafton, W. Va.	28 15	Rockwood, Pa.	26 05
Hagerstown, Md.	21 10	Somerset, Pa.	26 15
Harper's Ferry, W. Va.	20 20	Uniontown, Pa.	28 25
Havre de Grace, Md.	22 95	Washington, Pa.	31 20
Johnstown, Pa.	27 85	Wheeling, W. Va.	32 15
Keyser, W. Va.	25 00	Wilmington, Del.	24 50
McKeesport, Pa.	29 55	Winchester, Va.	21 80
Martinsburg, W. Va.	20 95		

Form Ex. 17.—Morganton, N. C. and Return.

Baltimore & Ohio R. R.	to Lexington.
Chesapeake & Ohio R. R.	to Lynchburg.
Richmond & Danville R. R.	to Morganton.

Returning, same route.

THROUGH RATES.

Baltimore, Md.	$19 50	Morgantown, W. Va.	$27 35
Bellaire, O.	29 75	Moundsville, W. Va.	29 00
Berkeley Springs, W. Va.	19 15	Mountain Lake Park, Md.	23 15
Cameron, W. Va.	28 30	Mt. Pleasant, Pa.	25 60
Charlestown, W. Va.	17 50	Newark, Del.	23 80
Chester, Pa.	25 00	New York, N. Y.	29 50
Clarksburg, W. Va.	26 35	Oakland, Md.	23 35
Connellsville, Pa.	25 10	Parkersburg, W. Va.	19 50
Cumberland, Md.	21 10	Philadelphia, Pa.	25 50
Deer Park, Md.	23 30	Piedmont, W. Va.	22 50
Fairmont, W. Va.	26 35	Pittsburgh, Pa.	27 10
Frederick, Md.	18 45	Rockwood, Pa.	23 35
Grafton, W. Va.	25 15	Somerset, Pa.	23 75
Hagerstown, Md.	18 50	Staunton, Va.	11 60
Harper's Ferry, W. Va.	17 50	Strasburg, Va.	17 50
Harrisonburg, Va.	15 90	Uniontown, Pa.	25 55
Havre de Grace, Md.	22 95	Washington, D. C.	17 50
Johnstown, Pa.	25 15	Washington, Pa.	28 50
Keyser, W. Va.	22 30	Wheeling, W. Va.	29 50
McKeesport, Pa.	26 85	Wilmington, Del.	24 50
Martinsburg, W. Va.	18 25	Winchester, Va.	17 50
Meyersdale, Pa.	22 00		

MT. KINEO HOUSE (MOOSEHEAD LAKE), ME.

FORM EX. 1011.—MT. KINEO HOUSE (MOOSEHEAD LAKE), ME., AND RETURN.

(Via rail, Bangor and Greenville; returning via Sound Lines.)

Baltimore & Ohio R. R.	to Philadelphia.
Rail Lines (see pages 50 to 55 for route)	to Boston.
Boston & Maine R. R.	to Portland.
Maine Central R. R.	to Dover and Foxcroft or Oldtown.
Bangor & Piscataquis R. R.	to Greenville.
Steamer on Moosehead Lake (20 miles)	to Mt. Kineo House.
Steamer on Moosehead Lake (20 miles)	to Greenville.
Bangor & Piscataquis R. R.	to Dover and Foxcroft or Oldtown.
Maine Central R. R.	to Portland.
Boston & Maine R. R.	to Boston.
Sound Lines (see pages 50 to 55 for route)	to New York.
Central R. R. of New Jersey	to Bound Brook.
Philadelphia & Reading R. R.	to Philadelphia.
Baltimore & Ohio R. R.	to starting point.

THROUGH RATES.

Baltimore, Md. . . . . . . $32 00 | Washington, D. C. $34 00
Philadelphia, Pa. 28 00

FORM EX. 1011.—MT. KINEO HOUSE (MOOSEHEAD LAKE), ME., AND RETURN.

(Via Sound Lines, Bangor and Greenville; returning via rail.)

Baltimore & Ohio R. R.	to Philadelphia.
Philadelphia & Reading R. R.	to Bound Brook.
Central R. R. of New Jersey	to New York.
Sound Lines (see pages 50 to 55 for route)	to Boston.
Boston & Maine R. R.	to Portland.
Maine Central R. R.	to Dover and Foxcroft or Oldtown.
Bangor & Piscataquis R. R.	to Greenville.
Steamer on Moosehead Lake (20 miles)	to Mt. Kineo House.
Steamer on Moosehead Lake (20 miles)	to Greenville.
Bangor & Piscataquis R. R.	to Dover and Foxcroft or Oldtown.
Maine Central R. R.	to Portland.
Boston & Maine R. R.	to Boston.
Rail Lines (see pages 50 to 55 for route)	to Philadelphia.
Baltimore & Ohio R. R.	to starting point.

THROUGH RATES.

Baltimore, Md. . . . . . . $32 00 | Washington, D. C. $34 00
Philadelphia, Pa. 28 00

FORM EX. 1011.—MT. KINEO HOUSE (MOOSEHEAD LAKE), ME., AND RETURN.

(Via Rail Lines, Bangor and Greenville, in both directions.)

Baltimore & Ohio R. R.	to Philadelphia.
Rail Lines (see pages 50 to 55 for route)	to Boston.
Boston & Maine R. R.	to Portland.
Maine Central R. R.	to Dover and Foxcroft or Oldtown.
Bangor & Piscataquis R. R.	to Greenville.
Steamer on Moosehead Lake (20 miles)	to Mt. Kineo House.

Returning, same route.

THROUGH RATES.

Baltimore, Md. . . . . . . $33 00 | Washington, D. C. $35 00
Philadelphia, Pa. 29 00

FORM EX. 1041. MT. KINEO HOUSE (MOOSEHEAD LAKE), ME., AND
RETURN.
(Via Sound Lines, Bangor and Greenville, in both directions.)

Baltimore & Ohio R. R.	to Philadelphia.
Philadelphia & Reading R. R.	to Bound Brook.
Central R. R. of New Jersey	to New York.
Sound Lines (see pages 0 to 55 for route)	to Boston.
Boston & Maine R. R.	to Portland.
Maine Central R. R.	to Dover and Foxcroft or Oldtown.
Bangor & Piscataquis R. R.	to Greenville.
Steamer on Moosehead Lake (20 miles)	to Mt. Kineo House.

Returning, same route.

THROUGH RATES.

Baltimore, Md.	$33 00	Washington, D. C.	$33 00
Philadelphia, Pa.	27 00		

MOUNTAIN LAKE PARK.

On the summit of the Alleghanies, between Deer Park and Oakland, is a summer resort entering upon its eighth successful season. Here one may reside with his family in perfect security, free from many objectionable associations such as are found in the ordinary fashionable establishments. Here is a summer city, protected from grave moral perils; a summer home, in the most salubrious of climates; a summer school, with competent instructors; a summer lyceum, with able lecturers; a summer resort, amid superb scenery; a public auditorium, where philanthropic, benevolent and religious subjects are presented, and where concerts and scenic representations are produced.

Here also is freedom from the annoyances of hay fever, malaria and liquors. Mosquitoes, rarely known, are feeble and degenerate representatives of the race that swarms the seaside resorts.

Railroad station, express, telegraph and post-offices on the grounds. Three mails; two accommodation and three express trains, with parlor cars and sleepers each way, east and west, every day. New York, Philadelphia, Baltimore and Wheeling newspapers on the day of issue.

Thousands of people visited Mountain Lake Park last year, and were delighted with its advantages. About one hundred cottages are built and occupied for the greater part by their owners. A few cottages are for rent. A first-class hotel (The Mountain Lake Park Hotel) is open all

MOUNTAIN LAKE PARK.

the season for those who do not wish to keep house. Other excellent hotels and boarding-houses accommodate guests. These buildings are not massed together in a narrow enclosure, but are scattered over a hundred acres, among beautiful oak groves. Each person may have almost absolute retirement or genial and refined company.

Here also is a branch of the great popular university, the Chautauqua Literary and Scientific Circle. Here are schools for drawing and painting, of oratory and elocution, and of amateur photography, with a skillful instructor, and facilities for developing negatives and printing pictures. The study of geology, amid surrounding rocks, and of botany, with a rich and varied flora, may be successfully prosecuted. A kindergarten for the little ones and a normal school for kindergarten training are also established.

Here one finds tennis and croquet, foot ball and base ball, for the playful; hammocks and shade for the idle; trout streams and boating for sporting; lectures for the thoughtful, and religious meetings for the devout. Rest, quiet and health for everybody.

Mountain Lake Park is a tract of eight hundred acres of forest and glade in the midst of the majestic and picturesque scenery of the Baltimore & Ohio Railroad. No one is compelled to do anything to which his taste does not incline him. In so large a territory everyone can have his choice of place and occupation. Only those things are forbidden which tend to disturb the rest and quiet of the community.

FORM EX. 97 OR EX. MOUNTAIN LAKE PARK, MD., AND RETURN.

Baltimore & Ohio R. R. . . . . to Mountain Lake Park.
Returning, same route.

THROUGH RATES.

Annapolis, Md.	$9 00	Grafton, W. Va.	$2 00
Baltimore, Md.	9 15	Hagerstown, Md.	7 00
Bellaire, O.	6 35	Harper's Ferry, W. Va.	5 95
Berkeley Springs, W. Va.	1 60	Harrisonburg, Va.	10 95
Cameron, W. Va.	1 85	Havre de Grace, Md.	10 60
Charlestown, W. Va.	6 15	Johnstown, Pa.	5 80
Chester, Pa.	12 65	Keyser, W. Va.	1 15
Clarksburg, W. Va.	2 30	Lexington, Va.	11 05
Connellsville, Pa.	5 75	McKeesport, Pa.	7 30
Cumberland, Md.	2 05	Martinsburg, W. Va.	5 15
Deer Park, Md.	15	Meyersdale, Pa.	3 55
Fairmont, W. Va.	2 00	Morgantown, W. Va.	3 90
Frederick, Md.	7 00	Moundsville, W. Va.	5 55

ROUTES AND RATES FOR SUMMER TOURS. 211

COTTAGE LIFE, MOUNTAIN LAKE PARK.

Mt. Pleasant, Pa.	$6 25	Somerset, Pa.	$4 40
Newark, Del.	11 45	Springfield, W. Va.	2 90
New York, N. Y.	17 45	Staunton, Va.	12 25
Oakland, Md.	45	Strasburg, Va.	8 90
Parkersburg, W. Va.	6 45	Uniontown, Pa.	6 20
Paw Paw, W. Va.	3 00	Washington, D. C.	8 45
Philadelphia, Pa.	13 45	Washington, Pa. (via Wheel	
Piedmont, W. Va.	95	ing, W. Va.)	7 35
Pittsburgh, Pa.	8 05	Wheeling, W. Va.	6 00
Rockwood, Pa.	4 00	Wilmington, Del.	12 45
Sir John's Run, W. Va.	1 05	Winchester, Va.	7 80

In addition to the season tickets for which rates are quoted above, special signature contract tickets, Form Ex. 802, will be sold from the following stations to Mountain Lake Park, Md., and return, for use going on train No. 3 on Fridays and all trains on Saturday of each week, good to return on any train leaving Mountain Lake Park on the following Monday.

EXCURSION RATES.

Baltimore, Md.	$5 00	Washington, D. C.	$5 00
Philadelphia, Pa.	8 00		

MOUNT WASHINGTON, N. H.

FORM EX. 1042. MOUNT WASHINGTON, N. H., AND RETURN.

(Via rail, Boston and Bethlehem Junction; returning via Glen House, North Conway and Sound Lines.)

Baltimore & Ohio R. R.	to Philadelphia.
Rail Lines (see pages 50 to 55 for route)	to Boston.
Boston & Maine R. R.	to Nashua.
Concord & Montreal R. R.	to Bethlehem June.
Profile & Franconia Notch R. R.	to Profile House.
Profile & Franconia Notch R. R.	to Bethlehem June.
Concord & Montreal R. R.	to Fabyan House.
Concord & Montreal R. R.	to Base.
Mt. Washington R. R.	to Summit.
Milliken's Stage Line (9 miles)	to Glen House.
Milliken's Stage Line (11 miles)	to Glen Station.
Maine Central R. R.	to North Conway.
Boston & Maine R. R.	to Boston.
Sound Lines (see pages 50 to 55 for route)	to New York.
Central R. R. of New Jersey	to Bound Brook.
Philadelphia & Reading R. R.	to Philadelphia.
Baltimore & Ohio R. R.	to starting point.

Transfer through Boston, returning, included.

THROUGH RATES.

Baltimore, Md.	$38 70	Washington, D. C.	$40 70
Philadelphia, Pa.	34 70		

FORM EX. 1042. MOUNT WASHINGTON, N. H., AND RETURN.

(Via Sound Lines, Boston and Bethlehem Junction; returning via Glen House, North Conway and rail.)

Baltimore & Ohio R. R.	to Philadelphia.
Philadelphia & Reading R. R.	to Bound Brook.
Central R. R. of New Jersey	to New York.
Sound Lines (see pages 50 to 55 for route)	to Boston.
Boston & Maine R. R.	to Nashua.
Concord & Montreal R. R.	to Bethlehem June.
Profile & Franconia Notch R. R.	to Profile House.
Profile & Franconia Notch R. R.	to Bethlehem June.
Concord & Montreal R. R.	to Fabyan House.
Concord & Montreal R. R.	to Base.

Mt. Washington R. R.	to Summit.
Milliken's Stage Line (9 miles)	to Glen House.
Milliken's Stage Line (11 miles)	to Glen Station.
Maine Central R. R.	to North Conway.
Boston & Maine R. R.	to Boston.
Rail Lines (see pages 50 to 55 for route)	to Philadelphia.
Baltimore & Ohio R. R.	to starting point.

THROUGH RATES.

Baltimore, Md. . . . . . $37 00 | Washington, D. C. $29 00
†Philadelphia, Pa. 33 00

Transfer through Boston, going, included.

FORM EX. 1012.—MOUNT WASHINGTON, N. H., AND RETURN.

(Via rail, Boston and Bethlehem Junction; returning via Glen House, North Conway and rail.)

Baltimore & Ohio R. R.	to Philadelphia.
Rail Lines (see pages 50 to 55 for route)	to Boston.
Boston & Maine R. R.	to Nashua.
Concord & Montreal R. R.	to Bethlehem June.
Profile & Franconia Notch R. R.	to Profile House.
Profile & Franconia Notch R. R.	to Bethlehem June.
Concord & Montreal R. R.	to Fabyan House.
Concord & Montreal R. R.	to Base.
Mt. Washington R. R.	to Summit.
Milliken's Stage Line (9 miles)	to Glen House.
Milliken's Stage Line (11 miles)	to Glen Station.
Maine Central R. R.	to North Conway.
Boston & Maine R. R.	to Boston.
Rail Lines (see pages 50 to 55 for route)	to Philadelphia.
Baltimore & Ohio R. R.	to starting point.

THROUGH RATES.

Baltimore, Md. . . . . . $40 45 | Washington, D. C. $42 45
†Philadelphia, Pa. 36 45

FORM EX. 1012.—MOUNT WASHINGTON, N. H., AND RETURN.

(Via Sound Lines, Boston and Bethlehem Junction; returning via Glen House, North Conway and Sound Lines.)

Baltimore & Ohio R. R.	to Philadelphia.
Philadelphia & Reading R. R.	to Bound Brook.
Central R. R. of New Jersey.	to New York.
Sound Lines (see pages 50 to 55 for route)	to Boston.
Boston & Maine R. R.	to Nashua.
Concord & Montreal R. R.	to Bethlehem June.
Profile & Franconia Notch R. R.	to Profile House.
Profile & Franconia Notch R. R.	to Bethlehem June.
Concord & Montreal R. R.	to Fabyan House.
Concord & Montreal R. R.	to Base.
Mt. Washington R. R.	to Summit.
Milliken's Stage Line (9 miles)	to Glen House.
Milliken's Stage Line (11 miles)	to Glen Station.
Maine Central R. R.	to North Conway.
Boston & Maine R. R.	to Boston.
Sound Lines (see pages 50 to 55 for route)	to New York.
Central R. R. of New Jersey.	to Bound Brook.
Philadelphia & Reading R. R.	to Philadelphia.
Baltimore & Ohio R. R.	to starting point.

THROUGH RATES.

Baltimore, Md. . . . . . $36 40 | Washington, D. C. $38 40
†Philadelphia, Pa. 32 40

Transfer through Boston, in both directions, included.

214 BALTIMORE & OHIO RAILROAD COMPANY

Form Ex. 1043. Mount Washington, N. H., and Return.

(Via rail, Boston, North Conway and Glen House; returning via Portland and Sound Lines.)

Baltimore & Ohio R. R.	to Philadelphia.
Rail Lines (see pages 50 to 55 for routes)	to Boston.
Boston & Maine R. R.	to North Conway.
Maine Central R. R.	to Glen Station.
Milliken's Stage (14 miles)	to Glen House.
Milliken's Stage (9 miles)	to Summit.
Mount Washington R. R.	to Base.
Concord & Montreal R. R.	to Fabyans.
Maine Central R. R.	to Portland.
Boston & Maine R. R.	to Boston.
Sound Lines (see pages 50 to 55 for routes)	to New York.
Central R. R. of New Jersey	to Bound Brook.
Philadelphia & Reading R. R.	to Philadelphia.
Baltimore & Ohio R. R.	to starting point.

THROUGH RATES.

Baltimore, Md. . . . . . $36 75 | Washington, D. C. $38 75
†Philadelphia, Pa. . . . 32 75 |

Transfer through Boston, returning, included.

Form Ex. 1045. Mount Washington, N. H., and Return.

(Via Sound Lines, Boston, North Conway and Glen House; returning via Portland and rail.)

Baltimore & Ohio R. R.	to Philadelphia.
Philadelphia & Reading R. R.	to Bound Brook.
Central R. R. of New Jersey	to New York.
Sound Lines (see pages 50 to 55 for routes)	to Boston.
Boston & Maine R. R.	to North Conway.
Maine Central R. R.	to Glen Station.
Milliken's Stage (14 miles)	to Glen House.
Milliken's Stage (9 miles)	to Summit.
Mount Washington R. R.	to Base.
Concord & Montreal R. R.	to Fabyans.
Maine Central R. R.	to Portland.
Boston & Maine R. R.	to Boston.
Rail Lines (see pages 50 to 55 for routes)	to Philadelphia.
Baltimore & Ohio R. R.	to starting point.

THROUGH RATES.

Baltimore, Md. . . . . . $37 35 | Washington, D. C. $39 35
†Philadelphia, Pa. . . . 33 35 |

Transfer though Boston, going, included.

Form Ex. 1045.—Mount Washington, N. H., and Return.

(Via rail, Boston, North Conway and Glen House; returning via Portland and rail.)

Baltimore & Ohio R. R.	to Philadelphia.
Rail Lines (see pages 50 to 55 for routes)	to Boston.
Boston & Maine R. R.	to North Conway.
Maine Central R. R.	to Glen Station.
Milliken's Stage (14 miles)	to Glen House.
Milliken's Stage (9 miles)	to Summit.
Mount Washington R. R.	to Base.
Concord & Montreal R. R.	to Fabyans.
Maine Central R. R.	to Portland.
Boston & Maine R. R.	to Boston.
Rail Lines (see pages 50 to 55 for routes)	to Philadelphia.
Baltimore & Ohio R. R.	to starting point.

THROUGH RATES.

Baltimore, Md. . . . . . $38 85 | Washington, D. C. $40 85
†Philadelphia, Pa. . . . 34 85 |

FORM EX. 1013.—MOUNT WASHINGTON, N. H., AND RETURN.

(Via Sound Lines, Boston, North Conway and Glen House; returning via Portland and Sound Lines.)

Baltimore & Ohio R. R. . . . . to Philadelphia.
Philadelphia & Reading R. R. . . . . to Bound Brook.
Central R. R. of New Jersey . . . . to New York.
Sound Lines (see pages 50 to 55 for route) . . to Boston.
Boston & Maine R. R. . . . . to North Conway.
Maine Central R. R. . . . . to Glen Station.
Milliken's Stage (1 miles) . . . . to Glen House.
Milliken's Stage (9 miles) . . . . to Summit.
Mount Washington R. R. . . . . to Base.
Concord & Montreal R. R. . . . . to Fabyans.
Maine Central R. R. . . . . to Portland.
Boston & Maine R. R. . . . . to Boston.
Sound Lines (see pages 50 to 55 for route) . . to New York.
Central R. R. of New Jersey . . . . to Bound Brook.
Philadelphia & Reading R. R. . . . . to Philadelphia.
Baltimore & Ohio R. R. . . . . to starting point.

THROUGH RATES.

Baltimore, Md. . . . . . $35 25   Washington, D. C. $37 25
*Philadelphia, Pa. 31 25

Transfer through Boston, in both directions, included.

FORM EX. 830.—MOUNT WASHINGTON, N. H., AND RETURN.

(Via rail, Boston, Portland and Glen House; returning via North Conway and Sound Lines.)

Baltimore & Ohio R. R. . . . . to Philadelphia.
Rail Lines (see pages 50 to 55 for route) . . . to Boston.
Boston & Maine R. R. . . . . to Portland.
Maine Central R. R. . . . . to Fabyans.
Concord and Montreal R. R. . . . . to Base.
Mt. Washington R. R. . . . . to Summit.
Milliken's Stage (9 miles) . . . . to Glen House.
Milliken's Stage (1 miles) . . . . to Glen Station.
Maine Central R. R. . . . . to North Conway.
Boston & Maine R. R. . . . . to Boston.
Sound Lines (see pages 50 to 55 for route) . . to New York.
Central R. R. of New Jersey . . . . to Bound Brook.
Philadelphia & Reading R. R. . . . . to Philadelphia.
Baltimore & Ohio R. R. . . . . to starting point.

THROUGH RATES.

Baltimore, Md. . . . . . $35 35   Washington, D. C. $37 35
*Philadelphia, Pa. 31 35

Transfer through Boston, returning, included.

FORM EX. 830.—MOUNT WASHINGTON, N. H., AND RETURN.

(Via Sound Lines, Boston, Portland and Glen House; returning via North Conway and Rail Lines.)

Baltimore & Ohio R. R. . . . . to Philadelphia.
Philadelphia & Reading R. R. . . . . to Bound Brook.
Central R. R. of New Jersey . . . . to New York.
Sound Lines (see pages 50 to 55 for route) . . to Boston.
Boston & Maine R. R. . . . . to Portland.
Maine Central R. R. . . . . to Fabyans.
Concord & Montreal R. R. . . . . to Base.
Mt. Washington R. R. . . . . to Summit.
Milliken's Stage (9 miles) . . . . to Glen House.
Milliken's Stage (1 miles) . . . . to Glen Station.
Maine Central R. R. . . . . to North Conway.

Boston & Maine R. R. . . . . to Boston.
Rail Lines (see pages 50 to 55 for route) . . . . . to Philadelphia.
Baltimore & Ohio R. R. . . . . to starting point.

THROUGH RATES.

Baltimore, Md. . . . . . . $34 75   Washington, D. C. $36 75
†Philadelphia, Pa. 30 75

Transfer through Boston, going, included.

FORM EX. 830. MOUNT WASHINGTON, N. H., AND RETURN.

(Via Rail Lines, Boston, Portland and Glen House; returning via
North Conway and Rail Lines.)

Baltimore & Ohio R. R. . . . . to Philadelphia.
Rail Lines (see pages 50 to 55 for route) . . . . . to Boston.
Boston & Maine R. R. . . . . to Portland.
Maine Central R. R. . . . . to Fabyans.
Concord & Montreal R. R. . . . . to Base.
Mt. Washington R. R. . . . . to Summit.
Milliken's Stage (9 miles) . . . . to Glen House.
Milliken's Stage (1 mile) . . . . to Glen Station.
Maine Central R. R. . . . . to North Conway.
Boston & Maine R. R. . . . . to Boston.
Rail Lines (see pages 50 to 55 for route) . . . . . to Philadelphia.
Baltimore & Ohio R. R. . . . . to starting point.

THROUGH RATES.

Baltimore, Md. . . . . . . $36 85   Washington, D. C. $38 85
†Philadelphia, Pa. 32 85

FORM EX. 839. MOUNT WASHINGTON, N. H., AND RETURN.

(Via Sound Lines, Boston, Portland and Glen House; returning via
North Conway and Sound Lines.)

Baltimore & Ohio R. R. . . . . to Philadelphia.
Philadelphia & Reading R. R. . . . . to Bound Brook.
Central R. R. of New Jersey . . . . to New York.
Sound Lines (see pages 50 to 55 for route) . . . . to Boston.
Boston & Maine R. R. . . . . to Portland.
Maine Central R. R. . . . . to Fabyans.
Concord & Montreal R. R. . . . . to Base.
Mt. Washington R. R. . . . . to Summit.
Milliken's Stage (9 miles) . . . . to Glen House.
Milliken's Stage (1 mile) . . . . to Glen Station.
Maine Central R. R. . . . . to North Conway.
Boston & Maine R. R. . . . . to Boston.
Sound Lines (see pages 50 to 55 for route) . . . . to New York.
Central R. R. of New Jersey . . . . to Bound Brook.
Philadelphia & Reading R. R. . . . . to Philadelphia.
Baltimore & Ohio R. R. . . . . to starting point.

THROUGH RATES.

Baltimore, Md. . . . . . . $33 25   Washington, D. C. $35 25
†Philadelphia, Pa. 29 25

Transfer through Boston, in both directions, included.

FORM EX. 1015. MOUNT WASHINGTON, N. H., AND RETURN.

(Via rail, Boston, Portland and Glen House; returning via Bethlehem
Junction and Sound Lines.)

Baltimore & Ohio R. R. . . . . to Philadelphia.
Rail Lines (see pages 50 to 55 for route) . . . . . to Boston.
Boston & Maine R. R. . . . . to Portland.
Maine Central R. R. . . . . to Glen Station.

Milliken's Stage Line (11 miles)	to Glen House.
Milliken's Stage Line (9 miles)	to Summit.
Mt. Washington R. R.	to Base.
Concord & Montreal R. R.	to Fabyan House.
Concord & Montreal R. R.	to Bethlehem Junc.
Profile & Franconia Notch R. R.	to Profile House.
Profile & Franconia Notch R. R.	to Bethlehem Junc
Concord & Montreal R. R.	to Nashua.
Boston & Maine R. R.	to Boston.
Sound Lines (see pages 50 to 55 for route)	to New York.
Central R. R. of New Jersey	to Philadelphia.
Philadelphia & Reading R. R.	to Bound Brook.
Baltimore & Ohio R. R.	to starting point.

THROUGH RATES.

Baltimore, Md. . . . . . . $20.00   Washington, D. C. $11.00
†Philadelphia, Pa. 25.00

Transfer through Boston, returning, included.

FORM EX. 1015. MOUNT WASHINGTON, N. H., AND RETURN.

(Via Sound Lines, Boston, Portland and Glen House; returning via Bethlehem Junction and rail.)

Baltimore & Ohio R. R.	to Philadelphia.
Philadelphia & Reading R. R.	to Bound Brook.
Central R. R. of New Jersey	to New York.
Sound Lines (see pages 50 to 55 for route)	to Boston.
Boston & Maine R. R.	to Portland.
Maine Central R. R.	to Glen Station.
Milliken's Stage Line (11 miles)	to Glen House.
Milliken's Stage Line (9 miles)	to Summit.
Mt. Washington R. R.	to Base.
Concord & Montreal R. R.	to Fabyan House.
Concord & Montreal R. R.	to Bethlehem Junc.
Profile & Franconia Notch R. R.	to Profile House.
Profile & Franconia Notch R. R.	to Bethlehem Junc.
Concord & Montreal R. R.	to Nashua.
Boston & Maine R. R.	to Boston.
Rail Lines (see pages 50 to 55 for route)	to Philadelphia.
Baltimore & Ohio R. R.	to starting point.

THROUGH RATES.

Baltimore, Md. . . . . . . $40.70 | Washington, D. C. $42.70
†Philadelphia, Pa. 36.70

Transfer through Boston, going, included.

FORM EX. 1015. MOUNT WASHINGTON, N. H., AND RETURN.

(Via rail, Boston, Portland and Glen House; returning via Bethlehem Junction and rail.)

Baltimore & Ohio R. R.	to Philadelphia.
Rail Lines (see pages 50 to 55 for route)	to Boston.
Boston & Maine R. R.	to Portland.
Maine Central R. R.	to Glen Station
Milliken's Stage Line (11 miles)	to Glen House.
Milliken's Stage Line (9 miles)	to Summit.
Mt. Washington R. R.	to Base.
Concord & Montreal R. R.	to Fabyan House.
Concord & Montreal R. R.	to Bethlehem Junc.
Profile & Franconia Notch R. R.	to Profile House.
Profile & Franconia Notch R. R.	to Bethlehem Junc.
Concord & Montreal R. R.	to Nashua.
Boston & Maine R. R.	to Boston.
Rail Lines (see pages 50 to 55 for route)	to Philadelphia.
Baltimore & Ohio R. R.	to starting point.

THROUGH RATES.

Baltimore, Md. . . . . . . $42.20   Washington, D. C. $44.20
†Philadelphia, Pa. 38.20

FORM EX. 1015.—MOUNT WASHINGTON, N. H., AND RETURN.

(Via Sound Lines, Boston, Portland and Glen House; returning via Bethlehem Junction and Sound Lines.)

Baltimore & Ohio R. R.	to Philadelphia.
Philadelphia & Reading R. R.	to Bound Brook.
Central R. R. of New Jersey	to New York.
Sound Lines (see pages 50 to 55 for route)	to Boston.
Boston & Maine R. R.	to Portland.
Maine Central R. R.	to Glen Station.
Milliken's Stage Line (1 mile)	to Glen House.
Milliken's Stage Line (9 miles)	to Summit.
Mt. Washington R. R.	to Base.
Concord & Montreal R. R.	to Fabyan House.
Concord & Montreal R. R.	to Bethlehem Junc.
Profile & Franconia Notch R. R.	to Profile House.
Profile & Franconia Notch R. R.	to Bethlehem Junc.
Concord & Montreal R. R.	to Nashua.
Boston & Maine R. R.	to Boston.
Sound Lines (see pages 50 to 55 for route)	to New York.
Central R. R. of New Jersey	to Bound Brook.
Philadelphia & Reading R. R.	to Philadelphia.
Baltimore & Ohio R. R.	to Starting Point.

THROUGH RATES.

Baltimore, Md. . . . . $38 40   Washington, D. C. . . . $40 40
Philadelphia, Pa. . . . 34 40

Transfer through Boston, in both directions, included.

FORM EX. 616. FABYAN HOUSE TO SUMMIT MT. WASHINGTON, N. H., AND RETURN.

Concord & Montreal R. R. Fabyan House to Base Mt. Washington.
Mt. Washington R. R. . . . . to Summit Mt. Washington.

Returning, same route.

Sold in connection with any ticket passing through or terminating at Fabyan House.

Rate $6 00

MUSKOKA LAKES, ONTARIO, CAN.

The Muskoka Lake and Georgian Bay region, of Canada, present a multitude of advantages to the seeker after summer pleasures. The fresh, pure air of this elevated region, with its picturesque surroundings of lakes and forest, cannot fail to invigorate exhausted physical nature. The peculiar softness of the limpid water and the resinous odor of the pine forests are potent health-creating agencies. The lovers of the water find sheltered lakes teeming with fish; while drives and rambles or more pretentious excursions by steamer afford the strongest weapons against ennui.

The Muskoka region, of which this sketch treats, comprises the three lakes, Muskoka, Rosseau and Joseph. The triplets extend a distance of fifty miles in a direct line, and furnish an irregular coast line of two hundred miles.

The waters of the lakes and their tributary streams abound in fish, the prevailing varieties being salmon, trout, whitefish, bass, pickerel and muskallonge.

FORM EX. 1035.— ALL ROUND MUSKOKA LAKES, ONT., AND RETURN.

Grand Trunk Ry. . . . . Niagara Falls to Muskoka Wharf.
Muskoka & Georgian Bay Navigation Co. . . . . to All Round Muskoka Lakes.
Returning, same route.

Sold in connection with any ticket passing through or terminating at Niagara Falls.

Rate $8.30

FORM EX. 1035. BALA, ONT.

Grand Trunk Ry. . . . . Niagara Falls to Muskoka Wharf.
Muskoka & Georgian Bay Navigation Co. . . . . to Bala.
Returning, same route.

Sold in connection with any ticket passing through or terminating at Niagara Falls.

Rate $7.40

FORM EX. 1036. PARRY SOUND, ONT.

Grand Trunk Ry. . . . . Niagara Falls to Penetanguishene or Midland.
North Shore Navigation Co. . . . . to Parry Sound.
Returning, same route.

Sold in connection with any ticket passing through or terminating at Niagara Falls.

Rate (meals included on steamer) $10.40

FORM EX. 1037. PARRY SOUND, ONT.

Grand Trunk Ry. . . . . Niagara Falls to Muskoka Wharf.
Muskoka & Georgian Bay Navigation Co. . . . . to Rossean.
Stage . . . . to Parry Sound.
North Shore Navigation Co. . . . . to Penetanguishene or Midland.
Grand Trunk Ry. . . . . to Niagara Falls.

FORM EX. 1084. PARRY SOUND, ONT.

Reverse of preceding excursion.

Rate $9.90

FORM EX. 1035. PORT COCKBURN, ONT.

Grand Trunk Ry. . . . . Niagara Falls to Muskoka Wharf.
Muskoka & Georgian Bay Navigation Co. . . . . to Port Cockburn.
Returning, same route.

Sold in connection with any ticket passing through or terminating at Niagara Falls.

Rate $8.40

FORM EX. 1035. ROSSEAU, ONT.

Grand Trunk Ry. . . . . Niagara Falls to Muskoka Wharf.
Muskoka & Georgian Bay Navigation Co. . . . . to Rossean.
Returning, same route.

Sold in connection with any ticket passing through or terminating at Niagara Falls.

Rate $8.45

NANTASKET BEACH, MASS.

FORM EX. 1016.—NANTASKET BEACH, MASS., AND RETURN.

(Via New York and Fall River; returning via Boston and New York.)

Baltimore & Ohio R. R.	to Philadelphia.
Philadelphia & Reading R. R.	to Bound Brook.
Central R. R. of New Jersey	to New York.
Old Colony Steamboat Co. (Fall River Line)	to Fall River.
Old Colony R. R. (Short Line)	to Nantasket Beach.
Old Colony R. R.	to Boston.
Old Colony R. R.	to Fall River.
Old Colony Steamboat Co. (Fall River Line)	to New York.
Central R. R. of New Jersey	to Bound Brook.
Philadelphia & Reading R. R.	to Philadelphia.
Baltimore & Ohio R. R.	to starting point.

FORM EX. 1017.—NANTASKET BEACH, MASS., AND RETURN.

Reverse of preceding excursion.

THROUGH RATES.

Baltimore, Md. . . . . $16 60   Washington, D. C. . . . $18 00
†Philadelphia, Pa. . . . 12 60

NANTUCKET, MASS.

FORM EX. 993.—NANTUCKET, MASS., AND RETURN.

Baltimore & Ohio R. R.	to Philadelphia.
Philadelphia & Reading R. R.	to Bound Brook.
Central R. R. of New Jersey	to New York.
Old Colony Steamboat Co. (Fall River Line)	to Fall River.
Old Colony R. R.	to New Bedford.
New Bedford, Martha's Vineyard & Nantucket Steamboat Line	to Nantucket.

Returning, same route.

THROUGH RATES.

Baltimore, Md. . . . . $16 25   Washington, D. C. . . . $18 25
†Philadelphia, Pa. . . . 12 25

FORM EX. 995.—NANTUCKET, MASS., AND RETURN.

Baltimore & Ohio R. R.	to Philadelphia.
Philadelphia & Reading R. R.	to Bound Brook.
Central R. R. of New Jersey	to New York.
Old Colony Steamboat Co. (Fall River Line)	to Fall River.
Old Colony R. R.	to New Bedford.
New Bedford, Martha's Vineyard & Nantucket Steamboat Line	to Nantucket.
New Bedford, Martha's Vineyard & Nantucket Steamboat Line	to Wood's Holl.
Old Colony R. R.	to Boston.
Old Colony R. R.	to Fall River.
Old Colony Steamboat Co. (Fall River Line)	to New York.
Central R. R. of New Jersey	to Bound Brook.
Philadelphia & Reading R. R.	to Philadelphia.
Baltimore & Ohio R. R.	to starting point.

THROUGH RATES.

Baltimore, Md. . . . . $18 75   Washington, D. C. . . . $20 75
†Philadelphia, Pa. . . . 14 75

NARRAGANSETT PIER.

This well-known seacoast resort is located on the eastern border of the town of South Kingstown on the mainland, just below the entrance to Narragansett Bay, facing the broad Atlantic. It is but a few years since it was comparatively unknown to the public, but of late it has grown rapidly in popular favor. From being a quiet, unobserved locality, surrounded by a farming district, it has quickly grown to be one of the most highly-favored summer resorts in the State.

This was the old "Narragansett Country," rich in Indian lore and the records of the romantic life of the early English settlers.

Attracted, perhaps, in part by these, together with certain natural features of the place, and, above all, by the beautiful beach washed by the open sea, a certain few families of wealth and refinement came hither a few years since to spend the summer months. The following season they returned and others came with them, and from this time on Narragansett Pier became rapidly and widely known. At first one or two hotels were built, which were soon filled to overflowing, and two or three years later some twelve or fifteen hotels, large and commodious, had been constructed, and all fully occupied by people gathered from all parts of the country. In addition to the hotels there are now many fine cottages, and many of these are occupied by permanent residents, constituting a pretty village.

The bathing facilities here are of the very best to be found anywhere. The beach stretches away for a mile or more in a graceful curve, is perfectly smooth and even, and has the great advantage of the unobstructed billows sweeping in majestically from the open sea.

The northern portion of this beach is sadly associated with several shipwrecks. The United States Government now maintains near the pier a life-station well equipped for its merciful work.

FORM EX. 626.—NARRAGANSETT PIER, R. I., AND RETURN.

Baltimore & Ohio R. R.	to Philadelphia.
Philadelphia & Reading R. R.	to Bound Brook.
Central R. R. of New Jersey,	to New York.
Stonington Line	to Stonington.
New York, Providence & Boston R. R.	to Kingston.
Narragansett Pier R. R.	to Narragansett Pier.

Returning, same route.

THROUGH RATES.

Baltimore, Md. . . . . . . $13.00   Washington, D. C. . . $15.00
†Philadelphia, Pa. 9.00

FORM EX. 627.—NARRAGANSETT PIER, R. I., AND RETURN.

Baltimore & Ohio R. R.	to Philadelphia.
Philadelphia & Reading R. R.	to Bound Brook.
Central R. R. of New Jersey,	to New York.
New York, New Haven & Hartford R. R.	to New London.
New York, Providence & Boston R. R.	to Kingston.
Narragansett Pier R. R.	to Narragansett Pier.

Returning, same route.

THROUGH RATES.

Baltimore, Md. . . . . . . $15.35   Washington, D. C. . . $17.35
†Philadelphia, Pa. 11.35

FORM EX. 628.—NARRAGANSETT PIER, R. I., AND RETURN.

Baltimore & Ohio R. R.	to Philadelphia.
Philadelphia & Reading R. R.	to Bound Brook.
Central R. R. of New Jersey,	to New York.
Providence Line	to Providence.
New York, Providence & Boston R. R.	to Kingston.
Narragansett Pier R. R.	to Narragansett Pier.

Returning, same route.

THROUGH RATES.

Baltimore, Md. . . . . . . $14.50   Washington, D. C. . . $16.50
†Philadelphia, Pa. 10.50

FORM EX. 629.—NARRAGANSETT PIER, R. I., AND RETURN.

Baltimore & Ohio R. R.	to Philadelphia.
Philadelphia & Reading R. R.	to Bound Brook.
Central R. R. of New Jersey	to New York.
Providence Line	to Providence.
New York, Providence & Boston R. R.	to Kingston.
Narragansett Pier R. R.	to Narragansett Pier.
Narragansett Pier R. R.	to Kingston.
New York, Providence & Boston R. R.	to New London.
New York, New Haven & Hartford R. R.	to New York.
Central R. R. of New Jersey	to Bound Brook.
Philadelphia & Reading R. R.	to Philadelphia.
Baltimore & Ohio R. R.	to starting point.

THROUGH RATES.

Baltimore, Md. . . . . . $15 70 | Washington, D. C. $17 70
(Philadelphia, Pa. . . . . 11 70 |

FORM EX. 636.—NARRAGANSETT PIER, R. I. AND RETURN.

Baltimore & Ohio R. R. . . . . to Philadelphia.
Philadelphia & Reading R. R. . . . . to Bound Brook.
Central R. R. of New Jersey . . . . to New York.
Stonington Line . . . . to Stonington.
New York, Providence & Boston R. R. . . . . to Kingston.
Narragansett Pier R. R. . . . . to Narragansett Pier.
Narragansett Pier R. R. . . . . to Kingston.
New York, Providence & Boston R. R. . . . . to New London.
New York, New Haven & Hartford R. R. . . . to New York.
Central R. R. of New Jersey . . . . to Bound Brook.
Philadelphia & Reading R. R. . . . . to Philadelphia.
Baltimore & Ohio R. R. . . . . to starting point.

THROUGH RATES.

Baltimore, Md. . . . . . $15 00 | Washington, D. C. $17 00
(Philadelphia, Pa. . . . . 11 00 |

NATURAL BRIDGE, VA.

FORM EX. 265.—NATURAL BRIDGE, VA.

Limited to six (6) months from date of sale.

Baltimore & Ohio R. R. . . . . to Lexington.
Chesapeake & Ohio R. R. . . . . to Natural Bridge Stn.
Stage (2 miles) . . . . to Natural Bridge.

Returning, same route.

THROUGH RATES.

Baltimore, Md.	$12 90	Morgantown, W. Va.	$18 45
Bellaire, O.	20 85	Moundsville, W. Va.	20 15
Berkeley Springs, W. Va.	10 65	Mountain Lake Park, Md.	14 00
Cameron, W. Va.	19 45	Mt. Pleasant, Pa.	16 70
Charlestown, W. Va.	8 90	Newark, Del.	15 20
Chester, Pa.	16 40	New York, N. Y.	20 90
Clarksburg, W. Va.	17 45	Oakland, Md.	14 70
Connellsville, Pa.	16 30	Parkersburg, W. Va.	20 55
Cumberland, Md.	12 50	Philadelphia, Pa.	16 90
Deer Park, Md.	14 45	Piedmont, W. Va.	13 65
Fairmont, W. Va.	17 45	Pittsburgh, Pa.	18 50
Frederick, Md.	9 95	Rockwood, Pa.	14 45
Grafton, W. Va.	16 55	Somerset, Pa.	14 85
Hagerstown, Md.	9 95	Staunton, Va.	1 10
Harper's Ferry, W. Va.	8 90	Strasburg, Va.	7 75
Harrisonburg, Va.	5 40	Uniontown, Pa.	16 65
Havre de Grace, Md.	11 35	Washington, D. C.	10 90
Johnstown, Pa.	16 25	Washington, Pa.	19 00
Keyser, W. Va.	13 45	Wheeling, W. Va.	20 55
McKeesport, Pa.	17 85	Wilmington, Del.	15 80
Martinsburg, W. Va.	9 35	Winchester, Va.	8 80
Meyersdale, Pa.	14 00		

FORM EX. 266.—NATURAL BRIDGE, VA.

Limited to six (6) months from date of sale.

Baltimore & Ohio R. R. . . . . to Shenandoah Junc.
Norfolk & Western R. R. . . . . to Natural Bridge Stn.
Stage (2 miles) . . . . to Natural Bridge.

Returning, same route.

THROUGH RATES.

Baltimore, Md.	$12 90	Morgantown, W. Va.	$18 45
Bellaire, O.	20 85	Moundsville, W. Va.	20 45
Berkeley Springs, W. Va.	10 65	Mountain Lake Park, Md.	14 60
Cameron, W. Va.	19 45	Mt. Pleasant, Pa.	16 70
Chester, Pa.	16 40	Newark, Del.	15 20
Clarksburg, W. Va.	17 45	New York, N. Y.	20 90
Connellsville, Pa.	16 20	Oakland, Md.	11 70
Cumberland, Md.	12 50	Parkersburg, W. Va.	20 55
Deer Park, Md.	11 45	Philadelphia, Pa.	16 90
Fairmont, W. Va.	17 45	Piedmont, W. Va.	13 65
Frederick, Md.	9 95	Pittsburgh, Pa.	18 50
Grafton, W. Va.	16 55	Rockwood, Pa.	14 45
Harper's Ferry, W. Va.	8 90	Somerset, Pa.	14 85
Havre de Grace, Md.	14 35	Uniontown, Pa.	16 65
Johnstown, Pa.	16 25	Washington, D. C.	10 90
Keyser, W. Va.	13 45	Washington, Pa.	19 00
McKeesport, Pa.	17 95	Wheeling, W. Va.	20 55
Martinsburg, W. Va.	9 35	Wilmington, Del.	15 90
Meyersdale, Pa.	14 00		

NATURAL BRIDGE STATION, VA.

FORM EX. 780.—NATURAL BRIDGE STATION, VA.

Limited to six (6) months from date of sale.

Baltimore & Ohio R. R. . . . . to Shenandoah June.
Norfolk & Western R. R. . . . . to Natural Bridge Stn.
  Returning, same route.

THROUGH RATES.

Baltimore, Md.	$14 90	Morgantown, W. Va.	$17 45
Bellaire, O.	19 85	Moundsville, W. Va.	19 45
Berkeley Springs, W. Va.	9 65	Mountain Lake Park, Md.	13 60
Cameron, W. Va.	18 45	Mt. Pleasant, Pa.	15 70
Chester, Pa.	15 40	Newark, Del.	14 20
Clarksburg, W. Va.	16 45	New York, N. Y.	19 90
Connellsville, Pa.	15 20	Oakland, Md.	13 70
Cumberland, Md.	11 50	Parkersburg, W. Va.	19 55
Deer Park, Md.	13 45	Philadelphia, Pa.	15 90
Fairmont, W. Va.	16 45	Piedmont, W. Va.	12 65
Frederick, Md.	8 95	Pittsburgh, Pa.	17 50
Grafton, W. Va.	15 55	Rockwood, Pa.	13 45
Harper's Ferry, W. Va.	7 90	Somerset, Pa.	13 85
Havre de Grace, Md.	13 35	Uniontown, Pa.	15 65
Johnstown, Pa.	15 25	Washington, D. C.	9 90
Keyser, W. Va.	12 45	Washington, Pa.	18 00
McKeesport, Pa.	16 95	Wheeling, W. Va.	19 55
Martinsburg, W. Va.	8 35	Wilmington, Del.	14 90
Meyersdale, Pa.	13 00		

NEW BEDFORD, MASS.

FORM EX. 753.—NEW BEDFORD, MASS., AND RETURN.

Baltimore & Ohio R. R. . . . . to Philadelphia.
Philadelphia & Reading R. R. . . . . to Bound Brook.
Central R. R. of New Jersey . . . . to New York.
Old Colony Steamboat Co. (Fall River Line) . . to Fall River.
Old Colony R. R. . . . . to New Bedford.
  Returning, same route.

THROUGH RATES.

Baltimore, Md.	$11 25	Washington, D. C.	$16 25
Philadelphia, Pa.	10 25		

NEWPORT, R. I.

Newport may justly be termed the metropolis of watering-places. It stands at the head of all the American resorts in point of age, and occupies the highest place in the social scale. The land on which the city is built is clothed with historic memories, reaching back to a date of which no authentic records remain; and the old stone mill, a relic of pre-historic days, has been the subject of much antiquarian research, and furnished a theme to song and story. But the glory of the present outshines the interest of the past. The light of social prominence, the radiance of wealth, and the brilliancy of fashion shed a glamour over the historic ground, which makes it the most highly-favored retreat of the American aristocracy. Nature has lavished her riches on the spot. There is a rare beauty in the land, its trees, grass, and shrubs; there is a surpassing charm in air and sky, and a fascination in the sea and its blue waters studded with gem-like isles. Its natural advantages alone would stamp it as a charming spot, yet the magic wand of wealth has touched and beautified its shores with princely villas, smiling gardens and lovely landscapes.

The city is laid out with great taste. The broad avenues, bordered with the grounds surrounding the summer habitations of moneyed princes, present a magnificent appearance when crowded with the gorgeous equipages and richly-dressed men and women who worship the goddess Fashion at this shrine. The walks and drive on the bluff overlooking the sea and bay have a charm that never fails to win the admiration of all who have gazed upon the view, and the picturesque bits of scenery on land and coast, with which the region abounds, would satisfy the demands of the most artistic imagination. It is a delightful place, and deserves to be visited by every lover of beauty as well as every student of social conditions.

FORM EX. 624. NEWPORT, R. I., AND RETURN.

Baltimore & Ohio R. R. . . . . to Philadelphia.
Philadelphia & Reading R. R. . . . . to Bound Brook.
Central R. R. of New Jersey . . . . to New York.
Old Colony Steamboat Co. (Fall River Line) . . to Fall River.

Old Colony R. R. . . . . to Newport.
Old Colony Steamboat Co. (Fall River Line) . . to New York.
Central R. R. of New Jersey . . . . to Bound Brook.
Philadelphia & Reading R. R. . . . . to Philadelphia.
Baltimore & Ohio R. R. . . . . to starting point.

THROUGH RATES.
Baltimore, Md. . . . . . . $14.50 | Washington, D. C. . . . $16.50
†Philadelphia, Pa. . . . . 10.50 |

FORM EX. 624. NEWPORT, R. I., AND RETURN.

Baltimore & Ohio R. R. . . . . to Philadelphia.
Philadelphia & Reading R. R. . . . . to Bound Brook.
Central R. R. of New Jersey . . . . to New York.
Old Colony Steamboat Co. (Fall River Line) . . to Newport.
Returning, same route.

THROUGH RATES.
Baltimore, Md. . . . . . . $14.00 | Washington, D. C. . . . $16.00
†Philadelphia, Pa. . . . . 10.00 |

FORM EX. 1048. NEWPORT, R. I., AND RETURN.
(Via New York, all rail in both directions.)

Baltimore & Ohio R. R. . . . . to Philadelphia.
Philadelphia & Reading R. R. . . . . to Bound Brook.
Central R. R. of New Jersey . . . . to New York.
New York, New Haven & Hartford R. R. . . . . . to New London.
New York, Providence & Boston R. R. . . . . . . to Wickford Junc.
Newport & Wickford R. R. & S. B. Line . . . . to Newport.
Returning, same route.

THROUGH RATES.
Baltimore, Md. . . . . . . $17.00 | Washington, D. C. . . . $19.00
†Philadelphia, Pa. . . . . 13.00 |

NEWPORT, VT.

FORM EX. 782.—NEWPORT, VT. AND RETURN.

Baltimore and Ohio R. R. . . . . to Philadelphia.
Philadelphia & Reading R. R. . . . . to Bound Brook.
Central R. R. of New Jersey . . . . to New York.
Providence Line . . . . to Providence.
New York, Providence & Boston R. R. (Wor. Div.) to Worcester.
Boston & Maine R. R. . . . . to Nashua.
Concord & Montreal R. R. . . . . to Wells River.
Boston & Maine R. R. . . . . to Newport.
Returning, same route.

THROUGH RATES.
Baltimore, Md. . . . . . . $23.50 | Washington, D. C. . . . $25.50
†Philadelphia, Pa. . . . . 19.50 |

FORM EX. 783. NEWPORT, VT. AND RETURN.

Baltimore & Ohio R. R. . . . . to Philadelphia.
Philadelphia & Reading R. R. . . . . to Bound Brook.
Central R. R. of New Jersey . . . . to New York.
New York, New Haven & Hartford R. R. . . . . . to Springfield.
Connecticut River R. R. . . . . to South Vernon.
Central Vermont R. R. . . . . to Brattleboro.
Vermont Valley R. R. . . . . to Windsor.
Central Vermont R. R. . . . . to White River Jc.
Boston & Maine R. R. . . . . to Newport.
Returning, same route.

THROUGH RATES.
Baltimore, Md. . . . . . . $24.50 | Washington, D. C. . . . $26.50
†Philadelphia, Pa. . . . . 20.50 |

FORM EX. 784—NEWPORT, VT., AND RETURN.

Baltimore and Ohio R. R.	to Philadelphia.
Philadelphia & Reading R. R.	to Bound Brook.
Central R. R. of New Jersey	to New York.
Norwich Line	to New London.
New York and New England R. R., N. & W. Div.	to Worcester.
Boston & Maine R. R.	to Nashua.
Concord & Montreal R. R.	to Wells River.
Boston & Maine R. R.	to Newport.

Returning, same route.

THROUGH RATES.

Baltimore, Md.	$23 50	Washington, D. C.	$25 50
Philadelphia, Pa.	19 70		

NEW RIVER, VA.

FORM EX. 89.—NEW RIVER, VA., AND RETURN.

Baltimore & Ohio R. R.	to Washington.
Transfer	B. & O. Depot to R. & D. Depot.
Richmond & Danville R. R.	to Lynchburg.
Norfolk & Western R. R.	to New River.

Returning, same route.

THROUGH RATES.

Baltimore, Md.	$14 90	Meyersdale, Pa.	$21 00
Bellaire, O.	27 85	Morgantown, W. Va.	25 15
Berkeley Springs, W. Va.	17 55	Moundsville, W. Va.	27 10
Cameron, W. Va.	26 40	Mountain Lake Park, Md.	21 05
Charlestown, W. Va.	16 40	Mt. Pleasant, Pa.	23 70
Chester, Pa.	18 40	Newark, Del.	17 20
Clarksburg, W. Va.	24 45	New York, N. Y.	22 90
Connellsville, Pa.	23 20	Oakland, Md.	21 15
Cumberland, Md.	19 50	Parkersburg, W. Va.	27 55
Deer Park, Md.	20 90	Philadelphia, Pa.	18 90
Fairmont, W. Va.	24 45	Piedmont, W. Va.	20 60
Frederick, Md.	15 70	Pittsburgh, Pa.	25 50
Grafton, W. Va.	23 55	Rockwood, Pa.	21 45
Hagerstown, Md.	16 50	Somerset, Pa.	21 85
Harper's Ferry, W. Va.	15 60	Uniontown, Pa.	23 65
Havre de Grace, Md.	16 35	Washington, Pa.	26 60
Johnstown, Pa.	23 25	Wheeling, W. Va.	27 55
Keyser, W. Va.	20 40	Wilmington, Del.	17 90
McKeesport, Pa.	24 95	Winchester, Va.	17 20
Martinsburg, W. Va.	16 35		

FORM EX. 191.—NEW RIVER, VA., AND RETURN.

Baltimore & Ohio R. R.	to Shenandoah Junc.
Norfolk & Western R. R.	to New River.

Returning, same route.

THROUGH RATES.

Baltimore, Md.	$14 90	Morgantown, W. Va.	$21 35
Bellaire, O.	23 75	Moundsville, W. Va.	23 05
Berkeley Springs, W. Va.	15 55	Mountain Lake Park, Md.	17 50
Cameron, W. Va.	22 55	Mt. Pleasant, Pa.	19 60
Chester, Pa.	18 40	Newark, Del.	17 20
Clarksburg, W. Va.	20 55	New York, N. Y.	22 90
Connellsville, Pa.	19 40	Oakland, Md.	17 60
Cumberland, Md.	15 40	Parkersburg, W. Va.	23 45
Deer Park, Md.	17 55	Philadelphia, Pa.	18 90
Fairmont, W. Va.	20 35	Piedmont, W. Va.	16 55
Frederick, Md.	13 15	Pittsburgh, Pa.	21 10
Grafton, W. Va.	19 45	Rockwood, Pa.	17 35
Harper's Ferry, W. Va.	12 65	Somerset, Pa.	17 55
Havre de Grace, Md.	16 35	Uniontown, Pa.	19 55
Johnstown, Pa.	19 15	Washington, D. C.	12 90
Keyser, W. Va.	16 35	Washington, Pa.	22 50
McKeesport, Pa.	20 85	Wheeling, W. Va.	23 45
Martinsburg, W. Va.	12 25	Wilmington, Del.	17 90
Meyersdale, Pa.	16 90		

NIAGARA FALLS.

It seems presumptuous to attempt a description of these world-renowned Falls in a meagre sketch, as volumes portraying their grandeur and magnificence might be written, and yet fail in conveying to the perception a clear and succinct outline of their wonderful proportions and great sublimity. To be properly appreciated they must be visited, and when once viewed the recollection of the visit will linger long in the memory. The Falls of Niagara are twenty-two miles from Buffalo. The hotels of this resort compare favorably with the ones at the eastern watering-places. The place abounds in objects of interest, and is visited annually by thousands of people from all parts of the world.

FORM EX. 324. — NIAGARA FALLS, N. Y., AND RETURN.

Baltimore & Ohio R. R. . . . . to Philadelphia.
Philadelphia & Reading R. R. . . . . to Bound Brook.
Central R. R. of New Jersey. . . . . to New York.
New York Central & Hudson River R. R. . . . to Troy.
Delaware & Hudson R. R. . . . . to Saratoga.
Delaware & Hudson R. R. . . . . to Schenectady.
New York Central & Hudson River R. R. . . . to Niagara Falls.
New York Central & Hudson River R. R. . . . to New York.
Central R. R. of New Jersey. . . . . to Bound Brook.
Philadelphia & Reading R. R. . . . . to Philadelphia.
Baltimore & Ohio R. R. . . . . to starting point.

THROUGH RATES.

Baltimore, Md. . . . . . $26 75 | Washington, D. C. $28 75
Philadelphia, Pa. . . . . 22 75 |

FORM EX. 325. — NIAGARA FALLS, N. Y., AND RETURN.

Baltimore & Ohio R. R. . . . . to Philadelphia.
Philadelphia & Reading R. R. . . . . to Bound Brook.
Central R. R. of New Jersey. . . . . to New York.
New York Central & Hudson River R. R. . . . to Albany.
Delaware & Hudson R. R. . . . . to C. & C. V. June.
Cooperstown & Charlotte Valley R. R. . . . . to Cooperstown.
Otsego Lake Steamer and Stage. . . . . to Richfield Springs
Delaware, Lackawanna & Western R. R. . . . to Utica.
New York Central & Hudson River R. R. . . . to Niagara Falls.
New York Central & Hudson River R. R. . . . to New York.
Central R. R. of New Jersey. . . . . to Bound Brook.
Philadelphia & Reading R. R. . . . . to Philadelphia.
Baltimore & Ohio R. R. . . . . to starting point.

THROUGH RATES.

Baltimore, Md. . . . . . $27 15 Washington, D. C. $29 15
Philadelphia, Pa. 23 15

Tickets between Cooperstown and Richfield Springs by the Otsego Lake Steamer and Stage, are for passage only; baggage will be charged extra.

FORM EX. 326. — NIAGARA FALLS, N. Y., AND RETURN.

Baltimore & Ohio R. R. . . . . to Philadelphia.
Philadelphia & Reading R. R. . . . . to Bound Brook.
Central R. R. of New Jersey. . . . . to New York.
New York Central & Hudson River R. R. . . . to Niagara Falls.
New York Central & Hudson River R. R. . . . to New York.
Central R. R. of New Jersey. . . . . to Bound Brook.
Philadelphia & Reading R. R. . . . . to Philadelphia.
Baltimore & Ohio R. R. . . . . to starting point.

THROUGH RATES.

Baltimore, Md. . . . . . . $25 00 | Washington, D. C. $27 00
(Philadelphia, Pa. . . . . 24 00 |

FORM EX. 307.—NIAGARA FALLS, N. Y., AND RETURN.

Baltimore & Ohio R. R. . . . . to Philadelphia.
Philadelphia & Reading R. R. . . . . to Bound Brook.
Central R. R. of New Jersey. . . . . to New York.
New York Central & Hudson River R. R. . . . to Niagara Falls.
New York, Lake Erie & Western R. R. . . . . . to New York.
Central R. R. of New Jersey. . . . . to Bound Brook.
Philadelphia & Reading R. R. . . . . to Philadelphia.
Baltimore & Ohio R. R. . . . . to starting point.

THROUGH RATES.

Baltimore, Md. . . . . . . $24 50 | Washington, D. C. $26 50
(Philadelphia, Pa. . . . . 20 50 |

FORM EX. 100.—NIAGARA FALLS, N. Y., AND RETURN.

Baltimore & Ohio R. R. . . . . to Philadelphia.
Philadelphia & Reading R. R. . . . . to Bound Brook.
Central R. R. of New Jersey. . . . . to New York.
New York Central & Hudson River R. R. . . . to Niagara Falls.
New York Central & Hudson River R. R. . . . to Schenectady.
Delaware & Hudson R. R. . . . . to Saratoga.
Delaware & Hudson R. R. . . . . to Troy.
New York Central & Hudson River R. R. . . . to New York.
Central R. R. of New Jersey. . . . . to Bound Brook.
Philadelphia & Reading R. R. . . . . to Philadelphia.
Baltimore & Ohio R. R. . . . . to starting point.

THROUGH RATES.

Baltimore, Md. . . . . . . $26 75 | Washington, D. C. $28 75
(Philadelphia, Pa. . . . . 22 75 |

FORM EX. 101.—NIAGARA FALLS, N. Y., AND RETURN.

Baltimore & Ohio R. R. . . . . to Philadelphia.
Philadelphia & Reading R. R. . . . . to Bound Brook.
Central R. R. of New Jersey. . . . . to New York.
New York Central & Hudson River R. R. . . . to Utica.
Delaware, Lackawanna & Western R. R. . . . to Richfield Springs.
Delaware, Lackawanna & Western R. R. . . . to Utica.
New York Central & Hudson River R. R. . . . to Niagara Falls.
New York Central & Hudson River R. R. . . . to New York.
Central R. R. of New Jersey. . . . . to Bound Brook.
Philadelphia & Reading R. R. . . . . to Philadelphia.
Baltimore & Ohio R. R. . . . . to starting point.

THROUGH RATES.

Baltimore, Md. . . . . . . $27 00 | Washington, D. C. $29 00
(Philadelphia, Pa. . . . . 23 00 |

FORM EX. 105.—NIAGARA FALLS, N. Y., AND RETURN.

Baltimore & Ohio R. R. . . . . to Philadelphia.
Philadelphia & Reading R. R. . . . . to Bound Brook.
Central R. R. of New Jersey. . . . . to New York.
New York Central & Hudson River R. R. . . . to Niagara Falls.
New York Central & Hudson River R. R. . . . to Utica.
Delaware, Lackawanna & Western R. R. . . . to Richfield Springs.
Otsego Lake Steamers and Stage . . . . to Cooperstown.

Cooperstown & Charlotte Valley R. R. . . . . . to C. & C. V. June.
Delaware & Hudson R. R. . . . . to Albany.
New York Central & Hudson River R. R. . . . to New York.
Central R. R. of New Jersey . . . . to Bound Brook.
Philadelphia & Reading R. R. . . . . to Philadelphia.
Baltimore & Ohio R. R. . . . . to starting point.

THROUGH RATES.

Baltimore, Md. . . . . . $27 15 | Washington, D. C. $29 15
Philadelphia, Pa. 23 15

Tickets between Cooperstown and Richfield Springs, by the Otsego Lake Steamers and Stage, are for passage only; baggage will be charged for extra.

FORM EX. 104.—NIAGARA FALLS, N. Y., AND RETURN.

Baltimore & Ohio R. R. . . . . to Philadelphia.
Philadelphia & Reading R. R. . . . . to Bound Brook.
Central R. R. of New Jersey . . . . to New York.
New York Central & Hudson River R. R. . . . to Niagara Falls.
New York Central & Hudson River R. R. . . . to Buffalo.
Lake Shore & Michigan Southern R. R. . . . . to Brocton.
Chautauqua Lake Ry. . . . . to Mayville.
Chautauqua Lake Ry. . . . . to Brocton.
Lake Shore & Michigan Southern R. R. . . . . to Buffalo.
New York Central & Hudson River R. R. . . . to New York.
Central R. R. of New Jersey . . . . to Bound Brook.
Philadelphia & Reading R. R. . . . . to Philadelphia.
Baltimore & Ohio R. R. . . . . to starting point.

THROUGH RATES.

Baltimore, Md. . . . . . $27 50 | Washington, D. C. $29 50
Philadelphia, Pa. 23 50

FORM EX. 106.—NIAGARA FALLS, N. Y., AND RETURN.

Baltimore & Ohio R. R. . . . . to Philadelphia.
Philadelphia & Reading R. R. . . . . to Bound Brook.
Central R. R. of New Jersey . . . . to New York.
New York Central & Hudson River R. R. . . . to Niagara Falls.
New York Central & Hudson River R. R. . . . to Buffalo.
Western New York & Pennsylvania R. R. . . . to Mayville.
Western New York & Pennsylvania R. R. . . . to Buffalo.
New York Central & Hudson River R. R. . . . to New York.
Central R. R. of New Jersey . . . . to Bound Brook.
Philadelphia & Reading R. R. . . . . to Philadelphia.
Baltimore & Ohio R. R. . . . . to starting point.

THROUGH RATES.

Baltimore, Md. . . . . . $27 00   Pittsburgh, Pa. $29 00
Parkersburg, W. Va. . . . 42 75   Washington, D. C. 29 00
Philadelphia, Pa. . . . . 23 00   Wheeling, W. Va. 42 75

FORM EX. 107.—NIAGARA FALLS, N. Y., AND RETURN.

Baltimore & Ohio R. R. . . . . to Philadelphia.
Philadelphia & Reading R. R. . . . . to Bound Brook.
Central R. R. of New Jersey . . . . to New York.
New York Central & Hudson River R. R. . . . to Niagara Falls.
New York Central & Hudson River R. R. . . . to Cayuga.
Cayuga Lake Steamers . . . . to Ithaca.
Delaware, Lackawanna & Western R. R. . . . . to New York.
Central R. R. of New Jersey . . . . to Bound Brook.
Philadelphia & Reading R. R. . . . . to Philadelphia.
Baltimore & Ohio R. R. . . . . to starting point.

THROUGH RATES.

Baltimore, Md.	$26 00	Pittsburgh, Pa.	$28 00
Parkersburg, W. Va.	14 75	Washington, D. C.	28 00
Philadelphia, Pa.	22 00	Wheeling, W. Va.	14 75

FORM EX. 198.—NIAGARA FALLS, N. Y., AND RETURN.

Baltimore & Ohio R. R. . . . . to Pittsburgh.
Transfer Baltimore & Ohio R. R. Depot . . . . to P. & L. E. R. R. Depot
Pittsburgh & Lake Erie R. R. . . . . to Youngstown.
Lake Shore & Michigan Southern Ry. . . . . . to Buffalo.
New York Central & Hudson River R. R. . . . to Niagara Falls.

Returning, same route.

THROUGH RATES.

Baltimore, Md.	$24 20	Martinsburg, W. Va.	$19 65
Bellaire, O.	13 90	Meyersdale, Pa.	15 00
Berkeley Springs, W. Va.	19 00	Morgantown, W. Va. (via Wheeling)	17 10
Cameron, W. Va. (via Wheeling)	14 40	Moundsville, W. Va. (via Wheeling)	13 75
Charlestown, W. Va.	20 80		
Chester, Pa.	27 10	Mountain Lake Park, Md. (via Cumberland)	18 55
Clarksburg, W. Va. (via Wheeling)	18 15	Mt. Pleasant, Pa.	13 10
Connellsville, Pa.	12 80	Newark, Del.	26 50
Cumberland, Md.	16 50	New York, N. Y.	31 10
Deer Park, Md. (via Cumberland)	18 40	Oakland, Md. (via Cumberland)	18 65
Fairmont, W. Va. (via Wheeling)	16 40	Philadelphia, Pa.	27 10
		Piedmont, W. Va.	17 60
Frederick, Md.	21 45	Rockwood, Pa.	14 55
Grafton, W. Va. (via Wheeling)	17 50	Somerset, Pa.	14 90
		Staunton, Va.	26 70
Hagerstown, Md.	21 45	Strasburg, Va.	23 05
Harper's Ferry, W. Va.	20 10	Uniontown, Pa.	13 50
Harrisonburg, Va.	25 40	Washington, D. C.	22 60
Havre de Grace, Md.	25 65	Washington, Pa.	12 00
Keyser, W. Va.	17 40	Wheeling, W. Va.	13 70
Lexington, Va.	28 50	Wilmington, Del.	27 10
McKeesport, Pa.	11 40	Winchester, Va.	22 00

FORM EX. 149.—NIAGARA FALLS, N. Y., AND RETURN.

Baltimore & Ohio R. R. . . . . to Philadelphia.
Philadelphia & Reading R. R. . . . . to Bound Brook.
Central R. R. of New Jersey . . . . to New York.
New York Central & Hudson River R. R. . . . to Niagara Falls.
New York Central & Hudson River R. R. . . . to Buffalo.
Delaware, Lackawanna & Western R. R. . . . to New York.
Central R. R. of New Jersey . . . . to Bound Brook.
Philadelphia & Reading R. R. . . . . to Philadelphia.
Baltimore & Ohio R. R. . . . . to starting point.

THROUGH RATES.

Baltimore, Md.	$24 50	Washington, D. C.	$26 50
Philadelphia, Pa.	20 50		

FORM EX. 150.—NIAGARA FALLS, N. Y., AND RETURN.

Baltimore & Ohio R. R. . . . . to Philadelphia.
Philadelphia & Reading R. R. . . . . to Bound Brook.
Central R. R. of New Jersey . . . . to New York.
West Shore R. R. . . . . to Niagara Falls.

Returning, same route.
Transfer through New York, in both directions, included.

THROUGH RATES.

Baltimore, Md.	$24 00	Washington, D. C.	$25 00
Philadelphia, Pa.	20 00		

234   BALTIMORE & OHIO RAILROAD COMPANY

Form Ex. 451.—Niagara Falls, N. Y., and Return.

Baltimore & Ohio R. R. . . . . to Philadelphia.
Philadelphia & Reading R. R. . . . . to Bound Brook.
Central R. R. of New Jersey . . . . to New York.
West Shore R. R. . . . . to Niagara Falls.
New York, Lake Erie & Western R. R. . . . . to New York.
Central R. R. of New Jersey . . . . to Bound Brook.
Philadelphia & Reading R. R. . . . . to Philadelphia.
Baltimore & Ohio R. R. . . . . to starting point.

Transfer through New York, going, included.

THROUGH RATES.

Baltimore, Md. . . . . . . $24 00 | Washington, D. C. $26 00
†Philadelphia, Pa. . . . . 20 00 |

Form Ex. 452.—Niagara Falls, N. Y., and Return.

Baltimore & Ohio R. R. . . . . to Philadelphia.
Philadelphia & Reading R. R. . . . . to Bound Brook.
Central R. R. of New Jersey . . . . to New York.
West Shore R. R. . . . . to Niagara Falls.
New York, Lake Erie & Western R. R. . . . . to Jamestown.
New York, Lake Erie & Western R. R. . . . . to Salamanca.
New York, Lake Erie & Western R. R. . . . . to New York.
Central R. R. of New Jersey . . . . to Bound Brook.
Philadelphia & Reading R. R. . . . . to Philadelphia.
Baltimore & Ohio R. R. . . . . to starting point.

Transfer through New York, going, included.

THROUGH RATES.

Baltimore, Md. . . . . . . $24 75 | Washington, D. C. $26 75
†Philadelphia, Pa. . . . . 20 75 |

Form Ex. 453.—Niagara Falls, N. Y., and Return.

Baltimore & Ohio R. R. . . . . to Philadelphia.
Philadelphia & Reading R. R. . . . . to Bound Brook.
Central R. R. of New Jersey . . . . to New York.
West Shore R. R. . . . . to Albany.
Delaware & Hudson R. R. . . . . to Saratoga.
Delaware & Hudson R. R. . . . . to South Schenectady.
West Shore R. R. . . . . to Niagara Falls.
West Shore R. R. . . . . to New York.
Central R. R. of New Jersey . . . . to Bound Brook.
Philadelphia & Reading R. R. . . . . to Philadelphia.
Baltimore & Ohio R. R. . . . . to starting point.

Transfer through New York, in both directions, included.

THROUGH RATES.

Baltimore, Md. . . . . . . $25 95 | Washington, D. C. $27 95
†Philadelphia, Pa. . . . . 21 95 |

Form Ex. 454.—Niagara Falls, N. Y., and Return.

Baltimore & Ohio R. R. . . . . to Philadelphia.
Philadelphia & Reading R. R. . . . . to Bound Brook.
Central R. R. of New Jersey . . . . to New York.
West Shore R. R. . . . . to Niagara Falls.
West Shore R. R. . . . . to Albany.
New York & Albany Day Line Steamers . . . . to New York.
Central R. R. of New Jersey . . . . to Bound Brook.
Philadelphia & Reading R. R. . . . . to Philadelphia.
Baltimore & Ohio R. R. . . . . to starting point.

Transfer through New York, going, included.

THROUGH RATES.

Baltimore, Md. . . . . . . $24 00 | Washington, D. C. $26 00
†Philadelphia, Pa. . . . . 20 00 |

ROUTES AND RATES FOR SUMMER TOURS. 235

FORM EX. 155.—NIAGARA FALLS, N. Y., AND RETURN.

Baltimore & Ohio R. R. . . . . to Philadelphia.
Philadelphia & Reading R. R. . . . . to Bound Brook.
Central R. R. of New Jersey . . . . to New York.
New York Central & Hudson River R. R. . . . to Niagara Falls.
New York Central & Hudson River R. R. . . . to Albany.
New York & Albany Day Line Steamers . . . . to New York.
Central R. R. of New Jersey . . . . to Bound Brook.
Philadelphia & Reading R. R. . . . . to Philadelphia.
Baltimore & Ohio R. R. . . . . to starting point.

THROUGH RATES.

Baltimore, Md. . . . . . . $24.50 | Washington, D. C. $26.50
(Philadelphia, Pa. . . . . 20.50 |

FORM EX. 156.—NIAGARA FALLS, N. Y., AND RETURN.

Baltimore & Ohio R. R. . . . . to Philadelphia.
Philadelphia & Reading R. R. . . . . to Bound Brook.
Central R. R. of New Jersey . . . . to New York.
West Shore R. R. . . . . to Niagara Falls.
West Shore R. R. . . . . to Rotterdam June.
Fitchburg R. R. . . . . to Boston.
Old Colony R. R. . . . . to Fall River.
Old Colony Steamboat Co. (Fall River Line) . to New York.
Central R. R. of New Jersey . . . . to Bound Brook.
Philadelphia & Reading R. R. . . . . to Philadelphia.
Baltimore & Ohio R. R. . . . . to starting point.
      Transfer through New York, going, included.

THROUGH RATES.

Baltimore, Md. . . . . . . $30.65 | Washington, D. C. $32.65
(Philadelphia, Pa. . . . . 26.65 |

FORM EX. 157.—NIAGARA FALLS, N. Y., AND RETURN.

Baltimore & Ohio R. R. . . . . to Philadelphia.
Philadelphia & Reading R. R. . . . . to Bound Brook.
Central R. R. of New Jersey . . . . to New York.
New York Central & Hudson River R. R. . . . to Niagara Falls.
New York Central & Hudson River R. R. . . . to Troy.
Fitchburg R. R. . . . . to Boston.
Old Colony R. R. . . . . to Fall River.
Old Colony Steamboat Co. (Fall River Line) . to New York.
Central R. R. of New Jersey . . . . to Bound Brook.
Philadelphia & Reading R. R. . . . . to Philadelphia.
Baltimore & Ohio R. R. . . . . to starting point.

THROUGH RATES.

Baltimore, Md. . . . . . . $31.45 | Washington, D. C. $33.45
(Philadelphia, Pa. . . . . 27.45 |

FORM EX. 158.—NIAGARA FALLS, N. Y., AND RETURN.

Baltimore & Ohio R. R. . . . . to Philadelphia.
Philadelphia & Reading R. R. . . . . to Bound Brook.
Central R. R. of New Jersey . . . . to New York.
West Shore R. R. . . . . to Niagara Falls.
West Shore R. R. . . . . to South Schenectady.
Delaware & Hudson R. R. . . . . to Saratoga.
Fitchburg R. R. . . . . to Boston.
Old Colony R. R. . . . . to Fall River.
Old Colony Steamboat Co. (Fall River Line) . to New York.
Central R. R. of New Jersey . . . . to Bound Brook.
Philadelphia & Reading R. R. . . . . to Philadelphia.
Baltimore & Ohio R. R. . . . . to starting point.
      Transfer through New York, going, included.

THROUGH RATES.

Baltimore, Md. . . . . . . $30.65 | Washington, D. C. $32.65
(Philadelphia, Pa. . . . . 26.65 |

236   BALTIMORE & OHIO RAILROAD COMPANY.

Form Ex. 159.—Niagara Falls, N. Y., and Return.

Baltimore & Ohio R. R.	to Philadelphia.
Philadelphia & Reading R. R.	to Bound Brook.
Central R. R. of New Jersey	to New York.
New York Central & Hudson River R. R.	to Niagara Falls.
New York Central & Hudson River R. R.	to Schenectady.
Delaware & Hudson R. R.	to Saratoga.
Fitchburg R. R.	to Boston.
Old Colony R. R.	to Fall River.
Old Colony Steamboat Co. (Fall River Line)	to New York.
Central R. R. of New Jersey	to Bound Brook.
Philadelphia & Reading R. R.	to Philadelphia.
Baltimore & Ohio R. R.	to starting point.

Through Rates.

Baltimore, Md.	$31 15	Washington, D. C.	$33 15
Philadelphia, Pa.	27 15		

Form Ex. 160.—Niagara Falls, N. Y., and Return.

Baltimore & Ohio R. R.	to Philadelphia.
Philadelphia & Reading R. R.	to Bound Brook.
Central R. R. of New Jersey	to New York.
West Shore R. R.	to Albany.
Delaware & Hudson R. R.	to C. & C. V. Junc.
Cooperstown & Charlotte Valley R. R.	to Cooperstown.
Otsego Lake Steamer and Stage	to Richfield Springs.
Delaware, Lackawanna & Western R. R.	to Utica.
West Shore R. R.	to Niagara Falls.
West Shore R. R.	to New York.
Central R. R. of New Jersey	to Bound Brook.
Philadelphia & Reading R. R.	to Philadelphia.
Baltimore & Ohio R. R.	to starting point.

Transfer through New York, in both directions, included.

Through Rates.

Baltimore, Md.	$28 70	Washington, D. C.	$30 70
Philadelphia, Pa.	24 70		

Tickets between Cooperstown and Richfield Springs, by the Otsego Lake Steamer and Stage, are for passage only; baggage will be charged extra.

Form Ex. 162.—Niagara Falls, N. Y., and Return.

Baltimore & Ohio R. R.	to Philadelphia.
Philadelphia & Reading R. R.	to Bound Brook.
Central R. R. of New Jersey	to New York.
West Shore R. R.	to Niagara Falls.
West Shore R. R.	to South Schenectady.
Delaware & Hudson R. R.	to Saratoga.
Delaware & Hudson R. R.	to Albany.
West Shore R. R.	to New York.
Central R. R. of New Jersey	to Bound Brook.
Philadelphia & Reading R. R.	to Philadelphia.
Baltimore & Ohio R. R.	to starting point.

Transfer through New York, in both directions, included.

Through Rates.

Baltimore, Md.	$25 95	Washington, D. C.	$27 95
Philadelphia, Pa.	21 95		

Form Ex. 163.—Niagara Falls, N. Y., and Return.

Baltimore & Ohio R. R.	to Philadelphia.
Philadelphia & Reading R. R.	to Bound Brook.
Central R. R. of New Jersey	to New York.
West Shore R. R.	to Utica.
Delaware, Lackawanna & Western R. R.	to Richfield Springs.
Delaware, Lackawanna & Western R. R.	to Utica.
West Shore R. R.	to Niagara Falls.
West Shore R. R.	to New York.
Central R. R. of New Jersey	to Bound Brook.
Philadelphia & Reading R. R.	to Philadelphia.
Baltimore & Ohio R. R.	to starting point.

Transfer through New York, in both directions, included.

THROUGH RATES.

Baltimore, Md.	$26 00	Washington, D. C.	$28 00
†Philadelphia, Pa.	22 00		

Form Ex. 164.—Niagara Falls, N. Y., and Return.

Baltimore & Ohio R. R.	to Philadelphia.
Philadelphia & Reading R. R.	to Bound Brook.
Central R. R. of New Jersey	to New York.
West Shore R. R.	to Niagara Falls.
West Shore R. R.	to Utica.
Delaware, Lackawanna & Western R. R.	to Richfield Springs.
Otsego Lake Steamers and Stage	to Cooperstown.
Cooperstown & Charlotte Valley R. R.	to C. & C. V. Junc.
Delaware & Hudson R. R.	to Albany.
West Shore R. R.	to New York.
Central R. R. of New Jersey	to Bound Brook.
Philadelphia & Reading R. R.	to Philadelphia.
Baltimore & Ohio R. R.	to starting point.

Transfer through New York, in both directions, included.

THROUGH RATES.

Baltimore, Md.	$26 65	Washington, D. C.	$28 65
†Philadelphia, Pa.	22 65		

Tickets between Cooperstown and Richfield Springs, by the Otsego Lake Steamer and Stage, are for passage only; baggage will be charged extra.

Form Ex. 167.—Niagara Falls, N. Y., and Return.

Baltimore & Ohio R. R.	to Philadelphia.
Philadelphia & Reading R. R.	to Bound Brook.
Central R. R. of New Jersey	to New York.
West Shore R. R.	to Niagara Falls.
New York Central & Hudson River R. R.	to Buffalo.
Western New York & Pennsylvania R. R.	to Mayville.
Western New York & Pennsylvania R. R.	to Buffalo.
West Shore R. R.	to New York.
Central R. R. of New Jersey	to Bound Brook.
Philadelphia & Reading R. R.	to Philadelphia.
Baltimore & Ohio R. R.	to starting point.

Transfer through New York, in both directions, included.

THROUGH RATES.

Baltimore, Md.	$26 50	Washington, D. C.	$28 50
†Philadelphia, Pa.	22 50		

238   BALTIMORE & OHIO RAILROAD COMPANY

FORM EX. 169. NIAGARA FALLS, N. Y., AND RETURN.

Baltimore & Ohio R. R. . . . . to Philadelphia.
Philadelphia & Reading R. R. . . . . to Bound Brook.
Central R. R. of New Jersey . . . . to New York.
West Shore R. R. to Niagara Falls.
New York Central & Hudson River R. R. . . . to Buffalo.
Delaware, Lackawanna & Western R. R. . . . . to New York.
Central R. R. of New Jersey . . . . to Bound Brook.
Philadelphia & Reading R. R. . . . . to Philadelphia.
Baltimore & Ohio R. R. . . . . to starting point.

Transfer through New York, going, included.

THROUGH RATES.

Baltimore, Md. . . . . . $24 00 | Washington, D. C. $26 00
†Philadelphia, Pa. 20 00

FORM EX. 170. NIAGARA FALLS, N. Y., AND RETURN.

Baltimore & Ohio R. R. . . . . to Philadelphia.
Philadelphia & Reading R. R. . . . . to Bound Brook.
Central R. R. of New Jersey . . . . to New York.
New York, Lake Erie & Western R. R. . . . . . to Niagara Falls.

Returning, same route.

THROUGH RATES.

Baltimore, Md. . . . . . $24 00 | Washington, D. C. $26 00
†Philadelphia, Pa. 20 00

FORM EX. 172. NIAGARA FALLS, N. Y., AND RETURN.

Baltimore & Ohio R. R. . . . . to Philadelphia.
Philadelphia & Reading R. R. . . . . to Bound Brook.
Central R. R. of New Jersey . . . . to New York.
New York, Lake Erie & Western R. R. . . . . . to Niagara Falls.
New York, Lake Erie & Western R. R. . . . . . to Binghamton.
Delaware & Hudson R. R. . . . . to Albany.
New York & Albany Day Line Steamers . . . . to New York.
Central R. R. of New Jersey . . . . to Bound Brook.
Philadelphia & Reading R. R. . . . . to Philadelphia.
Baltimore & Ohio R. R. . . . . to starting point.

THROUGH RATES.

Baltimore, Md. . . . . . $24 00 | Washington, D. C. $26 00
†Philadelphia, Pa. 20 00

FORM EX. 173. NIAGARA FALLS, N. Y., AND RETURN.

Baltimore & Ohio R. R. . . . . to Philadelphia.
Philadelphia & Reading R. R. . . . . to Bound Brook.
Central R. R. of New Jersey . . . . to New York.
New York, Lake Erie & Western R. R. . . . . . to Niagara Falls.
New York, Lake Erie & Western R. R. . . . . . to Binghamton.
Delaware & Hudson R. R. . . . . to C. & C. V. Junc.
Cooperstown & Charlotte Valley R. R. . . . . . to Cooperstown.
Cooperstown & Charlotte Valley R. R. . . . . . to C. & C. V. Junc.
Delaware & Hudson R. R. . . . . to Albany.
New York & Albany Day Line Steamers . . . . to New York.
Central R. R. of New Jersey . . . . to Bound Brook.
Philadelphia & Reading R. R. . . . . to Philadelphia.
Baltimore & Ohio R. R. . . . . to starting point.

THROUGH RATES.

Baltimore, Md. . . . . . $25 20 | Washington, D. C. $27 20
†Philadelphia, Pa. 21 20

Form Ex. 471.—Niagara Falls, N. Y., and Return.

Baltimore & Ohio R. R. . . . . to Philadelphia.
Philadelphia & Reading R. R. . . . . to Bound Brook.
Central R. R. of New Jersey . . . . to New York.
New York, Lake Erie & Western R. R. . . . . to Niagara Falls.
New York, Lake Erie & Western R. R. . . . . to Binghamton.
Delaware & Hudson R. R. . . . . to Sharon Springs.

Delaware & Hudson R. R. . . . . to Albany.
New York & Albany Day Line Steamers . . . . to New York.
Central R. R. of New Jersey . . . . to Bound Brook.
Philadelphia & Reading R. R. . . . . to Philadelphia.
Baltimore & Ohio R. R. . . . . to starting point.

THROUGH RATES.

Baltimore, Md. . . . . . . $21 50 | Washington, D. C. $23 50
Philadelphia, Pa. . . . . 20 50 |

FORM EX. 175.— NIAGARA FALLS, N. Y., AND RETURN.

Baltimore & Ohio R. R. . . . . to Philadelphia.
Philadelphia & Reading R. R. . . . . to Bound Brook.
Central R. R. of New Jersey . . . . to New York.
New York, Lake Erie & Western R. R. . . . . to Niagara Falls.
New York, Lake Erie & Western R. R. . . . . to Binghamton.
Delaware, Lackawanna & Western R. R. . . . to New York.
Central R. R. of New Jersey . . . . to Bound Brook.
Philadelphia & Reading R. R. . . . . to Philadelphia.
Baltimore & Ohio R. R. . . . . to starting point.

THROUGH RATES.

Baltimore, Md. . . . . . . $24 00 | Washington, D. C. $26 00
Philadelphia, Pa. . . . . 20 00 |

FORM EX. 176.— NIAGARA FALLS, N. Y., AND RETURN.

Baltimore & Ohio R. R. . . . . to Philadelphia.
Philadelphia & Reading R. R. . . . . to Bound Brook.
Central R. R. of New Jersey . . . . to New York.
New York, Lake Erie & Western R. R. . . . . to Niagara Falls.
New York Central & Hudson River R. R. . . to Albany.
New York & Albany Day Line Steamers . . . to New York.
Central R. R. of New Jersey . . . . to Bound Brook.
Philadelphia & Reading R. R. . . . . to Philadelphia.
Baltimore & Ohio R. R. . . . . to starting point.

THROUGH RATES.

Baltimore, Md. . . . . . . $24 00 | Washington, D. C. $26 00
Philadelphia, Pa. . . . . 20 00 |

FORM EX. 177.— NIAGARA FALLS, N. Y., AND RETURN.

Baltimore & Ohio R. R. . . . . to Philadelphia.
Philadelphia & Reading R. R. . . . . to Bound Brook.
Central R. R. of New Jersey . . . . to New York.
New York, Lake Erie & Western R. R. . . . . to Niagara Falls.
West Shore R. R. to Albany.
New York & Albany Day Line Steamers . . . to New York.
Central R. R. of New Jersey . . . . to Bound Brook.
Philadelphia & Reading R. R. . . . . to Philadelphia.
Baltimore & Ohio R. R. . . . . to starting point.

THROUGH RATES.

Baltimore, Md. . . . . . . $24 00 | Washington, D. C. $26 00
Philadelphia, Pa. . . . . 20 00 |

FORM EX. 178.— NIAGARA FALLS, N. Y., AND RETURN.

Baltimore & Ohio R. R. . . . . to Philadelphia.
Philadelphia & Reading R. R. . . . . to Bound Brook.
Central R. R. of New Jersey . . . . to New York.
New York, Lake Erie & Western R. R. . . . . to Niagara Falls.
New York Central & Hudson River R. R. . . to New York.
Central R. R. of New Jersey . . . . to Bound Brook.
Philadelphia & Reading R. R. . . . . to Philadelphia.
Baltimore & Ohio R. R. . . . . to starting point.

THROUGH RATES.

Baltimore, Md. . . . . . . $24 50 | Washington, D. C. $26 50
Philadelphia, Pa. . . . . 20 50 |

ROUTES AND RATES FOR SUMMER TOURS. 241

Form Ex. 179.—Niagara Falls, N. Y., and Return.

Baltimore & Ohio R. R. . . . . to Philadelphia.
Philadelphia & Reading R. R. . . . . to Bound Brook.
Central R. R. of New Jersey . . . . to New York.
New York, Lake Erie & Western R. R. . . . to Niagara Falls.
West Shore R. R. . . . . to New York.
Central R. R. of New Jersey . . . . to Bound Brook.
Philadelphia & Reading R. R. . . . . to Philadelphia.
Baltimore & Ohio R. R. . . . . to starting point.

Transfer through New York, returning, included.

THROUGH RATES.

Baltimore, Md. . . . . . $24 00 | Washington, D. C. $26 00
†Philadelphia, Pa. 20 00

Form Ex. 181.—Niagara Falls, N. Y., and Return.

Baltimore & Ohio R. R. . . . . to Philadelphia.
Philadelphia & Reading R. R. . . . . to Bound Brook.
Central R. R. of New Jersey . . . . to New York.
New York, Lake Erie & Western R. R. . . . to Niagara Falls.
West Shore R. R. . . . . to South Schenectady.
Delaware & Hudson R. R. . . . . to Saratoga.
Delaware & Hudson R. R. . . . . to Albany.
New York & Albany Day Line Steamers . . to New York.
Central R. R. of New Jersey . . . . to Bound Brook.
Philadelphia & Reading R. R. . . . . to Philadelphia.
Baltimore & Ohio R. R. . . . . to starting point.

THROUGH RATES.

Baltimore, Md. . . . . . $25 75 | Washington, D. C. $27 75
†Philadelphia, Pa. 21 75

Form Ex. 182.—Niagara Falls, N. Y., and Return.

Baltimore & Ohio R. R. . . . . to Philadelphia.
Philadelphia & Reading R. R. . . . . to Bound Brook.
Central R. R. of New Jersey . . . . to New York.
New York, Lake Erie & Western R. R. . . . to Niagara Falls.
New York Central & Hudson River R. R. . to Schenectady.
Delaware & Hudson R. R. . . . . to Saratoga.
Delaware & Hudson R. R. . . . . to Albany.
New York & Albany Day Line Steamers . . to New York.
Central R. R. of New Jersey . . . . to Bound Brook.
Philadelphia & Reading R. R. . . . . to Philadelphia.
Baltimore & Ohio R. R. . . . . to starting point.

THROUGH RATES.

Baltimore, Md. . . . . . $25 75 | Washington, D. C. $27 75
†Philadelphia, Pa. 21 75

Form Ex. 183.—Niagara Falls, N. Y., and Return.

Baltimore & Ohio R. R. . . . . to Philadelphia.
Philadelphia & Reading R. R. . . . . to Bound Brook.
Central R. R. of New Jersey . . . . to New York.
Delaware, Lackawanna & Western R. R. . . to Buffalo.
New York Central & Hudson River R. R. . to Niagara Falls.

Returning, same route.

THROUGH RATES.

Baltimore, Md. . . . . . $24 00 | Washington, D. C. $26 00
†Philadelphia, Pa. 20 00

FORM EX. 184.—NIAGARA FALLS, N. Y., AND RETURN.

Baltimore & Ohio R. R. . . . . to Philadelphia.
Philadelphia & Reading R. R. . . . . to Bound Brook.
Central R. R. of New Jersey . . . . to New York.
Delaware, Lackawanna & Western R. R. . . . . to Buffalo.
New York Central & Hudson River R. R. . . . to Niagara Falls.
New York Central & Hudson River R. R. . . . to New York.
Central R. R. of New Jersey . . . . to Bound Brook.
Philadelphia & Reading R. R. . . . . to Philadelphia.
Baltimore & Ohio R. R. . . . . to starting point.

THROUGH RATES.

Baltimore, Md. . . . . . . $24 50 | Washington, D. C. $26 50
Philadelphia, Pa. 20 50

FORM EX. 185.—NIAGARA FALLS, N. Y., AND RETURN.

Baltimore & Ohio R. R. . . . . to Philadelphia.
Philadelphia & Reading R. R. . . . . to Bound Brook.
Central R. R. of New Jersey . . . . to New York.
Delaware, Lackawanna & Western R. R. . . . . to Buffalo.
New York, Lake Erie & Western R. R. . . . . to Niagara Falls.
New York, Lake Erie & Western R. R. . . . . to New York.
Central R. R. of New Jersey . . . . to Bound Brook.
Philadelphia & Reading R. R. . . . . to Philadelphia.
Baltimore & Ohio R. R. . . . . to starting point.

THROUGH RATES.

Baltimore, Md. . . . . . . $24 00 | Washington, D. C. $26 00
Philadelphia, Pa. 20 00

FORM EX. 186.—NIAGARA FALLS, N. Y., AND RETURN.

Baltimore & Ohio R. R. . . . . to Philadelphia.
Philadelphia & Reading R. R. . . . . to Bound Brook.
Central R. R. of New Jersey . . . . to New York.
Delaware, Lackawanna & Western R. R. . . . . to Buffalo.
New York Central & Hudson River R. R. . . . to Niagara Falls.
New York Central & Hudson River R. R. . . . to Albany.
New York & Albany Day Line Steamers . . . . to New York.
Central R. R. of New Jersey . . . . to Bound Brook.
Philadelphia & Reading R. R. . . . . to Philadelphia.
Baltimore & Ohio R. R. . . . . to starting point.

THROUGH RATES.

Baltimore, Md. . . . . . . $24 00 | Washington, D. C. $26 00
Philadelphia, Pa. 20 00

FORM EX. 187.—NIAGARA FALLS, N. Y., AND RETURN.

Baltimore & Ohio R. R. . . . . to Philadelphia.
Philadelphia & Reading R. R. . . . . to Bound Brook.
Central R. R. of New Jersey . . . . to New York.
Delaware, Lackawanna & Western R. R. . . . . to Buffalo.
New York Central & Hudson River R. R. . . . to Niagara Falls.
New York Central & Hudson River R. R. . . . to Utica.
Delaware, Lackawanna & Western R. R. . . . . to Richfield Springs.
Delaware, Lackawanna & Western R. R. . . . . to New York.
Central R. R. of New Jersey . . . . to Bound Brook.
Philadelphia & Reading R. R. . . . . to Philadelphia.
Baltimore & Ohio R. R. . . . . to starting point.

THROUGH RATES.

Baltimore, Md. . . . . . . $27 15 | Washington, D. C. $29 15
Philadelphia, Pa. 23 15

FORM EX. 571.—NIAGARA FALLS, N. Y., AND RETURN.

Baltimore & Ohio R. R. . . . . to Philadelphia.
Philadelphia & Reading R. R. . . . . to Bethlehem.
Lehigh Valley R. R. . . . . to Waverly.
New York, Lake Erie & Western R. R. . . . . . to Niagara Falls.
    Returning, same route.

THROUGH RATES.

Baltimore, Md. . . . . $18 00 | Pittsburgh, Pa. $20 50
†Philadelphia, Pa. . . . . . 17 00 | Washington, D. C. 20 00

FORM EX. 572.—NIAGARA FALLS, N. Y., AND RETURN.

Baltimore & Ohio R. R. . . . . to Philadelphia.
Philadelphia & Reading R. R. . . . . to Williamsport.
Pennsylvania R. R. . . . . to Canandaigua.
New York Central & Hudson River R. R. . . . . to Niagara Falls.
    Returning, same route.

THROUGH RATES.

Baltimore, Md. . . . . $18 00 | Pittsburgh, Pa. $20 50
†Philadelphia, Pa. . . . . . 17 00 | Washington, D. C. 20 00

FORM EX. 573.—NIAGARA FALLS, N. Y., AND RETURN.

Baltimore & Ohio R. R. . . . . to Philadelphia.
Philadelphia & Reading R. R. . . . . to Williamsport.
Pennsylvania R. R. . . . . to Elmira.
New York, Lake Erie & Western R. R. . . . . . to Niagara Falls.
    Returning, same route.

THROUGH RATES.

Baltimore, Md. . . . . $18 00 | Pittsburgh, Pa. $20 50
†Philadelphia, Pa. . . . . . 17 00 | Washington, D. C. 20 00

FORM EX. 574.—NIAGARA FALLS, N. Y., AND RETURN.

Baltimore & Ohio R. R. . . . . to Philadelphia.
Philadelphia & Reading R. R. . . . . to Bethlehem.
Lehigh Valley R. R. . . . . to Waverly.
New York, Lake Erie & Western R. R. . . . . . to Elmira.
Pennsylvania R. R. . . . . to Watkins.
Pennsylvania R. R. . . . . to Elmira.
New York, Lake Erie & Western R. R. . . . . . to Niagara Falls.
New York, Lake Erie & Western R. R. . . . . . to Waverly.
Lehigh Valley R. R. . . . . to Bethlehem.
Philadelphia & Reading R. R. . . . . to Philadelphia.
Baltimore & Ohio R. R. . . . . to starting point.

THROUGH RATES.

Baltimore, Md. . . . . $18 00 | Pittsburgh, Pa. $20 50
†Philadelphia, Pa. . . . . . 17 00 | Washington, D. C. 20 00

FORM EX. 575.—NIAGARA FALLS, N. Y., AND RETURN.

Baltimore & Ohio R. R. . . . . to Philadelphia.
Philadelphia & Reading R. R. . . . . to Williamsport.
Pennsylvania R. R. . . . . to Watkins.
Seneca Lake Steam Navigation Co. . . . . to Geneva.
New York Central & Hudson River R. R. . . . . to Niagara Falls.
New York Central & Hudson River R. R. . . . . to Canandaigua.
Pennsylvania R. R. . . . . to Williamsport.
Philadelphia & Reading R. R. . . . . to Philadelphia.
Baltimore & Ohio R. R. . . . . to starting point.

THROUGH RATES.

Baltimore, Md. . . . . $18 00 | Pittsburgh, Pa. $20 50
†Philadelphia, Pa. . . . . . 17 00 | Washington, D. C. 20 00

FORM EX. 576.—NIAGARA FALLS, N. Y., AND RETURN.

Baltimore & Ohio R. R. . . . . to Philadelphia.
Philadelphia & Reading R. R. . . . . to Bethlehem.
Lehigh Valley R. R. . . . . to Waverly.
New York, Lake Erie & Western R. R. . . . . to Elmira.
Pennsylvania R. R. . . . . to Watkins.
Seneca Lake Steam Navigation Co. . . . . . to Geneva.
New York Central & Hudson River R. R. . . to Niagara Falls.
New York, Lake Erie & Western R. R. . . . . to Waverly.
Lehigh Valley R. R. . . . . to Bethlehem.
Philadelphia & Reading R. R. . . . . to Philadelphia.
Baltimore & Ohio R. R. . . . . to starting point.

THROUGH RATES.

Baltimore, Md. . . . . $18 00 | Washington, D. C. $20 00
Philadelphia, Pa. . . . . . 18 00 |

FORM EX. 577.—NIAGARA FALLS, N. Y., AND RETURN.

Baltimore & Ohio R. R. . . . . to Philadelphia.
Philadelphia & Reading R. R. . . . . to Bethlehem.
Lehigh Valley R. R. . . . . to Waverly.
New York, Lake Erie & Western R. R. . . . . to Niagara Falls.
New York Central & Hudson River R. R. . . to Geneva.
Seneca Lake Steam Navigation Co. . . . . . to Watkins.
Pennsylvania R. R. . . . . to Elmira.
New York, Lake Erie & Western R. R. . . . . to Waverly.
Lehigh Valley R. R. . . . . to Bethlehem.
Philadelphia & Reading R. R. . . . . to Philadelphia.
Baltimore & Ohio R. R. . . . . to starting point.

THROUGH RATES.

Baltimore, Md. . . . . $18 00 | Washington, D. C. $20 00
Philadelphia, Pa. . . . . . 18 00 |

FORM EX. 578.—NIAGARA FALLS, N. Y., AND RETURN.

Baltimore & Ohio R. R. . . . . to Philadelphia.
Philadelphia & Reading R. R. . . . . to Williamsport.
Pennsylvania R. R. . . . . to Watkins.
Seneca Lake Steam Navigation Co. . . . . . to Geneva.
New York Central & Hudson River R. R. . . to Niagara Falls.
New York, Lake Erie & Western R. R. . . . . to Waverly.
Lehigh Valley R. R. . . . . to Bethlehem.
Philadelphia & Reading R. R. . . . . to Philadelphia.
Baltimore & Ohio R. R. . . . . to starting point.

THROUGH RATES.

Baltimore, Md. . . . . $18 00 | Washington, D. C. $20 00
Philadelphia, Pa. . . . . . 18 00 |

FORM EX. 579.—NIAGARA FALLS, N. Y., AND RETURN.

Baltimore & Ohio R. R. . . . . to Philadelphia.
Philadelphia & Reading R. R. . . . . to Bethlehem.
Lehigh Valley R. R. . . . . to Waverly.
New York, Lake Erie & Western R. R. . . . . to Niagara Falls.
New York Central & Hudson River R. R. . . to Geneva.
Seneca Lake Steam Navigation Co. . . . . . to Watkins.
Pennsylvania R. R. . . . . to Williamsport.
Philadelphia & Reading R. R. . . . . to Philadelphia.
Baltimore & Ohio R. R. . . . . to starting point.

THROUGH RATES.

Baltimore, Md. . . . . $18 00 | Washington, D. C. $20 00
Philadelphia, Pa. . . . . . 18 00 |

ROUTES AND RATES FOR SUMMER TOURS   245

FORM EX. 580. NIAGARA FALLS, N. Y., AND RETURN.

Baltimore & Ohio R. R. . . . . to Philadelphia.
Philadelphia & Reading R. R. . . . . to Bethlehem.
Lehigh Valley R. R. . . . . to Sheldrake.
Cayuga Lake Steamers . . . . to Cayuga.
New York Central & Hudson River R. R. . . . to Niagara Falls.
New York Central & Hudson River R. R. . . . to Cayuga.
Cayuga Lake Steamers . . . . to Ithaca.
Lehigh Valley R. R. . . . . to Bethlehem.
Philadelphia & Reading R. R. . . . . to Philadelphia.
Baltimore & Ohio R. R. . . . . to starting point.

THROUGH RATES.

Baltimore, Md. . . . . . . $18 00 Washington, D. C. . . . $20 00
†Philadelphia, Pa. 17 00

FORM EX. 581.—NIAGARA FALLS, N. Y., AND RETURN.

Baltimore & Ohio R. R. . . . . to Philadelphia.
Philadelphia & Reading R. R. . . . . to Bethlehem.
Lehigh Valley R. R. . . . . to Waverly.
New York, Lake Erie & Western R. R. . . . . . to Niagara Falls.
New York Central & Hudson River R. R. . . . to Lyons.
Fall Brook Coal Co. R. R. . . . . to Williamsport.
Philadelphia & Reading R. R. . . . . to Philadelphia.
Baltimore & Ohio R. R. . . . . to starting point.

THROUGH RATES.

Baltimore, Md. . . . . . . $18 00 Washington, D. C. . . . $20 00
†Philadelphia, Pa. 18 00

FORM EX. 583. NIAGARA FALLS, N. Y., AND RETURN.

Baltimore & Ohio R. R. . . . . to Philadelphia.
Philadelphia & Reading R. R. . . . . to Williamsport.
Fall Brook Coal Co. R. R. . . . . to Lyons.
New York Central & Hudson River R. R. . . . to Niagara Falls.
New York Central & Hudson River R. R. . . . to Geneva (via Lyons)
Lehigh Valley R. R. . . . . to Bethlehem.
Philadelphia & Reading R. R. . . . . to Philadelphia.
Baltimore & Ohio R. R. . . . . to starting point.

THROUGH RATES.

Baltimore, Md. . . . . . . $18 00 Washington, D. C. . . . $20 00
†Philadelphia, Pa. 18 00

FORM EX. 584.—NIAGARA FALLS, N. Y., AND RETURN.

Baltimore & Ohio R. R. . . . . to Philadelphia.
Philadelphia & Reading R. R. . . . . to Bethlehem.
Lehigh Valley R. R. . . . . to Waverly.
New York, Lake Erie & Western R. R. . . . . . to Elmira.
Pennsylvania R. R. . . . . to Watkins.
Seneca Lake Steam Navigation Co. . . . . . . to Geneva.
New York Central & Hudson River R. R. . . . to Niagara Falls.
New York Central & Hudson River R. R. . . . to Albany.
New York & Albany Day Line Steamers . . . . to New York.
Central R. R. of New Jersey. . . . . to Bound Brook.
Philadelphia & Reading R. R. . . . . to Philadelphia.
Baltimore & Ohio R. R. . . . . to starting point.

THROUGH RATES.

Baltimore, Md. . . . . . $23 25 | Pittsburgh, Pa. $31 70
Parkersburg, W. Va. . . 34 50 | Washington, D. C 25 25
†Philadelphia, Pa. . . . 19 25 | Wheeling, W. Va. 34 50

246   BALTIMORE & OHIO RAILROAD COMPANY

FORM EX. 585. NIAGARA FALLS, N. Y., AND RETURN.

Baltimore & Ohio R. R. . . . . to Philadelphia.
Philadelphia & Reading R. R. . . . . to Bethlehem.
Lehigh Valley R. R. . . . . to Waverly.
New York, Lake Erie & Western R. R. . . . . to Niagara Falls.
New York Central & Hudson River R. R. . . . to Albany.
New York & Albany Day Line Steamers . . . . to New York.
Central R. R. of New Jersey . . . . to Bound Brook.
Philadelphia & Reading R. R. . . . . to Philadelphia.
Baltimore & Ohio R. R. . . . . to starting point.

THROUGH RATES.

Baltimore, Md. . . . . . . $23 25 | Pittsburgh, Pa. $31 70
Parkersburg, W. Va. . . . 31 50 | Washington, D. C. 25 25
†Philadelphia, Pa. . . . . 19 25 | Wheeling, W. Va. 31 50

FORM EX. 586. NIAGARA FALLS, N. Y., AND RETURN.

Baltimore & Ohio R. R. . . . . to Philadelphia.
Philadelphia & Reading R. R. . . . . to Williamsport.
Pennsylvania R. R. . . . . to Watkins.
Seneca Lake Steam Navigation Co. . . . . . . to Geneva.
New York Central & Hudson River R. R. . . . to Niagara Falls.
New York Central & Hudson River R. R. . . . to Albany.
New York & Albany Day Line . . . . to New York.
Central R. R. of New Jersey . . . . to Bound Brook.
Philadelphia & Reading R. R. . . . . to Philadelphia.
Baltimore & Ohio R. R. . . . . to starting point.

THROUGH RATES.

Baltimore, Md. . . . . . . $23 25 | Pittsburgh, Pa. $31 70
Parkersburg, W. Va. . . . 31 50 | Washington, D. C. 25 25
†Philadelphia, Pa. . . . . 19 25 | Wheeling, W. Va. 31 50

FORM EX. 587. NIAGARA FALLS, N. Y., AND RETURN.

Baltimore & Ohio R. R. . . . . to Philadelphia.
Philadelphia & Reading R. R. . . . . to Bound Brook.
Central R. R. of New Jersey . . . . to New York.
New York Central & Hudson River R. R. . . . to Niagara Falls.
New York Central & Hudson River R. R. . . . to Geneva.
Seneca Lake Steam Navigation Co. . . . . . . to Watkins.
Pennsylvania R. R. . . . . to Elmira.
New York, Lake Erie & Western R. R. . . . . to Waverly.
Lehigh Valley R. R. . . . . to Bethlehem.
Philadelphia & Reading R. R. . . . . to Philadelphia.
Baltimore & Ohio R. R. . . . . to starting point.

THROUGH RATES.

Baltimore, Md. . . . . . . $23 75 | Washington, D. C. $25 75
†Philadelphia, Pa. . . . . 19 75 |

FORM EX. 588. NIAGARA FALLS, N. Y., AND RETURN.

Baltimore & Ohio R. R. . . . . to Philadelphia.
Philadelphia & Reading R. R. . . . . to Williamsport.
Pennsylvania R. R. . . . . to Watkins.
Seneca Lake Steam Navigation Co. . . . . . . to Geneva.
New York Central & Hudson River R. R. . . . to Niagara Falls.
New York Central & Hudson River R. R. . . . to New York.
Central R. R. of New Jersey . . . . to Bound Brook.
Philadelphia & Reading R. R. . . . . to Philadelphia.
Baltimore & Ohio R. R. . . . . to starting point.

THROUGH RATES.

Baltimore, Md. . . . . . . $23 75 | Washington, D. C. $25 75
†Philadelphia, Pa. . . . . 19 75 |

FORM EX. 589.—NIAGARA FALLS, N. Y., AND RETURN.

Baltimore & Ohio R. R. . . . . to Philadelphia.
Philadelphia & Reading R. R. . . . . to Bound Brook.
Central R. R. of New Jersey . . . . to New York.
New York Central & Hudson River R. R. . . . . to Niagara Falls.
New York, Lake Erie & Western R. R. . . . . . to Waverly.
Lehigh Valley R. R. . . . . to Bethlehem.
Philadelphia & Reading R. R. . . . . to Philadelphia.
Baltimore & Ohio R. R. . . . . to starting point.

THROUGH RATES.

Baltimore, Md. . . . . . . $23 75 | Washington, D. C. $25 75
†Philadelphia, Pa. 19 75

FORM EX. 590.—NIAGARA FALLS, N. Y., AND RETURN.

Baltimore & Ohio R. R. . . . . to Philadelphia.
Philadelphia & Reading R. R. . . . . to Bethlehem.
Lehigh Valley R. R. . . . . to Waverly.
New York, Lake Erie & Western R. R. . . . . . to Niagara Falls.
New York Central & Hudson River R. R. . . . . to New York.
Central R. R. of New Jersey . . . . to Bound Brook.
Philadelphia & Reading R. R. . . . . to Philadelphia.
Baltimore & Ohio R. R. . . . . to starting point.

THROUGH RATES.

Baltimore, Md. . . . . . . $23 75 | Washington, D. C. $25 75
†Philadelphia, Pa. 19 75

FORM EX. 591.—NIAGARA FALLS, N. Y., AND RETURN.

Baltimore & Ohio R. R. . . . . to Philadelphia.
Philadelphia & Reading R. R. . . . . to Bethlehem.
Lehigh Valley R. R. . . . . to Waverly.
New York, Lake Erie & Western R. R. . . . . . to Niagara Falls.
New York, Lake Erie & Western R. R. . . . . . to New York.
Central R. R. of New Jersey . . . . to Bound Brook.
Philadelphia & Reading R. R. . . . . to Philadelphia.
Baltimore & Ohio R. R. . . . . to starting point.

THROUGH RATES.

Baltimore, Md. . . . . . . $23 25 | Washington, D. C. $25 25
†Philadelphia, Pa. 19 25

FORM EX. 592.—NIAGARA FALLS, N. Y., AND RETURN.

Baltimore & Ohio R. R. . . . . to Philadelphia.
Philadelphia & Reading R. R. . . . . to Bethlehem.
Lehigh Valley R. R. . . . . to Waverly.
New York, Lake Erie & Western R. R. . . . . . to Niagara Falls.
New York Central & Hudson River R. R. . . . . to Utica.
Rome, Watertown & Ogdensburg R. R. . . . . . to Trenton Falls.
Rome, Watertown & Ogdensburg R. R. . . . . . to Utica.
New York Central & Hudson River R. R. . . . . to Schenectady.
Delaware & Hudson R. R. . . . . to Albany.
New York & Albany Day Line . . . . to New York.
Central R. R. of New Jersey . . . . to Bound Brook.
Philadelphia & Reading R. R. . . . . to Philadelphia.
Baltimore & Ohio R. R. . . . . to starting point.

THROUGH RATES.

Baltimore, Md. . . . . . . $25 25 | Washington, D. C. $27 25
†Philadelphia, Pa. 21 25

218   BALTIMORE & OHIO RAILROAD COMPANY

Form Ex. 1050.—Niagara Falls, N. Y., and Return

For routes to Niagara Falls, see page 249.

New York C. & H. River R. R. . . . Niagara Falls to Lewiston.
Rome, Watertown & Ogdensburg R. R. . . . . . . to Norwood.
Central Vermont R. R. . . . . to Montpelier.
Montpelier & Wells River R. R. . . . . to Wells River.
Concord & Montreal R. R. . . . . to Nashua Junc.
Boston & Maine R. R. . . . . to Boston.
Sound or Rail Lines (see pages 50 to 55 for routes) to Philadelphia.
Baltimore & Ohio R. R. . . . . to starting point.

THROUGH RATES.

	Via Sound	Via Rail.
Baltimore, Md.	$31 65	$32 15
Philadelphia, Pa.	27 65	28 15
Washington, D. C.	33 65	34 15

The following Forms to Niagara Falls, N. Y., are used only in connection with Routes Beyond that Point and are given in order that passengers may have a choice of routes to Niagara Falls (rates are included in rate for routes mentioned):

Form Ex. 191. Niagara Falls, N. Y.

Baltimore & Ohio R. R.	to Philadelphia.
Philadelphia & Reading R. R.	to Williamsport.
Pennsylvania R. R.	to Canandaigua.
New York Central & Hudson River R. R.	to Niagara Falls.

Form Ex. 192. Niagara Falls, N. Y.

Baltimore & Ohio R. R.	to Philadelphia.
Philadelphia & Reading R. R.	to Williamsport.
Pennsylvania R. R.	to Watkins.
Seneca Lake Steam Navigation Co.	to Geneva.
New York Central & Hudson River R. R.	to Niagara Falls.

Form Ex. 193. Niagara Falls, N. Y.

Baltimore & Ohio R. R.	to Philadelphia.
Philadelphia & Reading R. R.	to Bethlehem.
Lehigh Valley R. R.	to Geneva.
New York Central & Hudson River R. R.	to Niagara Falls.

Form Ex. 194.—Niagara Falls, N. Y.

Baltimore & Ohio R. R.	to Philadelphia.
Philadelphia & Reading R. R.	to Bethlehem.
Lehigh Valley R. R.	to Waverly.
New York, Lake Erie & Western R. R.	to Elmira.
Pennsylvania R. R.	to Canandaigua.
New York Central & Hudson River R. R.	to Niagara Falls.

Form Ex. 195. Niagara Falls, N. Y.

Baltimore & Ohio R. R.	to Philadelphia.
Philadelphia & Reading R. R.	to Bethlehem.
Lehigh Valley R. R.	to Waverly.
New York, Lake Erie & Western R. R.	to Niagara Falls.

Form Ex. 196. Niagara Falls, N. Y.

Baltimore & Ohio R. R.	to Philadelphia.
Philadelphia & Reading R. R.	to Williamsport.
Fall Brook Coal Co. R. R.	to Lyons.
New York Central & Hudson River R. R.	to Niagara Falls.

Form Ex. 1067. Niagara Falls, N. Y.

Baltimore & Ohio R. R.	to Philadelphia.
Philadelphia & Reading R. R.	to Bethlehem.
Philadelphia & Reading R. R. (Lehigh Valley Div.)	to Niagara Falls.

NORTH CONWAY, N. H.

FORM EX. 762.—NORTH CONWAY, N. H., AND RETURN.

(Via Sound Lines and Boston in both directions.)

Baltimore & Ohio R. R. . . . . to Philadelphia.
Philadelphia & Reading R. R. . . . . to Bound Brook.
Central R. R. of New Jersey . . . . to New York.
Sound Lines (see pages 50 to 55 for route) . . . to Boston.
Boston & Maine R. R. . . . . to North Conway.

Returning, same route.

Transfer through Boston, in both directions, included.

THROUGH RATES.

Baltimore, Md. . . . . . $21 00 | Washington, D. C. $23 00
Philadelphia, Pa. . . . . 17 00 |

FORM EX. 762.—NORTH CONWAY, N. H., AND RETURN.

(Via Rail Lines and Boston in both directions.)

Baltimore & Ohio R. R. . . . . to Philadelphia.
Rail Lines (see pages 50 to 55 for route) . . . . to Boston.
Boston & Maine R. R. . . . . to North Conway.

Returning, same route.

THROUGH RATES.

Baltimore, Md. . . . . . $24 50 | Washington, D. C. $26 50
Philadelphia, Pa. . . . . 20 50 |

FORM EX. 762.—NORTH CONWAY, N. H., AND RETURN.

(Via Rail Lines and Boston; returning via Boston and Sound Lines.)

Baltimore & Ohio R. R. . . . . to Philadelphia.
Rail Lines (see pages 50 to 55 for route) . . . . to Boston.
Boston & Maine R. R. . . . . to North Conway.
Boston & Maine R. R. . . . . to Boston.
Sound Lines (see pages 50 to 55 for route) . . . to New York.
Central R. R. of New Jersey . . . . to Bound Brook.
Philadelphia & Reading R. R. . . . . to Philadelphia.
Baltimore & Ohio R. R. . . . . to starting point.

Transfer through Boston, returning, included.

THROUGH RATES.

Baltimore, Md. . . . . . $21 00 | Washington, D. C. $23 00
Philadelphia, Pa. . . . . 20 00 |

FORM EX. 762.—NORTH CONWAY, N. H., AND RETURN.

(Via Sound Lines and Boston; returning all rail.)

Baltimore & Ohio R. R. . . . . to Philadelphia.
Philadelphia & Reading R. R. . . . . to Bound Brook.
Central R. R. of New Jersey . . . . to New York.
Sound Lines (see pages 50 to 55 for route) . . . to Boston.
Boston & Maine R. R. . . . . to North Conway.
Boston & Maine R. R. . . . . to Boston.
Rail Lines (see pages 50 to 55 for route) . . . . to Philadelphia.
Baltimore & Ohio R. R. . . . . to starting point.

Transfer through Boston, going, included.

THROUGH RATES.

Baltimore, Md. . . . . . $21 00 | Washington, D. C. $23 00
Philadelphia, Pa. . . . . 20 00 |

FORM EX. 1051. NORTH CONWAY, N. H., AND RETURN.

(Via rail to Boston and Portland; returning via Sound Lines.)

Baltimore & Ohio R. R. . . . . to Philadelphia.
Rail Lines (see pages 50 to 55 for route) . . . . . to Boston.
Boston & Maine R. R. . . . . to Portland.
Maine Central R. R. . . . . to North Conway.
Maine Central R. R. . . . . to Portland.
Boston & Maine R. R. . . . . to Boston.
Sound Lines (see pages 50 to 55 for route) . . . . to New York.
Central R. R. of New Jersey . . . . to Bound Brook.
Philadelphia & Reading R. R. . . . . to Philadelphia.
Baltimore & Ohio R. R. . . . . to starting point.

THROUGH RATES.

Baltimore, Md. . . . . . $24 00 | Washington, D. C. $26 00
{Philadelphia, Pa. . . . . 20 00 }

Transfer through Boston, returning, included.

FORM EX. 1051. NORTH CONWAY, N. H., AND RETURN.

(Via Sound Lines, Boston and Portland; returning all rail.)

Baltimore & Ohio R. R. . . . . to Philadelphia.
Philadelphia & Reading R. R. . . . . to Bound Brook.
Central R. R. of New Jersey . . . . to New York.
Sound Lines (see pages 50 to 55 for route) . . . . to Boston.
Boston & Maine R. R. . . . . to Portland.
Maine Central R. R. . . . . to North Conway.
Maine Central R. R. . . . . to Portland.
Boston & Maine R. R. . . . . to Boston.
Rail Lines (see pages 50 to 55 for route) . . . . . to Philadelphia.
Baltimore & Ohio R. R. . . . . to starting point.

THROUGH RATES.

Baltimore, Md. . . . . . $24 00 | Washington, D. C. $26 00
{Philadelphia, Pa. . . . . 20 00 }

Transfer through Boston, going, included.

FORM EX. 1051.—NORTH CONWAY, N. H., AND RETURN.

(Via Rail Lines, Boston and Portland, in both directions.)

Baltimore & Ohio R. R. . . . . to Philadelphia.
Rail Lines (see pages 50 to 55 for route) . . . . . to Boston.
Boston & Maine R. R. . . . . to Portland.
Maine Central R. R. . . . . to North Conway.

Returning, same route.

THROUGH RATES.

Baltimore, Md. . . . . . $24 50 | Washington, D. C. $26 50
{Philadelphia, Pa. . . . . 20 50 }

FORM EX. 1051. NORTH CONWAY, N. H., AND RETURN.

(Via Sound Lines, Boston and Portland, in both directions.)

Baltimore & Ohio R. R. . . . . to Philadelphia.
Philadelphia & Reading R. R. . . . . to Bound Brook.
Central R. R. of New Jersey . . . . to New York.
Sound Lines (see pages 50 to 55 for route) . . . . to Boston.
Boston & Maine R. R. . . . . to Portland.
Maine Central R. R. . . . . to North Conway.

Returning, same route.

THROUGH RATES.

Baltimore, Md. . . . . . $21 00 | Washington, D. C. $23 00
{Philadelphia, Pa. . . . . 17 00 }

Transfer through Boston, in both directions, included.

OAKLAND, MD.

What has been said of Deer Park applies with equal force to its twin resort, Oakland, situated six miles westward on the mountain edge, under the shade of those monarchs of the forest that give to Oakland its name.

Illustrated descriptive pamphlets mailed free upon application to the Passenger Department of the Baltimore & Ohio R. R.

FORM EX. 6 OR EX. OAKLAND, MD., AND RETURN.

Baltimore & Ohio R. R. . . . . to Oakland.

Returning, same route.

DIRECT RATES.

Baltimore, Md.	$9 25	Meyersdale, Pa.	$5 65
Bellaire, O.	6 25	Morgantown, W. Va.	3 80
Berkeley Springs, W. Va.	4 65	Moundsville, W. Va.	5 45
Cameron, W. Va.	4 75	Mountain Lake Park, Md.	15
Charlestown, W. Va.	6 55	Mt. Pleasant, Pa.	6 35
Chester, Pa.	12 75	Newark, Del.	11 35
Clarksburg, W. Va.	2 80	New York, N. Y.	17 25
Connellsville, Pa.	5 85	Parkersburg, W. Va.	6 05
Cumberland, Md.	2 15	Philadelphia, Pa.	13 25
Deer Park, Md.	25	Piedmont, W. Va.	1 05
Fairmont, W. Va.	2 80	Pittsburgh, Pa.	8 15
Frederick, Md.	7 10	Rockwood, Pa.	4 40
Grafton, W. Va.	1 90	Somerset, Pa.	4 80
Hagerstown, Md.	7 10	Staunton, Va.	12 35
Harper's Ferry, W. Va.	6 05	Strasburg, Va.	8 70
Harrisonburg, Va.	11 05	Uniontown, Pa.	6 30
Havre de Grace, Md.	10 70	Washington, D. C.	8 25
Johnstown, Pa.	5 90	Washington, Pa. (via Wheeling, W. Va.)	7 25
Keyser, W. Va.	1 25		
Lexington, Va.	14 15	Wheeling, W. Va.	5 90
McKeesport, Pa.	7 60	Wilmington, Del.	12 25
Martinsburg, W. Va.	5 70	Winchester, Va.	7 65

In addition to the season tickets for which rates are quoted above, special signature contract tickets, Form Ex. 801, will be sold from the following stations to Oakland, Md., and return, for use going on train No. 3 on Fridays and all trains on Saturday and Sunday of each week, good to return on any train leaving Oakland on the following Monday:

EXCURSION RATES.

Baltimore, Md.	$5 00	Washington, D. C.	$5 00
Philadelphia, Pa.	8 00		

OCEAN GROVE (ASBURY PARK), N. J.

The origin of Ocean Grove was in this wise: A few years ago some of the ministers and members of the Methodist Episcopal Church in Pennsylvania, New Jersey and New York conceived the idea of establishing by the seaside a camping-ground and summer resort for Christian families. They secured a plot of ground six miles south of Long Branch, dedicated it to religious purposes, and commenced

OAKLAND, MD.

its improvement, under the title of "The Ocean Grove Camp-Meeting Association." The association was authorized to make its own laws, and these have been framed so as to secure, for all time, the purposes in view when the work began. No intoxicating liquors are allowed on the grounds. Boating, bathing and driving are prohibited on Sunday, and all behavior unbecoming such a place is quickly suppressed. These regulations, suiting the religious ideas of a large number of people, have made the place extremely popular with certain classes, who now visit it to the number of more than 500,000 every year. The foreigner, who wishes to see one of the most curious developments of American civilization, should not fail to visit Ocean Grove.

FORM EX. 385. OCEAN GROVE (ASBURY PARK), N. J., AND RETURN.

Baltimore & Ohio R. R. . . . . to Philadelphia.
Philadelphia & Reading R. R. . . . . to Bound Brook.
Central R. R. of N. J. . . . . to Ocean Grove (Asbury Park.)

Returning, same route.

THROUGH RATES.

Baltimore, Md. . . . . . . $8 00   Washington, D. C. $10 00
(Philadelphia, Pa. 1 00

In addition to the above excursion tickets, Form Ex. 385, Ocean Grove, N. J. (Asbury Park), may be sold from the following stations at rates as quoted below.
Tickets should be limited with an "L" punch to sixteen (16) days, including day of issue.

THROUGH RATES.

Baltimore, Md. . . . . . . $7 50   (Philadelphia, Pa. $8 50
Chester, Pa. . . . . 1 00   Washington, D. C. 9 50
Havre de Grace, Md. . . . 5 85   Wilmington, Del. 1 50
Newark, Del. 5 00

OHIO PYLE, PA.

The whole body of the Youghiogheny here pitches over the precipice, and to say that it seems to boil with rage, or that it writhes and fumes to a white heat, is to express but feebly the whirling caldron below. On one side the mountains exhibit a sheer height of hundreds of feet, and on the other is a romantic old mill, age-worn and moss-covered, and of that fashion of construction which artists' eyes love to behold.

FORM EX. 34. OHIO PYLE, PA., AND RETURN.

Baltimore & Ohio R. R. . . . . to Ohio Pyle.
Returning, same route.

THROUGH RATES.

Baltimore, Md.	$10 70		Meyersdale, Pa.	$1 55
Berkeley Springs, W. Va.	5 50		Morgantown, W. Va.	8 95
Charlestown, W. Va.	7 40		Mountain Lake Park, Md.	3 05
Chester, Pa.	14 20		Mt. Pleasant, Pa.	1 45
Clarksburg, W. Va.	7 95		Newark, Del.	13 00
Connellsville, Pa.	75		New York, N. Y.	18 70
Cumberland, Md.	3 00		Oakland, Md.	5 15
Deer Park, Md.	4 90		Parkersburg, W. Va.	11 05
Fairmont, W. Va.	7 95		Philadelphia, Pa.	11 70
Frederick, Md.	7 95		Piedmont, W. Va.	4 40
Grafton, W. Va.	7 05		Pittsburgh, Pa.	3 00
Hagerstown, Md.	7 95		Rockwood, Pa.	1 05
Harper's Ferry, W. Va.	6 90		Somerset, Pa.	1 45
Harrisonburg, Va.	11 90		Staunton, Va.	13 20
Havre de Grace, Md.	12 15		Strasburg, Va.	9 55
Johnstown, Pa.	2 90		Uniontown, Pa.	1 40
Keyser, W. Va.	3 90		Washington, D. C.	9 40
Lexington, Va.	15 00		Wilmington, Del.	13 70
McKeesport, Pa.	2 40		Winchester, Va.	8 50
Martinsburg, W. Va.	6 15			

FORM EX. 35. OHIO PYLE, PA., AND RETURN.

Baltimore & Ohio R. R. . . . . to Ohio Pyle.
Returning, same route.

THROUGH RATES.

Bellaire, O. . . . . $6 00 | Washington, Pa. $4 10
Cameron, W. Va. . . . . . . 6 50 | Wheeling, W. Va. 5 40
Moundsville, W. Va. 5 85

OLD ORCHARD, ME.,

Possesses one of the finest beaches in New England. It is smooth, firm, gently-shelving, and ten miles long; admirably adapted for either driving or bathing. Among the attractions of the place may be mentioned the Methodist National Camp Ground.

FORM EX. 525.—OLD ORCHARD, ME., AND RETURN.

(Via Rail Lines to Boston; returning via Sound Lines.)

Baltimore & Ohio R. R. . . . . to Philadelphia.
Rail Lines (see pages 50 to 55 for routes) . . . . . to Boston.
Boston & Maine R. R. . . . . to Old Orchard.
Boston & Maine R. R. . . . . to Boston.
Sound Lines (see pages 50 to 55 for routes) . . . . to New York.
Central R. R. of New Jersey . . . . to Bound Brook.
Philadelphia & Reading R. R. . . . . to Philadelphia.
Baltimore & Ohio R. R. . . . . to starting point.

THROUGH RATES.

Baltimore, Md. . . . . $21 00 | Washington, D. C. $23 00
†Philadelphia, Pa. 17 00

FORM EX. 525.—OLD ORCHARD, ME., AND RETURN.

(Via Sound Lines to Boston; returning all rail.)

Baltimore & Ohio R. R. . . . . to Philadelphia.
Philadelphia & Reading R. R. . . . . to Bound Brook.
Central R. R. of New Jersey . . . . to New York.
Sound Lines (see pages 50 to 55 for routes) . . . . to Boston.
Boston & Maine R. R. . . . . to Old Orchard.
Boston & Maine R. R. . . . . to Boston.
Rail Lines (see pages 50 to 55 for routes) . . . . . to Philadelphia.
Baltimore & Ohio R. R. . . . . to starting point.

THROUGH RATES.

Baltimore, Md. . . . . $21 00 | Washington, D. C. $23 00
†Philadelphia, Pa. 17 00

FORM EX. 525.—OLD ORCHARD, ME., AND RETURN.

(Via Rail Lines to Boston in both directions.)

Baltimore & Ohio R. R. . . . . to Philadelphia.
Rail Lines (see pages 50 to 55 for routes) . . . . . to Boston.
Boston & Maine R. R. . . . . to Old Orchard.
Returning, same route.

THROUGH RATES.

Baltimore, Md. . . . . $22 00 | Washington, D. C. $24 00
†Philadelphia, Pa. 18 00

FORM EX. 525.—OLD ORCHARD, ME., AND RETURN.

(Via Sound Lines to Boston in both directions.)

Baltimore & Ohio R. R. . . . . to Philadelphia.
Philadelphia & Reading R. R. . . . . to Bound Brook.
Central R. R. of New Jersey . . . . to New York.
Sound Lines (see pages 50 to 55 for routes) . . . . to Boston.
Boston & Maine R. R. . . . . to Old Orchard.

Returning, same route.

THROUGH RATES.

Baltimore, Md. $20 00
Philadelphia, Pa. 16 00
Washington, D. C. $22 00

OLD POINT COMFORT, VA.

FORM EX. 855.—OLD POINT COMFORT, VA., AND RETURN.

Limited to six (6) months from date of sale.

Baltimore & Ohio R. R. . . . . to Washington.
Knox Transfer Co. . . . . B. & O. R. R. Depot to N. & W.
                                       D. C. Steamboat Co.'s Wharf.
Norfolk & Washington, D. C., Steamboat Company . . . . to Old Point Comfort.

Returning, same route.

THROUGH RATES.

Baltimore, Md.	$6 00	Meyersdale, Pa.	$12 00
Bellaire, O.	19 45	Morgantown, W. Va.	17 05
Berkeley Springs, W. Va.	9 45	Moundsville, W. Va.	18 70
Cameron, W. Va.	18 00	Mountain Lake Park, Md.	12 65
Charlestown, W. Va.	7 70	Mt. Pleasant, Pa.	15 30
Chester, Pa.	8 50	Newark, Del.	8 30
Clarksburg, W. Va.	16 05	New York, N. Y.	13 00
Connellsville, Pa.	14 80	Oakland, Md.	12 75
Cumberland, Md.	11 10	Parkersburg, W. Va.	19 45
Deer Park, Md.	12 50	Philadelphia, Pa.	9 00
Fairmont, W. Va.	16 05	Piedmont, W. Va.	12 20
Frederick, Md.	7 30	Pittsburgh, Pa.	17 10
Grafton, W. Va.	15 45	Rockwood, Pa.	13 05
Hagerstown, Md.	8 40	Somerset, Pa.	13 45
Harper's Ferry, W. Va.	7 20	Uniontown, Pa.	15 25
Havre de Grace, Md.	6 45	Washington, Pa.	18 20
Johnstown, Pa.	14 85	Wheeling, W. Va.	19 45
Keyser, W. Va.	12 00	Wilmington, Del.	8 00
McKeesport, Pa.	16 55	Winchester, Va.	8 80
Martinsburg, W. Va.	7 95		

FORM EX. 564.—OLD POINT COMFORT, VA., AND RETURN.

Limited to six (6) months from date of sale.

Baltimore & Ohio R. R. . . . . to Baltimore.
Baltimore Steam Packet Co. . . . . to Old Point Comfort.

Returning, same route.

258   BALTIMORE & OHIO RAILROAD COMPANY

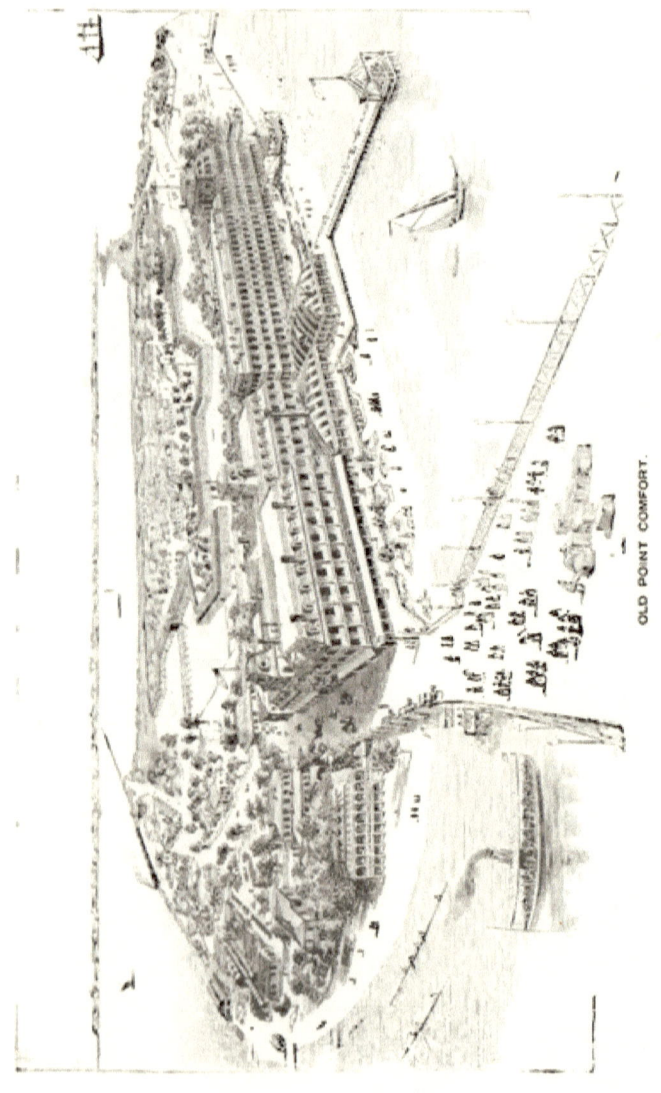

OLD POINT COMFORT.

THROUGH RATES.

Bellaire, O.	$21 05	Morgantown, W. Va.	$18 65
Berkeley Springs, W. Va.	10 75	Moundsville, W. Va.	20 40
Cameron, W. Va.	19 60	Mountain Lake Park, Md.	14 15
Charlestown, W. Va.	9 50	Mt. Pleasant, Pa.	16 50
Chester, Pa.	8 50	Newark, Del.	7 50
Clarksburg, W. Va.	17 65	New York, N. Y.	13 00
Connellsville, Pa.	16 40	Oakland, Md.	11 25
Cumberland, Md.	12 70	Parkersburg, W. Va.	20 75
Deer Park, Md.	14 00	Philadelphia, Pa.	9 00
Fairmont, W. Va.	17 60	Piedmont, W. Va.	13 80
Frederick, Md.	7 45	Pittsburgh, Pa.	18 70
Grafton, W. Va.	16 75	Rockwood, Pa.	14 65
Hagerstown, Md.	9 50	Somerset, Pa.	15 05
Harper's Ferry, W. Va.	8 80	Staunton, Va.	15 40
Harrisonburg, Va.	13 80	Strasburg, Va.	11 15
Havre de Grace, Md.	6 45	Uniontown, Pa.	16 85
Johnstown, Pa.	16 45	Washington, D. C.	7 00
Keyser, W. Va.	13 60	Washington, Pa.	19 80
Lexington, Va.	16 90	Wheeling, W. Va.	20 75
McKeesport, Pa.	18 45	Wilmington, Del.	8 00
Martinsburg, W. Va.	9 65	Winchester, Va.	10 40
Meyersdale, Pa.	14 20		

ONTARIO BEACH, N. Y.

This attractive summer resort is situated at Charlotte, on the shore of Lake Ontario, seven miles from the city of Rochester. The surrounding country is as fertile as a garden, and a ride or walk in the vicinity presents scenes of beauty and varied color that none can fail to admire and enjoy.

The village itself, with its well-shaded streets, tasteful houses and public spirited citizens, makes an ideal summer home.

Directly upon the shore of the lake, about a half mile distant from the village, is the commodious and elegant Hotel Ontario, which was erected in 1884 at great expense. It is handsomely furnished and fitted throughout, and contains all the latest appliances for the comfort and pleasure of patrons.

A large dancing pavilion, near the hotel, for the use of excursion parties, is connected with bowling alleys, billiard rooms, and the like, and though separate from the hotel itself, these means of recreation are close at hand. The beach, at the point where the hotel is located, is exceptionally fine for bathing, and the facilities for boating and fishing are unsurpassed.

FORM EX. 527. ONTARIO BEACH, N. Y., AND RETURN.

Baltimore & Ohio R. R. . . . . to Philadelphia.
Philadelphia & Reading R. R. . . . . to Bound Brook.
Central R. R. of New Jersey . . . . to New York.
New York Central & Hudson River R. R. . . to Ontario Beach.
Returning, same route.

THROUGH RATES.

Baltimore, Md. . . . . . . $25.75   Washington, D. C . . $26.75
†Philadelphia, Pa. 19.75

ORKNEY SPRINGS, VA.

Orkney has an unchallenged right to the plural. There are seven clearly defined waters, all possessing peculiar medicinal advantages. "Bear Wallow," the leading spring, has been known for nearly a century, and is richly entitled to a front rank among known mineral waters. Palatable, has no objectionable taste, unless it be slightly saline; cool, about 56°, and does not produce distention or weight in the stomach, even when freely used. It is a powerful water, and should be taken with discretion. A long line of obstinate chronic diseases have been conquered by it. The next may be mentioned Powder Spring, an alkaline sulphur water, effective in diseases of the stomach, bowels, kidneys and liver; also in cutaneous diseases, rheumatism, even in chronic state. The Healing Spring is a tonic and alterative water, and is beneficial in stomach derangements, also in inflammatory type of cutaneous diseases and lung trouble. The Iron Sulphur Spring is a combination of Bear Wallow and Powder Springs, and is a remedy in chronic diseases arising out of the torpidity of the secretive organs, complicated with nervous debility. It is an invigorating tonic. The Chalybeate Spring is almost a pure iron water, and a ferruginous tonic, pleasant in taste and popular. The Arsenic Spring—the therapeutic effect in the use of this water in acute and chronic tuberculosis, granular laryngitis, scrofula and all skin diseases is wonderful. This water should be used under the advice of a physician. In regulating the capillary circulation it removes splotches or freckles, ugly disfigurations and cloudiness and gives a clearness and brilliancy to the complexion. These facts, and they are facts, make the Arsenic Spring popular; for after all, "beauty is but *skin* deep." Alum water is brought daily from the Alum Springs, two miles distant.

The atmosphere at such an altitude is necessarily pure, dry and exhilarating, and is of itself calculated to be an effective agent in the restoration of impaired health and vigor. At Orkney one can take up his abode in the hotel, or a party sufficiently numerous may together occupy a row of buildings, and if it consist of a single family all the comforts of home may be found in a cottage. In the height of the season Orkney is somewhat like a little city. There are suitable accommodations for eight hundred guests, and almost no end of pleasure afforded for their entertainment.

FORM EX. 228. ORKNEY SPRINGS, VA., AND RETURN.

Baltimore & Ohio R. R. . . . . to Mt. Jackson.
Stage (12 miles) . . . . to Orkney Springs.
Returning, same route.

THROUGH RATES.

Baltimore, Md.	$10 45	Chester, Pa.		$15 95
Bellaire, O.	18 90	Clarksburg, W. Va.		15 30
Berkeley Springs, W. Va.	8 00	Connellsville, Pa.		11 25
Cameron, W. Va.	17 45	Cumberland, Md.		10 55
Charlestown, W. Va.	6 20	Deer Park, Md.		12 15

Fairmont, W. Va.	$15 50	Newark, Del.	$12 75
Frederick, Md.	7 70	New York, N. Y.	18 45
Grafton, W. Va.	11 00	Oakland, Md.	12 70
Hagerstown, Md.	7 70	Parkersburg, W. Va.	18 05
Harper's Ferry, W. Va.	6 65	Philadelphia, Pa.	11 45
Harrisonburg, Va.	4 30	Piedmont, W. Va.	11 65
Havre de Grace, Md.	11 90	Pittsburgh, Pa.	16 55
Johnstown, Pa.	11 30	Rockwood, Pa.	12 50
Keyser, W. Va.	11 45	Somerset, Pa.	12 90
Lexington, Va.	7 40	Staunton, Va.	5 60
McKeesport, Pa.	16 00	Strasburg, Va.	1 20
Martinsburg, W. Va.	7 40	Uniontown, Pa.	11 70
Meyersdale, Pa.	12 05	Washington, D. C.	8 85
Morgantown, W. Va.	16 50	Washington, Pa.	17 65
Moundsville, W. Va.	18 45	Wheeling, W. Va.	18 05
Mountain Lake Park, Md.	12 00	Wilmington, Del.	13 45
Mount Pleasant, Pa.	14 75	Winchester, Va.	5 10

OTTAWA, CANADA.

The erection of the vast and imposing buildings of the Canadian Parliament transformed this busy little lumbering town into a Mecca for a large and constantly augmented army of sight-seekers. Aside from the splendid piles of masonry, the picturesque falls of the Chaudiere River are worth seeing.

FORM EX. 528.—OTTAWA, ONT., AND RETURN.

Baltimore & Ohio R. R. . . . . to Philadelphia
Philadelphia & Reading R. R. . . . . to Bound Brook.
Central R. R. of New Jersey . . . . to New York.
New York Central & Hudson River R. R. . . . to Utica.
Rome, Watertown & Ogdensburg R. R. . . . . . to Morristown.
Ferry . . . . to Brockville.
Canadian Pacific Ry. . . . . to Ottawa.

Returning, same route.

THROUGH RATES.

Baltimore, Md. . . . . . . $28 50 | Washington, D. C. $30 50
†Philadelphia, Pa. 24 50

FORM EX. 529.—OTTAWA, ONT., AND RETURN.

Baltimore & Ohio R. R. . . . . to Philadelphia
Philadelphia & Reading R. R. . . . . to Bound Brook.
Central R. R. of New Jersey . . . . to New York.
New York Central & Hudson River R. R. . . . to Troy.
Delaware & Hudson R. R. . . . . to Rouse's Point.
Canada Atlantic R. R. . . . . to Ottawa.

Returning, same route.

THROUGH RATES.

Baltimore, Md. . . . . . . $28 50 | Washington, D. C. $30 50
†Philadelphia, Pa. 24 50

ORKNEY.

FORM EX. 520.—OTTAWA, ONT., AND RETURN.

Baltimore & Ohio R. R. . . . . to Philadelphia.
Philadelphia & Reading R. R. . . . . to Bound Brook.
Central R. R. of New Jersey . . . . to New York.
West Shore R. R. to Albany.
Delaware & Hudson R. R. . . . . to Rouse's Point.
Canada Atlantic R. R. . . . . to Ottawa.

Returning, same route.

Transfer through New York, in both directions, included.

THROUGH RATES.

Baltimore, Md. . . . . . . $28 50 | Washington, D. C. $30 50
‡Philadelphia, Pa. 24 50

FORM EX. 1052.—OTTAWA, ONT., AND RETURN.

Grand Trunk Ry. . . . . Montreal to Coteau Junction.
Canada Atlantic Ry. . . . . to Ottawa.

Returning, same route.

Sold in connection with any ticket passing through or terminating at Montreal.

Rate $5 00

Form Ex. 1052 must not be sold in connection with forms to or from Montreal reading via Canadian Pacific Ry.

FORM EX. 1053.—OTTAWA, CANADA, AND RETURN.

Canadian Pacific R. R. . . . . Montreal to Ottawa.

Returning, same route.

Sold in connection with any ticket passing through or terminating at Montreal.

Rate $5 00

Form Ex. 1053 must not be sold in connection with forms to or from Montreal reading via Grand Trunk Ry.

PATCHOGUE, LONG ISLAND, N. Y.

FORM EX. 1054.—PATCHOGUE, N. Y., AND RETURN.

(Via New York and Long Island City in both directions.)

Baltimore & Ohio R. R. . . . . to Philadelphia.
Philadelphia & Reading R. R. . . . . to Bound Brook.
Central R. R. of New Jersey. . . . . to New York.
Metropolitan Ferry Co., James' Slip, or 34th St.
 Ferry . . . . to Long Island City.
Long Island R. R. . . . . to Patchogue.

Returning, same route.

THROUGH RATES.

Baltimore, Md. . . . . . . $11 10 | Washington, D. C. $13 10
‡Philadelphia, Pa. 7 10

PLYMOUTH, N. H.

FORM EX. 1055.— PLYMOUTH, N. H., AND RETURN.

(Via rail and Boston; returning by Sound Lines.)

Baltimore & Ohio R. R. . . . . to Philadelphia.
Rail Lines (see pages 50 to 55 for route) . . . . . to Boston.
Boston & Maine R. R. . . . . to Nashua.
Concord & Montreal R. R. . . . . to Plymouth.
Concord & Montreal R. R. . . . . to Nashua.
Boston & Maine R. R. . . . . to Boston.
Sound Lines (see pages 50 to 55 for route) . . . . to New York.
Central R. R. of New Jersey . . . . to Bound Brook.
Philadelphia & Reading R. R. . . . . to Philadelphia.
Baltimore & Ohio R. R. . . . . to starting point.

THROUGH RATES.

Baltimore, Md. . . . . . $22 85 | Washington, D. C. $24 85
(Philadelphia, Pa. . . . . 18 85 |

Transfer through Boston, returning, included.

FORM EX. 1055.— PLYMOUTH, N. H., AND RETURN.

(Via Sound Lines and Boston; returning all rail.)

Baltimore & Ohio R. R. . . . . to Philadelphia.
Philadelphia & Reading R. R. . . . . to Bound Brook.
Central R. R. of New Jersey . . . . to New York.
Sound Lines (see pages 50 to 55 for route) . . . . to Boston.
Boston & Maine R. R. . . . . to Nashua.
Concord & Montreal R. R. . . . . to Plymouth.
Concord & Montreal R. R. . . . . to Nashua.
Boston & Maine R. R. . . . . to Boston.
Rail Lines (see pages 50 to 55 for route) . . . . to Philadelphia.
Baltimore & Ohio R. R. . . . . to starting point.

THROUGH RATES.

Baltimore, Md. . . . . . $22 85 | Washington, D. C. $24 85
(Philadelphia, Pa. . . . . 18 85 |

Transfer through Boston, going, included.

FORM EX. 1055.— PLYMOUTH, N. H., AND RETURN.

(Via Rail Lines and Boston in both directions.)

Baltimore & Ohio R. R. . . . . to Philadelphia.
Rail Lines (see pages 50 to 55 for route) . . . . . to Boston.
Boston & Maine R. R. . . . . to Nashua.
Concord & Montreal R. R. . . . . to Plymouth.

Returning, same route.

THROUGH RATES.

Baltimore, Md. . . . . . $23 10 | Washington, D. C. $25 10
(Philadelphia, Pa. . . . . 19 10 |

FORM EX. 1055.— PLYMOUTH, N. H., AND RETURN.

(Via Sound Lines and Boston in both directions.)

Baltimore & Ohio R. R. . . . . to Philadelphia.
Philadelphia & Reading R. R. . . . . to Bound Brook.
Central R. R. of New Jersey . . . . to New York.
Sound Lines (see pages 50 to 55 for route) . . . . to Boston.
Boston & Maine R. R. . . . . to Nashua.
Concord & Montreal R. R. . . . . to Plymouth.

Returning, same route.

THROUGH RATES.

Baltimore, Md. . . . . . $20 20 | Washington, D. C. $22 20
(Philadelphia, Pa. . . . . 16 20 |

Transfer through Boston, in both directions, included.

POLAND SPRINGS, ME.

FORM EX. 1036.—POLAND SPRINGS, ME., AND RETURN.
(Via rail, Boston and Portland; returning via Sound Lines.)

Baltimore & Ohio R. R. . . . . to Philadelphia.
Rail Lines (see pages 50 to 55 for routes) . . . to Boston.
Boston & Maine R. R. . . . . to Portland.
Maine Central R. R. . . . . to Danville June.
Stage (6 miles) . . . . to Poland Springs.

Stage (6 miles) . . . . to Danville June.
Maine Central R. R. . . . . to Portland.
Boston & Maine R. R. . . . . to Boston.
Sound Lines (see pages 50 to 55 for route) . . . . to New York.
Central R. R. of New Jersey . . . . to Bound Brook.
Philadelphia & Reading R. R. . . . . to Philadelphia.
Baltimore & Ohio R. R. . . . . to starting point.

THROUGH RATES.

Baltimore, Md. . . . . . . $23 00 | Washington, D. C. $25 00
†Philadelphia, Pa. . . . . 19 00 |

FORM EX. 1055. POLAND SPRINGS, ME., AND RETURN.

(Via Sound Lines, Boston and Portland; returning all rail.)

Baltimore & Ohio R. R. . . . . to Philadelphia.
Philadelphia & Reading R. R. . . . . to Bound Brook.
Central R. R. of New Jersey . . . . to New York.
Sound Lines (see pages 50 to 55 for route) . . . . to Boston.
Boston & Maine R. R. . . . . to Portland.
Maine Central R. R. . . . . to Danville June.
Stage (6 miles) . . . . to Poland Springs.
Stage (6 miles) . . . . to Danville June.
Maine Central R. R. . . . . to Portland.
Boston & Maine R. R. . . . . to Boston.
Rail Lines (see pages 50 to 55 for route) . . . . . to Philadelphia.
Baltimore & Ohio R. R. . . . . to starting point.

THROUGH RATES.

Baltimore, Md. . . . . . . $23 00 | Washington, D. C. $25 00
†Philadelphia, Pa. . . . . 19 00 |

FORM EX. 1056. POLAND SPRINGS, ME., AND RETURN.

(Via Rail Lines and Portland in both directions.)

Baltimore & Ohio R. R. . . . . to Philadelphia.
Rail Lines (see pages 50 to 55 for route) . . . . . to Boston.
Boston & Maine R. R. . . . . to Portland.
Maine Central R. R. . . . . to Danville June.
Stage (6 miles) . . . . to Poland Springs.

Returning, same route.

THROUGH RATES.

Baltimore, Md. . . . . . . $24 00 | Washington, D. C. $26 00
†Philadelphia, Pa. . . . . 20 00 |

FORM EX. 1056. POLAND SPRINGS, ME., AND RETURN.

(Via Sound Lines and Portland in both directions.)

Baltimore & Ohio R. R. . . . . to Philadelphia.
Philadelphia & Reading R. R. . . . . to Bound Brook.
Central R. R. of New Jersey . . . . to New York.
Sound Lines (see pages 50 to 55 for route) . . . . to Boston.
Boston & Maine R. R. . . . . to Portland.
Maine Central R. R. . . . . to Danville June.
Stage (6 miles) . . . . to Poland Springs.

Returning, same route.

THROUGH RATES.

Baltimore, Md. . . . . . . $22 00 | Washington, D. C. $24 00
†Philadelphia, Pa. . . . . 18 00 |

FORM EX. 1057.—POLAND SPRINGS, ME., AND RETURN.

Maine Central R. R. . . . . Portland to Danville June.
Stage (6 miles) . . . . to Poland Springs.

Returning, same route.

Rate $3 00

Sold in connection with Summer Excursion Tickets passing through or terminating at Portland, Me.

PORT KENT, N. Y.,

Lies on the western shore of Lake Champlain, nearly opposite Burlington, Vt., from which it is ten miles distant. It is the starting point for Au Sable Chasm. The new Keesville, Au Sable Chasm & Lake Champlain Railroad runs direct from Port Kent to the entrance to the chasm.

FORM EX. 1058. PORT KENT, N. Y., AND RETURN.

(Via rail in both directions.)

Baltimore & Ohio R. R. . . . . to Philadelphia.
Philadelphia & Reading R. R. . . . . to Bound Brook.
Central R. R. of New Jersey. . . . . to New York.
West Shore R. R. . . . . to Albany.
Delaware & Hudson R. R. (via Saratoga) . . . to Port Kent.

Returning, same route.

Transfer through New York in both directions, included.

THROUGH RATES.

Baltimore, Md. . . . . . $22 00   Washington, D. C. . . . $24 00
Philadelphia, Pa 18 00

FORM EX. 1059. PORT KENT, N. Y., AND RETURN.

(Via rail in both directions.)

Baltimore & Ohio R. R. . . . . to Philadelphia.
Philadelphia & Reading R. R. . . . . to Bound Brook.
Central R. R. of New Jersey. . . . . to New York.
New York Central & Hudson River R. R. . . . to Troy.
Delaware & Hudson R. R. (via Saratoga) . . . to Port Kent.

Returning, same route.

THROUGH RATES.

Baltimore, Md. . . . . . $22 00   Washington, D. C. . . . $24 00
Philadelphia, Pa 18 00

FORM EX. 1060. PORT KENT, N. Y., AND RETURN.

(Via Hudson River Steamers in both directions.)

Baltimore & Ohio R. R. . . . . to Philadelphia.
Philadelphia & Reading R. R. . . . . to Bound Brook.
Central R. R. of New Jersey. . . . . to New York.
Day or People's Line Steamers. . . . . to Albany.
Delaware & Hudson R. R. (via Saratoga) . . . to Port Kent.

Returning, same route.

THROUGH RATES.

Baltimore, Md. . . . . . $20 35   Washington, D. C. . . . $22 35
Philadelphia, Pa 16 35

PROFILE HOUSE, N. H.

The Profile House is the central point of the Franconia Mountains, a range scarcely less grand than the White Mountains, and separated from them by the Twin Mountain and Field Willing ranges. The view from Mt. Lafayette shows Katahdin (in Maine) and the White Mountains to the northeast, the lovely Pemigewasset Valley to the south, and the Green Mountains of Vermont to the west. In addition to innumerable beauties in the shape of tripping cascades and placid lakes, the Franconia region possesses two great natural curiosities, either one of which would make any other region famous. Profile Mountain forms the south side of Franconia Notch, and rises two thousand feet above the Pemigewasset River at its base. Eight hundred feet below its summit is to be seen the Profile, or Old Man of the Mountain, formed by the grouping of three distinct masses of rock.

The flume is a rocky chasm seven hundred feet long and sixty feet high, with an average breadth of twenty feet.

FORM EX. 525.— PROFILE HOUSE, N. H., AND RETURN.

(Via Rail and Boston; returning via Sound Lines.)

Baltimore & Ohio R. R., ... to Philadelphia.
Rail Lines (see pages 50 to 55 for route), ... to Boston.
Boston & Maine R. R., ... to Nashua.
Concord & Montreal R. R., ... to Bethlehem June.
Profile & Franconia Notch R. R., ... to Profile House.
Profile & Franconia Notch R. R., ... to Bethlehem June.
Concord & Montreal R. R., ... to Nashua.
Boston & Maine R. R., ... to Boston.
Sound Lines (see pages 50 to 55 for route), . . . to New York.
Central R. R. of New Jersey, ... to Bound Brook.
Philadelphia & Reading R. R., ... to Philadelphia.
Baltimore & Ohio R. R., ... to starting point.

Transfer through Boston, returning, included.

THROUGH RATES.

Baltimore, Md., ... $28 80 | Washington, D. C., ... $30 80
{Philadelphia, Pa., ... 24 80 |

FORM EX. 526.— PROFILE HOUSE, N. H., AND RETURN.

(Via Sound Lines and Boston; returning all rail.)

Baltimore & Ohio R. R., ... to Philadelphia.
Philadelphia & Reading R. R., ... to Bound Brook.
Central R. R. of New Jersey, ... to New York.
Sound Lines (see pages 50 to 55 for route), . . . to Boston.
Boston & Maine R. R., ... to Nashua.
Concord & Montreal R. R., ... to Bethlehem June.
Profile & Franconia Notch R. R., ... to Profile House.
Profile & Franconia Notch R. R., ... to Bethlehem June.
Concord & Montreal R. R., ... to Nashua.
Boston & Maine R. R., ... to Boston.
Rail Lines (see pages 50 to 55 for route), . . . to Philadelphia.
Baltimore & Ohio R. R., ... to starting point.

Transfer through Boston, going, included.

THROUGH RATES.

Baltimore, Md., ... $28 80 | Washington, D. C., ... $30 80
{Philadelphia, Pa., ... 24 80 |

FORM EX. 526.—PROFILE HOUSE, N. H., AND RETURN.
(Via Rail Lines and Boston in both directions.)

Baltimore & Ohio R. R. . . . . to Philadelphia.
Rail Lines (see pages 50 to 55 for route) . . . . . to Boston.
Boston & Maine R. R. . . . . to Nashua.
Concord & Montreal R. R. . . . . to Bethlehem June.
Profile & Franconia Notch R. R. . . . . to Profile House.
            Returning, same route.

THROUGH RATES.

Baltimore, Md. . . . . . $30 75 | Washington, D. C. . . . $32 75
‡Philadelphia, Pa. . . . 26 75 |

FORM EX. 526.—PROFILE HOUSE, N. H., AND RETURN.
(Via Sound Lines and Boston in both directions.)

Baltimore & Ohio R. R. . . . . to Philadelphia.
Philadelphia & Reading R. R. . . . . to Bound Brook.
Central R. R. of New Jersey . . . . to New York.
Sound Lines (see pages 50 to 55 for route) . . . . to Boston.
Boston & Maine R. R. . . . . to Nashua.
Concord & Montreal R. R. . . . . to Bethlehem June.
Profile & Franconia Notch R. R. . . . . to Profile House.
            Returning, same route.
Transfer through Boston, in both directions, included.

THROUGH RATES.

Baltimore, Md. . . . . . $25 00 | Washington, D. C. . . . $27 00
‡Philadelphia, Pa. . . . 21 00 |

FORM EX. 1061.—PROFILE HOUSE, N. H., AND RETURN.
(Via rail and Boston; returning via Sound Lines.)

Baltimore & Ohio R. R. . . . . to Philadelphia.
Rail Lines (see pages 50 to 55 for route) . . . . to Boston.
Boston & Maine R. R. . . . . to North Conway.
Maine Central R. R. . . . . to Zealand Junction.
Profile & Franconia Notch R. R. . . . . to Profile House.
Profile & Franconia Notch R. R. . . . . to Zealand Junction.
Maine Central R. R. . . . . to North Conway.
Boston & Maine R. R. . . . . to Boston.
Sound Lines (see pages 50 to 55 for route) . . . . to New York.
Central R. R. of New Jersey . . . . to Bound Brook.
Philadelphia & Reading R. R. . . . . to Philadelphia.
Baltimore & Ohio R. R. . . . . to starting point.

THROUGH RATES.

Baltimore, Md. . . . . . $29 40 | Washington, D. C. . . . $31 40
‡Philadelphia, Pa. . . . 25 40 |
Transfer through Boston, returning, included.

FORM EX. 1061.—PROFILE HOUSE, N. H., AND RETURN.
(Via Sound Lines and Boston; returning all rail.)

Baltimore & Ohio R. R. . . . . to Philadelphia.
Philadelphia & Reading R. R. . . . . to Bound Brook.
Central R. R. of New Jersey . . . . to New York.
Sound Lines (see pages 50 to 55 for route) . . . . to Boston.
Boston & Maine R. R. . . . . to North Conway.
Maine Central R. R. . . . . to Zealand Junction.
Profile & Franconia Notch R. R. . . . . to Profile House.
Profile & Franconia Notch R. R. . . . . to Zealand Junction.
Maine Central R. R. . . . . to North Conway.
Boston & Maine R. R. . . . . to Boston.
Rail Lines (see pages 50 to 55 for route) . . . . to Philadelphia.
Baltimore & Ohio R. R. . . . . to starting point.

THROUGH RATES.

Baltimore, Md. . . . . . $29 40 | Washington, D. C. . . . $31 40
‡Philadelphia, Pa. . . . 25 40 |
Transfer through Boston, going, included.

ROUTES AND RATES FOR SUMMER TOURS. 271

FORM EX. 1061. PROFILE HOUSE, N. H., AND RETURN.
(Via Rail Lines and Boston in both directions.)

Baltimore & Ohio R. R. . . . . to Philadelphia.
Rail Lines (see pages 50 to 55 for routes) . . . . . to Boston.
Boston & Maine R. R. . . . . to North Conway.
Maine Central R. R. . . . . to Zealand Junction.
Profile & Franconia Notch R. R. . . . . to Profile House.
Returning, same route.

THROUGH RATES.

Baltimore, Md. . . . . . . $30 75 | Washington, D. C. $32 75
† Philadelphia, Pa. . . . . . 26 75 |

FORM EX. 1061.—PROFILE HOUSE, N. H., AND RETURN.
(Via Sound Lines and Boston in both directions.)

Baltimore & Ohio R. R.	to Philadelphia.
Philadelphia & Reading R. R.	to Bound Brook.
Central R. R. of New Jersey	to New York.
Sound Lines (see pages 50 to 55 for routes)	to Boston.
Boston & Maine R. R.	to North Conway.
Maine Central R. R.	to Zealand Junction.
Profile & Franconia Notch R. R.	to Profile House.

Returning, same route.

THROUGH RATES.

Baltimore, Md. . . . . . $28 00   Washington, D. C. $28 00
Philadelphia, Pa. 22 00

Transfer through Boston, in both directions, included.

FORM EX. 1062.—PROFILE HOUSE, N. H., AND RETURN.
(Via rail and Boston; returning via Sound Lines.)

Baltimore & Ohio R. R.	to Philadelphia.
Rail Lines (see pages 50 to 55 for routes)	to Boston.
Boston & Maine R. R.	to Portland.
Maine Central R. R.	to Zealand Junction.
Profile & Franconia Notch R. R.	to Profile House.
Profile & Franconia Notch R. R.	to Zealand Junction.
Maine Central R. R.	to Portland.
Boston & Maine R. R.	to Boston.
Sound Lines (see pages 50 to 55 for routes)	to New York.
Central R. R. of New Jersey	to Bound Brook.
Philadelphia & Reading R. R.	to Philadelphia.
Baltimore & Ohio R. R.	to starting point.

THROUGH RATES.

Baltimore, Md. . . . . . $29 10   Washington, D. C. $31 10
Philadelphia, Pa. 25 10

Transfer through Boston, returning, included.

FORM EX. 1062.—PROFILE HOUSE, N. H., AND RETURN.
(Via Sound Lines and Boston; returning all rail.)

Baltimore & Ohio R. R.	to Philadelphia.
Philadelphia & Reading R. R.	to Bound Brook.
Central R. R. of New Jersey	to New York.
Sound Lines (see pages 50 to 55 for routes)	to Boston.
Boston & Maine R. R.	to Portland.
Maine Central R. R.	to Zealand Junction.
Profile & Franconia Notch R. R.	to Profile House.
Profile & Franconia Notch R. R.	to Zealand Junction.
Maine Central R. R.	to Portland.
Boston & Maine R. R.	to Boston.
Rail Lines (see pages 50 to 55 for routes)	to Philadelphia.
Baltimore & Ohio R. R.	to starting point.

THROUGH RATES.

Baltimore, Md. . . . . . $29 10   Washington, D. C. $31 10
Philadelphia, Pa. 25 10

Transfer through Boston, going, included.

FORM EX. 1062.—PROFILE HOUSE, N. H., AND RETURN.
(Via Rail Lines and Boston in both directions.)

Baltimore & Ohio R. R.	to Philadelphia.
Rail Lines (see pages 50 to 55 for routes)	to Boston.
Boston & Maine R. R.	to Portland.
Maine Central R. R.	to Zealand Junction.
Profile & Franconia Notch R. R.	to Profile House.

Returning, same route.

ROUTES AND RATES FOR SUMMER TOURS.   273

THROUGH RATES.
Baltimore, Md. . . . . . . $30 75   Washington, D. C. $32 75
†Philadelphia, Pa. 26 75

FORM EX. 1062.—PROFILE HOUSE, N. H., AND RETURN.
(Via Sound Lines and Boston in both directions.)

Baltimore & Ohio R. R. . . . . to Philadelphia.
Philadelphia & Reading R. R. . . . . to Bound Brook
Central R. R. of New Jersey . . . . to New York.
Sound Lines (see pages 50 to 55 for route) . . . to Boston.
Boston & Maine R. R. . . . . to Portland.
Maine Central R. R. . . . . to Zealand Junction
Profile & Franconia Notch R. R. . . . . to Profile House.
Returning, same route.

THROUGH RATES.
Baltimore, Md. . . . . . . $26 00   Washington, D. C. $28 00
†Philadelphia, Pa. 22 00
Transfer through Boston, in both directions, included.

FORM EX. 1063.—PROFILE HOUSE, N. H., AND RETURN.
(Via rail and Boston; returning via North Woodstock, Lake Winnipesaukee, Boston and Sound Lines.)

Baltimore & Ohio R. R. . . . . to Philadelphia
Rail Lines (see pages 50 to 55 for route) . . . . to Boston.
Boston & Maine R. R. . . . . to Portland.
Maine Central R. R. . . . . to Zealand June
Profile & Franconia Notch R. R. . . . . to Profile House
Pemigewasset Valley Stage Line . . . . to N. Woodstock.
Concord & Montreal R. R. . . . . to Weirs.
Steamer . . . . to Wolfboro.
Boston & Maine R. R. . . . . to Boston.
Sound Lines (see pages 50 to 55 for route) . . . to New York
Central R. R. of New Jersey . . . . to Bound Brook
Philadelphia & Reading R. R. . . . . to Philadelphia.
Baltimore & Ohio R. R. . . . . to starting point

THROUGH RATES.
Baltimore, Md. . . . . . . $30 25   Washington, D. C. $32 25
†Philadelphia, Pa. 26 25
Transfer through Boston, in both directions, included.

FORM EX. 1065.—PROFILE HOUSE, N. H., AND RETURN.
(Via Sound Lines and Boston; returning via North Woodstock, Lake Winnipesaukee, Boston and rail.)

Baltimore & Ohio R. R. . . . . to Philadelphia
Philadelphia & Reading R. R. . . . . to Bound Brook.
Central R. R. of New Jersey . . . . to New York.
Sound Lines (see pages 50 to 55 for route) . . . to Boston.
Boston & Maine R. R. . . . . to Portland
Maine Central R. R. . . . . to Zealand June
Profile & Franconia Notch R. R. . . . . to Profile House
Pemigewasset Valley Stage Line . . . . to N. Woodstock.
Concord & Montreal R. R. . . . . to Weirs.
Steamer . . . . to Wolfboro.
Boston & Maine R. R. . . . . to Boston.
Rail Lines (see pages 50 to 55 for route) . . . . to Philadelphia.
Baltimore & Ohio R. R. . . . . to starting point.

THROUGH RATES.
Baltimore, Md. . . . . . . $30 25   Washington, D. C. $32 25
†Philadelphia, Pa. 26 25
Transfer through Boston, going, included.

274   BALTIMORE & OHIO RAILROAD COMPANY

FORM EX. 1065.   PROFILE HOUSE, N. H., AND RETURN.

(Via Rail Lines and Boston; returning via North Woodstock, Lake Winnipesaukee and Boston.)

Baltimore & Ohio R. R. . . . . to Philadelphia
Rail Lines (see pages 30 to 35 for routes) . . . . . to Boston.
Boston & Maine R. R. . . . . to Portland.
Maine Central R. R. . . . . to Zealand June.
Profile & Franconia Notch R. R. . . . . to Profile House.
Pemigewasset Valley Stage Line . . . . to N. Woodstock.
Concord & Montreal R. R. . . . . to Weirs.
Steamer . . . . to Wolfboro.
Boston & Maine R. R. . . . . to Boston.
Rail Lines (see pages 30 to 35 for routes) . . . . . to Philadelphia
Baltimore & Ohio R. R. . . . . to starting point

THROUGH RATES.

Baltimore, Md. . . . . . . $34 10   Washington, D. C. . . . $35 10
{Philadelphia, Pa. 27 10

FORM EX. 1066.   PROFILE HOUSE, N. H., AND RETURN.

(Via Sound Lines and Boston; returning via North Woodstock, Lake Winnipesaukee and Boston.)

Baltimore & Ohio R. R. . . . . to Philadelphia
Philadelphia & Reading R. R. . . . . to Bound Brook
Central R. R. of New Jersey . . . . to New York.
Sound Lines (see pages 30 to 35 for routes) . . . . to Boston.
Boston & Maine R. R. . . . . to Portland.
Maine Central R. R. . . . . to Zealand June.
Profile & Franconia Notch R. R. . . . . to Profile House.
Pemigewasset Valley Stage Line . . . . to N. Woodstock.
Concord & Montreal R. R. . . . . to Weirs.
Steamer . . . . to Wolfboro.
Boston & Maine R. R. . . . . to Boston.
Sound Lines (see pages 30 to 35 for routes) . . . . to New York
Central R. R. of New Jersey . . . . to Bound Brook
Philadelphia & Reading R. R. . . . . to Philadelphia
Baltimore & Ohio R. R. . . . . to starting point

THROUGH RATES.

Baltimore, Md. . . . . . . $28 00   Washington, D. C. . . . $29 00
{Philadelphia, Pa. 21 00

Transfer through Boston, in both directions, included.

FORM EX. 634.   PROFILE HOUSE, N. H., AND RETURN.

Baltimore & Ohio R. R. . . . . to Philadelphia
Philadelphia & Reading R. R. . . . . to Bound Brook.
Central R. R. of New Jersey . . . . to New York.
New York, New Haven & Hartford R. R. . . . . to Springfield.
Connecticut River R. R. . . . . to South Vernon.
Central Vermont R. R. . . . . to Brattleboro.
Vermont Valley R. R. . . . . to Windsor.
Central Vermont R. R. . . . . to White River June
Boston & Maine R. R. . . . . to Wells' River.
Concord & Montreal R. R. . . . . to Bethlehem June.
Profile & Franconia Notch R. R. . . . . to Profile House.

Returning, same route.

THROUGH RATES.

Baltimore, Md. . . . . . . $27 00   Washington, D. C. . . . $28 00
{Philadelphia, Pa. 23 00

ROUTES AND RATES FOR SUMMER TOURS. 275

FORM EX. 632.— PROFILE HOUSE, N. H., AND RETURN.

Baltimore & Ohio R. R. . . . . to Philadelphia.
Philadelphia & Reading R. R. . . . . to Bound Brook.
Central R. R. of New Jersey . . . . to New York.
Old Colony Steamboat Co. (Fall River Line) . to Fall River.
Old Colony R. R. . . . . to Lowell.
Boston & Maine R. R. . . . . to Nashua.
Concord & Montreal R. R. . . . . to Bethlehem Junc.
Profile & Franconia Notch R. R. . . . . to Profile House.

Returning, same route.

THROUGH RATES.

Baltimore, Md. . . . . . $25 00 | Washington, D. C. $27 00
Philadelphia, Pa. . . . . 24 00 |

FORM EX. 633.— PROFILE HOUSE, N. H., AND RETURN.

Baltimore & Ohio R. R. . . . . to Philadelphia.
Philadelphia & Reading R. R. . . . . to Bound Brook.
Central R. R. of New Jersey . . . . to New York.
Old Colony Steamboat Co. (Fall River Line) . to Fall River.
Old Colony R. R. . . . . to Lowell.
Boston & Maine R. R. . . . . to Nashua.
Concord & Montreal R. R. . . . . to North Woodstock.
Pemigewasset Valley Stage Line . . . . to Profile House.

Returning, same route.

THROUGH RATES.

Baltimore, Md. . . . . . $25 00 | Washington, D. C. $27 00
Philadelphia, Pa. . . . . 24 00 |

FORM EX. 660.— PROFILE HOUSE, N. H., AND RETURN.

Profile & Franconia Notch R. R., Bethlehem Junc. to Profile House.

Returning, same route.

Sold in connection with any ticket passing through or terminating at Bethlehem Junction.

Rate $3 00

FORM EX. 661.— PROFILE HOUSE, N. H., AND RETURN.

Profile & Franconia Notch R. R., Zealand Junc., to Profile House.

Returning, same route.

Sold in connection with any ticket passing through Zealand Junction.

Rate $3 00

PEN-MAR, MD.

FORM EX. 840. PEN-MAR, MD., AND RETURN.

Baltimore & Ohio R. R. . . . . to Baltimore.
Transfer B. & O. R. R. Depot . . . . to West. Md. R. R. Fulton Station.
Western Maryland R. R. . . . . to Pen-Mar.

Returning, same route.

THROUGH RATES.

Baltimore, Md.	$3 00	Philadelphia, Pa.	$7 00
Chester, Pa.	7 10	Washington, D. C.	5 00
New York, N. Y.	11 00	Wilmington, Del.	6 00

FORM EX. 680. PEN-MAR, MD., AND RETURN.

Baltimore & Ohio R. R. . . . . to Hagerstown.
Transfer B. & O. R. R. Depot . . . . to West. Md. R. R. Depot.
Western Maryland R. R. . . . . to Pen-Mar.

Returning, same route.

THROUGH RATES.

Bellaire, O.	$11 05	Moundsville, W. Va.	$13 25
Berkeley Springs, W. Va.	3 70	Mountain Lake Park, Md.	7 70
Charlestown, W. Va.	2 85	Mt. Pleasant, Pa.	9 85
Clarksburg, W. Va.	10 00	Oakland, Md.	7 80
Connellsville, Pa.	9 35	Parkersburg, W. Va.	13 70
Cumberland, Md.	5 65	Piedmont, W. Va.	6 75
Deer Park, Md.	7 55	Pittsburgh, Pa.	11 65
Fairmont, W. Va.	10 00	Rockwood, Pa.	7 00
Grafton, W. Va.	9 70	Somerset, Pa.	8 00
Harper's Ferry, W. Va.	2 55	Staunton, Va.	8 65
Harrisonburg, Va.	7 35	Uniontown, Pa.	9 80
Johnstown, Pa.	9 10	Washington, D. C.	4 10
Keyser, W. Va.	6 55	Washington via Pittsb'g, Pa	12 75
Lexington, Va.	10 15	Wheeling, W. Va.	13 70
Meyersdale, Pa.	7 15	Winchester, Va.	3 95
Morgantown, W. Va.	11 00		

QUEBEC, P. Q.

One of the quaintest and most interesting cities on the continent of America. It is situated at the confluence of the St. Lawrence and St. Charles Rivers, and is divided into two portions, called the Upper Town and Lower Town, the former being perched on the summit of Cape Diamond, three hundred and thirty-three feet above the river, and comprises the vast fortifications of the Citadel, hotels, private dwellings, and churches. The Lower Town is the commercial section of the city.

FORM EX. 535. QUEBEC, P. Q. AND RETURN.

Baltimore & Ohio R. R. . . . . to Philadelphia.
Philadelphia & Reading R. R. . . . . to Bound Brook.
Central R. R. of New Jersey . . . . to New York.
New York Central & Hudson River R. R. . . . to Troy.
Delaware & Hudson R. R. . . . . to Rouse's Point.
Grand Trunk Ry. . . . . to Quebec.

Returning, same route.

THROUGH RATES.

Baltimore, Md.	$31 00	Washington, D. C.	$23 00
Philadelphia, Pa.	27 00		

FORM EX. 536. QUEBEC, P. Q., AND RETURN.

Baltimore & Ohio R. R. . . . . to Philadelphia.
Philadelphia & Reading R. R. . . . . to Bound Brook.
Central R. R. of New Jersey . . . . to New York.
West Shore R. R. . . . . to Albany.
Delaware & Hudson R. R. . . . . to Rouse's Point.
Grand Trunk Ry. . . . . to Quebec.

Returning, same route.

Transfer through New York, in both directions, included.

THROUGH RATES.

Baltimore, Md. . . . . $31 00 | Washington, D. C. $33 00
{Philadelphia, Pa. . . . . . 27 00 |

FORM EX. 537. QUEBEC, P. Q., AND RETURN.

Baltimore & Ohio R. R. . . . . to Philadelphia.
Philadelphia & Reading R. R. . . . . to Bound Brook.
Central R. R. of New Jersey . . . . to New York.
New York & Albany Day Line . . . . to Albany.
Delaware & Hudson R. R. . . . . to Rouse's Point.
Grand Trunk Ry. . . . . to Quebec.

Returning, same route.

THROUGH RATES.

Baltimore, Md. . . . . $29 00 | Washington, D. C. $31 00
{Philadelphia, Pa. . . . . . 25 00 |

FORM EX. 1015. QUEBEC, P. Q., AND RETURN.

Grand Trunk Railway or Richelieu and Ontario
Navigation Co. . . . . Montreal to Quebec.

Returning, same route.

Sold in connection with any ticket passing through or terminating at Montreal.

Rate. $5 00

Form Ex. 1015 must not be sold in connection with forms to or from Montreal, reading via Canadian Pacific Railway.

FORM EX. 1098. QUEBEC, P. Q., AND RETURN.

Canadian Pacific Railway . . . . , Montreal to Quebec.

Returning, same route.

Sold in connection with any ticket passing through or terminating at Montreal.

Rate. $5 00

Form Ex. 1098 must not be sold in connection with forms to or from Montreal, reading via Grand Trunk Railway.

FORM EX. 652. QUEBEC TO HA-HA BAY OR CHICOUTIMI, P. Q., AND RETURN.

Richelieu & Ontario Navigation Co. . . . , to Ha-Ha Bay or Chicoutimi.

Returning, same route.

Sold in connection with any excursion ticket passing through or terminating at Quebec.

Rate $8 00

Meals and berth extra.

FORM EX. 633. QUEBEC TO TADOUSAC, P. Q., AND RETURN.

Richelieu & Ontario Navigation Co. . . . . to Tadousac.
Returning, same route.
Sold in connection with any excursion ticket passing through or terminating at Quebec.

Rate. $5.00

Meals and berth extra.

FORM EX. 848. QUEBEC TO MURRAY BAY, P. Q., AND RETURN.

Richelieu and Ontario Navigation Co. . . . . . . to Murray Bay.
Returning, same route.
Sold in connection with any excursion ticket passing through or terminating at Quebec.

Rate. $4.00

Meals and berth extra.

FORM EX. 849. QUEBEC TO RIVIERE DU LOUP, P. Q., AND RETURN.

Richelieu and Ontario Navigation Co. . . . . . to Riviere du Loup, P. Q.
Returning, same route.
Sold in connection with any excursion ticket passing through or terminating at Quebec.

Rate. $4.00

Meals and berth extra.

RANDOLPH, VT.

Randolph is a thrifty little village in the foot-hills of the Green Mountains. The surrounding country is elevated and broken, presenting many picturesque views for which the higher peaks of the Green Mountains furnish a background.

FORM EX. 1065. RANDOLPH, VT., AND RETURN.

(Via New York, Springfield and Connecticut Valley in both directions.)

Baltimore & Ohio R. R. . . . . to Philadelphia.
Philadelphia & Reading R. R. . . . . to Bound Brook.
Central R. R. of New Jersey . . . . to New York.
New York, New Haven & Hartford R. R. . . . to Springfield.
Connecticut River R. R. . . . . to South Vernon.
Central Vermont R. R. . . . . to Brattleboro.
Vermont Valley R. R. . . . . to Windsor.
Central Vermont R. R. . . . . to Randolph.

Returning, same route.

THROUGH RATES.

Baltimore, Md. . . . . . $24.00   Washington, D. C. $25.00
Philadelphia, Pa. 17.00

RANGELEY LAKES, ME.

"Nowhere on earth," quotes a recent writer, "is presented such a remarkable chain of deep water lakes as exists in this far northern corner of our country. Connected

by streams which allow transportation from one to the other, six large Rangeleys, with their numerous ponds, join Umbagog and Parmachene through the wonderful Magalloway, all but unknown to a majority of even the citizens of Maine. Scattered all through this entire section are hunting and fishing grounds unsurpassed, recognized by the foremost hunters and anglers of our country as the home of the largest and gamest fish known to the rod and fly; and the home also of moose, caribou and deer." A veritable sportsman's paradise.

FORM EX. 1006. RANGELEY LAKES, ME. AND RETURN.

(Via rail and Farmington; returning by Sound Lines.)

Baltimore & Ohio R. R. . . . . to Philadelphia.
Rail Lines (see pages 50 to 55 for routes). . . . . to Boston.
Boston & Maine R. R. . . . . to Portland.
Maine Central R. R. . . . . to Farmington.
Sandy River R. R. . . . . to Phillips.
Phillips & Rangeley R. R. . . . . to Rangeley.
Phillips & Rangeley R. R. . . . . to Phillips.
Sandy River R. R. . . . . to Farmington.
Maine Central R. R. . . . . to Portland.
Boston & Maine R. R. . . . . to Boston.
Sound Lines (see pages 50 to 55 for routes). . . . to New York.
Central R. R. of New Jersey . . . . to Bound Brook.
Philadelphia & Reading R. R. . . . . to Philadelphia.
Baltimore & Ohio R. R. . . . . to starting point.

THROUGH RATES.

Baltimore, Md. . . . . . $30 00   Washington, D. C. $31 00
Philadelphia, Pa. 25 00

FORM EX. 1006. RANGELEY LAKES, ME. AND RETURN.

(Via Sound Lines and Farmington; returning by rail.)

Baltimore & Ohio R. R. . . . . to Philadelphia.
Philadelphia & Reading R. R. . . . . to Bound Brook.
Central R. R. of New Jersey . . . . to New York.
Sound Lines (see pages 50 to 55 for route) . . . . to Boston.
Boston & Maine R. R. . . . . to Portland.
Maine Central R. R. . . . . to Farmington.
Sandy River R. R. . . . . to Phillips.
Phillips & Rangeley R. R. . . . . to Rangeley.
Phillips & Rangeley R. R. . . . . to Phillips.
Sandy River R. R. . . . . to Farmington.
Maine Central R. R. . . . . to Portland.
Boston & Maine R. R. . . . . to Boston.
Rail Lines (see pages 50 to 55 for routes). . . . . to Philadelphia.
Baltimore & Ohio R. R. . . . . to starting point.

THROUGH RATES.

Baltimore, Md. . . . . . $30 00   Washington, D. C. $31 00
Philadelphia, Pa. 25 00

FORM EX. 1006. RANGELEY LAKES, ME. AND RETURN.

(Via Rail Lines and Boston in both directions.)

Baltimore & Ohio R. R. . . . . to Philadelphia.
Rail Lines (see pages 50 to 55 for routes). . . . . to Boston.
Boston & Maine R. R. . . . . to Portland.
Maine Central R. R. . . . . to Farmington.
Sandy River R. R. . . . . to Phillips.
Phillips & Rangeley R. R. . . . . to Rangeley.

Returning, same route.

THROUGH RATES.

Baltimore, Md. . . . . . $30 00   Washington, D. C. $32 00
Philadelphia, Pa. 26 00

FORM EX. 1056.—RANGELEY LAKES, ME., AND RETURN.
(Via Sound Lines and Boston in both directions.)

Baltimore & Ohio R. R. . . . . to Philadelphia.
Philadelphia & Reading R. R. . . . . to Bound Brook.
Central R. R. of New Jersey . . . . to New York.
Sound Lines (see pages 50 to 55 for routes) . . . to Boston.
Boston & Maine R. R. . . . . to Portland.
Maine Central R. R. . . . . to Farmington.
Sandy River R. R. . . . . to Phillips.
Phillips & Rangeley R. R. . . . . to Rangeley.

Returning, same route.

THROUGH RATES.

Baltimore, Md. . . . . . . $28 00   Washington, D. C. $30 00
Philadelphia, Pa. 24 00

RAWLEY SPRINGS, VA.

Rawley is situated eleven miles west of Harrisonburg, among the North Mountains, at an elevation of about 2,000 feet above the level of the sea. The atmosphere is dry, pure and invigorating, and free from prostrating heat, even in mid-summer. The scenery is wild and rugged, but grand and picturesque, and, contrary to the rule followed at most resorts, the buildings at Rawley Springs are not located upon a level at the foot of the range, but are set in the mountain gorge, and the beholder might easily imagine himself in Switzerland.

Dry River is a splendid trout stream. Bear, deer, wild turkeys, ruffled grouse, and other game abound. Rawley is fortunately located in the midst of the Appalachian hills of Virginia. From June to November the finest climate in America is that of the mountains of Virginia.

FORM EX. 214. RAWLEY SPRINGS, VA., AND RETURN.

Baltimore & Ohio R. R. . . . . to Harrisonburg.
Stage . . . . to Rawley Springs.

Returning, same route.

THROUGH RATES.

Baltimore, Md.	$11 80	Morgantown, W. Va.	$17 85
Bellaire, O.	20 25	Moundsville, W. Va.	19 50
Berkeley Springs, W. Va.	9 95	Mountain Lake Park, Md.	13 95
Cameron, W. Va.	18 80	Mt. Pleasant, Pa.	16 40
Charlestown, W. Va.	7 50	Newark, Del.	11 40
Chester, Pa.	15 30	New York, N. Y.	19 80
Clarksburg, W. Va.	16 85	Oakland, Md.	11 95
Connellsville, Pa.	15 60	Parkersburg, W. Va.	20 50
Cumberland, Md.	11 50	Philadelphia, Pa.	15 80
Deer Park, Md.	12 80	Piedmont, W. Va.	13 00
Fairmont, W. Va.	16 85	Pittsburgh, Pa.	17 50
Frederick, Md.	9 95	Rockwood, Pa.	15 85
Grafton, W. Va.	15 35	Somerset, Pa.	14 25
Hagerstown, Md.	9 60	Staunton, Va.	4 50
Harper's Ferry, W. Va.	8 00	Strasburg, Va.	5 70
Havre de Grace, Md.	13 25	Uniontown, Pa.	16 05
Johnstown, Pa.	15 65	Washington, D. C.	10 20
Keyser, W. Va.	12 80	Washington, Pa.	19 00
Lexington, Va.	6 40	Wheeling, W. Va.	20 00
McKeesport, Pa.	17 35	Wilmington, Del.	14 80
Martinsburg, W. Va.	8 75	Winchester, Va.	6 40
Meyersdale, Pa.	13 40		

RED SULPHUR SPRINGS, W. VA.

FORM EX. 69. RED SULPHUR SPRINGS, W. VA., AND RETURN.

Baltimore & Ohio R. R. . . . . to Shenandoah June
Norfolk & Western R. R. . . . . to Basic.
Chesapeake & Ohio Ry. . . . . to Lowell.
Stage (12 miles) . . . . to Red Sulphur Springs.

Returning, same route.

THROUGH RATES.

Baltimore, Md.	$19 75	New York, N. Y.	$27 75
Chester, Pa.	23 25	Philadelphia, Pa.	23 25
Havre de Grace, Md.	21 20	Washington, D. C.	17 75
Newark, Del.	22 65	Wilmington, Del.	22 75

ROUTES AND RATES FOR SUMMER TOURS. 283

FORM EX. 174. RED SULPHUR SPRINGS, W. VA., AND RETURN.

Baltimore & Ohio R. R.	to Staunton.
Chesapeake & Ohio Ry.	to Lowell.
Stage (12 miles)	to Red Sulphur Springs.

Returning, same route.

THROUGH RATES.

Baltimore, Md.	$19 75	Meyersdale, Pa.	$22 35
Bellaire, O.	29 20	Morgantown, W. Va.	26 80
Berkeley Springs, W. Va.	18 90	Moundsville, W. Va.	28 45
Cameron, W. Va.	27 75	Mountain Lake Park, Md.	22 50
Charlestown, W. Va.	16 45	Mt. Pleasant, Pa.	25 05
Chester, Pa.	23 25	Newark, Del.	22 05
Clarksburg, W. Va.	25 80	New York, N. Y.	27 75
Connellsville, Pa.	24 55	Oakland, Md.	23 00
Cumberland, Md.	20 85	Parkersburg, W. Va.	28 95
Deer Park, Md.	22 75	Philadelphia, Pa.	23 75
Fairmont, W. Va.	25 80	Piedmont, W. Va.	21 95
Frederick, Md.	18 00	Pittsburgh, Pa.	26 85
Grafton, W. Va.	24 90	Rockwood, Pa.	22 80
Hagerstown, Md.	18 00	Somerset, Pa.	23 20
Harper's Ferry, W. Va.	16 95	Strasburg, Va.	14 30
Harrisonburg, Va.	14 95	Uniontown, Pa.	25 00
Havre de Grace, Md.	21 20	Washington, D. C.	17 75
Johnstown, Pa.	24 00	Washington, Pa.	27 95
Keyser, W. Va.	21 75	Wheeling, W. Va.	28 95
Lexington, Va.	12 45	Wilmington, Del.	22 75
McKeesport, Pa.	26 30	Winchester, Va.	15 35
Martinsburg, W. Va.	17 70		

FORM EX. 316. RED SULPHUR SPRINGS, W. VA., AND RETURN.

Baltimore & Ohio R. R.	to Washington.
Transfer	B. & O. Depot to C. & O. Depot.
Chesapeake & Ohio Ry.	to Lowell.
Stage (12 miles)	to Red Sulphur Springs.

Returning, same route.

THROUGH RATES.

Baltimore, Md.	$19 75	Meyersdale, Pa.	$25 85
Bellaire, O.	32 70	Morgantown, W. Va.	30 30
Berkeley Springs, W. Va.	22 40	Moundsville, W. Va.	31 95
Cameron, W. Va.	31 25	Mountain Lake Park, Md.	25 40
Charlestown, W. Va.	20 45	Mt. Pleasant, Pa.	28 55
Chester, Pa.	23 25	Newark, Del.	22 05
Clarksburg, W. Va.	29 30	New York, N. Y.	27 75
Connellsville, Pa.	28 05	Oakland, Md.	26 00
Cumberland, Md.	24 35	Parkersburg, W. Va.	32 40
Deer Park, Md.	25 75	Philadelphia, Pa.	23 75
Fairmont, W. Va.	29 30	Piedmont, W. Va.	25 45
Frederick, Md.	20 55	Pittsburgh, Pa.	30 35
Grafton, W. Va.	28 40	Rockwood, Pa.	26 30
Hagerstown, Md.	21 55	Somerset, Pa.	26 70
Harper's Ferry, W. Va.	20 45	Uniontown, Pa.	28 50
Havre de Grace, Md.	21 20	Washington, Pa.	31 45
Johnstown, Pa.	28 10	Wheeling, W. Va.	32 40
Keyser, W. Va.	25 25	Wilmington, Del.	22 75
McKeesport, Pa.	29 80	Winchester, Va.	22 05
Martinsburg, W. Va.	21 20		

RICHFIELD SPRINGS.

These springs, long and favorably known, are in Otsego County, N. Y. Next to Saratoga Springs, they are, perhaps, the most widely known and enjoy the most liberal patronage. The hotels are numerous, and the attractions of the place are many and varied. The village of Richfield Springs is situated on a narrow plain near the head of Schuyler's Lake, which is five miles in length and a mile and a quarter at its greatest breadth. This little lake is surrounded by high hills, and, being but a mile from the springs, forms the principal attraction for visitors.

FORM EX. 538. RICHFIELD SPRINGS, N. Y., AND RETURN.

Baltimore & Ohio R. R. . . . . to Philadelphia
Philadelphia & Reading R. R. . . . . to Bound Brook.
Central R. R. of New Jersey . . . . to New York.
New York Central & Hudson River R. R. . . . to Utica.
Delaware, Lackawanna & Western R. R. . . . to Richfield Springs.
Returning, same route.

THROUGH RATES.

Baltimore, Md. . . . . . . $18 75 | Washington, D. C. $20 75
†Philadelphia, Pa. . . . . 14 75 |

ROUTES AND RATES FOR SUMMER TOURS. 285

FORM EX. 820. RICHFIELD SPRINGS, N. Y., AND RETURN.

Baltimore & Ohio R. R. . . . . to Philadelphia.
Philadelphia & Reading R. R. . . . . to Bound Brook.
Central R. R. of New Jersey . . . . to New York.
West Shore R. R. . . . . to Utica.
Delaware, Lackawanna & Western R. R. . . . to Richfield Springs.

Returning, same route.

Transfer through New York, in both directions, included.

THROUGH RATES.

Baltimore, Md. . . . . $18 75 | Washington, D. C. $20 75
Philadelphia, Pa. . . . . . . 14 75 |

FORM EX. 509. RICHFIELD SPRINGS, N. Y., AND RETURN.

Baltimore & Ohio R. R. . . . . to Philadelphia.
Philadelphia & Reading R. R. . . . . to Bound Brook.
Central R. R. of New Jersey . . . . to New York.
Delaware, Lackawanna & Western R. R. . . . to Richfield Springs.

Returning, same route.

THROUGH RATES.

Baltimore, Md. . . . . $18 75 | Washington, D. C. $20 75
Philadelphia, Pa. . . . . . . 14 75 |

FORM EX. 654. RICHFIELD SPRINGS, N. Y., AND RETURN.

Baltimore & Ohio R. R. . . . . to Philadelphia.
Philadelphia & Reading R. R. . . . . to Bethlehem.
Lehigh Valley R. R. . . . . to Waverly.
New York, Lake Erie & Western R. R. . . . . to Binghamton.
Delaware & Hudson R. R. . . . . to C. & C. V. Junc.
Cooperstown & Charlotte Valley R. R. . . . . to Cooperstown.
Otsego Lake Steamer and Stage . . . . to Richfield Springs.
Delaware, Lackawanna & Western R. R. . . . to Utica.
New York Central & Hudson River R. R. . . to New York.
Central R. R. of New Jersey . . . . to Bound Brook.
Philadelphia & Reading R. R. . . . . to Philadelphia.
Baltimore & Ohio R. R. . . . . to starting point.

THROUGH RATES.

Baltimore, Md. . . . . $24 30 | Washington, D. C. $25 30
Philadelphia, Pa. . . . . . . 17 30 |

Tickets between Cooperstown and Richfield Springs by the Otsego Lake Steamer and Stage are for passage only; baggage will be charged extra.

ROAN MOUNTAIN, TENN.

FORM EX. 36. ROAN MOUNTAIN, TENN., AND RETURN.

Baltimore & Ohio R. R. . . . . to Shenandoah Junc.
Norfolk & Western R. R. . . . . to Bristol.
East Tennessee, Virginia & Georgia R. R. . . . to Johnson City.
East Tennessee & Western North Carolina R. R. to Roan Mountain.

Returning, same route.

THROUGH RATES.

Baltimore, Md.	$22 85	Morgantown, W. Va.	$28 90
Bellaire, O.	31 50	Moundsville, W. Va.	30 00
Berkeley Springs, W. Va.	21 10	Mountain Lake Park, Md.	25 05
Cameron, W. Va.	29 90	Mt. Pleasant, Pa.	27 10
Chester, Pa.	26 35	Newark, Del.	25 15
Clarksburg, W. Va.	27 90	New York, N. Y.	30 85
Connellsville, Pa.	26 65	Oakland, Md.	25 15
Cumberland, Md.	22 95	Parkersburg, W. Va.	31 00
Deer Park, Md.	24 90	Philadelphia, Pa.	26 85
Fairmont, W. Va.	27 90	Piedmont, W. Va.	24 10
Frederick, Md.	20 70	Pittsburgh, Pa.	28 35
Grafton, W. Va.	27 00	Rockwood, Pa.	24 90
Harper's Ferry, W. Va.	19 60	Somerset, Pa.	25 90
Havre de Grace, Md.	24 50	Uniontown, Pa.	27 10
Johnstown, Pa.	26 70	Washington, D. C.	20 85
Keyser, W. Va.	23 90	Washington, Pa.	30 05
McKeesport, Pa.	28 10	Wheeling, W. Va.	31 00
Martinsburg, W. Va.	19 80	Wilmington, Del.	26 85
Meyersdale, Pa.	24 15		

ROBERVAL LAKE ST. JOHN, P. Q.

FORM EX. 1087.   ROBERVAL, P. Q., AND RETURN.

Quebec & Lake St. John Ry. . . . . Quebec to Roberval

Returning, same route.

Sold in connection with any excursion ticket passing through or terminating at Quebec.

Rate. $7 40

ROCKBRIDGE ALUM SPRINGS, VA.

Rockbridge Alum is spacious in its lay-out, nearly the whole of the valley in which it is situated being occupied by the principal buildings, cottages, bath-houses, &c. The view from the hotel portico is one that will make the guest content to remain. An almost unlimited number of spots may readily be found where the sun upon the hottest days of the year cannot penetrate, and where it is always cool and invigorating. Little suffering is ever experienced from the heat at Rockbridge Alum; the nights are invariably cool enough to require blankets, and except in actual mid-summer, fires are in frequent demand both evening and morning. Immediately adjoining Rockbridge Alum is Jordan Alum. Both of these well-known resorts were a year or two since consolidated into one. The location of the hotel at Jordan Alum is on the brow of a symmetrical hill, with a high mountain behind, and from this eminence a panorama many miles in extent may be brought within the range of vision. The water from the springs at Rockbridge as well as Jordan has long been popular in the markets of the country, as it is shipped in large quantities to the leading cities. The medicinal value of the springs is beyond estimate; they are simply unrivaled in the cure of scrofulous complaints, dyspepsia, and disordered secretions in general.

ROCKBRIDGE ALUM

FORM LX. 10. ROCKBRIDGE ALUM SPRINGS, VA., AND RETURN

Baltimore & Ohio R. R. . . . . to Washington.
Transfer . . . . B. & O. Depot to C. & O. Depot.
Chesapeake & Ohio Ry. . . . . to Goshen.
Victoria R. R. . . . . to Rockbridge Alum Springs.
Returning, same route.

THROUGH RATES.

Baltimore, Md.	$14 80	Meyersdale, Pa.	$20 00
Bellaire, O.	27 75	Morgantown, W. Va.	25 35
Berkeley Springs, W. Va.	17 15	Moundsville, W. Va.	27 00
Cameron, W. Va.	26 30	Mountain Lake Park, Md.	20 05
Charlestown, W. Va.	16 00	Mt. Pleasant, Pa.	23 60
Chester, Pa.	18 30	Newark, Del.	17 10
Clarksburg, W. Va.	24 35	New York, N. Y.	22 80
Connellsville, Pa.	23 10	Oakland, Md.	21 05
Cumberland, Md.	19 10	Parkersburg, W. Va.	27 15
Deer Park, Md.	20 80	Philadelphia, Pa.	18 80
Fairmont, W. Va.	24 35	Piedmont, W. Va.	20 50
Frederick, Md.	15 00	Pittsburgh, Pa.	25 10
Grafton, W. Va.	23 15	Rockwood, Pa.	21 35
Hagerstown, Md.	16 10	Somerset, Pa.	21 75
Harper's Ferry, W. Va.	15 50	Strasburg, Va.	17 10
Havre de Grace, Md.	16 25	Uniontown, Pa.	23 55
Johnstown, Pa.	23 15	Washington, Pa.	26 50
Keyser, W. Va.	20 30	Wheeling, W. Va.	27 15
McKeesport, Pa.	24 85	Wilmington, Del.	17 80
Martinsburg, W. Va.	16 25		

FORM EX. 79. ROCKBRIDGE ALUM SPRINGS, VA., AND RETURN.

Baltimore & Ohio R. R.	to Shenandoah June.
Norfolk & Western R. R.	to Basic.
Chesapeake & Ohio Ry.	to Goshen.
Victoria R. R.	to Rockbridge Alum Springs.

Returning, same route.

THROUGH RATES.

Baltimore, Md.	$14 80	New York, N. Y.	$22 80
Chester, Pa.	18 25	Philadelphia, Pa.	18 80
Havre de Grace, Md.	16 25	Washington, D. C.	12 80
Newark, Del.	17 10	Wilmington, Del.	17 80

FORM EX. 90. ROCKBRIDGE ALUM SPRINGS, VA., AND RETURN.

Baltimore & Ohio R. R.	to Staunton.
Chesapeake & Ohio Ry.	to Goshen.
Victoria R. R.	to Rockbridge Alum Springs.

Returning, same route.

THROUGH RATES.

Baltimore, Md.	$11 80	Meyersdale, Pa.	$16 10
Bellaire, O.	22 05	Morgantown, W. Va.	20 55
Berkeley Springs, W. Va.	12 65	Moundsville, W. Va.	22 20
Cameron, W. Va.	21 50	Mountain Lake Park, Md.	16 65
Charlestown, W. Va.	10 20	Mt. Pleasant, Pa.	18 80
Chester, Pa.	18 30	Newark, Del.	17 10
Clarksburg, W. Va.	19 55	New York, N. Y.	22 80
Connellsville, Pa.	18 30	Oakland, Md.	16 75
Cumberland, Md.	14 00	Parkersburg, W. Va.	22 70
Deer Park, Md.	16 50	Philadelphia, Pa.	18 80
Fairmont, W. Va.	19 55	Piedmont, W. Va.	15 70
Frederick, Md.	11 75	Pittsburgh, Pa.	20 00
Grafton, W. Va.	18 65	Rockwood, Pa.	16 55
Hagerstown, Md.	11 75	Somerset, Pa.	16 95
Harper's Ferry, W. Va.	10 70	Strasburg, Va.	8 05
Harrisonburg, Va.	5 70	Uniontown, Pa.	18 75
Havre de Grace, Md.	16 25	Washington, D. C.	12 80
Johnstown, Pa.	18 35	Washington, Pa.	21 70
Keyser, W. Va.	15 50	Wheeling, W. Va.	22 70
Lexington, Va.	6 20	Wilmington, Del.	17 80
McKeesport, Pa.	20 05	Winchester, Va.	9 10
Martinsburg, W. Va.	11 15		

ROCKBRIDGE BATHS, VA.

Form Ex. 92. Rockbridge Baths, Va., and Return.

Baltimore & Ohio R. R. . . . . to Timber Ridge
Stage (12 miles). . . . . to Rockbridge Baths
Returning, same route.

THROUGH RATES.

Baltimore, Md.	$12 55	Meyersdale, Pa.	$14 15
Bellaire, O.	21 00	Morgantown, W. Va.	18 00
Berkeley Springs, W. Va.	10 70	Moundsville, W. Va.	20 25
Cameron, W. Va.	19 55	Mountain Lake Park, Md.	11 70
Charlestown, W. Va.	8 25	Mt. Pleasant, Pa.	16 85
Chester, Pa.	16 05	Newark, Del.	11 85
Clarksburg, W. Va.	17 00	New York, N. Y.	20 55
Connellsville, Pa.	16 35	Oakland, Md.	11 80
Cumberland, Md.	12 65	Parkersburg, W. Va.	20 75
Deer Park, Md.	11 55	Philadelphia, Pa.	16 25
Fairmont, W. Va.	17 00	Piedmont, W. Va.	13 75
Frederick, Md.	9 80	Pittsburgh, Pa.	18 05
Grafton, W. Va.	16 70	Rockwood, Pa.	14 00
Hagerstown, Md.	9 80	Somerset, Pa.	15 00
Harper's Ferry, W. Va.	8 75	Staunton, Va.	2 45
Harrisonburg, Va.	3 75	Strasburg, Va.	6 10
Havre de Grace, Md.	11 00	Uniontown, Pa.	16 80
Johnstown, Pa.	16 40	Washington, D. C.	10 95
Keyser, W. Va.	13 55	Washington, Pa.	19 75
Lexington, Va.	1 40	Wheeling, W. Va.	20 75
McKeesport, Pa.	18 40	Wilmington, Del.	15 55
Martinsburg, W. Va.	9 50	Winchester, Va.	7 15

ROCK ENON SPRINGS, VA.

The location of Rock Enon Springs in a little valley surrounded by mountains, the gorge to the rear creating a current, ever preserving a delightful state of the atmosphere, renders this resort one of the most popular in the Shenandoah Valley.

Desirous of making this lovely spot in the mountains a permanent and attractive summer resort for the refined and intelligent who seek health, rest, pleasure, and freedom from the exacting demands of fashion, and greatly encouraged by the generous patronage heretofore extended, and the very great satisfaction expressed by the guests of the past seasons with the place and its management, the proprietor will put forth every effort for the comfort and pleasure of visitors the present year.

The hotel is abundantly supplied on every floor with pure water taken directly from the great "Cold Spring" on Pinnacle Mountain. The sanitary arrangements are complete, and will be found all that could be desired. Great improvements have been made in this respect; the house and grounds are kept scrupulously neat and clean.

THE BATHS.

The accommodations for bathing are all that could be desired. A large steam boiler has been put in place, from which the numerous baths are supplied with hot water, and the water in the immense swimming pool—75 by 25 feet, 5½ feet deep—can now be partially heated by steam. Separate hours for bathing are allotted to ladies, children, and gentlemen, and an hour for gentlemen and ladies. The bath-house is comparatively new; large additions have been made to it. At the suggestion of eminent physicians who have visited Rock Enon, the waters of the mineral springs have been utilized. New bath-rooms have been constructed, and are supplied with these invaluable waters.

The water of the "Old Capper" Spring is very delightful to bathe in; it renders the skin clear, soft, and beautiful; it is very healing in its nature, and has proved most efficacious in rheumatic complaints and diseases of the skin, and when combined with the "Chalybeate" water in the bath, as it may be, it is exceedingly strengthening to the whole system.

THE SPRINGS.

There are eight springs within a stone's-throw of the hotel, three of which are mineral and of very great efficacy. The pure spring water from five large springs is freestone. There is one large limestone spring on the premises.

THE CHALYBEATE SPRING

is one of the most valuable in the State. The water was analyzed by Professors Gale and Mew, of the Smithsonian Institution, who made the following report:—

Analysis of the Chalybeate Spring at Rock Enon. Its constituents per gallon are as follows:

Carbonate of lime	5.13 grs.
Carbonate of soda	1.21 "
Carbonate of protoxide of iron	14.26 "
Carbonate of protoxide of manganese	1.66 "
Sulphate of magnesia	12.89 "
Sulphate of lime	3.76 "
Chloride of magnesium	1.42 "
Alumina	0.80 "
Silica	0.42 "
	40.45 grs.

By spectrum analysis lithia was also found in it.

BROOK AND SPRING, ROCK ENON.

This spring is, in some very essential particulars, similar to the far-famed Pyrmont Spring in Waldeck, Germany, which has so long and so deservedly enjoyed a high reputation among physicians. It possesses a rare combination of tonic properties, with others existing in admirable proportion, calculated to free it from some of the too well-known causes of objection to chalybeate waters.

FORM EX. 56. ROCK ENON SPRINGS, VA., AND RETURN.

Baltimore & Ohio R. R. . . . . to Winchester.
Stage (17 miles), ... to Rock Enon Springs.
Returning, same route.

THROUGH RATES.

Baltimore, Md.	$9 00	Deer Park, Md.	$11 20
Bellaire, O.	18 35	Fairmount, W. Va.	11 95
Berkeley Springs, W. Va.	8 05	Frederick, Md.	7 15
Cameron, W. Va.	16 90	Grafton, W. Va.	11 05
Charlestown, W. Va.	5 90	Hagerstown, Md.	7 15
Chester, Pa.	13 40	Harper's Ferry, W. Va.	6 10
Clarksburg, W. Va.	14 85	Harrisonburg, Va.	7 90
Connellsville, Pa.	13 70	Havre de Grace, Md.	11 35
Cumberland, Md.	10 00	Johnstown, Pa.	15 75

Keyser, W. Va.	$10 90	Philadelphia, Pa.	$15 00
Lexington, Va.	11 00	Piedmont, W. Va.	11 40
McKeesport, Pa.	15 45	Pittsburgh, Pa.	16 00
Martinsburg, W. Va.	6 85	Rockwood, Pa.	11 95
Meyersdale, Pa.	11 50	Somerset, Pa.	12 35
Morgantown, W. Va.	15 95	Staunton, Va.	9 20
Moundsville, W. Va.	17 00	Strasburg, Va.	5 55
Mountain Lake Park, Md.	12 05	Uniontown, Pa.	14 15
Mt. Pleasant, Pa.	14 20	Washington, D. C.	8 30
Newark, Del.	12 20	Washington, Pa.	17 40
New York, N. Y.	17 90	Wheeling, W. Va.	18 40
Oakland, Md.	12 15	Wilmington, Del.	12 90
Parkersburg, W. Va.	18 40		

ROCKINGHAM MINERAL SPRINGS, VA.

Form Ex. 187.—Rockingham Mineral Springs, Va., and Return.

Baltimore & Ohio R. R. . . . . to Harrisonburg.
Stage (14 miles). . . . . to Rockingham Mineral Springs.

Returning, same route.

Through Rates.

Baltimore, Md.	$12 50	Morgantown, W. Va.	$18 35
Bellaire, O.	20 75	Moundsville, W. Va.	20 00
Berkeley Springs, W. Va.	10 45	Mountain Lake Park, Md.	14 45
Cameron, W. Va.	19 50	Mt. Pleasant, Pa.	16 60
Charlestown, W. Va.	8 00	Newark, Del.	14 60
Chester, Pa.	15 80	New York, N. Y.	20 50
Clarksburg, W. Va.	17 35	Oakland, Md.	14 55
Connellsville, Pa.	16 40	Parkersburg, W. Va.	20 50
Cumberland, Md.	12 40	Philadelphia, Pa.	16 50
Deer Park, Md.	14 30	Piedmont, W. Va.	13 50
Fairmont, W. Va.	17 35	Pittsburgh, Pa.	18 40
Frederick, Md.	9 55	Rockwood, Pa.	14 35
Grafton, W. Va.	16 25	Somerset, Pa.	14 75
Hagerstown, Md.	9 55	Staunton, Va.	1 80
Harper's Ferry, W. Va.	8 50	Strasburg, Va.	5 90
Havre de Grace, Md.	13 75	Uniontown, Pa.	16 55
Johnstown, Pa.	16 45	Washington, D. C.	10 70
Keyser, W. Va.	13 50	Washington, Pa.	19 50
Lexington, Va.	6 60	Wheeling, W. Va.	20 50
McKeesport, Pa.	17 85	Wilmington, Del.	15 30
Martinsburg, W. Va.	9 25	Winchester, Va.	6 90
Meyersdale, Pa.	13 90		

ROCKLAND, ME.

This marvelously picturesque town lies at the very entrance to Penobscot Bay, and is the diverging point from which travelers reach all the bay towns and the eastern shore.

The surroundings are charming as places for summer recreation, for the numerous inlets of the sea afford the best of fishing, boating and bathing.

294 BALTIMORE & OHIO RAILROAD COMPANY

FORM EX. 1068.—ROCKLAND, ME., AND RETURN.

(Via rail, returning by Sound Lines from Boston.)

Baltimore & Ohio R. R.	to Philadelphia.
Rail Lines (see pages 50 to 55 for route)	to Boston.
Boston & Maine R. R.	to Portland.
Maine Central R. R.	to Rockland.
Maine Central R. R.	to Portland.
Boston & Maine R. R.	to Boston.
Sound Lines (see pages 50 to 55 for route)	to New York.
Central R. R. of New Jersey	to Bound Brook.
Philadelphia & Reading R. R.	to Philadelphia.
Baltimore & Ohio R. R.	to starting point.

THROUGH RATES.

Baltimore, Md.	$25 00	Washington, D. C.	$27 00
Philadelphia, Pa.	24 00		

FORM EX. 1068.—ROCKLAND, ME., AND RETURN.

(Via Sound Lines, returning by rail from Boston.)

Baltimore & Ohio R. R.	to Philadelphia.
Philadelphia & Reading R. R.	to Bound Brook.
Central R. R. of New Jersey	to New York.
Sound Lines (see pages 50 to 55 for route)	to Boston.
Boston & Maine R. R.	to Portland.
Maine Central R. R.	to Rockland.
Maine Central R. R.	to Portland.
Boston & Maine R. R.	to Boston.
Rail Lines (see pages 50 to 55 for route)	to Philadelphia.
Baltimore & Ohio R. R.	to starting point.

THROUGH RATES.

Baltimore, Md.	$25 00	Washington, D. C.	$27 00
Philadelphia, Pa.	24 00		

FORM EX. 1068.—ROCKLAND, ME., AND RETURN.

(Via Rail Lines in both directions.)

Baltimore & Ohio R. R.	to Philadelphia.
Rail Lines (see pages 50 to 55 for route)	to Boston.
Boston & Maine R. R.	to Portland.
Maine Central R. R.	to Rockland.

Returning, same route.

THROUGH RATES.

Baltimore, Md.	$26 00	Washington, D. C.	$28 00
Philadelphia, Pa.	22 00		

FORM EX. 1068.—ROCKLAND, ME., AND RETURN.

(Via Sound Lines to Boston, and rail to Rockland in both directions.)

Baltimore & Ohio R. R.	to Philadelphia.
Philadelphia & Reading R. R.	to Bound Brook.
Central R. R. of New Jersey	to New York.
Sound Lines (see pages 50 to 55 for route)	to Boston.
Boston & Maine R. R.	to Portland.
Maine Central R. R.	to Rockland.

Returning, same route.

THROUGH RATES.

Baltimore, Md.	$24 00	Washington, D. C.	$26 00
Philadelphia, Pa.	20 00		

FORM EN. 1069. ROCKLAND, ME., AND RETURN.

(Via rail to Boston, thence by steamer; returning by Sound Lines from Boston.)

Baltimore & Ohio R. R. . . . . to Philadelphia.
Rail Lines (see pages 50 to 55 for routes) . . . . to Boston.
Boston & Bangor Steamship Line . . . . to Rockland.
Boston & Bangor Steamship Line . . . . to Boston.
Sound Lines (see pages 50 to 55 for route) . . . . to New York.
Central R. R. of New Jersey . . . . to Bound Brook.
Philadelphia & Reading R. R. . . . . to Philadelphia.
Baltimore & Ohio R. R. . . . . to starting point.

THROUGH RATES.

Baltimore, Md. . . . . $21 00 | Washington, D. C. $23 00
†Philadelphia, Pa. . . . . . 17 00 |

FORM EN. 1069.—ROCKLAND, ME., AND RETURN.

(Via Sound Lines to Boston, thence steamer from Boston; returning by rail from Boston.)

Baltimore & Ohio R. R. . . . . to Philadelphia.
Philadelphia & Reading R. R. . . . . to Bound Brook.
Central R. R. of New Jersey . . . . to New York.
Sound Lines (see pages 50 to 55 for route) . . . . to Boston.
Boston & Bangor Steamship Line . . . . to Rockland.
Boston & Bangor Steamship Line . . . . to Boston.
Rail Lines (see pages 50 to 55 for routes) . . . . to Philadelphia.
Baltimore & Ohio R. R. . . . . to starting point.

THROUGH RATES.

Baltimore, Md. . . . . $21 00 | Washington, D. C. $23 00
†Philadelphia, Pa. . . . . . 17 00 |

FORM EN. 1069. ROCKLAND, ME., AND RETURN.

(Via Rail Lines to Boston, thence steamer in both directions.)

Baltimore & Ohio R. R. . . . . to Philadelphia.
Rail Lines (see pages 50 to 55 for routes) . . . . to Boston.
Boston & Bangor Steamship Line . . . . to Rockland.

Returning, same route.

THROUGH RATES.

Baltimore, Md. . . . . $22 00 | Washington, D. C. $24 00
†Philadelphia, Pa. . . . . . 18 00 |

FORM EN. 1069.—ROCKLAND, ME., AND RETURN.

(Via Sound Lines and steamer in both directions.)

Baltimore & Ohio R. R. . . . . to Philadelphia.
Philadelphia & Reading R. R. . . . . to Bound Brook.
Central R. R. of New Jersey . . . . to New York.
Sound Lines (see pages 50 to 55 for route) . . . . to Boston.
Boston & Bangor Steamship Line . . . . to Rockland.

Returning, same route.

THROUGH RATES.

Baltimore, Md. . . . . $20 00 | Washington, D. C. $22 00
†Philadelphia, Pa. . . . . . 16 00 |

ROCKPORT, MASS.

FORM EX. 762. ROCKPORT, MASS., AND RETURN.

(Via Sound Lines and Boston in both directions.)

Baltimore & Ohio R. R. . . . . to Philadelphia.
Philadelphia & Reading R. R. . . . . to Bound Brook.
Central R. R. of New Jersey . . . . to New York.
Sound Lines (see pages 50 to 55 for routes) . . . . to Boston.
Boston & Maine R. R. . . . . to Rockport.

Returning, same route.

THROUGH RATES.

Baltimore, Md. . . . . . . $17 75 | Washington, D. C. $19 75
Philadelphia, Pa. . . . . . 13 75 |

FORM EX. 762. ROCKPORT, MASS., AND RETURN.

(Via Rail Lines and Boston in both directions.)

Baltimore & Ohio R. R. . . . . to Philadelphia.
Rail Lines (see pages 50 to 55 for routes) . . . . to Boston.
Boston & Maine R. R. . . . . to Rockport.

Returning, same route.

THROUGH RATES.

Baltimore, Md. . . . . . . $19 75 | Washington, D. C. $21 75
Philadelphia, Pa. . . . . . 15 75 |

FORM EX. 762. ROCKPORT, MASS., AND RETURN.

(Via Rail Lines and Boston; returning via Boston and Sound Lines.)

Baltimore & Ohio R. R. . . . . to Philadelphia.
Rail Lines (see pages 50 to 55 for routes) . . . . to Boston.
Boston & Maine R. R. . . . . to Rockport.
Boston & Maine R. R. . . . . to Boston.
Sound Lines (see pages 50 to 55 for routes) . . . . to New York.
Central R. R. of New Jersey . . . . to Bound Brook.
Philadelphia & Reading R. R. . . . . to Philadelphia.
Baltimore & Ohio R. R. . . . . to starting point.

THROUGH RATES.

Baltimore, Md. . . . . . . $18 75 | Washington, D. C. $20 75
Philadelphia, Pa. . . . . . 14 75 |

FORM EX. 762. ROCKPORT, MASS., AND RETURN.

(Via Sound Lines and Boston; returning all rail.)

Baltimore & Ohio R. R. . . . . to Philadelphia.
Philadelphia & Reading R. R. . . . . to Bound Brook.
Central R. R. of New Jersey . . . . to New York.
Sound Lines (see pages 50 to 55 for routes) . . . . to Boston.
Boston & Maine R. R. . . . . to Rockport.
Boston & Maine R. R. . . . . to Boston.
Rail Lines (see pages 50 to 55 for routes) . . . . to Philadelphia.
Baltimore & Ohio R. R. . . . . to starting point.

THROUGH RATES.

Baltimore, Md. . . . . . . $18 75 | Washington, D. C. $20 75
Philadelphia, Pa. . . . . . 14 75 |

ROUND KNOB, N. C.

FORM EX. 41. ROUND KNOB, N. C., AND RETURN.

Baltimore & Ohio R. R. . . . . to Washington.
Transfer . . . . B. & O. Depot to R. & D. Depot.
Richmond & Danville R. R. . . . . to Round Knob.
Returning, same route.

THROUGH RATES.

Baltimore, Md.	$21 25	Meyersdale, Pa.	$27 35
Bellaire, O.	31 20	Morgantown, W. Va.	31 80
Berkeley Springs, W. Va.	23 90	Moundsville, W. Va.	33 15
Cameron, W. Va.	32 75	Mountain Lake Park, Md.	27 10
Charlestown, W. Va.	22 15	Mt. Pleasant, Pa.	30 05
Chester, Pa.	21 75	Newark, Del.	23 55
Clarksburg, W. Va.	30 40	New York, N. Y.	29 25
Connellsville, Pa.	29 50	Oakland, Md.	27 50
Cumberland, Md.	25 85	Parkersburg, W. Va.	33 90
Deer Park, Md.	27 25	Philadelphia, Pa.	23 25
Fairmont, W. Va.	30 80	Piedmont, W. Va.	26 05
Frederick, Md.	22 05	Pittsburgh, Pa.	31 85
Grafton, W. Va.	29 30	Rockwood, Pa.	27 80
Hagerstown, Md.	22 85	Somerset, Pa.	28 20
Harper's Ferry, W. Va.	21 95	Uniontown, Pa.	30 00
Havre de Grace, Md.	22 70	Washington, Pa.	32 95
Johnstown, Pa.	29 00	Wheeling, W. Va.	33 90
Keyser, W. Va.	26 75	Wilmington, Del.	24 25
McKeesport, Pa.	31 20	Winchester, Va.	23 35
Martinsburg, W. Va.	22 70		

FORM EX. 48. ROUND KNOB, N. C., AND RETURN.

Baltimore & Ohio R. R. . . . . to Lexington.
Chesapeake & Ohio R. R. . . . . to Lynchburg.
Richmond & Danville R. R. . . . . to Round Knob.
Returning, same route.

THROUGH RATES.

Baltimore, Md.	$21 05	Meyersdale, Pa.	$24 65
Bellaire, O.	31 50	Morgantown, W. Va.	29 10
Berkeley Springs, W. Va.	21 20	Moundsville, W. Va.	30 75
Cameron, W. Va.	30 05	Mountain Lake Park, Md.	25 20
Chester, Pa.	21 75	Mt. Pleasant, Pa.	27 35
Clarksburg, W. Va.	28 10	Newark, Del.	23 55
Connellsville, Pa.	26 85	New York, N. Y.	29 25
Cumberland, Md.	23 15	Oakland, Md.	25 30
Deer Park, Md.	25 05	Parkersburg, W. Va.	31 25
Fairmont, W. Va.	28 10	Philadelphia, Pa.	23 25
Frederick, Md.	19 90	Piedmont, W. Va.	24 25
Grafton, W. Va.	27 20	Pittsburgh, Pa.	29 15
Hagerstown, Md.	20 25	Rockwood, Pa.	25 10
Harper's Ferry, W. Va.	19 25	Somerset, Pa.	25 50
Havre de Grace, Md.	22 70	Uniontown, Pa.	27 30
Johnstown, Pa.	26 30	Washington, D. C.	19 25
Keyser, W. Va.	24 05	Washington, Pa.	30 25
McKeesport, Pa.	28 00	Wheeling, W. Va.	31 25
Martinsburg, W. Va.	20 00	Wilmington, Del.	24 25

RYE BEACH, N. H.

Form Ex. 779. Rye Beach, N. H., and Return.

Baltimore & Ohio R. R.	to Philadelphia.
Philadelphia & Reading R. R.	to Bound Brook.
Central R. R. of New Jersey	to New York.
Sound Lines (see pages 50 to 55 for route)	to Boston.
Boston & Maine R. R.	to North Hampton.
Stage	to Rye Beach.

Returning, same route.

THROUGH RATES.

Baltimore, Md.	$19 50	Washington, D. C.	$21 50
Philadelphia, Pa.	15 50		

Form Ex. 779. Rye Beach, N. H., and Return.

Baltimore & Ohio R. R.	to Philadelphia.
Rail Lines (see pages 50 to 55 for route)	to Boston.
Boston & Maine R. R.	to North Hampton.
Stage	to Rye Beach.

Returning, same route.

THROUGH RATES.

Baltimore, Md.	$21 50	Washington, D. C.	$23 50
Philadelphia, Pa.	17 50		

Form Ex. 779. Rye Beach, N. H., and Return.

Baltimore & Ohio R. R.	to Philadelphia.
Rail Lines (see pages 50 to 55 for route)	to Boston.
Boston & Maine R. R.	to North Hampton.
Stage	to Rye Beach.
Stage	to North Hampton.
Boston & Maine R. R.	to Boston.
Sound Lines (see pages 50 to 55 for route)	to New York.
Central R. R. of New Jersey	to Bound Brook.
Philadelphia & Reading R. R.	to Philadelphia.
Baltimore & Ohio R. R.	to starting point.

THROUGH RATES.

Baltimore, Md.	$20 50	Washington, D. C.	$22 50
Philadelphia, Pa.	16 50		

Form Ex. 779. Rye Beach, N. H., and Return.

Baltimore & Ohio R. R.	to Philadelphia.
Philadelphia & Reading R. R.	to Bound Brook.
Central R. R. of New Jersey	to New York.
Sound Lines (see pages 50 to 55 for route)	to Boston.
Boston & Maine R. R.	to North Hampton.
Stage	to Rye Beach.
Stage	to North Hampton.
Boston & Maine R. R.	to Boston.
Rail Lines (see pages 50 to 55 for route)	to Philadelphia.
Baltimore & Ohio R. R.	to starting point.

THROUGH RATES.

Baltimore, Md.	$20 50	Washington, D. C.	$22 50
Philadelphia, Pa.	16 50		

ST. ANDREW'S, N. B., ON PASSAMA-
QUODDY BAY,

"just across the border," is a summer resort possessing rare attractions, and fitly described by the novelist as "a sleeping beauty."

Situated on Passamaquoddy Bay, which is seven miles wide and seventeen miles long, and only separated from the State of Maine by the St. Croix River, its location affords to the yachtsman and fisherman the best sport attainable. Its chains of fresh-water lakes, within twenty

minutes of the town, are filled with landlocked salmon and trout, while its driving-roads are the admiration of visitors. It has been demonstrated that to the hay fever sufferer St. Andrew's is an absolutely exempt district, the most obstinate and long-seated cases finding within forty-eight hours complete relief. The delightful cool climate, entire absence of malaria and mosquitoes, comparative freedom from fog, together with the restful, recuperative properties of the atmosphere, make St. Andrew's an extremely desirable resort.

"The Algonquin," a new and perfectly constructed summer hotel, opened to the public in 1889, received the encomiums of nearly 1400 guests. It is heated by steam and lighted by gas, has steam elevator and laundry, salt and fresh water (hot and cold) baths on each floor, billiard, smoking, and writing rooms, piazzas 340 feet long, from which uninterrupted views of seventy-five miles in extent are had, and in short is as nearly as may be—a perfect hotel in a perfect location.

St. Andrew's is reached directly by rail lines centering at Boston, Portland, the White Mountains, Montreal, and St. John, or by steamers from Boston, Bar Harbor, and St. John, and passengers are ticketed through from starting point to destination by agents of the B. & O. R. R.

FORM EX. 764.—ST. ANDREW'S, N. B., AND RETURN.

(Via Rail Lines and Boston, returning via Boston and Sound Lines.)

Baltimore & Ohio R. R.	to Philadelphia.
Rail Lines (see pages 50 to 55 for route)	to Boston.
Boston & Maine R. R.	to Portland.
Maine Central R. R.	to Vanceboro.
Canadian Pacific Ry.	to St. Andrew's.
Canadian Pacific Ry.	to Vanceboro.
Maine Central R. R.	to Portland.
Boston & Maine R. R.	to Boston.
Sound Lines (see pages 50 to 55 for route)	to New York.
Central R. R. of New Jersey	to Bound Brook.
Philadelphia & Reading R. R.	to Philadelphia.
Baltimore & Ohio R. R.	to starting point.

THROUGH RATES.

Baltimore, Md.	$32 00	Washington, D. C. $34 00
Philadelphia, Pa.	28 00	

FORM EX. 764.—ST. ANDREW'S, N. B., AND RETURN.

(Via Sound Lines to Boston, returning via Boston and Rail Lines.)

Baltimore & Ohio R. R.	to Philadelphia.
Philadelphia & Reading R. R.	to Bound Brook.
Central R. R. of New Jersey	to New York.
Sound Lines (see pages 50 to 55 for route)	to Boston.

Boston & Maine R. R.	to Portland.
Maine Central R. R.	to Vanceboro.
Canadian Pacific Ry.	to St. Andrew's
Canadian Pacific Ry.	to Vanceboro.
Maine Central R. R.	to Portland.
Boston & Maine R. R.	to Boston.
Rail Lines (see pages 50 to 55 for route)	to Philadelphia.
Baltimore & Ohio R. R.	to starting point.

THROUGH RATES.

Baltimore, Md.	$32 00	Washington, D. C.	$34 00
Philadelphia, Pa.	28 00		

FORM EX. 761.—ST. ANDREW'S, N. B. AND RETURN.

(Via Sound Lines and Boston in both directions.)

Baltimore & Ohio R. R.	to Philadelphia.
Philadelphia & Reading R. R.	to Bound Brook.
Central R. R. of New Jersey	to New York.
Sound Lines (see pages 50 to 55 for route)	to Boston.
Boston & Maine R. R.	to Portland.
Maine Central R. R.	to Vanceboro.
Canadian Pacific Railway	to St. Andrew's.

Returning, same route.

THROUGH RATES.

Baltimore, Md.	$31 00	Washington, D. C.	$33 00
Philadelphia, Pa.	27 00		

FORM EX. 762.—ST. ANDREW'S, N. B. AND RETURN.

(Via Rail Lines and Boston in both directions.)

Baltimore & Ohio R. R.	to Philadelphia.
Rail Lines (see pages 50 to 55 for route)	to Boston.
Boston & Maine R. R.	to Portland.
Maine Central R. R.	to Vanceboro.
Canadian Pacific Railway	to St. Andrew's.

Returning, same route.

THROUGH RATES.

Baltimore, Md.	$33 00	Washington, D. C.	$35 00
Philadelphia, Pa.	29 00		

ST. JOHNS, N. B.

FORM EX. 1000.—ST. JOHN, N. B., AND RETURN.

Baltimore & Ohio R. R.	to Philadelphia.
Philadelphia & Reading R. R.	to Bound Brook.
Central R. R. of New Jersey	to New York.
Mallory Steamship Line	to St. John.

Returning, same route.

THROUGH RATES.

Baltimore, Md.	$26 50	Washington, D. C.	$28 50
Philadelphia, Pa.	22 50		

Steamers of the Mallory Line will leave New York, Pier 21, East River, Saturdays at 5.00 P. M. for St. John, N. B. Rates include berth on steamer. State-rooms from $4.00 to $5.00 each extra, according to location. Meals, breakfast and supper, 75 cents; dinner, $1.00.

SACKETT'S HARBOR, N. Y.

FORM EX. 1070.—SACKETT'S HARBOR, N. Y., AND RETURN.

Baltimore & Ohio R. R. . . . . to Philadelphia.
Philadelphia & Reading R. R. . . . . to Bound Brook.
Central R. R. of New Jersey . . . . to New York.
New York Central & Hudson River R. R. . . . to Utica.
Rome, Watertown & Ogdensburg R. R. . . . . to Sackett's Harbor.
Returning, same route.

THROUGH RATES.

Baltimore, Md.	$22 25	Washington, D. C.	$21 25
Philadelphia, Pa.	18 25		

SALEM, VA.

FORM EX. 9.—SALEM (ROANOKE RED SULPHUR SPRINGS), VA.,
AND RETURN.

Baltimore & Ohio R. R. . . . . to Shenandoah June.
Norfolk & Western R. R. . . . . to Salem.
Returning, same route.

THROUGH RATES.

Baltimore, Md.	$15 00	Morgantown, W. Va.	$19 50
Bellaire, O.	21 00	Moundsville, W. Va.	21 00
Berkeley Springs, W. Va.	14 70	Mountain Lake Park, Md.	15 65
Cameron, W. Va.	20 50	Mt. Pleasant, Pa.	17 75
Chester, Pa.	16 50	Newark, Del.	15 50
Clarksburg, W. Va.	18 50	New York, N. Y.	21 00
Connellsville, Pa.	17 25	Oakland, Md.	15 75
Cumberland, Md.	15 55	Parkersburg, W. Va.	21 00
Deer Park, Md.	15 50	Philadelphia, Pa.	17 00
Fairmont, W. Va.	18 50	Piedmont, W. Va.	14 70
Frederick, Md.	11 30	Pittsburgh, Pa.	19 55
Grafton, W. Va.	17 00	Rockwood, Pa.	15 50
Harper's Ferry, W. Va.	10 20	Somerset, Pa.	15 90
Havre de Grace, Md.	11 15	Uniontown, Pa.	17 70
Johnstown, Pa.	17 30	Washington, D. C.	11 00
Keyser, W. Va.	14 50	Washington, Pa.	20 65
McKeesport, Pa.	19 00	Wheeling, W. Va.	21 00
Martinsburg, W. Va.	10 45	Wilmington, Del.	16 00
Meyersdale, Pa.	15 65		

Form Ex. 90.—Salem (Roanoke Red Sulphur Springs), Va., and Return.

Baltimore & Ohio R. R. . . . . to Washington.
Transfer . . . . B. & O. Depot to R. & D. Depot.
Norfolk & Western R. R. . . . . to Salem.

Returning, same route.

THROUGH RATES.

Baltimore, Md.	$15 00	Meyersdale, Pa.	$19 10
Bellaire, O.	25 95	Morgantown, W. Va.	25 55
Berkeley Springs, W. Va.	15 65	Moundsville, W. Va.	25 20
Cameron, W. Va.	24 50	Mountain Lake Park, Md.	19 15
Charlestown, W. Va.	14 20	Mt. Pleasant, Pa.	21 80
Chester, Pa.	16 50	Newark, Del.	15 30
Clarksburg, W. Va.	22 55	New York, N. Y.	21 00
Connellsville, Pa.	21 50	Oakland, Md.	19 25
Cumberland, Md.	17 60	Parkersburg, W. Va.	25 65
Deer Park, Md.	19 00	Philadelphia, Pa.	17 00
Fairmont, W. Va.	22 55	Piedmont, W. Va.	18 70
Frederick, Md.	15 80	Pittsburgh, Pa.	23 60
Grafton, W. Va.	21 65	Rockwood, Pa.	19 55
Hagerstown, Md.	14 60	Somerset, Pa.	19 96
Harper's Ferry, W. Va.	15 70	Uniontown, Pa.	21 75
Havre de Grace, Md.	14 45	Washington, Pa.	24 70
Johnstown, Pa.	21 35	Wheeling, W. Va.	25 65
Keyser, W. Va.	18 50	Wilmington, Del.	16 00
McKeesport, Pa.	23 05	Winchester, Va.	15 30
Martinsburg, W. Va.	14 45		

SALT SULPHUR SPRINGS, W. VA.

Form Ex. 49.—Salt Sulphur Springs, W. Va., and Return.

Baltimore & Ohio R. R. . . . . to Staunton.
Chesapeake & Ohio Ry . . . . to Fort Spring.
Stage (10 miles) . . . . to Salt Sulphar Springs

Returning, same route.

THROUGH RATES.

Baltimore, Md.	$18 00	Meyersdale, Pa.	$24 15
Bellaire, O.	28 00	Morgantown, W. Va.	25 60
Berkeley Springs, W. Va.	17 70	Moundsville, W. Va.	27 25
Cameron, W. Va.	26 55	Mountain Lake Park, Md.	21 70
Charlestown, W. Va.	15 25	Mt. Pleasant, Pa.	23 85
Chester, Pa.	21 50	Newark, Del.	20 30
Clarksburg, W. Va.	24 60	New York, N. Y.	26 00
Connellsville, Pa.	23 55	Oakland, Md.	21 80
Cumberland, Md.	19 65	Parkersburg, W. Va.	27 75
Deer Park, Md.	21 55	Philadelphia, Pa.	22 00
Fairmont, W. Va.	24 60	Piedmont, W. Va.	20 75
Frederick, Md.	16 80	Pittsburgh, Pa.	25 65
Grafton, W. Va.	23 70	Rockwood, Pa.	24 60
Hagerstown, Md.	16 80	Somerset, Pa.	22 00
Harper's Ferry, W. Va.	15 75	Strasburg, Va.	13 10
Harrisonburg, Va.	10 75	Uniontown, Pa.	23 80
Havre de Grace, Md.	19 45	Washington, D. C.	16 00
Johnstown, Pa.	23 40	Washington, Pa.	26 75
Keyser, W. Va.	20 55	Wheeling, W. Va.	27 75
Lexington, Va.	11 25	Wilmington, Del.	21 00
McKeesport, Pa.	25 10	Winchester, Va.	14 45
Martinsburg, W. Va.	16 50		

FORM EX. 71.—SALT SULPHUR SPRINGS, W. VA., AND RETURN.

Baltimore & Ohio R. R. . . . . to Shenandoah June.
Norfolk & Western R. R. . . . . to Basic.
Chesapeake & Ohio Ry. . . . . to Fort Spring.
Stage (10 miles) . . . . to Salt Sulphur Springs.

Returning, same route.

THROUGH RATES.

Baltimore, Md.	$18 00	New York, N. Y.	$26 00
Chester, Pa.	21 50	Philadelphia, Pa.	22 00
Havre de Grace, Md.	19 15	Washington, D. C.	16 00
Newark, Del.	20 30	Wilmington, Del.	21 00

SALTVILLE, VA.

FORM EX. 101.—SALTVILLE, VA., AND RETURN.

Baltimore & Ohio R. R. . . . . to Shenandoah June.
Norfolk & Western R. R. . . . . to Saltville.

Returning, same route.

THROUGH RATES.

Baltimore, Md.	$19 50	Morgantown, W. Va.	$25 25
Bellaire, O.	27 65	Moundsville, W. Va.	26 90
Berkeley Springs, W. Va.	17 45	Mountain Lake Park, Md.	21 10
Cameron, W. Va.	26 25	Mt. Pleasant, Pa.	23 50
Chester, Pa.	22 80	Newark, Del.	21 60
Clarksburg, W. Va.	24 25	New York, N. Y.	27 30
Connellsville, Pa.	23 00	Oakland, Md.	21 50
Cumberland, Md.	19 30	Parkersburg, W. Va.	27 35
Deer Park, Md.	21 25	Philadelphia, Pa.	23 30
Fairmont, W. Va.	24 25	Piedmont, W. Va.	20 15
Frederick, Md.	17 05	Pittsburgh, Pa.	25 20
Grafton, W. Va.	23 35	Rockwood, Pa.	24 25
Harper's Ferry, W. Va.	15 95	Somerset, Pa.	24 65
Havre de Grace, Md.	20 75	Uniontown, Pa.	23 45
Johnstown, Pa.	23 05	Washington, D. C.	17 50
Keyser, W. Va.	20 25	Washington, Pa.	26 10
McKeesport, Pa.	24 75	Wheeling, W. Va.	27 35
Martinsburg, W. Va.	16 15	Wilmington, Del.	22 30
Meyersdale, Pa.	20 80		

SARATOGA SPRINGS.

This "Queen of American Watering-places" is located within an hour's ride of Albany. Its resident population is about nine thousand, but during the season of pleasure travel, which extends from June 15th to September 15th, its population frequently exceeds thirty thousand. The name Saratoga (from the Indian, Saraghoga) signifies "The Place of the Herrings," which formerly passed up the Hudson into Saratoga Lake. In all, there are twenty-eight springs (including six spouting) at Saratoga; some chalybeate, others impregnated with iodine, sulphur, and magnesia, and all powerfully charged with carbonic acid gas.

The medicinal properties of these waters were known at an early date to the Indians, as has been demonstrated by subsequent events. Several of the springs are cathartic; some are taken as a tonic, while others are utilized for bathing. The wonderful cures effected by these springs induced their owners, several years since, to engage in the business of bottling the waters, until now the industry has assumed such immense proportions that the waters may be found in

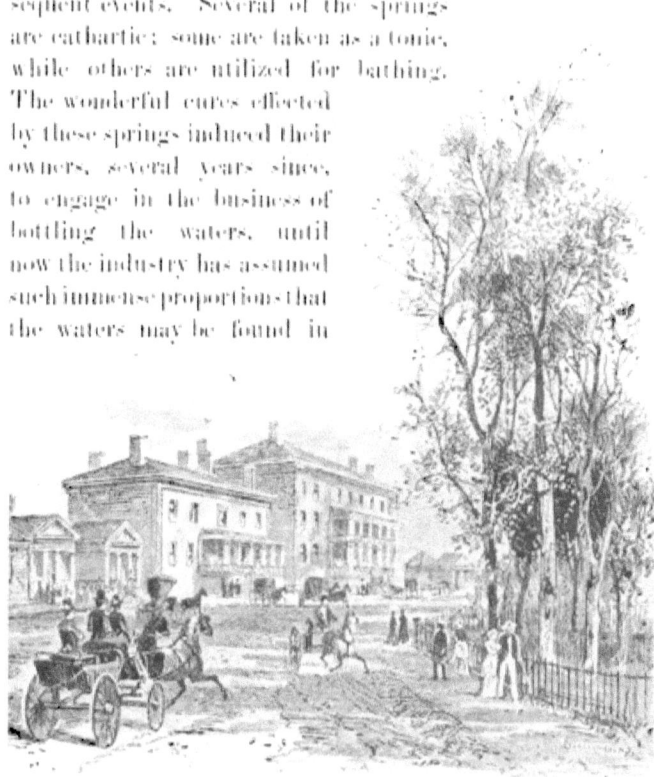

all parts of the country. But while the waters of Saratoga, and the clear, balmy atmosphere of the entire region, have proved valuable auxiliaries in the development of that far-famed resort, the magnificent hotels, of which there are many, have contributed largely to the name and fame of Saratoga. These hotels are located principally on Broadway, a broad and well-kept boulevard, lined on either side with tall and stately elms and picturesque promenades. The hotels are managed with great liberality, and are furnished throughout in the most sumptuous manner. At the height of the season hops are held at each of the large hotels every night, while from sunrise to sunset the sweet and melodious strains of music vibrate upon the ear at every turn, rendering a sojourn at this resort one of indescribable pleasure.

FORM EX. 541.—SARATOGA, N. Y., AND RETURN.

Baltimore & Ohio R. R. . . . . to Philadelphia.
Philadelphia & Reading R. R. . . . . to Bound Brook.
Central R. R. of New Jersey . . . . .to New York.
New York Central & Hudson River R. R. . . . . . to Troy.
Delaware & Hudson R. R. . . . . to Saratoga.

Returning, same route.

THROUGH RATES.

Baltimore, Md. . . . . . . $15 50 | Washington, D. C. $17 50
| Philadelphia, Pa. . . . . 11 50 |

FORM EX. 543.—SARATOGA, N. Y., AND RETURN.

Baltimore & Ohio R. R. . . . . to Philadelphia.
Philadelphia & Reading R. R. . . . . to Bound Brook.
Central R. R. of New Jersey . . . . .to New York.
West Shore R. R. . . . . to Albany.
Delaware & Hudson R. R. . . . . to Saratoga.

Returning, same route.

Transfer through New York, in both directions, included.

THROUGH RATES.

Baltimore, Md. . . . . . . $15 50 | Washington, D. C. $17 50
| Philadelphia, Pa. . . . . 11 50 |

FORM EX. 718.—SARATOGA, N. Y., AND RETURN.

Baltimore & Ohio R. R. . . . . to Philadelphia.
Philadelphia & Reading R. R. . . . . to Bound Brook.
Central R. R. of New Jersey . . . . .to New York.
People's Line Steamers . . . . to Albany.
Delaware & Hudson R. R. . . . . to Saratoga.

Returning, same route.

THROUGH RATES.

Baltimore, Md. . . . . . . $12 85 | Washington, D. C. $14 85
| Philadelphia, Pa. . . . . 8 85 |

FORM EX. 546.—SARATOGA, N. Y., AND RETURN.

Baltimore & Ohio R. R. . . . . to Philadelphia.
Philadelphia & Reading R. R. . . . . to Bound Brook.
Central R. R. of New Jersey . . . . .to New York.
New York & Albany Day Line . . . . to Albany.
Delaware & Hudson R. R. . . . . to Saratoga.

Returning, same route.

THROUGH RATES.

Baltimore, Md. . . . . . . $13 75 | Washington, D. C. $15 75
| Philadelphia, Pa. . . . . 9 75 |

FORM EX. 547. SARATOGA, N. Y., AND RETURN.

Baltimore & Ohio R. R. . . . . to Philadelphia.
Philadelphia & Reading R. R. . . . . to Bethlehem.
Central R. R. of New Jersey . . . . to Wilkesbarre.
Delaware & Hudson R. R. . . . . to Saratoga.

Returning, same route.

THROUGH RATES.

Baltimore, Md. . . . . . . $19 65   Washington, D. C. $21 65
Philadelphia, Pa. . . . . . 15 65 |

FORM EX. 1072.—SARATOGA SPRINGS, N. Y., AND RETURN.

(Via New York and Day Line Steamers; returning via Boston.)

Baltimore & Ohio R. R. . . . . to Philadelphia.
Philadelphia & Reading R. R. . . . . to Bound Brook.
Central R. R. of New Jersey . . . . to New York.
New York & Albany Day Line . . . . to Albany.
Delaware & Hudson R. R. . . . . to Saratoga.
Fitchburg R. R. . . . . to Boston.
Rail or Sound Lines (see pages 50 to 55 for route) to Philadelphia.
Baltimore & Ohio R. R. . . . . to starting point.

FORM EX. 1073.—SARATOGA SPRINGS, N. Y., AND RETURN.

Reverse of preceding excursion.

THROUGH RATES.

	Via Sound	Via Rail
Baltimore, Md.	$20 35	$21 35
Philadelphia, Pa.	16 35	17 35
Washington, D. C.	22 35	23 35

FORM EX. 1074.—SARATOGA SPRINGS, N. Y., AND RETURN.

(Via New York; returning via Boston.)

Baltimore & Ohio R. R. . . . . to Philadelphia.
Philadelphia & Reading R. R. . . . . to Bound Brook.
Central R. R. of New Jersey . . . . to New York.
New York Central & Hudson River R. R. . . . . to Troy.
Delaware & Hudson R. R. . . . . to Saratoga.
Fitchburg R. R. . . . . to Boston.
Rail or Sound Lines (see pages 50 to 55 for route) to Philadelphia.
Baltimore & Ohio R. R. . . . . to starting point.

FORM EX. 1075.—SARATOGA SPRINGS, N. Y., AND RETURN.

Reverse of preceding excursion.

THROUGH RATES.

	Via Sound	Via Rail
Baltimore, Md.	$21 35	$22 35
Philadelphia, Pa.	17 35	18 35
Washington, D. C.	23 35	24 35

FORM EX. 1076.—SARATOGA SPRINGS, N. Y., AND RETURN.

(Via West Shore Route and rail; returning via Boston.)

Baltimore & Ohio R. R. . . . . to Philadelphia.
Philadelphia & Reading R. R. . . . . to Bound Brook.
Central R. R. of New Jersey . . . . to New York.
West Shore R. R. . . . . to Albany.
Delaware & Hudson R. R. . . . . to Saratoga.
Fitchburg R. R. . . . . to Boston.
Rail or Sound Lines (see pages 50 to 55 for route) to Philadelphia.
Baltimore & Ohio R. R. . . . . to starting point.

Transfer through New York, going, included.

FORM EX. 1077.—SARATOGA SPRINGS, N. Y., AND RETURN.
Reverse of preceding excursion.
Transfer through New York, returning, included.

THROUGH RATES.

	Via Sound.	Via Rail.
Baltimore, Md.	$21 35	$22 35
†Philadelphia, Pa.	17 35	18 35
Washington, D. C.	23 35	24 35

FORM EX. 1078.—SARATOGA SPRINGS, N. Y., AND RETURN.
(Via New York and rail; returning via Hudson River Steamers.)

Baltimore & Ohio R. R.	to Philadelphia.
Philadelphia & Reading R. R.	to Bound Brook.
Central R. R. of New Jersey	to New York.
New York Central & Hudson River R. R.	to Troy.
Delaware & Hudson R. R.	to Saratoga.
Delaware & Hudson R. R.	to Albany.
New York & Albany Day Line	to New York.
Central R. R. of New Jersey	to Bound Brook.
Philadelphia & Reading R. R.	to Philadelphia.
Baltimore & Ohio R. R.	to starting point.

THROUGH RATES.

Baltimore, Md. . . . . . $15 40 Washington, D. C. . . . $17 40
†Philadelphia, Pa. 11 40

FORM EX. 1079.—SARATOGA SPRINGS, N. Y., AND RETURN.
(Via West Shore Route and rail; returning via Hudson River Steamers.)

Baltimore & Ohio R. R.	to Philadelphia.
Philadelphia & Reading R. R.	to Bound Brook.
Central R. R. of New Jersey	to New York.
West Shore R. R.	to Albany.
Delaware & Hudson R. R.	to Saratoga.
Delaware & Hudson R. R.	to Albany.
New York & Albany Day Line	to New York.
Central R. R. of New Jersey	to Bound Brook.
Philadelphia & Reading R. R.	to Philadelphia.
Baltimore & Ohio R. R.	to starting point.

Transfer through New York, going, included.

THROUGH RATES.

Baltimore, Md. . . . . . $15 40 Washington, D. C. . . . $17 40
†Philadelphia, Pa. 11 40

FORM EX. 1074.—SARATOGA SPRINGS, N. Y., AND RETURN.

Delaware & Hudson R. R. . . . . Albany to Saratoga.

Returning, same route.

Sold in connection with any ticket passing through Albany.

Rate $2 34

SCARBORO BEACH, ME.

FORM EX. 762.—SCARBORO BEACH, MAINE, AND RETURN.

Baltimore & Ohio R. R.	to Philadelphia.
Philadelphia & Reading R. R.	to Bound Brook.
Central R. R. of New Jersey	to New York.
Sound Lines (see pages 50 to 55 for route)	to Boston.
Boston & Maine R. R.	to Scarboro Beach.

Returning, same route.

THROUGH RATES.

Baltimore, Md. . . . . . $20 25 Washington, D. C. . . . $22 25
†Philadelphia, Pa. 16 25

FORM EX. 762.—SCARBORO BEACH, MAINE, AND RETURN.

Baltimore & Ohio R. R. . . . . to Philadelphia.
Rail Lines (see pages 50 to 55 for route) . . . . . to Boston.
Boston & Maine R. R. . . . . to Scarboro Beach.

Returning, same route.

THROUGH RATES.

Baltimore, Md. . . . . $22 25 | Washington, D. C. $21 25
Philadelphia, Pa. . . . . . 18 25 |

FORM EX. 762. SCARBORO BEACH, MAINE, AND RETURN.

Baltimore & Ohio R. R. . . . . to Philadelphia.
Rail Lines (see pages 50 to 55 for route) . . . . . to Boston.
Boston & Maine R. R. . . . . to Scarboro Beach.
Boston & Maine R. R. . . . . to Boston.
Sound Lines (see pages 50 to 55 for route) . . . . to New York.
Central R. R. of New Jersey . . . . to Bound Brook.
Philadelphia & Reading R. R. . . . . to Philadelphia.
Baltimore & Ohio R. R. . . . . to starting point.

THROUGH RATES.

Baltimore, Md. . . . . $21 25 | Washington, D. C. $23 25
Philadelphia, Pa. . . . . . 17 25 |

FORM EX. 762.—SCARBORO BEACH, MAINE, AND RETURN.

Baltimore & Ohio R. R. . . . . to Philadelphia.
Philadelphia & Reading R. R. . . . . to Bound Brook.
Central R. R. of New Jersey . . . . to New York.
Sound Lines (see pages 50 to 55 for route) . . . . to Boston.
Boston & Maine R. R. . . . . to Scarboro Beach.
Boston & Maine R. R. . . . . to Boston.
Rail Lines (see pages 50 to 55 for route) . . . . . to Philadelphia.
Baltimore & Ohio R. R. . . . . to starting point.

THROUGH RATES.

Baltimore, Md. . . . . $21 25 | Washington, D. C. $23 25
Philadelphia, Pa. . . . . . 17 25 |

SHARON SPRINGS.

This "Baden-Baden of America," as it has been recently denominated, is a favorite summer resort of easy access. It is situated in a narrow valley surrounded by high hills, and is noted for its mineral springs, of which the most prominent are chalybeate, magnesia, white sulphur, and blue sulphur. The magnesia and white sulphur springs bear a close resemblance to the White Sulphur Springs of Virginia, and the waters of the former are used freely. The specialty of the place, however, is its baths, of which there are a great variety, of wonderful curative power.

FORM EX. 518.—SHARON SPRINGS, N. Y., AND RETURN.

Baltimore & Ohio R. R. . . . . to Philadelphia.
Philadelphia & Reading R. R. . . . . to Bound Brook.
Central R. R. of New Jersey . . . . to New York.
New York Central & Hudson River R. R. . . . to Albany.
Delaware & Hudson R. R. . . . . to Sharon Springs.
Returning, same route.

THROUGH RATES.

Baltimore, Md. . . . . . . $16 85 | Washington, D. C. $18 85
| Philadelphia, Pa. . . . . 12 85 |

FORM EX. 519.—SHARON SPRINGS, N. Y., AND RETURN.

Baltimore & Ohio R. R. . . . . to Philadelphia.
Philadelphia & Reading R. R. . . . . to Bound Brook.
Central R. R. of New Jersey . . . . to New York.
West Shore R. R. . . . . to Albany.
Delaware & Hudson R. R. . . . . to Sharon Springs.
Returning, same route.
Transfer through New York, in both directions, included.

THROUGH RATES.

Baltimore, Md. . . . . . . $16 85 | Washington, D. C. $18 85
| Philadelphia, Pa. . . . . 12 85 |

FORM EX. 749.—SHARON SPRINGS, N. Y., AND RETURN.

Baltimore & Ohio R. R. . . . . to Philadelphia.
Philadelphia & Reading R. R. . . . . to Bound Brook.
Central R. R. of New Jersey . . . . to New York.
People's Line . . . . to Albany.
Delaware & Hudson R. R. . . . . to Sharon Springs.
Returning, same route.

THROUGH RATES.

Baltimore, Md. . . . . . . $15 85 | Washington, D. C. $15 85
| Philadelphia, Pa. . . . . 9 85 |

FORM EX. 550.—SHARON SPRINGS, N. Y., AND RETURN.

Baltimore & Ohio R. R. . . . . to Philadelphia.
Philadelphia & Reading R. R. . . . . to Bound Brook.
Central R. R. of New Jersey . . . . to New York.
New York & Albany Day Line . . . . to Albany.
Delaware & Hudson R. R. . . . . to Sharon Springs.
Returning, same route.

THROUGH RATES.

Baltimore, Md. . . . . . . $14 85 | Washington, D. C. $16 85
| Philadelphia, Pa. . . . . 10 85 |

SHELDRAKE, N. Y.

FORM EX. 597.—SHELDRAKE, N. Y., AND RETURN.

Baltimore & Ohio R. R. . . . . to Philadelphia.
Philadelphia & Reading R. R. . . . . to Bethlehem.
Lehigh Valley R. R. . . . . to Sheldrake.
Returning, same route.

THROUGH RATES.

Baltimore, Md. . . . . . . $14 00 | Washington, D. C. $16 00
| Philadelphia, Pa. . . . . 11 00 |

SHENANDOAH ALUM SPRINGS, VA.

A home-like resort, and just the place a man of family would like to summer with his wife and children.

The hotel and cottages front on a lawn, which is so shaded as to afford the coolest of spots for a retreat to while away the day. The provision for the enjoyment of children and the little folks, in the way of croquet and kindred out-door sports, is all the fondest of mothers could wish for.

There are no particular pretensions to style at Shenandoah, as the aim is to insure comfort and rest without carrying the dissipations of the winter over into the summer. It is a home-like resort, and those who avail themselves of its accommodations remain, as a rule, during the hot months.

and leave only when it becomes so cool as to require the use of double blankets at night. For health and rest it would be difficult to name a more advantageous locality. The main springs consist of alum, but there are also chalybeate, sulphur, iron, and arsenic; and invalids seeking the health-restoring qualities of nature's own remedies may consult their physician as to whether or not waters of this character are best adapted for their cases. No trouble can be experienced by any one in securing the pamphlets of the different resorts, which not only specify the varieties of springs, but also give rates for accommodation and other essential details.

FORM EX. 561. SHENANDOAH ALUM SPRINGS, VA., AND RETURN.

Baltimore & Ohio R. R. . . . . to Mt. Jackson.
Stage (42 miles) . . . . to Shenandoah Alum Springs.
Returning, same route.

THROUGH RATES.

Baltimore, Md.	$10 45	Meyersdale, Pa.	$12 00
Bellaire, O.	18 30	Morgantown, W. Va.	16 30
Berkeley Springs, W. Va.	8 60	Moundsville, W. Va.	18 15
Cameron, W. Va.	17 45	Mountain Lake Park, Md.	12 60
Charlestown, W. Va.	6 20	Mt. Pleasant, Pa.	14 75
Chester, Pa.	13 95	Newark, Del.	12 75
Clarksburg, W. Va.	15 30	New York, N. Y.	18 15
Connellsville, Pa.	11 25	Oakland, Md.	12 70
Cumberland, Md.	10 55	Parkersburg, W. Va.	18 65
Deer Park, Md.	12 15	Philadelphia, Pa.	14 15
Fairmont, W. Va.	15 30	Piedmont, W. Va.	11 65
Frederick, Md.	7 70	Pittsburgh, Pa.	16 55
Grafton, W. Va.	14 60	Rockwood, Pa.	12 50
Hagerstown, Md.	7 70	Somerset, Pa.	12 90
Harper's Ferry, W. Va.	6 65	Staunton, Va.	5 60
Harrisonburg, Va.	1 30	Strasburg, Va.	1 20
Havre de Grace, Md.	11 90	Uniontown, Pa.	11 70
Johnstown, Pa.	14 30	Washington, D. C.	8 85
Keyser, W. Va.	11 15	Washington, Pa.	17 65
Lexington, Va.	7 40	Wheeling, W. Va.	18 65
McKeesport, Pa.	16 00	Wilmington, Del.	13 15
Martinsburg, W. Va.	7 10	Winchester, Va.	5 10

SHELTER ISLAND, N. Y.

Shelter Island was originally the home of the Manhasset Indians. Settlements were made on it as early as 1652, and in 1730 it was incorporated as a town. The island, six miles long by four wide, is a picturesque and irregularly-shaped bit of land, situated at the eastern end of Long Island, between the waters of Peconic and Gardiner Bays.

The surface of the Island is diversified in a pleasing way by rolling hills, pretty valleys, fresh ponds and deep inlets. In the very midst of salt water it must needs be healthy.

FORM EX. 1080. SHELTER ISLAND, N. Y., AND RETURN.

Baltimore & Ohio R. R. . . . . to Philadelphia.
Philadelphia & Reading R. R. . . . . to Bound Brook.
Central R. R. of New Jersey . . . . to New York.
Metropolitan Ferry Co., James' Slip or 34th Street
 Ferry . . . . to Long Island City
Long Island R. R. . . . . to Greenport.
Shelter Island Ferry . . . . to Shelter Island.
Returning, same route.

THROUGH RATES.

Baltimore, Md. . . . . . . $13 45   Washington, D. C. . . . $13 45
|Philadelphia, Pa. 9 45

SORRENTO, ME.

Sorrento lies directly opposite Bar Harbor, upon the left as one leaves the ferry for Mt. Desert. This peninsula is three miles long, with an average width of a mile, and has borne until recently the name of "Waukeag Neck." It has six miles of water front, which has been divided into cottage lots rising gradually from the sea, terraced by the hand of nature. Now that Bar Harbor land has attained such fabulous prices, these neighboring lands are appreciating rapidly in value. Sorrento is destined in a not far distant future to become the terminus of the rail line to Mt. Desert, offering, by reason of its closer proximity to Bar Harbor, increased facilities for reaching that point by allowing the passage which now requires thirty minutes to be reduced by fully one-half. This, however, may not prove such a charm to the visitor, as the ferry journey forms one of the pleasantest features of the trip, leaving more, rather than a reduction, to be desired.

FORM EX. 1081 OR FORM SPL. EX. 1082. SORRENTO, ME., AND RETURN.

(Via rail to Sorrento; returning by same route to Boston, thence via Sound Lines from Boston.)

Baltimore & Ohio R. R. . . . . to Philadelphia.
Rail Lines (see pages 50 to 55 for route) . . . to Boston.
Boston & Maine R. R. . . . . to Portland.
Maine Central R. R. . . . . to Sorrento.
Maine Central R. R. . . . . to Portland.
Boston & Maine R. R. . . . . to Boston.
Sound Lines (see pages 50 to 55 for routes) . . to New York.
Central R. R. of New Jersey . . . . to Bound Brook.
Philadelphia & Reading R. R. . . . . to Philadelphia.
Baltimore & Ohio R. R. . . . . to starting point.

THROUGH RATES.

Baltimore, Md. . . . . . . $33 00   Washington, D. C. . . . $33 00
|Philadelphia, Pa. 27 00

Form Spl. Ex. 1082 is good for continuous passage only east of Portland, and the rates for same are $2.50 less than the rates for the regular excursion as quoted above.

FORM EX. 1081 OR FORM SPL. EX. 1082.—SORRENTO, ME., AND RETURN.

(Via Sound Lines to Boston, rail to Sorrento; returning by same route to Boston, thence via rail.)

Baltimore & Ohio R. R. . . . . to Philadelphia.
Philadelphia & Reading R. R. . . . . to Bound Brook.
Central R. R. of New Jersey . . . . to New York.
Sound Lines (see pages 50 to 55 for routes) . . . . to Boston.
Boston & Maine R. R. . . . . to Portland.
Maine Central R. R. . . . . to Sorrento.
Maine Central R. R. . . . . to Portland.
Boston & Maine R. R. . . . . to Boston.
Rail Lines (see pages 50 to 55 for route) . . . . to Philadelphia.
Baltimore & Ohio R. R. . . . . to starting point.

THROUGH RATES.

Baltimore, Md. . . . . . . $31 00 | Washington, D. C. . . . $33 00
†Philadelphia, Pa. . . . . . 27 00 |

Form Spl. Ex. 1082 is good for continuous passage only east of Portland, and the rates for same are $2.50 less than the rates for the regular excursion as quoted above.

FORM EX. 1081, OR FORM SPL. EX. 1082.—SORRENTO, ME., AND RETURN.

(Via Rail Lines to Sorrento in both directions.)

Baltimore & Ohio R. R. . . . . to Philadelphia.
Rail Lines (see pages 50 to 55 for routes) . . . . to Boston.
Boston & Maine R. R. . . . . to Portland.
Maine Central R. R. . . . . to Sorrento.

Returning, same route.

THROUGH RATES.

Baltimore, Md. . . . . . . $32 00 | Washington, D. C. . . . $34 00
†Philadelphia, Pa. . . . . . 28 00 |

Form Spl. Ex. 1082 is good for continuous passage only east of Portland, and the rates for same are $2.50 less than rates for the regular excursion as quoted above.

FORM EX. 1081, OR FORM SPL. EX. 1082.—SORRENTO, ME., AND RETURN.

(Via Sound Lines to Boston, rail to Sorrento, and return to Boston, thence via Sound Lines.)

Baltimore & Ohio R. R. . . . . to Philadelphia.
Philadelphia & Reading R. R. . . . . to Bound Brook.
Central R. R. of New Jersey . . . . to New York.
Sound Lines (see pages 50 to 55 for route) . . . . to Boston.
Boston & Maine R. R. . . . . to Portland.
Maine Central R. R. . . . . to Sorrento.

Returning, same route.

THROUGH RATES.

Baltimore, Md. . . . . . . $30 00 | Washington, D. C. . . . $32 00
†Philadelphia, Pa. . . . . . 26 00 |

Form Spl. Ex. 1082 is good for continuous passage only east of Portland, and the rates for same are $2.50 less than rates for same are the regular excursion as quoted above.

SOMERSET, PA.

SOMERSET, PA., AND RETURN.
Use Local Excursion-book Tickets.

THROUGH RATES.

Connellsville, Pa.	$2 30	Pittsburgh, Pa.	$4 40
Johnstown, Pa.	1 45	Rockwood, Pa.	40
McKeesport, Pa.	3 85	Uniontown, Pa.	2 65
Meyersdale, Pa.	85	Washington, Pa.	5 55
Mt. Pleasant, Pa.	2 00		

SOUTH HARPSWELL, ME.

Form Ex. 1083.—South Harpswell, Me., and Return.
(Via rail to Portland, thence steamer.)

Baltimore & Ohio R. R. . . . . to Philadelphia.
Rail Lines (see pages 50 to 55 for route) . . . . . to Boston.
Boston & Maine R. R. . . . . to Portland.
South Harpswell Steamboat Co. . . . . to South Harpswell.
        Returning, same route.

THROUGH RATES.

Baltimore, Md. . . . . . $23 25 | Washington, D. C. $25 25
†Philadelphia, Pa. . . . . 19 25 |

Form Ex. 1083.—South Harpswell, Me., and Return.
(Via Sound Lines to Boston and rail to Portsmouth, thence steamer.)

Baltimore & Ohio R. R. . . . . to Philadelphia.
Philadelphia & Reading R. R. . . . . to Bound Brook.
Central R. R. of New Jersey. . . . . to New York.
Sound Lines (see pages 50 to 55 for route) . . . . to Boston.
Boston & Maine R. R. . . . . to Portland.
South Harpswell Steamboat Co. . . . . to South Harpswell.
        Returning, same route.

THROUGH RATES.

†Philadelphia, Pa. . . . . $17 25 | Washington, D. C. $23 25
Baltimore, Md. . . . . . 21 25 |

Form Ex. 1083.—South Harpswell, Me., and Return.
(Via rail to Portsmouth, thence steamer; returning by Sound Lines from Boston.)

Baltimore & Ohio R. R. . . . . to Philadelphia.
Rail Lines (see pages 50 to 55 for route) . . . . . to Boston.
Boston & Maine R. R. . . . . to Portland.
South Harpswell Steamboat Co. . . . . to South Harpswell.
South Harpswell Steamboat Co. . . . . to Portland.
Boston & Maine R. R. . . . . to Boston.
Sound Lines (see pages 50 to 55 for route) . . . . to New York.
Central R. R. of New Jersey . . . . to Bound Brook.
Philadelphia & Reading R. R. . . . . to Philadelphia.
Baltimore & Ohio R. R. . . . . to starting point.

THROUGH RATES.

†Philadelphia, Pa. . . . . $18 25 | Washington, D. C. $24 25
Baltimore, Md. . . . . . 22 25 |

Form Ex. 1083.—South Harpswell, Me., and Return.
(Via Sound Lines to Portsmouth, thence steamer; returning by Rail Lines from Boston.)

Baltimore & Ohio R. R. . . . . to Philadelphia.
Philadelphia & Reading R. R. . . . . to Bound Brook.
Central R. R. of New Jersey . . . . to New York.
Sound Lines (see pages 50 to 55 for route) . . . . to Boston.
Boston & Maine R. R. . . . . to Portland.
South Harpswell Steamboat Co. . . . . to South Harpswell.
South Harpswell Steamboat Co. . . . . to Portland.
Boston & Maine R. R. . . . . to Boston.
Rail Lines (see pages 50 to 55 for route) . . . . . to Philadelphia.
Baltimore & Ohio R. R. . . . . to starting point.

THROUGH RATES.

†Philadelphia, Pa. . . . . $18 25 | Washington, D. C. $24 25
Baltimore, Md. . . . . . 22 25 |

STAUNTON, VA.

FORM EX. 98. STAUNTON, VA., AND RETURN.

Baltimore & Ohio R. R. . . . . to Staunton.
Returning same route.

LIST OF RATES.

Baltimore, Md.	$10 10	Meyersdale, Pa.	$11 70
Bellaire, O.	18 20	Morgantown, W. Va.	16 45
Berkeley Springs, W. Va.	8 25	Moundsville, W. Va.	17 80
Cameron, W. Va.	17 40	Mountain Lake Park, Md.	12 25
Charlestown, W. Va.	5 80	Mt. Pleasant, Pa.	14 40
Chester, Pa.	13 60	Newark, Del.	12 40
Clarksburg, W. Va.	15 15	New York, N. Y.	18 40
Connellsville, Pa.	13 90	Oakland, Md.	12 35
Cumberland, Md.	10 20	Parkersburg, W. Va.	18 20
Deer Park, Md.	12 40	Philadelphia, Pa.	14 40
Fairmont, W. Va.	15 15	Piedmont, W. Va.	11 20
Frederick, Md.	7 45	Pittsburgh, Pa.	16 20
Grafton, W. Va.	14 25	Rockwood, Pa.	12 45
Hagerstown, Md.	7 35	Somerset, Pa.	12 35
Harper's Ferry, W. Va.	6 30	Strasburg, Va.	3 65
Harrisonburg, Va.	1 20	Uniontown, Pa.	14 35
Havre de Grace, Md.	11 55	Washington, D. C.	8 20
Johnstown, Pa.	13 85	Washington, Pa.	17 20
Keyser, W. Va.	11 40	Wheeling, W. Va.	18 20
Lexington, Va.	1 80	Wilmington, Del.	13 40
McKeesport, Pa.	15 65	Winchester, Va.	4 70
Martinsburg, W. Va.	7 05		

STOCKBRIDGE, BERKSHIRE HILLS, MASS.

This village has a reputation as a summer resort which attracts to its well-kept hotels—the principal hostelry, the Stockbridge House, having the well-earned reputation of being one of the best hotels in the country—its cottages and fine homes, hosts of admiring guests, whose numbers increase with every passing year.

With the country villas and cottages thrown open and the hotels well filled, the summer life here is one of most sensible enjoyment. An extensive public park has lately been laid out on the hill to the northward, by Cyrus W. Field, a native of Stockbridge. The village neatness is the wonder of every stranger. The main street is from one hundred and twenty to one hundred and fifty feet wide, and all the streets outside the wagon-way are kept closely mown and clean. Almost every house in town has a handsome lawn around it and flowers before it. One of the most noted scenic beauties of Stockbridge is its famous "Bowl," in the extreme northerly part of the town, and so close to the line which divides it from Lenox that it is often thought to belong to the latter town.

The prospect from around the rim of the "Bowl" is very fine indeed, and attracts many visitors. Walks about town are in numerous directions. A favorite one is to Ice Glen, a cleft across the spur of Bear Mountain, a short distance from the village. Here, in a deep, cool, shady, wild ravine of irregular formation, is a luxurious retreat on a hot day, where ice is found all summer down among the fallen rocks. Beyond Ice Glen a magnificent mountain outlook is had from Laura's Rest. Here the range of vision extends wide into Connecticut, New York and Vermont, on nearly every side of the observer, and the beauties that are spread before him are transcendent.

Fine sidewalks from the centre of the village from one-half to three-quarters of a mile in every direction, and these, well shaded, make delightful strolls. Prospect Hill, just above the village, commands one of the choicest views of beauty in the world. Laurel Hill, on the edge of the village, is the object of another walk. A walk to "Cherry Cottage" is often taken by those who want to go three miles. But the stranger in Stockbridge needs no direction to find the beautiful. It is everywhere!

FORM EX. 981.—STOCKBRIDGE, (BERKSHIRE HILLS) MASS.

Baltimore & Ohio R. R. . . . . to Philadelphia.
Philadelphia & Reading R. R. . . . . to Bound Brook.
Central R. R. of New Jersey . . . . to New York.
New York, New Haven & Hartford R. R. . . . to South Norwalk.
Housatonic R. R. . . . . to Stockbridge.
Returning, same route.

THROUGH RATES.

Baltimore, Md. . . . . . . $13 70 | Washington, D. C. $15 70
†Philadelphia, Pa. 9 70

Limited to continuous passage on Housatonic R. R., and not good on Sunday trains over that line.

FORM EX. 982.—STOCKBRIDGE, (BERKSHIRE HILLS) MASS.

Baltimore & Ohio R. R. . . . . to Philadelphia.
Philadelphia & Reading R. R. . . . . to Bound Brook.
Central R. R. of New Jersey . . . . to New York.
New York, New Haven & Hartford R. R. . . . to Bridgeport.
Housatonic R. R. . . . . to Stockbridge.
Returning, same route.

THROUGH RATES.

Baltimore, Md. . . . . . . $14 80 | Washington, D. C. $16 80
†Philadelphia, Pa. 10 80

Limited to continuous passage on Housatonic R. R., and not good on Sunday trains over that line.

STRIBLING SPRINGS, VIRGINIA.

These springs are located in the Shenandoah Mountains, at the western edge of Virginia's famous valley, at an elevation of 1650 feet above tidewater. Besides continued general improvements, including a swimming pool, a few novel features for the entertainment and amusement of guests will be added, such as an eyrie in the pine tops on Buck Hill, and a camp on the summit of Hankey Mountain, at an altitude of 3500 feet, whence may be obtained a grand view of mountain, stream, and valley, and of the sunrise. This camp will be found a great convenience to fishing parties. To the eastward is the wondrously beautiful and fertile valley of the Shenandoah, traversed in all directions by well-built roads which wind their sinuous way in picturesque beauty through cultivated farms and quaint villages so famously portrayed by Porte Crayon, now and then rising to cross quite lofty points, from which far-reaching and resplendent views delight the eager eye.

The healthfulness of this enchanting section has become proverbial, and nowhere, perhaps, would quinine be so likely to sell at a discount as at Stribling Springs. The location of the springs offers no vantage ground whereon malaria can secure a hold, and the absence of this and kindred diseases greatly enhances the value of the springs, not alone to those in search of health, but to lovers of nature, and to devotees of beauty and tranquility.

The mineral springs, situated on the hotel grounds, contain alum, sulphur, and chalybeate waters, the efficacy of which as remedial agents in certain abnormal conditions of the system is already too familiar to the public to need reiteration.

Their value as therapeutical remedies in renovating a reduced system has long since been recognized by the medical faculty, and it is sufficient to bear in mind the wide circle of their application made possible by their alternation and combination under the special conditions indicated.

Each water enumerated is in itself a most potent agent in forms of temporary or chronic physical disease, and each has formed the subject of the most favorable comment by eminent physicians and skillful analysts throughout the country. It is conceded that the close proximity of waters of such varied and valuable properties renders the springs of unusual interest and attractiveness to those seeking the recuperation of injured health in the healing influence of these mountain waters.

Analysis of the waters of Stribling Springs. Made by the analytical chemist, University of Virginia. The table gives the contents, in grains, of an imperial gallon.

Alum Springs.

	No. 1.	No. 2.	No. 3.
Silicic acid	2,512	2,539	2,532
Sulphate of iron	11,117	13,781	15,515
Sulphate of alumina	20,052	21,254	16,020
Sulphate of lime	17,501	20,292	22,950
Sulphate of magnesia	.631	.415	7,880
Sulphate of potassa	.639	1,087	1,200
Sulphate of soda	.700	2,812	2,110
Free sulphuric acid	6,052	11,700	7,841
Organic matter	1,506	...	...
	61,049	76,180	106,170
Specific gravity	1.00	1.001	1.00

Sulphur and Chalybeate Springs.

	CHALYBEATE.		SULPHUR
	No. 1.	No. 3.	No. 2.
Silicic acid	1,325	1,091	.761
Sulphate of lime	.250	3,509	1,494
Carbonate of iron	.091	.136	.149
Carbonate of lime	1,806	1,253	11,559
Carbonate of magnesia	1,173	1,322	2,112
Bicarbonate of soda	1,203	1,701	10,749
Bicarbonate of potassa	.544	1,201	.885
Free carbonic acid	11,175	7,982	5,959
Chloride of sodium	...	...	.770
Sulphuretted hydrogen	...	...	.122
	20,947	18,208	34,908

FORM EX. 515.—STRIBLING SPRINGS, VA., AND RETURN.

Baltimore & Ohio R. R. . . . . to Staunton.
Stage . . . . to Stribling Springs.
Returning, same route.

THROUGH RATES.

Baltimore, Md.	$12 40	Meyersdale, Pa.	$13 70
Bellaire, O.	20 55	Morgantown, W. Va.	18 15
Berkeley Springs, W. Va.	10 25	Moundsville, W. Va.	19 80
Cameron, W. Va.	19 40	Mountain Lake Park, Md.	11 25
Charlestown, W. Va.	7 80	Mt. Pleasant, Pa.	16 40
Chester, Pa.	15 00	Newark, Del.	11 40
Clarksburg, W. Va.	17 15	New York, N. Y.	20 40
Connellsville, Pa.	15 80	Oakland, Md.	11 35
Cumberland, Md.	12 20	Parkersburg, W. Va.	20 20
Deer Park, Md.	11 40	Philadelphia, Pa.	16 40
Fairmont, W. Va.	17 15	Piedmont, W. Va.	13 20
Frederick, Md.	9 35	Pittsburgh, Pa.	18 20
Grafton, W. Va.	16 25	Rockwood, Pa.	11 15
Hagerstown, Md.	9 55	Somerset, Pa.	11 55
Harper's Ferry, W. Va.	8 30	Strasburg, Va.	5 65
Harrisonburg, Va.	3 30	Uniontown, Pa.	16 35
Havre de Grace, Md.	13 55	Washington, D. C.	10 20
Johnstown, Pa.	15 95	Washington, Pa.	19 20
Keyser, W. Va.	13 40	Wheeling, W. Va.	20 30
Lexington, Va.	3 80	Wilmington, Del.	15 40
McKeesport, Pa.	17 65	Winchester, Va.	6 70
Martinsburg, W. Va.	9 05		

FORM EX. 29.—STRIBLING SPRINGS, VA., AND RETURN.

Baltimore & Ohio R. R. . . . . to Shenandoah June.
Norfolk & Western R. R. . . . . to Basic.
Chesapeake & Ohio Ry. . . . . to Staunton.
Stage . . . . to Stribling Springs.
Returning, same route.

THROUGH RATES.

Baltimore, Md.	$12 40	New York, N. Y.	$20 40
Chester, Pa.	15 00	Philadelphia, Pa.	16 40
Havre de Grace, Md.	13 55	Washington, D. C.	10 20
Newark, Del.	11 40	Wilmington, Del.	15 40

SWEET CHALYBEATE SPRINGS, VA.

FORM EX. 50. SWEET CHALYBEATE SPRINGS, VA., AND RETURN.

Baltimore & Ohio R. R. . . . . to Staunton.
Chesapeake & Ohio Ry. . . . . to Alleghany Station.
Stage (9 miles) . . . . to Sweet Chalybeate Springs.
Returning, same route.

THROUGH RATES.

Baltimore, Md.	$16 00	Meyersdale, Pa.	$18 80
Bellaire, O.	25 65	Morgantown, W. Va.	23 25
Berkeley Springs, W. Va.	15 35	Moundsville, W. Va.	24 00
Cameron, W. Va.	24 20	Mountain Lake Park, Md.	19 35
Charlestown, W. Va.	12 90	Mt. Pleasant, Pa.	21 50
Chester, Pa.	19 50	Newark, Del.	18 30
Clarksburg, W. Va.	22 25	New York, N. Y.	21 00
Connellsville, Pa.	21 00	Oakland, Md.	19 45
Cumberland, Md.	17 30	Parkersburg, W. Va.	26 40
Deer Park, Md.	19 50	Philadelphia, Pa.	20 00
Fairmont, W. Va.	22 25	Piedmont, W. Va.	18 40
Frederick, Md.	14 45	Pittsburgh, Pa.	23 30
Grafton, W. Va.	21 35	Rockwood, Pa.	19 25
Hagerstown, Md.	14 15	Somerset, Pa.	19 65
Harper's Ferry, W. Va.	13 40	Strasburg, Va.	10 75
Harrisonburg, Va.	8 40	Uniontown, Pa.	21 45
Havre de Grace, Md.	17 45	Washington, D. C.	14 00
Johnstown, Pa.	21 05	Washington, Pa.	24 40
Keyser, W. Va.	18 20	Wheeling, W. Va.	25 10
Lexington, Va.	8 90	Wilmington, Del.	19 00
McKeesport, Pa.	22 75	Winchester, Va.	11 80
Martinsburg, W. Va.	14 15		

FORM EX. 73. SWEET CHALYBEATE SPRINGS, VA., AND RETURN.

Baltimore & Ohio R. R. . . . . to Shenandoah June.
Norfolk & Western R. R. . . . . to Basic.
Chesapeake & Ohio Ry. . . . . to Alleghany Station.
Stage (9 miles) . . . . to Sweet Chalybeate Springs.
Returning, same route.

THROUGH RATES.

Baltimore, Md.	$16 00	New York, N. Y.	$24 00
Chester, Pa.	19 50	Philadelphia, Pa.	20 00
Havre de Grace, Md.	17 15	Washington, D. C.	14 00
Newark, Del.	18 50	Wilmington, Del.	19 00

FORM EX. 130.—SWEET CHALYBEATE SPRINGS, VA., AND RETURN.

Baltimore & Ohio R. R.	. . . to Washington.
Transfer	B. & O. to C. & O. Depot.
Chesapeake & Ohio Ry.	to Alleghany Station.
Stage (9 miles)	to Sweet Chalybeate Springs

Returning, same route.

THROUGH RATES.

Baltimore, Md.	$16 00	Meyersdale, Pa.	22 10
Bellaire, O.	28 95	Morgantown, W. Va.	26 35
Berkeley Springs, W. Va.	18 65	Moundsville, W. Va.	28 30
Cameron, W. Va.	27 50	Mountain Lake Park, Md.	22 15
Charlestown, W. Va.	17 20	Mt. Pleasant, Pa.	24 80
Chester, Pa.	19 50	Newark, Del.	18 50
Clarksburg, W. Va.	25 35	New York, N. Y.	24 00
Connellsville, Pa.	24 20	Oakland, Md.	22 25
Cumberland, Md.	20 60	Parkersburg, W. Va.	28 65
Deer Park, Md.	22 00	Philadelphia, Pa.	20 00
Fairmont, W. Va.	25 35	Piedmont, W. Va.	21 70
Frederick, Md.	16 80	Pittsburgh, Pa.	26 00
Grafton, W. Va.	24 65	Rockwood, Pa.	22 55
Hagerstown, Md.	17 60	Somerset, Pa.	22 95
Harper's Ferry, W. Va.	16 70	Uniontown, Pa.	24 75
Havre de Grace, Md.	17 15	Washington, D. C.	27 70
Johnstown, Pa.	24 35	Wheeling, W. Va.	28 65
Keyser, W. Va.	21 50	Wilmington, Del.	19 00
McKeesport, Pa.	26 05	Winchester, Va.	18 30
Martinsburg, W. Va.	17 15		

SWEET SPRINGS, W. VA.

The location of Sweet Springs is in a more open country than is generally the rule in mountain districts. The springs themselves flow from a valley of surpassing loveliness and fertility, surrounded by mountain scenery of wondrous beauty. The water is powerfully tonic, diuretic, mildly cathartic, and alterative. As a tonic it is applicable to all cases of debility, general or local, and to many forms of dyspepsia, and cases of functional disease of the stomach and bowels. In cases of chronic diarrhœa and dysentery it is often used with signal benefit. In rheumatic and neuralgic affections, in diseases of the kidneys and urinary passages, and in calculus affections it stands probably without a rival. In amenorrhœa and the diseases peculiar to females, the happiest results are frequently obtained. There are many other diseased conditions to which the waters are applicable which the limits of a brief notice prevent enumerating.

The high standard of the cuisine which the Sweet Springs Hotel has obtained will be fully maintained in every respect.

ROUTES AND RATES FOR SUMMER TOURS. 325

Visitors are conveyed from the station to the Springs over a smooth and well-graded road, through romantic mountain scenery, in comfortable four-horse Concord coaches. The teams are exceptionally fine, and the drivers polite, careful and experienced. Coaches are always awaiting the arrival of all trains at the Alleghany Station, so that there is no delay in the conveyance of passengers.

FORM EX. 69. SWEET SPRINGS, W. VA., AND RETURN.

Baltimore & Ohio R. R. . . . . to Staunton.
Chesapeake & Ohio Ry. . . . . to Alleghany Station
Stage (10 miles) . . . . to Sweet Springs.
Returning, same route.

THROUGH RATES.

Baltimore, Md.	$16 00	Meyersdale, Pa.	$18 80
Bellaire, O.	25 65	Morgantown, W. Va.	23 25
Berkeley Springs, W. Va.	15 35	Moundsville, W. Va.	24 10
Cameron, W. Va.	24 20	Mountain Lake Park, Md.	19 35
Charlestown, W. Va.	12 10	Mount Pleasant, Pa.	21 00
Chester, Pa.	19 70	Newark, Del.	18 30
Clarksburg, W. Va.	22 25	New York, N. Y.	24 00
Connellsville, Pa.	21 00	Oakland, Md.	19 45
Cumberland, Md.	17 30	Parkersburg, W. Va.	25 10
Deer Park, Md.	19 20	Philadelphia, Pa.	20 00
Fairmont, W. Va.	22 25	Piedmont, W. Va.	18 50
Frederick, Md.	14 45	Pittsburgh, Pa.	23 30
Grafton, W. Va.	21 35	Rockwood, Pa.	19 25
Hagerstown, Md.	14 45	Somerset, Pa.	19 65
Harper's Ferry, W. Va.	13 10	Strasburg, Va.	10 75
Harrisonburg, Va.	8 10	Uniontown, Pa.	21 65
Havre de Grace, Md.	17 45	Washington, D. C.	14 00
Johnstown, Pa.	21 05	Washington, Pa.	24 40
Keyser, W. Va.	18 20	Wheeling, W. Va.	25 40
Lexington, Va.	8 40	Wilmington, Del.	19 00
McKeesport, Pa.	22 75	Winchester, Va.	11 80
Martinsburg, W. Va.	14 45		

FORM EX. 72. SWEET SPRINGS, W. VA., AND RETURN.

Baltimore & Ohio R. R. . . . . to Shenandoah June.
Norfolk & Western R. R. . . . . to Basic.
Chesapeake & Ohio Ry. . . . . to Alleghany Station.
Stage (10 miles) . . . . to Sweet Springs.
Returning, same route.

THROUGH RATES.

Baltimore, Md.	$16 00	New York, N. Y.	$24 00
Chester, Pa.	19 50	Philadelphia, Pa.	20 00
Havre de Grace, Md.	17 45	Washington, D. C.	14 00
Newark, Del.	18 30	Wilmington, Del.	19 00

FORM EX. 128. SWEET SPRINGS, W. VA., AND RETURN.

Baltimore & Ohio R. R. . . . . to Washington.
Transfer . . . . B. & O. Depot to C. & O. Depot.
Chesapeake & Ohio R. R. . . . . to Alleghany.
Stage (10 miles) . . . . to Sweet Springs.
Returning, same route.

THROUGH RATES.

Baltimore, Md.	$16 00	Meyersdale, Pa.	$22 10
Bellaire, O.	28 95	Morgantown, W. Va.	26 55
Berkeley Springs, W. Va.	18 65	Moundsville, W. Va.	28 20
Cameron, W. Va.	27 50	Mountain Lake Park, Md.	22 15
Charlestown, W. Va.	17 20	Mt. Pleasant, Pa.	24 80
Chester, Pa.	19 50	Newark, Del.	18 20
Clarksburg, W. Va.	25 55	New York, N. Y.	24 00
Connellsville, Pa.	24 50	Oakland, Md.	22 25
Cumberland, Md.	20 02	Parkersburg, W. Va.	28 65
Deer Park, Md.	22 00	Philadelphia, Pa.	20 00
Fairmont, W. Va.	25 55	Piedmont, W. Va.	21 70
Frederick, Md.	16 80	Pittsburgh, Pa.	26 00
Grafton, W. Va.	24 65	Rockwood, Pa.	22 55
Hagerstown, Md.	17 60	Somerset, Pa.	22 95
Harper's Ferry, W. Va.	16 70	Uniontown, Pa.	24 75
Havre de Grace, Md.	17 45	Washington, Pa.	27 70
Johnstown, Pa.	24 55	Wheeling, W. Va.	28 65
Keyser, W. Va.	21 50	Wilmington, Del.	19 00
McKeesport, Pa.	25 05	Winchester, Va.	18 20
Martinsburg, W. Va.	17 45		

SWITCHBACK, PA.

"The Switchback" is a gravity road running from Mauch Chunk to Summit Hill and return, a distance of eighteen miles, in the heart of the coal regions of Pennsylvania, "The Switzerland of America."

The scenery in this section is well worthy of note. Mauch Chunk itself is hid from view among the mountains, and bursts on one's sight like a picture from which the curtain is suddenly lifted, adding an additional charm to this picturesque mountain city.

Glen Onoko, about two miles distant, is a perfect gem, and the tourist should not leave this enchanting region without paying it a visit.

FORM EX. 326. SWITCHBACK, PA., AND RETURN.

Baltimore & Ohio R. R.	to Philadelphia.
Philadelphia & Reading R. R.	to Bethlehem.
Lehigh Valley R. R.	to Mauch Chunk.
Switchback R. R.	to Summit Hill.

Returning, same route.

THROUGH RATES.

Baltimore, Md.	$8 50	Washington, D. C.	$10 50
Philadelphia, Pa.	4 50		

Transfer through Mauch Chunk 25 cents in each direction.

GLEN ONOKO.

ONAL VISTA

FORM EX. 604. SWITCHBACK, PA., AND RETURN.

Baltimore & Ohio R. R. . . . . to Philadelphia.
Philadelphia & Reading R. R. . . . . to Bethlehem.
Central R. R. of New Jersey . . . . to Mauch Chunk.
Switchback R. R. . . . . to Summit Hill.

Returning, same route.

THROUGH RATES.

Baltimore, Md. . . . . $8 50 | Washington, D. C. $10 50
Philadelphia, Pa. 4 50

Transfer through Mauch Chunk 25 cents in each direction.

TWIN MOUNTAIN HOUSE, N. H.

Form Ex. 1086.—Twin Mountain House, N. H., and Return.

(Via rail and Boston; returning via Boston and Sound Lines.)

Baltimore & Ohio R. R. . . . . to Philadelphia.
Rail Lines (see pages 50 to 55 for routes) . . . to Boston.
Boston & Maine R. R. . . . . to North Conway.
Maine Central R. R. . . . . to Twin Mountain House.
Maine Central R. R. . . . . to North Conway.
Boston & Maine R. R. . . . . to Boston.
Sound Lines (see pages 50 to 55 for routes) . . . to New York.
Central R. R. of New Jersey . . . . to Bound Brook.
Philadelphia & Reading R. R. . . . . to Philadelphia.
Baltimore & Ohio R. R. . . . . to starting point.

THROUGH RATES.

Baltimore, Md. . . . . . . $26 10 | Washington, D. C. $28 10
{Philadelphia, Pa. 22 10

Transfer through Boston, returning, included.

Form Ex. 1086.—Twin Mountain House, N. H., and Return.

(Via Sound Lines and Boston; returning via Boston, all rail.)

Baltimore & Ohio R. R. . . . . to Philadelphia.
Philadelphia & Reading R. R. . . . . to Bound Brook.
Central R. R. of New Jersey . . . . to New York.
Sound Lines (see pages 50 to 55 for routes) . . to Boston.
Boston & Maine R. R. . . . . to North Conway.
Maine Central R. R. . . . . to Twin Mountain House.
Maine Central R. R. . . . . to North Conway.
Boston & Maine R. R. . . . . to Boston.
Rail Lines (see pages 50 to 55 for routes) . . . to Philadelphia.
Baltimore & Ohio R. R. . . . . to starting point.

THROUGH RATES.

Baltimore, Md. . . . . . . $26 10 | Washington, D. C. $28 10
{Philadelphia, Pa. 22 10

Transfer through Boston, going, included.

Form Ex. 1086.—Twin Mountain House, N. H., and Return.

(Via Rail Lines and Boston in both directions.)

Baltimore & Ohio R. R. . . . . to Philadelphia.
Rail Lines (see pages 50 to 55 for routes) . . . to Boston.
Boston & Maine R. R. . . . . to North Conway.
Maine Central R. R. . . . . to Twin Mountain House.

Returning, same route.

THROUGH RATES.

Baltimore, Md. . . . . . . $27 75 | Washington, D. C. $29 75
{Philadelphia, Pa. 23 75

Form Ex. 1086.—Twin Mountain House, N. H., and Return.

(Via Sound Lines and Boston in both directions.)

Baltimore & Ohio R. R. . . . . to Philadelphia.
Philadelphia & Reading R. R. . . . . to Bound Brook.
Central R. R. of New Jersey . . . . to New York.
Sound Lines (see pages 50 to 55 for routes) . . to Boston.
Boston & Maine R. R. . . . . to North Conway.
Maine Central R. R. . . . . to Twin Mountain House.

Returning, same route.

THROUGH RATES.

Baltimore, Md. . . . . . . $23 00 | Washington, D. C. $25 00
{Philadelphia, Pa. 19 00

Transfer through Boston, in both directions, included.

FORM EX. 1087.—TWIN MOUNTAIN HOUSE, N. H., AND RETURN.
(Via rail and Boston; returning via Boston and Sound Lines.)

Baltimore & Ohio R. R. . . . . to Philadelphia,
Rail Lines (see pages 50 to 55 for routes) . . to Boston,
Boston & Maine R. R. . . . . to Portland,
Maine Central R. R. . . . . to Twin Mountain House,
Maine Central R. R. . . . . to Portland,
Boston & Maine R. R. . . . . to Boston,
Sound Lines (see pages 50 to 55 for routes) . . to New York,
Central R. R. of New Jersey . . . . to Bound Brook,
Philadelphia & Reading R. R. . . . . to Philadelphia,
Baltimore & Ohio R. R. . . . . to starting point.

THROUGH RATES.

Baltimore, Md. . . . . . . $26 10   Washington, D. C. $28 10
†Philadelphia, Pa. 22 10

Transfer through Boston, returning, included.

FORM EX. 1087.—TWIN MOUNTAIN HOUSE, N. H., AND RETURN.
(Via Sound Lines and Boston; returning via Boston, all rail.)

Baltimore & Ohio R. R. . . . . to Philadelphia,
Philadelphia & Reading R. R. . . . . to Bound Brook,
Central R. R. of New Jersey . . . . to New York,
Sound Lines (see pages 50 to 55 for routes) . . to Boston,
Boston & Maine R. R. . . . . to Portland,
Maine Central R. R. . . . . to Twin Mountain House,
Maine Central R. R. . . . . to Portland,
Boston & Maine R. R. . . . . to Boston,
Rail Lines (see pages 50 to 55 for routes) . . to Philadelphia,
Baltimore & Ohio R. R. . . . . to starting point.

THROUGH RATES.

Baltimore, Md. . . . . . . $26 10   Washington, D. C. $28 10
†Philadelphia, Pa. 22 10

Transfer through Boston, going, included.

FORM EX. 1087.—TWIN MOUNTAIN HOUSE, N. H., AND RETURN.
(Via Rail Lines and Boston in both directions.)

Baltimore & Ohio R. R. . . . . to Philadelphia,
Rail Lines (see pages 50 to 55 for routes) . . to Boston,
Boston & Maine R. R. . . . . to Portland,
Maine Central R. R. . . . . to Twin Mountain House,
Returning, same route.

THROUGH RATES.

Baltimore, Md. . . . . . . $27 75   Washington, D. C. $29 75
†Philadelphia, Pa. 23 75

FORM EX. 1087.—TWIN MOUNTAIN HOUSE, N. H., AND RETURN.
(Via Sound Lines and Boston in both directions.)

Baltimore & Ohio R. R. . . . . to Philadelphia,
Philadelphia & Reading R. R. . . . . to Bound Brook,
Central R. R. of New Jersey . . . . to New York,
Sound Lines (see pages 50 to 55 for routes) . . to Boston,
Boston & Maine R. R. . . . . to Portland,
Maine Central R. R. . . . . to Twin Mountain House,
Returning, same route.

THROUGH RATES.

Baltimore, Md. . . . . . . $23 00   Washington, D. C. $25 00
†Philadelphia, Pa. 19 00

Transfer through Boston, in both directions, included.

ROUTES AND RATES FOR SUMMER TOURS.   334

FORM EX. 108S.—TWIN MOUNTAIN HOUSE, N. H., AND RETURN.
(Via rail and Boston; returning via Boston and Sound Lines.)

Baltimore & Ohio R. R. . . . . to Philadelphia.
Rail Lines (see pages 50 to 55 for routes) . . . to Boston.
Boston & Maine R. R. . . . . to Nashua.
Concord & Montreal R. R. . . . . to Twin Mountain House.
Concord & Montreal R. R. . . . . to Nashua.
Boston & Maine R. R. . . . . to Boston.
Sound Lines (see pages 50 to 55 for routes) . . to New York.
Central R. R. of New Jersey . . . . to Bound Brook.
Philadelphia & Reading R. R. . . . . to Philadelphia.
Baltimore & Ohio R. R. . . . . to starting point.

THROUGH RATES.

Baltimore, Md. . . . . . . $25 85 | Washington, D. C. $27 85
†Philadelphia, Pa. 24 85

Transfer through Boston, returning, included.

FORM EX. 108S.—TWIN MOUNTAIN HOUSE, N. H., AND RETURN.
(Via Sound Lines and Boston; returning via Boston, all rail.)

Baltimore & Ohio R. R. . . . . to Philadelphia.
Philadelphia & Reading R. R. . . . . to Bound Brook.
Central R. R. of New Jersey . . . . to New York.
Sound Lines (see pages 50 to 55 for routes) . . to Boston.
Boston & Maine R. R. . . . . to Nashua.
Concord & Montreal R. R. . . . . to Twin Mountain House.
Concord & Montreal R. R. . . . . to Nashua.
Boston & Maine R. R. . . . . to Boston.
Rail Lines (see pages 50 to 55 for routes) . . . to Philadelphia.
Baltimore & Ohio R. R. . . . . to starting point.

THROUGH RATES.

Baltimore, Md. . . . . . . $25 85 | Washington, D. C. $27 85
†Philadelphia, Pa. 24 85

Transfer through Boston, going, included.

FORM EX. 108S.—TWIN MOUNTAIN HOUSE, N. H., AND RETURN.
(Via Rail Lines and Boston in both directions.)

Baltimore & Ohio R. R. . . . . to Philadelphia.
Rail Lines (see pages 50 to 55 for routes) . . . to Boston.
Boston & Maine R. R. . . . . to Nashua.
Concord & Montreal R. R. . . . . to Twin Mountain House.
Returning, same route.

THROUGH RATES.

Baltimore, Md. . . . . . . $27 75 | Washington, D. C. $29 75
†Philadelphia, Pa. 26 75

FORM EX. 108S.—TWIN MOUNTAIN HOUSE, N. H., AND RETURN.
(Via Sound Lines and Boston in both directions.)

Baltimore & Ohio R. R. . . . . to Philadelphia.
Philadelphia & Reading R. R. . . . . to Bound Brook.
Central R. R. of New Jersey . . . . to New York.
Sound Lines (see pages 50 to 55 for routes) . . to Boston.
Boston & Maine R. R. . . . . to Nashua.
Concord & Montreal R. R. . . . . to Twin Mountain House.
Returning, same route.

THROUGH RATES.

Baltimore, Md. . . . . . . $22 50 | Washington, D. C. $24 50
†Philadelphia, Pa. 18 50

Transfer through Boston, in both directions, included.

VALLEY VIEW SPRINGS, VA.

Form Ex. 1874. Valley View Springs, Va., and Return.

Baltimore & Ohio R. R. . . . . to New Market.
Stage . . . . to Valley View Springs.
Returning, same route.

THROUGH RATES.

Baltimore, Md.	$9 85	Meyersdale, Pa.	$11 15
Bellaire, O.	18 30	Morgantown, W. Va.	15 90
Berkeley Springs, W. Va.	8 00	Moundsville, W. Va.	17 55
Cameron, W. Va.	16 85	Mountain Lake Park, Md.	12 00
Charlestown, W. Va.	5 55	Mt. Pleasant, Pa.	11 15
Chester, Pa.	13 55	Newark, Del.	12 15
Clarksburg, W. Va.	14 90	New York, N. Y.	17 85
Connellsville, Pa.	13 65	Oakland, Md.	12 40
Cumberland, Md.	9 95	Parkersburg, W. Va.	18 05
Deer Park, Md.	11 85	Philadelphia, Pa.	13 85
Fairmont, W. Va.	14 90	Piedmont, W. Va.	11 05
Frederick, Md.	7 40	Pittsburgh, Pa.	15 95
Grafton, W. Va.	14 00	Rockwood, Pa.	11 50
Hagerstown, Md.	7 10	Somerset, Pa.	12 30
Harper's Ferry, W. Va.	6 05	Staunton, Va.	1 25
Harrisonburg, Va.	2 95	Strasburg, Va.	3 55
Havre de Grace, Md.	11 20	Uniontown, Pa.	11 10
Johnstown, Pa.	13 70	Washington, D. C.	8 25
Keyser, W. Va.	10 85	Washington, Pa.	17 05
Lexington, Va.	6 05	Wheeling, W. Va.	18 05
McKeesport, Pa.	15 40	Wilmington, Del.	12 85
Martinsburg, W. Va.	6 80	Winchester, Va.	4 45

VIRGINIA BEACH, VA.

Form Ex. 860. Virginia Beach, Va.
Limited to six (6) months from date of sale.

Baltimore & Ohio R. R. . . . . to Washington.
Knox Transfer Co. . . . . B. & O. R. R. Depot to Norfolk & Washington, D. C., Steamboat Co.'s Wharf.
Norfolk & Washington, D. C., Steamboat Company . . . . to Norfolk.
Norfolk & Portsmouth Transfer Co., N. & W. D. C. S. Co.'s Wharf to N., A. & A. R. R. Depot.
Norfolk, Albemarle & Atlantic R. R. . . to Virginia Beach.
Returning, same route.

THROUGH RATES.

Baltimore, Md.	$7 25	Meyersdale, Pa.	$13 85
Bellaire, O.	20 70	Morgantown, W. Va.	18 30
Berkeley Springs, W. Va.	10 40	Moundsville, W. Va.	19 95
Cameron, W. Va.	19 25	Mountain Lake Park, Md.	13 40
Charlestown, W. Va.	8 95	Mt. Pleasant, Pa.	16 55
Chester, Pa.	9 75	Newark, Del.	8 55
Clarksburg, W. Va.	17 30	New York, N. Y.	14 25
Connellsville, Pa.	16 05	Oakland, Md.	14 00
Cumberland, Md.	12 35	Parkersburg, W. Va.	20 40
Deer Park, Md.	13 75	Philadelphia, Pa.	10 25
Fairmont, W. Va.	17 30	Piedmont, W. Va.	13 45
Frederick, Md.	8 55	Pittsburgh, Pa.	18 35
Grafton, W. Va.	16 40	Rockwood, Pa.	14 30
Hagerstown, Md.	9 55	Somerset, Pa.	14 70
Harper's Ferry, W. Va.	8 45	Uniontown, Pa.	16 50
Havre de Grace, Md.	7 70	Washington, Pa.	19 45
Johnstown, Pa.	16 10	Wheeling, W. Va.	20 40
Keyser, W. Va.	13 25	Wilmington, Del.	9 25
McKeesport, Pa.	17 80	Winchester, Va.	10 05
Martinsburg, W. Va.	9 20		

FORM EX. 758.—VIRGINIA BEACH, VA.

Limited to six (6) months from date of sale.

Baltimore & Ohio R. R. . . . . to Baltimore.
Baltimore Steam Packet Co. . . . . to Norfolk.
Norfolk, Albemarle & Atlantic R. R. . . . . . . to Virginia Beach.

Returning, same route.

THROUGH RATES.

Bellaire, O.	$21 80	Morgantown, W. Va.	$19 10
Berkeley Springs, W. Va.	11 50	Moundsville, W. Va.	20 15
Cameron, W. Va.	20 35	Mountain Lake Park, Md.	11 90
Charlestown, W. Va.	10 05	Mt. Pleasant, Pa.	17 65
Chester, Pa.	9 25	Newark, Del.	8 05
Clarksburg, W. Va.	18 10	New York, N. Y.	13 75
Connellsville, Pa.	17 15	Oakland, Md.	15 00
Cumberland, Md.	13 15	Parkersburg, W. Va.	21 50
Deer Park, Md.	14 75	Philadelphia, Pa.	9 75
Fairmont, W. Va.	18 35	Piedmont, W. Va.	14 55
Frederick, Md.	8 20	Pittsburgh, Pa.	19 15
Grafton, W. Va.	17 50	Rockwood, Pa.	15 10
Hagerstown, Md.	10 25	Somerset, Pa.	15 80
Harper's Ferry, W. Va.	9 55	Strasburg, Va.	12 20
Harrisonburg, Va.	14 55	Uniontown, Pa.	17 60
Havre de Grace, Md.	7 20	Washington, D. C.	7 75
Johnstown, Pa.	17 20	Washington, Pa.	20 55
Keyser, W. Va.	14 35	Wheeling, W. Va.	21 50
McKeesport, Pa.	18 90	Wilmington, Del.	8 75
Martinsburg, W. Va.	10 40	Winchester, Va.	11 15
Meyersdale, Pa.	14 35		

FORM EX. 694.—VIRGINIA BEACH, VA.

Limited to six (6) months from date of sale.

Baltimore Steam Packet Co., Old Point Comfort, to Norfolk.
Norfolk, Albemarle & Atlantic R. R. . . . . . . to Virginia Beach.

Returning, same route.

Transfer through Norfolk included.

To be sold only in connection with Summer Excursion Tickets passing through or terminating at Old Point Comfort, Va.

Rate $1 75

WARM SPRINGS, VA.

FORM EX. 71.—WARM SPRINGS, VA., AND RETURN.

Baltimore & Ohio R. R. . . . . to Shenandoah June.
Norfolk & Western R. R. . . . . to Basic.
Chesapeake & Ohio Ry. . . . . to Hot Springs.
Stage Line . . . . to Warm Springs.

Returning, same route.

THROUGH RATES.

Baltimore, Md.	$18 00	New York, N. Y.	$26 00
Chester, Pa.	21 50	Philadelphia, Pa.	22 00
Havre de Grace, Md.	19 15	Washington, D. C.	16 00
Newark, Del.	20 50	Wilmington, Del.	21 00

FORM EX. 80.—WARM SPRINGS, VA., AND RETURN.

Baltimore & Ohio R. R. . . . . to Staunton.
Transfer . . . . B. & O. R. R. Depot to C. & O. R. R. Depot.
Chesapeake & Ohio Ry. . . . . to Hot Springs.
Stage Line . . . . to Warm Springs.

Returning, same route.

WARM SPRINGS.

ROUND TRIP RATES.

Baltimore, Md.	$18 00		Meyersdale, Pa.	$20 40
Bellaire, O.	27 25		Morgantown, W. Va.	24 85
Berkeley Springs, W. Va.	16 95		Moundsville, W. Va.	26 70
Cameron, W. Va.	25 80		Mountain Lake Park, Md.	20 95
Charlestown, W. Va.	14 50		Mt. Pleasant, Pa.	23 40
Chester, Pa.	24 50		Newark, Del.	20 30
Clarksburg, W. Va.	23 85		New York, N. Y.	26 00
Connellsville, Pa.	22 60		Oakland, Md.	24 05
Cumberland, Md.	18 90		Parkersburg, W. Va.	27 00
Deer Park, Md.	20 80		Philadelphia, Pa.	22 00
Fairmont, W. Va.	23 85		Piedmont, W. Va.	20 00
Frederick, Md.	16 05		Pittsburgh, Pa.	24 90
Grafton, W. Va.	22 95		Rockwood, Pa.	20 85
Hagerstown, Md.	16 05		Somerset, Pa.	21 25
Harper's Ferry, W. Va.	15 00		Strasburg, Va.	12 35
Harrisonburg, Va.	10 00		Uniontown, Pa.	23 05
Havre de Grace, Md.	19 45		Washington, D. C.	16 00
Johnstown, Pa.	22 65		Washington, Pa.	26 00
Keyser, W. Va.	19 80		Wheeling, W. Va.	27 00
Lexington, Va.	10 50		Wilmington, Del.	21 00
McKeesport, Pa.	24 35		Winchester, Va.	13 40
Martinsburg, W. Va.	15 75			

FORM EX. 623. WARM SPRINGS, VA., AND RETURN.

Baltimore & Ohio R. R.	to Washington.
Transfer	B. & O. R. R. Depot to C. & O. R. R. Depot.
Chesapeake & Ohio Ry.	to Hot Springs.
Stage Line	to Warm Springs.

Returning, same route.

THROUGH RATES.

Baltimore, Md.	$18 00	New York, N. Y.	$25 00
Chester, Pa.	21 50	Philadelphia, Pa.	22 00
Havre de Grace, Md.	19 45	Wilmington, Del.	21 00
Newark, Del.	20 50		

WATCH HILL, R. I.

FORM EX. 725. WATCH HILL, R. I., AND RETURN.

Baltimore & Ohio R. R.	to Philadelphia.
Philadelphia & Reading R. R.	to Bound Brook.
Central R. R. of New Jersey	to New York.
Norwich Line	to New London.
Steamer	to Watch Hill.

Returning, same route.

THROUGH RATES.

Baltimore, Md.	$11 40	Washington, D. C.	$13 40
Philadelphia, Pa.	7 40		

FORM EX. 725. WATCH HILL, R. I., AND RETURN.

Baltimore & Ohio R. R.	to Philadelphia.
Philadelphia & Reading R. R.	to Bound Brook.
Central R. R. of New Jersey	to New York.
Stonington Line	to Stonington.
Steamer	to Watch Hill.

Returning, same route.

THROUGH RATES.

Baltimore, Md.	$11 40	Washington, D. C.	$13 40
Philadelphia, Pa.	7 40		

FORM EX. 724. WATCH HILL, R. I., AND RETURN.

Baltimore & Ohio R. R.	to Philadelphia.
Philadelphia & Reading R. R.	to Bound Brook.
Central R. R. of New Jersey	to New York.
New York, New Haven & Hartford R. R.	to New London.
Steamer	to Watch Hill.

Returning, same route.

THROUGH RATES.

Baltimore, Md.	$14 35	Washington, D. C.	$16 35
Philadelphia, Pa.	10 35		

WATKINS GLEN, N. Y.

The lovely village of Watkins, at the head of Seneca Lake, is the Mecca of a vast pilgrimage of those who halt here to explore its peerless glen. This remarkable canyon—a water-worn rift in the mountain-side—is entered from its lower portals, just at the head of the village. The coaches of the several hotels of the place are always at the landing upon the arrival of boats.

The many picturesque features of Watkins Glen have been described by a thousand pens. "T were a pity that any one passing through this region, to whom the glen is not familiar, should go from Seneca Lake without having set foot in this temple of Nature's handiwork. The glen may be "done," with a good pair of lungs and equally good legs, in a couple of hours. It *ought* to occupy one a full day.

FORM EX. 551.— WATKINS, N. Y., AND RETURN.

Baltimore & Ohio R. R. . . . . to Philadelphia.
Philadelphia & Reading R. R. . . . . to Bound Brook.
Central R. R. of New Jersey . . . . to New York.
New York Central & Hudson River R. R. . . . to Geneva.
Fall Brook Coal Co. R. R. . . . . to Watkins.
Returning, same route.

THROUGH RATES.

Baltimore, Md. . . . . . . $21 00 | Washington, D. C. . . . $23 00
Philadelphia, Pa. . . . . . 17 00 |

FORM EX. 552.— WATKINS, N. Y., AND RETURN.

Baltimore & Ohio R. R. . . . . to Philadelphia.
Philadelphia & Reading R. R. . . . . to Bound Brook.
Central R. R. of New Jersey . . . . to New York.
West Shore R. R. . . . . to Syracuse.
New York Central & Hudson River R. R. . . . to Geneva.
Fall Brook Coal Co. R. R. . . . . to Watkins.
Returning, same route.
Transfer through New York, in both directions, included.

THROUGH RATES.

Baltimore, Md. . . . . . . $21 00 | Washington, D. C. . . . $23 00
Philadelphia, Pa. . . . . . 17 00 |

FORM EX. 553.— WATKINS, N. Y., AND RETURN.

Baltimore & Ohio R. R. . . . . to Philadelphia.
Philadelphia & Reading R. R. . . . . to Bound Brook.
Central R. R. of New Jersey . . . . to New York.
New York Central & Hudson River R. R. . . . to Geneva.
Seneca Lake Steam Navigation Co. . . . . . . to Watkins.
Returning, same route.

THROUGH RATES.

Baltimore, Md. . . . . . . $21 00 | Washington, D. C. . . . $23 00
Philadelphia, Pa. . . . . . 17 00 |

WATKINS GLEN.

FORM EX. 602.—WATKINS, N. Y., AND RETURN.

Baltimore & Ohio R. R. . . . . to Philadelphia.
Philadelphia & Reading R. R. . . . . to Bethlehem.
Lehigh Valley R. R. . . . . to Waverly.
New York, Lake Erie & Western R. R. . . . . to Elmira.
Pennsylvania R. R. . . . . to Watkins.

Returning, same route.

THROUGH RATES.

Baltimore, Md. . . . . . $13 15 | Washington, D. C. . . . $15 15
†Philadelphia, Pa. . . . 11 60 |

FORM EX. 603.—WATKINS, N. Y., AND RETURN.

Baltimore & Ohio R. R. . . . . to Philadelphia.
Philadelphia & Reading R. R. . . . . to Williamsport.
Pennsylvania R. R. . . . . to Watkins.

Returning, same route.

THROUGH RATES.

Baltimore, Md. . . . . . $13 15 | Washington, D. C. . . . $15 15
†Philadelphia, Pa. . . . 11 60 |

FORM EX. 604.—WATKINS, N. Y., AND RETURN.

Baltimore & Ohio R. R. . . . . to Philadelphia.
Philadelphia & Reading R. R. . . . . to Williamsport.
Fall Brook Coal Co. R. R. . . . . to Watkins Glen.
Stage . . . . to Watkins.

Returning, same route.

THROUGH RATES.

Baltimore, Md. . . . . . $13 15 | Washington, D. C. . . . $15 15
†Philadelphia, Pa. . . . 11 60 |

FORM EX. 605.—WATKINS, N. Y., AND RETURN.

Baltimore & Ohio R. R. . . . . to Philadelphia.
Philadelphia & Reading R. R. . . . . to Bethlehem.
Lehigh Valley R. R. . . . . to Waverly.
New York, Lake Erie & Western R. R. . . . . to Elmira.
Pennsylvania R. R. . . . . to Watkins.
Pennsylvania R. R. . . . . to Williamsport.
Philadelphia & Reading R. R. . . . . to Philadelphia.
Baltimore & Ohio R. R. . . . . to starting point.

THROUGH RATES.

Baltimore, Md. . . . . . $17 40 | Washington, D. C. . . . $19 40
†Philadelphia, Pa. . . . 13 40 |

FORM EX. 606.—WATKINS, N. Y., AND RETURN.

Baltimore & Ohio R. R. . . . . to Philadelphia.
Philadelphia & Reading R. R. . . . . to Williamsport.
Pennsylvania R. R. . . . . to Watkins.
Pennsylvania R. R. . . . . to Elmira.
New York, Lake Erie & Western R. R. . . . . to Waverly.
Lehigh Valley R. R. . . . . to Bethlehem.
Philadelphia & Reading R. R. . . . . to Philadelphia.
Baltimore & Ohio R. R. . . . . to starting point.

THROUGH RATES.

Baltimore, Md. . . . . . $17 40 | Washington, D. C. . . . $19 40
†Philadelphia, Pa. . . . 13 40 |

FORM EX. 007.—WATKINS, N. Y., AND RETURN.

Baltimore & Ohio R. R.	to Philadelphia.
Philadelphia & Reading R. R.	to Bethlehem.
Lehigh Valley R. R.	to Waverly.
New York, Lake Erie & Western R. R.	to Elmira.
Pennsylvania R. R.	to Watkins.
Pennsylvania R. R.	to Elmira.
New York, Lake Erie & Western R. R.	to New York.
Central R. R. of New Jersey	to Bound Brook.
Philadelphia & Reading R. R.	to Philadelphia.
Baltimore & Ohio R. R.	to starting point.

THROUGH RATES.

Baltimore, Md.	$19 00	Washington, D. C.	$21 00
Philadelphia, Pa.	15 00		

The following forms of tickets, reading Geneva to Watkins and return, are to be issued in connection with forms of summer excursion tickets passing through or terminating at Geneva, N. Y., as a side trip, at rates quoted:

FORM EX. 398.—GENEVA TO WATKINS, N. Y., AND RETURN.

Fall Brook Coal Co. R. R.	to Watkins.
Fall Brook Coal Co. R. R.	to Geneva.
Rate from Geneva	$1 50

FORM EX. 399.—GENEVA TO WATKINS, N. Y., AND RETURN.

Seneca Lake Steam Navigation Co.	to Watkins.
Seneca Lake Steam Navigation Co.	to Geneva.
Rate from Geneva	$1 25

WAYNESVILLE, N. C.

FORM EX. 12.—WAYNESVILLE, N. C., AND RETURN.

Baltimore & Ohio R. R.	to Washington.
Transfer	B. & O. depot to R. & D. Depot.
Richmond & Danville R. R.	to Waynesville.

Returning, same route.

THROUGH RATES.

Baltimore, Md.	$23 50	Meyersdale, Pa.	$29 00
Bellaire, O.	36 45	Morgantown, W. Va.	31 05
Berkeley Springs, W. Va.	26 15	Mountsville, W. Va.	35 70
Cameron, W. Va.	35 00	Mountain Lake Park, Md.	29 65
Charlestown, W. Va.	24 70	Mt. Pleasant, Pa.	32 20
Chester, Pa.	27 00	Newark, Del.	25 80
Clarksburg, W. Va.	33 00	New York, N. Y.	31 20
Connellsville, Pa.	31 80	Oakland, Md.	29 75
Cumberland, Md.	28 10	Parkersburg, W. Va.	36 15
Deer Park, Md.	29 70	Philadelphia, Pa.	27 70
Fairmont, W. Va.	33 05	Piedmont, W. Va.	29 20
Frederick, Md.	24 30	Pittsburgh, Pa.	31 10
Grafton, W. Va.	32 15	Rockwood, Pa.	30 65
Hagerstown, Md.	25 10	Somerset, Pa.	30 15
Harper's Ferry, W. Va.	24 20	Uniontown, Pa.	32 25
Havre de Grace, Md.	24 95	Washington, Pa.	35 20
Johnstown, Pa.	31 85	Wheeling, W. Va.	36 15
Keyser, W. Va.	30 00	Wilmington, Del.	26 50
McKeesport, Pa.	33 55	Winchester, Va.	25 80
Martinsburg, W. Va.	24 95		

FORM EX. 512.— WAYNESVILLE, N. C., AND RETURN.

Baltimore & Ohio R. R. . . . . to Lexington.
Chesapeake & Ohio R. R. . . . . to Lynchburg.
Richmond & Danville R. R. . . . . to Waynesville.

Returning, same route.

THROUGH RATES.

Baltimore, Md.	$23 50	Morgantown, W. Va.	$31 05
Bellaire, O.	33 45	Moundsville, W. Va.	32 75
Berkeley Springs, W. Va.	23 25	Mountain Lake Park, Md.	27 30
Cameron, W. Va.	32 05	Mt. Pleasant, Pa.	29 50
Charlestown, W. Va.	24 50	Newark, Del.	25 80
Chester, Pa.	27 00	New York, N. Y.	31 50
Clarksburg, W. Va.	30 05	Oakland, Md.	27 30
Connellsville, Pa.	28 80	Parkersburg, W. Va.	32 45
Cumberland, Md.	25 40	Philadelphia, Pa.	27 50
Deer Park, Md.	27 05	Piedmont, W. Va.	26 25
Fairmont, W. Va.	30 05	Pittsburgh, Pa.	31 10
Frederick, Md.	22 45	Rockwood, Pa.	27 05
Grafton, W. Va.	29 45	Somerset, Pa.	27 45
Hagerstown, Md.	21 50	Staunton, Va.	18 80
Harper's Ferry, W. Va.	21 50	Strasburg, Va.	21 50
Harrisonburg, Va.	20 40	Uniontown, Pa.	29 25
Havre de Grace, Md.	24 95	Washington, D. C.	21 50
Johnstown, Pa.	28 85	Washington, Pa.	32 50
Keyser, W. Va.	26 05	Wheeling, W. Va.	33 45
McKeesport, Pa.	30 55	Wilmington, Del.	26 50
Martinsburg, W. Va.	24 95	Winchester, Va.	21 50
Meyersdale, Pa.	26 60		

WERNERSVILLE, PA.

FORM EX. 513. WERNERSVILLE, PA., AND RETURN.

Baltimore & Ohio R. R. to Philadelphia.
Philadelphia & Reading R. R. . . . . to Wernersville.

Returning, same route.

THROUGH RATES.

	Limit.	Rate.		Limit.	Rate.
Baltimore, Md.	11 days	$6 68	*Philadelphia, Pa.	6 days	$2 68
Chester, Pa.	6 days	3 48	Washington, D. C.	11 days	8 68
Havre de Grace, Md.	6 days	5 03	Wilmington, Del.	6 days	3 68
Newark, Del.	6 days	4 48			

WEST END, N. J.

FORM EX. 660. WEST END, N. J., AND RETURN.

Baltimore & Ohio R. R. . . . . to Philadelphia.
Philadelphia & Reading R. R. . . . . to Bound Brook.
Central R. R. of New Jersey . . . . to West End.

Returning, same route.

THROUGH RATES.

Baltimore, Md. . . . . . . $8 00 | Washington, D. C. $10 00
†Philadelphia, Pa. . . . . 1 00 |

In addition to the above, excursion tickets, Form Ex. 660, West End, N. J., may be sold from the following stations at rates as quoted below.
Tickets should be limited with an "L" punch to sixteen (16) days, including day of issue.

THROUGH RATES.

Baltimore, Md. . . . . $7 50 | †Philadelphia, Pa. $3 50
Chester, Pa. . . . . 1 00 | Washington, D. C. 9 50
Havre de Grace, Md. . . . 5 85 | Wilmington, Del. 1 50
Newark, Del. . . . . 5 00 |

WEST OSSIPEE, N. H.

FORM EX. 762. WEST OSSIPEE, N. H., AND RETURN.

(Via Sound Lines and Boston in both directions.)

Baltimore & Ohio R. R. . . . . to Philadelphia.
Philadelphia & Reading R. R. . . . . to Bound Brook.
Central R. R. of New Jersey . . . . to New York.
Sound Lines (see pages 50 to 55 for route) . . . to Boston.
Boston & Maine R. R. . . . . to West Ossipee.

Returning, same route.

THROUGH RATES.

Baltimore, Md. . . . . . . $20 50   Washington, D. C. $22 50
†Philadelphia, Pa. 16 50

FORM EX. 762. WEST OSSIPEE, N. H., AND RETURN.

(Via Rail Lines and Boston in both directions.)

Baltimore & Ohio R. R. . . . . to Philadelphia.
Rail Lines (see pages 50 to 55 for route) . . . . to Boston.
Boston & Maine R. R. . . . . to West Ossipee.

Returning, same route.

THROUGH RATES.

Baltimore, Md. . . . . . . $23 40 | Washington, D. C. $25 40
†Philadelphia, Pa. . . . . 19 40 |

FORM EX. 762. WEST OSSIPEE, N. H., AND RETURN.

(Via Rail Lines and Boston; returning via Boston and Sound Lines.)

Baltimore & Ohio R. R. . . . . to Philadelphia.
Rail Lines (see pages 50 to 55 for route) . . . . to Boston.
Boston & Maine R. R. . . . . to West Ossipee.
Boston & Maine R. R. . . . . to Boston.
Sound Lines (see pages 50 to 55 for route) . . . to New York.
Central R. R. of New Jersey . . . . to Bound Brook.
Philadelphia & Reading R. R. . . . . to Philadelphia.
Baltimore & Ohio R. R. . . . . to starting point.

THROUGH RATES.

Baltimore, Md. . . . . . . $22 50 | Washington, D. C. $24 50
†Philadelphia, Pa. . . . . 18 50 |

FORM EX. 762.—WEST OSSIPEE, N. H., AND RETURN.
(Via Sound Lines and Boston; returning all rail.)

Baltimore & Ohio R. R.	to Philadelphia.
Philadelphia & Reading R. R.	to Bound Brook.
Central R. R. of New Jersey	to New York.
Sound Lines (see pages 50 to 55 for route)	to Boston.
Boston & Maine R. R.	to West Ossipee.
Boston & Maine R. R.	to Boston.
Rail Lines (see pages 50 to 55 for route)	to Philadelphia.
Baltimore & Ohio R. R.	to starting point.

THROUGH RATES.

Baltimore, Md. .... $22.50   Washington, D. C. $24.50
†Philadelphia, Pa. 18.50

WEST POINT, N. Y.

FORM EX. 732.—WEST POINT, N. Y., AND RETURN.

Baltimore & Ohio R. R.	to Philadelphia.
Philadelphia & Reading R. R.	to Bound Brook.
Central R. R. of New Jersey	to New York.
Steamer "Mary Powell"	to West Point.

Returning, same route.

THROUGH RATES.

Baltimore, Md. .... $9.00   Washington, D. C. $11.00
†Philadelphia, Pa. 5.00

FORM EX. 1080.—WEST POINT, N. Y., AND RETURN.

Baltimore & Ohio R. R.	to Philadelphia.
Philadelphia & Reading R. R.	to Bound Brook.
Central R. R. of New Jersey	to New York.
Day Line Steamers	to West Point.

Returning, same route.

THROUGH RATES.

Baltimore, Md. .... $9.00   Washington, D. C. $11.00
†Philadelphia, Pa. 5.00

WHITEFIELD, N. H.

FORM EX. 1094.—WHITEFIELD, N. H., AND RETURN.

(Via rail and Boston; returning by Sound Lines.)

Baltimore & Ohio R. R.	to Philadelphia.
Rail Lines (see pages 50 to 55 for route)	to Boston.
Boston & Maine R. R.	to Nashua.
Concord & Montreal R. R.	to Whitefield.
Concord & Montreal R. R.	to Nashua.
Boston & Maine R. R.	to Boston.
Sound Lines (see pages 50 to 55 for route)	to New York.
Central R. R. of New Jersey	to Bound Brook.
Philadelphia & Reading R. R.	to Philadelphia.
Baltimore & Ohio R. R.	to starting point.

THROUGH RATES.

Baltimore, Md. .... $25.85   Washington, D. C. $27.85
†Philadelphia, Pa. 21.85

Transfer through Boston, returning, included.

344   BALTIMORE & OHIO RAILROAD COMPANY

Form Ex. 1001.—WHITEFIELD, N. H., AND RETURN.
(Via Sound Lines and Boston; returning all rail.)

Baltimore & Ohio R. R.	to Philadelphia.
Philadelphia & Reading R. R.	to Bound Brook.
Central R. R. of New Jersey.	to New York.
Sound Lines (see pages 50 to 55 for route)	to Boston.
Boston & Maine R. R.	to Nashua.
Concord & Montreal R. R.	to Whitefield.
Concord & Montreal R. R.	to Nashua.
Boston & Maine R. R.	to Boston.
Rail Lines (see pages 50 to 55 for route)	to Philadelphia.
Baltimore & Ohio R. R.	to starting point.

THROUGH RATES.

Baltimore, Md. . . . . . $25 85 | Washington, D. C. $27 85
(Philadelphia, Pa. . . . 24 85

Transfer through Boston, going, included.

Form Ex. 1001.—WHITEFIELD, N. H., AND RETURN.
(Via Rail Lines and Boston in both directions.)

Baltimore & Ohio R. R.	to Philadelphia.
Rail Lines (see pages 50 to 55 for route)	to Boston.
Boston & Maine R. R.	to Nashua.
Concord & Montreal R. R.	to Whitefield.

Returning, same route.

THROUGH RATES.

Baltimore, Md. . . . . . $27 75 | Washington, D. C. $29 75
(Philadelphia, Pa. . . . 26 75

Form Ex. 1001.—WHITEFIELD, N. H., AND RETURN.
(Via Sound Lines and Boston in both directions.)

Baltimore & Ohio R. R.	to Philadelphia.
Philadelphia & Reading R. R.	to Bound Brook.
Central R. R. of New Jersey.	to New York.
Sound Lines (see pages 50 to 55 for route)	to Boston.
Boston & Maine R. R.	to Nashua.
Concord & Montreal R. R.	to Whitefield.

Returning, same route.

THROUGH RATES.

Baltimore, Md. . . . . . $22 50 | Washington, D. C. $24 50
(Philadelphia, Pa. . . . 18 50

Transfer through Boston, in both directions, included.

Form Ex. 1002.—WHITEFIELD, N. H., AND RETURN.
(Via rail to Whitefield; returning by same route to Boston, thence via Sound Lines from Boston.)

Baltimore & Ohio R. R.	to Philadelphia.
Rail Lines (see pages 50 to 55 for route)	to Boston.
Boston & Maine R. R.	to North Conway.
Maine Central R. R.	to Whitefield.
Maine Central R. R.	to North Conway.
Boston & Maine R. R.	to Boston.
Sound Lines (see pages 50 to 55 for route)	to New York.
Central R. R. of New Jersey.	to Bound Brook.
Philadelphia & Reading R. R.	to Philadelphia.
Baltimore & Ohio R. R.	to starting point.

THROUGH RATES.

Baltimore, Md. . . . . . $26 10 | Washington, D. C. $28 10
(Philadelphia, Pa. . . . 22 10

Transfer through Boston, returning, included.

FORM EX. 1062. WHITEFIELD, N. H., AND RETURN.

(Via Sound Lines to Boston, rail to Whitefield; returning by same route to Boston, thence via rail.)

Baltimore & Ohio R. R. . . . . to Philadelphia.
Philadelphia & Reading R. R. . . . . to Bound Brook.
Central R. R. of New Jersey . . . . to New York.
Sound Lines (see pages 50 to 55 for route) . . . to Boston.
Boston & Maine R. R. . . . . to North Conway.
Maine Central R. R. . . . . to Whitefield.
Maine Central R. R. . . . . to North Conway.
Boston & Maine R. R. . . . . to Boston.
Rail Lines (see pages 50 to 55 for route) . . . . . to Philadelphia.
Baltimore & Ohio R. R. . . . . to starting point.

THROUGH RATES.

Baltimore, Md. . . . . . . $26 10 | Washington, D. C. . . $28 10
{Philadelphia, Pa. . . . . 22 10 |

Transfer through Boston, going, included.

FORM EX. 1062. WHITEFIELD, N. H., AND RETURN.

(Via Rail Lines to Whitefield in both directions.)

Baltimore & Ohio R. R. . . . . to Philadelphia.
Rail Lines (see pages 50 to 55 for route) . . . . . to Boston.
Boston & Maine R. R. . . . . to North Conway.
Maine Central R. R. . . . . to Whitefield.

Returning, same route.

THROUGH RATES.

Baltimore, Md. . . . . . . $27 75 | Washington, D. C. . . $29 75
{Philadelphia, Pa. . . . . 23 75 |

FORM EX. 1062.—WHITEFIELD, N. H., AND RETURN.

(Via Sound Lines to Boston, rail to Whitefield and return to Boston, thence via Sound Lines.)

Baltimore & Ohio R. R. . . . . to Philadelphia.
Philadelphia & Reading R. R. . . . . to Bound Brook.
Central R. R. of New Jersey . . . . to New York.
Sound Lines (see pages 50 to 55 for route) . . . to Boston.
Boston & Maine R. R. . . . . to North Conway.
Maine Central R. R. . . . . to Whitefield.

Returning, same route.

THROUGH RATES.

Baltimore, Md. . . . . . . $23 00 | Washington, D. C. . . $25 00
{Philadelphia, Pa. . . . . 19 00 |

Transfer through Boston, in both directions, included.

FORM EX. 1063.—WHITEFIELD, N. H., AND RETURN.

(Via rail to Whitefield; returning by same route to Boston, thence via Sound Lines from Boston.)

Baltimore & Ohio R. R. . . . . to Philadelphia.
Rail Lines (see pages 50 to 55 for route) . . . . . to Boston.
Boston & Maine R. R. . . . . to Portland.
Maine Central R. R. . . . . to Whitefield.
Maine Central R. R. . . . . to Portland.
Boston & Maine R. R. . . . . to Boston.
Sound Lines (see pages 50 to 55 for route) . . . to New York.
Central R. R. of New Jersey. . . . . to Bound Brook.
Philadelphia & Reading R. R. . . . . to Philadelphia.
Baltimore & Ohio R. R. . . . . to starting point.

THROUGH RATES.

Baltimore, Md. . . . . . . $26 10 | Washington, D. C. . . $28 10
{Philadelphia, Pa. . . . . 22 10 |

Transfer through Boston, returning, included.

FORM EX. 1686.—WHITEFIELD, N. H., AND RETURN.

(Via Sound Lines to Boston, rail to Whitefield; returning by same route to Boston, thence via rail.)

Baltimore & Ohio R. R. . . . . to Philadelphia.
Philadelphia & Reading R. R. . . . . to Bound Brook.
Central R. R. of New Jersey. . . . . to New York.
Sound Lines (see pages 50 to 55 for route) . . . to Boston.
Boston & Maine R. R. . . . . to Portland.
Maine Central R. R. . . . . to Whitefield.
Maine Central R. R. . . . . to Portland.
Boston & Maine R. R. . . . . to Boston.
Rail Lines (see pages 50 to 55 for route) . . . . to Philadelphia.
Baltimore & Ohio R. R. . . . . to starting point.

THROUGH RATES.

Baltimore, Md. . . . . . $28 10   Washington, D. C. $28 10
(Philadelphia, Pa. 22 10

Transfer through Boston, going, included.

FORM EX. 1686.—WHITEFIELD, N. H., AND RETURN.

(Via Rail Lines to Whitefield in both directions.)

Baltimore & Ohio R. R. . . . . to Philadelphia.
Rail Lines (see pages 50 to 55 for route) . . . . to Boston.
Boston & Maine R. R. . . . . to Portland.
Maine Central R. R. . . . . to Whitefield.

Returning, same route.

THROUGH RATES.

Baltimore, Md. . . . . . $27 75   Washington, D. C. $29 75
(Philadelphia, Pa. 23 75

FORM EX. 1686.—WHITEFIELD, N. H., AND RETURN.

(Via Sound Lines to Boston, rail to Whitefield, and return to Boston, thence via Sound Lines.)

Baltimore & Ohio R. R. . . . . to Philadelphia.
Philadelphia & Reading R. R. . . . . to Bound Brook.
Central R. R. of New Jersey. . . . . to New York.
Sound Lines (see pages 50 to 55 for route) . . . to Boston.
Boston & Maine R. R. . . . . to Portland.
Maine Central R. R. . . . . to Whitefield.

Returning, same route.

THROUGH RATES.

Baltimore, Md. . . . . . $25 00   Washington, D. C. $25 00
(Philadelphia, Pa. 19 00

Transfer through Boston, in both directions, included.

WHITE SULPHUR SPRINGS, W. VA.

FORM EX. 28.—WHITE SULPHUR SPRINGS, W. VA., AND RETURN.

Baltimore & Ohio R. R. . . . . to Shenandoah June.
Norfolk & Western R. R. . . . . to Basic.
Chesapeake & Ohio Ry. . . . . to White Sulphur Springs.

Returning, same route.

THROUGH RATES.

Baltimore, Md. . . . . . $14 00   New York, N. Y. $22 00
Chester, Pa. . . . . 17 50   Philadelphia, Pa. 18 00
Havre de Grace, Md . . 15 45   Washington, D. C. . . . 12 00
Newark, Del. . . . . . . 16 50   Wilmington, Del. 17 00

ROUTES AND RATES FOR SUMMER TOURS. 347

FORM EX. 54.—WHITE SULPHUR SPRINGS, W. VA., AND RETURN.

Baltimore & Ohio R. R. . . . . to Staunton.
Chesapeake & Ohio Ry. . . . . to White Sulphur Springs.
Returning, same route.

WHITE SULPHUR.

THROUGH RATES.

Baltimore, Md.	$14 00	Havre de Grace, Md.	$15 15
Bellaire, O.	24 05	Johnstown, Pa.	19 45
Berkeley Springs, W. Va.	13 75	Keyser, W. Va.	16 00
Cameron, W. Va.	22 60	Lexington, Va.	7 50
Charlestown, W. Va.	11 30	McKeesport, Pa.	21 15
Chester, Pa.	17 50	Martinsburg, W. Va.	12 55
Clarksburg, W. Va.	20 65	Meyersdale, Pa.	17 20
Connellsville, Pa.	19 40	Morgantown, W. Va.	21 65
Cumberland, Md.	15 70	Moundsville, W. Va.	23 30
Deer Park, Md.	17 60	Mountain Lake Park, Md.	17 75
Fairmont, W. Va.	20 65	Mt. Pleasant, Pa.	19 90
Frederick, Md.	12 65	Newark, Del.	16 30
Grafton, W. Va.	19 75	New York, N. Y.	22 00
Hagerstown, Md.	12 85	Oakland, Md.	17 85
Harper's Ferry, W. Va.	11 80	Parkersburg, W. Va.	23 80
Harrisonburg, Va.	6 80	Philadelphia, Pa.	18 00

Piedmont, W. Va.	$16 80	Washington, D. C.	$12 00
Pittsburgh, Pa.	21 70	Washington, Pa.	22 80
Rockwood, Pa.	17 65	Wheeling, W. Va.	23 80
Somerset, Pa.	18 05	Wilmington, Del.	17 00
Strasburg, Va.	9 15	Winchester, Va.	10 20
Uniontown, Pa.	19 85		

FORM EX. 339. WHITE SULPHUR SPRINGS, W. VA., AND RETURN.

Baltimore & Ohio R. R. . . . . to Washington.
Transfer. . . . . B. & O. Depot to C. & O. Depot.
Chesapeake & Ohio Ry. . . . . to White Sulphur Springs.
Returning, same route.

THROUGH RATES.

Baltimore, Md.	$14 00	Meyersdale, Pa.	$20 10
Bellaire, O.	26 95	Morgantown, W. Va.	21 55
Berkeley Springs, W. Va.	16 65	Moundsville, W. Va.	26 30
Cameron, W. Va.	25 50	Mountain Lake Park, Md.	20 15
Charlestown, W. Va.	15 20	Mt. Pleasant, Pa.	22 80
Chester, Pa.	17 50	Newark, Del.	16 30
Clarksburg, W. Va.	23 55	New York, N. Y.	22 00
Connellsville, Pa.	22 20	Oakland, Md.	20 25
Cumberland, Md.	18 60	Parkersburg, W. Va.	26 65
Deer Park, Md.	20 00	Philadelphia, Pa.	18 00
Fairmont, W. Va.	23 55	Piedmont, W. Va.	19 70
Frederick, Md.	11 80	Pittsburgh, Pa.	24 60
Grafton, W. Va.	22 65	Rockwood, Pa.	20 55
Hagerstown, Md.	15 60	Somerset, Pa.	20 95
Harper's Ferry, W. Va.	14 70	Uniontown, Pa.	22 75
Havre de Grace, Md.	15 15	Washington, Pa.	25 70
Johnstown, Pa.	22 55	Wheeling, W. Va.	26 65
Keyser, W. Va.	19 50	Wilmington, Del.	17 00
McKeesport, Pa.	24 05	Winchester, Va.	16 30
Martinsburg, W. Va.	15 15		

WILLOW GROVE, VA.

FORM EX. 14.—WILLOW GROVE, VA., AND RETURN.

Baltimore & Ohio R. R. . . . . to Willow Grove.
Returning, same route.
Transfer of twenty-five cents, in each direction, not included.

THROUGH RATES.

Baltimore, Md.	$7 00	Meyersdale, Pa.	$8 00
Bellaire, O.	15 15	Morgantown, W. Va.	13 05
Berkeley Springs, W. Va.	5 15	Moundsville, W. Va.	14 70
Cameron, W. Va.	14 00	Mountain Lake Park, Md.	9 15
Charlestown, W. Va.	2 70	Mt. Pleasant, Pa.	11 30
Chester, Pa.	10 50	Newark, Del.	9 20
Clarksburg, W. Va.	12 05	New York, N. Y.	15 00
Connellsville, Pa.	10 80	Oakland, Md.	9 25
Cumberland, Md.	7 10	Parkersburg, W. Va.	15 20
Deer Park, Md.	9 00	Philadelphia, Pa.	11 00
Fairmont, W. Va.	12 05	Piedmont, W. Va.	8 20
Frederick, Md.	4 25	Pittsburgh, Pa.	13 10
Grafton, W. Va.	11 15	Rockwood, Pa.	9 05
Hagerstown, Md.	4 25	Somerset, Pa.	9 45
Harper's Ferry, W. Va.	3 20	Staunton, Va.	3 15
Harrisonburg, Va.	1 85	Strasburg, Va.	65
Havre de Grace, Md.	8 15	Uniontown, Pa.	11 25
Johnstown, Pa.	10 55	Washington, D. C.	5 40
Keyser, W. Va.	8 00	Washington, Pa.	14 30
Lexington, Va.	4 95	Wheeling, W. Va.	15 20
McKeesport, Pa.	12 55	Wilmington, Del.	10 00
Martinsburg, W. Va.	3 95	Winchester, Va.	1 60

WINTER HARBOR, ME.

FORM EX. 1094 OR FORM SPL. EX. 1095. WINTER HARBOR, ME., AND RETURN.

(Via rail to Bar Harbor, thence steamer; returning by same route to Boston, thence via Sound Lines from Boston.)

Baltimore & Ohio R. R.	to Philadelphia.
Rail Lines (see pages 50 to 55 for routes)	to Boston.
Boston & Maine R. R.	to Portland.
Maine Central R. R.	to Bar Harbor.
Steamer "Silver Star"	to Winter Harbor.
Steamer "Silver Star"	to Bar Harbor.
Maine Central R. R.	to Portland.
Boston & Maine R. R.	to Boston.
Sound Lines (see pages 50 to 55 for routes)	to New York.
Central R. R. of New Jersey	to Bound Brook.
Philadelphia & Reading R. R.	to Philadelphia.
Baltimore & Ohio R. R.	to starting point.

THROUGH RATES.

Baltimore, Md. . . . . . . $31.50 | Washington, D. C. $33.50
† Philadelphia, Pa. 27.50

Form Spl. Ex. 1095 is good for continuous passage only east of Portland, and the rates for same are $2.50 less than the rates for the regular excursion as quoted above.

FORM EX. 1094 OR FORM SPL. EX. 1095.—WINTER HARBOR, ME., AND RETURN.

(Via Sound Lines to Boston, rail to Bar Harbor, thence steamer; returning by same route to Boston, thence via rail.)

Baltimore & Ohio R. R.	to Philadelphia.
Philadelphia & Reading R. R.	to Bound Brook.
Central R. R. of New Jersey	to New York.
Sound Lines (see pages 50 to 55 for routes)	to Boston.
Boston & Maine R. R.	to Portland.
Maine Central R. R.	to Bar Harbor.
Steamer "Silver Star"	to Winter Harbor.
Steamer "Silver Star"	to Bar Harbor.
Maine Central R. R.	to Portland.
Boston & Maine R. R.	to Boston.
Rail Lines (see pages 50 to 55 for routes)	to Philadelphia.
Baltimore & Ohio R. R.	to starting point.

THROUGH RATES.

Baltimore, Md. . . . . . . $31.50 | Washington, D. C. $33.50
† Philadelphia, Pa. 27.50

Form Spl. Ex. 1095 is good for continuous passage only east of Portland, and the rates for same are $2.50 less than rates for the regular excursion as quoted above.

FORM EX. 1094 OR FORM SPL. EX. 1095.—WINTER HARBOR, ME., AND RETURN.

(Via Rail Lines to Bar Harbor, thence steamer in both directions.)

Baltimore & Ohio R. R.	to Philadelphia.
Rail Lines (see pages 50 to 55 for routes)	to Boston.
Boston & Maine R. R.	to Portland.
Maine Central R. R.	to Bar Harbor.
Steamer "Silver Star"	to Winter Harbor.

Returning, same route.

THROUGH RATES.

Baltimore, Md. . . . . . . $32.50 | Washington, D. C. $34.50
† Philadelphia, Pa. 28.50

Form Spl. Ex. 1095 is good for continuous passage only east of Portland, and the rates for same are $2.50 less than rates for the regular excursion as quoted above.

FORM EX. 1034 OR FORM SPL. EX. 1035. WINTER HARBOR, ME., AND
RETURN.

(Via Sound Lines to Boston, rail to Bar Harbor, thence steamer, and
return to Boston, thence via Sound Lines.)

Baltimore & Ohio R. R. . . . . to Philadelphia.
Philadelphia & Reading R. R. . . . . to Bound Brook.
Central R. R. of New Jersey . . . . to New York.
Sound Lines (see pages 50 to 55 for route) . . . to Boston.
Boston & Maine R. R. . . . . to Portland.
Maine Central R. R. . . . . to Bar Harbor.
Steamer "Silver Star" . . . . to Winter Harbor.

Returning, same route.

THROUGH RATES.

Baltimore, Md. . . . . . . $30.50   Washington, D. C. $32.50
Philadelphia, Pa. 26.50

Form Spl. Ex. 1035 is good for continuous passage only east of Portland, and the rates for same are $2.50 less than rates for the regular excursion as quoted above.

WYTHEVILLE, VA.

FORM EX. 94. WYTHEVILLE (SHARON SPRINGS), VA., AND RETURN.

Baltimore & Ohio R. R. . . . . to Washington.
Transfer . . . . B. & O. Depot to R. & D. Depot
Richmond & Danville R. R. . . . . to Lynchburg.
Norfolk & Western R. R. . . . . to Wytheville.

Returning, same route.

THROUGH RATES.

Baltimore, Md.	$16.65	Meyersdale, Pa.	$22.75
Bellaire, O.	29.00	Morgantown, W. Va.	27.20
Berkeley Springs, W. Va.	19.30	Moundsville, W. Va.	28.85
Cameron, W. Va.	28.15	Mountain Lake Park, Md.	22.80
Charlestown, W. Va.	17.85	Mt. Pleasant, Pa.	25.15
Chester, Pa.	20.45	Newark, Del.	18.95
Clarksburg, W. Va.	26.20	New York, N. Y.	21.65
Connellsville, Pa.	24.95	Oakland, Md.	22.90
Cumberland, Md.	21.25	Parkersburg, W. Va.	29.30
Deer Park, Md.	22.65	Philadelphia, Pa.	20.65
Fairmont, W. Va.	26.20	Piedmont, W. Va.	23.35
Frederick, Md.	17.15	Pittsburgh, Pa.	27.25
Grafton, W. Va.	25.30	Rockwood, Pa.	23.20
Hagerstown, Md.	18.25	Somerset, Pa.	23.60
Harper's Ferry, W. Va.	17.35	Uniontown, Pa.	25.40
Havre de Grace, Md.	18.40	Washington, Pa.	28.35
Johnstown, Pa.	25.00	Wheeling, W. Va.	29.30
Keyser, W. Va.	22.15	Wilmington, Del.	19.65
McKeesport, Pa.	26.70	Winchester, Va.	18.95
Martinsburg, W. Va.	18.40		

FORM EX. 246.—WYTHEVILLE (SHARON SPRINGS), VA., AND RETURN.

Baltimore & Ohio R. R. . . . . to Shenandoah June.
Norfolk & Western R. R. . . . . to Wytheville.

Returning, same route.

THROUGH RATES.

Baltimore, Md.	$16 65	Morgantown, W. Va.	$22 85
Bellaire, O.	25 25	Moundsville, W. Va.	21 55
Berkeley Springs, W. Va.	15 05	Mountain Lake Park, Md.	19 00
Cameron, W. Va.	23 85	Mt. Pleasant, Pa.	24 10
Chester, Pa.	20 15	Newark, Del.	18 95
Clarksburg, W. Va.	21 80	New York, N. Y.	21 65
Connellsville, Pa.	20 90	Oakland, Md.	19 10
Cumberland, Md.	16 90	Parkersburg, W. Va.	24 95
Deer Park, Md.	18 85	Philadelphia, Pa.	20 65
Fairmont, W. Va.	21 85	Piedmont, W. Va.	18 05
Frederick, Md.	14 65	Pittsburgh, Pa.	22 90
Grafton, W. Va.	20 95	Rockwood, Pa.	18 85
Harper's Ferry, W. Va.	13 55	Somerset, Pa.	19 25
Havre de Grace, Md.	18 40	Uniontown, Pa.	21 65
Johnstown, Pa.	20 65	Washington, D. C.	14 65
Keyser, W. Va.	17 85	Washington, Pa.	24 00
McKeesport, Pa.	22 55	Wheeling, W. Va.	24 95
Martinsburg, W. Va.	15 75	Wilmington, Del.	19 65
Meyersdale, Pa.	18 10		

YORK BEACH, ME.

FORM EX. 780.—YORK BEACH, MAINE, AND RETURN.

Baltimore & Ohio R. R.	to Philadelphia.
Philadelphia & Reading R. R.	to Bound Brook.
Central R. R. of New Jersey	to New York.
Sound Lines (see pages 30 to 35 for route)	to Boston.
Boston & Maine R. R.	to Portsmouth.
York Harbor & Beach R. R.	to York Beach.

Returning, same route.

THROUGH RATES.

Baltimore, Md.	$20 00	Washington, D. C.	$22 00
Philadelphia, Pa.	16 00		

FORM EX. 780.—YORK BEACH, MAINE, AND RETURN.

Baltimore & Ohio R. R.	to Philadelphia.
Rail Lines (see pages 30 to 35 for route)	to Boston.
Boston & Maine R. R.	to Portsmouth.
York Harbor & Beach R. R.	to York Beach.

Returning, same route.

THROUGH RATES.

Baltimore, Md.	$22 00	Washington, D. C.	$24 00
Philadelphia, Pa.	18 00		

FORM EX. 780.—YORK BEACH, MAINE, AND RETURN.

Baltimore & Ohio R. R.	to Philadelphia.
Rail Lines (see pages 30 to 35 for route)	to Boston.
Boston & Maine R. R.	to Portsmouth.
York Harbor & Beach R. R.	to York Beach.
York Harbor & Beach R. R.	to Portsmouth.
Boston & Maine R. R.	to Boston.
Sound Lines (see pages 30 to 35 for route)	to New York.
Central R. R. of New Jersey	to Bound Brook.
Philadelphia & Reading R. R.	to Philadelphia.
Baltimore & Ohio R. R.	to starting point.

THROUGH RATES.

Baltimore, Md.	$21 00	Washington, D. C.	$23 00
Philadelphia, Pa.	17 00		

FORM EX. 780.—YORK BEACH, MAINE, AND RETURN.

Baltimore & Ohio R. R. . . . . to Philadelphia.
Philadelphia & Reading R. R. . . . . to Bound Brook.
Central R. R. of New Jersey . . . . to New York.
Sound Lines (see pages 50 to 55 for routes) . . . . to Boston.
Boston & Maine R. R. . . . . to Portsmouth.
York Harbor & Beach R. R. . . . . to York Beach.
York Harbor & Beach R. R. . . . . to Portsmouth.
Boston & Maine R. R. . . . . to Boston.
Rail Lines (see pages 50 to 55 for routes) . . . . to Philadelphia.
Baltimore & Ohio R. R. . . . . to starting point.

THROUGH RATES.

Baltimore, Md. . . . . . . $21 00 | Washington, D. C. $23 00
Philadelphia, Pa. . . . . . 17 00 |

YORK HARBOR, ME.

FORM EX. 811.—YORK HARBOR, ME., AND RETURN.

(Via rail and Boston; returning by Sound Lines.)

Baltimore & Ohio R. R. . . . . to Philadelphia.
Rail Lines (see pages 50 to 55 for routes) . . . . to Boston.
Boston & Maine R. R. . . . . to Portsmouth.
York Harbor & Beach R. R. . . . . to York Harbor.
York Harbor & Beach R. R. . . . . to Portsmouth.
Boston & Maine R. R. . . . . to Boston.
Sound Lines (see pages 50 to 55 for routes) . . . to New York.
Central R. R. of New Jersey . . . . to Bound Brook.
Philadelphia & Reading R. R. . . . . to Philadelphia.
Baltimore & Ohio R. R. . . . . to starting point.

THROUGH RATES.

Baltimore, Md. . . . . . . $20 65 | Washington, D. C. $22 65
Philadelphia, Pa. . . . . . 16 65 |

FORM EX. 811.—YORK HARBOR, ME., AND RETURN.

(Via Sound Lines and Boston; returning by rail.)

Baltimore & Ohio R. R. . . . . to Philadelphia.
Philadelphia & Reading R. R. . . . . to Bound Brook.
Central R. R. of New Jersey . . . . to New York.
Sound Lines (see pages 50 to 55 for routes) . . . to Boston.
Boston & Maine R. R. . . . . to Portsmouth.
York Harbor & Beach R. R. . . . . to York Harbor.
York Harbor & Beach R. R. . . . . to Portsmouth.
Boston & Maine R. R. . . . . to Boston.
Rail Lines (see pages 50 to 55 for routes) . . . . to Philadelphia.
Baltimore & Ohio R. R. . . . . to starting point.

THROUGH RATES.

Baltimore, Md. . . . . . . $20 65 | Washington, D. C. $22 65
Philadelphia, Pa. . . . . . 16 65 |

FORM EX. 811.—YORK HARBOR, ME., AND RETURN.

(Via Rail Lines and Boston in both directions.)

Baltimore & Ohio R. R. . . . . to Philadelphia.
Rail Lines (see pages 50 to 55 for routes) . . . . to Boston.
Boston & Maine R. R. . . . . to Portsmouth.
York Harbor & Beach R. R. . . . . to York Harbor.

Returning, same route.

THROUGH RATES.

Baltimore, Md. . . . . . . $21 65 | Washington, D. C. $23 65
Philadelphia, Pa. . . . . . 17 65 |

ROUTES AND RATES FOR SUMMER TOURS. 353

FORM EX. 811.—YORK HARBOR, ME., AND RETURN.
(Via Sound Lines and Boston in both directions.)

Baltimore & Ohio R. R.	to Philadelphia.
Philadelphia & Reading R. R.	to Bound Brook.
Central R. R. of New Jersey	to New York.
Sound Lines (see pages 30 to 35 for route)	to Boston.
Boston & Maine R. R.	to Portsmouth.
York Harbor & Beach R. R.	to York Harbor.

Returning, same route.

THROUGH RATES.

Baltimore, Md.	$19 65	Washington, D. C.	$21 65
Philadelphia, Pa.	15 65		

Rates from Washington, D. C., to points on the Norfolk & Western R. R. and East Tennessee, Virginia & Georgia R. R. Blank excursion forms, as indicated below, will be used in ticketing tourists to these points:

FORM EX. 787.

To	Rate.	To	Rate.
Basic, Va.	$7 60	Foster Falls, Va.	$14 80
Bluefield, W. Va.	16 80	Marion, Va.	16 00
Bramwell, W. Va.	16 65	Pocahontas, Va.	16 60
Bristol, Tenn.	18 00	Pulaski, Va.	13 60
Buchanan, Va.	10 80	Radford, Va.	12 85
Buena Vista, Va.	9 75	Roanoke, Va.	10 80
Chilhowie, Va.	16 50	Rural Retreat, Va.	15 30
Cloverdale, Va.	10 80	Seven Mile Ford, Va.	16 35
Dublin, Va.	13 25	Tazewell, Va.	17 40
Elliston (Big Springs), Va.	11 65		

FORM EX. 788.

To	Rate.	To	Rate.
Greenville, Tenn.	$20 00	Jonesboro, Tenn.	$19 65
Johnson's City, Tenn.	19 25	Morristown, Tenn.	20 00

Elizabethton 19.85 Tate Spring, Tenn 20.75

AROUND AND ABOUT HARPER'S FERRY.

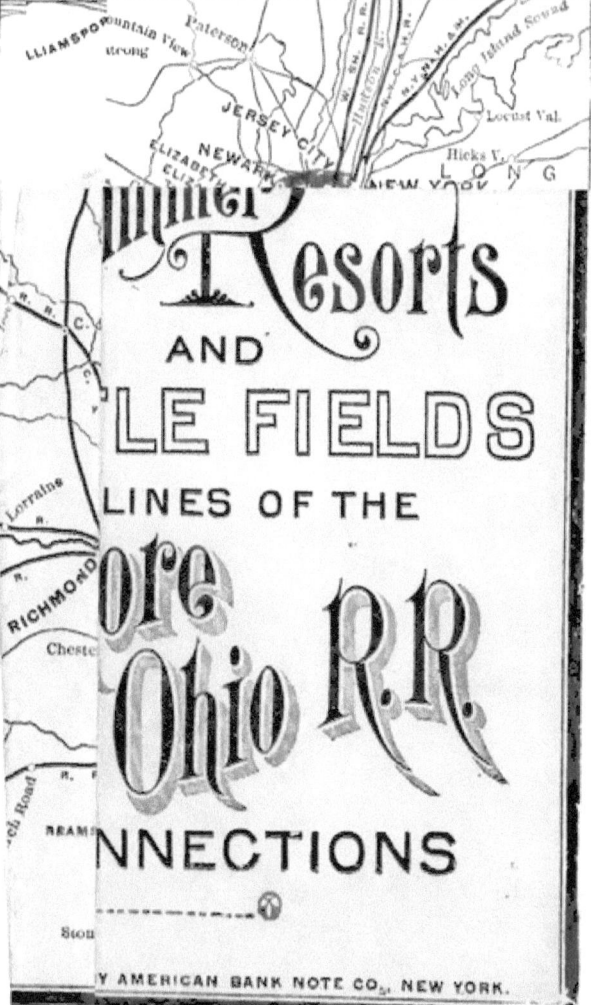

MOVEMENTS OF STEAMER LINES, SEASON 1892.

Subject to Change.

BALTIMORE STEAM PACKET COMPANY.
(Bay Line Steamers.)

The "Georgia," "Virginia" and "Carolina" run, except Sundays, all the year. Leave Baltimore, Union Dock, 6.30 P. M., Canton 7.00 P. M.; arrive Old Point Comfort 7.00 A. M., Norfolk and Portsmouth 8.00 A. M. Leave Norfolk and Portsmouth 6.15 P. M., Old Point Comfort 7.15 P. M.; arrive Baltimore 7.00 A. M. Passenger capacity, 300. Meals, $1.00. State-rooms, $1.00, $1.50, $2.00 and $2.50.

BLOCK ISLAND STEAMERS.

The steamer "Block Island" commences running on or about July 2d daily (Sundays excepted), leaving New London 10.00 A. M., or on arrival of train from New York, and arriving at Block Island 1.00 P. M., touching at Watch Hill. Returning, leave Block Island 2.00 P. M., stopping at Watch Hill, and arriving at New London 5.15 P. M.

BOSTON & BANGOR STEAMSHIP LINE.

Palace steamers "Penobscot," "Lewiston" and "Katahdin" leave Boston from June 16th to September 5th daily (Sunday excepted), at 5.00 o'clock P. M., for Bangor, Southwest Harbor and Bar Harbor (Mt. Desert), and all towns and summer resorts on Penobscot river and bay. Leave Bangor at 11.00 A. M., Bar Harbor at 1.00 P. M., Southwest Harbor at 2.00 P. M., same days for Boston. About 100 state-rooms on each steamer. Capacity, 500. Meals on board.

Mount Desert Line.—Steamer "Mt. Desert" leaves Rockland, Me., for Bar Harbor at 6.30 A. M., arriving at Bar Harbor at 11.00 A. M., returning every day (except Sunday) at 1.00 P. M., arriving in Rockland at 5.00 P. M. Close connection at Rockland with Boston steamers. Large state-rooms, $2.00 and $3.00. Meals on board.

BOSTON & PORTSMOUTH STEAMSHIP COMPANY.

The steamer "John Brooks" leaves Boston from June 15th to October 1st on week days at 9.00 A. M., and arrives at Isles of Shoals 1.00 P. M. Leaves Boston on Sundays 10.30 A. M. On return trip, steamer leaves Isles of Shoals, week days, at 2.30 P. M., and arrives at Boston 6.30 P. M.

The steamer "Baltimore" leaves Isles of Shoals, week days, at 6.15 and 9.35 A. M., 1.00 and 3.40 P. M., and arrives at Portsmouth 7.05 and 10.15 A. M., 2.10 and 4.15 P. M., respectively. Leaves Portsmouth for Isles of Shoals 8.15 and 11.30 A. M., 2.35 and 5.35 P. M., and arrives at Isles of Shoals 9.10 and 12.20 A. M., 1.05 and 6.30 P. M., respectively. On Sundays this steamer leaves Isles of Shoals at 9.00 A. M., 2.35 and 6.00 P. M., and arrives at Portsmouth 10.00 A. M., 3.10 and 7.00 P. M., respectively. Returning, leaves Portsmouth for Isles of Shoals at 10.30 A. M., 4.00 and 7.30 P. M.

CAYUGA LAKE STEAMER.
(Cayuga Lake Transportation Company, Limited.)

Steamer "Frontenac" commences running May 19th and ceases about November 1st, leaving Ithaca at 10.00 A. M. for Cayuga Bridge, allowing stopover at Glenwood, Taughannock Falls (220 feet high), Frontenac Beach, Kidders, Cayuga Lake Hotel, Sheldrake and Aurora, arriving at Cayuga about 2.00 P. M., and returning leave Cayuga on arrival of east and west bound trains, reaching Ithaca about 7.15 P. M. Passenger capacity, 500. Meals served on board at 50 cents. Trains of Delaware, Lackawanna & Western Railroad run direct to steamer.

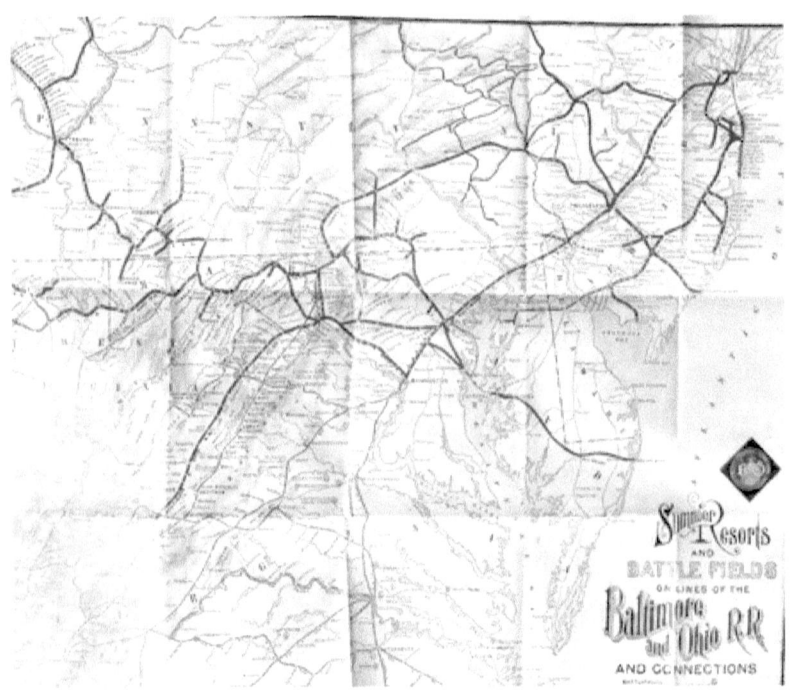

CHAMPLAIN TRANSPORTATION COMPANY.

The steamers "Vermont" and "Chateaugay" ply as follows: The "Vermont" commences June 1st and ceases about October 15th, sailing between Fort Ticonderoga and Plattsburgh, landing at Bluff Point, Port Kent, Burlington, Essex, Westport, Port Henry, Fort Frederick, Crown Point and Larrabee's. Leave Plattsburgh 7.00 A. M. Leave Fort Ticonderoga 1.30 P. M. Trip occupies five hours. Passenger capacity, 1,500. Dinner, $1.00; breakfast and supper, 75 cents each.

The "Chateaugay" runs during the entire season of navigation, April to December, between Essex, Cedar Beach, Burlington, Port Kent, Bluff Point, Plattsburgh and the Islands, touching at Port Jackson, Grand Isle and North Hero. Leaves Burlington, June to October, 9.00 A. M.; arrives 5.00 P. M. Trip occupies 3½ hours. Passenger capacity, 1,500.

CHAUTAUQUA STEAMBOAT COMPANY.

(RED STACK AND PEOPLES' LINE CONSOLIDATED.)

OWNING AND OPERATING ALL STEAMERS ON CHAUTAUQUA LAKE.

Steamers "City of New York," "City of Chicago," "City of Cincinnati," "City of Cleveland," "City of Buffalo," "City of Pittsburgh," "City of Erie," "City of Jamestown," run from May 1st to November 1st between Jamestown, Lakewood, Greenhurst, Griffith's Point, Bemus Point, Long Point, Maple Springs, Point Whiteside, Point Chautauqua, Chautauqua (the great assembly grounds) and Mayville. Connection is made at Mayville with all trains on the Western New York & Pennsylvania Railroad and Chautauqua Lake Railroad, at Lakewood with all trains on the New York, Pennsylvania & Ohio Railroad, at Jamestown with all trains on the New York, Pennsylvania & Ohio Railroad, New York, Lake Erie & Western Ry. and Branches, and Dunkirk, Allegheny Valley & Pittsburgh Railroad, giving direct connection with New York Central and Hudson River Railroad.

CITIZENS' LINE STEAMERS.

(TROY NIGHT BOATS.)

The "Saratoga" and "City of Troy" commence running as soon as navigation on the Hudson River opens, and cease in December, plying between New York (Pier 16, North River, second pier above Christopher street); Steamboat Square, Albany; and foot of Broadway, Troy.

Leave New York daily, except Saturday, at 6.00 P. M., arriving at Troy daily, except Sunday, at 6.00 A. M. Leave Troy daily, except Saturday, about 7.30 P. M. (Sundays at 6.00 P. M.); arrive at New York 7.00 A. M.

Land at Albany, going north, on Monday (Sunday night trip) only, 5.30 A. M., and going south, on Sunday (Sunday night trip) only, at 7.00 P. M. Passenger capacity, 350. Meals served on European plan. Berths in cabin, 50 cents. State-rooms, $1.00 and $2.00.

DAY LINE STEAMERS.

(HUDSON RIVER LINE.)

Steamers "New York" and "Albany" commence their trips from New York about May 29th. Cease running about October 15th. Ply between New York and Albany as follows: Leave Desbrosses Street Pier, North River 8.40 A. M., and Twenty-second Street Pier 9.00 A. M. Arrive at Hamilton street, Albany, 6.10 P. M. Leave Albany 8.30 A. M.; arrive Twenty-second street, New York, 5.30 P. M., Desbrosses street 6.00 P. M. Landings are made at Yonkers, West Point, Newburg, Poughkeepsie, Rhinebeck, Catskill and Hudson. Passenger capacity, 2,000. Breakfast and dinner *a la carte*, also *table de Hote* dinner at $1.00. Drawing-rooms for parties. Morning and afternoon concerts on each steamer.

EASTERN STEAMBOAT CO.'S BATH AND BOOTHBAY MAIL LINE.

Steamers "Wiwurna," "Nahanada," "Winter Harbor" and "Samoset" run daily the year round between Bath and Boothbay Harbor and Islands, a distance of from 15 to 48 miles. All inside smooth-water navigation. During the summer season three or four trips daily to Boothbay Harbor and Islands, and three or four trips weekly to Heron Island and Pemaquid Harbor.

FALL RIVER LINE.

(OLD COLONY STEAMBOAT COMPANY.)

The steamers of this line consist of the "Puritan," "Pilgrim," "Plymouth" and "Providence." Trips are made every day in the year, Sunday trips being omitted only from January to March inclusive. A double service is maintained during the summer months, two steamers being run week days and one on Sundays from Pier 28 North River, New York, to Newport and Fall River. Returning, two every day (Saturdays one only) Sundays included. Leave New York at 5.00 P. M. until about the middle of June. Touch at Newport at about 3.00 A. M. and arrive Fall River about 5.00 A. M., there connecting with express trains leaving about 5.25 and 7.30 A. M., arriving Boston about 6.50 and 9.00 A. M. Returning, train leaves Boston 6.00 P. M. week days, 7.00 P. M. Sundays, connecting with steamers leaving Fall River 7.30 P. M. week days, 8.30 P. M. Sundays; touching at Newport 8.30 P. M. week days, 9.30 P. M. Sundays, arriving New York about 7.00 A. M.

SCHEDULE OF DOUBLE SERVICE, IN EFFECT ABOUT JUNE 15TH TO OCTOBER 1ST.

DIRECT FALL RIVER LINE. Steamer leaves New York at 5.30 P. M. daily, Sundays included, due at Fall River 5.00 A. M., there connecting with Boston trains leaving the wharf at 5.25 and 7.30 A. M., and due to arrive about 6.50 and 9.00 A. M. respectively. Returning, the latest train leaves Boston 7.00 P. M. daily, Sundays included, connecting with steamers leaving Fall River at 8.30 P. M., and due at New York about 7.00 A. M. The Sunday steamer from New York will touch at Newport Monday mornings about 3.00 A. M.

FALL RIVER VIA NEWPORT. Steamer leaves New York at 6.15 P. M. week days only, and is due to arrive at Newport about 3.45 A. M.; Fall River 7.00 A. M.; there connecting with 7.30 A. M. Boston train, due to arrive at Boston 9.00 A. M. Returning, train leaves Boston 6.00 P. M. week days and Sundays, connecting with steamer leaving Fall River 7.30 P. M.; touching at Newport 8.30 P. M., and due at New York about 7.00 A. M.

Meals on steamers served a la carte. Berths free. State-rooms, $1.00 and $2.00 each. Parlor rooms, $3.00 to $8.00. Passenger capacity of steamers as follows: "Puritan," 1,500; "Pilgrim," 1,250; "Plymouth," 1,250; "Providence," 1,000.

Music is a prominent feature of this line, an orchestra being attached to each steamer all the year round.

Passengers for Cape Cod, Martha's Vineyard and Nantucket take 5.30 P. M. boat from New York.

Steamers leave New York at 5.00 P. M. beginning about October 1st, or when the double service is discontinued.

INTERNATIONAL STEAMSHIP COMPANY.

(BETWEEN BOSTON, PORTLAND, EASTPORT AND ST. JOHN.)

The steamers of this company are the "Cumberland," "State of Maine" and the "New Brunswick," side-wheel seagoing steamers of 1,600, 1,400 and 900 tons respectively, and the only side-wheel passenger steamers running to and from the Provinces.

Sailing days from Boston, from July 4th to September 4th, will be Monday, Tuesday, Thursday and Friday at 5.00 P. M., and from Portland Wednesday and Saturday at 5.00 P. M.

On Wednesday and Saturday through connection is made by taking the Boston & Maine Railroad 12.30 or 1.00 P. M. train, connecting with the steamer at Portland.

This arrangement makes daily service, except Sunday, to and from Eastport and St. John. State-rooms are $1.00 and $2.00, according to location. Cabin berths are free. Meals are 50 cents for breakfast and supper, and 75 cents for dinner.

During spring and early fall the steamers leave Boston at 8.30 A. M., three times each week, Mondays, Wednesdays and Fridays, and Portland Mondays and Fridays only. This line is operated the year round, but the number of trips is increased or diminished according to the demands of the business.

LAKE GEORGE STEAMERS.
(LAKE GEORGE STEAMBOAT LINE.)

The "Horicon" will commence running about June 1st and cease about October 15th. Will leave Caldwell on arrival of train from Albany, about 9.15 A. M., landing at Assembly Point, Cleverdale, Sheldon's, Kattskill, Trout Pavilion, Marion, Bolton, Green Island, Fourteen-Mile Island, Hundred Islands, Pearl Point, Hulett's, Sabbath-Day Point, Silver Bay, Hague and Roger's Rock, reaching Baldwin about 12.30 P. M. Returning, leave Baldwin on arrival of train from Lake Champlain 1.00 P. M., making above landings; arrive Caldwell about 4.30 P. M., connecting with train for the South.

The "Ticonderoga" will be brought out about July 1st, and will run until about September 20th. Will leave Caldwell at 1.30 P. M., on arrival of New York train, making above landings. Arrive Baldwin 7.30 P. M. Returns in morning, leaving at 7.15. Reaches Caldwell at 10.30 A. M. to connect with train leaving at that hour.

The "Horicon" will also leave Caldwell Saturday nights (after July 1st) on arrival of train from South 10.30 P. M., making landings as far down as Pearl Point. Will lay at Pearl Point, leaving there at 7.00 Sunday evening, making all landings, reaching Caldwell to connect with sleeper for New York, leaving at 10.00 P. M.

LAKE WINNIPESAUKEE STEAMER.
(CONCORD & MONTREAL R. R.)

The "Lady of the Lake" commences running June 20th and ceases October 15th, plying between Weir's, Wolfeboro and Centre Harbor, connecting with the day express trains. Lunches are served on board at rate of fifty cents. Passenger capacity, 600. The trip consumes one hour to Centre Harbor and one and one-half hours to Wolfeboro.

NEW BEDFORD, MARTHA'S VINEYARD & NANTUCKET STEAMBOAT LINE.
SUMMER SCHEDULE IN EFFECT COMMENCING JUNE 15th AND SUBJECT TO CHANGE.

Steamers will be due to leave New Bedford for Cottage City (Martha's Vineyard), week days, 7.05, 10.00 A. M., 1.50 and 4.30 P. M., and arrive Cottage City at 9.00 A. M., 12.30, 4.00 and 7.15 P. M. Sundays, leave New Bedford at 8.15 A. M.; arrive Cottage City at 10.30 A. M. Returning, leave Cottage City, week days, at 6.15, 9.50 A. M., 1.00 and 3.00 P. M.; arrive New Bedford at 8.25 and 11.40 A. M., 3.10 and 5.25 P. M. Sundays, leave Cottage City at 4.45 P. M.; arrive New Bedford at 6.50 P. M.

Leave New Bedford for Nantucket, week days, at 7.05 A. M. and 1.50 P. M.; arrive Nantucket at 11.30 A. M. and 6.15 P. M. Sundays, leave New Bedford at 8.15 A. M.; arrive Nantucket at 1.20 P. M. Returning, leave Nantucket, week days, at 7.00 A. M. and 12.30 P. M.; arrive New Bedford at 11.40 A. M. and 5.25 P. M. Sundays, leave Nantucket at 2.15 P. M.; arrive New Bedford at 6.50 P. M.

Leave Wood's Holl for Cottage City, week days, at 11.10 A. M., 3.15 and 6.30 P. M.; arrive Cottage City at 12.30, 4.00 and 7.15 P. M. Sundays, leave Wood's Holl at 10.10 A. M.; arrive Cottage City at 10.40 A. M. Returning, leave Cottage City, week days, at 6.15 and 9.30 A. M. and 5.00 P. M.; arrive Wood's Holl at 7.00 and 10.10 A. M. and 5.50 P. M. Sundays, leave Cottage City at 4.45 P. M.; arrive Wood's Holl at 5.25 P. M.

Leave Wood's Holl for Nantucket, week days, at 3.45 P. M.; arrive Nantucket at 6.15 P. M. Sundays, leave Wood's Holl at 10.10 A. M.; arrive Nantucket at 1.20 P. M. Returning, leave Nantucket, week days, at 7.00 A. M. and 12.30 P. M.; arrive Wood's Holl at 10.10 A. M. and 3.50 P. M. Sundays, leave Nantucket at 2.15 P. M.; arrive Wood's Holl at 5.25 P. M.

NIAGARA NAVIGATION COMPANY.

The steamers "Ongiara," "Chicora" and "Cibola" commence their trips middle of May and cease in October, plying between Lewiston, N. Y., Niagara and Toronto, Canada, week days only. The steamer leaves Lewiston on arrival of morning and afternoon trains of the New York Central Railroad. Leave Toronto 7.00 and 11.00 A. M., 2.00 and 1.45 P. M. Close connection at Toronto for steamers on St. Lawrence River. Passenger capacity, 800 and 1,200.

NORFOLK & WASHINGTON (D. C.) STEAMBOAT COMPANY.

The new palace steamers "Washington" and "Norfolk" are in daily service between Washington, D. C., Fortress Monroe and Norfolk. Steamers will leave Washington at 7.00 P. M.; arrive at Fortress Monroe 6.30 and Norfolk 7.30 next morning. Steamers will leave Norfolk at 6.10 P. M. daily, Old Point Comfort 7.20 P. M.; arrive at Washington 6.30 next morning.

NORWICH LINE.

The "City of Worcester," "City of New York," and "City of Boston" ply all the year between New York and New London, and the "City of Lawrence" between New York and Norwich. Leave New York daily, Sundays excepted, from old Pier 40, North River, adjoining Desbrosses Street Ferry, 5.30 P. M., connecting at New London with trains for Boston, first train arriving at 7.30 A. M. Leave Boston 6.55 P. M., Worcester 7.40 P. M., New London 10.55 P. M., and arrive at New York 7.00 A. M. Meals on European plan. Cabin berths free. State-rooms, $1.00 and $2.00. Passenger capacity, 1,200.

OTSEGO LAKE STEAMER.
(OTSEGO LAKE STEAMBOAT AND STAGE LINE.)

The "Natty Bumppo" and connecting Stage Line commence June 1st and cease October 1st; the former between Cooperstown and Island Cottage and the latter between Island Cottage and Richfield Springs (seven miles). The boat makes landings at Three-Mile Point (Thayer's) and Five-Mile Point (Tunnicliff) on signal or request.

Leave Cooperstown 9.30 A. M. and 1.30 P. M. for Richfield. Leave Richfield for Cooperstown 9.00 A. M. and 3.45 P. M. The trip on lake, one hour; stage, one and a half hours. The passenger capacity of the steamer is about 100. Runs made daily, except Sunday.

PEOPLE'S LINE STEAMERS.
(ALBANY NIGHT BOATS.)

The "Dean Richmond" and "Drew" run daily, except Sundays, from March 25th to December 1st, between New York and Albany, making no intermediate stops.

Leave Pier 41, North River (foot of Canal street), 6.00 P. M. daily, except Sundays. Arrive at Albany 6.00 A. M. Leave Albany, except Sundays, at 8.00 P. M., arrive in New York 7.00 A. M. Passenger capacity, 800. Meals on European plan. State-rooms, $1.00, $2.00 and $3.00. Berths in cabin, 50 cents.

PEOPLE'S WASHINGTON & NORFOLK STEAMBOAT COMPANY.

The steamer "Jane Moseley" or "Lady of the Lake" plies between Washington, Fortress Monroe and Norfolk, stopping at Alexandria in both directions. They leave Washington, from Sixth Street Wharf, Sundays, Wednesdays and Fridays at 5.00 P. M.; returning, leave Norfolk Mondays, Thursdays and Saturdays at 4.00 P. M.

PORTLAND, MT. DESERT & MACHIAS STEAMBOAT LINE.

The steamer "City of Richmond" will make two round trips per week between Portland, Bar Harbor and Machias-port, leaving Portland every Tuesday and Friday at 11.00 P. M., or after arrival of train leaving Boston at 7.00 P. M., touching at Rockland, Hesboro, Castine, Deer Isle, Sedgwick, Southwest Harbor, Northeast Harbor, Bar Harbor, Milbridge, Jonesport, and arrive at Machiasport Wednesdays and Saturdays at 8.00 P. M. Returning, will leave Machias-port Mondays and Thursdays at 4.00 A. M., touching at Jonesport and Milbridge, and arriving at Bar Harbor at 10.00 A. M., connecting with trains of the Maine Central Railroad for Portland and Boston. After leaving Bar Harbor she touches at the same ports as on her eastward trip, arriving in Portland Tuesdays and Fridays at 4.00 A. M., connecting with early morning trains for Boston.

PORTLAND STEAM PACKET LINE.

The new steamers "Tremont" and "Portland" run every evening except Sunday throughout the year between Boston and Portland. Leave India Wharf, Boston, 7.00 P. M.; Leave Franklin Wharf, Portland, 7.00 P. M., the trip being made in about eight hours. Sunday trips from each port at 7.00 P. M., from June 19th to September 11th inclusive. Passenger capacity, 500. State-rooms, $1.00, $1.50 and $2.00. Meals served on the boats.

PROVIDENCE LINE.

(PROVIDENCE & STONINGTON S. S. CO.)

Steamers "Connecticut" and "Massachusetts" commence running about May 1st and cease about November 1st. Leave New York from Pier 29, North River (foot of Warren street), 5.30 P. M., arrive Fox Point Wharf, Providence, at 5.30 A. M., connecting with express train with parlor cars leaving 6.00 A. M., arriving Boston 7.45 A. M.; also, with through White Mountain Express, with parlor cars attached, leaving steamer wharf at 7.15 A. M., arriving Fabyan's 4.30 P. M. Returning, leave Boston Park Square Station 6.30 P. M., Providence 7.30 P. M.; arrive New York 7.00 A. M. Passenger capacity, 1,000. Meals on board on European plan. State-rooms, $1.00, $2.00, $3.00 and $4.00. Berths in cabin free. Steamers make no intermediate stops.

RICHELIEU & ONTARIO NAVIGATION COMPANY, CLAYTON & MONTREAL LINE.

(IN CONNECTION WITH B. W. & O. R. R.)

The steamers of this company commence running June 2d and cease September 30th. The "Passport," "Spartan," "Corsican" and "Algerian" between Clayton and Montreal. Capacity, 300 to 500. In addition to these the beautiful new palace steamer "Columbia," capacity 800, will be placed on the route between Kingston and Montreal about July 4th, leaving Kingston on Mondays, Wednesdays and Fridays. Landings will be made at Thousand-Island Park, Round-Island Park, Alexandria Bay, Brockville and Prescott. Meals are served on board the boats. A steamboat express train, leaving Niagara Falls daily 8.40 P. M., Rochester 10.55 P. M., with through sleeping cars attached, arrives at Clayton 5.50 A. M., running direct to steamboat dock, and connecting without transfer with steamers for Alexandria Bay and Montreal. In addition to regular service between Montreal and Quebec, commencing about June 20th and continuing until about September 15th, a Sunday service will be inaugurated, and steamers will leave Montreal and Quebec respectively at 5.00 P. M., calling at intermediate ports, thus affording passengers the opportunity of leaving either point on Saturday and returning on Sunday.

THE RICHELIEU & ONTARIO NAVIGATION COMPANY'S STEAMERS

Between Toronto and Montreal consists of the "Spartan," "Corsican," "Passport" and "Algerian," leaving both places daily (Sundays excepted)—the former place at 2.00 P. M.,—from the 1st of June to the 15th of September inclusive, calling at Port Darlington (Bowmanville), Port Hope, Cobourg, Kingston, Clayton, Round Island, Thousand Island Park, Alexandria Bay, Brockville, Prescott, Cornwall, and arriving at Montreal at 6.30 P. M., connecting with the steamers for Quebec. The line between Montreal and Quebec is composed of the magnificent steamers "Quebec" and "Montreal," leaving Montreal every evening, commencing May 1st (Sundays excepted) at 7.00 o'clock, calling at Sorel, Three Rivers and Batiscan, arriving at Quebec at about 6.00 A. M., connecting with the Intercolonial Railway for maritime provinces, and with steamers "Canada" and "Saguenay" for the Saguenay and lower St. Lawrence watering places. Returning, steamers leave Quebec for Montreal 5.00 P. M. daily, except Sunday. The Quebec steamers run from the opening of navigation to its close.

RICHELIEU & ONTARIO NAVIGATION CO'S STEAMERS.

(SAGUENAY RIVER LINE.)

The steamers "Canada" and "Saguenay" commence running between Quebec and Chicoutimi about May 4th, leaving Quebec Tuesdays and Fridays at 7.30 A. M. until November 15th. From June 20th to September 15th steamers leave Quebec on Wednesdays and Saturdays; also, at 7.30 A. M.; Murray Bay 2.00 P. M., Riviere du Loup 5.00 P. M., Tadousac 7.00 P. M., L'Anse St. Jean 9.30 P. M., arriving at Ha-Ha Bay 5.00 A. M., and Chicoutimi according to tide. Returning, leave Tadousac at 2.30 P. M., Riviere du Loup 5.00 P. M., Murray Bay 10.00 P. M., arriving at Quebec 7.00 A. M. Meals on board, 50 and 75 cents. Sleeping accommodations at moderate rates.

SCHROON LAKE STEAMBOAT LINE.

Steamers on Schroon Lake commence running about June 25th and cease operations about September 15th, connecting with trains of the Adirondack Railway by stage from Riverside station, passing through Pottersville.

BLUE MOUNTAIN & RAQUETTE LAKE STEAMBOAT LINE.

Steamers on Blue Mountain and Raquette Lakes commence running about June 20th and cease October 1st, connecting with trains of Adirondack Railway by stage from North Creek station.

SENECA LAKE STEAMERS.

(SENECA LAKE STEAM NAVIGATION LINE.)

The "Onondaga," "Schuyler," "W. B. Dunning" and "Otetiani" ply between Watkins and Geneva, stopping at Glenora, Peach Orchard, North Hector, Severne, Lamoreaux, Starkey, Himrods, Lodi, Highlands, Long Point Hotel, Ovid, Willard, Dresden, Glen Gowen and Deyes Landing. From November 1st to June 1st leave Watkins 12.00 noon, Leave Geneva 8.40 A. M. June 1st to 20th leave Watkins 7.00 A. M. and 12.00 noon; leave Geneva 7.47 A. M. and 12.30 P. M. June

20th to September 29th leave Watkins 7.00 A. M., 12.00 noon and 5.00 P. M.; leave Geneva 8.10 A. M., 12.30 and 5.32 P. M. September 30th to November 1st leave Watkins 7.00 A. M. and 12.00 noon; leave Geneva 8.10 A. M. and 4.30 P. M. Trip occupies 3½ hours. Passenger capacity, 800. Leaving and arriving at Watkins in connection with Northern Central Railway and at Geneva with New York Central & Hudson River Railroad, Lehigh Valley and Fall Brook Railroads. Free transfer of baggage at terminal points. Meals on steamers. The above is subject to changes for correction without notice.

SHELTER ISLAND FERRY.

The boats between Greenport and Shelter Island run during the summer season in connection with all trains to and from Greenport, stopping at both Manhansett and Shelter Island Heights.

STEAMER EMPRESS OF INDIA.

The steamer "Empress of India" runs between Port Dalhousie and Toronto from May until November. A train leaves Niagara Falls on arrival of morning trains of the New York, Lake Erie & Western Railroad, making direct connection at the steamboat wharf, returning from Toronto in the afternoon. Passenger capacity, 750.

STEAMER FROM CLAYTON TO ALEXANDRIA BAY.

The steamers "St. Lawrence," "J. F. Maynard" and "Islander" commence running June 1st and cease October 1st, plying between Clayton and Alexandria Bay, viz: Leave Clayton 5.30, 10.20 A. M., 2.20 10.20 P. M. Returning, leave Alexandria Bay 7.20 and 11.55 A. M., 3.20 and 5.30 P. M. Stops are made at Round Island, S. B. Grenell's Island, Thousand-Island Park, Wellesley House, Central Park and Alexandria Bay. Trip occupies from one hour to an hour and a quarter. The above steamers connect at Alexandria Bay with ferry for Westminster Park. The steamer "St. Lawrence" makes forty-mile trips among the Thousand Islands, leaving Clayton at 8.45 A. M. and 2.00 P. M.

STEAMER FROM BABYLON TO FIRE ISLAND.

This boat commences her trips between Babylon and Fire Island about June 15th and ceases about October 1st. Trips are made every week day in connection with morning and afternoon trains from Long Island City.

STEAMER "MARY POWELL."

The "Mary Powell" commences her trips about May 21st and ceases about October 20th. Leave New York, except Sundays, from Desbrosses Street Pier, North River, 3.45 P. M. (Twenty-second street, 3.30 P. M.); arrive Cranston's 6.00 P. M., West Point 6.10 P. M., Cornwall 6.30 P. M., Newburg 6.45 P. M., Poughkeepsie 7.15 P. M., Kingston 8.30 P. M. Leave Kingston 5.30 A. M., Poughkeepsie 6.30 A. M., Newburg 7.30 A. M., Cornwall 7.45 A. M., West Point 8.05 A. M. and Cranston's 8.10 A. M.; arrive New York 10.45 A. M. Passenger capacity, 1,800. Meals at all hours *a la carte*. On Saturdays only the "Powell" will leave Desbrosses Street Pier at 1.45, and Twenty-second street at 2.00 P. M.

STEAMER "WATCH HILL."

(STONINGTON & WATCH HILL FERRY.)

Steamer will ply between Stonington and Watch Hill, commencing about June 15th and continuing until about September 15th, connecting with "Shore Line" trains for New York, Boston, Providence, Worcester, etc., also with "Stonington Line" to and from New York.

STONINGTON LINE.

(PROVIDENCE & STONINGTON S. S. CO.)

Steamer "Rhode Island" and new steamers "Maine" and "New Hampshire" ply between New York and Stonington all the year, making no intermediate stops. Leave new Pier 36, North River, New York (one block above Canal Street, reached by street cars direct from Liberty Street Ferry), in summer, 5.00 P. M., connecting at Stonington with three trains for Boston (first train arriving at 6.00 A. M.) and with transfer steamer for Watch Hill and with through car for Narragansett Pier. Returning, leave Boston 6.30 P. M., Stonington 9.30 P. M., and arrive at New York 6.00 A. M. Passenger capacity, 500. Meals on board on European plan. Staterooms, $1.00, $2.00, $3.00 and $4.00. Berths in cabin, free.

SCENERY.

THE grandeur and beauty of the scenery along the line of the Baltimore and Ohio Railroad is world-renowned, and has gained for this route the sobriquet of

Picturesque B. & O.

In no distance of equal length on the continent is there such variety of views of mountain, valley and stream, and nowhere are the surroundings invested with greater historic interest. One has but to repeat the names of Potomac, Shenandoah, Harper's Ferry, to have come trooping upon the memory a legion of events and incidents that crowd the pages of the later history of the Republic. Much of the region traversed by the B. & O.

INDIAN CREEK.

WILLS CREEK.

was, during the civil war, the debatable land over which the contending hosts marched and fought, alternately pursuers and pursued. At Harper's Ferry the old brick fort from which John Brown bade defiance to Virginia's pride and power, still stands in full view from the car windows as the train glides on to the graceful bridge that here spans the Potomac. It is at this point the historic river, disdaining impediment, has literally cleft its way through the Blue Ridge Mountains, whose rock ribbed walls rise sheer, for a thousand feet, from the water's edge. This is but one picture. The entire line, from Washington to the Ohio River, is a living gallery of views that prove a source of present delight to the traveler, and become a cherished recollection in after years.

HOMES

IF YOU WANT

A Farm,
Manufacturing Site,
Valuable Water Power,
Choice Coal Lands,
Hunting Preserve,
Stock or Sheep Ranch,
Mine of Richest Iron Ore,
Bank of Brick or Fire Clay,
Bed of Finest Glass Sand,
Belt of Magnificent Timber,
Superb Location for Truck Farm,
Desirable Point for Creamery,
Unsurpassed Place for Apiary,
Unequalled Spot for Vineyard,
Magnificent Summer Resort,
Delightful Winter Home,
Elegant Site for Suburban Residence,
Home in Genial and Healthful Climate,

Then come to the Upper Southern States, Virginia, West Virginia and Maryland, where ALL Branches of Agricultural Industry can be successfully engaged in; where Manufacturing Possibilities exist on the Grandest Scale, and Prosperity and Happiness join hands with Energy and Industry.

If you desire information of the Bonanza Agricultural, Manufacturing and Commercial Section, Par Excellence of the United States, call on or address,

M. V. RICHARDS,
Land and Immigration Agent, B. & O. R. R.,
Baltimore, Maryland.

ON THE B. & O.

Cottages ✦ ✦

THE location of DEER PARK, at an altitude of about three thousand feet above the level of the sea, its surroundings, its pure air and salubrious climate, the character of the accommodations and entertainment it can offer its guests, its nearness to the great commercial and business centres of the Union, and the facility with which it can be reached over the B. & O. R. R., entitle it to be called

"The Summer Capital"

of the United States. The Railroad Company owns a tract of land at this point, comprising several hundred acres. They have platted the grounds that overlook the hotel and railroad, and offer lots at nominal figures to persons who will erect cottages. The lots are large, varying from one-half to one acre in size. The streets are so conveniently shaped as to afford beautiful miniature parks, magnificent drives and walks.

Liberal concessions will be made by the Company in freight rates, on material used in the construction of cottages, etc.

The undersigned will be pleased to give full information to persons contemplating the erection of Summer Cottages. Plats of the Park will be furnished on application.

The Baltimore and Ohio Railroad Company have their own employees the year around on the grounds, so that when cottages are not occupied they are carefully guarded. Address

M. V. RICHARDS,

Land and Immigration Agent,

B. & O. R. R., Baltimore, Md.

AT ✦ DEER ✦ PARK.

Vestibuled Trains.

Through the Vestibule

THE chief merit claimed for the Vestibule appliance is that it effectually prevents telescoping cars in case of collision, and the second great advantage lies in the fact that the new device entirely overcomes the swaying motion imparted to ordinary trains when rounding curves at high speed.

The Limited Express Trains

Running via B. & O. R. R. between St. Louis, Cincinnati Washington and Baltimore, between Chicago, Washington and Baltimore, and between Washington, Baltimore, Philadelphia and New York are composed entirely of Vestibuled Cars, the Baggage Cars, Day Coaches and Pullman Sleepers and Dining Cars all being fitted with Pullman's Patent Vestibules.

Investments

THE attention now being devoted to the South in the section of country traversed by the B. & O., and the rapidly growing towns along its lines, are surprises to the "oldest inhabitant," and those who had the foresight to make investments here in the past are now reaping an abundant harvest in the shape of good dividends, and the rise in values has just commenced.

Put your money where it will do the most good, and invest it in properties on this line of Railroad. The Land and Immigration Department of the B. & O. R. R. is prepared to show good openings for the manufacturer, business man or farmer, and will take pleasure in giving information concerning these at any and all times.

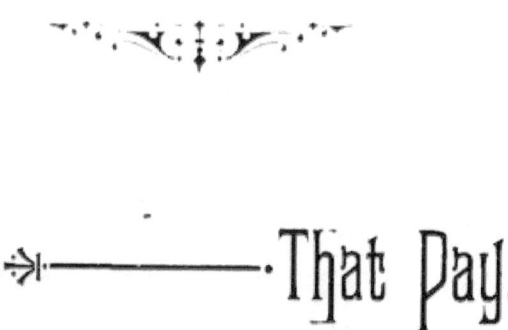

ROYAL · BLUE · LINE

BETWEEN

New York, Philadelphia, Baltimore
and Washington via

Baltimore & Ohio R. R.

FASTEST, FINEST AND SAFEST TRAINS IN THE WORLD.

The entire equipment is brand new, and consists of the finest Baggage
Cars, Coaches, Parlor, Sleeping and Dining Cars ever built by
the Pullman Company. The trains are vestibuled from
end to end and protected by Pullman's improved

ANTI-TELESCOPING DEVICE.

ALL THE CARS IN ALL THE TRAINS ARE
HEATED BY STEAM AND LIGHTED BY PINTSCH GAS.

MEMORANDA.

MEMORANDA.

MEMORANDA.

MEMORANDA.

CHAS. O. SCULL, General Passenger Agent,
Baltimore, Md.

R. F. BOND, Division Passenger Agent,
Baltimore, Md.

BALTIMORE & OHIO RAILROAD COMPANY.

PASSENGER DEPARTMENT.

S. B. HEGE,
   City Passenger Agent.
H. B. BOWSER, Ticket Agent.
   619 Pennsylvania Ave.

Washington, D. C. ___189

Calston

6.95

MEMORANDA.

BALTIMORE & OHIO RAILROAD COMPANY.

Washington, D. C.

www.ingramcontent.com/pod-product-compliance
Lightning Source LLC
Chambersburg PA
CBHW022111290426
44112CB00008B/630